Communications
in Computer and Information Sc̣ ̣ ̣ ̣ ̣ ̣ ̣ ̣ ̣ ⌄⊥ᴛ

Mohammad S. Obaidat
José L. Sevillano   Joaquim Filipe (Eds.)

E-Business and Telecommunications

International Joint Conference, ICETE 2011
Seville, Spain, July 18-21, 2011
Revised Selected Papers

 Springer

Volume Editors

Mohammad S. Obaidat
Monmouth University, Department of Computer Science
West Long Branch, NJ 07764, USA
E-mail: obaidat@monmouth.edu

José L. Sevillano
University of Seville
C/S. Fernando, 4, C.P. 41004 Sevilla, Spain
E-mail: sevi@atc.us.es

Joaquim Filipe
INSTICC – IPS
Department of Systems and Informatics
Rua do Vale de Chaves - Estefanilha, 2910-761 Setúbal, Portugal
E-mail: joaquim.filipe@estsetubal.ips.pt

ISSN 1865-0929   e-ISSN 1865-0937
ISBN 978-3-642-35754-1   e-ISBN 978-3-642-35755-8
DOI 10.1007/978-3-642-35755-8
Springer Heidelberg Dordrecht London New York

Library of Congress Control Number: 2012954173

CR Subject Classification (1998): C.2.1, C.2.4-5, K.4.4, K.6.5, C.5.3, H.3.5, H.5.1, H.5.5, I.4.2, E.3, J.1

Typesetting: Camera-ready by author, data conversion by Scientific Publishing Services, Chennai, India

Printed on acid-free paper

Springer is part of Springer Science+Business Media (www.springer.com)

Preface

The present book includes extended and revised versions of a set of selected best papers from the 8th International Joint Conference on e-Business and Telecommunications (ICETE), which was held in July 2011, in Seville, Spain. This conference reflects a continuing effort to increase the dissemination of recent research results among professionals who work in the areas of e-business and telecommunications. ICETE is a joint international conference integrating four major areas of knowledge that are divided into six corresponding conferences: DCNET (International Conference on Data Communication Networking), ICE-B (International Conference on e-Business), OPTICS (International Conference on Optical Communication Systems), SECRYPT (International Conference on Security and Cryptography), WINSYS (International Conference on Wireless Information Systems), and SIGMAP (International Conference on Signal Processing and Multimedia).

The program of this joint conference included several outstanding keynote lectures presented by internationally renowned distinguished researchers who are experts in the various ICETE areas. Their keynote speeches contributed to heightening the overall quality of the program and significance of the theme of the conference.

The conference topic areas define a broad spectrum in the key areas of e-business and telecommunications. This wide-view reporting made ICETE appealing to a global audience of engineers, scientists, business practitioners, ICT managers, and policy experts. The papers accepted and presented at the conference demonstrated a number of new and innovative solutions for e-business and telecommunication networks and systems, showing that the technical problems in these closely related fields are challenging and worthwhile approaching with an interdisciplinary perspective such as that promoted by ICETE.

ICETE 2011 received 409 papers in total, with contributions from 59 different countries, on all continents, which really shows the success and global dimension of the conference. To evaluate each submission, a double-blind paper evaluation method was used; each paper was reviewed by at least two experts from the International Program Committee, and most papers received three reviews or even more. In the end, 118 papers were selected for oral presentation and publication, corresponding to a 28.8% acceptance ratio. Of these, only 52 were accepted as full papers (12.7% of submissions) and 66 as short papers. Additionally, 52 papers were accepted for poster presentation.

We hope that you will find this collection of the best ICETE 2011 papers an excellent source of inspiration as well as a helpful reference for research in the afore-mentioned areas.

May 2012

Mohammad S. Obaidat
José L. Sevillano
Joaquim Filipe

Organization

Conference Co-chairs

Mohammad S. Obaidat   Monmouth University, USA
Jose Luis Sevillano   University of Seville, Spain

Program Co-chairs

DCNET

Mohammad S. Obaidat   Monmouth University, USA
Jose Luis Sevillano   University of Seville, Spain

ICE-B

David A. Marca   University of Phoenix, USA
Boris Shishkov   IICREST, Bulgaria
Marten van Sinderen   University of Twente, The Netherlands

OPTICS

Eusebi Calle Ortega   University of Girona, Spain

SECRYPT

Javier Lopez   University of Malaga, Spain
Pierangela Samarati   Università degli Studi di Milano, Italy

SIGMAP

Alejandro Linares Barranco   University of Seville, Spain
George Tsihrintzis   University of Piraeus, Greece

WINSYS

Rafael Caldeirinha   Polytechnic Institute of Leiria, Portugal
Mohammad S. Obaidat   Monmouth University, USA

Organizing Committee

Sérgio Brissos, INSTICC, Portugal
Helder Coelhas, INSTICC, Portugal
Vera Coelho, INSTICC, Portugal
Andreia Costa, INSTICC, Portugal
Patrícia Duarte, INSTICC, Portugal
Bruno Encarnação, INSTICC, Portugal
Liliana Medina, INSTICC, Portugal
Carla Mota, INSTICC, Portugal
Raquel Pedrosa, INSTICC, Portugal

Vitor Pedrosa, INSTICC, Portugal
Daniel Pereira, INSTICC, Portugal
Cláudia Pinto, INSTICC, Portugal
Mónica Saramago, INSTICC, Portugal

José Varela, INSTICC, Portugal
Pedro Varela, INSTICC, Portugal

DCNET Program Committee

Julio Barbancho, Spain
Alejandro Linares Barranco, Spain
Fernando Beltrán, New Zealand
Christos Bouras, Greece
Roberto Bruschi, Italy
Christian Callegari, Italy
Tomaso De Cola, Germany
Franco Davoli, Italy
Hala ElAarag, USA
Pingyi Fan, China
Sebastià Galmés, Spain
Jose Daniel Garcia, Spain
Orhan Gemikonakli, UK
Katja Gilly, Spain
Sami Habib, Kuwait
Abdelhakim Hafid, Canada
Carlos Juiz, Spain
Dimitris Kanellopoulos, Greece
Randi Karlsen, Norway
Abdallah Khreishah, USA

Andy (Zhenjiang) Li, USA
Pascal Lorenz, France
S. Kami Makki, USA
Rami Melhem, USA
Pascale Minet, France
Carlos León de Mora, Spain
Fei Nan, USA
Mohammad S. Obaidat, USA
Elena Pagani, Italy
Georgios Papadimitriou, Greece
Michal Pioro, Poland
Joel Rodrigues, Portugal
Alex Sprintson, USA
Vicente Traver, Spain
Pere Vilà, Spain
Manuel Villen-Altamirano, Spain
Bernd E. Wolfinger, Germany
Cliff C. Zou, USA

DCNET Auxiliary Reviewers

Ramon Alcarria, Spain
M. Soledad Escolar, Spain
Javier Fernandez, Spain
Isaac Lera, Spain

Mariusz Mycek, Poland
Shan Wang, China

ICE-B Program Committee

Anteneh Ayanso, Canada
Morad Benyoucef, Canada
Indranil Bose, Hong Kong
Rebecca Bulander, Germany
Wojciech Cellary, Poland
Soon Chun, USA

Michele Colajanni, Italy
Rafael Corchuelo, Spain
Peter Dolog, Denmark
Erwin Fielt, Australia
Flavius Frasincar, The Netherlands
José María García, Spain

Paul Grefen, The Netherlands
Andreas Holzinger, Austria
Ela Hunt, Switzerland
Arun Iyengar, USA
Anton Lavrin, Slovak Republic
Yung-Ming Li, Taiwan
Sebastian Link, New Zealand
David Marca, USA
Tokuro Matsuo, Japan
Gavin McArdle, Ireland
Adrian Mocan, Germany
Ali Reza Montazemi, Canada
Maurice Mulvenna, UK
Daniel O'Leary, USA
Krassie Petrova, New Zealand

Pak-Lok Poon, China
Philippos Pouyioutas, Cyprus
Sofia Reino, UK
Ana Paula Rocha, Portugal
Erik Rolland, USA
Gustavo Rossi, Argentina
Jarogniew Rykowski, Poland
Boris Shishkov, Bulgaria
Marten van Sinderen, The Netherlands
Zhaohao Sun, Australia
Laurentiu Vasiliu, Ireland
Michael Weiss, Canada
Qi Yu, USA
Lina Zhou, USA

ICE-B Auxiliary Reviewers

Marco Comuzzi, The Netherlands
Bhavik Pathak, USA

Yanbin Tu, Brazil
Jochem Vonk, The Netherlands

OPTICS Program Committee

Girish Saran Agarwal, USA
Anjali Agarwal, USA
Víctor López Álvarez, Spain
Davide Careglio, Spain
Adolfo Cartaxo, Portugal
Walter Cerroni, Italy
Marco Genoves, Italy
Masahiko Jinno, Japan
Miroslaw Klinkowski, Poland
Franko Küppers, USA
Xavier Masip-Bruin, Spain

Yesid Donoso Meisel, Colombia
Amalia Miliou, Greece
Jordi Perelló, Spain
João Rebola, Portugal
Mehdi Shadaram, USA
Surinder Singh, India
Wolfgang Sohler, Germany
Salvatore Spadaro, Spain
NaoyaWada, Japan
Xiaohua Ye, USA

OPTICS Auxiliary Reviewers

José Morgado, Portugal
Oscar Pedrola, Spain

SECRYPT Program Committee

Claudio Ardagna, Italy
Josang Audun, Norway
Ken Barker, Canada
Giampaolo Bella, Italy
Marina Blanton, USA
Carlo Blundo, Italy
Pino Caballero-Gil, Spain
David Chadwick, UK
Jorge Cuellar, Germany
Frédéric Cuppens, France
Paolo D'arco, Italy
Jorge Davila, Spain
Josep Domingo-ferrer, Spain
Eduardo B. Fernandez, USA
Eduardo Fernández-medina, Spain
Alberto Ferrante, Switzerland
Josep-Lluis Ferrer-Gomila, Spain
Simone Fischer-Hübner, Sweden
Sara Foresti, Italy
Keith Frikken, USA
Steven Furnell, UK
Amparo Fúster-Sabater, Spain
R. M. Gasca, Spain
Antonio Gómez-skarmeta, Spain
Dimitris Gritzalis, Greece
Yong Guan, USA
Ragib Hasan, USA
Jordi Herrera, Spain
Jiankun Hu, Australia
Michael Huth, UK
Cynthia Irvine, USA
Sokratis Katsikas, Greece
Stefan Katzenbeisser, Germany
Costas Lambrinoudakis, Greece
Bo Lang, China

Olivier Markowitch, Belgium
Vashek Matyas, Czech Republic
Carlos Maziero, Brazil
Jorge Guajardo Merchan,
    The Netherlands
Chris Mitchell, UK
Marco Casassa Mont, UK
David Naccache, France
Juan Gonzalez Nieto, Australia
Eiji Okamoto, Japan
Rolf Oppliger, Switzerland
Stefano Paraboschi, Italy
Gerardo Pelosi, Italy
Rene Peralta, USA
Günther Pernul, Germany
Alessandro Piva, Italy
Joachim Posegga, Germany
Kui Ren, USA
Carlos Ribeiro, Portugal
Pierangela Samarati, Italy
Miguel Soriano, Spain
Neeraj Suri, Germany
Willy Susilo, Australia
Juan Tapiador, UK
Marianthi Theoharidou, Greece
Sabrina de Capitani di Vimercati, Italy
Lingyu Wang, Canada
Yang Xiang, Australia
Alec Yasinsac, USA
Nicola Zannone, The Netherlands
Justin Zhan, USA
Jianying Zhou, Singapore
Bo Zhu, Canada

SECRYPT Auxiliary Reviewers

Gianpiero Costantino, Italy
Angel Perez del Pozo, Spain
Kenneth Radke, Australia

Yanjiang Yang, Singapore
Ge Zhang, Sweden

SIGMAP Program Committee

Harry Agius, UK
João Ascenso, Portugal
Pradeep K. Atrey, Canada
Oscar Au, Hong Kong
Ramazan Aygun, USA
Arvind Bansal, USA
Alejandro Linares Barranco, Spain
Adrian Bors, UK
Enrique Cabello, Spain
Wai-Kuen Cham, China
Chin-Chen Chang, Taiwan
Shu-Ching Chen, USA
Wei Cheng, Singapore
Ryszard S. Choras, Poland
Rob Evans, Australia
Jianping Fan, USA
Quanfu Fan, USA
Clement Farabet, USA
Lorenzo Granai, Switzerland
William Grosky, USA
Malka Halgamuge, Australia
Hermann Hellwagner, Austria
Richang Hong, Singapore
Wolfgang Hürst, The Netherlands
Razib Iqbal, Canada
Mohan Kankanhalli, Singapore
Sokratis Katsikas, Greece
Constantine Kotropoulos, Greece
Jing Li, UK
Zhu Li, USA
Zhu Liu, USA

Mathias Lux, Austria
Hong Man, USA
Ketan Mayer-Patel, USA
Klaus Moessner, UK
Sebastien Mondet, Norway
Arturo Morgado-Estevez, Spain
Alejandro Murua, Canada
Mokhtar Nibouche, UK
Pietro Pala, Italy
Ioannis Paliokas, Greece
Gang Qian, USA
Maria Paula Queluz, Portugal
Rudolf Rabenstein, Germany
Matthias Rauterberg, The Netherlands
Pedro Real, Spain
Mei-Ling Shyu, USA
Gamhewage Chaminda de Silva, Japan
George Tsihrintzis, Greece
Andreas Uhl, Austria
Steve Uhlig, Germany
Zhiyong Wang, Australia
Michael Weber, Germany
Lei Wu, USA
Changsheng Xu, China
Kim-hui Yap, Singapore
Chengcui Zhang, USA
Tianhao Zhang, USA
Yongxin Zhang, USA
Ce Zhu, Singapore

SIGMAP Auxiliary Reviewers

Vineetha Bettaiah, USA
Catarina Brites, Portugal
Yi Chen, USA
Wen Jin, USA
Viorica Patraucean, France

Jun Qian, USA
Teng Wang, USA
Xin Xin, USA
Tianzhu Zhang, China

WINSYS Program Committee

Vicente Alarcon-Aquino, Mexico
Josephine Antoniou, Cyprus
Francisco Barcelo Arroyo, Spain
Bert-Jan van Beijnum,
    The Netherlands
Luis Bernardo, Portugal
Raffaele Bolla, Italy
Matthias R. Brust, USA
Iñigo Cuiñas, Spain
Amit Dvir, Hungary
David Ferreira, Portugal
Patrik Floreen, Finland
Chuan Heng Foh, Singapore
Matthias Hollick, Germany
Jehn-Ruey Jiang, Taiwan
Eduard Jorswieck, Germany

Abdelmajid Khelil, Germany
Imad Mahgoub, USA
S. Kami Makki, USA
Klaus Moessner, UK
Daniele Riboni, Italy
António Rodrigues, Portugal
Jörg Roth, Germany
Manuel García Sánchez, Spain
Christian Schindelhauer, Germany
Kuei-Ping Shih, Taiwan
George Tombras, Greece
Enrique Vazquez, Spain
Dimitrios D. Vergados, Greece
IssacWoungang, Canada

WINSYS Auxiliary Reviewers

Ahmed Badi, USA
Cliff Kemp, USA
Marcelino Minero-Muñoz, UK
Stefanos Nikolidakis, Greece

Aggeliki Sgora, Greece
Michael Slavik, USA
Dimitris J. Vergados, Greece

Invited Speakers

Han-Chieh Chao, National Ilan University, Taiwan
Vincenzo Piuri, Università degli Studi di Milano, Italy
Enrique Cabello, Universidad Rey Juan Carlos, Spain
Winfried Lamersdorf, University of Hamburg, Germany

Table of Contents

Invited Speakers

Part I: Data Communication Networking

Part II: e-Business

Part III: Optical Communication Systems

Part IV: Security and Cryptography

Part V: Signal Processing and Multimedia Applications

Part VI: Wireless Information Networks and Systems

Invited Speakers

Biometric Privacy Protection:
Guidelines and Technologies

Ruggero Donida Labati, Vincenzo Piuri, and Fabio Scotti

Universit degli Studi di Milano, Department of Information Technology,
via Bramante 65, I-26013 Crema (CR), Italy
{ruggero.donida,vincenzo.piuri,fabio.scotti}@unimi.com
http://www.dti.unimi.it

Abstract. Compared with traditional techniques used to establish the identity of
a person, biometric systems offer a greater confidence level that the authenticated
individual is not impersonated by someone else. However, it is necessary to consider different privacy and security aspects in order to prevent possible thefts and
misuses of biometric data. The effective protection of the privacy must encompass different aspects, such as the perceived and real risks pertaining to the users,
the specificity of the application, the adoption of correct policies, and data protection methods as well. This chapter focuses on the most important privacy issues
related to the use of biometrics, it presents actual guidelines for the implementation of privacy-protective biometric systems, and proposes a discussion of the
methods for the protection of biometric data.

Keywords: Biometrics, Privacy, Security, Template protection.

1 Introduction

Traditional techniques used to establish the identity of a person are based on surro-
gate representations of his/her identity, such as passwords, keys, tokens, and identity
cards. In many situations, these representations cannot guarantee a sufficient level of
security because they can be shared, misplaced or stolen. Biometric recognition systems, instead, are based on physiological or behavioral characteristics of the individual,
which are univocally related to their owner, cannot be shared or misplaced, and are
more difficult to be stolen. The use of biometric systems is continuously increasing in
different applicative scenarios [46] and the related market is showing a significant positive trend. In 2011, it reached the amount of 5 billion dollars and it is expected to reach
12 billion dollars by the end of 2015 [1]. Typical applicative scenarios are: physical access control (critical areas, public buildings, sport arenas, bank caveau, transportations,
etc.); surveillance (private buildings, public areas, etc.); government applications (identity cards, passports, driving licenses, immigration control, health cards, access control
to online government services, etc.); forensic applications (body identification, crime
investigation, searching of disappeared childrens, kinships, intelligence, etc.); logical
access control to data, networks and services (home banking, ATM, supermarkets,
e-commerce, mobile phones, computers, etc.).

M.S. Obaidat, J.L. Sevillano, and J. Filipe (Eds.): ICETE 2011, CCIS 314, pp. 3–19, 2012.

In order to prevent possible thefts and misuses of biometric data, it is necessary to consider different privacy and security aspects. Security and privacy are two different concepts because the privacy protection is more restrictive than the security protection. The security ensures: authentication, data integrity, confidentiality, and non-repudiation. Differently, the privacy requires also the data protection.

The protection from privacy abuses is very important in biometric systems. For example, if the biometric data related to an individual are stolen, this person can be impersonated for a long period of time and it is not easy to modify or substitute the compromised data. This is due to the fact that biometric traits are unique for each individual and strictly associated to their owner. Moreover, biometric traits are irrevocable, in the sense that the association cannot be changed during the human life.

The public acceptance of a biometric system is strictly related to the privacy risks perceived by the users. Usually, these risks are different from the real risks associated to a biometric system. In general, the most important perceived risk is related to possible identity thefts. Other perceived risks are related to misuses of the personal data, for example for tracing all the activities of the individuals or for operating proscription lists. Real risks should be evaluated considering different factors associated to the applicative context and used biometric traits. Examples of these aspects are the modalities adopted for storing the personal data, the owner of the system, the used recognition modality (authentication or identification in a biometric database), the durability of the used traits, and the class of the trait (physiological or compartmental).

It is possible to consider a privacy-protective biometric system as a system that drastically reduce the real risks associated to the use of biometric data. In order to properly design a privacy-protective biometric system, it is not sufficient to evaluate only aspects related to performances, costs, acceptability, and applicative conditions, but it is necessary to follow a set of guidelines for the use of biometric data [32]. These guidelines permit to effectively reduce the risks related to possible misuses of personal data.

In order to protect the privacy of the users, it is also necessary to consider the possible attacks that can be performed to a biometric system. In general, biometric systems are composed by four modules: sensor, feature extractor, database, and matcher. Each module can be subject to adversary attacks. As shown in Fig. 1, it is possible to distinguish eight distinct classes of attacks to the different modules [19,44,47]: (I) fake biometric at the sensor, (II) resubmission of old digitally stored biometrics signal, (III) override feature extractor, (IV) tampering with the feature representation; (V) override matcher, (VI) tampering with stored templates, (VII) channel attack between stored templates and the matcher, (VIII) decision override.

There are different classes of techniques that should be used to protect the privacy of the users also from possible attacks. Every component of the biometric system should in fact be protected by using properly methods. Important classes of techniques are: liveness detection methods, physical and cryptographic methods for the channel protection, secure code execution practices, template protection methods [25].

In this chapter, the most treated class of techniques for the protection of biometric systems regards the template protection methods. In a biometric application, the template is an abstract representation of the physiological or behavioral features, extracted from the acquired biometric samples (signals, images, or frame sequences).

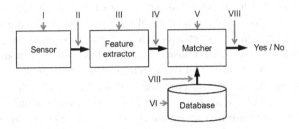

Fig. 1. Points of attack in a biometric system

Template protection methods permit to perform the recognition by using a protected representation of the biometric templates. In the literature, there are different methods for the biometric template protection: methods based on the transformation of the template (cancelable biometrics), methods based on cryptographic algorithms that perform the recognition by comparing cryptographic keys (biometric cryptosystems), methods based on cryptographic techniques that permits to perform a set of operations without converting the data in the plain domain (cryptographically secure methods).

The chapter discusses the privacy issues related to the use of biometrics and presents some of the most advanced techniques available today for the privacy protection of biometric data. Section 2 presents the problems related to the privacy risks, describes a possible classification of the privacy protection levels, and overviews the guidelines for the design of privacy-protective biometric systems. Section 3 proposes a brief review of the template protection techniques in the literature, while the last section is devoted to conclusions.

2 Privacy in Biometric Systems

Traditional authentication methods are based on somewhat known (e.g. a password) or a possessed object (e.g. a key or a token). If passwords or keys are theft of stolen, it is easy to revoke or replace them. Differently, biometric traits are univocally related to their owners and cannot be replaced or modified. If data related to a biometric trait are stolen, the owner of the trait can be impersonated in many different biometric systems and for a long period of time or the individual can be included in different biometric systems without explicit consents. For this reason, it is particularly important to protect biometric data.

It is possible to distinguish three different perspectives about the privacy in biometrics. The first perspective is related to the risks perceived by the users and should be considered in order to evaluate the acceptability of the system itself. The second perspective regards the application context in which the biometric system should be exploited and permits to properly design privacy protection techniques. The last aspect that should be considered is the used biometric trait. Each biometric trait, in fact, presents different propriets.

The evaluation of the risks perceived by users is a complex task because the risk perception is different for every person. Generally speaking, one of the most important perceived risks is related to the fact that the persons consider the acquisition of the biometric traits as an exact permanent filing of their activities and behaviors, and the idea that the biometric systems can guarantee a recognition accuracy equal to 100% is very common. Other perceived risks consist in the use of the collected biometric data for malicious purposes, and for tracing all the activities of the individuals or for operating proscription lists. Another important perceived risk is the fact that the acquisition of some biometric traits can be dangerous for the health. For example, the iris images are usually captured by using infrared illuminators, which can be erroneously considered as harmful). This psychological aspects should been taken into account, and, during the deployment of the biometric system, it is very important to inform the users about the real risks for the health and for the privacy, as well as all the procedures designed and applied to protect the biometric data.

The evaluation of the application context permits to determine some real risks of privacy invasiveness. Table 1 plots a qualitative representation of the privacy risks versus ten different application features, according to the International Biometric Group [32]:

1. *Covert* recognition systems (for example surveillance applications) are more privacy invasive than *overt* biometric systems. In some cases, covert applications can use biometric data without any knowledge or explicit consent of the individuals.
2. Applications that require a *mandatory* use of biometric systems are more invasive for the user's privacy than applications in which the use of biometric technologies is *optional*. In this case, the users can decide to not be checked by a biometric system, and they can adopt a different authentication method.
3. *Identification* systems perform the biometric recognition by comparing the acquired biometric data with N identities stored in a database. *Authentication* systems consider only the acquired biometric data and the declared identity, performing a 1 to 1 comparison. In most of the cases, the biometric database used for performing the identification is situated in a physical place different from the one in which the biometric sensors is located. For these reasons, identifications present more privacy risks than authentications.
4. It is possible to distinguish systems that use biometric data for a *fixed period* and systems that can use these information for *indefinite* time. Policies that define the storing duration of biometric data can reduce privacy risks.
5. Usually, biometric applications in the *public sector* are considered to be more susceptible to privacy invasiveness than applications in the *private sector*. An important fear of the users is related to possible government abuses.
6. The role of the individuals that use the biometric system has great impact on the privacy. The privacy risks are associated to the rights of the individuals over the stored biometric data, and are lower in the case when the users retain usage rights. For example, there are more privacy risks for *employees and citizens* than *individuals and costumers*.
7. The applications in which private or public *institutions* own the used biometric data are more privacy invasive than the applications in which the users (*enrollee*) own their data. The user control of the data is not possible in all the biometric applications.
8. Biometric systems that use databases of biometric data (*database storage*) present more privacy risks with respect to systems based on data stored in smartcard or

Table 1. Applicative aspects concerning the privacy according to the IBG (Iternational Biometric Group)

Lower Risk	Question	Greater Risk
Overt	Is the system deployed overtly or covertly?	Covert
Optional	Is the system optional or mandatory?	Mandatory
Verification	Is the system used for Identification or Verification?	Identification
Fixed Period	Is the system deployed for a fixed period of time?	Indefinite
Private Sector	Is the system deployed in the private or public sector?	Public Sector
Individual/Customer	In what role is the user interacting with the system?	Employee/Citizen
Enrollee	Who owns the biometric information?	Institution
Personal storage	Where is the biometric data stored?	Database Storage
Behavioral	What type of biometric technology is being deployed?	Physiological
Templates	Does the system use templates, samples or both?	Sample/Images

memory devices possessed by the users (*personal storage*) because the use of personal memory devices can prevent possible abuses.

9. The use of *physiological* biometric traits presents more privacy risks than the use of *behavioral* traits. In most of the cases, physiological traits can obtain more recognition accuracy, are more harder to mask or alter, and can be acquired with less user cooperation.

10. Biometric systems that store *samples and images* are more subject to privacy risks than systems that store biometric *templates*. This is due to the fact that templates reveal more limited information.

In order to determine the real risks of privacy invasiveness, it is also necessary to consider the adopted biometric traits because they can introduce different kinds of risks. Four important features related to the tecnologies associated to the different biometric traits are presented in [32]:

1. The first feature is the possibility to use the biometric trait in *identification* systems. Not all the biometric traits can be used for the identification because this process requires high performances in terms of accuracy and speed. Examples of biometric traits that can be used for performing the identification are the iris and fingerprint. In general, systems based on traits that can be used in identification are more invasive for the user's privacy.

2. The second feature is associated to the possibility of the trait to be used in *covert* systems. For example, the face trait can be more easily used in covert recognition systems with respect to the fingerprint trait. Covert systems present more privacy risks than overt systems.

3. The third feature evaluates how much biometric traits can be considered as *physiological or behavioral*. Not all the biometric traits can be considered as completely physiological or behavioral. The face trait, for example, can be considered as physiological but can be modified by the user's behaviors (expressions, make up, etc.). Behavioral traits can be considered as more privacy compliant because they can be modified by the users and are less permanent then physiological traits.

4. The forth feature is the *database compatibility* and is related to two points: the technology interoperability between systems based on different databases, and the presence of numerous and/or large biometric databases. An example of trait with high

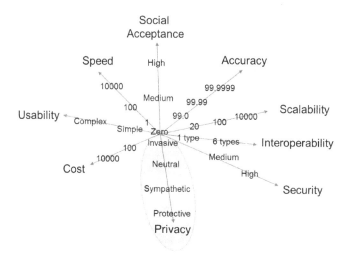

Fig. 2. Evaluative aspects of biometric systems

database interoperability is the fingerprint since there are many large databases containing standardized templates related to this trait. Traits characterized by a lower technology interoperability can be considered as more privacy compliant.

Performing a weighted mean of these features, it is possible to classify the overall risk level related to the technologies based on a specific biometric trait. Examples of traits that present a high risk level are the face and fingerprint. A medium risk can be assigned to the iris and retina, and traits characterized by low risks for the privacy are the hand, voice, keystroke, and signature.

Considering the different characteristics of the traits and application contexts, the development and deployment of biometric systems requires the analysis of at least nine different aspects: cost, usability, speed, social acceptance, accuracy, scalability, interoperability, security, and privacy. Different biometric technologies can provide good performances in one or more of these aspects. The choice of the adopted technology should be done by considering the most import characteristics for the evaluated application. As shown in Fig. 2, the nine main evaluative aspects can be quantized and plotted in a nine-dimensional space (e.g., in a spider diagram), where a specific application is represented by a point in this space.

Considering the privacy aspect, it is possible to define four different classes: protective, sympathetic, neutral, invasive [32]:

1. *Privacy-protective applications* use biometrics in order to protect personal information that might otherwise be compromised. In this case, the use of biometric recognition techniques provide a mean for an individual to establish a trusted identity, and permits to limit the accesses to sensible data. Examples of privacy-protective applications are systems for the enterprise security and accountholder verification:
2. *Privacy-sympathetic applications* are designed to protect the biometric data from unauthorized access and usage. All the elements of these applications are designed

considering privacy protection techniques. Most of the current applications can incorporate privacy-sympathetic elements.

3. *Privacy-neutral applications* use biometrics without considering privacy aspects. In these applications, the privacy impact is usually slight. Examples of privacy-neutral applications are some access control technologies and authentication systems for electronic devices (personal computers, mobile phones, etc.).

4. A *Privacy-invasive applications* permit the use of personal data in a fashion that is contrary to privacy principles. Applications that use biometrics without any knowledge or explicit consent of the individuals and systems that use biometric data for undisclosed purposes or beyond the initial scope appertain to this class. Surveillance applications and some national ID services can be considered as privacy-invasive.

In order to design privacy-sympathetic and privacy-protective systems, it is necessary to follow a set of guidelines [32]. These guidelines are related to: scope and capabilities of the system; user control of personal data; disclosure, auditing and accountability of the biometric system; data protection techniques:

1. The *scope and capabilities* of the system should be declared to the users and should not be extended during the life of the system. Biometric data should also be deleted from the database after a period of time known by the users. The storage of biometric data is particularly critical. In order to protect the privacy of the individuals, in fact, it is necessary to store only the minimum quantity of information necessary to perform the biometric recognition. For this reason, no other data should be saved and the system should store only biometric templates deleting raw data (images, signals, and frame sequences) as soon as possible. Moreover, no other personal data should be integrated into the biometric template biometric templates should not be used as unique identifiers.

2. The user should have the *control* of the biometric data. The use of the biometric system should be voluntary. The user should also have the possibilities to be unrolled and to change or modify her data. Users should also be enrolled with some degrees of anonymity.

3. A *disclosure* regarding the biometric system should be provided. This document should regard the system purpose, enrollment modalities, matching modalities, optional or mandatory use of the biometric recognition, individuals who are responsible for the system, the data protection system. In fact, it is important to let users know when the biometric system is used, especially when enrolment and verification or identification phases are carried on. Each operator should also be made *accountable* in order to detect possible errors or misuses. Moreover, the owner of the biometric system and the operators should be to provide a clear and effective process of *auditing* when an institution or a third party entity need to perform a critical review of all the modules which compose the biometric system.

4. The system should also provide mechanisms for the *protection* of all the steps performed by the biometric system from possible attacks. Aspects that should be considered are: use of encryption primitives, adoption of private networks, design and management of algorithms and infrastructures based on the state of the art best practices, placement of the biometric system in a secure and controlled area. These

aspects should be maintained throughout the life cycle of the of the system and the results of every performed recognition recognitions should also be protected. Another important practice is to limit the access to the biometric data to a defined number of operators. Template protection techniques should also be adopted in order to improve the user acceptance of the system and to overcame legal issues related to the respect of privacy protection laws that are currently ruling in several countries.

3 Technologies for Biometric Privacy

In the literature, there are many different methods for the protection of biometric templates. An ideal biometric template protection method should satisfy four properties [24,25]:

1. *diversity:* the secure template must not allow cross-matching across databases;
2. *revocability:* compromised template can be revoked;
3. *security:* the estimation of the plain template from the secure template must be computationally hard;
4. *performance:* the accuracy of the biometric system must not be degraded by the biometric template protection method.

These four proprieties cannot be guaranteed by encrypting the templates with standard methods (e.g. RSA, AES, etc.). In fact, using these methods, the intraclass variability (biometric data captured from the same biometric trait look different from one another) does not allow to perform the matching in the encrypted domain. Therefore, it is necessary to decrypt the templates during every recognition attempt. This approach is not secure and it is necessary to adopt methods designed for the protection of biometric data.

In the literature, most of the biometric template protection methods are based on two different classes of techniques: cancelable biometrics, and biometric cryptosystems [25,45]. Recent researches also proposed other approaches based on cryptographically secure methods [11].

3.1 Cancelable Biometrics

Cancelable biometrics are based on intentional, repeatable distortions of biometric data. The used transformations permit to perform comparisons of biometric templates in the transformed domain [42]. During the enrollment phase, the biometric data T is modified by applying a transformation function F with parameters K obtained by a random key or a password. The transformed template $F(T, K)$ is then stored in the database. The authentication step applies the same transformation to the query data Q and directly matches the transformed templates $F(Q, K)$ and $F(T, K)$. Fig. 3 schematizes the described process.

The main advantage of this technique is that, if a transformed template is compromised, cancelable biometrics permit to easily substitute the stored transformed template by changing the transformation parameters. The design of the transformation functions

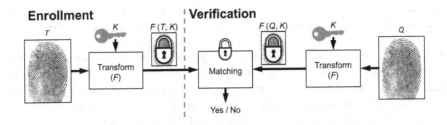

Fig. 3. Cancelable biometrics: enrollment and verification

is particularly critical because it is necessary to adopt functions that are robust to intra-class variations in order to do not reduce the accuracy of the biometric system. Another aspect that should be considered is that the correlation of transformed templates should not reveal information about the transformation function. Transformation functions can be applied to biometric samples (e.g. face images [2]), processed signals (e.g. the iris pattern [12]) or templates (e.g. features extracted from a face image [53]). It is possible to distinguish two different classes of methods: biometric salting, non-invertible transforms.

Usually, systems based on the biometric salting transform features using an invertible function defined by a user-specific key or password. Considering that the used transformation is invertible, the password must be securely stored by the user and presented during each authentication. The principal advantage of the biometric salting is that it is possible to use multiple templates for the same biometric trait because the keys are specified by the users. An important limitation of methods based on keys or passwords is that they are not usable in identification systems. Moreover, if the key is known, it is possible to obtain the original template. In the literature, one of the most used methods based on the biometric salting is the BioHashing [2,54,39]. This method is designed for the fingerprint trait and is divisible in two steps [27]: an invariant and discriminative transform of the biometric data, with a moderate degree offset tolerance; a discretization of the data. There are also methods designed for face recognition systems. One of these methods uses the Fisher discriminant analysis and then performs a transformation of the obtained vectors by using a randomly selected set of orthogonal directions [53]. Differently, the method proposed in [49] is based on minimum average correlation energy filters. Salting methods can also be applied to different biometric traits (e.g. iris [12], palmprint, and dynamic handwriting [36]).

In the literature, many methods secure the templates by using non-invertible transformation functions. Non-invertible transformation refers to a one-way function that is computable in polynomial time and hard to invert. The main advantage of this class of methods is that the protection of the plain biometric template is more secure than the one offered by the methods appertaining to the salting class. In fact, if the key and/or the transformed template are known, the estimation of the plain template is a computationally hard task (considering a brute force attack). Another advantage of these methods is that diversity and revocability can be achieved by using different transformation functions. The main problem is that it is difficult to design transformation functions that satisfy both the discriminability and the non-invertibility. For example, a study on the measurement of the real non-invertibility of methods based on the fingerprint is presented in [37]. Another important aspect is that the transformation function depends on the biometric features to be used in a specific application. Moreover, similarly to the biometric salting, the adoption of keys obtained by passwords or tokens does not permit to use methods based on non-invertible transformation functions in identification systems. In the literature, there are methods based on non-invertible transformation functions designed for different biometric traits. For example, fingerprint [28], face [56,55], and signature [35]. A general schema is proposed in [42] and is based on a non-invertible function designed to transform a point pattern by using high order polynomials. This method can be used in fingerprint based on minutiae features, and voice recognition systems. Also the approach proposed in [43] is designed for fingerprint recognition systems and proposes three different functions (Cartesian, Polar, and functional) in order to transform minutiae templates. A different schema called Biotope is proposed in [6,7]. This schema transforms the original biometric data by using cryptographic primitives and supports a robust distance metric in order to perform the matching. The approach supports both transforms that are public-key cryptographically invertible and/or using cryptographic one-way functions (such as MD5). The Biotope schema can be applied to different biometric traits, such as face [6] and fingerprint [7].

3.2   Biometric Cryptosystems

Biometric cryptosystems was originally designed in order to secure cryptographic keys by using biometric information or to directly compute cryptographic keys from biometric data [25]. Nowadays, these techniques are also used for the privacy protection of biometric templates. Biometric cryptosystems store public data regarding the biometric trait, called helper data. During the authentication process, the helper data is used in order to extract a cryptographic key from the biometric query sample. The matching step checks the validity of the obtained key in order to verify the identity. It is possible to divide the biometric cryptosystems in two different classes: key-binding biometric cryptosystem, and key-generating biometric cryptosystem.

Key-binding biometric cryptosystems store helper data by biding the template with a chosen cryptographic key. The binding process obtains a helper data considerable as a single entity that embeds both the key and the template without revealing information about them. In fact, it is computationally hard to estimate the key or the template without knowing the user's biometric data. The authentication is performed by using the query template in order to retrieve the cryptographic key from the helper data. Usually, this task is based on error correction algorithms. If the obtained key corresponds to the correct cryptographic key, the result of the authentication is a match value. Fig. 4 shows a general schema of the key-binding biometric cryptosystem. This class of methods has two main advantages. First, the helper data does not reveal much information about the key or the biometric data. Moreover, this approach is tolerant to intra-user variations. The main limitation consists in the degradation of the accuracy of the biometric system caused by the substitution of the original matching algorithms with error correction schemes. Moreover, these methods do not guarantee diversity and revocability. The firstly proposed key-binding biometric cryptosystems based on fingerprints are Mytec1 and Mytec2 [40], which are based on the correlation between filter functions

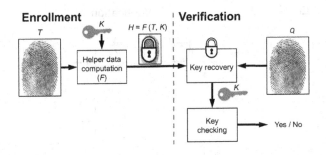

Fig. 4. Key-binding biometric cryptosystem: enrollment and verification

and the biometric images. Another well-known approach in the literature is the fuzzy commitment scheme [30]. This approach combines error correcting codes algorithms and cryptography techniques in order to achieve a cryptographic primitive called fuzzy commitment. During the enrollment, a biometric template x composed by a fixed length feature vector and a codeword w of an error correction schema C are bound. The helper data (fuzzy commitment) consists in $x - w$ and $h(w)$, where h is a hash function. The biometric matching tries to reconstruct w starting from a biometric query x'. First, the stored value $x - w$ is subtracted from x', obtaining $w' = w + \delta$, where $w' = x' - x$. If the value w is obtained by applying the error correction schema C to w', the result of the matching step is positive. The fuzzy vault [29] approach uses a set A to lock a secret key k, yielding a vault V_A. If the key k is reconstructed by using a set B that is sufficiently similar to A, the vault V_A is unlocked. This approach is based on polynomial encoding and error correction algorithms. Examples of other approaches appertaining to this class are the shielding functions [21] and distributed source coding [16]. In the literature, there are methods based on different biometric traits. For example, face [22], fingerprint [38], iris [31], and signature [33].

Key generating biometric cryptosystems compute a cryptographic key directly from the biometric data. The recognition process performed by biometric systems based on key generating biometric cryptosystems is similar to the one executed by using key-binding biometric cryptosystems but do not requires external keys. The schema of this process is shown in Fig. 5. The main advantage of these methods is that the obtained cryptographic keys can be used in many applications. However, an important problem is that it is difficult to generate keys with high stability and entropy [23,9]. Two well-known approaches are the secure sketch and fuzzy extractor [15]. Secure sketches solve the problem of error tolerance, enabling the computation of a public key P from a biometric reading r, such as from another reading r' sufficiently close to r it is possible to reconstruct the original one. Fuzzy extractors address the problem of non-uniformity by associating a random uniform string R to the public string P still keeping all the properties of secure sketches. Indeed, fuzzy extractors can be built out of secure sketches and enable to recovering of the secret uniform random string R, from the knowledge of the public string P and a reading r' sufficiently close to r. A syndrome-based key-generating scheme called PinSketch is presented in [15]. Similarly to the fuzzy vault, this method is based on polynomial interpolation. Compared with the fuzzy vault, the

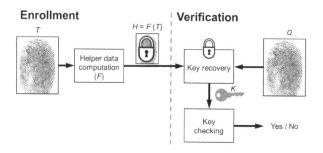

Fig. 5. Key generating biometric cryptosystem: enrollment and verification

PinSketch scheme reduces the computational time, and length of the public key. During the enrollment phase, a syndrome based on polynomial interpolation is computed and stored as helper data. During the recognition phase, an error vector is computed from the query biometric sample and the helper data to recover the enrolled biometric. An approach based on multiple biometric traits is presented in [13]. This method is based on the fuzzy commitment scheme. During the enrollment phase, one biometric reading is xored with a random bit string obtained after a pseudo random permutation from the other biometric reading. Differently, during the verification phase, the process is inverted and the second biometric template is reconstructed in order to be used as preliminary check (by comparing the computed hash with the value stored into the identifier) and as input of the matching module. In the literature, there are also other types of key-binding biometric cryptosystem [52,34].

3.3   Cryptographically Secure Methods

The recognition accuracy of systems based on cancelable biometrics can be decreased by the applied transformation functions. Similarly, in biometric cryptosystems it is not possible to always adopt the best matching functions used in the plain domain and, as a consequence, the accuracy can be worsened. As a solution to this problem, in the literature there are template protection techniques specifically designed with the aim to perform the biometric recognition without applying transformations of the biometric data and without modifying the matching functions designed for the adopted templates. These methods can directly perform the matching using the encrypted data and are usually based on homomorphic cryptosystems.

In homomorphic cryptosystems, given a set M (resp., C) of the plaintexts (resp., ciphertexts), for any given encryption key k the encryption function E satisfies

$$\forall m_1, m_2 \in M, \quad E\left(m_1 \odot_M m_2\right) \leftarrow E\left(m_1\right) \odot_C E\left(m_2\right)$$

for some operators $\odot_M$ in M and $\odot_C$ in C, where $\leftarrow$ means "can be directly computed from", that is, without any intermediate decryption [20].

The main advantage of these systems is that the accuracy obtained by using the transformed templates is very similar to the accuracy obtained by using the plain data. Usually, a decreasing of the performance can be caused by an excessive quantization or

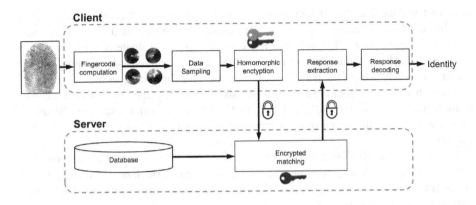

Fig. 6. Example of a cryptographically secure method based on fingerprints. The biometric matching algorithm is processed in the encripted domain exploiting a homomorphic cryptosystem.

data reduction [5]. The main disadvantage is that it is difficult to adopt homomorphic cryptosystems in biometric systems that require complex matching functions. Homomorphic cryptosystems are also computationally expensive.

A cryptographically secure method designed for distributed architectures is proposed in [4,3]. This method is based on the fingerprint biometric trait and uses a feature representation called Fingercode [26], which consists in a set of numeric values obtained by applying Gabor filters with different orientations to the fingerprint image. The cryptographic protocol strongly relies on the notion of additively homomorphic encryption and uses two encryption schemes: the Paillier's encryption scheme [41] and a variant of the El Gamal encryption scheme [17] ported on Elliptic Curves. On the client side, the template is computed, quantized and encrypted using the public-key of the client. The server computes the match score in the encrypted domain by exploiting the homomorphic properties of the adopted cryptosystem. The match score consists in the quadratic Euclidean distance between the evaluated templates. During the final task of the recognition process, the server interacts with the client in order to select, in the ciphertext domain, the enrolled identities with the related distances that are below a fixed threshold. Fig. 6 shows the schema of this method.

A similar approach that use the homomorphic encryption is presented in [18,48] and is designed for face recognition systems. In the literature, there are also approaches based on homomorphic encryption methods and designed for biometric systems that compute the match score as the Hamming distance between feature vectors (e.g. Iriscode [14]): the system in [51] is based on the Blum-Goldwasser cryptosystem, the system in [10] on the Goldwasser-Micali scheme, the system in [8] on the method on homomorphic properties of Goldwasser-Micali and Paillier cryptosystems, the system in [50] on the ElGamal scheme and Garbled Circuits.

4   Conclusions

Relevant privacy and security aspects have to be considered during the design phase and the deployment of biometric systems in order to prevent possible thefts and misuses of biometric data. The use of biometric data, in fact, presents different privacy risks. Usually, the risks perceived by the users are different from the real risks related to a biometric application. The perceived risks are difficult to evaluate because they are different for each individual. In general, the perceived risks are related to identity thefts and to improperly uses of the personal data (for example, for tracing all the activities of the individuals or for operating proscription lists). Differently, the real risks are related to the applicative context and are determined by different factors, such as the used storage techniques, the owner of the system, the used biometric traits, and other design choices.

In order to properly design a privacy-protective biometric system, it is necessary to follow specific guidelines regarding the treatment of biometric data. These guidelines consider the storage modalities, rights of the users, responsibilities of the operators, and data protection techniques.

In the literature, there are different methods for the protection of biometric data. Most of these methods are designed for the protection of the biometric templates, which are abstract representations of the distinctive features extracted from the biometric samples (signals, images or frame sequences). Template protection methods permit to perform the identity comparison by using protected representations of the biometric templates, and can be divided in three different classes: cancelable biometrics (based on transformations of the templates), biometric cryptosystems (based on cryptographic algorithms that perform the recognition by comparing cryptographic keys), and cryptographically secure methods (based on cryptographic techniques that permits to perform a set of operations without converting the data in the plain domain). The use of these methods can effectively increase the security of the biometric systems, but can reduce the obtained performances in terms of accuracy and computational time. The transformation functions used by cancelable biometrics, in fact, can decrease the accuracy of the recognition system. Similarly, in biometric cryptosystems, it is not possible to always adopt the best matching functions used in the plain domain and, as a consequence, the accuracy can be worsened. Cryptographically secure methods are designed to solve these problems, but are usually based on computationally expansive algorithms and can require a data reduction step in order to increase the speed of the recognition process.

References

1. International Biometrics Group, http://www.ibgweb.com
2. Cancellable biometrics and annotations on biohash. Pattern Recognition 41(6), 2034–2044 (2008)
3. Barni, M., Bianchi, T., Catalano, D., Raimondo, M.D., Donida Labati, R., Failla, P., Fiore, D., Lazzeretti, R., Piuri, V., Scotti, F., Piva, A.: A privacy-compliant fingerprint recognition system based on homomorphic encryption and fingercode templates. In: IEEE Fourth International Conference on Biometrics: Theory, Applications and Systems (BTAS) (September 2010)
4. Barni, M., Bianchi, T., Catalano, D., Raimondo, M.D., Labati, R.D., Failla, P., Fiore, D., Lazzeretti, R., Piuri, V., Scotti, F., Piva, A.: Privacy-preserving fingercode authentication. In: 12th ACM Multimedia and Security Workshop (2010)

5. Bianchi, T., Turchi, S., Piva, A., Donida Labati, R., Piuri, V., Scotti, F.: Implementing fingercode-based identity matching in the encrypted domain. In: IEEE Workshop on Biometric Measurements and Systems for Security and Medical Applications (BIOMS), pp. 15–21 (September 2010)
6. Boult, T.: Robust distance measures for face-recognition supporting revocable biometric tokens. In: International Conference on Automatic Face and Gesture Recognition, pp. 560–566 (April 2006)
7. Boult, T., Schdrer, W., Woodworth, R.: Revocable fingerprint biotokens: Accuracy and security analysis. In: IEEE Conference on Computer Vision and Pattern Recognition (CVPR), pp. 1–8 (June 2007)
8. Bringer, J., Chabanne, H.: An Authentication Protocol with Encrypted Biometric Data. In: Vaudenay, S. (ed.) AFRICACRYPT 2008. LNCS, vol. 5023, pp. 109–124. Springer, Heidelberg (2008)
9. Bringer, J., Chabanne, H., Cohen, G., Kindarji, B., Zemor, G.: Theoretical and practical boundaries of binary secure sketches. IEEE Transactions on Information Forensics and Security 3(4), 673–683 (2008)
10. Bringer, J., Chabanne, H., Izabachène, M., Pointcheval, D., Tang, Q., Zimmer, S.: An Application of the Goldwasser-Micali Cryptosystem to Biometric Authentication. In: Pieprzyk, J., Ghodosi, H., Dawson, E. (eds.) ACISP 2007. LNCS, vol. 4586, pp. 96–106. Springer, Heidelberg (2007)
11. Cavoukian, A., Stoianov, A.: Biometric encryption. In: Encyclopedia of Cryptography and Security, 2nd edn., pp. 90–98 (2011)
12. Chin, C.S., Jin, A.T.B., Ling, D.N.C.: High security iris verification system based on random secret integration. Computer Vision and Image Understanding 102, 169–177 (2006)
13. Cimato, S., Gamassi, M., Piuri, V., Sassi, R., Cimato, F.S., Scotti, F.: A biometric verification system addressing privacy concerns. In: International Conference on Computational Intelligence and Security, pp. 594–598 (December 2007)
14. Daugman, J.: How iris recognition works. In: Proceedings of the International Conference on Image Processing, vol. 1, pp. 33–36 (2002)
15. Dodis, Y., Ostrovsky, R., Reyzin, L., Smith, A.: Fuzzy extractors: How to generate strong keys from biometrics and other noisy data. SIAM Journal on Computing 38(1), 97–139 (2008)
16. Draper, S., Khisti, A., Martinian, E., Vetro, A., Yedidia, J.: Using distributed source coding to secure fingerprint biometrics. In: IEEE International Conference on Acoustics, Speech and Signal Processing, vol. 2, pp. 29–132 (April 2007)
17. El Gamal, T.: A Public Key Cryptosystem and a Signature Scheme Based on Discrete Logarithms. In: Blakely, G.R., Chaum, D. (eds.) CRYPTO 1984. LNCS, vol. 196, pp. 10–18. Springer, Heidelberg (1985)
18. Erkin, Z., Franz, M., Guajardo, J., Katzenbeisser, S., Lagendijk, I., Toft, T.: Privacy-Preserving Face Recognition. In: Goldberg, I., Atallah, M.J. (eds.) PETS 2009. LNCS, vol. 5672, pp. 235–253. Springer, Heidelberg (2009)
19. Faundez-Zanuy, M.: On the vulnerability of biometric security systems. IEEE Aerospace and Electronic Systems Magazine 19(6), 3–8 (2004)
20. Fontaine, C., Galand, F.: A survey of homomorphic encryption for nonspecialists. EURASIP Journal on Information Security, 1–15 (2007)
21. Huixian, L., Man, W., Liaojun, P., Weidong, Z.: Key binding based on biometric shielding functions. In: International Conference on Information Assurance and Security, vol. 1, pp. 19–22 (August 2009)
22. Ignatenko, T., Willems, F.: Information leakage in fuzzy commitment schemes. IEEE Transactions on Information Forensics and Security 5(2), 337–348 (2010)

23. Ignatenko, T., Willems, F.: Information leakage in fuzzy commitment schemes. IEEE Transactions on Information Forensics and Security 5(2), 337–348 (2010)
24. Jain, A.K., Maltoni, D.: Handbook of Fingerprint Recognition. Springer-Verlag New York, Inc., Secaucus (2003)
25. Jain, A.K., Nandakumar, K., Nagar, A.: Biometric template security. EURASIP Journal on Advances in Signal Processing, 1–17 (2008)
26. Jain, A.K., Prabhakar, S., Hong, L., Pankanti, S.: Filterbank-based fingerprint matching. IEEE Transactions on Image Processing 9, 846–859 (2000)
27. Jin, A.T.B., Ling, D.N.C., Goh, A.: Biohashing: two factor authentication featuring fingerprint data and tokenised random number. Pattern Recognition 37(11), 2245–2255 (2004)
28. Jin, Z., Teoh, A., Ong, T.S., Tee, C.: Generating revocable fingerprint template using minutiae pair representation. In: International Conference on Education Technology and Computer, vol. 5 (June 2010)
29. Juels, A., Sudan, M.: A fuzzy vault scheme. In: IEEE International Symposium on Information Theory, p. 408 (2002)
30. Juels, A., Wattenberg, M.: A fuzzy commitment scheme. In: Sixth ACM Conference on Computer and Communications Security, pp. 28–36 (1999)
31. Lee, Y.J., Park, K.R., Lee, S.J., Bae, K., Kim, J.: A new method for generating an invariant iris private key based on the fuzzy vault system. IEEE Transactions on Systems, Man, and Cybernetics, Part B: Cybernetics 38(5), 1302–1313 (2008)
32. LLC International Biometric Group: Bioprivacy initiative (2003), http://www.bioprivacy.org/
33. Maiorana, E., Campisi, P.: Fuzzy commitment for function based signature template protection. IEEE Signal Processing Letters 17(3), 249–252 (2010)
34. Maiorana, E., Campisi, P.: Fuzzy commitment for function based signature template protection. IEEE Signal Processing Letters 17(3), 249–252 (2010)
35. Maiorana, E., Campisi, P., Fierrez, J., Ortega-Garcia, J., Neri, A.: Cancelable templates for sequence-based biometrics with application to on-line signature recognition. IEEE Transaction on Systems, Man and Cybernetic, Part A: Systems and Humans 40(3), 525–538 (2010)
36. Makrushin, A., Scheidat, T., Vielhauer, C.: Towards robust biohash generation for dynamic handwriting using feature selection. In: International Conference on Digital Signal Processing, pp. 1–6 (July 2011)
37. Nagar, A., Jain, A.: On the security of non-invertible fingerprint template transforms. In: First IEEE International Workshop on Information Forensics and Security (WIFS), pp. 81–85 (2009)
38. Nandakumar, K., Jain, A., Pankanti, S.: Fingerprint-based fuzzy vault: Implementation and performance. IEEE Transactions on Information Forensics and Security 2(4), 744–757 (2007)
39. Nanni, L., Lumini, A.: Empirical tests on biohashing. Neurocomputing 69, 2390–2395 (2006)
40. Nichols, R.K.: Icsa Guide to Cryptography. McGraw-Hill Professional (1998)
41. Paillier, P.: Public-Key Cryptosystems Based on Composite Degree Residuosity Classes. In: Stern, J. (ed.) EUROCRYPT 1999. LNCS, vol. 1592, pp. 223–238. Springer, Heidelberg (1999)
42. Ratha, N.K., Connell, J.H., Bolle, R.M.: Enhancing security and privacy in biometrics-based authentication systems. IBM Systems Journal 40(3), 614–634 (2001)
43. Ratha, N.K., Chikkerur, S., Connell, J.H., Bolle, R.M.: Generating cancelable fingerprint templates. IEEE Transaction on Pattern Analysis and Machine Intelligence 29(4), 561–572 (2007)

44. Ratha, N.K., Connell, J.H., Bolle, R.M.: An Analysis of Minutiae Matching Strength. In: Bigun, J., Smeraldi, F. (eds.) AVBPA 2001. LNCS, vol. 2091, pp. 223–228. Springer, Heidelberg (2001)
45. Rathgeb, C., Uhl, A.: A survey on biometric cryptosystems and cancelable biometrics. EURASIP Journal on Information Security (1) (2011)
46. RNCOS (ed.): Electronics Security: Global Biometric Forecast to 2012 (2010)
47. Sabena, F., Dehghantanha, A., Seddon, A.: A review of vulnerabilities in identity management using biometrics. In: Second International Conference on Future Networks (CFN), pp. 42–49 (January 2010)
48. Sadeghi, A., Schneider, T., Wehrenberg, I.: Efficient Privacy-Preserving Face Recognition. In: Lee, D., Hong, S. (eds.) ICISC 2009. LNCS, vol. 5984, pp. 229–244. Springer, Heidelberg (2010)
49. Savvides, M., Vijaya Kumar, B., Khosla, P.: Cancelable biometric filters for face recognition. In: International Conference on Pattern Recognition, vol. 3, pp. 922–925 (August 2004)
50. Schoenmakers, B., Tuyls, P.: Computationally Secure Authentication with Noisy Data, pp. 141–149. Springer, Heidelberg (2007)
51. Stoianov, A.: Cryptographically secure biometrics. In: Kumar, B.V.K.V., Prabhakar, S., Ross, A.A. (eds.) Biometric Technology for Human Identification VII, vol. 7667, p. 76670C. SPIE (2010)
52. Sutcu, Y., Li, Q., Memon, N.: Protecting biometric templates with sketch: Theory and practice. IEEE Transactions on Information Forensics and Security 2(3), 503–512 (2007)
53. Teoh, A., Goh, A., Ngo, D.: Random multispace quantization as an analytic mechanism for biohashing of biometric and random identity inputs. IEEE Transactions on Pattern Analysis and Machine Intelligence 28(12), 1892–1901 (2006)
54. Teoh, A., Jin, B., Connie, T., Ngo, D., Ling, C.: Remarks on biohash and its mathematical foundation. Information Processing Letters 100, 145–150 (2006)
55. Wang, Y., Hatzinakos, D.: On random transformations for changeable face verification. IEEE Transaction on Systems, Man and Cybernetic, Part B: Cybernetics 41(3), 840–854 (2011)
56. Wang, Y., Plataniotis, K.N.: An analysis of random projection for changeable and privacy-preserving biometric verification. IEEE Transaction on Systems, Man and Cybernetic, Part B: Cybernetics 40, 1280–1293 (2010)

Face Recognition in Uncontrolled Environments, Experiments in an Airport

Cristina Conde, Isaac Martin de Diego, and Enrique Cabello

Universidad Rey Juan Carlos, C/ Tulipan s/n, 28933 Mostoles, Spain
{cristina.conde,isaac.martin,enrique.cabello}@urjc.es

Abstract. This paper presents and an evaluation of results obtained from a face recognition system in a real uncontrolled localization. The involved infrastructure is Barajas Airport (the international airport in Madrid, Spain). The use of this infrastructure during normal operation hours has imposed some constrains. It was not allowed to change or to add new cameras and passengers should not be disturbed by any means. Passengers should not be aware of the presence of the system, so no request should be done to change their normal behavior. To fulfill these requirements, three video surveillance cameras were selected: two in the corridor areas and one in a control point. Images were acquired and processed with illumination changes, several quality levels, collaborative and non-collaborative subjects and during three weeks. The influence of data compression method and classificator has been detailed in the paper. Three scenarios were simulated: first one is a normal operational mode, second one is a high security mode and last one is a friendly or soft-recognition mode. Four data compression methods were considered in the paper: 1dpca (1d principal components analysis), 2dpca (2d principal components analysis), 2dlda (2d linear discriminant analysis) and csa (coupled subspace analysis). Csa has obtained the best performance. For classificatory purpoises, svm (support vector machines) were selected with excellent results. The overall analysis shows that the approach taken will lead to excellent results given the hard conditions of a real scenario such an airport.

Keywords: Face recognition, Uncontrolled environment and airport.

1 Introduction

In modern societies we are under continuous video surveillance, sometimes we are aware of it and we modify our normal behavior but others not. Cameras are placed in public locations to help in vandalism detection (for example in a parking area) or in indoor locations like banks for instance. An airport is a public space in which a subject knows that are under some kind of video surveillance. The subject is not worried by the fact that the airport is completely full of cameras. The behavior of the subject do not change due to the presence of such cameras, since their primary focus is not to stay there but to move to or from an airplane as soon as possible. In this task the airport is just seen as the connection building in which spend the minimum time. All

M.S. Obaidat, J.L. Sevillano, and J. Filipe (Eds.): ICETE 2011, CCIS 314, pp. 20–32, 2012.
© Springer-Verlag Berlin Heidelberg 2012

airports have cameras in almost all halls and corridors, with the main focus in video surveillance and this infrastructure is usually managed by the security personnel.

The usual way to perform a face verification system in an airport is to add some cameras, specifically devoted to this task. One of the requirements of this paper was not to modify airport infrastructure. And a different approach was considered. No new cameras were added and existing video surveillance cameras were used to perform face recognition in the uncontrolled environment. Therefore the performance of these cameras was evaluated for a face verification task.

Barajas airport (the international airport in Madrid, Spain) was selected to obtain data. During three weeks in September 2008, interviews with Spanish police department (Guardia Civil) and with airport management (AENA) were conduced to select the cameras and to design most useful experiments. As a pilot study one constraint was that passengers were not disturbed. This requirement was fulfilled with the selection of face verification over other technologies (like fingerprint or iris). Even more, technology selected is not invasive and subjects could be not collaborative.

The paper is divided in the following parts: in section 2 a short state of the art is presented, section 3 is devoted to the experiment description, the face verification system is explained in section 4, section 5 will show results and discussions and section 6 conclude. The acknowledgements and references will end the paper.

2   State of the Art

Person identification and recognition in uncontrolled environments is one of the most significant fields of research in the recent years. Few results of face verification in open public spaces have been presented in the literature. Face verification is performed usually in lab conditions or near-lab conditions, but not in uncontrolled situations. In this environment the most usual characterization of a subject have been done based on gait [1]; [2];[3]. In face recognition and verification a significant advance has been done in the last years. In the FRGC competition [4] one of the testing scenarios was uncontrolled environments. Uncontrolled environments could correspond to outdoor or indoor situations but in all cases, subject is collaborative and is aware that the face is acquired for verification purpoises.

Face recognition is one of the three biometrics modalities chosen by ICAO (the International Civil Aviation Organization) for inclusion in machine-readable travel documentation [21]. Face recognition applications in airports have been mainly focused in Automatic Border Checks (ABC) systems [5]; [6]. Face, fingerprint or iris is matched against stored data in these systems. In the case of face, usual situation is an ABC point in which camera is closed to the subject, illumination is controlled and subject is collaborative. The usual match is live photo against passport photo. Commercial systems are used in this tasks and only commercial information is available, without the scientific details needed to be compared and reported.

In automatic video surveillance systems [7], face recognition has received little interest. When used, it is added to a bag of characteristics in the so-called soft-biometrics recognition [8]; [9]. In systems in which face recognition is fussed with gait recognition [11]; [12]; [13], the usual hardware considered is two cameras or a camera in which zoom is changed. Other requirements could include calibrated cameras [14];

[15] that are not easy to implement in crowded spaces or in huge number. The use of camera arrays are also considered in robust systems to pose and partial occlusion of subjects such [16]; [17]; [18]. In multicamera systems, face recognition is also combined with tracking frameworks [19]; [20]. Requirements of these systems may include overlapping cameras or at least a clear view of subjects during the tracking stage.

There are some experiments reported in scientific literature taking place in airports, like SCface database [10] but new infrastructure is considered and only high quality images are selected, so more than an uncontrolled system is likely to an access control.

3   Experiment Description

The main goal was focused in studying the viability of a face recognition system in an uncontrolled environment such as an airport. There were several restrictions imposed by the security officer: no new sensors or cameras could be added (so only the presented infrastructure in the airport could be used), and under no circumstances the movement of the passengers could be altered. In this scenario cameras are working in stressed conditions: working 24/7, with high temperature variations, variable humidity and atmospheric conditions. In the airport, there are more than 2.000 cameras installed. Due to legislation requirements, images are stored during two weeks and then, deleted. To maintain a reasonable amount of stored data, cameras are working with a 640x480 pixels resolution and 4 frames per second. During small amounts of time, this resolution and frame rate can be increased, but stored data were used in the experiment.

The first task was the selection of the cameras between all available in airport to achieve the desired face recognition task. In an environment such as an airport, the number of cameras is huge. Some cameras were discarded because they were focused in places with few or even no persons present (like outside areas). In the indoor environment, the main objective of the cameras is video surveillance. These cameras try to show a complete vision of an area, not a closed vision of subjects. This will limit the number of cameras that can be considered. Since one of the requirements was that only existing infrastructure were considered, camera selection was on crucial step.

In an airport there are cameras of different image qualities. Some cameras are not placed in an optimum position, others has been degraded due to the used time. If only cameras with good image quality were considered, great part of the airport environment will be not considered. Also, ideal situation was the selection of cameras with good field of view. But is a usual situation that once a camera is placed; some elements could be added to the scenario (signals, illumination and information elements) that limits the field of view or generates light spots or high illumination contrasts. Therefore, to cover a normal operation situation, cameras of different qualities should be selected.

One interesting experiment that turned out very hard to achieve was the use of two different cameras to identify the same subject simultaneously. There are few areas in which two cameras overlap in a huge area in a way that allows a face verification process.

At the end, to cover a huge range of normal scenarios in an airport, three cameras were selected in three extreme situations.

First one was selected in a huge hostile environment. This is called "Corridor 1". Subjects are moving in a belt and there are a surveillance camera very degraded due to time. Corridor is scarcely illuminated. The subjects were moving in the foreground and the background is very illuminated. So face is very dark and few face details are visible. Fig 1 shows an image acquired with this camera.

Fig. 1. Image taken from Corridor 1

Second one is a similar condition than the previous one but in better conditions. Camera is placed focused a corridor with good illumination conditions and camera has enough resolution to acquire good images. This will be called "Corridor 2". One example of this camera is shown in Fig. 2.

Fig. 2. Image taken from Corridor 2

In these two situations subjects are developing normal behaviors, so occlusions due to mobile phones appear; high face rotation degrees are present.

Third one is a camera focused in an arc detector gate; this will be called "Control Point". Subjects usually cross the gate in almost frontal position, no occlusion is present and illumination is quite uniform. The main task in this situation was to find an existing camera in which face can be captured with enough quality to be processed. One image of the selected camera is presented in Fig. 3.

Fig. 3. Image taken from Control Point

In an airport, it can be required several security levels in different areas. There are restricted areas in which a strict control system is mandatory (high security level). There are other areas in which only registered passengers can access (normal situation) and the last case is the public area in which a friendly security system could be considered. To simulate these situations, the confusion matrix of the classificator was taken into account, see Table 1. From Table 1 it is possible to obtain the two parameters that represent the accuracy of the system. First one is the False Acceptance Rate (see Eq. 1) and second one is the False Rejection Rate (see Eq. 2). Both errors have associated different risk conditions and since both errors are related, increasing one of them will imply that the other one will decrease. These errors and the corresponding risk involved a cost for each situation. Therefore to describe a situation, we have to present the error rate, the risk and the error cost. There are two extreme and one normal situation that can be considered. First one is a high FAR which means that FRR will be low. In this case, few subjects are disturbed, but the cost present is that few criminals will be identified. This is a friendly system and it could be applied for instance in the case of VIP or preregistered passengers for marketing reasons or to obtain special benefits. Second one is a system in which FAR is low and therefore FRR is high. This system identifies correctly the suspicious, but the cost associate is that innocent citizens will be disturbed (probably they will be rejected frequently and has to start the process several times). This is a high security system, with a clear purpose of suspicious or criminal detection for example. The third situation is the normal one. In this system, the FAR is equal to the FRR; this is called the Equal Error Rate (EER) point. It is an intermediate situation in which criminals were identified but some citizens were disturbed.

Three scenarios were selected in this paper. First one is the normal situation in which the operational point for the classificator was the point in which the False Acceptance Rate (FAR) was equal to the False Rejection Rate (FRR), that is, the Equal Error Rate point. Second one was a friendly situation in which the FRR was maintained deliberately low, so FAR increases. The point in which FAR was five times higher than FRR was selected. Third one was a secure environment in which FAR was maintained low, so FRR increases. FRR was five times higher than FRR in the selected point.

Table 1. Confusion matrix of a classificator

		Predicted	
		Class A	Class B
Truth	Class A	True Negative (TN)	False Positive (FP)
	Class B	False Negative (FN)	True Positive (TP)

$$FAR = \frac{FP}{FP + TN} \qquad (1)$$

$$FRR = \frac{FN}{FN + TP} \qquad (2)$$

During all experiments legal regulations about data protection [22] were strictly followed.

4 Face Verification System

The face verification system is split in three parts: face detection and location, face representation and face verification. All these three processes are applied sequentially and are described in the following sections

4.1 Face Detection and Location

The face detection and location system is based in the well known Viola and Jones method [23]. The method allows the detection of faces in uncontrolled environments in a very efficient way.

The size of the faces varies from 43x43 to 76x76 pixels. Even the selected method can detect faces with low resolution, 43x43 pixels are a good resolution to perform face recognition tasks. An intermediate situation of 70x70 pixels were chosen to standardize face dimensions among the different cameras. In this stage the low level image processing is also considered, face image is equalized and converted to a gray-level image. Results obtained in the three uncontrolled environments are shown in Table 2.

Table 2. Face location percentage in unsupervised conditions

DataBase	Time considered	Number of detected subjects	Number of subjects in the scenes	Correct detection percentage
Control Point	20 min	34	34	100
Corridor 1	26 min	137	250	54
Corridor 2	20 min	158	238	66

Results show the well known characteristics of the method: in frontal or almost frontal situations the performance is quite well and in non-frontal situations or in the presence of occlusions the performance is degraded. As pointed before, "Corridor 1" has a light in the background, so the foreground is dark and faces are more difficult detected.

4.2   Face Representation

Once the face is detected, the next step is to represent the face in a compact way. Optimal characteristics selection for data representation is a broad field in pattern recognition research with many different approximations. Our implementation is a straight forward approximation. The huge number of cameras present in an airport will lead to high processing resources if algorithms selected are complex. Therefore only methods with low computing time could be selected. Face resolution considered is enough for verification if global methods are selected, local methods implies more processing resources and high quality images.

For low resolution images the traditional face representation methods (information reduction) requires that 2D face images are considered as 1D row vectors [24]. Other techniques have been developed for bidimensional data feature extraction like Two-Dimensional PCA (2DPCA) [25]; [26], Two-Dimensional LDA (2DLDA) [27]; [28] and Coupled Subspace Analysis (CSA) [29]. These methods are based on 2D matrices rather than 1D vector, preserving spatial information. As base line method Principal Component Analysis [30] has been used.

4.3   Face Verification

Support vector machines (SVM) is a method of learning and separating binary classes [31], it is superior in classification performance and is a widely used technique in pattern recognition and especially in face verification tasks [32]. SVM offers excellent results in 2-class problems. This classifier could be easily used in verification problems (recognizing one subject against rest). Linear kernels were considered and not special effort was done to optimize the kernel [33] or to increase the accuracy performing optimal parameter estimation.

5   Results and Discussion

As explained before, three experiments were performed: normal, friendly and high security situations. This situations were applied to the three cameras selected (Corridor 1, Corridor 2 and Control Point). Each experiment is analyzed in detail in this section. All results present are obtained applying the entire algorithm to the images of the video individually considered. Results could be better if some information is passed to one image to perform a fusion of information algorithm (even so simple such as a voting algorithm). Any of these improvements was considered, because the main objective was performance evaluation of the face verification system in such a complex real situation like an airport.

For each camera train and test sets were obtained. Both sets have no common images. Train set were done with the first elements of the video and test set were done with the last elements of the video. The algorithm were applied first to each camera, the train set were used to obtain projection matrices and to train the SVM classifier. Then test set were considered to obtain the Receiver Operating Characteristics (ROC) curve and the EER point. This test set was changed from the three cameras to obtain cross validation. All this results were individually reported.

5.1   Normal Situation

In this normal operation simulation, the desired operation point is the Equal Error Rate (EER). In this point, the FAR (False Acceptance Rate) and the FRR (False Rejection Rate) percentages have the same value. It could be said that the importance given to the FAR is the same than FRR. Results of the FAR are shown in Table 3.

Table 3. Equal Error Rate (Fals Accepntace Rate = False Rejection Rate) for the database

Train	Test	1dpca	2dpca	2dlda	csa
	Corridor 1	9,56	14,60	12,00	9,00
Corridor 1	Corridor 2	26,00	23,45	24,00	22,91
	Control Point	30,00	27,31	34,37	23,64
	Corridor 1	38,00	33,20	38,73	34,89
Corridor 2	Corridor 2	1,20	2,67	1,60	0,67
	Control Point	24,04	34,17	36,25	28,00
	Corridor 1	30,72	30,00	37,78	27,97
Control Point	Corridor 2	25,50	32,92	26,88	27,50
	Control Point	15,80	13,75	6,80	8,33

Train and test with data obtained from the same camera obtains best results than training with images from one camera and testing with the others. Train and test with Corridor2 obtains best results. It can be observed that for the nine cases (train-test) the best EER is achieved by the algorithm Coupled Subspace Analysis (CSA) in five situations, 1dpca in two cases and there are one situation for 2dpca and another one for 2dlda.

Figure 4 plots the ROC curve for all the algorithms when trained and tested with images of Corridor1. It can be shown that results from the different methods are in a short variation range. Images from this camera have low quality, and results are not very degraded even for this condition.

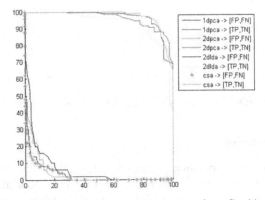

Fig. 4. ROC curve, train set and test set are from Corridor 1

Figure 5 shows the ROC curve when trained and tested with Corridor 2 images. Results achieved in this curve are similar to produced in lab conditions. The quality of this images is high and scene has good illumination conditions. Taking into account that system is not optimized and the methods selected are not high processing demand, this video surveillance camera is a good candidate to perform a face verification task.

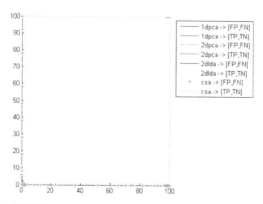

Fig. 5. ROC curve, train set and test set are from Corridor 2

Figure 6 shows results with images obtained in the Control Point, both for train and test. CSA and 2DPCA has a good performance, better than PCA and 2DLDA. In this camera, selection of the method is a critical step. If a face verification system should be considered here, it is advice that optimization phase could be required.

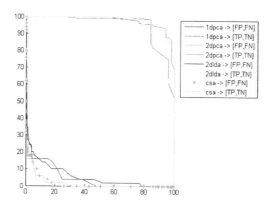

Fig. 6. ROC curve, train set and test set are from Control Point

5.2   Friendly Operation

In this situation, a friendly operation is simulated. In this case the desired False Acceptance Rate (FAR) will be five times higher than the False Rejection Rate (FRR). So, there will be few cases of rejection but the number of false acceptance will be higher. This could be a situation in which there is a previous control and the objective is to perform a soft check control near the plane, for example. The main requirement in this system is that almost no passenger will be disturbed. The cost associated with this soft verification procedure is that almost no suspicious will be identified. Table 4 shows the False Acceptance Rate percentage.

Table 4. FAR in a friendly situation. (FRR is five times smaller than FAR shown)

Train	Test	1dpca	2dpca	2dlda	csa
	Corridor 1	28,21	22,22	16,29	22,07
Corridor 1	Corridor2	70,00	50,00	50,43	57,73
	Control Point	47,85	52,50	63,28	49,22
	Corridor 1	75,34	67,75	64,18	65,42
Corridor 2	Corridor2	1,428	10,00	1,90	0,91
	Control Point	62,50	62,50	75,69	54,05
	Corridor 1	51,97	85,90	65,06	54,89
Control Point	Corridor2	75,00	62,50	100,0	76,35
	Control Point	24,47	30,40	13,33	16,15

In Table 4 it can be shown than training and testing with data acquired from the same camera obtains better results than training with one camera and testing with the others. It can be observed that the FAR has been increased over results present in Table 3, so there could be more "suspicious" that can pass our system without raising an alarm. FRR has lower values, so very scarcely one subject will be rejected and required to perform the identification procedure again. In this friendly situation case, training and testing with Corridor 2 images offers good results, acceptable as a face verification control access system.

5.3   High Security Operation

The last situation simulated is the use of the video surveillance cameras to simulate a high security environment. In this case FAR was selected to be five times lower than the FRR. The number of FRR is increased, and it will be more common the situation in which a subject is rejected and required to initiate again the face recognition procedure. The advantage gain is that almost all criminal persons will be identified. In other words, if this system is used for an access control, only registered subjects will be allowed to enter. Table 5 shows the False Acceptance Rate percentage in this situation.

Table 5 shows than training and testing with data acquired from the same camera obtains better results than training with one camera and testing with the others. It can be observed that the FAR has been decreased over results present in Table 3. FRR has higher values, so frequently one subject will be rejected and required to perform the identification procedure again. In this secure situation case, training and testing with Corridor 2 images offers results comparable to reported in lab conditions, even considering that images are acquired in uncontrolled environments.

Table 5. FAR in a secure system (FRR is five times higher than FAR shown)

Train	Test	1dpca	2dpca	2dlda	csa
Corridor 1	Corridor 1	3,38	5,53	5,11	3,14
	Corridor2	9,20	9,60	8,92	7,18
	Control Point	10,00	8,00	13,33	7,88
Corridor 2	Corridor 1	12,00	11,41	11,60	11,56
	Corridor2	0,66	1,59	0,67	0,28
	Control Point	7,76	15,44	10,43	8,41
Control Point	Corridor 1	9,88	13,50	12,31	8,65
	Corridor2	8,12	10,38	10,89	8,45
	Control Point	4,11	4,00	3,20	3,60

6   Conclusions

This paper presents an analysis results obtained from a face recognition system in a real uncontrolled localization. The involved infrastructure is Barajas Airport (the international airport in Madrid, Spain). The use of this infrastructure during normal operation hours has imposed some constrains. It was not allowed to change or to add new cameras and passengers should not be disturbed by any means. Passengers should not be aware of the presence of the system, so no request should be done to change their normal behavior. Face recognition using computer vision techniques with the existing video surveillance cameras has satisfied these requirements.

In a real infrastructure there are cameras with several conditions (from new to old ones). Working environment is very hostile and image quality is degraded faster than in other locations. Three video surveillance cameras were selected with different locations and images qualities: two cameras in the corridor areas and one in a control point. Images were acquired during three weeks in September 2008.

Three scenarios were simulated: first one is a normal operational mode, second one is a high security mode and last one is a friendly or soft-recognition mode. In all cases has been proven that training and testing the system with data obtained from the same camera shows better results that training with images from one camera and testing with the others. In all cases the intersection of testing and training sets are void.

Four data compression methods were considered in the paper: 1dpca (1d principal components analysis), 2dpca (2d principal components analysis), 2dlda (2d linear discriminant analysis) and csa(coupled subspace analysis). Csa has obtained the best performance than the others. For classificatory purpoises, svm (support vector machines) were selected with excellent results.

It can be concluded that the application of a face verification system in an airport is possible, but several restrictions have to be considered. In first place, the camera-system presented in critical infrastructures is not oriented to face verification, but videosurveillance. This situation impose a carefully selection of the cameras selected to the face verification process because in most cases the present cameras will not be appropriate for this purpose. In second place, the scenario selected has to be previously analyzed: not all areas in an airport are suitable for face recognition: frontal images and with few illumination changes are desired. Finally, system parameters must be fixed for the operational mode selected.

Acknowledgements. The support of the IUISI (Instituto Universitario de Investigacion en Seguridad Interior) from UNED (Universidad Nacional de Eduacion a Distancia), AENA (Spanish airports and air navigation) and Guardia Civil (Spanish police) is gratefully recognized. Also, thanks to the work of Beatriz Rodriguez-Lobo.

References

1. Gafurov, D.: Security analysis of impostor attempts with respect to gender in gait biometrics. In: IEEE International Conference on Biometrics: Theory, Applications and Systems (BTAS), Washington D.C., USA, September 27-29 (2007)
2. Kale, A., Cuntoor, N., Yegnanarayana, B., Rajagopalan, A.N., Chellappa, R.: Gait Analysis for Human Identification. In: Kittler, J., Nixon, M.S. (eds.) AVBPA 2003. LNCS, vol. 2688, pp. 706–714. Springer, Heidelberg (2003)
3. Sundaresan, A., RoyChowdhury, A., Chellappa, R.: A hidden Markov model based framework for recognition of humans from gait sequences. In: Int. Conf. on Image Processing ICIP 2003, vol. 3, pp. 93–96 (2003)
4. Phillips, J., Todd Scruggs, W., O'Toole, A.J., Flynn, P.J., Bowyer, K.W., Schott, C.L., Sharpe, M.: FRVT 2006 and ICE 2006 Large-Scale Results. NISTIR 7408 (March 2007)
5. CEN. Recommendations for using Biometrics in European ABC. CEN/TC 224/WG 18
6. Frontex Technical Report. BIOPASS II Automated Biometric Border Crossing Systems Based on Electronic Passports and Facial Recognition: RAPID and SmartGate (2010)
7. Krahnstoever, N., Tu, P., Sebastian, T., Perera, A., Collins, R.: Multiview detection and tracking of travelers and luggage in mass transit environments. In: Ninth IEEE International Workshop on Performance Evaluation of Tracking and Surveillance, PETS (2006)
8. Dantcheva, A., Dugelay, J.-L., Elia, P.: Soft biometrics systems: Reliability and asymptotic bounds. In: Fourth IEEE Int. Conference on Biometrics: Theory Applications and Systems, BTAS (2010)
9. Okumura, M., Iwama, H., Makihara, Y., Yagi, Y.: Performance evaluation of vision-based gait recognition using a very large-scale gait database. In: Fourth IEEE Int. Conference on Biometrics: Theory Applications and Systems, BTAS (2010)
10. Grgic, M., Delac, K., Grgic, S.: SCface - surveillance cameras face database. Multimedia Tools and Applications Journal 51(3), 863–879 (2011)
11. Wheeler, F.W., Weiss, R.L., Tu, P.H.: Face recognition at a distance system for surveillance applications. In: Fourth IEEE Int. Conference on Biometrics: Theory Applications and Systems, BTAS (2010)
12. Zhou, X., Collins, R., Kanade, T., Metes, P.: A master-slave system to acquire biometric imagery of humans at distance. In: ACM International Workshop on Video Surveillance (December 2003)
13. Marchesotti, L., Marcenaro, L., Regazzoni, C.: Dual camera system for face detection in unconstrained environments. In: Proc. International Conference on Image Processing (2003)
14. Hampapur, A., Pankanti, S., Senior, A., Tian, Y.-L., Brown, L., Bolle, R.: Face cataloger: multi-scale imaging for relating identity to location. In: IEEE Conference on Advanced Video and Signal Based Surveillance (AVSS), pp. 13–20 (July 2003)

15. Senior, A., Hampapur, A., Lu, M.: Acquiring multi-scale imagesby pan-tilt-zoom control and automatic multi-camera calibration. In: IEEE Workshop on Application of Computer Vision (WACV), vol. 1, pp. 433–438 (January 2005)
16. Prince, S., Elder, J., Warrell, J., Felisberti, F.: Tied factor analysisfor face recognition across large pose differences. IEEE Trans. on Pattern Analysis and Machine Intelligence 30, 970–984 (2008)
17. Prince, S., Elder, J., Hou, Y., Sizinstev, M., Olevsky, E.: Towardsface recognition at a distance. In: IET Conf. on Crimeand Security, pp. 570–575 (June 2006)
18. Elder, J.H., Prince, S., Hou, Y., Sizintsev, M., Oleviskiy, Y.: Preattentiveand attentive detection of humans in wide-field scenes. Int. J. Computer Vision 72, 47–66 (2007)
19. Bellotto, N., Sommerlade, E., Benfold, B., Bibby, C., Reid, I., Roth, D., Fernandez, C., Gool, L.V., Gonzalez, J.: A distributed camerasystem for multi-resolution surveillance. In: ACM/IEEEIntl. Conf. on Distributed Smart Cameras, ICDSC (2009)
20. Krahnstoever, N., Yu, T., Lim, S.-N., Patwardhan, K., Tu, P.: Collaborativereal-time control of active cameras in large scale surveillancesystems. In: Workshop on Multi-camera and Multi-modal SensorFusion Algorithms and Applications (M2SFA2) (October 2008)
21. International Civil Aviation Organization. Machine Readable Travel Document. Doc 9303 (2008)
22. SpanishParliament. Ley Organica 15/1999 de protección de datos de caracter personal. BOE (1999)
23. Viola, P., Jones, M.J.: Robust real-time face detection. International Journal of Computer Vision 57(2), 151–173 (2004)
24. Pang, S., Kim, D., Bang, S.Y.: Membership authentication in the dynamic group by face classification using SVM ensemble. Pattern Recognition Letters 24, 215–225 (2003)
25. Yang, J., Yang, J.: From image vector to matrix: a straightforward image projection technique–IMPCA vs. PCA. Pattern Recognition 35, 1997–1999 (2002)
26. Yang, J., Zhang, D., Frangi, F., Yang, J.: Two-Dimensional PCA: A new approach to apperance-based face representation and recognition. IEEE Transacctions on Pattern Recognition and Machine Intelligence 26, 131–137 (2004)
27. Li, M., Yuan, B.Z.: A novel statistical linear discriminant analysis for image matrix: two-dimensional fisherfaces. In: Proceedings of the International Conference on Signal Processing, pp. 1419–1422 (2004)
28. Chen, S., Zhu, Y., Zhang, D., Yang, J.: Feature extraction approaches based on matrix pattern: MatPCA and MatFLDA. Pattern Recognition Letters 26(8), 1157–1167 (2005)
29. Xu, D., Yan, S., Zhang, L., Liu, Z., Zhang, H.: Coupled subspace analysis. Technical Report MSR-TR-2004-106, Microsof Research (2004)
30. Turkand, M., Pentland, A.: Eigenfaces for recognition. Journal of Cognitive Neuroscience 3, 71–86 (1999)
31. Cortes, C., Vapnik, V.: Support vector network. Machine Learning 20, 273–297 (1995)
32. Martín de Diego, I., Serrano, Á., Conde, C., Cabello, E.: Face Verification with a Kernel Fusion Method. Pattern Recognition Letters 31(9), 837–844 (2010)
33. Joachims, T.: Making large scale support vector machine learning practical. In: Advances in Kernel Methods: Support Vector Machines. MIT Press, Cambridge (1998)

Paradigms of Distributed Software Systems: Services, Processes and Self-organization[*]

Winfried Lamersdorf

Distributed Systems, Informatics Department, University of Hamburg,
Vogt-Kölln-Straße 30, D-22527 Hamburg, Germany
Winfried.Lamersdorf@informatik.uni-hamburg.de

1 Introduction

Due to the high availability of communications networks of many kinds, most modern IT applications are today *distributed* – either at larger-scale (e.g. Internet-based) or as part of the growing number of local "networks of things" (i.e. intelligent devices, sensors and smart applications etc.). Therefore, any new software infrastructure – as well as software development – for such applications has to adequately adapt to that.

For instance, state-of-the-art distributed software systems and applications such as, e.g., e-commerce, e-business, e-services applications, usually extend over a variety of physical locations, computer nodes, application programs and/or organizational units. In order to adequately address both the underlying complexity as well as to provide the necessary flexibility for dynamically changing co-operations, these applications are increasingly structured based on the paradigm of distributed software or application *services*. In addition, such environments are intrinsically heterogeneous – a fact which requires specific technical software support for such applications based on commonly agreed interface and protocol *standards*.

These issues can be addressed both at the application side – where applications are more and more modular, interact in rather flexible ways, and such co-operations patterns change dynamically over time – as well as for structuring the necessary software support. In both cases, the overall *"Service-Oriented Architecture"* (SOA) has paved the way for a still increasing number of many detailed standards which altogether help to realize open distributed service co-operations – most prominently expressed in the form of the so called "Web Services" (or: "Wx"-) standards (for a profound technical overview on that see, e.g., [6].)

In general, such services may already exist (e.g. in so called legacy software or application components) or may be newly developed for specific (new) application purposes. They are able to interact in many ways – also and predominantly in open and heterogeneous distributed environments – based on standardized interfaces and interconnection protocols as, e.g., provided by related "Web Services" standards. And, finally, they can be combined in different ways out of any other services – in ways which are described by rules and policies beforehand but are often executed not before runtime.

[*] The research leading to these results has received funding from the European Community's Seventh Framework Program under grant agreement 215483 (NoE S-Cube) and from the German National Research Foundation (Deutsche Forschungsgemeinschaft).

M.S. Obaidat, J.L. Sevillano, and J. Filipe (Eds.): ICETE 2011, CCIS 314, pp. 33–40, 2012.

State-of-the-art research on what is generally called "service engineering" is actually coordinated and conducted jointly be 16 different European research institutions in the ongoing EU Network of Excellence "S-Cube" (for: Software Services and Systems) in the 7th EU research framework program. As an S-Cube result brochure states: "Service-based systems and their corresponding software services require fundamental changes to the way software is developed and maintained. The use of software services implies that software is no longer owned by its users and that it is no longer running in the place where users are interacting with it. This distributed ownership of the software opens up a whole range of research challenges, including its design, evolution, adaptation and quality assurance. But while many organizations across Europe are investigating some of those very challenges, so far there has been little or no concerted effort to explore challenges that cut across different research disciplines. This is where the S-Cube project comes in." [http://www.s-cube-network.eu/pdfs/s-cube-results-brochure.pdf, accessed in December 2011]. For an overview of its partner institutions see Figure 1.

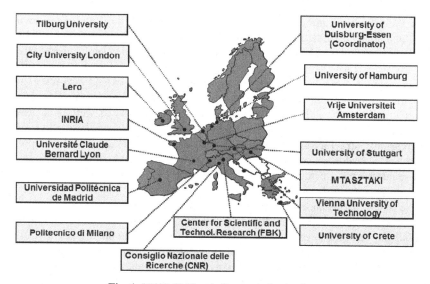

Fig. 1. EU NoE "S-cube": partner institutions

2   Software Support for Modern Application Organization

On the application side, advanced service-based software systems reflect (e.g. business) scenarios which are increasingly structured as sets of distributed co-operating entities (as opposed to earlier mostly function-oriented business organizations). Such so called "service-" or "process-"oriented applications typically involve several and heterogeneous component services from various sources – internally as well as from external sites. Further on, based on such elementary services, more complex business processes or procedures can be built up in order to help to realize more complex business semantics by *service compositions* – even in dynamically changing environments – according to predefined (functional as well as non-functional) application needs.

Technically, services-based applications first profited from the Internet and its increasing commercial use (e.g. for all kinds of e-commerce/ e-business applications). This then lead from "business to consumer (B2C) to "business to business" (B2B) applications and nowadays to several kinds of (also increasing professional) use of the still fast-growing set of "social networks" (For service-oriented e-government and e-business applications see also [2]).

On the programming side of IT history, "structured programming" languages and paradigms first lead to "object-orientation" and then via structured "software components" (and their systematic composition) finally to "service-orientation".

According to that, software support for service- or process-oriented distributed applications can profit substantially from a service-oriented software architecture. Such an architecture can provide appropriate architectural patterns for the sophisticated and flexible development of information systems that can easily interoperate, change components and therefore cope with the high complexity, dynamicity and demands of modern business environments. In dynamic service-oriented scenarios, services may typically (dis-) appear at any time and may, furthermore, change their configuration, e.g. their commitment towards a certain application or their respective costs, dynamically. A behavior like that can, for example, be found in particular in domains that use market-based pricing for negotiating contracts between respective consumers and providers of such services. Here, the inherent dynamics of the underlying market-based systems complicates the runtime management of applications that are composed of different services considerably and, thus, requires solutions that are capable of coping with these challenges as *autonomously* as possibly.

3   Actual Research Issues in Service Engineering

Among several other issues of service-oriented software development (such as, e.g., requirement engineering, application design, adaptation and monitoring etc.) the research part of the ongoing EU Network of Excellence "S-Cube" concentrates on three major aspects of the service-oriented software development process: Business Management, Service Composition, and an according Service Infrastructure. In these areas, two main research fields have been identified for main co-operative activities: "Engineering and Adaptation Methodologies for Service-based Systems" (Joint Research Activity, JRA, 1) and "Distributed System Realization Mechanisms for Service-based Systems" (Joint Research Activity, JRA, 2).

As an example for such research activities, consider the area of "Adaptable Coordinated Service Compositions" as part of JRA 2: Here, a distributed process execution is considered and the goal of this research activity is to make it robust and adaptive to all kinds of changes which may occur during execution of such a process in a (e.g.) dynamically changing and instable distributed environment. An actual solution for that concentrates on specifying all (i.e. functional as well as non-functional) characteristics of such a process in an environment-independent way (e.g. based on a so called "abstract machine").

Next, during process execution, all environment changes which are relevant for this process have to be monitored. And, finally, the resulting monitoring data has to be used to manage this process such that it may continue to run (e.g. on different machines) as long as it is somehow possible in the combined distributed environment.

For an example overview of a distributed process execution see Figure 2; and for further details of this research approach also see, e.g., [3] or [4].

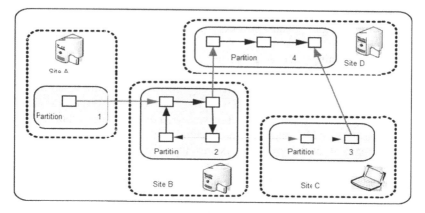

Fig. 2. Distributed process execution

Another recent concept for making distributed processes adaptable also in *mobile environments* is based on so called "migrating processes" which can be executed on any available network node which provides the necessary (functional and non-functional) characteristics as specified based on the abstract machine description of that process. This then leads to the concept of a "mobile process as a service" in a service-oriented environment which can be specified (statically) in an environment-independent way and (maybe later on and by other users) accessed and executed in a way which provides – despite potential dynamic environment changes – as much robustness as possible on the basis of all accessible distributed resources. A vision of a business process model (BPM) in a (future) distributed "cloud service" environment is depicted in Figure 3.

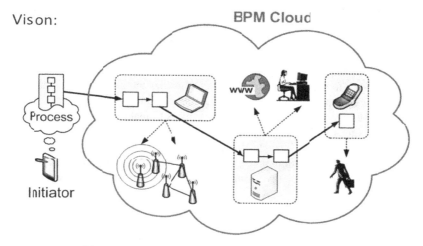

Fig. 3. Overall application scenario: "Cloud" services

Further details on context-based distributed and dynamic mobile process management and migration can be found in references [11], [12] and [13].

Remaining challenges includes management service issues aiming at (e.g.) changing such a process at runtime on users requests (e.g. commands like: "stop that process" or: "run my process as fast as possible"), enforcing additional security requests (such as: "execute this process only on nodes xyz") or budget constraints (such as: "execute this process as long as there is still budget for it").

4   Managing Self-organizing Applications

The final important challenge in managing distributed processes in dynamically changing environment as mentioned here addresses the issue of "self-management" of software applications, systems, and/or components. For example, think of a computer manufacturer who needs to acquire different well-defined and standardized sub-components like hard-disks, keyboards, RAM etc. for his production line regularly. It acquires these components from a number of complementary as well as competing providers whose characteristics (such as, e.g., availability, stability, trustworthiness, costs etc.) changes dynamically over time. In such a scenario, it would be very desirable to just state the necessary components as well as some goals for non-functional requirements (such as, e.g., time or financial restrictions) and then let the system infrastructure manage the whole process accordingly. This means that, for such kinds of applications, a clear demand for a so called *"autonomous" management* of (e.g.) such a supply process is necessary. It takes into account different functional and non-functional aspects and (dynamically) selects the most appropriate service provider at any time in a constantly changing environment (see Figure 4 as cited from [9]).

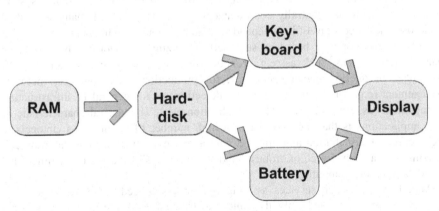

Fig. 4. PC configuration application example

Furthermore, not only the selection but also the execution of the selected service should be automatically monitored and managed – such that, for instance in the case of a service-breakdown, appropriate actions, e.g. instantiation of a new selection process, should be initiated automatically. In such an approach, service consumers are enabled to adaptively select service providers at run-time where selection criteria are based on the cost of a service provision as constantly and dynamically evaluated based on its reputation, i.e. its evaluated track record of meeting its respective service commitments. Related papers (see, e.g., [1], [5] or [9] for that) discusses design and operating principles of such an automatic service selection middleware extension as well as its ability to balance different quality criteria for service selection, such as its cost vs. its reliability, together with a first empirical evaluation based on a multi-agent platform approach.

The ongoing DFG-funded project "SodekoVS" (for an overview see [5]) aims at coordination support for such self-organizing processes on the basis of a system software infrastructure which distinguishes functional and coordination aspects of a process and then tries to provide coordination strategies (and related systems software) which are re-usable, exchangeable and based on separately identifiable design elements. Application examples include motor highway (e.g. congestion) management, production line management (as indicated by the small example cited before) or "trust-based" dynamic service selection (for example aiming "always selecting the most relevant service providers in dynamically changing environments" (for details for such an approach see [9]).

5   (Multi-) Agent-Based Implementation and Simulation of Self-organizing Systems and Applications

In general, the concept of self-organization is derived from examples in nature – such as, e.g., physical structures (like liquids, magnets or laser light), biological systems (like, e.g., swarms) or also social systems (like, e.g., urban development or the ever increasing social media networks). It aims a an overall stable ("macroscopic") system behavior which is not centrally coordinated but just the result of many individual ("microscopic") decisions of its independent ("autonomous") components.

Software development based on such self-organizing behavior can be applied in many different areas, such as, e.g.: robotics (e.g. for motion control and/or self-assembly), production management (e.g. for production lines, logistics), network management (e.g. for routing or intrusion detection) or for general IT infrastructure management (as, e.g., for green IT, virtualization etc.). The general characteristic of such applications is that they consist of a high number of autonomous elements, a high degree of distribution and aim a decentralized coordination of scalable overall systems with a high degree of "robust" and "autonomous" behavior (sometimes also called "autonomic computing").

And, finally, if such services as well as business procedures increasingly self-organize – especially in highly dynamical distributed environments – appropriate system software is needed which supports that. If such service become more and more "independent" and act "autonomously", the software paradigm of rather independent (software) *"agents"* has proven to be rather adequate for modeling (and later also simulating and implementing) co-operation pattern which aim at achieving a specific (abstract) goal – rather than specifying how to reach that in full technical detail. An according system infrastructure provides support for many such agents ("multi-agent system") and can be implemented as part of a distributed system middleware.

A practically relevant examples for such "multi-agent systems" ("Jadex") has been developed and implemented at Hamburg University in recent years and is currently used to realize and support self-organizing system environments based on the BDI agent model (for further details on how to use that infrastructure for specifying, realizing, simulating and evaluating such applications can be found in [7] and [8]). In practical experimentation, it could be demonstrated, that software (multi-) agent systems can be used for that – both at the modeling as well as at the simulation and/or implementation level.

For example, this system is currently used in a realistic (car manufacturing) environment in order to first specify (model), analyze, simulate and evaluate specific application processes (resp. alternatives) before the "real" (and expensive!) production processes are actually implemented. This way, expensive real test scenarios (as traditionally used e.g. for car production systems) can be substituted by (relatively inexpensive but still rather extensive) agent-based simulations and application-specific evaluations

6   Summary and Conclusions

In conclusion, this contribution argued first that state-of-the-art distributed applications are increasingly *service-* and *process-oriented* and, thus, based on distributed services and processes. The SOA software architecture (including its currently predominant web service-based implementations) provides an appropriate framework for realizing such applications – also in open and heterogeneous service-based distributed environments. Research issues in this area include question of how to best implement service compositions – especially in dynamically changing (e.g. mobile) environments.

Another important issue, specifically for distributed service-based processes and systems in dynamically changing environments, is the goal to make them increasingly *self-organizing* – i.e. independently aiming a predefined goals based on a given set of (functional as well as non-functional) specifications. A promising approach to implement such systems is based on the (software) paradigm of independently acting (multi-) *agents*. In its most recent form, an example system implementation as described in [8] provides both adequate specification as well as software development methods and a rich set of tools as also an according simulation environment which can be used to, e.g., simulate, test and evaluate different implementation scenarios before the corresponding systems are actually implemented.

This way, both service-oriented and self-organizing characteristics of new distributed processes can be addressed and corresponding systems can be specified, realized as well as evaluated in a common software development scenario.

Besides continuous system improvements, future extensions of this research shall address adequate inclusion of *event-based* strategies of specifying, implementing and adequately supporting such – increasingly important – aspects of distributed applications as well.

References

1. Jander, K., Lamersdorf, W.: GPMN-Edit: High-level and Goal-oriented Workflow Modeling. In: Hellbrück, H., Luttenberger, N., Turau, V. (eds.) Proc. Workshops of the German National Conference on Communication in Distributed Systems, Electronic Communications of the EASST, pp. 146–157 (April 2011)
2. Janssen, M., Lamersdorf, W., Pries-Heje, J., Rosemann, M.: E-Government, E-Services and Global Processes, p. 259. Springer, Heidelberg (2010)
3. Kunze, C.P., Zaplata, S., Turjalei, M., Lamersdorf, W.: Enabling context-based cooperation: A generic context model and management system. In: Abramowicz, W., Fensel, D. (eds.) BIS 2008. LNBIP 7, pp. 459–470. Springer, Heidelberg (2008)
4. Meiners, M., Zaplata, S., Lamersdorf, W.: Structured Context Prediction: A Generic Approach. In: Eliassen, F., Kapitza, R. (eds.) DAIS 2010. LNCS, vol. 6115, pp. 84–97. Springer, Heidelberg (2010)
5. Sudeikat, J., Braubach, L., Pokahr, A., Renz, W., Lamersdorf, W.: Systematically Engineering Self-organizing systems: The SodekoVS Approach. Electronic Communications of the EASST 17 (2009)
6. Papazoglou, M.P.: Web Services: Principles and Technology. Pearson Education Ltd., UK (2008)
7. Pokahr, A., Braubach, L., Jander, K.: Unifying Agent and Component Concepts. In: Dix, J., Witteveen, C. (eds.) MATES 2010. LNCS, vol. 6251, pp. 100–112. Springer, Heidelberg (2010)
8. Pokahr, A., Braubach, L., Jander, K.: Unifying Agent and Component Concepts – Jadex Active Components. In: Dix, J., Witteveen, C. (eds.) MATES 2010. LNCS, vol. 6251, pp. 100–112. Springer, Heidelberg (2010)
9. Vilenica, A., Hamann, K., Lamersdorf, W., Sudeikat, J., Renz, W.: An Extensible Framework for Dynamic Market-Based Service Selection and Business Process Execution. In: Felber, P., Rouvoy, R. (eds.) DAIS 2011. LNCS, vol. 6723, pp. 150–164. Springer, Heidelberg (2011)
10. Vilenica, A., Lamersdorf, W.: Simulation Management for Agent-Based Distributed Systems. In: Filipe, J., Cordeiro, J. (eds.) ICEIS 2010. LNBIP, vol. 73, pp. 477–492. Springer, Heidelberg (2011)
11. Zaplata, S., Kunze, C.P., Lamersdorf, W.: Context-based Cooperation in Mobile Business Environments: Managing the Distributed Execution of Mobile Processes. In: Business & Information Systems Engineering (BISE), vol. 4, pp. 301–314. Gabler-Verlag, Wiesbaden (2009)
12. Zaplata, S., Kottke, K., Meiners, M., Lamersdorf, W.: Towards Runtime Migration of WS-BPEL Processes. In: Dan, A., Gittler, F., Toumani, F. (eds.) ICSOC/ServiceWave 2009. LNCS, vol. 6275, pp. 477–487. Springer, Heidelberg (2010)
13. Zaplata, S., Meiners, M., Lamersdorf, W.: Designing future-context-aware dynamic applications with structured context prediction. In: Software: Practice and Experience, Wiley & Sons Ltd., Hoboken (2011) Wiley Online Library, doi:10.1002/spe.1126

Part I
Data Communication Networking

A Wildfire Prediction Based on Fuzzy Inference System for Wireless Sensor Networks

V.G. Gasull[1], D.F. Larios[1], J. Barbancho[1], C. León[1] and M.S. Obaidat[2]

[1] Department of Electronic Technology, University of Seville, Seville, Spain
[2] Department of Computer Science & Software Engineering, Monmouth University,
W. Long Branch, NJ 07764, U.S.A.
{vgasull,dflarios}@dte.us.es, {jbarbancho,cleon}@us.es,
obaidat@monmouth.edu

Abstract. The study of forest fires has been traditionally considered as an important application due to the inherent danger that this entails. This phenomenon takes place in hostile regions of difficult access and large areas. Introduction of new technologies such as Wireless Sensor Networks (WSNs) has allowed us to monitor such areas. In this paper, an intelligent system for fire prediction based on wireless sensor networks is presented. This system obtains the probability of fire and fire behavior in a particular area. This information allows firefighters to obtain escape paths and determine strategies to fight the fire. A firefighter can access this information with a portable device on every node of the network. The system has been evaluated by simulation analysis and its implementation is being done in a real environment.

Keywords: Fuzzy System, Wireless Sensor Networks, Forest Fire, Simulation.

1   Introduction

Usually, a wireless sensor networks is composed of multiple nodes spatially distributed in an area. These nodes obtain information on the environment such as temperature, pressure, humidity or pollutants, and send this information to a base station. A wide variety of applications for such networks often apply some kind of supervision, event detection, tracking or control, among others [1]. In [2] a large-scale deployment of these networks has been used for the supervision of wildlife habitats.

Most applications of sensor networks in forest fires are based on the detection of fires, such as [3] which uses a WSN based on a swarm-inspired system for detecting wildfires. Reference [4] shows an algorithm based on fuzzy logic for detecting events. In this case, the event is fire detection. The nodes are equipped with various sensors such as temperature, humidity, light intensity and carbon monoxide. In [5], a satellite monitoring system with a WSN is used to detect a forest fire. In [6] an implementation scheme of communication oriented WSN and monitoring computer is presented. The work in reference [7] reduces the consumption of the transmission using the information gathered by analyzing the Fire Weather Index (FWI) System. Reference [8] uses data from a WSN in the FARSITE simulator for fire detecting.

M.S. Obaidat, J.L. Sevillano, and J. Filipe (Eds.): ICETE 2011, CCIS 314, pp. 43–59, 2012.

Other papers are related to the use of WSN to improve the security on evacuations [9]. Reference [10] deals with the use of WSN to improve the information gathering for firefighters, in order to better perform when extinguishing a fire.

Some other research work is related to the study of fire evolution [11] or also fire prevention [12]. Others do real experiments with WSNs in order to evaluate its robustness against real conditions of a wildfire [13].

Traditionally, most wireless sensor networks are used for monitoring meteorological variables, with the final purpose of detecting the occurrence of fires. Only a few distributed approaches are proposed, like the one in [14], where the remote nodes process information of multiple sensors (temperature and smoke) sending alarm to a base station if a node detects an incident.

However, the scope of these networks can be increased by using distributed processing techniques and computational intelligence. In this paper, we propose a novel system for prediction of fire as well as the prediction its evolution. One advantage of this system is the real time processing of environmental variables, and then the information is available in real time, knowing at all times the current state of forests. Hence, if a fire brigade is currently operating in the area, it can choose the escape route or know which attacking side has to put out the fire.

The proposed system, called ISFPWSN (Intelligent System for Fire Prediction using Wireless Sensor Networks), is based on a distributed processing, that transmits information to neighboring nodes and does not need a base station. Centralized algorithms could be a problem in real situations because with a fire, one or more nodes could be burned, so the path to the base station could disappear.

The purpose of ISFPWSN is evaluating the risk of fire as 95% of wildfires are caused by humans [15]. It is necessary to consider sociological information, not only environmental conditions. Apart from the risk of fire, other goal of ISFPWSN is to offer information about the behavior and evolution of the fire in case of wildfire. It reduces the risk of the people exposed and improves the fire detection because it offers information about secure ways of escape and permits evaluation of a strategy for fire extinguishing.

ISFPWSN is based on computational intelligence algorithms that use fuzzy inference systems. It is because a fuzzy system has many advantages for WSN applications [166], such as its simplicity, which permits execution on devices with limited capabilities, or its ability to manage imprecise and uncertain information. All of these characteristics allow us to obtain a robust system without a high computational load.

The remainder of this paper is organized as follow. Section 2 presents the proposed system ISFPWSN. In Section 3, the simulator developed for testing the system is described. The results are presented in Section 4. Finally, Section 5 contains the concluding remarks and provides a discussion for future works.

2   Proposed System

2.1   Hardware Infrastructure of ISFPWSN

The system is designed to be used in a wireless sensor network, such as the one illustrated in Figure 1. This Figure shows a common network made by anchor nodes, but in this case there is no base station. The portable device, which is carried by qualified personnel, acts as base station, gathering the information of the nodes. A brief description about them is given below.

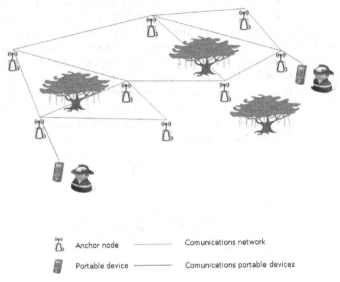

Fig. 1. The ISFPWSN network

Anchor Nodes. Anchor nodes are made up of wireless sensors that form a wireless sensor network. These devices can communicate among each other using the appropriate routing protocols. The nodes execute all the algorithms of ISFPWSN. Every Anchor node obtains the next measurements of sensor which include: temperature, wind direction, wind velocity, daily rain and humidity.

This information can be obtained from a small and cheaper weather station attached to each node, where the node can gather the information through a communication port, such as RS232-C or RS-485. It is interesting to provide power for these systems using renewable energy sources, such as solar panels or wind energy means.

Portable Devices. The other devices used in the project are the measurement apparatus devices. They are small and portable devices used by the fire-fighters to obtain environmental information. These devices can access all information on the state of the fire and can help in case of fire to provide information about its future evolution. This information is useful both to the extenuation and to determine secured ways for an escape; increasing worker safety.

2.2   Descriptions of ISFPWSN Algorithms

The nodes of the network execute their local processing algorithms to obtain the local estimates. Then they send these local estimates to other nodes in the network. Every node of the network gathers its information and executes the distributed processing algorithms. Subsequently, all the nodes share their information about the risk of fire or, in case of a forest fire, its evolution. ISFPWSN does not need a base station to gather the information. This increases the robustness of the network in case of wildfire because if some nodes were damaged in the fire, it is possible that they will not find a route to send the information to the base station.

Figure 2 sums up a flowchart of the main algorithm of the system. This figure shows several processes which will be explained later. In order to save energy, extending the lifetime of the network, the refresh rate (i.e., the frequency at which measurements are taken from the environment and therefore communicating with neighboring nodes), of this algorithm will automatically adjust as a function of the risk of fire. In this approach, each node executes one or other processes depending if a fire has occurred. If there is a fire, it will run algorithms to study their evolution, Fire Behavior (FB) and Prediction of Direction and Velocity of Fire (PD) at the maximum refresh rate. On the contrary, if there is no fire, it will run the prediction process, Probability of Fire (PF) and Risk of Fire (RF).

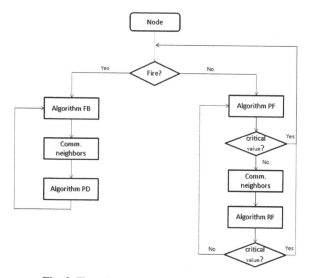

Fig. 2. Flowchart of the main algorithm

If there is a wildfire all nodes are aware and they update their data and communications quickly; obtaining the desired information in the rest of the nodes in real time. In this case, a firefighter can access the data available to the system at any time, and reacts appropriately using the parameters displayed from the nodes in the network.

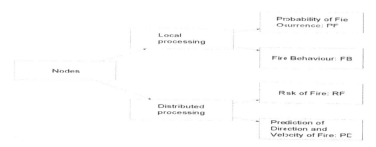

Fig. 3. Processing types

ISFPWSN is based on two main processes: a local process and a distributed process, as shown in Figure 3. These processes shared information between them as well as with the other nodes that form the network.

One goal of our approach is that a firefighter can access this information anywhere on the network, due to the fact that all nodes share information concerning the estimation or the behavior of the fire.

2.3   Local Processing

Local processing is executed on every node of the network. Nodes evaluate the environment with the information provided by each sensor. The local processing offers a partial solution of the global state of the system since this method only uses local information to get the results. This proposed processing is basically a fusion and data aggregation algorithm.

Within local processing there are two algorithms; an algorithm to obtain the probability of fire occurrence (PF) and an algorithm to obtain the behavior of fire (BF).

Probability of Fire Occurrence (PF). This algorithm determines the risk of fire in the environment in the neighborhood of the node.

The output of the PF algorithm is in [0-100] range, which indicates the probability of ignition of a forest fire after normalization. This algorithm is divided up into two blocks: an environmental processing and a sociological processing. Both methods are based on a fuzzy logic engine (Figure 4), and have as outputs fuzzy sets with functions summarized in Table 1.

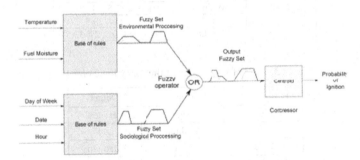

Fig. 4. Algorithm of the probability of fire

Table 1. Fuzzy sets of the outputs of environmental and sociological processing

Name	Membership function
Very low	Trapezoid (-20,0,10,17)
Low	Triangle (13,25,37)
Medium	Triangle (35,47,59)
High	Triangle (57,69,81)
Very high	Trapezoid (79,90,100,120)

Environmental Processing. This processing method obtains the fire likelihood as a function of the environmental variables. This is the classic assumption considered in other fire simulators, such as Behave Plus and FARSITE [17]. These simulators base their approximations on the Rothermel model [18] or the FWI index [19].

To determine the input functions of the fuzzy logic system, a preliminary study of the importance of the climate variables in the generation and evolution of a fire has been done. Therefore, due to historical data of wildfires, temperature and the fuel moisture has been considered as input variables. These magnitudes appear as the most relevant ones.

Fuel moisture is the dead fine fuel moisture. Within it, other variables such as humidity, shading from the sun, slope and terrain exposure has been considered.

The fuzzy sets of the inputs variables are shown in Table 2.

The parameters of fuzzy logic engine have been obtained by ANFIS (Adaptive Neuro Fuzzy Inference Systems) techniques which allows us obtain more accurately membership functions. This fuzzy logic engine has the knowledge base described in Table 3. Because there are 25 rules, this table only shows a small sample sufficient for comprehension.

Table 2. Fuzzy sets of the inputs of the environmental processing

Name	Set	Membership function
	Very-low	Triangle (-62, -40, -18)
	Low	Triangle (-40, -18, 4)
Temperature	Medium	Triangle (-18, 4, 26)
	High	Triangle (4, 26, 48)
	Very-high	Triangle (26, 48, 709
	Very-low	Triangle (-5.5, 1, 7.5)
	Low	Triangle(1, 7.5, 14)
Fuel Moisture	Medium	Triangle (7.5, 14, 20.5)
	High	Triangle (14, 20.5, 27)
	Very-high	Triangle (20.5, 27, 33.5)

Table 3. Base of knowledge of the fuzzy logic engine

Temperature	F. Moisture	Output
Low	High	Very low
Low	Medium	Low
Low	Low	Medium
Medium	High	Low
Medium	Medium	Medium
Medium	Low	High
High	High	Medium
High	Medium	High
High	Low	Very High

Figure 5 shows the probability of fire occurrence. This surface shows the probability for different values of temperature and fuel moisture used in simulations. Temperatures are in [-40 to 49] °C ranges and fuel of moisture [1 to 27] % range. As it can be seen, when temperature increases and fuel of moisture decreases, the probability of fire occurrence increases, reaching very-high values (around 90-100%).

Sociological Processing. This processing obtains the fire likelihood as a function of the sociological variables, such as weekends or holydays.

As an example, Figure 6 shows the causes of forest fires in Spain during the period 1992-2002. As it can be seen, man causes approximately 95% of wildfires. Moreover, a great percentage of these wildfires are produced during holidays.

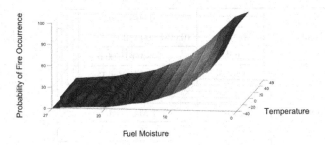

Fig. 5. Probability of fire occurrence

Because of this, it is necessary to consider sociological variables to estimate the risk of fire. As example, we consider that the number of visitor to the natural park is as important as the environmental variables. Despite its importance, fire simulators do generally not consider this kind of information, because it is difficult to assess it.

Sociological behavior is uncertain and it is not easy to model with classic techniques. Fuzzy logic is a good approach to evaluate this kind of behavior. Considering this information is the main objective of sociological processing. It is implemented with a fuzzy logic engine.

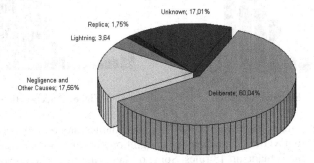

Fig. 6. Causes of wildfires

The input variables are day of week, month and hour time. Its fuzzy sets are summarized in Table 4. These fuzzy sets can be obtained from the past fire information of a region. In this case, we have considered a Spanish report with the information of the fires that took place during the years 1992 – 2002 [15]. Figures 7 and 8 show the fire occurred during this period.

Sixty percent (67%) of forest fires occurred in the months of July, August and September and the time of detection is 73% for fall time slots between 12:00 and 20:00. A low season for park visits is considered between November and April, while the high season considered between June and September. Low visit hours represent times when it is cold during the day (0:00 – 10:00h), while high visit hours are the hours when it is hot during the day (13:00 -19:00h); medium visit hours are all other times. For days of a week, all weekdays were considered low, Saturday or before holidays were considered high and on Sunday or holidays were medium.

Table 4. Fuzzy sets of the inputs of the sociological processing

	Low	0:00-10:00 h.	
Hours	Medium	10:00-13:00 and 19:00-23:00.h	Triangle
	High	13:00-19:00 h	
	Very-low	Jan. Feb. Nov.Dec	
	Low	Mar. Apr.	
Months	Medium	May. Oct.	Triangle
	High	Jun. Sep	
	Very-high	Jul. Aug	
	Low	Working day	
Days of Week	Medium	Sunday	Gaussian
	High	Saturday	

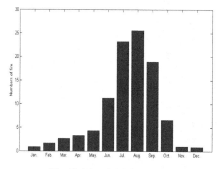

Fig. 7. Month of detection

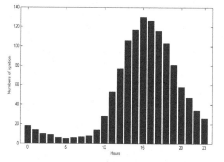

Fig. 8. Detection time

The proposed fuzzy logic engine has 3 input variables; hours, months and days of week and 1 output variable; probability of ignition for sociological variables. This base of knowledge is made up 13 rules. Some of these rules are listed below:

—If hour is Low then Probability of Ignition (PI) is Very-low.
—If months Low then PI is Very-low.
—If hour is Low and month is high then PI is Medium.
—If hour is High and month is Medium then PI is Medium.
—If Day of Week is Medium then PI is High.

Figure 9 shows the different values of the probability of ignition of sociological variables. This area is a surface of probabilities for the input variable hours and months.

It is important to mention that this fuzzy system is designed to apply to Spain, where the dry months are between April and November. For other regions, it would be necessary to change the fuzzy logic engine.

Fire Behavior (FB). This algorithm obtains the direction of the fire front and its velocity in an area around the node. It does not consider the topology of the terrain; it is used on the distributed algorithm for prediction of direction and velocity of the fire.

This algorithm considers the nodes as isolated devices with their local information of wind direction and velocity, temperature, humidity and daily rain. This algorithm is executed only in case of occurrence of fire.

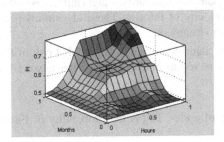

Fig. 9. Probability of ignition for sociological variables

The velocity of propagation of the fire is calculated using the formula below:

$$V = a(U + 1)b \tag{1}$$

Where V is the velocity of propagation of fire (m/min), U is the wind velocity (m/s), a=0.233 and b=1.332 for a "Pinnus Pinea" forest, as we considered this in this work. The direction of propagation can be obtained as follows.

If wind velocity = 0 Km/h: The fire follows a radial pattern, with the same velocity on all direction.

For other cases, the fire front has the direction of the wind and will trace an ellipse.

This algorithm also implements an alarm system for risk of great fires, according to the rule of 30% [15]. This rule says that a great forest fire can be produced with the conditions described on Table 5.

Table 5. Rule of 30%

Parameter	Value
Temperature	> 30%
Humidity	< 30%
Wind velocity	> 30km/h
Days without rain	> 30

When two or more values are above the threshold, the system considers that there are critical values (Figure2). Instead of taking the system back to the continuous capture of data from the environment, it verifies previously if a fire occurred.

2.4 Distributed Processing

The distributed processing is executed on each node of the network with the information gathered from the broadcast messages sent by the others nodes. This permits checking the global state of the environment without the need for a base station that collects all the information. This is especially useful for the study of wildfire as the route between any nodes to the base station can disappear if any node is burned by the wildfire. Moreover, this allows obtaining the global information, anywhere into the network. It can help firefighters who would only need a small portable device to check the evolution of the wildfire.

The distributed processing scheme combines all the partial solutions from the local processing of the nodes throughout two algorithms: risk of fire and prediction of the direction and the velocity of the fire. These algorithms provide results to assess the overall state of the environment.

Risk of Fire (RF). This algorithm evaluates the global risk of fire in the environment. In this case, it combines the results of every node in the network using the next formula:

$$RF = \frac{\sum_{i=1}^{n} PF_n}{n} \tag{2}$$

Where n is the number of nodes, PF_n is the Probability of Fire of each node and RF represents the risk of fire.

The output of this algorithm is a value [0 to 100] range, which will be encoded in one of five possible risk levels that have been considered. Values above 60 represent a high risk of forest fire; see Table 6.

As described in section 2, the output of this algorithm is the information considered in the refresh rate. This algorithm determines the global characteristic of the wildfire. This information is useful for the firefighters in order to determine the best way to extinguish a fire and the route of escape to be used, which increases the safety aspect of the approach.

Prediction of Direction and Velocity of the Fire (PD). This algorithm determines the global characteristic of the wildfire. This information is useful for the firefighters in order to determine the best way to extinguish a fire and the route to escape to be used, which increases the safety aspect of the approach.

Table 6. Evaluation of the risk of fire

Value RF	Probability of Fire
RF $\leq$ 10	Very Low
10 < RF $\leq$ 30	Low
30 < RF $\leq$ 40	Medium
40 < RF $\leq$ 60	High
RF > 60	Very High

This algorithm is based on a fuzzy logic system and offers two classes of outputs: the directions of the fire and its velocity.

As appears in Figure 10, the direction of fire is divided into 8 directions (D1 to D8), with 45 degrees between them. D1 represents if the direction of the node with the maximum slope (90°) in relation with a considered node. Every Di variable has two possible values: on or off. On signifies that the fire is going to advance in its direction. Off signifies that fire is not going to advance in its direction.

The velocity of propagation is represented throughout five values: very low, low, medium, high and very high.

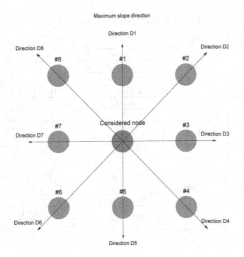

Fig. 10. Considered directions of the fire

As inputs, this algorithm uses the local estimations of the Fire Behavior (FB) algorithm, the speed of the wind and its velocity and the topography of the terrain. The proposed fuzzy logic system is shown on Figure 11.

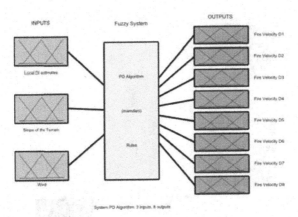

Fig. 11. Representation of the PD algorithm

The fuzzy system uses two internal parameters calculated based on the local estimation of the direction of fire: the consensus direction of fire (DFc) and the consensus velocity of fire (VFc). Both are evaluated as the medium of the local estimations of the system.

Table 7 summarizes the implementation rules. Due to the large number of rules, we only show some of them. All others rules can be obtained along the same lines shown in this table.

Table 7. Rules of PD Algorithms

DFc	VIc	Slope	Outputs
DFc= D1	Low	D1=low	D1, V1 = very low
		D1=medium	D1, V1 = low
		D1=high	D1, V1 = medium
	Medium	D1=low	D1, V1 = low
		D1=medium	D1, V1 = medium
		D1=high	D1, V1 = high
	High	D1=low	D1, V1 = high
		D1=high	D1, V1 = very high
DFc= D4	High	D1=low	D1 = off
		D1=medium	D1, V1 = low
		D1=high	D1, V1 = medium
		D3=low	D3, V3 = low
		D3=medium	D3, V3 = medium
		D3=high	D3, V3 = high
			D4, V4= very high

3   System Simulator

In order to test the proposed algorithms a C++ ad-hoc simulator has been developed. Figure 12 shows a functional diagram of the system architecture. Different Graphical User Interfaces (GUI) are described below.

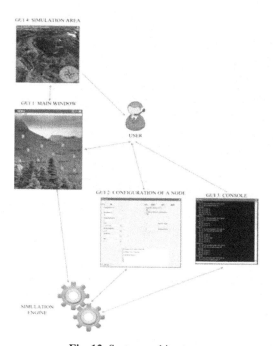

Fig. 12. System architecture

- GUI 1: This is the main window. This GUI shows the distribution of nodes in the environment and the connectivity of each one. This interface is where the user choo-ses the algorithm to perform.
- GUI 2: In this interface, the user can change the configuration of the sensors. This window appears when the user double clicks over a sensor in the main window (GUI 1).
- GUI 3: This is the console. All the partial and global results of the simulations can be obtained in the console window.
- GUI 4: This is the simulation scenario/area. For the first study we have considered localization on the "Pinsapar", a natural park of Grazalema, Cádiz, Spain

This simulator has two classes of inputs: static inputs and dynamic inputs. Static in-puts represent characteristic of the terrain and the topology of the network. These variables cannot change on execution time. Dynamic inputs are the measures of the sensors in every node. The information can be changed in the window of configura-tion of the sensors (GUI 2).

This simulator shows a graphic representation of the risk of fire (Figure 13) and the direction of fire (Figure 14).

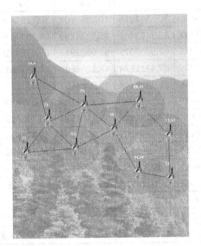 

Fig. 13. Representation of the risk of fire   **Fig. 14.** Representation of the direction of a fire

With this simulator, ISFPWSN algorithm has been verified. In all of the simulated scenarios, ISFPWSN offers a correct response. Its response is similar to that obtained by BehavePlus simulator using the same inputs.

4   Results

To test our system, it has been compared with the results obtained from the Behave Plus Simulator. In Figures 15 and 16, we check the similarity of the probability of fire obtained through our system as well as the probability of ignition obtained by the Simulator Behave respectively. Both figures show the probability as a function of temperature [40 to 49]°C and fuel moisture [1 to 27]%. Tables 8 and 9 show a brief summary of the information reflected in these figures. They show the values of the probability of ignition with ISFPWSN and the probability calculated with Behave simulator, for temperatures between 20-30°C and fuel moisture values 1-27%.

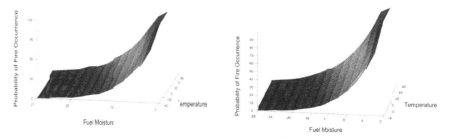

Fig. 15. PI our system   **Fig. 16.** PI behave plus

Table 8. Probability of ignition, ISFPWSN

Temp/F.Moisture	20	22	24	26	28	30
1	100,154494	100,181871	100,1669	100,111936	100,198908	100,281496
3	80,1878456	80,9286738	81,6457107	82,3462467	83,3241299	84,3033896
5	60,5096055	61,3377787	62,1608225	62,9909075	64,0302917	65,0768419
7	45,2412002	45,9520141	46,6763205	47,4311174	48,1266698	48,8351635
9	33,6203125	34,1887625	34,7703746	35,3870143	35,9384252	36,5022355
11	24,4977716	24,9673453	25,4434935	25,952969	26,4805139	27,0178309
13	18,0825517	18,484547	18,8865327	19,3201445	19,8108575	20,3087161
15	12,37531	12,6156812	12,8562432	13,1335065	13,4524117	13,7775382
17	8,76267436	9,00411181	9,25271814	9,54987376	9,83493396	10,1269967
19	6,07831408	6,31704863	6,56993062	6,8832077	7,10697667	7,33852943
21	3,60197221	3,7504699	3,91668668	4,15173726	4,23018887	4,31962861
23	2,3919787	2,50390544	2,62689982	2,81694903	2,8504334	2,9053503
25	1,51162377	1,59762167	1,68803563	1,84372173	1,80011255	1,78838043
27	0,96091963	1,03163123	1,10010715	1,23206876	1,07923855	0,96873003

To check the accuracy of our system, we calculated the absolute errors (ε). This error is calculated for each pair of values temperature-fuel moisture between the output of our system (PI_{IFPWSN}) and the Behave Simulator (PI_{Behave}). Table 10 shows a subset of these errors for certain values of temperature and fuel moisture.

$$\varepsilon = error = |PI_{IFPWSN} - PI_{Behave}|$$

As shown in Table 10, the values of the errors are very close to 0. This means that our system is quite reliable. The errors of the system can be summarized as:

— Maximum error = 1.8317 (For the 48°C temperature and 3% fuel moisture)
— Minimum error = 0.0119 (For the 48°C temperature and 17% fuel moisture)
— Average error = 0.3588

Table 9. Probability of ignition, Behave Plus

Temp/F.Moisture	20	22	24	26	28	30
1	100	100	100	100	100	100
3	80	81	82	83	84	85
5	60	61	62	63	64	65
7	45	46	47	47	48	49
9	34	34	35	35	36	37
11	25	25	26	26	27	27
13	18	18	19	19	19	20
15	13	13	13	14	14	14
17	9	9	9	10	10	10
19	6	6	6	6	7	7
21	4	4	4	4	4	5
23	2	2	3	3	3	3
25	1	1	2	2	2	2
27	1	1	1	1	1	1

Table 10. Absolute error

Temp/F.Moisture	20	22	24	26	28	30
1	0,1544943	0,1818710	0,1668996	0,1119361	0,1989078	0,2814956
3	0,1878456	0,0713262	0,3542893	0,6537533	0,6758701	0,6966104
5	0,5096054	0,3377786	0,1608225	0,0090925	0,0302916	0,0768419
7	0,2412001	0,0479858	0,3236794	0,4311173	0,1266697	0,1648365
9	0,3796875	0,1887624	0,2296254	0,3870142	0,0615748	0,4977644
11	0,5022284	0,0326547	0,5565065	0,0470310	0,5194860	0,0178308
13	0,0825516	0,4845469	0,1134672	0,3201445	0,8108574	0,3087161
15	0,6246899	0,3843188	0,1437568	0,8664935	0,5475882	0,2224618
17	0,2373256	0,0041118	0,2527181	0,4501262	0,1650660	0,1269967
19	0,0783140	0,3170486	0,5699306	0,8832077	0,1069766	0,3385294
21	0,3980277	0,2495301	0,0833133	0,1517372	0,2301888	0,6803713
23	0,3919787	0,5039054	0,3731001	0,1830509	0,1495666	0,0946497
25	0,5116237	0,5976216	0,3119643	0,1562782	0,1998874	0,2116195
27	0,0390803	0,0316312	0,1001071	0,2320687	0,0792385	0,0312699

Expanding the selection of temperatures throughout the range used [-40 to 49] °C, the error obtained for each pair (temperature-fuel moisture) are shown is Figure 17 and Figure 18. Figure 17 shows the histogram error; with higher values it is around "0" and it decrease as we move away from the center. Figure 18 shows a three-dimensional view of the error for each pair of temperature-fuel moisture used in the simulations.

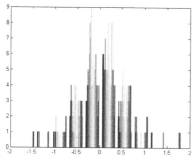

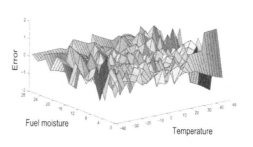

Fig. 17. Histogram error   **Fig. 18.** Dimensional error

5   Conclusions and Future Work

In this work, our ISFPWSN system is presented. This system is based on wireless sensor networks. In order to obtain the probability of fire and fire behavior prediction we use computational intelligence schemes in each of the nodes that belong to the network. One aim of the proposed wireless sensor networks is to be economical, permitting the development of the system in a huge area with a low cost.

The proposed algorithms employ collaborative processing techniques in order to cooperate with the wildfire fighting based on fuzzy logic processing. This system can act in two ways: first, it can determinate the risk of fire and, in such a case, this network gives useful information to the firefighters.

In case of fire, the system gives information about the location and direction of the fire fronts. This information can be used to study in an effective way how to control the fire and how to design escape routes in order to enhance workers' safety.

The results obtained with the proposed system have been compared with the outputs from the Behave simulator, which proved the accuracy of our system.

Currently, we are designing a real prototype version of the system, to be developed in a real environment in order to validate the proposed algorithms. The authors are currently working to develop neural network system to verify the fire behavior algorithms proposed in our scheme.

Acknowledgements. This work has been supported by the Consejería de Innovación, Ciencia y Empresa, Junta de Andalucía, Spain, through the excellence project ARTICA (reference number P07-TIC-02476) and project eSAPIENS (reference number TIC-5705). The authors would like to thank the Doñana Biological Station – EBD (Spanish Council for Scientific Research CSIC) and the Doñana Biological Reserve ICTS (Doñana Natural Space, Almonte, Huelva) for their collaboration and support.

References

1. Akyildiz, I.F., Su, W., Sankarasubramaniam, Y., Cayirci, E.: Wireless sensor networks: A survey. Computer Networks 38(4), 393–422 (2002)

2. Mainwaring, A., Polastre, J., Szewczyk, R., Culler, D., Anderson, J.: Wireless sensor networks for habitat monitoring. In: Proceedings of the International Workshop on Wireless Sensor Networks and Applications, pp. 88–97 (2002)
3. Ramachandran, C., Misra, S., Obaidat, M.S.: A probabilistic zonal approach for swarm-inspired wildfire detection using sensor networks. International Journal of Communication Systems 21(10), 1047–1073 (2008)
4. Manjunatha, J., Verma, A.K., Srividya, A.: Multi-Sensor data fusion in cluster based wireless sensor networks using fuzzy logic method. In: Proceedings of the International Conference on Industrial and Information Systems (2008)
5. Zhang, J., Li, W., Yin, Z., Liu, S., Guo, X.: Forest Fire Detection System based on Wireless Sensor Network. In: 4th IEEE Conference on Industrial Electronics and Applications, pp. 520–523 (2009)
6. Li, W., Zhang, J., Zhang, J., Xia, Z., Wang, G.: The monitoring of host computer for forest fire detection system based on wireless sensor network. In: 5th International Conference on Wireless Communications, Networking and Mobile Computing, pp. 1–4 (2009)
7. Hefeeda, M., Bagheri, M.: Wireless sensor networks for early detection of forest fires. In: IEEE International Conference on Mobile Adhoc and Sensor Systems, pp. 1–6 (2007)
8. Kosucu, B., Irgan, K., Kucuk, G., Baydere, S.: FireSenseTB: A wireless sensor networks testbed for forest fire detection. In: 6th International Conference on Wireless Communications and Mobile Computing: Connecting the World Wirelessly, pp. 1173–1177 (2009)
9. Cherniak, A., Zadorozhny, V.: Towards adaptive sensor data management for distributed fire evacuation infrastructure. In: 11th International Conference on Mobile Data Management, pp. 151–156 (2010)
10. García, E.M., Serna, M.A., Bermúdez, A., Casado, A.: Simulating a WSN-based wildfire fighting support system. In: International Symposium on Parallel and Distributed Processing with Application, pp. 896–902 (2008)
11. Lei, Z., Lu, J.: Distributed coverage of forest fire border based on WSN. In: 2nd International Conference on Industrial and Information Systems, pp. 341–344 (2010)
12. Obregón, P.D.P., Sondón, S., Sañu, S., Masson, F., Mandolesi, P.S., Julián, P.M.: System Based on Sensor Networks for Application in Forest Fire Prevention. In: Micro-Nanoelectronics, Technoloy and Applications, pp. 61–65 (2009)
13. Antoine-Santoni, T., Santucci, J.F., de Gentili, E., Silvani, X., Morandini, F.: Performance of a protected wireless sensor network in a fire: analysis of fire spread and data transmission. Sensors 9(8), 5878–5893 (2009)
14. Liu, S., Tu, D., Zhang, Y.: Multiparameter fire detection based on wireless sensor network. In: IEEE International Conference on Intelligent Systems, pp. 203–206 (2009)
15. Plan INFOCA 2003. Cap I-VIII, http://www.juntadeandalucia.es
16. Marin-Perianu, M., Havinga, P.: D-FLER – A Distributed Fuzzy Logic Engine for Rule-Based Wireless Sensor Networks. In: Ichikawa, H., Cho, W.-D., Satoh, I., Youn, H.Y. (eds.) UCS 2007. LNCS, vol. 4836, pp. 86–101. Springer, Heidelberg (2007)
17. Fire: Public domain software for the wildlandfire community (2008), http://www.fire.org
18. Rothermel, R.C.: How to predict the spread and intensity of forest and range fires. US Department of Agriculture, Forest Service, General Technical Report, INT-143 (1983)
19. Canadian Forest Fire Danger Rating System (CFFDRS), Equations and FORTRAN program for the Canadian forest fire weather index system (1985)

Evaluating Super Node Selection and Load Balancing in P2P VoIP Networks Using Stochastic Graph Transformation

Ajab Khan[1] and Reiko Heckel[2]

[1] Department of Computer Science, University of Malakand, Pakistan
[2] Department of Computer Science, University of Leicester, U.K.
ajabkhan@uom.edu.pk, reiko@mcs.le.ac.uk

Abstract. Super nodes have been introduced to improve the performance of structured P2P networks. The resulting heterogeneity benefits efficiency without compromising the decentralised nature. However, this only works as long as there are enough super nodes and the distribution of clients among them is roughly even. With the increase in the number of users or organisations preventing the use of their clients as super nodes, the overall number of candidate super nodes is limited. Thus selection and load balancing strategies are critical, especially in voice-over-IP (VoIP) networks where poor connectivity results in immediate loss of audio quality.

To evaluate different strategies we model the dynamics of P2P systems by graph transformations, a visual rule-based formalism supported by stochastic simulation. Considering P2P VoIP applications such as Skype, we model two alternative strategies one with static super node selection and load balancing and one based on dynamic selection and promotion, and compare their performance in ensuring client satisfaction.

Keywords: P2P VoIP networks, Load balancing, Static and dynamic super node selection, Stochastic modelling and simulation, Graph transformation.

1 Introduction

Peer-to-Peer (P2P) networks are distinguished from classical distributed systems by the concept of peers collaborating equally without central authority or infrastructure. To achieve this, peers have to pool resources such as CPU power, storage capacity, network bandwidth, and content [1]. Networks may be large (up to millions of peers), widely distributed, and subject to high degrees of peer dynamics churn resulting in frequent reconfiguration of their topology.

It comes as no surprise that, with large scale, geographic distribution, and high degrees of churn, the designer of a P2P network is faced with a number of challenges to ensure reliable service. Peers and their resources are contributed by participants who have full control of their system and can change the policies regarding their participation in the network at any time. The underlying network infrastructure can degrade or fail. When this happens, the communication topology needs to be updated to reroute connections, transfer administrative tasks, etc. To achieve this a dynamic, self-organised

M.S. Obaidat, J.L. Sevillano, and J. Filipe (Eds.): ICETE 2011, CCIS 314, pp. 60–73, 2012.

overlay topology is used, where peers make decisions based on local knowledge of the network only [2].

At the infancy stage of the P2P approach, most applications deployed over the internet were lacking a specific mechanism for enforcing a particular topology [4]. This resulted in the adoption of inefficient schemes such as flooding, or maintenance of large numbers of overlay connections with other participating peers. Today, most approaches realise the importance of selecting, constructing and maintaining appropriate overlay topologies for the implementation of efficient, reliable and robust P2P systems [4,3,5,7].

P2P VoIP services are gaining in popularity because they are apparently free. However, they still consume network bandwidth, resulting in hidden expenses for the client or Internet Service Provider (ISP). Most of these applications have use structured topologies, separating nodes into two classes, such as peers and super peers. Among these applications, Skype [12,14,6] is considered the most successful, contributing currently bout 8% of the total VoIP traffic. Skype distinguishes its nodes into Skype clients and super nodes [6]. This results in a two-level hierarchy: Nodes with powerful CPU, more free memory and greater bandwidth take on server-like responsibilities for the Skype clients. This approach enables a decentralised network to perform more efficiently by exploiting heterogeneity and putting the load on those clients that can handle the burden. At the same time it overcomes problems with the centralised client-server model, such as lack of scalability and a single point of failure, by using a distributed network of servers.

However, building and maintaining a super node-based overlay topology is not a simple task. Specifically, the selection strategy for super nodes turns out to be more and more critical because the number of clients available to be used as super nodes is limited. Apart from clients having limited resources, ISPs may impose bandwidth limitations. For example, the bandwidth available to a super node with cable/DSL connection is limited by the upstream link bandwidth of its host. As network address translation (NAT) and firewalls are on the rise, more standard nodes depend on super nodes to obtain VoIP services. The quality of Skype may degrade when the bandwidth demand of active sessions exceeds the available access capacity of the Skype super node network. At the same time super nodes may be subject to autonomous systems policy constraints such as the *no valley* routing policy [9] which prevents a customer from relaying traffic for other users. Super nodes relaying traffic for Skype clients violate this policy [10]. For this reason, some universities have already banned Skype from their campuses [11]. Consequently, P2P networks require efficient protocols to deliver a good the Quality of Service (QoS) in the face of scarce resources such as limited numbers of super nodes. Due to the dynamic nature of P2P, this includes the self reconfiguration of the overlay topology to react to events such as nodes joining or leaving the network in selfish or cooperative ways, crashing, or changing their resource characteristics. Where P2P is used for VoIP traffic, the network needs to reconfigure fast enough so that the QoS is not affected [19,23].

Questions about the quality of P2P VoIP network protocols therefore include the following. What is the effect on QoS if there are not enough super nodes? Can we predict if an existing super node will be capable of providing VoIP services to all its connected clients? How does it effect QoS if the load is not balanced, so that some super nodes are overloaded by clients and others are free? How many super nodes should a network have? The overall QoS of a protocol can be measured by counting the clients that are provided with a good quality connection, i.e., that are happy with their current selection of super node.

Based on this measurement, we are going to evaluate existing strategies: [16] propose a simple algorithm for load balancing by uniformly distributing load on peers; [17] explore the space of load-balancing algorithms that use a notion of virtual servers; [18] propose distributed and cooperative scheduling mechanism for dynamic load balancing in a large-scale distributed computing environment; [21] propose load balancing by moving clients from overloaded to free super nodes; [4] present a super node overlay topology algorithm and validated the approach using the Psim simulator; [15] propose to maintain redundant links between peers; [20] propose three different approaches for the selection of super node.

However, it is difficult and expensive to validate solutions directly on real networks. Geographic distribution of peers, network dynamics and lack of central control make testing difficult and costly. The simulation provides an alternative, but in particular load balancing and associated architectural reconfiguration is not easy either as existing simulators provide limited support for networks with dynamic topology [19,22,23].

We propose to model load balancing and architectural reconfigurations in P2P VoIP networks by means of graph transformation systems and use a new approach to the stochastic simulation of such systems to evaluate the performance of network protocols. We consider the P2P network architecture as a graph, in which network nodes are represented by graph vertices and graph edges represent network connections. Reconfiguration in such a network can be naturally modelled by graph transformation in a visual and rule-based formalism [19,23,15]. Stochastic simulation techniques [19] can be used to analyse performance questions such as those discussed above. In this paper we are going to use this approach to analyse, based on a model of the Skype VoIP application, different protocols for super node selection and load balancing.

2   Case Study: Skype Network

Skype is a P2P VoIP application developed in 2003 by KaZaA, currently claiming more than 200 million users. Statistics shows that an average of 20 million [27] users are usually online. Due to Skype's popularity, its architecture is receiving interest from the P2P research community as well as Telecom operators, resulting in a number of studies [6,13], but proprietary protocols, and sophisticated anti reverse-engineering techniques [14] mean that many interesting question are still unanswered.

The core architecture of the network remains largely unchanged. The Skype network consists of Skype clients and super nodes [6]. The nodes are heterogeneous in terms of network locality, CPU power, memory, and most importantly network bandwidth and type of internet connection. Skype clients with sufficient resources can be promoted to super node while continuing their primary role of client for the human user [6,13]. Super nodes form an overlay network among themselves, where each client first has to register with a central registration server and then subsequently select one of the super nodes as their host or point of contact[6]. The client will use its super node not only for searching for contacts, but use it for relaying actual traffic if the client is behind

NAT or firewall. The registration server is responsible for storing user information, including passwords, authenticating users on login and providing clients with super node addresses. All relevant information regarding on-line users and their current status is stored in a distributed fashion, which improves scalability and stability, even if the information is sometime out of date.

The population of super nodes in the network is not determined by demand, but based on the availability of bandwidth and reachability [13]. A network may have more super nodes than strictly necessary if these resources are plentiful. Due to the proprietary nature of Skype, little information is available about codecs but the in [6] author claims that Skype uses *5 Kbps* to *16 Kps* bandwidth, however a bandwidth of *25 kbps* is consumed whenever a VoIP call is in progress. If a Skype client is behind NAT or firewall, the actual call traffic will be relayed by the super node. The client sends keep-alive messages to the super node in order to check whether the super node still exists. In case the super node has left the network, the client has to reconfigure and try another super node for establishing a connection. The super node, based on the available free bandwidth, may allow or refuse new connections. Both clients and super nodes can leave the network either by shutting down selfishly or by using collaborative exit procedures.

3   A Graph-Based Model for Skype

We use graph transformations to model the structural evolution of the Skype network. Graphs provide are a natural representation for all kinds of structures, including network topologies. Formally, a graph consists of a set of vertices V and a set of edges E such that each edge $e \in E$ has source and target vertex $s(e)$ and $t(e)$ in V, respectively. More advanced notions allow for nodes and edges to be attributed with textual, boolean or numeric data [24]. Graphs occur at two levels, the type level and the instance level. A type-level graph is comparable to a class or ER diagram, containing types of nodes and edges, declarations of attributes, etc. Instance graphs represent the states of the system, typed over the type graph. With graphs as states, transformation rules provide state changing operations [15,19].

The type graph TG in Fig. 1 represents a model of the Skype architecture as described above. It defines types for registration server (RS), super node (SN), Skype client (SC) and their common super type. LK nodes are used to model links between SC and SN nodes while OV represents the connection between existing SN nodes, to model the overlay topology. Call and RouteCall are used to model two different call types. Edges of type *offline* are used to show that a user is registered but not currently in the network, while *online* shows that a user is successfully authenticated. The *overlay-index* models the connection between SNs and the RS, while *route* shows that a call is routed through an SN. Edge types *caller* and *callee* refer to the two parties in a call.

VoIP calls are modelled on the assumption that current codecs use 60 *Kbps* of bandwidth. The model supports direct calls as relayed calls. We randomly update the bandwidth of the nodes in order to model background traffic. If an SN leaves the network either by crashing or cooperative exit, we reconfigure the client to connect to a new SN.

We model two strategies for load balancing and super node selection, called static and the dynamic VoIP protocols [28]. In Fig. 2 we use a feature model to illustrate the

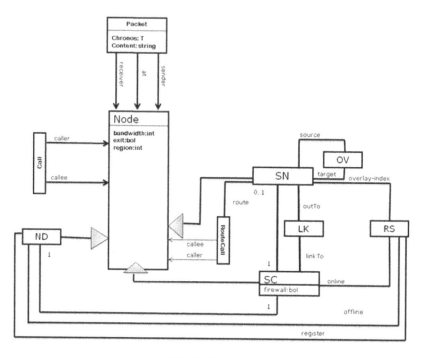

Fig. 1. Type graph

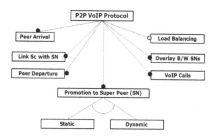

Fig. 2. Feature tree for P2P VoIP Protocol

options. In the static protocol, selection of SNs takes place only when peers are joining the network, provided that their bandwidth is at least 1.5 *Mbps*. The static protocol incorporates the optional feature of load balancing, allowing to transfer clients from an overloaded SN (with bandwidth less than 800 Kbps) to another SN. This action of the SN is based on its local awareness of its own bandwidth.

The dynamic VoIP protocol does not support this behaviour, but instead will promote (and demote) SCs to SNs at any time in their life, thus optimising the number and quality of SNs. The strategy enables this protocol to react to fluctuations of bandwidth, allowing promotion of SCs that have entered with low bandwidth and improved more recently.

The objective of modelling these two variants is to be able to evaluate them against each other through simulation. We will gather information about the numbers of SNs and SCs created as well as the proportion of connected and "happy" (i.e., well-connected) clients.

4   Network Operations as Graph Transformations

Reconfiguration steps are modelled by graph transformation rules $p : L \longrightarrow R$ consisting of a name p and a pair of TG-typed instance graphs L, R such that their intersection $L \cap R$ is well defined. The left-hand side L represents the preconditions of the rule whereas the right-hand side R describes the postconditions. Their intersection represents the elements that are required, but not destroyed, by the transformation. Graph transformation rules also use negative application conditions (NACs). A NAC assures that the rule will only be applied if pattern specified does *not* match the given graph. Graph transformation rules also allow computations on node attributes, enabling the rule to impose constraints in preconditions and to update them in the postcondition. A graph transformation system $\mathcal{G} = (TG, P)$ consists of a type graph TG and a set of rules P over TG.

Of the two graph transformation systems modelling, respectively, the static and dynamic protocols, due to space limitations we only introduce the rules for super node selection and load balancing. Operations for connecting SCs to SNs, crashing and controlled exits, etc. are described in our previous work [29,23]. However, for the simulation all these rules are required to provide a functioning model.

Static Protocol for Super Peer Promotion. The rule in Fig. 3 is used for static promotion from SC to SN. In this rule, a recently online Skype client SC will be promoted to super node SN, only if SC's current bandwidth is more than 1.5 Mbps and if connected to the Internet without firewall. After promotion to the new role SC will retain the primary role of client for its owner user while at the same time serving other SCs. Once successfully promoted, SC informs server RS about the recent change to its role in the network.

Dynamic Protocol for Super Peer Promotion. The rule in Fig. 4 along with that in Fig. 3 are used to implement the dynamic protocol for SC. This promotes an SC to SN at the start or later on. A SC may not have sufficient bandwidth at the start as, but later on may improve due to completion of other running tasks.

In this approach, the rule in Fig. 4 is used to promote a client which is already using the network. A client x with sufficient bandwidth and connected to the Internet without firewall which, is not leaving the network in a cooperative exit procedure, can be promoted to SN. Once selected for promotion, the client terminates its connection with its SN and informs the server RS regarding the new assignment.

Load Balancing. The rule in Fig. 5 models the operation where an SN, based on its local awareness of bandwidth, transfers some of its dependent SCs to other SNs in order to distribute the load more fairly. This is triggered if the SNs current bandwidth is less then 800 kbps, as long as there are other SNs with bandwidth more than 1.0 Mbps. This rule will make sure that an SC is only disconnected from the current SN. When the other SN has accepted a new connection. It is only used with the static variant.

The experiments in this paper are using 33 GT rules. Both the models link an SC with SN based on random SN selection approach as presented in [23,29]. Further, both model use control exit procedure and uncontrolled exit procedure for clients [23,29].

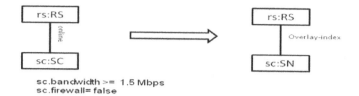

sc.bandwidth >= 1.5 Mbps
sc.firewall= false

Fig. 3. SC promotion to SN at start of joining

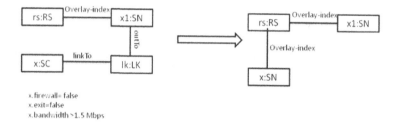

x.firewall= false
x.exit=false
x.bandwidth >1.5 Mbps

Fig. 4. Linked SC promotion to SN

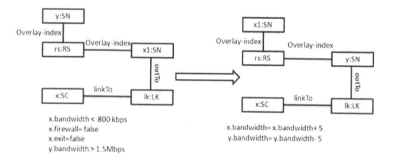

x.bandwidth < 800 kbps
x.firewall= false
x.exit=false
y.bandwidth > 1.5Mbps

x.bandwidth= x.bandwidth+ 5
y.bandwidth= y.bandwidth- 5

Fig. 5. Load balancing by transferring clients from overloaded

5   Stochastic Simulation of Graph Transformation System

Stochastic graph transformation allows to model, in conjunction with dynamic reconfiguration, non-functional qualities such as performance and reliability. In order to reason stochastically about a stochastic GTS (SGTS), we associate with each rule a distribution function governing the timing of the corresponding step. In this study we use log-normal and exponential distributions.

We say that $S = \langle G, F \rangle$ is a *stochastic graph transformation system* whenever G is a GTS and $F : P \to (R \to [0,1])$ is a function which associates with every rule in G a continuous distribution function.

Our interest in stochastic graph transformation systems is closely associated with their simulation, where the stochastic aspect is useful in order to resolve the non-deterministic character of ordinary GTS. We rely on standard notions of stochastic process and discrete event system [30]. The behaviour of a stochastic GTS can be described as a stochastic process over continuous time, where reachable graphs form a discrete state space, the application of transformation rules defines state transitions as instantaneous events, and interevent times, determined by the application of transformation rules, are dominated by continuous probability distributions. More precisely, we associate each rule, as it becomes enabled by a match, with an independent random variable (*timer*) which represents the time expected to elapse (*scheduled delay*) before the rule is applied to the match.

We simulate our model using the GraSS (Graph-based Stochastic Simulation) tool [8]. In GraSS a GTS is represented as a VIATRA model, consisting of a model space with the current graph and the transformation rules. Moreover, GraSS takes as input an XML file with the definitions of the distributions associated with transformation rules as well as general simulation parameters. Rules with empty post-conditions, called probes, are used to count the numbers of occurrences of certain patterns, such as connected or disconnected peers, for statistical purposes.

In our experiments we have used exponential distributions as well as log-normal distribution to control the delays of rule applications. We have used log-normal distribution for all rules modelling operations with a defined duration. For example [13] states that an SC takes from 10 seconds to 30 seconds to link to an SN. We have derived a log-normal distribution for this rule with corresponding mean and variance. At the same time we can not predict when a user will start using the network. For such external operations we use exponential distribution. The GT rules modelling static and the dynamic protocols are assigned exponential distributions because promotion does not depend on user choice. Once a peer satisfies the constraint or bandwidth requirement of 1.5 Mbps, the protocol could select that SC for promotion. However, with load balancing the super peer promotes one of its client. The super peer takes an average 50 seconds to promote a local client and transfer the load. Hence, log-normal distributions are assigned to the GT rules modelling this feature.

We have run several simulations of each of the two protocols, varying the rate for the client arrival rule in both protocols across $\{2, 3, 4, 5, 6\}$. With a unit of *per day* that means, a client will on average join the network every $\{8, 6, 4.8, 4\}$ hours. The total number of clients in model space is 1000. The aim behind the varying rate is to produce similar numbers of average clients online as in the real network [27] over a period of 24 hours.

In order to measure scale and quality of the network, we use probe rules to count SCs, SNs, linked SCs. The rule in Fig. 6 is used to count the number of clients happy with their current selection of SN. In our experiments, an SC is happy with its SN if this has more than 1 Mbps available bandwidth. While running individual simulations, GraSS computes statistics of these probes by collecting average, maximum, minimum and standard deviation values for each of them. Over each batch of runs, GraSS computes average, standard deviation and a confidence interval for each variable.

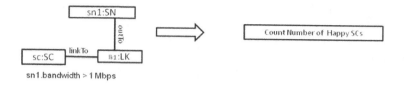

Fig. 6. Probe rule counting the number of clients happy with their SN

The rule in Fig. 6 is rewritten in to VIATRA2 code for use in the simulation tool GraSS.

```
gtrule Rule_SC_Happy_with_SN_Bandwidth() =
    {
        precondition pattern lhs(SC,LK,SN,BW) =
            {
            SN(SN);
            SC(SC);
            LK(LK);
            find LK_LinkTo(LK,SC);
            find LK_OutTo(LK,SN);
            find SN_Bandwidth(SN,BW);
            check((toInteger(value(BW)))>1000);
            }
        action {
                println("SC is happy with existing SN");
                }
    }
```

6   Simulation Results

We compare the static and dynamic protocols, each running through 4 variations of rate x for clients joining the network. For each variation we performed 6 runs with a time limit of 19.2 hours. The results are presented by graphs. The simulations in this paper are based on the time unit of 24 hours with a simulation time of 19.2 hours. We run the simulation with a batch size of 6 runs. The simulation time was selected based on steady state experiments. We simulated all models and observed that after 12 hours simulation time every model was in a steady state. Fig. 7 shows that the model is in a steady state for client joining at rate 2, 3, 4, 5 and 6.

Fig. 8 shows that the dynamic protocol and the static protocol with optional load balancing (LB) result in similar online client populations. This provides comparable input to the model and enables us to evaluate the output. The average number of SNs in both models are presented in Fig. 9. It shows that at joining rate 3 the average numbers of SNs are not much different, but at joining rates 5 and 6 this changes significantly.

In order to comment on performance, we evaluate both models on the basis of the numbers of SCs linked and the percentages of happy SCs. Fig. 10 shows the average number of SCs linked with SN. The graph shows that both protocols have similar averages at joining rate 2, 3, 5 and 6. Fig. 11 shows the percentages of happy peers in

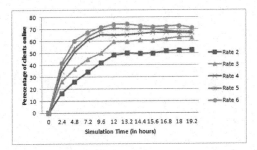

Fig. 7. Steady state of random SN selection

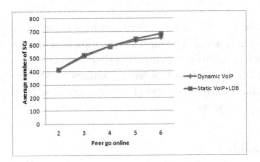

Fig. 8. Average number of SCs

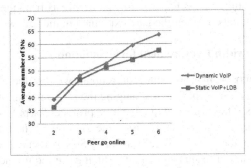

Fig. 9. Average number of SNs

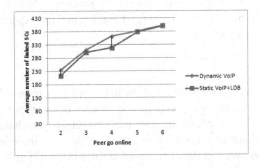

Fig. 10. Average number of SCs linked with SNs

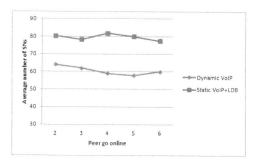

Fig. 11. Average number of SCs happy with SNs

the network. The static protocol with independent load balancing is performing much better than the dynamic protocol. The number of happy SCs is stable under increase of the joining rate, which confirms the scalability of the protocol.

These simulation results confirm that large numbers of SNs do not guarantee that the load will be balanced fairly. Therefore, local load transfer decisions can result in a greater number of happy clients.

7   Threats to Validity

In this section, we are going to discuss the possible threats to the validity of the simulation results. The case study in this paper is subject to threats from the modelling to the encoding stage. The threats we identified are explained in the following subsections.

7.1   Reducing Bandwidth Requirement for Promotion

In order to see the impact of bandwidth requirement, we develop a new set of rules for the SC connection to SN experiment, changing the requirement for promotion from 1.5 Mbps to 1.0 Mbps. These rule use the dynamic protocol for promotion. We run the simulation with joining rate 3 and simulation time 2.4 hours. The batch size is 6. We observe the average number of SCs, SNs, SCs, happy SCs, percentage of happy SCs and linked SCs. The simulation results show that reducing the requirement for promotion has affected the number of SNs in the model. The number has increased at joining rate 3. The SNs availability has improved the connection process and linking a large number of clients. The results shown in Fig. 12 suggest that beyond the expected improvement, the overall trends remain the same.

7.2   Start Graph

In order to see the effect of the start graph on the simulation results. We perform two experiments. The start graph in first experiment consists of one super peer and a single registration server. To analyse how the choice of start graph can change the result, we develop a second start graph that consists of five super peers, a single registration server and two online clients. We run the experiment again with all GT rules using the same distributions and rates. The simulation time is 2.4 hours and batch size is 6. We run

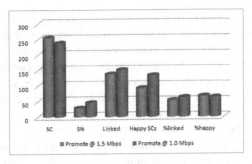

Fig. 12. Impact of reducing bandwidth constraint

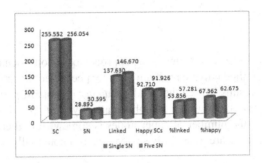

Fig. 13. Simulation results for two different start graphs

the simulation at joining rate 3 on both start graphs and observe using probe rules the number of SCs, the number of SNs, the number of SCs happy with the current selection of SN, the percentage of happy and linked peers. The simulation results show that despite the average number of SCs remaining the same, the start graph with more SNs has managed to link slightly more clients. The reason behind this could be that, as the number of SNs increases in the model, the chance of accepting a new connection also increases. The results are shown in Fig. 13. Overall difference is small.

8   Model Validation and Verification

Verification and validation of the simulation model is one of the core activities in modelling and simulation. There are various methods in the literature for this purpose [32,33]. In this study, we have used static and dynamic verification techniques in order to make sure that the model has correctly been converted into VIATRA2. The static technique has ensured that model and rules are error free and the right syntax has been followed. The dynamic verification technique has ensured that each rule does the task it was suppose to do.

Similarly for the purpose of model validation, we have used animation, face validation, event validation as well as compared the model with real system data [32,33]. In order to conclude this testing process and confirm the rates and distributions associated with GT rules, we performed a comparison with the output data of the real system. Although collection of real statistics from Skype's proprietary protocol is complex, previous authors not only provided crucial data for model development but have given enough statistics to help to validate the model. Apart from their work, forums like [27] provide Skype statistics with 15 second intervals as well as weekly, monthly and three monthly global statistics. The author in [31] states that in December 2010 there were 1.4 million super peers and 25 million users online, when the Skype network crashed due to non availability of super peers. This figure confirms that almost 6% of the on-line users were super peers, and still the Skype network crashed. This supports that the Skype super peer population must be over 6% of the online users, in order to make the network stable. The simulation results show the percentage of clients that go online is between 22% to 47% and super peer population is over 6%, which confirms the real statistics and previous experimental results.

9   Conclusions

In this paper we have outlined our simulation approach based on stochastic graph trans-formation. We have applied it to the problem of super peer selection and load balancing. From our simulation results we see that load balancing is more important to achieving high levels of client satisfaction than a sophisticated dynamic protocol for promotion and demotion, even if the number of super nodes is somewhat higher in this case. As candidates for super nodes are potentially scarce, this is a potentially important insight.

References

1. Li, Y., Cheng, D., Jhang-Li, J.: Building cooperation in VoIP network through a reward mechanism. In: Proc. 12th Pacific Asia Conference on Information Systems (PACIS 2008), Suzhou, China, pp. 799–808 (July 2008)
2. Chun Ji, L.: Computation in Peer-to-Peer Networks. Department of Computer Science, University of Saskatchewan, Canada, Tech. Report (2001)
3. Dabek, F., Brunskill, E., Frans Kaashoek, M., Karger, D., Morris, R., Stoica, I., Balakrishnan, H.: Building Peer-to-Peer Systems with Chord, a Distributed Lookup Service. In: Proc. of the 8th IEEE Workshop on Hot Topics in Operating Systems, HotOS-VIII (2001)
4. Montresor, A.: A robust Protocol for Building Superpeer Overlay Topologies. Department of Computer Science, University of Bologna, Italy, Technical Report UBLCS-2004-8 (May 2004)
5. Rowstron, A., Druschel, P.: Pastry: Scalable, Decentralized Object Location and Routing for Large-Scale Peer-to-Peer Systems. In: Proc. of the 18th Int. Conf. on Distributed Systems Platforms, Germany (November 2001)
6. Baset, S.A., Schulzrinne, H.G.: An analysis of the skype Peer-to-Peer internet telephony protocol. In: Proc. of the 25th IEEE International Conference on Computer Communications, pp. 1–11 (April 2006)
7. Zhao, B.Y., Huang, L., Stribling, J., Rhea, S.C., Joseph, A.D., Kubiatowicz, J.D.: Tapestry: A Resilient Global-scale Overlay for Service Deployment. IEEE Journal on Selected Areas in Communications 22, 41–53 (2003)
8. Torrini, P., Heckel, R., Ráth, I.: Stochastic Simulation of Graph Transformation Systems. In: Rosenblum, D.S., Taentzer, G. (eds.) FASE 2010. LNCS, vol. 6013, pp. 154–157. Springer, Heidelberg (2010)
9. Gao, L., Rexford, J.: Stable Internet routing without global coordination. In: Proceedings of SIGMETRICS, Santa Clara, CA (June 2000)

10. Seetharaman, S., Ammar, M.: Characterizing and mitigating inter-domain policy violations in overlay routes. In: Proc. of the 2006 IEEE International Conference on Network Protocols (2006)
11. Paul, R.: More Universities banning Skype (September 2006), http://arstechnica.com/news.ars/post/20060924-7814.html
12. Skype, http://www.skype.com
13. Guha, S., Daswani, N., Jain, R.: An Experimental Study of the Skype Peer-to-Peer VoIP System. In: Proc. of the IPTPS 2006 (2006)
14. Biondi, P., Desclaux, F.: Silver Needle in the Skype. EADS Corporate Research Centre, Suresnes, France (2006)
15. Heckel, R.: Stochastic Analysis of Graph Transformation Systems: A Case Study in P2P Networks. In: Van Hung, D., Wirsing, M. (eds.) ICTAC 2005. LNCS, vol. 3722, pp. 53–69. Springer, Heidelberg (2005)
16. Karger, D.R., Ruhl, M.: Simple Efficient Load Balancing Algorithms for Peer-to-Peer Systems. In: Proc. of the Sixteenth Annual ACM Symposium on Parallelism in Algorithms and Architectures (2004)
17. Surana, S., Godfrey, B., Lakshminarayanan, K., Karp, R., Stoica, I.: Load balancing in dynamic structured peer-to-peer systems. Performance Evaluation 63(3) (March 2006)
18. Murata, Y., Inaba, T., Takizawa, H.: A distributed and cooperative load balancing mechanism for large-scale P2P systems. In: Proc. of the International Symposium on Applications on Internet Workshops (2006)
19. Khan, A., Torrini, P., Heckel, R.: Model-based simulation of VoIP network reconfigurations using graph transformation systems. In: ICGT-DS 2009. ECEASST, vol. 16 (2009)
20. Lo, V., Zhou, D., Liu, Y., Dickey, C.G., Li, J.: Scalable super node selection in peer-to-peer overlay networks. In: Proc. of the Second International Workshop on Hot Topics in Peer-to-Peer Systems (2005)
21. Pournaras, E., Exarchakos, G., Antonopoulos, N.: Load-driven neighbourhood reconfiguration of gnutella overlay. Computer Communications 31(13), 3030–3039 (2008)
22. ISI, University of Southern California. The Network Simulator-NS2 (2008)
23. Khan, A., Heckel, R., Torrini, P., Ráth, I.: Model-Based Stochastic Simulation of P2P VoIP Using Graph Transformation System. In: Al-Begain, K., Fiems, D., Knottenbelt, W.J. (eds.) ASMTA 2010. LNCS, vol. 6148, pp. 204–217. Springer, Heidelberg (2010)
24. de Lara, J., Bardohl, R., Ehrig, H., Ehrig, K., Prange, U., Taentzer, G.: Attributed graph transformation with node type inheritance. Theor. Comput. Sci. 376(3), 139–163 (2007)
25. Heckel, R., Lajios, G., Menge, S.: Stochastic Graph Transformation Systems. In: Ehrig, H., Engels, G., Parisi-Presicce, F., Rozenberg, G. (eds.) ICGT 2004. LNCS, vol. 3256, pp. 210–225. Springer, Heidelberg (2004)
26. Bergmann, G., Ökrös, A., Ráth, I., Varró, G.: Incremental pattern matching in the VIATRA model transformation system. In: Proc. of the Third International Workshop on Graph and Model Transformations. ACM, New York (2008)
27. Skype Statistics, http://aaytch.com
28. Khan, A., Heckel, R.: Model-based Stochastic Simulation of Super Peer Promotion in P2P VoIP using Graph Transformation. In: Proc. of the DCNET 2011 in Seville Spain (2011)
29. Khan, A.: Stochastic Simulation of P2P VoIP Network Reconfiguration using Graph Transformation, PhD Thesis, University of Leicester, UK (2011)
30. Cassandras, C.G., Lafortune, S.: Introduction to discrete event systems. Kluwer (2008)
31. Wolff, P.: 1.4 Million Skype supernodes crashed, http://skypejournal.com/blog/?s=skype+crashed (accessed on October 10, 2011)
32. Sargent, R.G.: Verifying and Validating Simulation Models. In: Proc. of the 28th Conference on Winter Simulation. IEEE Computer Society, Washington (1996)
33. Whitner, B., Balci, O.: Guidelines for selecting and using Simulation model verification techniques. In: Proc. of the 21st Conference on Winter Simulation (1989)

Shared Security: How Wireless Sensor Networks Can Benefit from Threshold Cryptography

Manuel Koschuch[1], Matthias Hudler[1], Michael Krüger[1], Peter Lory[2],
and Jürgen Wenzl[3]

[1] Competence Centre for IT-Security, FH Campus Wien, University of Applied Science,
Favoritenstrasse 226, Vienna, Austria
{manuel.koschuch,matthias.hudler,
michael.krueger}@fh-campuswien.ac.at
http://www.fh-campuswien.ac.at/en/it-security
[2] Institut für Wirtschaftsinformatik, Universität Regensburg,
Universitätsstrasse 31, Regensburg, Germany
peter.lory@wiwi.uni-regensburg.de
http://www-wiwi.uni-regensburg.de/Home/index.html.en
[3] TMMO GmbH, Vilsgasse 25, Kallmünz, Germany
juergen.wenzl@gmx.de

Abstract. Wireless sensor networks consist of a huge number of small nodes, communicating wirelessly, to transmit any sort of measured data, like temperature, radiation, etc. At the air interface, unprotected messages can be easily intercepted and modified by an attacker. Traditionally, symmetric cryptography is deployed in sensor networks, due to the nodes being constrained in terms of energy, processing power and memory. If an attacker is now able to extract the secret symmetric key from a single node, the entire (or a huge subset of the) network is compromised. Threshold cryptography is an attractive approach to this problem: by separating the secret into several parts, an attacker has to compromise at least $t + 1$ nodes to be able to extract a meaningful value. In this work we investigate computational optimizations to the multiparty multiplication protocol of Gennaro, Rabin, and Rabin, thereby improving the running time of certain protocol steps by a factor of up to 6.

Keywords: Sensor networks, Threshold cryptography, Efficient implementation, Multiparty multiplication protocol of Gennaro, Rabin, and Rabin.

1 Introduction

Wireless Sensor Networks (WSNs), where a (potentially huge) number of small, resource-constrained sensor nodes is deployed in a large area to measure a wide variety of parameters and communicate them wirelessly in a hop-to-hop manner to a base station for evaluation, are still an emerging field of technology. They can be used to efficiently monitor things like water quality, temperature distribution or radioactive particles in areas where approaches using wired devices are too costly or even impossible.

The current challenge when dealing with wireless sensor networks is the difficulty to achieve confidential and authenticated communication over the air interface. Common techniques against eavesdropping, message forgery and manipulation that can easily be

M.S. Obaidat, J.L. Sevillano, and J. Filipe (Eds.): ICETE 2011, CCIS 314, pp. 74–81, 2012.
© Springer-Verlag Berlin Heidelberg 2012

deployed on stationary PCs usually do not work in WSNs, due to the huge constraints in terms of available memory, computing power and energy of the individual nodes. The usual way to secure WSNs today is to use symmetric cryptographic techniques, which in general can be evaluated much more efficiently than their asymmetric counterparts. The problem with this approach is the storage and distribution of the keys: two sensor nodes can only communicate when they share a common symmetric key. But due to the special structure of WSNs, the loss or malicious removal of single nodes goes largely undetected, so that an attacker can easily try to extract the secret key from a captured node. To avoid the whole network becoming compromised by such an attack, usually only a certain number of nodes share the same key, which raises the new problem of key distribution and/or cluster building. A general overview of different key management techniques usable in WSNs can be found in [20].

Given these special challenges, the approach used in threshold cryptography becomes attractive: instead of storing the secret key on a single node, a number $t + 1$ of uncompromised nodes must cooperate to generate a valid secret. Capturing a single node is now useless for an attacker, he has to gain access to at least $t+1$ nodes to extract the individual shares of the secret and combine them. There is a multitude of threshold cryptography schemes proposed in the literature, their main problem usually being the computational complexity.

In this work we extend our previous work on the subject by further accelerating the multiparty multiplication protocol of Gennaro, Rabin and Rabin (GRR) [13], thereby improving the applicability of this protocol in the context of sensor networks. Multiplication is the most important non-linear operation. The multiparty computation of non-linear functions is much less straightforward than the multiparty calculation of linear functions. In the usual case of a linear secret scheme (e.g. Shamir's [23]) the latter can be accomplished by purely local computations of each participant.

The remainder of this paper is structured as follows: Section 2 gives a general introduction to the protocol of Gennaro, Rabin and Rabin and details of our optimizations. Section 3 then presents our current experimental results, while finally Section 4 gives a short overview of possible applications of such a protocol in WSNs and an outlook on our next steps planned.

2   The Protocol of Gennaro, Rabin and Rabin

Classical theoretical results [2,7,14,26] show that any multiparty computation can be performed securely if the number of corrupted participants does not exceed certain bounds. For a survey of these results the reader is referred to the article of Cramer and Damgård [8].

Unfortunately, without further optimizations these results are not easily applicable in real world applications. One of the most prominent examples for the efforts to accelerate these approaches is the paper of Gennaro, Rabin and Rabin [13]. Among other results, it presents a more efficient variant of the Ben-Or, Goldwasser and Wigderson [2] multiplication protocol. It gives a protocol for the fast multiparty multiplication of two polynomially shared values over $\mathbb{Z}_q$ with a public prime number q.

Polynomial sharing refers to the threshold scheme originally proposed by Shamir [23], which assumes that n players share a secret α in a way that each player

P_i ($1 \leq i \leq n$) owns the function value $f_\alpha(i)$ of a polynomial f_α with degree at most t and $\alpha = f_\alpha(0)$. Then any subset of $t + 1$ participants can retrieve the secret α (for example by Lagrange's interpolation formula). At the beginning of the multiplication protocol each player P_i holds as input the function values $f_\alpha(i)$ and $f_\beta(i)$ of two polynomials f_α and f_β with maximum degree t and $\alpha = f_\alpha(0), \beta = f_\beta(0)$. At the end of the protocol each player owns the function value $H(i)$ of a polynomial H with maximum degree t as his share of the product $\alpha\beta = H(0)$. Multiplication protocols of this type are important cryptographic primitives. In particular, they play a decisive role in comparing shared numbers [11] and in the shared generation of an RSA modulus by a number of participants such that none of them knows the factorization [1,5].

The multiplication protocol of Gennaro, Rabin and Rabin [13] consists of two steps and requires one round of communication and $O(n^2k \log n + nk^2)$ bit-operations per player, where k is the bit size of the prime q and n is the number of players.

In step 1 player P_i ($1 \leq i \leq 2t + 1$) computes $f_\alpha(i)f_\beta(i)$ and shares this value by choosing a random polynomial $h_i(x)$ of maximum degree t, such that $h_i(0) = f_\alpha(i)f_\beta(i)$. He then gives player P_j ($1 \leq j \leq n$) the value $h_i(j)$.

In [19] a modification of this step is given, which reduces its complexity from $O(n^2k \log n)$ to $O(n^2k)$ (and thus the complexity of the entire protocol to $O(n^2k + nk^2)$) by utilization of Newton's scheme of divided differences.

However, in many practical situations (e. g. the above mentioned shared generation of an RSA modulus) k (typically $k = 1024$) will exceed n and the $O(nk^2)$-term will still dominate. For these cases, in [18] a protocol is given, which modifies step 2 to require only $O(n^2k)$ bit-operations per player. All of the above mentioned optimizations were also implemented and subsumed in [17].

In this work, we perform an additional investigation of step 2: in this step, each player P_j($1 \leq j \leq n$) determines his share $H(j)$ of $\alpha\beta$ by locally computing the linear combination

$$H(j) = \sum_{i=1}^{2t+1} \lambda_i h_i(j), \tag{1}$$

where the values $h_i(j)$ have been communicated to him by players P_i($1 \leq i \leq 2t + 1$) during step 1. Here, the λ_i are the coefficients of Lagrange's interpolation formula of degree $2t$, which interpolate the support abscissas $i = 1, 2, ..., 2t + 1$ to 0. In general, for a polynomial of degree $d - 1$ and support abscissas $i = 1, 2, ..., d$ these known non-zero-constants are given by

$$\lambda_i^{(d)} = \prod_{\substack{1 \leq k \leq d \\ k \neq i}} \frac{k}{k - i} \bmod q. \tag{2}$$

Expanding the unreduced coefficients gives

$$\lambda_i^{(d+1)} = \frac{1 \cdot 2 \cdot ... \cdot (i-1) \cdot (i+1) \cdot ... \cdot d \cdot (d+1)}{(-(i-1)) \cdot (-(i-2)) \cdot ... \cdot (-1) \cdot 1 \cdot 2 \cdot ... \cdot (d-i) \cdot (d+1-i)}$$
$$= (-1)^{i-1} \frac{(d-i+2) \cdot (d-i+3) \cdot ... \cdot d \cdot (d+1)}{2 \cdot 3 \cdot ... \cdot i}.$$

Consequently

$$|\lambda_i^{(d+1)}| = \frac{(d-i+2)\cdot(d-i+3)\cdot...\cdot d\cdot(d+1)}{2\cdot 3\cdot...\cdot i},$$

$$|\lambda_i^{(d)}| = \frac{(d-i+1)\cdot(d-i+2)\cdot...\cdot(d-1)\cdot d}{2\cdot 3\cdot...\cdot i},$$

$$|\lambda_{i-1}^{(d)}| = \frac{(d-i+2)\cdot(d-i+3)\cdot...\cdot(d-1)\cdot d}{2\cdot 3\cdot...\cdot(i-1)},$$

and

$$
\begin{aligned}
|\lambda_{i-1}^{(d)}| + |\lambda_i^{(d)}| &= \frac{i\cdot(d-i+2)\cdot(d-i+3)\cdot...\cdot(d-1)\cdot d}{2\cdot 3\cdot...\cdot i} + \frac{(d-i+1)\cdot(d-i+2)\cdot...\cdot(d-1)\cdot d}{2\cdot 3\cdot...\cdot i} \\
&= \frac{(d-i+2)\cdot(d-i+3)\cdot...\cdot(d-1)\cdot d}{2\cdot 3\cdot...\cdot i} * \frac{(i+d-i+1)}{1} \\
&= \frac{(d-i+2)\cdot(d-i+3)\cdot...\cdot(d-1)\cdot d\cdot(d+1)}{2\cdot 3\cdot...\cdot i} \\
&= |\lambda_i^{(d+1)}|.
\end{aligned}
$$

From this it follows that for equidistant support abscissas $i = 1, 2, ..., d$ (as they are used in the GRR protocol) the unreduced coefficients $\lambda_i^{(d)}$ of Lagrange's interpolation formula of degree $d - 1$ obey the recursion

$$|\lambda_i^{(d+1)}| = |\lambda_{i-1}^{(d)}| + |\lambda_i^{(d)}| \tag{3}$$

This and trivial initial values demonstrate that the $\lambda_i^{(d)}$ are always integers.

This fact has the consequence that the reduced coefficients as given by Equation (2) can be calculated very easily, because no computation of a modular inverse is necessary. In order to keep the absolute values of the coefficients low, the reduction should not be done into $\mathbb{Z}_q = \{x \in \mathbb{Z} | 0 \leq x < q\}$. Rather, the coefficients should be from $\mathbb{Z}_q := \{x \in \mathbb{Z} | -q/2 < x \leq q/2\}$ [1]. For small values of $d = 2t + 1$ this guarantees small absolute values for the coefficients and saves computing time.

3 Preliminary Results

Table 1 gives the comparison between step 2 of the unmodified GRR protocol with the modifications made in [18] and in this work for different bitlengths and participating players. The first version is the straightforward implementation of the unoptimized GRR protocol, with coefficients λ_i in the interval $\mathbb{Z}_q$; the second version is designed for small values of n as presented in [18] and implemented in [17]; the third version finally exploits the observations of the present work and uses coefficients λ_i from $\mathbb{Z}_q$.

All the computations use the GNU multiple precision arithmetic library [1] in version 5.0.1 and are on an AMD Athlon64 X2 5200+ with one physical core deactivated, fixed to 1.0GHz. The results obtained on this setup can obviously not be compared to those achievable on actual sensor hardware, but if the cycle count on this test setup is already far too large, the proposed solution will obviously not scale favorably down to sensor nodes.

---

[1] http://gmplib.org

Table 1. Comparison of the running time in milliseconds of step 2 of the unmodified GRR protocol, our optimizations of this protocol, as published in [17], and the additional optimizations from this work

Bitlength	Players	original GRR	Version from [17]	Reduction to $\mathcal{Z}_q$
$k = 160$	$n = 5$	0.007	0.012	0.006
	$n = 9$	0.020	0.053	0.016
	$n = 33$	0.239	1.187	0.172
	$n = 129$	5.744	98.157	5.279
$k = 521$	$n = 5$	0.019	0.015	0.006
	$n = 9$	0.062	0.062	0.018
	$n = 33$	0.867	2.146	0.259
	$n = 129$	17.137	120.734	8.954
$k = 1,024$	$n = 5$	0.045	0.018	0.009
	$n = 9$	0.154	0.081	0.027
	$n = 33$	2.217	2.847	0.373
	$n = 129$	40.772	154.080	13.058

Our new approach with reduction to $\mathcal{Z}_q$ improves the running times significantly, up to a factor of 6, depending on the bitlength and the number of players, when compared to an unmodified GRR implementation. In addition it can be assumed that this reduction also results in significantly less memory requirements during protocol execution for storing intermediate values, although this still remains to be proven by complementary measurements.

4 Applications and Outlook

Damgård et al. [11] have presented a protocol that computes, in constant rounds and with unconditional security, sharings of the bits of a shared value $a \in \mathbb{Z}_q$ with some prime q. Their protocol works for any linear secret sharing scheme with a multiplication protocol. In particular, this applies to Shamir's secret sharing scheme [23] with the multiplication protocol of Gennaro, Rabin, and Rabin and its accelerated modifications presented in Section 2. The complexity of the protocol in [11] is $O(d \log_2 k)$ invocations of the multiplication protocol for the underlying secret sharing scheme, where k is the bit size of q. Clearly, the protocol benefits from any improvement of the multiplication protocol as presented in the preceding sections.

Distributed signature schemes are another application that could be directly deployed in the context of wireless sensor networks: distributed versions of the Miller-Rabin primality test [21,22] can be built from the above mentioned protocols. For details see [1,5]. This allows the distributed generation of a shared RSA modulus N being the product of two primes or of two safe primes without the need for a trusted dealer. The subsequent distributed generation of shares of the private exponent is much less computationally involved. In particular, Boneh and Franklin [4] and Catalano, Gennaro and Halevi [6] present efficient protocols to accomplish this.

We already implemented a prototype of [4] for the use with embedded Intel 8051-based microcontrollers. The biggest challenge in this environment is to eliminate most of the communication overhead, since sending/receiving packets is quite taxing for a sensor node in terms of required energy.

One of the main applications of these results is the construction of threshold variants of signature schemes. In such a scheme n parties hold a $(t + 1)$-out-of-n sharing of the secret key. Only when at least $t + 1$ of them cooperate they can sign a given message. In the context of sensor networks, this would prevent malicious nodes from injecting wrong data into the network, as long as every (important) sensor reading has to be committed upon by a subset of nodes. The reader is referred to [6], where two such signature schemes are constructed. The first is an appropriate variant of the signature scheme of Gennaro, Halevi and Rabin [12]; the second relies on the signature scheme of Cramer and Shoup [9]. As all these protocols employ distributive multiplication as an essential part, they significantly benefit from the reduction of complexity detailed above.

Our preliminary results look promising and clearly indicate an additional performance improvement when using the optimizations proposed in this work. The next steps will be to replace the GMP library with our own code, optimized for constrained devices and much smaller than the GNU library and finally porting the protocol to a sensor node to get the timings on real hardware. An additional observation we made when implementing algorithms from [4] and [27] was the necessity to optimize the number of messages required for a successful completion of a protocol run: the time spent for transmitting, receiving and processing protocol messages scales unfavorably with the numbers of participating players, often even outweighing the time spent for actual computations. So our next steps will also focus on exploring whether the existence of a single entity that usually deploys the sensor network - and therefore can be treated like an a priori trusted party - could be used to offload some of the required communications.

Acknowledgements. Manuel Koschuch, Matthias Hudler, and Michael Krüger are supported by the MA27 - EU-Strategie und Wirtschaftsentwicklung - in the course of the funding programme "Stiftungsprofessuren und Kompetenzteams für die Wiener Fachhochschul-Ausbildungen". Peter Lory is supported by the European Regional Development Fund - Europäischer Fonds für regionale Entwicklung (EFRE).

References

1. Algesheimer, J., Camenisch, J., Shoup, V.: Efficient Computation Modulo a Shared Secret with Application to the Generation of Shared Safe-Prime Products. In: Yung, M. (ed.) CRYPTO 2002. LNCS, vol. 2442, pp. 417–432. Springer, Heidelberg (2002)
2. Ben-Or, M., Goldwasser, S., Wigderson, A.: Completeness theorems for non-cryptographic fault-tolerant distributed computation. In: Proceedings of the 20th Annual Symposium on Theory of Computing (STOC 1988), pp. 1–10. ACM Press, New York (1988)
3. Bogetoft, P., Damgård, I., Jakobsen, T., Nielsen, K., Pagter, J., Toft, T.: A Practical Implementation of Secure Auctions Based on Multiparty Integer Computation. In: Di Crescenzo, G., Rubin, A. (eds.) FC 2006. LNCS, vol. 4107, pp. 142–147. Springer, Heidelberg (2006)
4. Boneh, D., Franklin, M.: Efficient Generation of Shared RSA Keys. In: Kaliski Jr., B.S. (ed.) CRYPTO 1997. LNCS, vol. 1294, pp. 425–439. Springer, Heidelberg (1997)

5. Catalano, D.: Efficient distributed computation modulo a shared secret. In: Catalano, D., Cramer, R., Damgård, I., Di Crescenco, G., Pointcheval, D., Takagi, T. (eds.) Contemporary Cryptology. Advanced Courses in Mathematics - CRM Barcelona, pp. 1–39. Birkhäuser, Basel (2005)

6. Catalano, D., Gennaro, R., Halevi, S.: Computing Inverses over a Shared Secret Modulus. In: Preneel, B. (ed.) EUROCRYPT 2000. LNCS, vol. 1807, pp. 190–206. Springer, Heidelberg (2000)

7. Chaum, D., Crépeau, C., Damgård, I.: Multiparty unconditionally secure protocols. In: Proceedings of the 20th Annual Symposium on Theory of Computing (STOC 1988), pp. 11–19. ACM Press, New York (1988)

8. Cramer, R., Damgård, I.: Multiparty computation, an introduction. In: Catalano, D., Cramer, R., Damgård, I., Di Crescenco, G., Pointcheval, D., Takagi, T. (eds.) Contemporary Cryptology. Advanced Courses in Mathematics - CRM Barcelona, pp. 41–87. Birkhäuser, Basel (2005)

9. Cramer, R., Shoup, V.: Signature schemes based on the Strong RSA Assumption. ACM Transactions on Information and System Security (ACM TISSEC) 3(3), 161–185 (2000)

10. Damgård, I.: Theory and Practice of Multiparty Computation. In: De Prisco, R., Yung, M. (eds.) SCN 2006. LNCS, vol. 4116, pp. 360–364. Springer, Heidelberg (2006)

11. Damgård, I., Fitzi, M., Kiltz, E., Nielsen, J., Toft, T.: Unconditionally Secure Constant-Rounds Multi-party Computation for Equality, Comparison, Bits and Exponentiation. In: Halevi, S., Rabin, T. (eds.) TCC 2006. LNCS, vol. 3876, pp. 285–304. Springer, Heidelberg (2006)

12. Gennaro, R., Halevi, S., Rabin, T.: Secure Hash-and-Sign Signatures without the Random Oracle. In: Stern, J. (ed.) EUROCRYPT 1999. LNCS, vol. 1592, pp. 123–139. Springer, Heidelberg (1999)

13. Gennaro, R., Rabin, M.O., Rabin, T.: Simplified VSS and fast-track multiparty computations with applications to threshold cryptography. In: Proceedings of the 17th ACM Symposium on Principles of Distributed Computing (PODC 1998), pp. 101–111. ACM Press, New York (1998)

14. Goldreich, O., Micali, S., Wigderson, A.: How to play any mental game. In: Proceedings of the 19th Annual Symposium on Theory of Computing (STOC 1987), pp. 218–229. ACM Press, New York (1987)

15. Hairer, E., Wanner, G.: Analysis by Its History, 2nd edn. Springer, Berlin (2008)

16. Knuth, D.: The Art of Computer Programming, vol. 2. Addison-Wesley (1998)

17. Koschuch, M., Hudler, M., Krüger, M., Lory, P., Wenzl, J.: Applicability of Multiparty Computation Schemes for Wireless Sensor Networks - Position Paper. In: Sevillano, J.L., Obaidat, M.O., Nicopolitidis, P. (eds.) DCNET 2010 - International Conference on Data Communication Networking - Proceedings of DCNET and OPTICS 2010, pp. 125–128. SciTePress - Science and Technology Publications (2010)

18. Lory, P.: Secure distributed multiplication of two polynomially shared values: Enhancing the efficiency of the protocol. In: Proceedings of the Third International Conference on Emerging Security Information, Systems and Technologies (SECURWARE 2009), pp. 486–491. IEEE Computer Society (2009)

19. Lory, P.: Reducing the complexity in the distributed multiplication protocol of two polynomially shared values. In: Proceedings of the 21st International Conference on Advanced Information Networking and Applications (AINA 2007), pp. 404–408. IEEE Computer Society (2007)

20. Der Merwe, J.V., Dawoud, D., McDonald, S.: A survey on peer-to-peer key management for mobile ad hoc networks. ACM Computing Surveys (CSUR) 39(1), 1–45 (2007)

21. Miller, G.L.: Riemann's Hypothesis and tests for primality. In: Proceedings of Seventh Annual ACM Symposium on Theory of Computing, STOC 1975, pp. 234–239. ACM, New York (1975)
22. Rabin, M.O.: Probabilistic algorithms for testing primality. Journal of Number Theory 12, 128–138 (1980)
23. Shamir, A.: How to share a secret. Communications of the ACM 22(11), 612–613 (1979)
24. Stoer, J., Bulirsch, R.: Introduction to Numerical Analysis, 3rd edn. Springer, Berlin (2002)
25. Wenzl, J.: Laufzeitanalyse dreier Versionen eines Mehrparteien-Multiplikationsprotokolls. In: Regensburger Diskussionsbeiträge zur Wirtschaftswissenschaft 440. Institut für Wirtschaftsinformatik, Universität Regensburg (2010)
26. Yao, A.C.: How to generate and exchange secrets. In: Proceedings of the 27th IEEE Symposium on Foundations of Computer Science (FOCS 1986), pp. 162–167. IEEE Computer Society (1986)
27. Yiliang, H., Xiaoyuan, Y., Jun, S., Delong, L.: Verifiable threshold cryptosystems based on elliptic curve. In: International Conference on Computer Networks and Mobile Computing, ICCNMC 2003, pp. 334–337. IEEE Computer Society (2003)

Part II
e-Business

Selection of Information-Intensive Services:
A Multi-criteria Decision Model

Tobias Mettler[1] and Markus Eurich[2]

[1] University of St. Gallen, Institute of Information Management, St. Gallen, Switzerland
[2] ETH Zurich, D-MTEC, Technology and Innovation Management, Zurich, Switzerland
`tobias.mettler@unisg.ch, meurich@ethz.ch`

Abstract. The diffusion of the Internet fosters the development and provisioning of large amounts of information-intensive services. Methods and techniques such as heuristics, policy-based approaches, reputation- and trust-based selection techniques, multi-criteria decision analysis, UDDI-extensions, and ontology-based preference modeling approaches have been developed to facilitate the description, discovery, composition, and consumption of these services. Still, consumers face difficulties in selecting the services that best fit their needs. An assessment of the identified techniques suggests that multi-criteria decision analyses are best suited for the selection of information-intensive services. On this basis, a multi-dimensional service selection model is developed, which includes social, technological, economic, and political considerations. The application of this model is demonstrated by means of an exemplary case. This model with the inclusion of decision categories and sub-categories can help service consumers in selecting complex, information-intensive services.

Keywords: Analytic Hierarchy Process, Decision Model, Information-intensive Services, IT-business Value, Service Selection, STEP, Web Services.

1 Responsibilities of Service Providers and Service Consumers

Providers of information-intensive services still face problems in regard to the collaboration with globally distributed business partners. High demands on service accessibility and reliability, lack of widely accepted standards for service definition and orchestration, complicated pricing models as well as language problems are some of the reasons why the global provisioning of services has not yet become commonplace [1].

Different connotations and meanings for the term 'service' exist in distinct disciplines such as information systems, business administration or computer science [2]. In this paper we use the term service as "the application of specialized competences (knowledge and skills) through deeds, processes, and performances for the benefit of another entity or the entity itself" [3]. By that definition a wide range of possible manifestations of services are opened, for example: tangible (products) and intangible services; automated, IT-reliant and non-automated services; customized, semi-customized and non-customized services; personal and impersonal services; repetitive and non-repetitive services; and services with varying degrees of self-service responsibilities [4].

M.S. Obaidat, J.L. Sevillano, and J. Filipe (Eds.): ICETE 2011, CCIS 314, pp. 85–99, 2012.
© Springer-Verlag Berlin Heidelberg 2012

The different definitions of the service term usually have in common, that they distinguish between service providers and service consumers (cf. Fig. 1). These two basic roles typically hold distinct responsibilities as described in the subsequent sections.

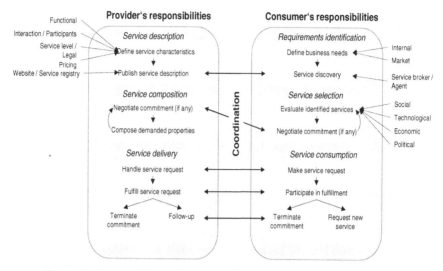

Fig. 1. Service provider's and consumer's responsibilities adapted from [5]

1.1   Service Provider's Responsibilities

With respect to information-intensive services the Organization for the Advancement of Structured Information Standards has defined the Unified Service Description Language (USDL) in order to help service providers describe technical and business-related properties. In contrast to the former Web Service Description Language (WSDL), which focused on a pure technical characterization of the service concept, USDL includes information about the participants, interaction between these parties, a delineation of the service level and pricing and legal as well as functional aspects. These service descriptions can then be published in public or closed community repositories, service registries, or the provider's website in order to enable consumers to discover the offered services. According to [5], there is still the need for negotiated commitments, under which a service is to be delivered several times. Flexibility, quality, and thoroughness of negotiated mutual commitments is thus a key determinant of whether long term service agreements will fully meet the consumers' needs [6].

1.2   Consumer's Responsibilities

Consumers on their part, may they be individuals, groups or organizations, thus have to define (or at least have an idea of) what their exact business needs are. This may be driven from an inside-out perspective, e.g., derived from the corporate strategy, or from an outside-in perspective, e.g., induced by market trends. Once the requirements are clear, a consumer has to find services, which may satisfy the identified needs. In doing so, a consumer may refer to search engines and software agents, rely on professional service brokers or word of mouth. However, the key challenge for consumers is not discovery, but selection. In accordance with [7], the key issue is that in most instances, service descriptions are given from the perspective of providers and do not necessarily include information relevant for the consumers. The selection of a particular service may not only be motivated by the best technical features or the lowest price, but by multiple criteria such as cultural fit or ethical and legal aspects [8]. Nevertheless, matchmaking mechanisms or algorithms for selecting information-intensive services (e.g. [9, 10, 11]) still mainly rely on technology-oriented criteria.

1.3 Objective

Due to the increase of the number of available services offered on vendor websites, service registries, or electronic marketplaces, we see a necessity of having an informed approach for service selection that also takes business, cultural, and legal considerations into account. It is the aim of this paper to address the problem of service selection in a holistic manner by defining a multi-dimensional decision model. To this end, the paper is organized as follows: after this introduction, we first provide an examination of the related work on general service selection techniques and discuss their suitability with respect to information-intensive services. In the section that follows, we describe potential criteria for service selection for each of the mentioned dimensions. Subsequently, the decision-making procedure is presented and illustrated by means of a comprehensive case study. Finally, we present some concluding remarks and offer some suggestions for future research.

2 Related Work

There is a wide range of research conducted in the field of service discovery and selection. Comparing and categorizing these works is not an easy job as one service is not like another and the measurement, especially of the quality of a service, is not trivial either.

In order to establish a semblance of order in our literature review, we focused on service selection and on information-intensive services. First, whereas 'service discovery' refers to the process of finding and retrieving services that fulfil the wanted functionality, we define 'service selection' as the process of choosing one service among several with adequate functionality on the basis of different criteria. Over the further course of this paper we focus on the latter. Second, services vary in their complexity. Following [12], services can be placed on a spectrum between 'professional services' on the one extreme and 'mass services' on the other. Professional services are characterized by a formal relationship, the importance of the service for the overall welfare of the customer, a high customization, the importance of a critical judgment, and a centring on people. Mass services are on the contrary: in other words, there is no formal relationship, no importance of the service for the overall welfare of the customer, no customization, no importance of a critical judgment, and the services are equipment-based [13, 14]. In this article, we will concentrate more on professional services, which we call 'complex services', and which we basically understand as information-intensive services. We refer to simple services or commodities as mass services. With this background, several techniques qualify for a more detailed appraisal, including heuristics, policy-based approaches, reputation- and trust-based selection techniques, multi-criteria decision analysis, UDDI-extensions, and ontology-based preference modelling approaches.

An optimal service can only be selected if an optimal service actually exists as well as a strategy to find it. If this is not the case, *heuristics* can help in choosing services that are good enough. In [15] an overview of fast and frugal heuristics can be found, which stop the search immediately if a factor allows it. The factors need to be retrieved in order of their importance. This has the advantage that a fast and frugal tree only has n + 1 leaves whereas a full tree has 2n leaves, which can make a full tree computationally intractable. Heuristic approaches for service selection are described, for instance, in [16, 17]. Heuristics are useful for service selection problems, where no optimal solution exists or where finding the solution is too expensive or even computationally intractable. They are less suitable for multi-criteria decisions and may have some weaknesses if the selection decision is made by a human. One weak spot is the base-rate fallacy, which is the finding that "people are relatively insensitive to consensus information presented in the form of numerical base rates" [18].

Similar to heuristics are *policy-driven approaches* for service selection, which are based on the specification of non-functional requirements coded in a Quality of Service (QoS) policy model [19]. The QoS policy model contains the service requestor's policies like preferences and restrictions. Policy-based approaches are outlined, for instance in [20] or [21]. Just like for heuristics one disadvantage is the difficulty in translating non-functional criteria to allow computation. The formulization of non-functional criteria is time-consuming and tricky, as the criteria have to be formulated as numbers or in another format. In principle, policy-based approaches could be applied for basic service selection as well as for a complex one.

Policy-based approaches – like most approaches for services selection – select the service on the basis of information provided by the service provider and try to match this information with the service requestor's selection criteria. Yet, a major difference of *reputation- and trust-based selection techniques* is the introduction of a trusted third party. Reputation- and trust-based selection approaches are genuinely meant for service selection, while most other approaches can also be used – or are indeed even designed – for service discovery. Some literature is summarized in [19], of which [22] and [23] can be recommended for further reading. The advantages of these approaches are that they can be used for any arbitrarily complex service and that non-functional requirements like legal issues, reliability, or availability parameters can also be incorporated into the selection process. On the downside, there is no real deployment of this approach in the real world yet due its high complexity (one service is not like another) and the enormous amount of time needed to establish a "trust and reputation"-community. Another drawback is the potential of manipulation of evaluations.

Another kind of service selection is *multi-criteria decision analysis*, which qualifies for numerous and possibly conflicting evaluations. Multi-criteria decision analysis methods are particularly well suited for complex service selection, for which several criteria need to be judged. Multi-criteria decision analysis methods include Analytic Hierarchy Process (AHP) and its successor Analytic Network Process (ANP), goal programming, and weighted product or sum models. The AHP is, for example, used for a QoS-based web service selection in [24]. It is also applicable as a decision support model for managers to understand the trade-offs between different criteria by group properties and thus structuring the decision (e.g. [25]). Advantages of the AHP include the support of both subjective and objective criteria, the accommodation of multiple criteria, the facilitation of participation, and its simple and intuitive character. A disadvantage might be the lengthy duration of the process.

Universal Description, Discovery and Integration (UDDI) is a directory service that provides a mechanism to register and locate web services. The UDDI repository basically consists of three components: the white pages (similar to a phone book, which gives information about the service providers supplying the service), the yellow pages (similar to the "Yellow Pages", which provide a classification of the services), and the green pages which are used to describe how to access a service and which control the congruency between the service provider's offers and the requestor's needs). While standard UDDI can be used for service discovery, *UDDI-extensions* aim at supporting service selection. For example in [26] the introduction of a quality broker in the service-oriented architecture between the service requestor and the UDDI repository is proposed. The quality broker monitors the performance, safety, and price of services, which are registered in the UDDI repository. In [19] also UDDI-based approaches for service selection are assessed, coming to the conclusion that there are two disadvantages: (1) information about the quality and service data are separated, and (2) there is no extensible service quality model, i.e., the selections are limited to few predefined criteria. Another weakness of this approach is its limited focus: there is an overemphasis on technical aspects while, e.g., legal aspects are neglected.

Other ways of service selection are *ontology-based preference modeling approaches*. In computer and information science, "an ontology refers to an engineering artifact, constituted by a specific vocabulary used to describe a certain reality, plus a set of explicit assumptions regarding the intended meaning of the vocabulary words" [27]. Adopting this definition implies two important premises: (a) the ontology is specified in form (syntax) and content (semantics), and (b) the ontology is appropriate to represent a consolidated world-view of a delimited domain (pragmatics). Consequently, for service selection, the selection criteria of a service requestor are formalized with semantic vocabulary and a domain structure for the classification. For example, in [26] user profiles with their preferences are described by means of an ontology. Similarly, a preference ontology for service selection and ranking is defined in [28]. An ontological model related to the service requestor's preferences and some criteria for service selection are discussed in [19]. This approach makes it possible to define weights for the preferences either by the service requestor or by the system to handle emergent behavior. An advantage of this ontology-based preference modeling approaches is that it is automatically interpretable by machines. A lot of advantages stem from the functions reasoning, inference, and validation, which basically means that new relationships can automatically be derived from concepts of the ontology. Still, major disadvantages are the difficulties in mapping ontologies and the effort to define an ontology and to keep it up to date.

As mentioned before, in our literature review we focused on service selection for information-intensive and compared several selection techniques (Table 1). A good comparison of service selection methods is also presented in [19] on the basis of seven requirements for web service selection approaches, which are: model for non-functional properties, hierarchical properties, user preferences, evaluation of preferences, dynamic aggregation, automation, and scalability and accuracy.

Table 1. Techniques for complex service selection

Service Selection Technique	Pro	Contra
Heuristics	Fast / cheap / often good enough/ suitable for simple service selection	Unsuitable for multi-criteria or multi-person decisions
Policy-based	Considers preferences and limitations of the requestor	Translation of policies (to make them machine readable) is complex and time-consuming
Reputation-/ trust-based	Decision can be based on own and others' experiences	Long time to build up reputation- and trust community / potential of manipulation of evaluations
Multi-criteria decision analysis	Accommodation of multiple criteria, facilitation of participation, simple and intuitive character	Lengthy duration of the process / boost of effort with increasing number of criteria
UDDI-extensions	Monitoring the performance, safety, and price of services	Limited focus: overemphasize on technical aspects / quality information and service data are separated
Ontology-based preference modeling	Automatically interpretable / ability to automatically derive new relationships between concepts of your ontology	Difficulties in mapping ontologies / big effort to define an ontology

As summarized in Table 1, all discussed service selection techniques have advantages and disadvantages. While heuristics might be the easiest and most convenient method for simple service selection, we consider multi-criteria decision analysis - and in particular AHP – as a superior technique for complex service selection. One major drawback of AHP is its lengthy process. However, once set-up, the process can be automated and several software tools are available to support the decision process. The application of AHP for service selection is not new and has been adopted for many different settings (e.g., selection of ERP vendor or communications service provider [29]). With this paper we want to extend the current field of application and show how AHP generally can be applied for decision-making in the complex area of information-intensive services.

3   Criteria for Selecting Information-Intensive Services

The selection of the right information on intensive service involves the balancing of a series of multi-dimensional and often interrelated aspects. The STEP (Social, Technological, Economic, Political) approach, also referred to as PEST [30], STEEP (second 'E' stands for 'Environmental' [31]), or PESTLE ('L' stands for 'Legal' [32]), offers a proven, integral framework for guiding a complex decision-making process. A general assumption is that not only directly assignable effects, such as the price or defined service levels, but also external or indirect circumstances, such as the image of the service provider, or cultural fit with the company, are likely to influence organizational investment decisions. To identify these influencing factors and get a 'satellite view' for a holistic choice, the decision-making process is based on four dimensions: technological, social, economic, and political. In order to identify the most relevant decision criteria for selecting information-intensive services, our literature review adheres to this classification and thus can be designated as 'concept-centric' [33].

3.1   Technological Dimension

The main focus of service selection is often more or less limited to the technological dimension and a great part of current service selection techniques mainly uses QoS-metrics (e.g. [11, 34]) as basis for decision-making. In particular under the label of QoS, characteristics of technological usability as a basis for service selection have been widely discussed (e.g. [10, 21]). Because QoS is defined and measured in different ways, we do not want to rehash a discussion about the subject, but rather focus on the three major concepts of usability as defined by the International Organization for Standardization (ISO-9241).

The first central concept to render usability is efficiency, which is commonly referred to as the level of resources consumed in performing a specific task. In regard to information-intensive services, efficiency can be quantified by a service's processing time (throughput), response time (latency), or capacity (guaranteed performance).

Effectiveness is the second fundamental concept for quantifying the quality of a service. According to [35], effectiveness is comprised of two aspects, namely the number of tasks the user completes and the quality of the goals the user achieves (output). With respect to the quantity, the scalability of a service is of major importance, since it represents a service provider's capability of increasing his capacity and ability to process more service consumer requests, operations, or transactions in a given time interval [36]. In regard to quality, criteria such as robustness (the degree of quality provided even in the presence of invalid, incomplete or conflicting inputs), reliability (the ability to perform a service under the stated conditions for a specified time interval), integrity (consistency of information and processing), and timeliness (actuality of information and punctuality of provision) can be used as units of measurement.

Finally, the service consumer's subjective satisfaction with using the technology is another inherent concept for service selection. From a technological point of view, satisfaction or perceived usefulness of the rendered service is positively influenced by its ease of use [37]. For example, this might be assessed by inspecting a service's integration possibilities (e.g. integration into regular tasks), adaptability (e.g. possibility to readjust service levels), or exception handling.

3.2   Social Dimension

QoS-metrics are often restricted to characteristics of technological usability (as described in the previous sub-section) and do not consider social aspects for service selection. No matter where information-intensive services are used – be it business-to-business or business-to-consumer - concepts such as trust (e.g. [38, 39]), reputation (e.g. [40, 41]) and cultural fit (e.g. [42]) play an important role in decision-making.

The concept of trust as basic principle for establishing business relationships and social phenomenon has been widely investigated in the past years (e.g. [43]). According to [44], trust can be gained by the service provider's competence, disposition, persistence, as well as the belief on his dependence, cooperation willingness, and

self-confidence. Reference points for assessing the trustworthiness of a service provider of an information-intensive service are, for instance, a transaction history [45], a sociability index [46] or a competency index [47].

Another concept that is central from a social perspective is reputation, which generally can be defined as the "public's opinion about the character or standing (such as honesty, capability, reliability) of an entity" [22]. Like trust, it is based on the long-term experiences that the different service consumers have made when collaborating with a particular service provider. However, in contrast to trust, which can be allocated on different levels (e.g., trust in the service itself, trust in the service provider), reputation is merely focused on a private or legal person and thus can be independent from a service offer. In this sense, not the quality of the service is in focus, but the quality of the service provider. Useful means to ascertain the reputation of a service provider could be a rating history [11] or the electronic word-of-mouth in online platforms [48].

Although several studies report a significant interrelation between culture and user interaction (e.g. [49]), the concept of cultural fit is often neglected in service selection techniques. Reasons for this are probably the difficulty in capturing 'culture' in tangible terms as well as the diversity of divergent understandings that are attributed to this concept. In a broad sense, culture can be conceived as a collective phenomenon that is manifested in several ways such as by common symbols, heroes, rituals, values, and practices [50]. For instance, it was discovered that there is a considerable difference in the way how Finish and French users interact with IT-based services [51]. Consequently, it can be assumed that cultural differences play an important role when selecting a particular service. In order to include it in the decision-making process for selecting a service, it must be narrowed down to concrete conceptions such as for example linguistic affiliation (e.g., does the service provider support all the different languages that are spoken in the company), professionalism (e.g., does the service provider certify a certain capability level), philosophy (e.g., does the service provider share the same values with respect to specific subjects), or business conduct (e.g., does the service provider apply the same or similar standards to business transactions).

3.3   Economic Dimension

In QoS policy models, the price is often the only economic criterion for service selection (e.g. [21]). However, especially in the context of information-intensive services, not only the costs, but also the benefits of utilizing the service (instead of accomplishing the required output on one's own or resigning) are important.

With respect to costs, a differentiation between non-recurring costs, ongoing costs (the price typically is a combination of both) as well as switching costs is needed. Non-recurring costs are, for instance, the purchase of a commercial software license, payment of a registration or activation fee, or one-time investment costs for infrastructure and training in order to effectively using the service. On the other hand, exemplary ongoing costs are subscription fees, utility-based maintenance and support costs, or user-based cost additions for using special service characteristics. Finally, when changing a service provider, switching costs must be considered, too. According to [52], switching costs may be transactional (e.g. returning of equipment), contractual (e.g. exit fees) as well as search and learning costs (e.g. retraining of employees). In addition, psychological, emotional, and social costs may incur.

Considerable research is available on how to assess the economic benefits of IT; however, it is less common to specifically study them in relation to information-intensive services. Following [53], advantages may occur on a strategic (e.g. enhanced customer relations), informational (e.g. improved decision-making), and transactional dimension (e.g. money savings or productivity increases).

3.4   Political Dimension

Although having an exceptional great impact on the final decision, political considerations are often neglected in current service selection techniques. One reason for this is that a wide mix of issues must be addressed, which usually makes it difficult to replace human intervention through programmatic means such as UDDI-extensions or QoS-algorithms. Accordingly, different stakeholders might be involved [54]. Among other considerations, the concepts of dependability and regulatory compliance play a major role.

Unlike the technological connotation of dependability, which generally uses this term to describe the trustworthiness of an IT-system based on its availability, reliability, safety, integrity, or maintainability [22, 55], we rather associate the service consumer's subservience to a particular condition of a service provider's offer with it (commonly referred to as lock-in). In the context of information-intensive services this might come to light when a service provider's market power is high enough to circumvent the compatibility or interoperability of a service by proprietary characteristics or to enforce additional obligations. Not least, a service should be also assessed whether it is capable to comply with national and/or international regulations (e.g. standard services directive) as well as with the own needs for privacy protection.

4   Decision-Making with AHP and STEP

The Analytical Hierarchy Process (AHP) was devised by [56] and became one of the most – or even the most – prevalent model for multi-criteria decision-making. The AHP provides a framework for solving multi-criteria decision problems based on the relative importance of the criteria assigned to each criterion in achieving the overall goal (e.g. [25]). The AHP technique is particularly suitable for multi-criteria and also multi-person decision making, in which subjective managerial opinions are present. The advantages of AHP over the other methods are: its applicability in vast variety of different areas (e.g. [25, 57]), its reliance on easy-to-get managerial data, its ability to reconcile inconsistencies in managerial perceptions, and the existence of various software tools [25] (see also section 2).

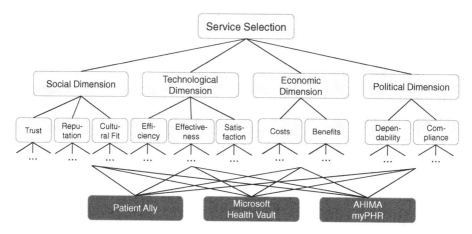

Fig. 2. A Multi-criteria decision model based on AHP and STEP

We describe the basics of the AHP technique in a four step approach (on basis of [24, 25, 56]), but as our approach suggests suitable sub-criteria, we mainly focus on the second abstraction level (for detailed information on the other levels please refer to [56]). Indications therefore are discussed in the previous section. In order to exemplarily explain the AHP and especially the second abstraction level, the illustration is based on the example of personal health records (PHR) as we think that the choice of a suitable PHR is complex and includes many technical (e.g., provision of interfaces to mobile devices, security and accessibility mechanisms) as well as non-technical considerations (e.g., credibility of provider, benefits of electronic vs. paper-based health records). However, our proposition is applicable to a wide area of domains. As basis for this comparison we chose three exemplary services: Patient Ally (PA), Microsoft Health Vault (MHV), and AHIMA my Personal Health Record (myPHR).

Step 1: Construction of the Hierarchy: All stakeholders can jointly construct the AHP hierarchy, for instance, physically in a workshop or over the Internet, e.g. on a Wiki [24]. The AHP hierarchy typically consists of three or four levels (can be extended to more levels, if applicable): the goal (service selection), the relevant criteria (cf. "STEP"), the relevant sub-criteria (as introduced in the previous section), and the alternatives to be evaluated (in this example: PA, MHV, and myPHR; see Figure 2). The decision makers need to agree on and describe the characteristics of the components in the hierarchy.

Step 2: Pair-wise Comparison and Estimation of Priorities: The stakeholders need to determine a priority for each alternative (Step 2.1) and each criterion (Step 2.2). The priority is a numerical measurement of the power of a node in relation to the other nodes on the same level and with respect to the node(s) above it.

Step 2.1: Priorities of Alternatives: Each alternative is pair-wise compared to all other alternatives with respect to all related sub-criteria and assigned weights, which reflect the relative intensity of importance. The decision makers can (among other variants) use a scale from 1 to 9: 1 being equally important, i.e., the two criteria contribute equally to the objective and 9 referring to favoring one criterion extremely over the other one; see Table 2).

Table 2. Alternatives compared with respect to TRUST

PA	5	MHV	1	Wrt TRUST PA is fairly favored over MHV
MHV	1	myPHR	7	myPHR strongly more trusted than MHV
myPHR	4	PA	1	myPHR is moderately more trusted than PA

There should be some evidence for the judgment and weighting: the evidence could stem from, e.g., past experience or the use of trial versions. The weights are then transferred into matrices for each sub-criterion: for each pair-wise comparison, the number that represents the greater weight (of a pair-wise comparison) is directly rendered into the matrix, whereas the reciprocal of that number is transferred to matrix instead of the smaller number. Then, for each sub-criterion priorities are calculated for the alternatives by mathematically processing the matrices. The estimation of priorities can be accomplished in many ways (Table 3).

Table 3. Priorities of alternatives with respect to TRUST

	PA	MHV	myPHR	Priority
PA	1	5	1/4	0.24
MHV	1/5	1	1/7	0.07
myPHR	4	7	1	0.69

Following [56] using a normalized eigenvector approach is recommended, which is a proven method for estimating the priorities [57]. Other approaches are discussed, for instance, in [58]. Software tools can take over the task of the calculation.

Step 2.2: Priorities of Sub-criteria: The same procedure is applied to get the priorities for the sub-criteria. That is to say, the sub-criteria are first pair-wise compared with respect to their super-criterion/criteria (see connecting lines between sub-criteria and criteria in Figure 2) and relative weights assigned. The weights are then transferred to matrices, from which the priorities for each sub-criterion are extracted.

Step 2.3: Priorities of Criteria: The same process as for the sub-criteria is applied to the criteria, resulting in one matrix that depicts the comparison of the criteria with respect to the goal, the service selection decision. Out of this matrix relative weights are calculated.

Step 3: Calculation of the Weight of each Alternative with Respect to the Goal: In this step the weights are multiplied and summated. The priorities of the alternatives are multiplied with the priorities of the sub-criteria and with those of the criteria, which results in the overall priorities of each alternative with respect to the goal. The priorities of each alternative with respect to the goal are summated over all criteria.

Step 4: Decision-making: In accordance to the AHP method, the alternative with the highest sum should be chosen: that is the alternative with the highest overall priority with respect to the goal. For example, if a priority of 0.38 is calculated for PA, 0.11 for MHV, and 0.51 for myPHR, the service myPHR should be selected.

5   Conclusions

The decision on selecting the right information-intensive service should be made in a holistic manner. We realized that the technological dimension tends to be overemphasized. Therefore, we suggest a multi-dimensional decision model for complex service selection that dynamically assigns relative importance to the social, technological, economic and political dimension. Even if a service may be ever so suitable from a technical perspective, it may be ruled out due to a legal issue. Another usual shortcoming is the limited perception of different decision criteria. For instance, economical considerations tend to be incomplete by focusing too much on single issues such as the purchase of a license, or the payment of a registration or activation fee. A complete cost-benefit ratio can offer valuable clues for complex service selection. For this reason, we devised a framework for relevant second level criteria: social (trust, reputation, cultural fit), technological (efficiency, effectiveness, satisfaction), and economic (costs, benefits), and political (dependability, compliance).

Advantages of the method include the accommodation of multiple criteria, the facilitation of participation, the provision of a model to learn from, to debate about, and to present to others, as well as its simple and intuitive character and its mathematical rigor. On the downside, the technique can lead to a lengthy process, in particular if further abstraction levels are added. To ensure a target-aiming decision making process, one needs to be careful not to end up with an information overload. The proposed method is therefore most suitable for the selection of complex services with sweeping consequences, e.g., if the service is very expensive, if the service cannot be changed later on or if many processes depend on the services. For a simple service selection, heuristics may be the method of choice as it is the cheapest and fastest way to come to a decision that is good enough. Future work should be directed to automate repetitive decision-making as good as possible. Still, it should be noted that automated decision-making and the suggested method is no substitute for clear thinking! The actual process of the analysis can support the decision makers in organizing and representing their thoughts, but only clear thinking can prevent them from an information overload and support them in quick decisions.

References

1. Schroth, C.: The internet of services: Global industrialization of information intensive services. In: Proceedings of the 2nd International Conference on Digital Information Management, Lyon, France, pp. 635–642 (2007)

2. Baida, Z., Gordijn, J., Omelayenko, B.: A shared service terminology for online service provisioning. In: Proceedings of the 6th International Conference on Electronic Commerce, Delft, The Netherlands, pp. 1–10 (2004)
3. Vargo, S.L., Lusch, R.F.: The four service marketing myths. Journal of Service Research 6, 324–335 (2004)
4. Alter, S.: Service systems fundamentals: Work system, value chain, and life cycle. IBM Systems Journal 47, 71–85 (2008)
5. Alter, S.: Service responsibility tables: a new tool for analyzing and designing systems. In: Proceedings of the 13th Americas Conference on Information Systems, Keystone, USA, pp. 1–10 (2007)
6. Cullen, S., Seddon, P., Willcocks, L.: Managing outsourcing: the life cycle imperative. MIS Quarterly Executive 4, 229–246 (2005)
7. Sreenath, R.M., Singh, M.P.: Agent-based service selection. Web Semantics: Science, Services and Agents on the World Wide Web 1, 261–279 (2004)
8. Krishna, S., Sahay, S., Walsham, G.: Managing cross-cultural issues in global software outsourcing. Communications of the ACM 47, 62–66 (2004)
9. Yu, T., Zhang, Y., Lin, K.-J.: Efficient algorithms for Web services selection with end-to-end QoS constraints. ACM Transactions on the Web 1, 1–26 (2007)
10. Zeng, L., Benatallah, B., Dumas, M., Kalagnanam, J., Sheng, Q.Z.: Quality driven web services composition. In: Proceedings of the 12th International Conference on World Wide Web. ACM, Budapest (2003)
11. Maximilien, E.M., Singh, M.P.: A framework and ontology for dynamic Web services selection. IEEE Internet Computing 8, 84–93 (2004)
12. Kugyt, R., Šliburyt, L.: Astandardized model of service provider selection criteria for different service types: A consumer-oriented approach. Inzinerine Ekonomika-Engineering Economics 3, 56–63 (2005)
13. Collier, D., Meyer, S.: An empirical comparison of service matrices. International Journal of Operations & Production Management 20, 705–729 (2000)
14. Ettenson, R., Turner, K.: An exploratory investigation of consumer decision making for selected professional and nonprofessional services. Journal of Services Marketing 11, 91–104 (1997)
15. Gigerenzer, G.: Gut Feelings: The Intelligence of the Unconscious. Penguin Books, New York (2007)
16. Menascé, D., Casalicchio, E., Dubey, V.: A heuristic approach to optimal service selection in service oriented architectures. In: Proceedings of the 7th International Workshop on Software and Performance, Princeton, NJ, USA (2008)
17. Menascé, D., Casalicchio, E., Dubey, V.: On optimal service selection in Service Oriented Architectures. Performance Evaluation 67, 659–675 (2010)
18. Brehm, S., Kassin, S., Fein, S.: Social Psychology. Houghton Mifflin, Boston (2002)
19. Yu, H., Reiff-Marganiec, S.: Non-functional property based service selection: A survey and classification of approaches. In: Proceedings of the 2nd Non Functional Properties and Service Level Agreements in Service Oriented Computing Workshop, Dublin, Ireland (2008)
20. Janicke, H., Solanki, M.: Policy-driven service discovery. In: Proceedings of the 2nd European Young Researchers Workshop on Service-Oriented Computing, Leicester, UK, pp. 56–62 (2007)
21. Liu, Y., Ngu, A.H., Zeng, L.Z.: QoS computation and policing in dynamic web service selection. In: Proceedings of the 13th International Conference on World Wide Web, Budapest, Hungary (2004)

22. Wang, Y., Vassileva, J.: Toward trust and reputation based web service selection: A survey. International Transactions on Systems Science and Applications 3, 118–132 (2007)

23. Galizia, S., Gugliotta, A., Domingue, J.: A trust based methodology for web service selection. In: Proceedings of International Conference on Semantic Computing, Irvine, CA, pp. 193–200 (2007)

24. Wu, C., Chang, E.: Intelligent web services selection based on AHP and Wiki. In: Proceedings of the IEEE/WIC/ACM International Conference on Web Intelligence, Fremont, CA, pp. 767–770 (2007)

25. Handfield, R., Walton, S.V., Sroufe, R., Melnyk, S.A.: Applying environmental criteria to supplier assessment: A study in the application of the analytical hierarchy process. European Journal of Operational Research 141, 70–87 (2002)

26. Seo, Y.-J., Jeong, H.-Y., Song, Y.-J.: A Study on Web Services Selection Method Based on the Negotiation Through Quality Broker: A MAUT-based Approach. In: Wu, Z., Chen, C., Guo, M., Bu, J. (eds.) ICESS 2004. LNCS, vol. 3605, pp. 65–73. Springer, Heidelberg (2005)

27. Guarino, N.: Formal ontology and information systems. In: Proceedings of the International Conference on Formal Ontology in Information Systems, Trento, Italy (1998)

28. García, J., Ruiz, D., Ruiz-Cortés, A.: A Model of User Preferences for Semantic Services Discovery and Ranking. In: Aroyo, L., Antoniou, G., Hyvönen, E., ten Teije, A., Stuckenschmidt, H., Cabral, L., Tudorache, T. (eds.) ESWC 2010, Part II. LNCS, vol. 6089, pp. 1–14. Springer, Heidelberg (2010)

29. Wei, C., Chien, C., Wang, M.: An AHP-based approach to ERP system selection. International Journal of Production Economics 96, 47–62 (2005)

30. Peng, G.C., Nunes, M.B.: Using PEST analysis as a tool for refining and focusing context for information systems research. In: Proceedings of the 6th European Conference on Research Methodology for Business and Management Studies, Lisbon, Portugal, pp. 229–236 (2007)

31. Voros, J.: Reframing environmental scanning: An integral approach. Foresight 3, 533–551 (2001)

32. Warner, A.G.: Strategic analysis and choice: A structured approach. Business Expert Press, New York (2010)

33. Webster, J., Watson, R.T.: Analyzing the past to prepare for the future: Writing a literature review. MIS Quarterly Executive 26, 13–23 (2002)

34. Tian, M., Gramm, A., Nabulsi, M., Ritter, H., Schiller, J.H., Voigt, T.: QoS Integration in Web Services. In: Proceedings of the Berlin XML Days 2003, Berlin, Germany, pp. 460–466 (2003)

35. Rengger, R., Macleod, M., Bowden, R., Drynan, A., Blaney, M.: Music performance measurement hand book. National Physical Laboratory, Teddington (1993)

36. W3C Group: QoS for web services: Requirements and possible approaches, http://www.w3c.or.kr/kr-office/TR/2003/ws-qos

37. Wixom, B., Todd, P.A.: A theoretical integration of user satisfaction and technology acceptance. Information Systems Research 16, 85–102 (2005)

38. Billhardt, H., Hermoso, R., Ossowski, S., Centeno, R.: Trust-based service provider selection in open environments. In: Proceedings of the 2007 ACM Symposium on Applied Computing, Seoul, Korea (2007)

39. Liu, W.: Trustworthy service selection and composition: Reducing the entropy of service-oriented web. In: Proceedings of the 3rd IEEE International Conference on Industrial Informatics, Perth, Australia, pp. 104–109 (2005)

40. Ding, Q., Li, X., Zhou, X.H.: Reputation based service selection in grid environment. In: Proceedings of the 2008 International Conference on Computer Science and Software Engineering, Wuhan, China, pp. 58–61 (2008)
41. Wang, P., Chao, K.-H., Lo, C.-C., Farmer, R., Kuo, P.-T.: A reputation-based service selection scheme. In: Proceedings of the IEEE International Conference on e-Business Engineering, Macau, China, pp. 501–506 (2009)
42. Javalgi, R.G., White, D.S.: Strategic challenges for the marketing of services internationally. International Marketing Review 19, 563–581 (2002)
43. McEvily, B., Perrone, V., Zaheer, A.: Trust as an organizing principle. Organization Science 14, 91–103 (2003)
44. Castelfranchi, C., Falcone, R.: Principles of trust for MAS: Cognitive anatomy, social importance, and quantification. In: Proceedings of the 3rd International Conference on Multiagent Systems, Paris, France, pp. 72–79 (1998)
45. Manchala, D.W.: E-commerce trust metrics and models. IEEE Internet Computing 4, 36–44 (2000)
46. Smoreda, Z., Thomas, F.: Social networks and residential ICT adoption and use. In: Proceedings of the EURESCOM Summit 2001, Heidelberg, Germany, pp. 900–903 (2001)
47. Hao, H.: Research on building key post competency model. In: Proceedings of the 2010 International Conference on E- Product, E-Service and E-Entertainment, Henan, China, pp. 1–5 (2010)
48. Hennig-Thurau, T., Gwinner, K.P., Walsh, G., Gremler, D.D.: Electronic word-of-mouth via consumer- opinion platforms: What motivates consumers to articulate themselves on the Internet. Journal of Interactive Marketing 18, 38–52 (2004)
49. Birukou, A., Blanzieri, E., D'Andrea, V., Giorgini, P., Kokash, N., Modena, A.: IC-service: a service- oriented approach to the development of recommendation systems. In: Proceedings of the 2007 ACM Symposium on Applied Computing, Seoul, Korea, pp. 1683–1688 (2007)
50. Hofstede, G., Hofestede, G.J.: Cultures and organizations: Software of the mind. McGraw-Hill, New York (2005)
51. Forest, F., Arhippainen, L.: Social acceptance of proactive mobile services: observing and anticipating cultural aspects by a sociology of user experience method. In: Proceedings of the 2005 Joint Conference on Smart Objects and Ambient Intelligence, Grenoble, France (2005)
52. Farrell, J., Klemperer, P.: Coordination and lock-in: Competition with switching costs and network effects. In: Armstrong, M., Porter, R. (eds.) Handbook of Industrial Organization, vol. 3, pp. 1967–2072. Elsevier, Amsterdam (2007)
53. Mirani, R., Lederer, A.L.: An instrument for assessing the organizational benefits of IS projects. Decision Sciences 29, 803–838 (1998)
54. Chatterjee, S., Webber, J.: Developing enterprise web services: An architect's guide. Prentice-Hall, Upper Saddle River (2004)
55. Avizienis, A., Laprie, J.-C., Randell, B., Landwehr, C.: Basic concepts and taxonomy of dependable and secure computing. IEEE Transactions on Dependable and Secure Computing 1, 11–33 (2004)
56. Saaty, T.L.: The analytic hierarchy process. McGraw-Hill, New York (1980)
57. Golden, B.L., Wasil, E.A., Harker, P.T., Alexander, J.M.: The analytic hierarchy process: Applications and studies. Springer, Berlin (1989)
58. Choo, E., Wedley, W.: A common framework for deriving preference values from pairwise comparison matrices. Computers & Operations Research 31, 893–908 (2004)

Territorial Safety Networks

Martin Steinhauser, Andreas C. Sonnenbichler, and Andreas Geyer-Schulz

Karlsruhe Institute of Technology, Kaiserstrasse 12, Karlsruhe, Germany
martin.steinhauser@student.kit.edu,
{andreas.sonnenbichler,andreas.geyer-schulz}@kit.edu

Abstract. It has been shown that crime and fear of crime are related to a loss of social control in large cities. Furthermore, the by-stander effect might prevent help for people in need in the case of an emergency. In this paper we suggest the Community Watch Service. It is a conceptional IT-framework to enable citizens create and/or join virtual, territorial communities. We define virtual, territorial communities as virtual communities which are linked to certain territorial aspects, e.g. a community for a certain city district, a specific street, a small town, a administrative border or any other territorial district. The Community Watch Service enriches each territory with certain software services offering functionality like reporting damage to public property, receiving information from public authorities or organizing help in the neighborhood. The Community Watch Service framework aims to improve social control in a positive way and to increase public safety in large cities. The framework is demonstrated with a prototype. It is available for standard web browsers and Android-based mobile phones.

1 Introduction

Crime in public places, unfortunately, happens everywhere and often. A 17-year old girl was injured by another girl in Karlsruhe. The incident was witnessed by several bystanders [16]. In Munich, business man Dominik Brunner was beaten to death while defending young people against attackers [28]. Also in Munich senior citizen Bruno Hubertus was attacked by two young men, because he stared at them [27]. All three cases have in common that the offenders are young people committing the crimes due to negligible causes. The attacks have taken place in large cities with lots of bystanders around. None of them provided help.

In the article [22] an online service is described how to use one's personal social network to receive help in an emergency situation. This Emergency Alert Service (EAS) collects data from the user's own contacts and calculates a friendship network. This network is used in case of an emergency. By making use of geo-location data of the victim, friends close enough to provide help and authorities (e.g. police) are alerted through their mobile phones. The EAS has been designed on a peer-to-peer mechanism and is based on mobile applications. The success of the EAS critically depends on the size of one's social network, the local proximity of one's social groups, and the strength of the social norms leading to help (social control). Therefore, in this paper we extend the Emergency Alert Service to a service bundle of territory-based social services. The motivation for this is that territory-based social services lead to an improvement in

M.S. Obaidat, J.L. Sevillano, and J. Filipe (Eds.): ICETE 2011, CCIS 314, pp. 100–114, 2012.
© Springer-Verlag Berlin Heidelberg 2012

'real-life' social groups building in one's neighborhood and thus improve the social relations and reinforce a positive social control.

Our service framework integrates territories in social networks: People register with their home location to be able to join local territories. They can also create territories on their own. These territories and the services on top are used to pass on 'territorial' information. Different kinds of services are possible: chat functionality, broken windows or damage to public property can be reported to authorities, and municipal administration can contact citizens, up to people in need that can ask for help.

With our work we aim to integrate and enable citizens to take over (more) responsibility for their place of living. We hope to create more of a feeling of ownership and commitment in the neighborhood. To achieve this, we focus on the power of social networks, pervasive computers and internet technology.

In section 2 we motivate our service by giving basic information when and how people feel secure and how safety in places, e.g. cities, can be achieved. Section 3 reviews current scientific work and applications in this field. In section 4 we describe our conceptual architecture for a territorial safety service framework and present its implementation as a prototype in section 5. We round up this paper in section 6 by a conclusion and look out for future work.

2   Fundamentals and Challenges

In 2010 for the first time worldwide more people lived in cities than in the rural area [7, p.47]. The consequences of that trend have been analyzed by Urban 21, the experts' report on the future of cities [15, p.205]. For mature cities the report predicts, for example, the proceeding separation of rich and poor people in urban areas and increasing conflicts between them. Crimes as a consequence of social tensions due to poverty are regarded as the classical theory in criminology [9, p.39-41]. Statistics prove a higher occurrence of criminality in cities than in rural areas (e.g. [4, p.46]). For the reasons for having an urban-rural gap in criminality we refer to Oberwittler and Koellisch [21, p.135]:

- There are more opportunities and incentives to commit crime in a conurbation of a big city compared to the rural area.
- The emergence of social hot spots in conurbations promotes social deviant behaviour.
- In rural areas there is stricter informal social control[1].
- In a rural area a high amount of deviant behaviors are handled underneath the citizens, whereas in the city often complaints are written.

Not only is the criminality higher in big cities but also the fear of crime. Surveys from 1999 (compare [5, p.48] among others) show a remarkable difference in the categories 'felt insecurity' and 'going to be a victim soon' depending on the size of the population [29, p.59]. Especially street crimes like the ones mentioned in section 1 have a considerable effect on the sense of security, due to a high number of possibilities to commit a

---

[1] Informal social control tries to reach behavioral conformity of members of a family, neighborhood, in an association or similar social groups [25, p.19].

crime on the one hand and the few chances to avoid such crimes on the other hand [17, p.6ff].

According to Boers, the reasons for a higher fear of crime can be broken down in three categories [6, p.45ff]: (1) A person fears crime more after being a victim (victimization perspective), (2) the fear of crime increases with the loss of informal social control (social-control perspective), (3) and media, politics, and official institutions influence the perception of the security (social-problem perspective). The theory of the social control perspective is closely related to the Broken Windows Theory by Wilson and Kelling [19, p.144].

Since informal social control plays a major role in crime as well as in the fear of crime, it is worth to be investigated more deeply. Fassmann [10] describes the differences between urban and rural areas, also focusing on social relationships. In a big city it is not possible to know all people by their names, characteristics and history. The traditional interaction with neighbors through knowing and caring for them is replaced by anonymous and often changing contacts to a big circle of acquaintances. Regarding to Simmel [26, p.122], townspeople can't face others with the same emotionalism (participating, understanding) and they build up a shield against many of the stimuli in a city. Townspeople do not only react differently to their environment, but they also notice only parts of the reality around them (e.g. people in need).

The characteristics of people living in a city also affect the emergency process. Whether citizens are willing to help people in need depends on a number of criteria explained by Darley and Latane in the social help process (see figure 1). For a detailed analysis, especially focusing on the bystander effect, the main reason for unhelpful crowds, we refer to [13].

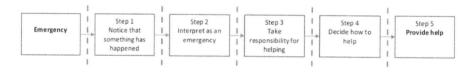

Fig. 1. Social Help Process according to Darley and Latane ([18, p.152-155] and [8, p.367])

Studies also show that people help more often, if they know the area. A person, who has fallen down, gets less help in an airport than at a subway station [19, p.154]. We argue that the criteria 'known environment' influences helpfulness.

One main point of our suggested territory-based service framework is the aim to strengthen the informal social control of citizens since this reduces the fear of crime as well as crime itself.

3   Related Work

This section takes a look at the latest concepts dealing with crime, participation of citizens and using information and communication technologies.

Fig. 2. Crime Map LAPD and corresponding Basic Car area [1]

The region of Brandenburg (Germany) offers a portal offering persons, registered by email, the possibility to report issues to the city administration. Messages are categorized (waste, vandalism, ...), contain a description, a postal address, the possibility to add pictures and a processing status. The issues can be tracked by users and employees. Employees of the city administration update the issues. This leads to an increased transparency [20]. FixMyStreet[2] follows a similar approach.

To inform their citizens about crime, the Los Angeles Police Department (LAPD) publishes a crime map (see figure 2). The crime map is part of an E-Policing strategy which applies the community policing ideas through the internet. A police district includes several 'Basic Car'-districts. Citizens have the possibility to engage as Senior Lead Officer who is the contact person for the local inhabitants. His task is to watch local criminality and to inform the police and the citizens about news[3]. German newspapers have started to track the level of crime on a map, too[4].

Video surveillance has been used for years to prevent crime on streets and public places. Many of the cities in Great Britain are using the closed circuit television-technology. A critical point of video surveillance is the monitoring of recorded videos [11, p.6-7]. A concept for an involvement of citizens in monitoring is offered by the company Internet Eyes Ltd. People all over the world have the chance to watch randomly selected surveillance cameras without knowing their actual location. By reporting an incident they gain points and receive prices[5].

The company Innovative Support To Emergencies Diseases and Disasters (InSTEDD)[6] has published the concept paper 'Watchfire'. It deals with emergencies (e.g. storms, fire, earthquakes and epidemics) in which inhabitants can not expect fast help from official aid organizations, but must rely on help from neighbors [3].

---

[2] http://www.fixmystreet.com

[3] http://www.lapdcrimemaps.org

[4] see the 'Blaulichtkurier' at http://www.berliner-kurier.de

[5] http://interneteyes.co.uk

[6] http://instedd.org

Fig. 3. Screenshot of the Watchfire site [3, p.3]

A screenshot is depicted in figure 3. As potential users InSTEDD especially addresses participants of neighborhood watch organizations. After signing up a user can see other users and their whereabouts on a map. Users can chat with each other and can send messages through mobile phones. Watchfire can be connected to professional aid organizations, but is primarily designed as local alert system for neighbors.

4   The Concept of the Community Watch Service

In section 3 we described some ways of dealing with crime and fear of crime. A recurring element is the focus on social-control. Social-control is hard to promote, especially in larger anonymous cities. Most of the existing concepts have territorial aspects included: Segregation, urban development of territories, neighborhood watch organizations, the police who is responsible for a district, reporting issues to the local city administration or a chat functionality to talk to neighbors. But also concepts like "Getting Help In A Crowd" (see [13]) which are independent of setting up a territory are possible. All of them have in common that there needs to be a motivation why persons participate in crime prevention or the emergency response process.

The main idea of the concept, named 'Community Watch Service' (CWS), is to create and improve relationships between neighbors. We do this by offering territory-based services in which only residents can participate. One consequence out of that is to know and verify the residence of a user. Another is, to map services to arbitrarily shaped territories. By this, we aim to strengthen the identification of persons with 'their' territories since only in-territory-people (in-group) may join. Furthermore, services can be offered in well-defined territories only, making sure that only local users can participate. We have to ensure that privacy of personal data, especially geo-locations of users. We expect people do not want to see personal information like their address being public information. Therefore, we do not show geo-positions of users but ensure only, that they can join only those territories their place belongs to. Furthermore, we use pseudonyms.

The creation of a relationship between people often starts with the fact that they live next to each other. This closeness can result in the feeling of belonging together as a group. Living next to each other creates common interests (e.g. talking about city topics, shared problems with vandalism, traffic related issues, fear of crime, ...) and opportunities to help each other (e.g. borrowing milk, receiving parcels, recommending a restaurant, taking care of children, ...) which could be channeled and supported by information and communication technology. The hypothesis is: Shared interests, opportunities for mutual help and the size of one's social network strengthens the motivation to engage locally even to the point that help is provided in the case of an emergency.

We do not restrict territory-based services to crime-related topics: Results of research on neighborhood watch programs show that services only motivated by crime related issues tend to get inactive over time [12, p.336]. Therefore, we offer a mixed bundle of services which can be crime related but need not to. The question which needs to be answered is, how to enable citizens to make use of multiple services in an easy way. Right now there are a lot of services available, offered by police, city administration or others. To be appealing, the Community Watch Service must offer its services in an easy, automated and structured way.

The living situation of a citizen can be very different. There are mini-neighborhoods with one-family-houses and block constructions. People in both places may have different attitudes and possibilities to engage in their neighborhood. Therefore, offered territory-based services may differ as well. E.g. in a highly anonymous environment, a local chat functionality may be a good starting point. A rescue service asking residents for help in the case of an emergency may be futile at first. Nevertheless, an increasing number of people using local services offered through CWS may improve the relevancy (acceptance) of such an emergency service later: First, people start with chats, then make use of something like FixMyStreet. Later a network with a Senior Lead Officer can evolve and then the willingness to participate in more demanding services like a local rescue service may rise. In other words – to reach the aim of 'Supporting Safety Through Social Territorial Networks' one must start with non-safety relevant services first and one can build upon that later.

The shape of a territory is determined by the offered service. A FixMyStreet-like service territory needs to be set up according to the administrative area of the city administration. Reported issues in territories are forwarded to the responsible employee by the service. The size and shape of territories may follow 'official' boundaries like city limits, districts, 911 service areas, or can be defined freely by the users' needs. For architectural reasons for territory shaping, we refer also to the book of Christopher Alexander [2]. In any case, the owner of the territory has the power to shape it. To simplify the shaping of territories, the company Urban Mapping Inc. offers official boundaries which may then be applied[7]. They can be used as orientation for owners of territories in order to shape them. Figure 4 shows an example from the prototype described in section 5.

A resident (whose actual location is hidden for data protection reasons) is the owner of the grey, inner most, smallest circle territory. It is linked to an emergency response service, where the user participates as emergency helper (the latter information is not

---

[7] http://www.urbanmapping.com

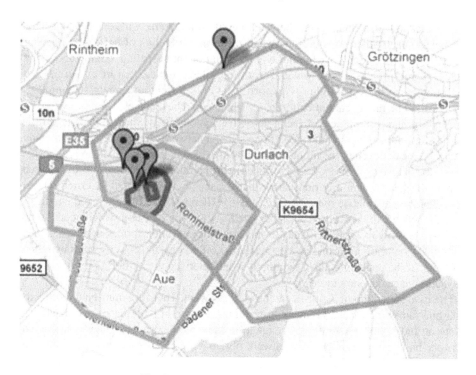

Fig. 4. Combination of different territories

depicted in the figure). The same person is registered in the territory 'Neighbors and friends' (brown, small circle) and 'fixmystreet' (turquoise, large on the left). There is another territory for which he is not registered (purple, large territory on the right). Detailed information about territories, linked services, owner, subscription state, etc., on pops up when moving the mouse over the territory marker (see figure 5).

Generally, a user can create his own territories and link them to services. Furthermore, a user can sign up to existing services covering his registered place of living. The sign-up process may include the approval of the territory owner. The CWS framework supports general functions. These include among others the registration of a new user with checking his residence, creating and editing territories and linking them to services, searching for them and editing user settings. The service itself might be offered by third parties. A territory is always linked to exactly one service. Otherwise, users registered for a service would have to sign-up for new services attached to the same territory again. Nevertheless, the shape of a territory can be (technically) reused for another territory (with the same shape) but linked to another service. The idea is to have encapsulated services with a given set of functionality. The conceptional augmented service models of Groenroos can be applied to differentiate core services [14, p.163ff]. 'Small and similar' functionality can extend an existing core service (attached to a territory) but (different) new core functionality would lead to a new service.

We expect CWS being successful only if valuable services are provided for territories. Therefore, the following list of examples is dedicated to give some examples of

Fig. 5. Editing territories in the CWS framework

territorial services. The order of examples reflects the degree of commitment or participation level of the citizens. Services with a lower requirement level are listed first.

– Information service of the city.
  The city informs selective territories about planned construction sites, street festivals, cultural events, ...
– Information service of the police.
  The Police provides general information about crime in the territory, crime prevention activities, and specific information on crime prosecution. The Police publishes mug shots in the newspaper or on the police's homepage. Those mug shots can be published promptly and selectively even on the mobile if offered.
– Chat functionality.
  People talk to people nearby about neighborhood gossip (weather, found a cat), but can also talk about security relevant stuff: an open car in front of the house, persons loitering in front of the house.

- Fixmystreet similar service.
  Either the city administration offers this service and deals with issues (Customer-ToAdministration) or people in the neighborhood take care themselves (Customer-ToCustomer).
- Local emergency helper.
  In the field of medical emergencies there are already first respondent concepts in place in which people agree to do locally voluntary work. The German red cross association has built up local first respondent teams to bridge the gap until professional help of aid organizations arrives. Those teams are integrated in the rescue chain and get informed by the headquarter [24, p.1]. The local emergency helper is a service where the helper is registered for a territory and others using this service push a button on their mobile which locates themselves and informs helpers registered in the callers territory.

In addition to these more security related services the CWS framework offers the freedom to be extended with other applications. A lot of room for creativity exists: a territory for finding people to go out with, organizing a street festival, offering mutual help, or other services which improve social interactions in the neighborhood are possible.

From these requirements it follows that people may want to be informed about new territories/services in their environment. Nevertheless, too much information would possibly be considered as spam. To deal with excessive generation of territories the territory creation and user perspective must be analyzed. One solution is to collect notifications of new territories and send out personalized newsletters once a month.

5   Prototype

Our CWS prototype includes the basic functions of the described concepts. This includes registering for CWS, creating and editing territories, finding territories and joining them. The prototype is currently available for standard personal computers through a web browser and also for mobile phones based on Android[8].

To make use of (backend) services already available, we used a web service technology for our implementation. Pautasso et al. [23] discuss the difference between big web service (WS-*) and REST. Their result is, that REST needs less architectural decisions to make but 'lead[s] to significant development efforts and technical risk, for example the design of the exact specification of the resources and their URI addressing scheme' [23, p.813]. Since CWS wants to be an open framework for services with territorial aspects, for an encapsulated application the full complexity of WS-* services can be used. Figure 6 shows the components and their connections, the communication interfaces and protocols of the chosen architecture. The main intention of the figure is to give an overview of the needed components. The components can be related to the lanes of the process description in figure 7 – the sub processes in the lane 'User' are implemented by 'Mobile' and 'Portal of a city'.

A key issue in the CWS concept is the residence of a user. This location is verified during the sign-up process of a user. This can be done by trusted third parties like the

---

[8] http://www.android.com

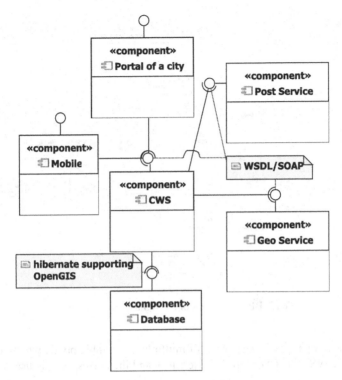

Fig. 6. Architecture of the CWS prototype

city administration who maintain the city register listing all residents. If trusted third parties lack an API or the permission to access these kind of data, a validation process as used e.g. by credit card companies can be applied. The CWS prototype integrates the services offered by 'Postal Methods'[9] to send letters to an address of a user. The letter contains an activation key which secures that the user really lives at the specified address. Only after activation, the user registration process for territories is finished successfully.

To be able to do calculations with the address of a user, the address is translated to spatial data for which the geo-referencing service of the "Via Michelin"[10] service is used. Of course, the user data and, especially, the location must be stored on a database level. Since later on there will be frequently requests for users of a territory, spatial data is directly saved in the OpenGIS format to be able to execute this request on the database level.

Figure 7 shows the different steps that are executed during user registration as a BPMN diagram (SOAP messages are shown as a postal symbol). After a successful activation, the user can create, edit and delete own territories by using map functionality. Google Maps[11] offers the Google Maps API. The API allows creating polygons in all

---

[9] http://www.postalmethods.com

[10] http://www.viamichelin.com

[11] http://maps.google.com

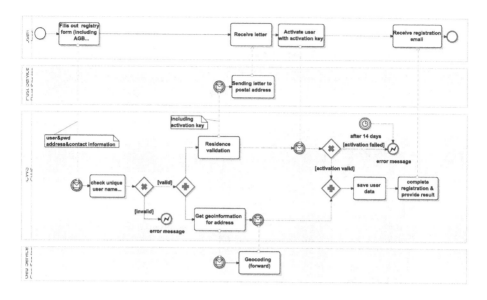

Fig. 7. BPMN process of a CWS user registration

desired shapes. Such polygons consist of multiple geographic points which are transferred to the CWS. The CWS saves the territory and the corresponding user data in its database.

Furthermore, a user can search for territories and is notified by email if new territories are created 'on top of' him. The territory search makes use of the hibernate criteria technology to efficiently execute complex searches (combination of multiple search criteria over many databases). By doing so, the user can explore different parts of the city and their social cohesion. Territories can be assigned properties like 'isHidden' to allow citizens to exclude their territory and the linked service from public view. This feature may be used e.g. in the service 'senior citizen partnership' which would otherwise give criminals easy targets.

The search function supports owner-related, location-related and service-related attributes. When a new territory is created, users with their residence inside this territory are identified. If these users have activated email notification, they are informed by email to explore the new territory. Figure 8 shows how the underlying ER-diagram looks like to store the necessary data. A user may also join existing territories. He can only join, if the territory related to the service includes the user's residence.

6   Conclusions and Future Work

Public crime and fear of crime is common in larger cities. In section 2 we have presented some fundamentals, how a low level of social control correlates with the size of the population. Besides other aspects, this is an important factor in crime and felt crime level. Furthermore, the bystander effect may prevent help in the case of emergencies.

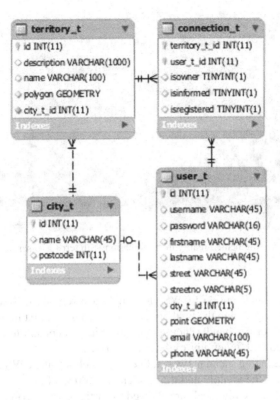

Fig. 8. Entity Relation diagram of the CWS prototype

To strengthen social control we suggest the Community Watch Service (CWS) Framework. The service framework enables citizens to form territorial communities. Every participant in the CWS can join communities related to his place or create his own territories. Such a community is linked with a certain functionality. For example, in one community, information about planned construction sites is distributed to the participants by the city administration. Another community service deals with damage to public property: Citizens report damage while employees of the city administration track these issues and fix them. A third possibility is local emergency helpers, who respond to help requests.

In this article we described the conceptual architecture of the Community Watch Service and its realization as a first prototype.

The mobile aspect of CWS has not been discussed in this paper that much but holds a significant potential. There are many appliances possible. A very sophisticated way of integrating CWS in a mobile application (next to just locate yourself and show the map on the Android-based mobile phone) is shown in figure 9.

The user sees through a camera display the real world with a digital overlay of territories above him – he might feel safer since he is walking through the supervised neighborhood 'NW-Block 17'.

Fig. 9. Augmented reality in combination with territorial services

Also, a full implementation of CWS and a field test remain for future work. Even without a full CWS system in the field, user surveys can give a first indication of how a concrete territorial service bundle should look like. First acceptance tests with residents could be conducted with mock-ups of the user interface.

With regard to existing social networks, like e.g. Facebook, the CWS concentrates on real social relations: the identity and the residential address of persons participating in the CWS are validated. Only locals are allowed to participate in territories. The aspects of belonging together present in local neighborhoods, local commitment, and informal social control are strengthened.

From a technological point of view, CWS is an open framework (available for standard web browsers and Android based mobile phones) which is using different existing web-services. CWS and all the web-services employed rely on flexible rights management services which handle location and group-based access requests. Today, none of the existing commercial social networks provides this functionality. The independence of an existing commercialized social network with given APIs leaves the freedom of developing completely new functionality, like searching for new services/territories nearby. Yet, CWS could be coupled with or added to the existing functionality of a social network – provided the rights management services of the social network are flexible enough and extended with territorial functionality – because in the end – the people that are assigned to local territories, connected with each other indirectly, are potential customers of a social network.

Acknowledgements. The research leading to these results has received funding from the European Community's 7th Framework Program FP7/2007-2013 under grant agreement n°215453 – WeKnowIt.

References

1. Crime Map LAPD and corresponding Basic Car area (2010),
   `http://www.lapdcrimemaps.org`
2. Alexander, C.: The Timeless Way of Building. Center for Environmental Structure Series,
   vol. 1. Oxford University Press, New York (1979)
3. Beckman, L., Rasmussen, E.: WATCHFIRE: Neighborhood Watch 2.0. In: STEDD
   (2010), `http://www.cmu.edu/silicon-valley/dmi/workshop/position-`
   `paper/beckman-pp.pdf` (last accessed: August 19, 2010)
4. Polizeiliche Kriminalstatistik (2007), bundeskriminalamt, `http://www.bka.de/pks/`
   `pks2007/download/pks-jb_2007_bka.pdf` (last accessed: July 12, 2010)
5. Polizeiliche Kriminalstatistik (1999), bundeskriminalamt,
   `http://www.bka.de/pks/pks1999/docs.zip` (last accessed: July 12, 2010)
6. Boers, K.: Kriminalitaetsfurcht: ueber den Entstehungszusammenhang und die Folgen
   eines sozialen Problems. Hamburger Studien zur Kriminologie, vol. 12. Centaurus-
   Verlagsgesellschaft, Hamburg (1991)
7. Verstaedterung: Stadt- und Landbevoelkerung in absoluten Zahlen und in Prozent der Welt-
   bevoelkerung (2010), bundeszentrale fuer politische Bildung,
   `http://www.bpb.de/files/HBW2V2.pdf` (last accessed: July 02, 2010)
8. Brehm, S.S., Kassin, S.M., Fein, S.: Social psychology, 6. aufl. edn. Houghton Mifflin, New
   York (2005)
9. Eisner, M.: Das Ende der zivilisierten Stadt? In: Die Auswirkungen von Modernisierung und
   urbaner Krise auf Gewaltdelinquenz. Campus-Verl., Frankfurt (1997)
10. Fassmann, H.: Stadtgeographie, Allgemeine Stadtgeographie, 2. neubearbeitete aufl. edn.,
    vol. 1. Westermann, Braunschweig (2009)
11. Floeting, H.: Can Technology Keep Us Safe? In: New Security Systems, Technological-
    Organizational Convergence, Developing Urban Security Regimes (2007),
    `http://edoc.difu.de/edoc.php?id=N403LKI7`
12. Garofalo, J., McLeod, M.: The structure and operations of neighborhood watch programs in
    the United States. Crime & Delinquency 35(3), 326 (1989)
13. Geyer-Schulz, A., Ovelgoenne, M., Sonnenbichler, A.: Getting help in a crowd – a social
    emergency alert service. In: Proceedings of the International Conference on e-Business.
    INSTICC, Athens (2010)
14. Groenroos, C.: Service management and marketing: customer management in service com-
    petition, 3rd edn. Wiley, Chichester (2007)
15. Hall, P., Pfeiffer, U.: Urban 21: der Expertenbericht zur Zukunft der Staedte. Menschen,
    Medien, Maerkte. Dt. Verl.-Anst., Stuttgart (2000)
16. Durch Messerstiche verletzt (2006), KA-News GmbH, `http://www.ka-news.de/`
    `region/karl-sruhe/Durch-Messerstiche-verletzt;art6066,50552?`
    `show=tfr200661-1352K` (last accessed: June 29, 2010)
17. Koetzsche, H., Hamacher, H.W.: Lehr- und Studienbriefe Kriminalistik, Kriminalistik, vol. 8.
    Verlage Deutsche Polizeiliteratur, Hilden (1990)
18. Latane, B., Darley, J.: The unresponsive bystander. Appleton-Century-Crofts, New York
    (1970)
19. Luedemann, C., Ohlemacher, T.: Soziologie der Kriminalitaet: Theoretische und empirische
    Perspektiven. Grundlagentexte der Soziologie, Juventa (2002)
20. eGovernment-Wettbewerb: Buerger machen mit, Maerker Brandenburg (2007), ministerium
    des Innern des Landes Brandenburg, `http://www.egovernment-wettbewerb.de/`
    `praesentatio-nen/2010/maerker_-online.pdf` (last accessed: August 19,
    2010)

21. Oberwittler, D., Koellisch, T.: Jugendkriminalitaet in Stadt und Land. In: Raithel, J., Mansel, J. (eds.) Kriminalitaet und Gewalt im Jugendalter: Hell- und Dunkelfeldbefunde im Vergleich, Juventa, Weinheim, Muenchen, pp. 135–161 (2003)

22. Ovelgoenne, M., Sonnenbichler, A., Geyer-Schulz, A.: Social emergency alert service - a Location-Based Privacy-Aware personal safety service. In: Proceedings of the 2010 Fourth International Conference on Next Generation Mobile Applications, Services and Technologies (NGMAST), pp. 84–89 (2010), doi:10.1109/NGMAST.2010.27

23. Pautasso, C., Zimmermann, O., Leymann, F.: Restful web services vs. 'big' web services: making the right architectural decision. In: WWW 2008: Proceeding of the 17th International Conference on World Wide Web, pp. 805–814. ACM, New York (2008)

24. Schoechlin, J., Ayasse, F.: 10 Jahre First-Responder-Teams: Erfahrungen beim DRK Mörsch. Rettungsdienst 27, 230–237 (2004)

25. Schwind, H.D.: Kriminologie: Eine praxisorientierte Einfuehrung mit Beispielen, 19th edn. neubearbeitete und erweiterte aufl. edn. Kriminalistik Verlag Heidelberg, Heidelberg (2009)

26. Simmel, G.: Die Grossstaedte und das Geistesleben. Zahn & Jaensch (1903)

27. Was labert der mich an (2007), Spiegel Online GmbH, http://www.spiegel.de/panorama/justiz/0,1518,-525153,00.html (last accessed: June 29, 2010)

28. Protokoll einer Eskalation (2010), Spiegel Online GmbH, http://www.spiegel.de/spiegel/print/d-68785414.html (last accessed: July 12, 2010)

29. Wurtzbacher, J.: Urbane Sicherheit und Partizipation: Stellenwert und Funktion buergerschaftlicher Beteiligung an kommunaler Kriminalpraevention. VS Verlag fuer Sozialwissenschaften, Wiesbaden (2008)

Killer Applications for Fiber to the Home Networks: Market Potential, Time Horizons and User Groups

Tom Evens[1], Elke Boudry[1], Pieter Verdegem[1], Lieven De Marez[1], Erik Vanhauwaert[2],
Koen Casier[2], Jan Van Ooteghem[2], and Sofie Verbrugge[2]

[1] Research Group for Media & ICT, Interdisciplinary Institute for Broadband Technology
(IBBT), Ghent University, Korte Meer 7-9-11, Belgium
[2] Internet Based Communication and Services Research Group,
Interdisciplinary Institute for Broadband Technology (IBBT), Ghent University,
Gaston Crommenlaan 8 bus 201, 9050 Ghent, Belgium
```
{Tom.Evens,Elke.Boudry,Pieter.Verdegem,
            Lieven.DeMarez}@UGent.be
{Erik.Vanhaewaert,Koen.Casier,Jan.VanOoteghem,
        Sofie.Verbrugge}@intec.UGent.be
```

Abstract. Telecom operators in cooperation with utility companies and public institutions are deploying fiber to the home infrastructure. The roll-out of these networks is justified by the supposed increasing user demand for high-bandwidth applications. Starting from a user-oriented perspective, this paper considers the utility of these networks for future users and explores those killer applications that could convince end-users to migrate to high-bandwidth connections. B y means of an international expert survey, the paper identifies value-added services that benefit from fiber's network potential in terms of high speed, symmetry and low delay.

Keywords: Value-added Services, Fiber to the Home (FTTH), Bandwidth Requirements, Expert Study, Nielsen's Law, Gilder' Law.

1   Introduction

Countries and cities all over the world currently are in the process of developing large-scale projects in the internet broadband sector. In most cases, these initiatives are driven by public-private partnerships (PPP), that align the interests of different private and public players. Typical examples of private players in such cooperation are network operators and service providers. Public parties involved are often local communities, municipalities and governments. With these considerable investments in upgrading network infrastructure, all stakeholders are eager to provide innovative and advanced broadband services to various user groups and tap into a new pool of revenues [1]. Public parties justify the roll-out and deployment of next-generation networks (NGN) by the desire to improve the 'quality of place' for citizens and enterprises. This high-speed network infrastructure should not only function as an economic engine for attracting more companies and creating new job opportunities, but is sometimes believed to close the persistent social and digital divides. Although this

M.S. Obaidat, J.L. Sevillano, and J. Filipe (Eds.): ICETE 2011, CCIS 314, pp. 115–128, 2012.
© Springer-Verlag Berlin Heidelberg 2012

belief seems a bit techno-optimistic and is worth a discussion (see [2]), the debate lies not within the scope of this paper.

Another, and probably more powerful, argument for rationalizing the vast investments in large-scale network infrastructure projects is the increasing user demand for high-bandwidth applications. According to Nielsen's Law, postulated in 1998, the available bandwidth to high end-users increases with fifty percent per annum on average and the mass market lags the high end-user by two-three years [3]. This law predicts that 100 Mbps will be available in 2015 and 1 Gbps in 2020. Thanks to the increased deployment of next-generation network infrastructure (such as fiber), a growing number of countries are already providing services to the residential market with a bandwidth higher than anticipated by this law (albeit on a small scale). In Sweden, for example, 100 Mbps connections are available since 2004 in several areas of the country. Given the extensive residential fiber deployment and the growing rivalry among internet service providers (ISPs) in terms of pricing and capacity, Sweden is expected to pass the 1 Gbps milestone already in the near future [4]. These developments also confirm Gilder's Law that was proposed by new media prophet Georg Gilder in 1997. According to this law, total bandwidth of communication systems would triple every year for the following 25 years.

In 1964, McLuhan stated that '*the medium is the message*' by which he meant that content is defined by the nature of its distribution mode [5]. Following the rationale behind this phrase, the availability of high-bandwidth capacity should thus eventually result in the supply and consumption of bandwidth-intensive services and applications. However, it may be clear from the past that end-users are only willing to adopt new technology if this provides them with perceived added value and benefits (the so-called chicken-and-egg problem). With regard to fiber networks, Noam notes that '*it is common to rush into talk of technology or rollout strategy without first considering the utility to users. If one builds an oil pipe one must first be sure that there is an oil supply at one end and demand for it at the other. The economic case for investment in super-broadband must rest on its meeting a demand/price combination that is not satisfied today*' [6]. Especially in Europe, this demand for fiber networks is still mainly unproven. Whether the network operators' goal is to migrate existing DSL (or cable) customers to fiber or to position fiber as a superfast high-end offer, fiber technology is not yet a widespread success in Europe [7]. In general, the number of homes passed is still small and commercially available offers have not yet fully convinced potential customers, which seem satisfied with their existing connection, to migrate to fiber. Although prices for superfast broadband access are in line with or slightly higher than those charged for regular access, end-users are reluctant to switch to NGN providing more bandwidth capacity these days. If the perceived utility for end-users is not in access prices, the supply of value-added services will certainly have to provide this utility.

In this paper the focus is on the supply and demand for bandwidth-intensive applications. Following a user-oriented approach – instead of the more technological deterministic perspective – the paper tries to identify those services that offer added value and that benefit from fiber networks' potential in terms of high speed, symmetry, low delay and low jitter. Based on opinions of 21 international experts, this paper explores business opportunities for a limited set of services and applications, which might help in convincing end-users to switch from regular to ultra-broadband internet connections. In order to be sure that these services need NGN (in this case fiber), it is questioned whether or not existing infrastructure will suffice to deliver these applications with similar 'quality of service' (QoS) and 'quality of experience' (QoE) [8].

2   Do We Really Need Fiber?

'If you build it, they will come'. This technology-centered 'adage' is often heard when talking about an innovative product or service. It implies that supply automatically evokes demand and that each innovation finds its way to the end-user. As this reasoning merely is an illustration of technological-deterministic approach, it does not provide sufficient arguments to convince operators to invest into expensive infrastructure in the short term. Currently, there is a lot of debate among experts whether fiber's bandwidth is excessive for services' requirements and whether existing network infrastructure would suffice to offer ultra-broadband applications. Hence, this section provides a brief overview of this debate – including some of the arguments held by fiber advocates and opponents – but also aims at going beyond this mainly theoretical discussion by offering technical application requirements and more quantitative argumentation of why fiber is an appropriate solution for realizing value-added services.

2.1   Fiber Deployment

Whereas previously Digital Subscriber Line (DSL) and Hybrid Fiber Coax (HFC) were among the most prominent technologies to provide homes and multi-dwelling buildings with access to telecommunications services, fiber is increasingly used to deliver signals from the operators' switching equipment to houses or offices. 'Fiber' is the generic term for any broadband network architecture that uses optical fiber to replace all or part of the existing metal local loop used for last mile internet communications. With regard to the distance between the optical fiber and the connected end-user (the shorter this distance, the faster the connection), distinct configurations can be distinguished:

- Fiber to the node (FTTN): fiber is terminated in a street cabinet up to 300 meter from the average end-user while the final last mile is connected by alternative distribution methods (wireless, copper, coax)
- Fiber-to-the-curb (FTTC): fiber is terminated in a street cabinet closer than 300 meter from the average end-user
- Fiber-to-the-building (FTTB): fiber terminates at the boundary of the building, the in-house connection continues over alternative in-building technologies
- Fiber to the home (FTTH): fiber continues indoors and reaches the living and working spaces

Compared to traditional infrastructure, the most obvious benefit optical fiber provides is speed. Fiber networks carry data by transmitting pulses of light, usually created by lasers, which turn these light signals on and off very quick. As these lasers are getting ever faster, higher speed data transmission is possible via the same network without the need to replace the fiber. Additionally, in contrast to other existing network media, the optical fiber is a medium with very low attenuation and dispersion of the signal. This allows optical networks to carry much higher bandwidths over longer distances with less loss and deformation of the signal (and content as such). Traditional upgraded network infrastructure (e.g. VDSL, DOCSIS) offers more problems for increasing bandwidths and current implementations typically ranging from 3 to 30 Mbps downstream and from 0.25 and 4.5 Mbps upstream capacity. Currently fiber offers downstream and upstream bandwidth of 100 Mbps even up to even 1 Gbps on the residential market. Business customers are often provided with much higher bandwidths over the same fiber network. Along with speed, symmetry – identical downstream and upstream bandwidth – is an important fiber benefit. The combination of speed and symmetry allows for low latency and as a result improved interactivity. Finally, fiber networks allow for a more reliable and consistent signal. As fiber is almost immune to electromagnetic interference and eavesdropping, its connection is perceived more stable than traditional network infrastructure. From a user perspective, this ultra-broadband network infrastructure should result in enhanced services and an increased QoE.

However, a small amount of authors believes that existing network infrastructure will suffice to deliver enhanced applications and services to end-users in the future. Fredebeul-Krein and Knoben [9], for example, argue that research shows limited evidence for increasing demand for high-bandwidth capacity and that people are rather reluctant to pay a price premium for fiber connections. In addition, telecom operators are facing regulatory uncertainty regarding future wholesale (*i.e.* will first movers be forced to open up their network to alternative access-seeking operators?), while technical progress may allow the current networks to deliver higher bandwidth. They claim that for telecom operators there are no obvious guarantees for a viable business case [10]. Noam also questions the viability of high-bandwidth content providers, which would have to invest heavily in developing innovative services without any guarantees considering return on investment [7].

This view is largely disproved by true broadband believers, who consider current networks incapable of meeting future bandwidth requirements, even if network operators would strongly invest to improve existing infrastructure. According to Huigen and Cave [11], *'the question is not so much whether a massive increase in bandwidth over fixed access networks is necessary, but rather when and how it will be realized'*. As the majority of applications demanding high-bandwidth is still to be developed, fiber is often said to be the most 'future-proof' technology. Referring to the traditional chicken-and-egg problem new platforms face, it is important to note that the availability of high-capacity services necessitates improved network infrastructure, while investments in upgrading networks may stimulate the development of capacity-sensitive applications [12]. This might mean that cities and countries can benefit from an 'accumulation effect'. The more homes and buildings are passed with fiber, the higher penetration rates will be and the more novel applications will be developed. In this regard, the development and provision of services could benefit from economies of scale, both on the supply and the demand side.

2.2   Applications Requirements

In order to evaluate the technical requirements for ultra-broadband applications with regard to existing and next-generation networks, one has to consider some properties of online communication networks [13]. The best-known network parameter is the provided bandwidth, which defines the amount of information sent over the network (expressed in bits/second). A distinction should be made between download and upload capacity, and between average and peak bit rates that are processed over a digital communication network. In terms of bandwidth, video applications obviously require more capacity to send over a network compared to text files. While it takes about 5Mb to share PDF e-books, sharing full-length high-definition quality movies requires up to several Gbs. Depending on its duration and quality level, high-definition video such as internet-protocol television (IPTV) content streams require about 12.5 to 20 Mbps [14]. For this reason, video-related applications should definitely benefit from increased bandwidth of next-generation networks such as fiber to the home.

Apart from bandwidth, delay and jitter are also important design and performance characteristics of a telecommunications network. Delay specifies the time needed for a bit to travel from one node to the other (typically measured in fractions of seconds) while jitter refers to the variance in this delay. These parameters are only critical in case of bi-directional and real-time applications such as video telephony and streaming. A smooth conversation requires that one hears the other with a delay of less than 100ms. Jitter is even more important than delay and can cause severe quality degradations, and is often solved by providing a buffer at the receiving end with a given average fill rate. These buffers however will also result in additional delay.

Table 1. Next-generation network quality parameters

Service class	Delay	Jitter
Real time	< 5ms	< 1ms
Streaming	< 40ms	< 10ms
Transactional	< 100ms	N.A.

This overview of critical network parameters allows us to indicate the technical requirements for fiber-networked applications and to identify value-added services with market potential. In Table 1, the NGN quality parameters (in this case delay and jitter) are summarized. It is obvious that bandwidth-intensive applications relying on real time, streaming or/and transactional functionalities will capture fiber's full benefits.

Table 2. Bandwidth requirements for end-user services (minimum case, in Mbps) [14]

Service	2010	2020	2030
Voice	0.15	0.15	0.15
Video telephony	0.5-2	4	10
High speed gaming	0.25-2	4	60
Video on demand	1-3	20	200
Cloud computing	2-2.5	18	150
Live streaming	4-10	12.5	160
IPTV channel	4-10	12.5	160
IPTV zapping	5-15	15	208

In terms of end-users services, Table 2 provides an overview of the current and future requirements for broadband services as estimated in the EU-supported OASE project. It becomes clear that current networks with limited bandwidth will hardly suffice for these future services' requirements taking into account technological developments (e.g. the expected shift towards super high-definition and for some purposes 3D quality). In the case of video telephony (think of video conferencing and e-learning platforms), there should ideally be a two-way path high-quality video stream. Additional information (such as documents) can be shared as well, but as previously mentioned, the latter have considerably lower impact on bandwidth requirements. The current required impact for video telephony is estimated at 2 Mbps mounting up to 4 to 10 Mbps (both for upload and download) in the next decades. In addition, video telephony is very sensitive to delay and jitter. Considering a video surveillance application, delay and jitter will be less of a problem. A number of cameras (both in-house and out-house) could send high-quality video to a central server simultaneously, where the data stream is analyzed and suspicious activity triggers an alarm. Assuming six cameras (ca. 12.5Mbps per stream) to cover all relevant areas inside and around homes and offices, an upload capacity of 75 Mbps is required. Another promising application is IPTV (digital TV), requiring 12.5 Mbps for each channel being watched or recorded (though in practice this can increase up to 20 Mbps). This requirement could mount up to 600 Mbps with ultra-high definition (UHD, Super Hi-Vision) and 3D quality in the future. Finally, online back-up and content management systems could create added value to the end-user. By using cloud computing, media files created by the user can be safeguarded online instead of stored on a local space (requiring tens of gigabytes). As delay is less important for this service, network bandwidth is an important bottleneck. Unlike other applications, the bandwidth use of this application is less continuous, but occurs in burst in sync with the user's activity. For example, after shooting, a photographer wants to upload 400 high-quality photos (about 2 Gbs). At an upload speed of 5 Mbps, it takes close to one hour while it takes about ten minutes at a speed of 25 Mbps. As the user wants to browse his pictures after uploading, it takes two seconds to load each photo, which feels very slow and unresponsive. To reach a response time lower than half a second, a download speed of 100 Mbps is required, and bandwidths of 500 Mbps or above can give the user an instantaneous feeling of the application for viewing his photographs.

2.3   Existing vs. Next-gen Solutions

The first mentioned discussion on fiber deployment could lead to the conclusion that existing network infrastructure should suffice to deliver some of the aforementioned services to end-users with a more or less optimal QoS and QoE. However, this discussion on bandwidth-intensive applications and the related technical requirements may be quite artificial. In real life, these applications will be used simultaneously within a family context. Assume a family household of four members where the father watches a particular television channel on the regular screen (while recording another one via the set-top box), and the son is viewing a football game via his tablet-pc. At the same time, the daughter is safeguarding her pictures online while the mother is making a video call with her sister living abroad. In this imaginary case, a download bit rate of over 50 Mbps is required (100+ is recommended) whereas the upload speed would have to be 17.5 Mbps (30+ is recommended) to guarantee an optimal QoS and QoE. Not to mention that some of these applications are sensitive to delay and jitter, which the users will experience in case the network is working at (close to) full capacity.

As delay and jitter in the network are not only determined by the access technology, but also by several elements in the network infrastructure, they have not been quantified within this study. Still, every buffer that has a faster connection (*i.e.* fiber) can contribute to a lower delay. Similarly, jitter is only expected to increase by fiber solutions when the newly provided applications seem so popular that the relative load on the network is increased significantly. Hence, the rest of this section will focus on bandwidth.

There is currently no large-scale fiber to the home network deployed in the Belgian market. The major players that dominate the market (Belgacom and Telenet) are experimenting with FTTH pilots, but no roll-out is planned to date. Regarding bandwidth, Table 3 – showing a typical and high-end service – indicates that the existing infrastructure in Belgium (as well as in many other countries) may prove insufficient to deliver the services discussed in this paper. It should be noted that in the Telenet case video is broadcast in a separate RF-channel not impacting downstream or upstream traffic. Additionally, it is necessary to note that the up- and downstream bandwidth is shared amongst all customers of the same coax line. In the Belgacom case, the bandwidth is dedicated per customer, but is used for both internet and video.

Table 3. Bandwidth of Belgian ISPs (bandwidth capacity in Mbps, prices in Euros)

	Telenet (cable)		Belgacom (xDSL)	
	Normal	High	Normal	High
Down	15	100	12	30
Up	1	5	1.5	4.5
Price	30	99	33	58

Table 4. FTTH bandwidth offerings

Country	Down (Mbps)	Up (Mbps)
the Netherlands	50	50
Sweden	1000	100
France	100	100
Portugal	200	20
United States	50	20
Japan	100	100
Korea	100	100

The overview shows that the upgraded network infrastructure (DOCSIS 3.0 and VDSL for Telenet and Belgacom respectively) hardly guarantees the optimal QoS and QoE for high-bandwidth services. While the download speed of the high-end solution of Telenet could suffice, the upload speed – just like the other solutions – fails to meet future bandwidth requirements. Since end-users attach great value to file-sharing and user-generated content, applications increasingly require symmetrical bandwidth [15].

It should be mentioned that these offers are theoretical values. Telenet states on its website that measurements indicate that realistic speeds of both Telenet and Belgacom connections are about 75 percent of the bandwidths officially indicated. The lack of fiber to the home solutions in Belgium heavily contrasts with the 100 Mbps solutions offered in several other countries and parts of the world (in terms of penetration, Asia is the undisputable forerunner in deploying FTTH services) [7]. The Belgian demand for, and large-scale roll-out of fiber to the home remains to date mere speculation. This is perhaps not because of limited demand and willingness to pay and demand, but has much to do with the existing duopoly in the broadband market. This dominance may depress investments in network optimization and at the same time hamper entrance of alternative operators, who are likely to reduce investments and seek access to the incumbents' improved networks.

3   Research Method

The results are based on the interdisciplinary TERRAIN project (*Techno-Economic Research for futuRe Access Infrastructure Networks*), which focuses on a better cooperation between all public and private actors that are involved to optimize the roll-out of new telecom and utility networks, and to align the operational processes in a more consistent way. All deployment issues will be analyzed from a techno-economic point of view, considering the technical, regulatory, economic and user-related problems. In the remaining part of this paper, the focus will be on user studies.

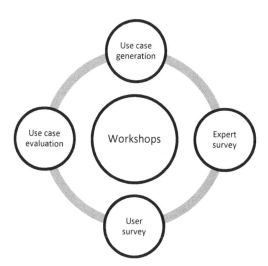

Fig. 1. Research design

In essence, the user studies within the project aim at identifying which applications and services have the potential to drive future adoption of fiber to the home networks, and which of these applications are fully appropriate to reap the fruits of superfast and high-bandwidth network infrastructure. As the focus of our first efforts was on exploring business opportunities, the primary goal of this study was to draw up and eventually evaluate a long list of high-bandwidth and fiber-sensitive applications (use cases). This has resulted in valuable input for the next stages of the project including a large-scale end-user survey both to residential and business customers.

Based on existing projects combined with literature research, a brainstorm session was organized to generate ideas for high-bandwidth applications. As a result, a long list of likely services was drawn up. This list was further discussed and refined in an interdisciplinary workshop with project partners. Eventually, a shortlist consisting of ten use cases was drafted:

- Surveillance cameras
- Virtual classrooms
- Health monitoring system
- Online multiplayer gaming
- Content storage and management
- Future Internet-protocol television (UHDTV and 3D)
- Video telephony
- Desktop sharing
- On-demand video streaming
- Immersive 3D tourist environment

To get a better picture of genuine drivers and use cases for FTTH solutions, it was deemed essential to take expert views and opinions into account. Therefore, a qualitative survey among international experts on fiber services and roll-outs was organized. A panel of international experts was derived from literature and personal contacts. All project partners were also invited to join the panel. All experts were sent a personal e-mail in which they were asked to complete an online questionnaire. In this questionnaire, the experts were asked about each service's likelihood, time horizons (in terms of technological feasibility, and reach of mass market) and most likely end-user groups.

A total of 21 experts completed the survey. Some 53 percent of respondents is working in public sector (especially research institutions) while the rest of the experts are mainly in the employ of equipment vendors and telecom operators. Most of them have a rather technical background, but a considerable part also indicated expertise in regulatory issues, content & applications and business models. In total, people from 8 countries participated in the expert survey.

4   Results

4.1   Overall Use Case Popularity

In the survey, the experts were asked to choose their personal three most convincing services and to rank them subsequently. Based on their ranking, use cases were given five (ranked first), three (ranked second) and one (ranked third) point(s). These points were then summed resulting in a total score. Rather than the absolute scores for each application, the relative position of each service is more interesting.

The resulting ranking brings to light some very interesting and perhaps unexpected conclusions. Health monitoring systems and online content management are clearly deemed most convincing, considering their high score and the fact that three experts rated them most convincing of all applications. The top three is completed by desktop sharing, beating an e-learning application and online multiplayer gaming. Without labeling these services as 'killer applications', they should be at least considered by service providers when rolling out fiber network infrastructure. These findings are somehow surprising since all the traditional video delivery applications – which were expected to benefit from fiber's high-bandwidth capacity – were found less convincing by the experts.

Table 5. Ranking of applications

Rank	Use case	Score	#1
1	Health monitoring system	18	3
2	Content storage/management	16	3
2	Desktop sharing	16	1
4	Virtual classroom	15	1
5	Online multiplayer gaming	14	2
6	Video telephony	11	2
6	Surveillance cameras	11	1
8	Internet-protocol television	6	0
8	On-demand video streaming	6	0
10	3D tourism environment	0	0

4.2   Time Horizons

In other parts of the survey, experts were asked about the time horizon along which the different use cases are expected to be available from a technical point of view and when they will reach mass market (*i.e.* be adopted by the early majority segments). With this, the study aimed to gather expert forecasts of the development and break-through of these services.

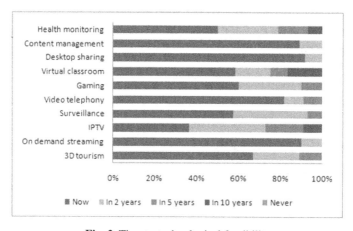

Fig. 2. Time to technological feasibility

With regard to the underlying technology of the use cases, experts consider that most of the applications can be launched at this moment or within two years except for 3D internet-protocol television (Figure 2). None of the applications' underlying technology is said to be infeasible. Four use cases were found market-ready, amongst other content management and desktop sharing systems, respectively ranked as number two and three in the former 'killer application' ranking. Surprisingly, health monitoring systems – identified as the most promising service – were seen as less market-ready. Future television is considered the least plausible use case as the minority of experts indicated the current readiness of technology. These findings may suggest that technology will not be the main barrier for the deployment of high-bandwidth applications. Experts confirm that most applications can be brought to market within two years; only the future television services are considered to be more long-term.

Regarding market acceptance and penetration, it is remarkable that the three most technologically feasible services (*i.e.* content management, desktop sharing and on-demand video streaming) should be able to reach mass market already today, although the time horizon for user adoption is less positive compared to its technological feasibility. According to the experts, technology is expected to come ahead of the market (Figure 3). While about 50 percent of the experts think that health monitoring systems are market-ready, only 25 percent estimates that there is a market for such a service at this moment. Hence, a time lag is expected between the actual possibility to enable an application from a technological stance and the time needed to reach critical mass (about 15 percent of the market). Generally, the time lag seems bigger for less popular use cases than for the most likely services – albeit that a considerable part of the experts expect health monitoring systems no sooner than within ten years.

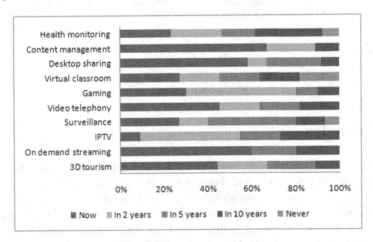

Fig. 3. Time to mass market

4.3   End-User Groups

After identifying promising services that are feasible from a technological as well as from a market-oriented perspective, experts were asked whether they believe an application is primarily a B2B or B2C scenario or both. Evidently, service providers are eager to offer services with market potential that can be used both for business and consumer purposes. In this context, applications identified as most promising are scoring rather well.

Figure 4 clearly shows that content management applications and surveillance cameras are considered appropriate for business as well as for consumer use. Health monitoring, online gaming, internet-protocol television and on-demand video streaming are seen as applications almost only relevant for consumer markets. In contrast, video telephony and desktop sharing are identified as business applications. Apart from this analysis, most use cases can be utilized by private as well as business end-users, which holds prospects in the light of the further development of these applications. As the development of these services will be subject to economies of scale on the supply and demand side, a larger sales potential should eventually lead to a cheaper and even faster development process.

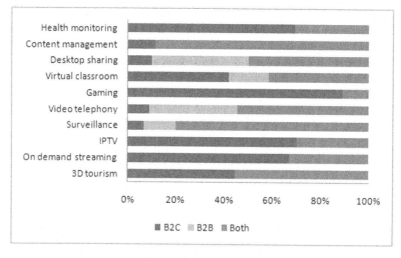

Fig. 4. End-user groups

5   Conclusions

In this paper, the focus was on the identification of applications that can generate added value to fiber networks and that can convince internet users to migrate from their existing connection to high-performance broadband networks. Since new technology is often developed and deployed without even knowing user requirements, a user-oriented approach was used in this project. In contrast to the belief that demand follows supply, a user-oriented approach allows us to identify what future users want, whether they are willing to pay for these services and when these services will be able to reach critical mass. As almost everything is possible from a technological perspective, service adoption is often slowed down by regulatory issues (e.g. privacy), unviable business models or products that fail to meet user requirements (pricing, features, added value, etc.). Hence, a plea is made for more interdisciplinary research on information technology looking beyond technical aspects but also taking into account economic, legal and social dimensions of new ICT applications.

The outcome of such a user-oriented approach is sometimes surprising since it may tackle taken-for-granted beliefs and provide refreshing insights that let arise new perspectives and inspiring solutions to old problems. Regarding fiber services, the literature – which is scarce – indicates video-based services as killer applications to fully benefit from fiber's higher bandwidth and speed. However, according to the experts consulted, high-quality video hardly seems convincing for end-users to switch to next-generation networks. Instead, health monitoring, content management and desktop sharing are identified as the most convincing use cases for connecting to fiber networks. In terms of time horizons, however, health monitoring lags behind as experts think its underlying technology is currently not ready while critical mass is expected within two years or at the earliest.

The findings should be considered explorative as they are only based on the views and opinions of 21 international experts. However, the results indicate which services are identified as value-added services and which create business opportunities for service providers. Thereby, the results provide valuable information for next research steps, including the construction of an end-user survey (both residential and business). Afterwards, it will be interesting to verify whether expert views correspond with end-user requirements and whether the most promising services will prove convincing to end-users.

Acknowledgements. This research was carried out as part of the IBBT TERRAIN project (2010-2012). This project is co-funded by IBBT, IWT and Acreo AB, Alcatel-Lucent, Comsof, Deutsche Telekom Laboratories, Digipolis, FTTH Council Europe, Geosparc, Stad Gent, TMVW, TE Connectivity, UNET and WCS Benelux BV.

References

1. Nucciarelli, A., Sadowski, B.M., Achard, P.O.: Emerging models of public-private interplay for European broadband access: evidence from the Netherlands and Italy. Telecommunications Policy 34(9), 513–527 (2010)
2. Dolente, C., Galea, J.J., Leporelli, C.: Next generation access and digital divide: opposites of the same coin? In: 21st European Regional ITS Conference, Copenhagen (2010)
3. Nielsen, J.: Nielsen's law of Internet bandwidth (1998),
   http://www.useit.com/alertbox/980405.html
4. Ventura Team LLP: Study to assess broadband bandwidth usage and key trends in Europe (2008), http://www.vandenberg.nl/publicaties/ftthrapport.pdf
5. McLuhan, M.: Understanding media: the extensions of man. McGraw Hill, New York (1964)
6. Noam, E.M.: If fiber is the medium, what is the message? Next-generation content for next-generation networks. Communications & Strategies, 19–34 (2008)
7. IDATE: FTTx 2010. Markets & Trends. Facts & Figures. IDATE, Montpellier (2010)
8. De Moor, K., De Marez, L.: The challenge of user- and QoE-centric research and product development in today's ICT-environment. In: Pierson, J., Mante-Meijer, E., Loos, E., Sapio, B. (eds.) Innovating for and by Users, pp. 77–90. Office for Official Publications of the European Communities, Luxembourg (2008)

 9. Fredebeul-Krein, M., Knoben, W.: Long term risk sharing contracts as an approach to establish public-private partnerships for investment into next generation access networks. Telecommunications Policy 34(9), 528–539 (2010)
10. Fredebeul-Krein, M., Steingröver, M.: Next-generation access networks: why is there a higher risk of investment and how to deal with it? In: Kruse, J., Dewenter, R. (eds.) Wettbewerbsprobleme im Internet, pp. 83–101. Hamburger Forum Medenökonomie, Hamburg (2008)
11. Huigen, J., Cave, M.: Regulation and the promotion of investment in next generation networks – A European dilemma. Telecommunications Policy 32(11), 713–721 (2008)
12. Falch, M., Henten, A.: Public private partnerships as a tool for stimulating investments in broadband. Telecommunications Policy 34(9), 496–504 (2010)
13. Comer, D.E.: Computer networks and internets. Prentice Hall, London (2009)
14. Charbonnier, B.: End-user future services in access, mobile and inbuilding networks (2008), http://www.ict-alpha.eu/upload/uafh%C3%A6ngige%20centre/webmap/alpha_d1%201p.pdf
15. Cave, M., Martin, I.: Motives and means for public investment in nationwide next generation networks. Telecommunications Policy 34(9), 505–512 (2010)

To Bid or Not To Bid?
Investigating Retail-Brand Keyword Performance in Sponsored Search Advertising

Tobias Blask, Burkhardt Funk, and Reinhard Schulte

Leuphana University of Lüneburg, Scharnhorststr. 1, 21335 Lüneburg, Germany
{blask,funk,schulte}@uni.leuphana.de
http://www.leuphana.de/ieg

Abstract. In Sponsored Search Advertising companies pay Search Engines for displaying their text advertisements in the context of selected queries on their Search Engine Results Pages (SERPs). The position of the ads is auctioned among all interested advertisers every time a query is executed by a user. The results are displayed separately from the organic results. Whether it is profitable for advertisers to pay for advertisements in the context of directly retail-brand related queries is a heated debate in practice between media agencies and budget responsible managers in companies. Anecdotal evidence implies that users who are searching for a specific retail-brand are conducting navigational searches and would end up on the brand owners website anyway, especially when the company is already placed prominently in the organic search results. The objective of the present research is to determine whether and under what circumstances it makes sense, in economic terms, for brand owners to pay for sponsored search ads for their own brand keywords. Using an exclusively available dataset from a major European internet-pharmacy we describe a non reactive method that is based on an A/B-test which enables us to investigate the economic value of the described behaviour. We are able to prove that the advertiser benefits significantly from these additional Sponsored Search ads which enable the company to generate more visitors (> 10 %), resulting in higher sales volumes at relatively low advertising costs even when the company is already listed in first position in the organic part of the respective SERP.

Keywords: Sponsored search, Search engine marketing, Paid search, Brand marketing, E-Commerce, Keyword selection, Branded keywords.

1 Introduction

In the information society, Internet search engines play a key role. They serve the information needs of their users and are an important source for advertising companies in terms of customer acquisition and activation [11]. Search engine companies like Google generate most of their revenue through sponsored search [10]. At the interface of computer science, economics, business administration, and behavioral sciences, search engine marketing has been established as an interdisciplinary research topic and has seen a growing and diverse number of publications during the last years [6][17][19][20]. Selected decision problems are examined from the perspective of three stakeholder groups

M.S. Obaidat, J.L. Sevillano, and J. Filipe (Eds.): ICETE 2011, CCIS 314, pp. 129–140, 2012.
© Springer-Verlag Berlin Heidelberg 2012

(i) users, (ii) search engines and (iii) advertising companies [24]. Beside the optimal bidding behavior in sponsored search auctions [13], one of the key decision problems for advertisers is the selection of keywords appropriate for their campaigns [1][7].

So far little research has been conducted on the use of brand names in sponsored search [14]. What is the subject of a heated debate in business practice is whether companies should bid on their own brand name or whether this only substitutes clicks from organic listings on the SERP. To answer this question, we apply a non-reactive experimental method and use it in a case study of an online pharmacy that is ranked first with its brand name in the organic search results in Google [18].

The contribution of this paper is the development and application of a method for measuring the impact of bidding on brand names in a partially controlled experiment. From a theoretical point of view, we make a contribution to understanding keyword selection in blended search. We begin with a review of the literature on the competitive importance of brands in search engine marketing. On this basis we derive four hypotheses which we examine using the methods described in chapter 4. In chapter 5 we discuss outcomes and business implications of this paper and finally give an outlook in chapter 6.

2   Literature Review

There are two streams of research which are important for our work. The first studies bidding behavior of competitors in sponsored search. The second stream blended search analyses user preferences for organic and sponsored results as well as the interactions between them.

2.1   Brand Bidding and Piggybacking

Although brand terms bidding behavior is of great relevance in business practice, there have only been very few scientific publications on the topic. As a first step, a distinction has to be drawn between the bids on the own brand and those on other companies brands. Previous research on sponsored search brand keyword advertising by Jansen and Rosso [14], which was based on the global top 100 brands included in the well-known WPP BrandZ survey, reveals that 2/3 of the brand names examined were used by other firms while only 1/3 of the brand owners analyzed advertise in the context of their own brand names on SERPs. Bidding on other companies brand names is referred to as piggybacking, for which three different types of motivation have been isolated: (i) competitive: piggybacking by an obvious, direct competitor; (ii) promotional: e.g. by a reseller; and (iii) orthogonal: e.g. by companies that offer complementary services and products for the brand owners products. While retail, fast food and consumer goods brands are greatly affected by piggybacking, this practice is rarely observed in the field of luxury brands and technology [14][15].

The Assimilation-Contrast Theory (ACT) [16] and the Mere Exposure Effect [25] are models that offer an explanation of the circumstances under which bids on ones own or third party brand names could be economically valuable. In sponsored search advertising the use of other companies brand names seems to be advantageous when the perceived difference between the own and other brands is low from a users point of view (ACT), while the value of bidding on own brand terms depends on the degree of the Exposure Effect, i.e. the display frequency that a brand needs in order to influence the purchasing decisions of users positively. Until now the empirical validations of these models for brand-bidding have been based on user surveys (Shin, 2010) and can therefore be subject to the problem of method bias. However, for the first time we are able to present results that are based on data that were collected in a non-reactive setup.

2.2   Blended Search

From the search engines perspective, the question is about the extent to which the free presentation of results in the organic part of the SERP counteracts their own financial interests in sponsored search as they generate essential parts of their profits in this area [22]. While a high perceived quality in the organic search results helps search engines to distinguish themselves from their competitors and to gain new customers, it is exactly this high quality in the organic results that may lead to cannibalization effects between organic and sponsored results [21].

From the users point of view, the question has to be asked which preferences and intentions they have when making their choice whether to use organic or sponsored results. Depending on their personal experience of this particular advertising channel and their motivation to search, Gauzette [8] shows that consumers do not only tolerate sponsored search as just one more channel for advertising on the Internet but do sometimes even consider these sponsored results more relevant than the organic ones. This is particularly true for transactional-intended queries, i.e. the so-called commercial-navigational search, in which the search engine is used instead of manually typing the URL into the browsers address bar. The same strong preference for sponsored results can also be found in the context of, for advertisers even more attractive, commercial-informational queries where users, although they have a strong intention to buy, are nevertheless still looking for the best matching result for their specific commercial interest [2].

Along with the multiplicity of intentions that individual users have when typing queries into search engines, there are significant variances of key performance indicators (KPI) that search engines and advertisers pay attention to. Ghose and Yang [9] compare organic and sponsored search results in respect to conversion rate, order value and profitability. In fact, the authors note that both conversion rate and order values are significantly higher through traffic that has been generated by sponsored search results than those generated by visitors that have clicked on organic results. It seems that the combination of relevance and the clearly separated presentation of organic and sponsored results as well as their explicit labeling are factors that lead to a greater credibility of the search engine and thus increases the willingness to click on the sponsored results, which are often not inferior to organic results [4].

Studies on the interaction between these two types of results indicate that their simultaneous presence in both the organic and sponsored results leads to a higher overall click probability [12]. More specifically, a high similarity between the content in the respective snippets leads to a higher click probability in the context of informational queries while users who are searching with transactional intentions seem to be more likely to click on one of the results when the similarity is low [5]. Ghose and Yang [23] confirm this observation and point out that this effect is much more pronounced in the context of brand-keywords with only little competition (e.g. retail brands / names of online retailers) than it is in a highly competitive environment.

In conclusion, and in contrast to a widely held opinion in business practice it has to be noted that previous research indicates that the placement of advertisements on SERPs is useful for advertisers even where the company is already represented in the organic results for the respective keyword. For the special - and for e-commerce queries most interesting - case of commercially intended queries, these studies indicate that the simultaneous occurrence in both result lists increases the overall probability to be clicked. The verification of these findings to brand terms has however not been accomplished so far and is the key contribution of this paper.

3   Hypothesis

The following hypotheses are formulated with reference to the online search and buying process. We assume that, when a user searches for the brand name of a company, both organic as well as sponsored results are displayed. These results contain links to the brand owners website as well as links to other companies websites. The user has three options to choose from (as shown in figure1): he may click on one of the two links that lead to the website of the company or click on a link that takes him to a different website, which makes him leave the area of observation of the study.

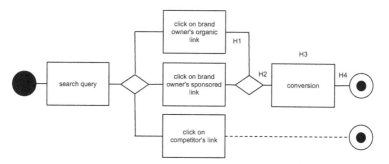

Fig. 1. Hypotheses of this study in the search and buying process from a users perspective

Due to partial substitution effects, the following hypothesis is almost self-evident as the studied brand occupies the first result in the organic part of the SERP for queries that contain the brand name:

> **H1:** The number of visitors from organic search results decreases when brand owners engage in sponsored search for their own brand keywords.

In his paper [12] Jansen assumes that the simultaneous appearance in the organic and the sponsored results has a positive impact on the overall click rate of the companies advertisements. This leads to:

H2: The overall number of visitors through brand name queries from a search engine increases when companies engage in sponsored search for respective keywords.

It is important to point out again that this statement is by no means self-evident, since it would be possible that the sponsored clicks generated through a brand term advertisement would merely substitute organic clicks that would come for free when no sponsored search is employed. In business practice it is exactly this point that is the subject of an intense and controversial debate between advertisers, agencies, and search engines. In their study (Ghose & Yang, 2008), Ghose and Yang point out that the conversion rate of commercial-navigationally intended queries is higher for sponsored than for organic results. Consequently, the following hypotheses can be derived:

H3: The conversion rate of keyword traffic from own brand keywords decreases when companies decide not to place sponsored search ads for these keywords.

Based on hypotheses H2 and H3 and other things being equal the following hypothesis on the number of sales and revenue derived from brand oriented search can be made:

H4: The overall number of sales and the respective revenue increase when companies bid on their own brand names in sponsored search.

Table 1. Brand keyword clicks and revenues (with standard deviations) in the reference period (data are disguised to ensure confidentiality)

Weekday	Mon	Tue	Wed	Thu	Fri	Sat	Sun
Ad Status	OFF	ON	OFF	ON	OFF	ON	OFF
Sum of all visiors	562.3	543.6	497.2	452.2	376	283	431.6
Standard Deviation	93.7	99.9	101.7	119.8	89.2	69.7	103.2
Revenue in €	8285	7119	6855	6162	4771	3843	7627
Standard Deviation	2117	1924	2022	1903	1630	1608	2537

4 Case Study

The study covers a 14 day test period in which sponsored search for brand keywords is switched on and off on alternate days. Below, the respective states in the test period are called ON (sponsored search for brand keywords is employed) and OFF" days. A full two weeks test period was chosen to allow us to monitor each weekday in both of the two possible states to ensure an acceptable consideration of the well-known weekday variations in e-commerce. The test period does not contain any holidays or other predictable events which could be relevant for the search engine traffic and conversions in this time span.

The company we study uses Google Analytics to collect data on the number and origin of users (organic as well as the sponsored results). In order to leverage existing data as a reference we decided to also use Google Analytics for our study. The reference period (Table 1) stretches from April 2009 to August 2010 with the omission of the test period which was chosen to be from April 12, 2010 till April 25, 2010, starting with an "OFF" day (Monday). The alternation of OFF" and "ON" in the test period was executed manually each morning at eight o'clock.

Google Analytics assigns recognized re-visitors to the origin of their first visit. For example, a user who first reached the company's website on an ON" day via a sponsored search result would also be associated with this type of result for his future visits and will thus be assigned to the sponsored search visitors regardless of whether he arrives via an organic search result or by typing the address into browser manually. This is the main reason why there are sponsored search visitors on "OFF" days. To derive statements on the effect of self-bidding, the data from the test period is compared with a reference period that has no overlap with the test period and contains continuous self-bidding activities for the brand keyword. As will be argued in the next section, the main question about the data is whether the results are statistically significant. Using a Monte-Carlo-Simulation, we examine the validity of the observations especially with respect to hypotheses H2.

Even though the applied method does obviously influence the behavior of involved users and could therefore be categorized as reactive in terms of social sciences, it shares common criteria with non-reactive methods since individual users have no knowledge of the investigation of his behavior.

5   Results

5.1   Testing the Hypotheses

Hypothesis H1 predicts that the placement of sponsored search ads for the own brand name leads to a substitution of clicks that would have otherwise been generated without costs through clicks on organic results. This is clearly confirmed in the data. The magnitude and significance of this effect is clearly illustrated in figure 2. Comparing the composition of the sum of all clicks generated on "ON" days with the clicks on those days without self-bidding activities, we find more than double the number of organic clicks on "OFF" days (2392 clicks) than on "ON" days (1060 clicks).

Table 2. Brand keyword visits, conversion rates and revenues in the test period (data are disguised to ensure confidentiality)

Day	04/13	04/14	04/15	04/16	04/17	04/18	04/19	04/20	04/21	04/22	04/23	04/24	04/25
Weekday	Mon	Tue	Wed	Thu	Fri	Sat	Sun	Mon	Tue	Wed	Thu	Fri	Sat
Ad status	ON	OFF	ON	OFF	ON	OFF	ON	OFF	ON	OFF	ON	OFF	ON
Paid visitors	376	56	340	64	184	44	436	92	340	108	292	68	252
Org. visitors	204	340	124	292	88	396	176	436	248	304	124	136	96
Sum visitors	580	396	464	356	272	440	612	528	588	412	416	204	348
Rev in €	5736	4704	6420	3328	3096	3720	8928	7796	6280	5832	4620	1112	7064
CVR	19%	22%	23%	19%	16%	12%	24%	23%	17%	17%	19%	10%	36%

It is, again, noticeable, and illustrated in figure 2, that we find sponsored clicks in the data that were generated on "OFF" days where we actually would not expect any. This can be explained by two effects: first, the status change was made manually from ON to

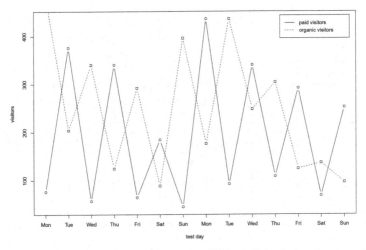

Fig. 2. Organic (dashed line) vs. sponsored (solid line) clicks during the test period

OFF and vice versa every day at eight o'clock in the morning in the test-period so that sponsored search advertisements were served until eight o'clock in the morning even on OFF days, accounting for the minor part of these clicks. Second, as argued before the cookie based tracking contributes to the occurrence of sponsored clicks on OFF days. It is obvious that the existence of sponsored search clicks on OFF days could never generate or strengthen but would on the contrary weaken the findings that are presented in this paper, since they tend to blur a potential effect.

In summary, it is clear that these findings are consistent with the expectation of a substitution of organic by sponsored search results (H1).

The second hypothesis H2 deals with the question of whether the sum of all sponsored and organic clicks that are generated through the use of the brand name as keyword in search engines can be increased through the use of sponsored search advertising. For this, we compare data from the test period with the data of the reference period (figure 3).

Beginning with an "OFF" day, figure 3 shows the values that were generated on a daily basis in the test period as well as the weekday values of the reference period, both representing the sum of sponsored and organic traffic via the brand keyword from the Google SERPs. The observations of the test period mainly fall into the 50% percentiles of the reference period and thus follow the overall weekday cycle.

However, one can clearly recognize an overlaying pattern in the test period that is most likely driven by the alternation of the status of "OFF" and "ON". Overall, the expected pattern of more clicks on "ON" days than on the surrounding "OFF" days could be observed in 11 of 13 possible daily changes.

What is the likelihood that this pattern occurs by chance? To answer this question we conduct a Monte-Carlo-Simulation, in which 1,000,000 random 14-day samples were generated, each representing a random test period. To generate each 14-day time series, we use the Poisson distribution and take weekday means from the reference period as the mean of the distribution. What is remarkable is that a fraction of only 0.2% of the randomly generated test periods fit the observed (alternating) pattern with at least 11

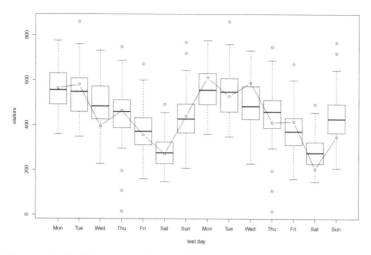

Fig. 3. Daily sum of all clicks, generated through the search engine via the brand term in the test period (solid line) compared to the weekday values in the reference period. The boxes contain 50% of the values from the reference period.

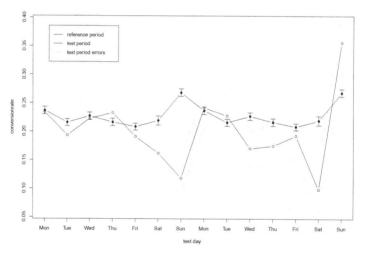

Fig. 4. Conversion rates observed in the test period (solid red line) with standard errors vs. average conversion rates with standard errors on a given weekday (solid line) in the reference period

or more changes. Employing this measure, it can be concluded with a probability of 99.8% that the placement of sponsored search advertisements for the own brand name actually leads to an increase in the total number of visitors for this keyword.

From the third hypotheses (H3), we would expect the conversion rate to be lower on days without sponsored search advertising than on the other days in the test. Given the average conversion rate of 22.7 % 0.3% in the reference period (figure 4) we find a lower conversion rate for the test period of 20.1% 1.6%, consistent with the study of Ghose and Yang (Ghose & Yang, 2008) , who observed a lower conversion rate for traffic from organic listings. It should be mentioned, that due to the low number

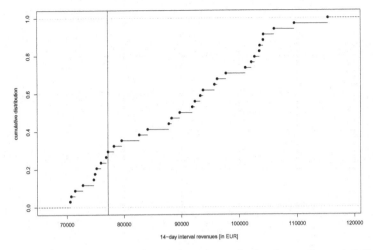

Fig. 5. Empirical cumulative distribution of the revenues in the observation period (14-day intervals, containing the reference- as well as the test period), the test period is indicated by the vertical line

of transactions per day (and the corresponding statistical error) we cannot observe a consistent difference of the conversion rate between ON and OFF days as for the overall clicks (figure 3).

Following the proven hypothesis H2 (more visitors through sponsored search advertising for the brand name) and the lower conversion rate observed in the context of hypothesis H3, we expect less sales and reduced revenues in the test period. In fact, the revenue via the brand keyword in the test period (€ 77,200) is lower than 70% of all comparable 14-day intervals in the reference period (figure 5).

Considering the revenue trend over the reference period, the relatively low revenue in the test period becomes significant since the revenue in the reference period shows a rising trend as shown in figure 6 (two-week revenue mean after New Years Eve without the test period: € 99,130 with a standard deviation of ± € 6,107.89). A similar reduction of sales can only be observed in the two-week period around Christmas and New Year's Eve 2009 corresponding to observation point 19 in figure 6. Thus, we interpret the lower revenue as a consequence of not employing sponsored search for brand keywords.

5.2 Economic Impact

We now estimate the economic value of sponsored search for own brand names. During the test period each weekday was observed in both states, "ON" and "OFF". The number of additional visitors can be estimated by the sum of all clicks on "ON" days minus the sum of all clicks on "OFF" day in the test period equal the total number of additional visitors for one week. In the current study, this results in 380 additional visitors per week. This is a significant growth of more than 10% achievable through sponsored search for own brand keywords.

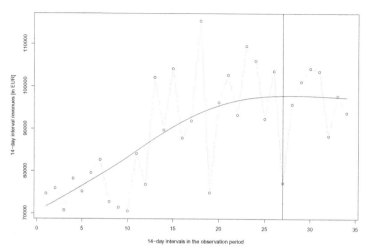

Fig. 6. Time series of revenues (14-day intervals) during the reference period (dashed line), including the test period (observation point 27, indicated by the vertical line) and a trend line (solid line)

Given the average conversion rate of 22.7% (reference period) and an average value per transaction of € 60.88 this leads to an increase in sales of about € 275,000 per year. The average cost per click for the brand keyword in the test period was € 0.03, leading to additional costs of about € 600 per year. To sum up: Even if there were only very moderate margins for online pharmacies we would recommend the use of sponsored search advertising for brand keywords.

In general, it seems to be likely that sponsored search for own brands lead to more visitors and accordingly to more sales and higher revenues for the brand owner. The low prices per click for brand keywords and a higher conversion rate make brand name advertising economically profitable in the context of sponsored search.

6   Conclusions and Outlook

It is plausible to argue that users who search for a specific retail brand name in a search engine have already decided where their search is going to end (the website of the retailer). Yet, evidence from this study suggests that this is not the case for all users. Some users apparently find other advertisements or organic results on the SERP more interesting so that they can get lost for the brand owner if he is not present in the sponsored search results.

We expect that the extent to which the described effect occurs in practice for other companies depends on a number of factors. E.g., the intensity of competition defined by the number of competitors who are also bidding on the brand name is likely to have an influence on the observed effect. This is of special interest, because since September 2010 (in the European Union) companies can not ban other advertisers to bid for their brand keywords (Bechtold, 2011) which will lead to a more intense competition. In the light of this change the present research gains in importance for a whole range of advertisers. Other factors may be the price level of sponsored search clicks, the reputation and brand value of the advertiser and product characteristics.

Considerably more research is needed to determine the extent to which these factors have an impact on the described effect. Besides that, the authors currently work on a project that will help to understand user behavior in this context.

References

1. Abhishek, V., Hosanagar, K.: Keyword generation for search engine advertising using semantic similarity between terms. In: Proceedings of the Ninth International Conference on Electronic Commerce, pp. 89–94 (2007)
2. Ashkan, A., Clarke, C.L., Agichtein, E., Guo, Q.: Classifying and Characterizing Query Intent. In: Boughanem, M., Berrut, C., Mothe, J., Soule-Dupuy, C. (eds.) ECIR 2009. LNCS, vol. 5478, pp. 578–586. Springer, Heidelberg (2009)
3. Bechtold, S.: Google AdWords and European trademark law. Communications of the ACM 54(1), 30–32 (2011), http://dl.acm.org/citation.cfm?id=1866749
4. Brown, A., Jansen, B., Resnick, M.: Factors relating to the decision to click on a sponsored link. Decision Support Systems 44(1), 46–49 (2007)
5. Danescu-Niculescu-Mizil, C., Broder, A.Z., Gabrilovich, E., Josifovski, V., Pang, B.: Competing for users attention. In: Proceedings of the 19th International Conference on World wide Web, WWW 2010, pp. 291–300 (2010)
6. Edelman, B., Ostrovsky, M., Schwarz, M.: Internet Advertising and the Generalized Second-Price Auction: Selling Billions of Dollars Worth of Keywords. American Economic Review 97(1), 242–259 (2007)
7. Fuxman, A., Tsaparas, P., Achan, K., Agrawal, R.: Using the wisdom of the crowds for keyword generation. In: Proceeding of the 17th International Conference on World Wide Web, WWW 2008, pp. 61–70 (2008)
8. Gauzente, C.: Information search and paid resultsproposition and test of a hierarchy-of- effect model. Electronic Markets 19(2), 163–177 (2009)
9. Ghose, A., Yang, S.: Comparing performance metrics in organic search with sponsored search advertising. In: Proceedings of the 2nd International Workshop on Data Mining and Audience Intelligence for Advertising, ADKDD 2008, pp. 18–26 (2008)
10. Hallerman, D.: Search Engine Marketing: User and Spending Trends. eMarketer (2008), http://www.emarketer.com/Reports/All/Emarketer_2000473.aspx
11. Jansen, B.J., Mullen, T.: Sponsored search: an overview of the concept, history, and technology. International Journal of Electronic Business 6(2), 114–131 (2008)
12. Jansen, B.J.: The comparative effectiveness of sponsored and nonsponsored links for Web e-commerce queries. ACM Transactions on the Web 1(1) (2007)
13. Kitts, B., Leblanc, B.: Optimal bidding on keyword auctions. Electronic Markets 14(3), 186–201 (2004)
14. Rosso, M., Jansen, B.J.: Brand Names as Keywords in Sponsored Search Advertising. Communications of the Association for Information Systems 27, Article 6 (2010)
15. Rosso, M., Jansen, B.J.: Smart marketing or bait & switch: competitors brands as keywords in online advertising. In: Proceedings of the 4th Workshop on Information Credibility, pp. 27–34 (2010)
16. Sherif, M., Hovland, C.: Social judgment:assimilation and contrast effects in communication and attitude change. Yale University Press (1961)
17. Skiera, B.: Stichwort Suchmaschinenmarketing. DBW Die Betriebswirtschaft (68), 113–117 (2008)

18. Unrau, E.: Wechselwirkungen zwischen bezahlter Suchmaschinenwerbung und dem organischen Index. Master Thesis, Leuphana University (2010) (unpublished)
19. Varian, H.: Position auctions. International Journal of Industrial Organization 25(6), 1163–1178 (2007)
20. Varian, H.R.: Online ad auctions. American Economic Review 99(2), 430–434 (2009)
21. White, A.: Search Engines: Left Side Quality Versus Right Side Profits (2008) SSRN, `http://ssrn.com/abstract=1694869`
22. Xu, L., Chen, J., Whinston, A.B.: Interplay Between Organic Listing and Sponsored Bidding in Search Advertising. McCombs Research Paper Series No. IROM-13-09 (2009)
23. Yang, S., Ghose, A.: Analyzing the Relationship Between Organic and Sponsored Search Advertising: Positive, Negative or Zero Interdependence? Marketing Science 29(4), 602–623 (2010)
24. Yao, S., Mela, C.F.: Sponsored Search Auctions: Research Opportunities in Marketing. Foundations and Trends in Marketing 3(2), 75–126 (2009)
25. Zajonc, R.B.: Attitudinal effects of mere exposure. Pers. Soc. Psycho. 9(2. part 2), 1–27 (1968)

Client-Oriented Preferences Model for QoS Aggregation in Service-Based Applications

Nabil Fakhfakh, Frédéric Pourraz, Hervé Verjus, and Patrice Moreaux

LISTIC, University of Savoie, 5 Chemin de Bellevue, Annecy Le Vieux, France
firstname.name@univ-savoie.fr

Abstract. Client satisfaction is considered today as one of the main concern to be ensured by enterprises, especially in e-business, where client position is central. With the spread of concurrency and the increase of functionally equivalent services, QoS became an important criterion, which is closely related to client satisfaction. In this context, we propose an approach to determine the satisfaction degree corresponding to the QoS of service-based applications, with regard to client's QoS expectations. Our approach is based on a preferences model, which is built only on the basis of client provided information. This preferences model is also based on the 2-additive Choquet operator that supports preferential dependencies. We present a study that compares the results obtained from our preferences model with those of related work, and shows that our approach provides more accurate results in the way that it represents more precisely client satisfaction.

Keywords: Preferences model, QoS aggregation, Service orchestration, Satisfaction degree measurement, The Choquet integral.

1 Introduction

Electronic business or e-business can be defined as the use of the technology of the Web to do business. There is a variety of e-business models. Among them, we found the Business to Client (B2C) and Business to Business to Client (B2B2C) [14]. Enterprises based on these models put much importance to *client's satisfaction* in the development of their e-business applications, as it is recommended by the standard ISO 9001:2008 [11] related to quality management. For this purpose, enterprises have to provide e-business applications with high Quality of Service (QoS) to be more competitive and to reach client's satisfaction. In this paper, we propose a method to measure client's satisfaction related to QoS of the e-business application. We focus in this paper on e-business applications supported through orchestrated e-services. When developing their e-business applications, enterprises aim to respect client's *QoS expectations* specified on the service orchestration. QoS expectations are defined by the upper and lower bounds of the QoS levels that the service orchestration must meet to guarantee client's satisfaction. The upper QoS level bound is denoted *desired QoS level* [13], and represents the QoS level that satisfies the best the client. Whereas, the lower QoS level bound is denoted *adequate QoS level* [13], and represents the minimum QoS level that satisfies the client. We denote also the measured QoS level on the client's side at run-time

M.S. Obaidat, J.L. Sevillano, and J. Filipe (Eds.): ICETE 2011, CCIS 314, pp. 141–155, 2012.

by *the perceived QoS level* [13]. Hereafter, we define a QoS level as a vector of QoS attributes values denoted $(q_1, ..., q_n)$, where q_j $(1 \leq j \leq n)$ is the jth QoS attribute value. However, during services life cycle, perceived QoS attributes values of the services may change. This leads to a variation of the perceived QoS level of the service orchestration into the range of QoS expectations. Besides, the client's satisfaction of the e-business application will be impacted. Therefore, clients exploiting the e-business application need to know how much they are satisfied in terms of QoS.

Various works dealing with evaluation of service orchestration's QoS attributes exist in the literature [4,2,15]. Their approaches fail when we try to appreciate the overall QoS of service orchestrations, especially if we consider several QoS attributes. The satisfaction degree of service orchestration is a high level information, which makes easier the interpretation of QoS related to the service orchestration. For this purpose, we use a Multi-Criteria Decision Making (MCDM) method to build a preferences model related to the client, which takes into account preferential dependencies [8] and also client's preferences.

The remainder of this paper is organized as follows. Section 2 discusses related work. In Sect. 3, we present our approach for the measurement of service orchestrations satisfaction degree. Section 4 discusses the results of our preferences model with regard to the related work, while Sect. 5 concludes the paper.

2 Related Work

In this section, we overview related works on QoS evaluation and highlight their limitations, that we target to improve in this paper.

Various works [4,2,15,6] deal with the evaluation of each QoS attribute for the overall service orchestration (e.g., giving response time values for all services involved in the orchestration, how to compute the response time of the overall orchestration ?). These works are based on *workflow pattern-based aggregation rules* approach. This approach consists in defining aggregation rules for QoS attributes and for each pair of workflow (control-flow) patterns [1]. A pair of workflow patterns, called hereafter *composition pattern* [2,15], is composed of "one split pattern" (e.g., AND-split) and "one join (synchronisation) pattern" (e.g., XOR-join) except the *sequence* and the *loop* patterns, which are considered individually. The advantage of this approach is that it can support a large set of QoS attributes. Moreover, it is extensible: *(i)* more composition patterns could be added and *(ii)* new QoS attributes could be integrated. For that reason, we exploit a workflow pattern-based approach in our proposal. However, all these works are based on the first result of Workflow Pattern Initiative (WPI) research, which consists in 20 workflow patterns [1]. Note that there exists a review of these patterns that resulted in 43 patterns [16]. Thus, composition patterns should be expressed with these last patterns rather than with the first ones, in order to cover wider spectrum of service orchestration models. Besides, the number of proposed composition patterns varies from one work to another (e.g., 9 composition patterns supported in [2], whereas 5 in [4] and 4 in [15]). As each of these works supports a different set of QoS attributes, some QoS attributes do not have aggregation rules for all composition patterns. In this context, we analyse all composition patterns existing in the related works, we propose a set of composition patterns expressed with the 43 patterns and we define missing aggregation rules (see Sect. 3). On the other hand, when changes affect positively or negatively some QoS attributes values, it becomes difficult to interpret these values and to estimate how much the whole orchestration fits client's expectations and satisfaction, especially when we have several QoS attributes. Thus, it would be useful to have a high-level information about the overall service orchestration quality. From this perspective, some works [18,17,10] have defined utility functions and used an aggregation operator (e.g., Weighted Arithmetic Mean, WAM) respectively in order to normalize QoS attributes values and to aggregate QoS attributes, which are heterogeneous (e.g., response time, availability and reliability). The aim is to have only one information that allows to discriminate services from QoS point of view, especially in service selection area. Nevertheless, most of these works defined linear utility functions (except [17]) for the normalization, which represents the satisfaction felt by the client over the QoS attributes values. This may lead to a wrong representation of client satisfaction that may be non linear. Therefore, the provided results (e.g., in service selection) will be erroneous regardless the considered aggregation operator. Although authors of [17] exploit client preferences for the normalization, their approach is based on the WAM aggregation operator, which does not enable preferential dependencies representation. Once again, the resulted scores may be not precise enough. To overcome these limitations, we use in our approach a combination of the MACBETH method [7] and the 2-additive Choquet integral operator [5,12]. This allows us to build, only on the basis of client preferences, both utility functions and aggregation function, called hereafter preferences model. We show in Sect. 4 how our preferences model improves the related works.

3   QoS Aggregation Proposal

In this section, we introduce our proposal for aggregating QoS attributes values, which is divided in two phases (see Fig. 1). In the first phase, we use workflow pattern aggregation rules, while in the second phase we use a MCDM method based on the MACBETH method extended to the 2-additive Choquet Integral. Each service S_i has a QoS level $(q_1, ..., q_n)_{S_i}$. Given these QoS levels of all orchestrated services, they are firstly aggregated in phase 1 using workflow pattern aggregation rules. This results in one QoS level of the service orchestration $(q_1, ..., q_n)_{orch}$ (see Fig. 1). As we said above (see Sect. 2), the interpretation of this QoS level may be a hard task when the number n of QoS attributes increases. To overcome this limitation, we propose to aggregate the QoS attributes values of the QoS level in phase 2 using a MCDM method. This provides us a sole and consolidated value, which is the satisfaction degree of the service orchestration. We define *the satisfaction degree of a service orchestration* as the assessment of client satisfaction with regard to the overall QoS of the orchestration, compared to client expectations and his preferences over QoS attributes.

Before detailing the two phases of our approach, we present a car insurance e-business application supported through a service orchestration described in Fig. 2. We will use this B2C service orchestration model to illustrate our approach.

The process starts by asking some information to the client (client age, driving license, car type and model, etc.). Such information is firstly analysed for a decision:

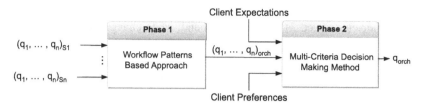

Fig. 1. Main phases of the QoS aggregation approach

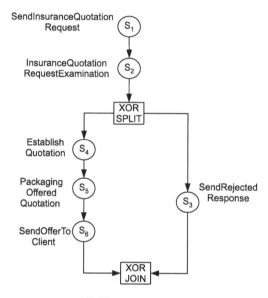

Fig. 2. B2C services orchestration

either the quotation request is accepted, either it is immediately rejected. When accepted, a quotation is established taking into account client provided information. Then, a commercial offer is packaged comprising the car insurance quotation and some commercial and promotional offers (life insurance, house insurance, etc.). The commercial offer is sent to the client.

3.1 Phase 1: Aggregation Based on Workflow Patterns Rules

In this first phase (see Fig. 1), we use aggregation rules based on workflow patterns to compute each QoS attribute value of the service orchestration. This consists in applying step-wisely rules in order to aggregate QoS attributes values. The applied rules are those corresponding to the composition patterns involved in the service orchestration model. Beginning from the most nested composition pattern, the orchestration model is parsed

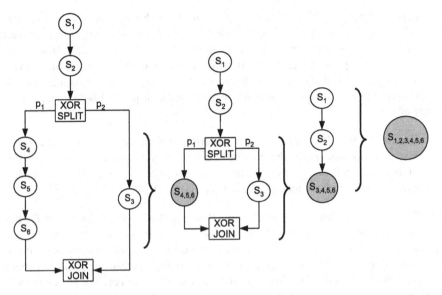

Fig. 3. Service orchestration reduction steps

and aggregation rules for each QoS attribute in the QoS level are progressively applied. This terminates when the whole service orchestration is reduced to a single node, as outlines Fig. 3. The resulted QoS attributes values of the resulting node compose the QoS level of the overall service orchestration. This approach is relevant for each QoS attribute that has aggregation rules for the involved composition patterns. In this context, we present our composition pattern selection based on our study of related works. The following exposed composition patterns are expressed with the last review of workflow patterns [16].

CP1: Sequence / Interleaved Parallel Routing / Interleaved Routing: this pattern describes the execution of a set of services, in a given order (Sequence), in a partial order (Interleaved Parallel Routing) or in any order (Interleaved Routing). However, two services can not be executed simultaneously.

CP2: Structured Loop: this pattern expresses the ability to execute a service repeatedly. In general, the number of iterations is denoted by l.

CP3: Exclusive Choice / Deferred Choice + Simple Merge / Synchronizing Merge / Multi-Merge / Local Merge / General Synchronizing Merge: this pattern is often denoted by *XOR-XOR* in [2,15,4]. It describes the choice of one of several services to be executed. The choice depends on the runtime orchestration data (Exclusive Choice) or on external data to the orchestration (Deferred Choice). At design-time, we annotate this composition pattern with probabilities p_i, $1 \leq i \leq n$ (n is the number of services in parallel), representing the probability that a service i is chosen to be executed at runtime.

CP4: Parallel Split + Synchronization / Structured Synchronization Merge / Generalised AND-Join / Local Synchronizing Merge / General Synchronizing Merge, Thread Split + Thread Merge: this pattern is often denoted *AND-AND* in [2,15,4]. In this pattern, all services in parallel start their execution simultaneously. Note that the convergence in this pattern is made with synchronization, i.e., the service following this pattern waits for the end of execution of all services made in parallel before starting its execution.

CP5: Parallel Split + Multi-Merge: this pattern represents the case of convergence without synchronization unlike the previous pattern. This means that the services following this pattern are executed each time when a service from the parallel branches finish its execution. We have identified this pattern in [6,9].

CP6: Parallel Split + Structural Partial Join / Blocking Partial Join / Cancelling Partial Join: among n services running simultaneously, a number m $(m < n)$ services are required for synchronization. Therefore, the service following this pattern is executed when m services have finished their execution. [4] describes this composition pattern as a fault tolerance pattern. In this case, the services made in parallel, are equivalent functionally. This is useful for critical processes to verify the results (services response) and ensure the continuity of the process. This pattern is denoted *AND-m out of n* in [2]. The number of possible combinations (upon convergence) of m services among n is $N = \binom{n}{m}$. At runtime, only one services combination, denoted S, will be executed. Thus, we denote by p_i, the probability that the services combination S_i will be executed at runtime.

CP7: Parallel Split + Structured Discriminator / Blocking Discriminator / Cancelling Discriminator: from n services executed simultaneously, the first service, which ends its execution, enables the execution of the service following the pattern, the other services are ignored. This pattern is denoted *AND-XOR* in [2]. Similarly, we denote by p_i, the probability that the service i will finish the first its execution at runtime.

CP8: Multi-Choice + Synchronizing Merge / Structured Synchronizing Merge / Generalised AND-Join / Local Synchronizing Merge / General Synchronizing Merge: this pattern is denoted *OR-OR* in [2]. Among n parallel services, a number k $(1 \leq k \leq n)$ of services is selected, according to a given condition, to run concurrently. The convergence of the selected services is performed with synchronization. This pattern is like the pattern CP4 except that only services that were selected during the divergence, are required for synchronization. At runtime, one of $(2^n - 1)$ possible services combinations will be executed. Let $\mathbb{K}$ be the set of possible combinations. The cardinal of $\mathbb{K}$, denoted $|\mathbb{K}|$, is equal to $(2^n - 1)$. Also note by $S = (s_1, ..., s_k)$ an element belonging to $\mathbb{K}$. The execution of this composition pattern consists in the choice of one S among all $\mathbb{K}$, which will be executed. Subsequently, we denote p_i $(1 \leq i \leq 2^n - 1)$, the probability that an element S_i of all $\mathbb{K}$ is chosen.

CP9: Multi-Choice + Multi-Merge: this pattern differs from the previous one in the type of convergence. The convergence of services that were selected during the divergence to run simultaneously is done without synchronization in this case. This pattern is also similar to pattern CP5 except that a k ($1 \leq k \leq n$) services is chosen at the divergence instead of the n parallel services.

CP10: Multi-Choice + Structural Partial Join / Blocking Partial Join / Cancelling Partial Join: this pattern is represented by *OR-m out of n* in [2]. Among n parallel services, a number k of services are selected at the time of divergence to run concurrently ($m \leq k \leq n$). Among the k started executing services, a subset of m services is required for synchronization. For this composition pattern, the number of possible combinations is $N_1 = \sum_{i=m}^{n} \binom{n}{i}$ for the divergence, while it is $N_2 = \sum_{j=m}^{k} \binom{k}{j}$ for the convergence. In this sense, we denote by (1) p_i^1, the probability that a services combination S_i is selected at the divergence and (2) p_j^2, the probability that a services combination S_j^i is selected at the convergence, where S_j^i is a subset of S_i.

CP11: Multi-Choice + Structured Discriminator / Blocking Discriminator / Cancelling Discriminator: this pattern is denoted *OR-XOR* in [2]. Among n parallel services, k ($1 \leq k \leq n$) services are selected at runtime. The first service which ends its execution, triggers the execution of the service following this composition pattern, the other services are ignored. This pattern is similar to the pattern CP7 except that we consider the k services at the divergence instead of n.

These 11 composition patterns have never been taken into account together in the literature. Therefore, if we consider for example three QoS attributes like *response time* (q_{rt}), *reliability* (q_{rel}) and *availability* (q_{av}), there are some composition patterns that do not have still aggregation rules for these QoS attributes. Tables 1 and 2 summarize aggregation rules for these three QoS attributes (see [4,6] for details and notation corresponding to CP6 reliability aggregation rule). From the presented rules, we proposed 7 aggregation rules for the response time corresponding to patterns CP5 to CP11, which were undefined in related works. We also proposed novel aggregation rules for reliability and availability corresponding to patterns CP5, CP7, CP8, CP9, CP10 and CP11. Note that for patterns CP5 and CP9, as the synchronization is not required for the convergence, we considered a service s_B, which represents the following part in the service orchestration model.

The checked composition patterns and their corresponding aggregation rules, allow us to evaluate QoS attributes for a large service orchestration models. As an example, if we apply the reduction steps shown in Fig. 3, we obtain at the end the following QoS attributes values for the overall service orchestration:

$$q_{rt}(\text{orch}) = \sum_{i=1}^{2} q_{rt}(S_i) + p_1 \sum_{i=4}^{6} q_{rt}(S_i) + p_2 \, q_{rt}(S_3) \tag{1}$$

$$q_{rel}(\text{orch}) = \prod_{i=1}^{2} q_{rel}(S_i) \left(p_1 \prod_{i=4}^{6} q_{rel}(S_i) + p_2 \, q_{rel}(S_3) \right) \tag{2}$$

$$q_{av}(\text{orch}) = \prod_{i=1}^{2} q_{av}(S_i) \left(p_1 \prod_{i=4}^{6} q_{av}(S_i) + p_2 \, q_{av}(S_3) \right) . \tag{3}$$

Table 1. Aggregation rules for response time

Composition pattern	Aggregation rules
CP1- Sequence	$\sum_{i=1}^{n} q_{\mathrm{rt}}(s_i)$
CP2- Loop	$l.q_{\mathrm{rt}}(s_i)$
CP3- XOR-XOR	$\sum_{i=1}^{n} p_i.q_{\mathrm{rt}}(s_i)$
CP4- AND-AND	$\max\{q_{\mathrm{rt}}(s_1),...,q_{\mathrm{rt}}(s_n)\}$
CP5- AND-AND (no synch.)	$\max\{q_{\mathrm{rt}}(s_1)+q_{\mathrm{rt}}(s_{\mathrm{B}}),...,q_{\mathrm{rt}}(s_n)+q_{\mathrm{rt}}(s_{\mathrm{B}})\}$
CP6- AND-m/n	$\sum_{k=1}^{N} p_k \max_{s\in S_k}\{q_{\mathrm{rt}}(s)\}$
CP7- AND-XOR	$\min\{q_{\mathrm{rt}}(s_1),...,q_{\mathrm{rt}}(s_n)\}$
CP8- OR-OR	$\sum_{i=1}^{2^n-1} p_i.\max\{q_{\mathrm{rt}}(S_i)\}$
CP9- OR-OR (no synch.)	$\sum_{i=1}^{2^n-1} p_i.\max\{q_{\mathrm{rt}}(S_i)+q_{\mathrm{rt}}(s_{\mathrm{B}})\}$
CP10- OR-m/n	$\sum_{k=1}^{N_1} p_k^1\left(\sum_{j=1}^{N_2} p_j^2 \max_{s\in S_j^i}\{q_{\mathrm{rt}}(s)\}\right)$
CP11- OR-XOR	$\sum_{k=1}^{N} p_k \min_{s\in S_k}\{q_{\mathrm{rt}}(s)\}$

Table 2. Aggregation rules for reliability and availability

Composition pattern	Aggregation rules
CP1- Sequence	$\prod_{i=1}^{n} q_{\mathrm{rel}}(s_i)$
CP2- Loop	$\left(q_{\mathrm{rel}}(s_i)\right)^l$
CP3- XOR-XOR	$\sum_{i=1}^{n} p_i.q_{\mathrm{rel}}(s_i)$
CP4- AND-AND	$\prod_{i=1}^{n} q_{\mathrm{rel}}(s_i)$
CP5- AND-AND (no synch.)	$\prod_{i=1}^{n} q_{\mathrm{rel}}(s_i).\left(q_{\mathrm{rel}}(s_{\mathrm{B}})\right)^n$
CP6- AND-m/n	$\sum_{i_1=0}^{1}\cdots\sum_{i_n=0}^{1} u\left(\sum_{j=1}^{n} \delta(i_j-1)-m\right)$ $\prod_{j=1}^{n}(\delta(i_j-1)q_{\mathrm{rel}}(s_j)+\delta(i_j)(1-q_{\mathrm{rel}}(s_j))$
CP7- AND-XOR	$1-\prod_{i=1}^{n}(1-q_{\mathrm{rel}}(s_i))$
CP8- OR-OR	$\sum_{i=1}^{2^n-1} p_i \prod_{s\in S_i} q_{\mathrm{rel}}(s)$
CP9- OR-OR (no synch.)	$\sum_{i=1}^{2^n-1} p_i \prod_{s\in S_i} q_{\mathrm{rel}}(s).\left(q_{\mathrm{rel}}(s_{\mathrm{B}})\right)^{|S_i|}$
CP10- OR-m/n	$\sum_{k=1}^{N_1} p_k^1\left(\sum_{i_1=0}^{1}\cdots\sum_{i_{|S_k|}=0}^{1} u\left(\sum_{j=1}^{k} \delta(i_j-1)-m\right)\right.$ $\left.\prod_{j=1}^{|S_k|}(\delta(i_j-1)q_{\mathrm{rel}}(s_j)+\delta(i_j)(1-q_{\mathrm{rel}}(s_j)))\right)$
CP11- OR-XOR	$\sum_{k=1}^{2^n-1} p_k.\left(1-\prod_{s\in S_k}(1-q_{\mathrm{rel}}(s))\right)$

This resulting values are those that compose the QoS level of the whole service orchestration $(q_{\mathrm{rt}}, q_{\mathrm{rel}}, q_{\mathrm{av}})_{\mathrm{orch}}$ and are the input of the phase 2 (Fig. 1).

3.2   Phase 2: Aggregation Using the 2-Additive Choquet Integral

The goal of this phase is to aggregate different values (obtained from (1), (2) and (3)) in the QoS level of the service orchestration (i.e., $(q_{rt}, q_{rel}, q_{av})_{orch}$) in order to provide a measure of the satisfaction degree of the services orchestration (q_{orch}) (see Fig. 1). For this purpose, we need to build a preferences model related to the client in order to represent the best his satisfaction. In this context, we use the MACBETH [7] method extended to 2-additive Choquet integral [5,12] to construct both the utility functions (for normalization) and the aggregation function that compose our preferences model. The MACBETH method is used for because it is based only on client information (preferences) to construct the preferences model, while the 2-additive Choquet integral enables the support of preferential dependencies. In this way, we consider that the final preferences model, maps client's satisfaction.

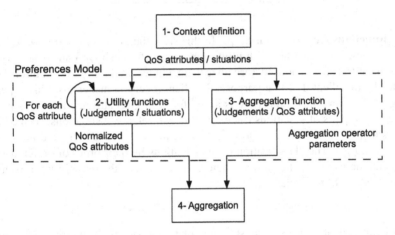

Fig. 4. The main steps of the MACBETH method

The MACBETH method defines four main steps (Fig. 4) to build the preferences model and then aggregate values in the QoS level.

Context Definition Step. The first step consists in identifying the criteria on which the comparison will be based. In our context, criteria are QoS attributes (e.g., response time, reliability, availability). Secondly, situations that will be compared are defined. In our case, situations are represented by QoS levels. If we consider the example of the e-business process cited above, the situations to be compared are the QoS level of the overall service orchestration ($q_{rt}, q_{rel}, q_{av})_{orch}$ (i.e., resulting from workflow patterns aggregation rules, see (1), (2) and (3)) and two reference situations, called *good situation* and *neutral situation*, which are required in the MACBETH method to determine respectively the scores 1 and 0. In order to take into account client expectations, we assign the desired and the adequate QoS levels to these two reference situations respectively. Note that these three situations are sufficient to apply our approach and to obtain the satisfaction degree corresponding to the QoS level of the service orchestration [8].

However, in order to compare our preferences model with existing works, we will consider 6 instead of 3 situations (e.g., from historic of executions) to be compared by the client (see Table 3).

Table 3. Example of situations for utility functions construction

QoS Levels	Response Time	Reliability	Availability
$S_1 = S^{\text{good}}$	50	1	1
S_2	58	0.8	0.6
S_3	60	0.7	0.7
S_4	62	0.1	0.95
S_5	66	0.85	0.3
$S_6 = S^{\text{neutral}}$	70	0.2	0.2

Utility Functions Construction Step. In this step, the goal is to normalize QoS attributes values, i.e., construct each utility function u_i for each QoS attribute i. We do not use linear transformations to normalize them, but we preferably exploit information provided by the client. For that purpose, the client (decision maker) uses his expertise to judge given situations. Firstly, he is asked for each QoS attribute about his preferences between pairs of situations (including the two reference situations). If the client prefers situation S^i to S^j for a QoS attribute k, this is noted $S^i \succ S^j$ and means that $u_k(q_k^i) > u_k(q_k^j)$. The classification of the situations by their order of preference depending on the values of the QoS attribute k. In the case of the reliability for example, the classification of the situations is:

$$S^1 \succ S^5 \succ S^2 \succ S^3 \succ S^6 \succ S^4 \ . \tag{4}$$

Secondly, the client expresses his strengths of preference about the difference of attractiveness between the same situations. The strengths of preference are characterized with seven levels in the MACBETH method: *0=null, 1=very weak, 2=weak, 3=moderate, 4=strong, 5=very strong, 6=extreme*. For a QoS attribute k, the client prefers the situation S^i to S^j with a difference of attractiveness characterized by a strength $h_m \in \{0, ..., 6\}$. This preference relation is denoted by $S^i \succ^{\mathbf{h_m}} S^j$ and is equivalent to:

$$q_k^i - q_k^j = h_m \alpha \ . \tag{5}$$

where α is the graduation on the utility function scale.

When all the strengths of preference between situations are provided [8], a system of equations can be extracted. Each strength of preference expressed on pair of situations gives an equation like (5). By solving this system of equations, we determine the utility function u_i (i.e., the normalized values of QoS attributes). For example, assume that the client expresses the following strengths of preference:

$$S^1 \succ^5 S^5 \succ^1 S^2 \succ^4 S^3 \succ^6 S^6 \succ^1 S^4 \ . \tag{6}$$

Then, we can extract an equations system to determine the utility function u_{rel} of the reliability. Note that S^1 and S^6 correspond to situations good and neutral (see Table 3), thus $u_{\mathrm{rel}}(q_{\mathrm{rel}}^1) = 1$ and $u_{\mathrm{rel}}(q_{\mathrm{rel}}^6) = 0$. Due to lack of space, we give directly the solution of the utility function (see [8] for more details):

$$u_{\mathrm{rel}}(q_{\mathrm{rel}}^2) = 0.625 \quad u_{\mathrm{rel}}(q_{\mathrm{rel}}^3) = 0.375 \quad u_{\mathrm{rel}}(q_{\mathrm{rel}}^4) = -0.0625 \quad u_{\mathrm{rel}}(q_{\mathrm{rel}}^5) = 0.6875 \ . \tag{7}$$

In the same way, we construct utility functions related to response time and availability. By defining utility functions for each QoS attribute, which map the satisfaction of the client over each QoS value, we determine the first part of the preferences model.

Aggregation Function Construction Step. The 2-additive Choquet Integral operator is defined by the following aggregation formula [5,12]:

$$q_{\mathrm{orch}} = \sum_{i=1}^{n} \nu_i . q_i - \frac{1}{2} \sum_{j=1}^{n} I_{ij} . |q_i - q_j| \ . \tag{8}$$

and involves 2 types of parameters:

1. Shapley parameters ν_i, which are the weights of each QoS attribute, with $\sum_{i=1}^{n} \nu_i = 1$,
2. Interaction parameters I_{ij} that quantify mutual interaction between criteria i and j, with $I_{ij} \in [-1, 1]$ and, $\forall i \in [1, n]$, $j \neq i$, $\left(\nu_i - \frac{1}{2} \sum_{j=1}^{n} |I_{ij}| \right) \geq 0$. These parameters ($I_{ij}$) may be:
   (a) positive, which implies that there is a contradiction between the pairs of criteria. So the aggregated value of QoS attributes (q_{orch}) decreases,
   (b) negative, which implies that there is a positive synergy between the pairs of criteria. Thus, the aggregated value of QoS attributes (q_{orch}) increases,
   (c) null, which implies that the pairs of criteria are independent. Therefore, the 2-additive Choquet Integral becomes equivalent to the weighted mean operator.

The aggregation function, which consists in the 2-additive Choquet Integral, is completely defined by its parameters (i.e., ν_i and I_{ij}). Therefore, in the case of three QoS attributes $(q_{\mathrm{rt}}, q_{\mathrm{rel}}, q_{\mathrm{av}})$, we have to determine 6 parameters: $\nu_{\mathrm{rt}}, \nu_{\mathrm{rel}}, \nu_{\mathrm{av}}, I_{\mathrm{rt-rel}}, I_{\mathrm{rt-av}}$ and $I_{\mathrm{rel-av}}$. The determination of these parameters is also based on client preferences, so that, the importance of QoS attributes from the client point of view and his preferential dependencies are well represented. For this purpose, the client has to express his strengths of preference over particular situations: binary situations. In the case of 3 QoS attributes, these situations are: $(1, 1, 1), (1, 1, 0), (0, 1, 1), (1, 0, 1), (1, 0, 0), (0, 1, 0),$ $(0, 0, 1), (0, 0, 0)$. Once the strengths of preference are expressed, a system of equations can be extracted in the same way as (5), and then solved. For example, let us consider the strengths of preferences: $S^{(1,1,1)} \succ^2 S^{(0,1,1)} \succ^4 S^{(1,1,0)} \succ^2 S^{(0,1,0)} \succ^2$ $S^{(1,0,1)} \succ^3 S^{(1,0,0)} \succ^3 S^{(0,0,1)} \succ^1 S^{(0,0,0)}$. The corresponding system of equations is:

$$q_{\text{orch}}^{(1,1,1)} - q_{\text{orch}}^{0,1,1)} = 2\alpha = \nu_{\text{rt}} + 0.5I_{\text{rt-rel}} + 0.5I_{\text{rt-av}}$$

$$q_{\text{orch}}^{(0,1,1)} - q_{\text{orch}}^{(1,1,0)} = 4\alpha = -\nu_{\text{rt}} + \nu_{\text{av}} - 0.5I_{\text{rt-rel}} + 0.5I_{\text{rel-av}}$$

$$q_{\text{orch}}^{(1,1,0)} - q_{\text{orch}}^{(0,1,0)} = 2\alpha = \nu_{\text{rt}} + 0.5I_{\text{rt-rel}} - 0.5I_{\text{rt-av}}$$

$$q_{\text{orch}}^{(0,1,0)} - q_{\text{orch}}^{(1,0,1)} = 3\alpha = -\nu_{\text{rt}} + \nu_{\text{rel}} - \nu_{\text{av}} \qquad (9)$$

$$q_{\text{orch}}^{(1,0,1)} - q_{\text{orch}}^{(1,0,0)} = 3\alpha = \nu_{\text{av}} + 0.5I_{\text{rt-av}} - 0.5I_{\text{rel-av}}$$

$$q_{\text{orch}}^{(1,0,0)} - q_{\text{orch}}^{(0,0,1)} = \alpha = \nu_{\text{rt}} - \nu_{\text{av}} - 0.5I_{\text{rt-rel}} + 0.5I_{\text{rel-av}}$$

$$q_{\text{orch}}^{(0,0,1)} - q_{\text{orch}}^{(0,0,0)} = 2\alpha = \nu_{\text{av}} - 0.5I_{\text{rt-av}} - 0.5I_{\text{rel-av}} \ .$$

The resolution of (9) with the constraint that the Shapley parameters must verify $(\sum_{i=1}^{n} \nu_i = 1)$, gives: $\nu_{\text{rt}} = 0.21$, $\nu_{\text{rel}} = 0.56$, $\nu_{\text{av}} = 0.23$, $I_{\text{rt-rel}} = -0.18$, $I_{\text{rt-av}} = 0.06$ and $I_{\text{rel-av}} = 0.23$.

At the end of this step, the aggregation function is well defined and therefore the preferences model related to the client is built.

Aggregation Step. The QoS attributes values being normalized and the Choquet Integral parameters being computed, we can now aggregate the QoS levels related to the service orchestration by applying (8). The obtained values from the aggregation represent the satisfaction degrees of the QoS levels with regard to client expectations and preferences. Let us consider the QoS levels presented in Table 3 and compute their satisfaction degrees based on our preferences model: $q_{\text{orch}}(S^1) = 1$, $q_{\text{orch}}(S^2) = 0.53$, $q_{\text{orch}}(S^3) = 0.4$, $q_{\text{orch}}(S^4) = 0.14$, $q_{\text{orch}}(S^5) = 0.41$, $q_{\text{orch}}(S^6) = 0$. If we assume that these QoS levels correspond to perceived QoS levels (after execution) related to different executions of the same orchestration, the satisfaction degrees allow us to analyse these executions from the QoS point of view. On the other hand, if these QoS levels correspond to "theoretical" QoS levels (i.e., at design time) of different service orchestrations supporting the same business process [8], the satisfaction degrees are useful to determine the best one that satisfies client's expectations.

4   Discussions

As we discussed in Sect. 2, there are existing works that exploit utility functions and aggregation operator (called hereafter preferences model regardless the method used) for aggregating QoS. In this section, we focus on the comparison of our preferences model with those ones. In this context, we base our study on 4 different preferences models that we identified:

1. preferences model based on the WAM operator and linear utility functions [18,3];
2. preferences model based on the WAM operator and utility functions built using preferences expression [17];
3. preferences model based on the 2-additive Choquet integral and linear utility functions [10];
4. Our preferences model based on the 2-additive Choquet integral and utility functions built using preferences expression.

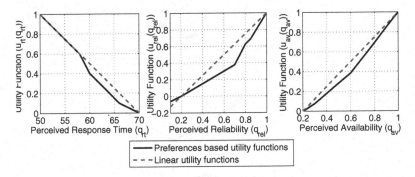

Fig. 5. Comparison between preference-based utility functions and linear utility functions

The study is based on comparison of satisfaction degrees related to QoS levels given in Table 3. In other words, we normalize the QoS levels and aggregate their values following each preferences model presented above. The results are shown in Figs. 5 and 6. Figure 5 highlights the difference between normalization based on linear utility functions (dashed line) used in the first and the third preferences models, and the normalization based on client preferences (continuous line) used in the second and fourth preferences models. We can notice that client satisfaction over each QoS attribute is usually non linear and linear utility functions often present an over-estimation of client satisfaction, which is the case for availability. The case of reliability for example presents a mix of over-estimation and under-estimation of client satisfaction. Indeed, linear utility functions present an under-estimation of client satisfaction for the bad values ($q_{rel} < 0.2$) and an over-estimation otherwise (see Fig. 5). For the response time, we can observe that client satisfaction is quasi-linear for good values, whereas linear utility functions show an over-estimation of client satisfaction for higher values. These errors, that occur due to the use of linear utility functions, may impact the determined satisfaction degree of service orchestration. Therefore, decisions based on this satisfaction degree can also be impacted (e.g., comparison between several service orchestration [8], service selection [18], etc) can also be impacted. Figure 6 outlines this impact. Indeed, we can notice the difference, which is important ($> 20\%$) for some QoS levels (e.g., for S^2, S^3 and S^5), between black and gray curves representing respectively preferences models using preference-based utility functions and those based on linear utility functions. On the other hand, if we analyse the situation (QoS level) S^4, we observe a difference between continuous and dashed curves representing respectively preferences models based on the WAM operator and those based on the 2-additive Choquet integral. The first ones express an over-estimation of the client satisfaction with regard to the latter ones. This over-estimation is due to the preferential dependencies that exist in the expressed preferences, which cannot taken into account in the first models [8] (i.e., WAM based preferences models).

To summarize, we consider that our preferences model presents a good precision to represent client satisfaction. This is performed thanks not only to the support of preferential dependencies with the use of the 2-additive Choquet integral operator, but also to the construction of preference-based utility functions (for normalization).

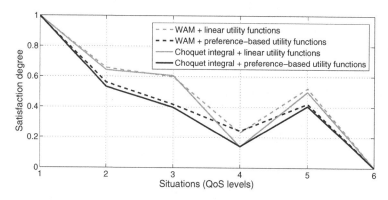

Fig. 6. QoS levels satisfaction degrees resulted from different preferences models

5 Conclusions

This paper presents an approach that measures the satisfaction degree of service orchestrations related to the client's QoS expectations. The approach newly combines workflow patterns aggregations rules and the 2-additive Choquet Integral. Besides, we have studied existing composition patterns in the literature and proposed a set of 11 patterns expressed with the last review of workflow patterns [16]. This allows us to support more service orchestration models. We have also defined previously missing aggregation rules for some composition patterns. On the other hand, we have presented our preferences model, which is used in the evaluation of the satisfaction. We have shown that our preferences model, compared to those existing in related work, represents more precisely client satisfaction. This is realised thanks to the MACBETH method combined to the 2-additive Choquet integral that *(i)* constructs the utility functions (and the aggregation function) only from client preferences, and *(ii)* supports preferential dependencies through interaction parameters.

Our future work aims to exploit this approach in the context of service orchestration runtime supervision. We aim to evaluate the satisfaction degree of the service orchestration throughout its execution and to predict the deviation of perceived the QoS level inside the QoS expectations range. Whenever we detect potential deviation, we will try to recover it by dynamic adaptation of the service orchestration.

Acknowledgements. This work is partially funded by the FEDER MES project granted by the French Rhône-Alpes Region.

References

1. van der Aalst, W., ter Hofstede, A., Kiepuszewski, B., Barros, A.: Workflow patterns. Distributed and Parallel Databases 14(1), 5–51 (2003)
2. Jaeger, C.: Optimising Quality-of-Service for the Composition of Electronic Services. Ph.D. thesis, Berlin University, Germany (2007)

3. Canfora, G., Di Penta, M., Esposito, R., Villani, M.L.: A framework for qos-aware binding and re-binding of composite web services. J. Syst. Softw. 81, 1754–1769 (2008)
4. Cardoso, J., Miller, J., Sheth, A., Arnold, J.: Modeling quality of service for workflows and web service processes. Journal of Web Semantics 1, 281–308 (2002)
5. Cliville, V., Berrah, L., Mauris, G.: Quantitative expression and aggregation of performance measurements based on the macbeth multi-criteria method. International Journal of Production Economics 105(1), 171–189 (2007)
6. Coppolino, L., Romano, L., Mazzocca, N., Salvi, S.: Web services workflow reliability estimation through reliability patterns. In: Security and Privacy in Communications Networks and the Workshops (2007)
7. Bana e Costa, Corte, J., Vansnick, J.: On the mathematical foundation of MACBETH. In: Multiple Criteria Decision Analysis: State of the Art Surveys, International Series in Operations Research & Management Science, vol. 78, pp. 409–437. Springer, New York (2005)
8. Fakhfakh, N., Pourraz, F., Verjus, H.: Quality of service aggregation in e-business applications. In: Proceedings of ICE-B 2011 International Conference on e-Business, pp. 100–110. SciTePress, Sevilla (2011)
9. He, Q., Yan, J., Jin, H., Yang, Y.: Adaptation of Web Service Composition Based on Workflow Patterns. In: Bouguettaya, A., Krueger, I., Margaria, T. (eds.) ICSOC 2008. LNCS, vol. 5364, pp. 22–37. Springer, Heidelberg (2008)
10. Herssens, C., Jureta, I.J., Faulkner, S.: Capturing and Using QoS Relationships to Improve Service Selection. In: Bellahsène, Z., Léonard, M. (eds.) CAiSE 2008. LNCS, vol. 5074, pp. 312–327. Springer, Heidelberg (2008)
11. ISO/TC 176: Quality management systems – requirements (November 2008)
12. Mayag, B., Grabisch, M., Labreuche, C.: A characterization of the 2-additive choquet integral through cardinal information. In: Fuzzy Sets and Systems (2010) (in press, corrected proof)
13. Parasuraman, A., Zeithaml, V.A., Berry, L.L.: Alternative scales for measuring service quality: A comparative assessment based on psychometric and diagnostic criteria. Journal of Retailing 70(3), 201–230 (1994)
14. Qi, M., Huang, X.: The design and analysis of three-dimensional e-business model. In: Proceedings of the 7th International Conference on Electronic Commerce, ICEC 2005, pp. 136–138. ACM, New York (2005)
15. Rosenberg, F.: QoS-Aware Composition of Adaptive Service-Oriented Systems. Ph.D. thesis, Technical University Vienna, Austria (June 2009)
16. Russell, N., Arthur, van der Aalst, W.M.P., Mulyar, N.: Workflow control-flow patterns: A revised view. Tech. rep., BPMcenter.org (2006)
17. Szydlo, T., Zielinski, K.: Method of Adaptive Quality Control in Service Oriented Architectures. In: Bubak, M., van Albada, G.D., Dongarra, J., Sloot, P.M.A. (eds.) ICCS 2008, Part I. LNCS, vol. 5101, pp. 307–316. Springer, Heidelberg (2008)
18. Taher, L., Basha, R., El Khatib, H.: Qos information & computation (qos-ic) framework for qos-based discovery of web services. UPGRADE 6(4) (August 2005)

An Answer to "Who Needs a Stylus?"
on Handwriting Recognition on Mobile Devices

Andreas Holzinger[1], Gig Searle[1], Bernhard Peischl[2], and Matjaz Debevc[3]

[1] Medical University Graz, A-8036 Graz, Austria
Institute for Medical Informatics, Statistics and Documentation, Research Unit HCI4MED
{andreas.holzinger,gig.searle}@medunigraz.at
[2] Softnet Austria, A-8010 Graz, Austria
bernhard.peischl@ist.tugraz.at
[3] University of Maribor, Faculty of Electrical Engineering and Computer Science,
SI-2000 Maribor, Slovenia
matjaz.debevc@uni-mb.si

Abstract. "Who needs a stylus?" asked the late Steve Jobs during his introduction of the iPhone. Interestingly, just at this time, Apple had made a patent application in handwriting and input recognition via pen, and Google and Nokia followed. So, "who needs a stylus then?" According to our experience in projects with mobile devices in the "real-world" we noticed that handwriting is still an issue, e.g. in the medical domain. Medical professionals are very accustomed to use a pen, whereas touch devices are rather used by non-medical professionals and definitely preferred by elderly people. During our projects on mobile devices, we noticed that both handwriting and touch has certain advantages and disadvantages, but that both are of equal importance. So to concretely answer "Who needs a stylus?" we can answer: Medical professionals for example. And this is definitely a large group of users.

Keywords: Handwriting recognition, Pen-based input, Mobile computer, Human-computer interaction.

1   Introduction

The late Steve Jobs argued in 2007 "Who need a stylus?", interestingly Apple has made a patent application on it [1], which was already in the mind for the Apple Newton [2].

Undoubtedly, it is true that touch input is well accepted and easy to learn, even amongst non-computer literate people and elderly people [3, 4]. Devices with touchscreens are useful in hospitals, where patients can, for example, fill out questionnaires while they are waiting for their examination, for the reception by the doctor, or during other spare times [5]. Direct input of questionnaire answers by the patients makes the error prone and time consuming copying of completed paper sheets unnecessary. This saves time, which can be used for direct contact with the patient, thereby improving the overall quality of the interaction between doctors and

M.S. Obaidat, J.L. Sevillano, and J. Filipe (Eds.): ICETE 2011, CCIS 314, pp. 156–167, 2012.
© Springer-Verlag Berlin Heidelberg 2012

their patients. Although touch is a very intuitive way of interaction, it was shown that in a professional medical context, styluses are preferred over finger-based input [6].

Input via stylus has the advantage of being more precise and the action is similar to the user's accustomed writing on sheets of paper – and paper is still a preferred medium in the hospital [7]. For addressing the problem of imprecise touch, using fingers, Vogel & Baudisch [8] developed a system called Shift, which makes it possible to make more precise selections using a finger. Shift shows a copy of the touched screen location and shows a pointer representing the selection point of the finger if the finger is placed over a small target. However, for further improving the precision of touch input via finger it must be better understood how people touch touchscreens [9].

Another problem with touch input using fingers is that the user's "fat fingers" also cover the areas the user intends to touch. To circumvent this problem [10] developed a mobile device which can be operated from the back. In addition, by using back-of-device interaction, it is possible to create very small touch devices [11].

Despite all these facts, medical professionals (medical doctors, nurses, therapists, first responders etc.) are more familiar with dictation and handling a stylus, since they are used to handling a pen all the time [6], [12], despite the issue of poor handwriting in medicine generally [13].

Let us take a short look at the mobile market: Worldwide sales of mobile devices totaled 440.5 million units in the third quarter of 2011, up 5.6 percent from the same period last year, according to Gartner, Inc. Smartphone sales to end users reached 115 million units in the third quarter of 2011, up 42 percent from the third quarter of 2010 and accounted to accounted for 26 percent of all mobile phone sales. In the third quarter of 2011, Android OS accounted 52.5% of worldwide smartphone sales to end users (compared to 25.3% a year earlier) whereas Symbian accounted for 16.9% (36.3% a year earlier), iOS accounted 15.0% (16.6 a year earlier) and Research In Motion accounted 11.0% (15.4% a year earlier) according to Gartner [14]. The majority of smartphones are tailored toward the business-to-consumer (B2C) market, thus the predominant input technique for mobile devices is the multi-touch concept (Wang & Ren, 2009). The majority of smartphones are tailored toward the business-to-consumer (B2C) market, thus the predominant input technique for mobile devices is the multi-touch concept [15].

Moreover, a press release from IDC in September 2011 stated: *By 2015, more U.S. Internet users will access the Internet through mobile devices than through PCs or other wireline devices. As smartphones begin to outsell simpler feature phones, and as media tablet sales explode, the number of mobile Internet users will grow by a compound annual growth rate (CAGR) of 16.6% between 2010 and 2015.*

As regards input technology, the most recent development on the mobile market is at contrast to the preferred input technique of professionals in the medical domain. Whereas, from the view-point of Human-Computer Interaction (HCI), handwriting can be seen as a very natural input technology [16], studies have shown that a recognition rate below 97% is not acceptable to end users [17]. The challenge in developing such a system is the fact that the art of handwriting is very individual for everybody, making a universal recognition of all handwriting particularly demanding [18].

A typical example is the case of incoming patients in the triage (aka EBA: first clinical examination),, where it is similar to an emergency: Rapid patient information collection is crucial. Promptly and accurately recorded and well communicated vital patient data can make the difference between life and death [19], [20]. Consequently, the data acquisition should have as little disruptive effect on the workflow of the medical professionals as possible. In the past, solutions for data input on mobile applications have been tested in the field [21], [16], [22], [23], [6], [18], [24].

Due to the fact that emergencies are usually complicated by difficult physical situations, special attention has to be given to the design of information technology for emergencies [25]. A key issue of any such information system is the acquisition of textual information. However, extensive text entry on mobile devices is principally to be avoided and a simple and easy to use interface, in accordance with the maxim: *less is more*, is a supreme necessity [23].

The basic evidence is that entering data onto a mobile device via a stylus is slower, more erroneous and less satisfactory for end users than entering data via a QWERTZ (de) or QUERTY (us) keyboard, as has been demonstrated in some studies [26], [27], however, the use of a stylus is much faster and more accurate than using finger touch [6].

2   State-of-the-Art in Handwriting Recognition Methodologies

Handwriting recognition is still considered an open research problem, mainly due to the substantial individual variation in appearance, consequently the challenges include the distortion of handwritten characters, since different people may use different style of handwriting, direction etc. [28].

If a system needs to deal with the input of different end users, a training phase is required to enable the system to understand the user's art of writing. The data received in this phase is stored in a database. During the recognition process, the system compares the input with the stored data and calculates the output.

Basically, handwriting recognition can be separated into online and offline recognition.

I) Offline Handwriting Recognition. Offline recognizers have not received the same attention as online recognizers [29].

There are several problem areas (e.g. postal address recognition) where offline handwriting recognizers are very useful due to the large amount of hand written text.

These systems have the ability to convert text into image form. The main disadvantage is that there is no possibility of obtaining information about the type of the input.

First, the text has to be separated into characters or words. With Hidden Markov Models or Neural Networks these words are matched to a sequence of data [30]. Most recently a work based on hybrid statistical features has been published [31].

II) Online Handwriting Recognition. These systems collect data during the process of input. The advantage is that specific information, such as the number of used strokes, can be collected. The result is calculated in real time [32].

This kind of recognition is used mostly in communication devices, such as Smartphones or PDAs. In this paper, we concentrate on the online handwriting recognition technique   [33] and present a detailed review of techniques and applications for online cursive handwriting recognition.

The first part of this article deals with the review of the main approaches employed in character recognition, since most of these are also used in cursive character recognition.

III) Recognition Process. Most recognition systems comprise of four distinct recognition phases [32]:

(1) Preprocessing: In this step, noise and other undesirable effects are reduced to improve the data for the recognition process [32]. Typically, some form of noise reduction and size normalization is applied.

Noise Reduction: During the input, undesired data can also be registered. For example, if the user accidently touches the screen. Such "wild points" have to be corrected.

Size Normalization: During the input the size of a character can vary. For a better recognition the characters have to be normalized to a general size.

(2) Feature Extraction: In this step, the relevant information from the input is extracted. The challenge is to extract a minimal set with maximum data recognition.

(3) Classification and (4) Recognition: The goal is to find the optimal letter to a given sequence of observations. The letter corresponding to the maximum probability is reported as the recognized letter [34], [35]. Compared with other techniques, Neural Networks and Hidden Markov Models are more often used for handwriting recognition [36].

Basically, we distinguish between statistical methods (relying on Hidden Markov models or neural networks) and structured and rule-based methods including the following:

Statistical Methods

Hidden Markov Model: HMMs consist of two processes. The underlying process is hidden and contains the state. The observable process contains the output which is visible.

The states have probability distributions over the possible output tokens. The further behavior of the system depends on its present state [34].

HMMs based on word models have the problem that the model set can grow quite large. Because of this, systems using letter models have become very popular.

Neural Networks (NNs): This method for classification has become popular since the 1980s [30]. NNs consist of multiple layers (input, output and hidden). Feed-forward neural networks are mostly used. The ability to train an NN and the back propagation of errors are the main advantages. A comparative study regarding NNs for online handwritten character recognition was conducted by [37].

Fuzzy Logic (FL): Each Fuzzy system is realized in three steps.

1) Fuzzification: Based on the features extracted in the further step the fuzzy sets could be generated easily.

2) Rule Application: The fuzzy sets are evaluated with the rules written for the system.

3) Defuzzification: In the last phase the output is generated [38], [39].

3   State-of-the-Art in Handwriting Recognition Applications

In the following, we briefly discuss the work in relation to the most notable products in handwriting recognition and list the major advantages and drawbacks.

Calligrapher SDK: The application, which we have developed and present in this paper is based on the use of Calligrapher SDK [40].

This recognition technology uses fuzzy logic and neuronal networks. Calligrapher is based on an integrated dictionary, which is used for the modeling process. It recognizes dictionary words from its main user-defined dictionary, as well as non-dictionary words, such as names, numbers and mixed alphanumeric combinations. The Calligrapher SDK provides automatic segmentation of handwritten text into words and automatically differentiates between vocabulary and non-vocabulary words, and between words and arbitrary alphanumeric strings. Further it supports several styles of handwriting, such as cursive, print and a mixed cursive/print style.

Advantages: The application provides many possibilities for the end user.

Disadvantages: The main problem is that it cannot be adapted to a specific end user.

Microsoft Tablet PC: This recognizer works with the Optical Character Recognition and the Convolutional Neural Networks. Such Neural Networks do not need feature vectors as input. The Tablet PC is also able to adapt to a new user during a training phase [41].

Advantages: The system provides many possibilities. There is a higher recognition rate of subsequently entered words because the detection depends on an integrated Dictionary.

Disadvantages: Users are given many unsolicited hints in order to use the device properly. This suggests that the adjustment to the user is not working very well and disrupts smooth functioning.

WritePad: This is a handwriting recognition system developed for iPhone, iPod and iPad Touch devices. The user can write directly onto the display using a finger or an AluPen. WritePad can recognize all styles of writing. It adapts to the user's style of writing, so it takes time until the user can use it with a lower error rate. Furthermore, it has an integrated shorthand feature, which allows the user to enter frequently used text quickly. To use the system properly, Apple offers an exhaustive tutorial. The user has to write largely and clearly for a correct translation. WritePad also includes an auto-corrector; however, this currently supports only English (Phatware, 2008). Meanwhile, Phatware launched an improved version of their advanced handwriting recognition Android app, WritePad in the Android Market (for less than 5 EUR). It supports different handwriting styles such as print, cursive or mixed. It supports the new pen-enabled tablets, such as Samsung Galaxy Note and HTC Jetstream.

Advantages: Through the training phase, the system can adapt to the writing style of the user.

Disadvantages: The user needs patience because the learning process can take longer in some circumstances.

HWPen: HWPen is a handwriting recognition tool which has already been published in 2008 for Apple devices. The software was developed by the company Hanwang.com.cn, mainly for the Chinese language. The system is heavily based on Graffiti. The adjustment period is longer because the user has first to learn the art of writing. However, similar to Graffiti, the system works very efficiently once mastered (Bailey 2008) (HWPen 2008).

Advantages: Since all characters differ greatly, HWPen has a very good detection.

Disadvantages: The user has to learn a new way of writing.

CellWriter: This is an open source HWR-System for Linux. CellWriter is based on the user's style of writing.

Therefore, a training session must be completed before use. Each character must be written in a separate cell. The system provides a drop-down list of other matches if the recognized result is wrong [42].

Advantages: It provides a word recognition feature.

Disadvantages: CellWriter is only available for Linux.

MyScriptStylus: This HWR-System is based on the latest version of MyScript and can run on Windows, Mac and Linux. The software can recognize about 26 different languages. It provides a lot of different modes, such as Writing Pad mode, in which all kinds of writing (cursive, digit, hand printed) can be recognized. For a better recognition the Character Pad mode can be used, which works similar to CellWriter, whereby the user has to input the letters in cells. Even if the system can work without a training phase, a personal dictionary should be created for better accuracy. This software also provides a list of alternatives in the case of a wrong recognition [43].

Advantages: A lot of language packages and different styles are provided.

Disadvantages: The activation code for the use costs about 40 EUR (without the calculator module).

Except for Graffiti and HWPen, all of the described systems try to give the user as much freedom in writing as possible. However, this leads to an accuracy rating worse than that of strict systems.

On the other hand, the big disadvantage of recognition systems like Graffiti is that the user has to learn a totally new art of writing.

No matter which path one follows, in both cases the user has to work with the device for some time to learn how to write clearly and precisely. This is the reason why HWR-Systems are not widely accepted, as the majority of the users typically do not want to spend much time for the learning phase.

In the following we present some Android Apps:

Writepad Stylus: Writepad Stylus is made specifically for stylus handwriting on a tablet. The software only records the writing done with a stylus, recognition of words written with a finger is not addressed by WritePad Stylus. The app offers convenience features like lasso erase (drawing a closed path to erase everything inside the this path), full zoom (holding the zoom button enables pinch zooming to any magnification), tablet flip and an out-scroll button. The stylus being used is required to have a soft rubber tip.

Advantages: No lag or jitter between the stylus movement and screen response, lots of convenience features, supports thicker tip styluses as well.

Disadvantages: Only records the writing with a stylus, no support for writing with finger.

Graffiti Pro: Graffiti Pro is a keyboard replacement for Android that uses the stroke-based handwriting recognition system text input system made popular by Palm™ PDAs running PalmOS™. With Graffiti, a user no longer types but draws Graffiti characters with your finger or a compatible stylus. Graffiti characters are mostly single-stroke drawings that closely match the usual alphabet, but are simplified to make entry faster and easier. For example, the letter "A" is entered with a stroke that looks like an upside-down "V", saving time that you do not need to cross the "A" in the middle. Same for the letter "T", which is entered almost like a "7". There are text and numeric input areas, improving the recognition of your input. Strokes drawn in the text area will only be interpreted as letters; strokes in the numeric area will be interpreted as numbers.

Advantages: Due to the use of so-called Graffitis, the app supports achieving a good compromise between speed and precision. It supports stylus as well as finger writing. For a comparison between unistrokes and Graffiti see [44], [45].

Disadvantages: Potential users have to learn the Graffiti alphabet, which is supported by a specific help feature.

DioPen™ Handwriting & Keyboard: DioPen™ is an input method editor that supports natural handwriting styles with high accuracy, developed by Diotek. In addition to the handwriting support the app provides a full QWERTY keyboard and supports a variety of languages (including English, Spanish, Italian, Korean, German, Durch, French). DioPen™ can be used with pen and fingers (even on a small display).

Advantages: Supports writing with finger on a small display as well as a number of languages.

Disadvantages: Many users report that the app is difficult to use when writing with a finger on a small device, moreover, many users reported that the app crashes.

MobileWrite: MobileWrite intends to fully allow for entering text by handwriting on the screen instead of typing on the keyboard. Text is entered by handwriting either printed or Graffiti letters, instead of typing on the keyboard. It's an alternative to onscreen keyboard and the real keyboard. Using a stylus improves the speed and accuracy. Notably all keyboard letters and keyboard symbols are supported.

Advantages: Supports handwriting and Graffiti letters and is a alternative to an onscreen or real keyboard. All keyboard letters are supported.

Disadvantages: Potential users have to learn the Graffiti alphabet.

SCUT gPen: SCUT gPen is a handwriting input method released by SCUT-HCII Laboratory of South China University of Technology (http://www.hcii-lab.net/gpen). gPen supports Chinese character sets, English letters, numbers and punctuations and more than 100 types of handwriting symbols. gPen also implements phrase association and an English keyboard.

Advantages: Supports the complex Chinese character set.

Disadvantages: Some of the users have complained about the overall usability.

4   Conclusions and Future Outlook

Generally the interest in using handwriting recognition will rather drop in the future (c.f. with Steve Jobs "who needs a stylus") – although Apple has made a new patent application in handwriting and input recognition via pen [1]

The reason for not using a stylus is twofold:

1) the finger is an accepted natural input medium [46], and

2) touch-based computers have gained a tremendous market success.

In future, communication and interaction on the basis of Natural Language Processing (NLP) will become more important.

However, within the professional area of medicine and health care, stylus-based interaction is still a topic of interest, because medical professionals prefer, and are accustomed to the use of a pen, therefore a stylus [6] is a more familiar writing tool.

Consequently, research in that area is still promising.

Although much research in the field of handwriting recognition has been done, recognition algorithms still do not achieve 100% of the high expectations of the users. Handwriting is very individual to every person and identifying characters is still very hard – as described a long time ago by [47].

Nowadays, many people, especially younger people, are connected to social networks, including Facebook, especially by using their smart phones – where today the user interface consists of a touch screen. Data acquisition is mostly realized with improved, intelligent virtual keyboards; e.g. with the implementation of a regional error correction [48]. Often they are connected with tactile feedback for touch screen widgets [49], which can improve performance and usability of virtual keyboards on small screens. Handwriting is taught from elementary school on and nearly everyone learns handwriting at school. Therefore, handwriting recognition is a very important technology for the input interfaces of mobile computers. However, today, even children get used to the QWERTY layout keyboard from elementary school. Consequently, interface designers can assume that nearly everyone is experienced in using a QWERTY layout keyboard.

Acknowledgements. This work is partly based on studies with support of FERK-Systems. We cordially thank Lamija Basic, who worked on the implementation of experiments, and the engineering team of FERK-Systems for their industrial support of this work. The research was partially funded by the Austrian Research Promotion Agency (FFG) within one, Innovationsscheck Österreich".

References

1. Yaeger, L.S., Fabrick, R.W., Pagallo, G.M.: Method and Apparatus for Acquiring and Organizing Ink Information in Pen-Aware Computer Systems 20090279783, Patent issued
2. Yaeger, L.S., Webb, B.J., Lyon, R.F.: Combining Neural Networks and Context-Driven Search for Online, Printed Handwriting Recognition in the Newton. In: Orr, G.B., Müller, K.-R. (eds.) NIPS-WS 1996. LNCS, vol. 1524, pp. 275–298. Springer, Heidelberg (1998)
3. Holzinger, A.: User-Centered Interface Design for Disabled and Elderly People: First Experiences with Designing a Patient Communication System (PACOSY). In: Proceedings of the 8th International Conference on Computers Helping People with Special Needs, pp. 33–40 (2002)
4. Holzinger, A.: Finger Instead of Mouse: Touch Screens as a Means of Enhancing Universal Access. In: Carbonell, N., Stephanidis, C. (eds.) UI4ALL 2002. LNCS, vol. 2615, pp. 387–397. Springer, Heidelberg (2003)
5. Holzinger, A., Kosec, P., Schwantzer, G., Debevc, M., Hofmann-Wellenhof, R., Frühauf, J.: Design and Development of a Mobile Computer Application to Reengineer Workflows in the Hospital and the Methodology to evaluate its Effectiveness. Journal of Biomedical Informatics 44(6), 968–977 (2011)
6. Holzinger, A., Höller, M., Schedlbauer, M., Urlesberger, B.: An Investigation of Finger versus Stylus Input in Medical Scenarios. In: Luzar-Stiffler, V., Dobric, V.H., Bekic, Z. (eds.) ITI 2008: 30th International Conference on Information Technology Interfaces, pp. 433–438. IEEE (2008)
7. Holzinger, A., Baernthaler, M., Pammer, W., Katz, H., Bjelic-Radisic, V., Ziefle, M.: Investigating paper vs. screen in real-life hospital workflows: Performance contradicts perceived superiority of paper in the user experience. International Journal of Human-Computer Studies 69(9), 563–570 (2011)
8. Vogel, D., Baudisch, P.: Shift: a technique for operating pen-based interfaces using touch. In: Proceedings of the SIGCHI Conference on Human Factors in Computing Systems, pp. 657–666 (2007)
9. Holz, C., Baudisch, P.: Understanding touch. In: Proceedings of the 2011 Annual Conference on Human Factors in Computing Systems, pp. 2501–2510 (2011)
10. Wigdor, D., Forlines, C., Baudisch, P., Barnwell, J., Shen, C.: Lucid touch: a see-through mobile device. In: Proceedings of the 20th Annual ACM Symposium on User Interface Software and Technology, pp. 269–278 (2007)
11. Baudisch, P., Chu, G.: Back-of-device interaction allows creating very small touch devices. In: Proceedings of the 27th International Conference on Human Factors in Computing Systems, pp. 1923–1932 (2009)

12. Holzinger, A., Hoeller, M., Bloice, M., Urlesberger, B.: Typical Problems with developing mobile applications for health care: Some lessons learned from developing user-centered mobile applications in a hospital environment. In: Filipe, J., Marca, D.A., Shishkov, B., Sinderen, M.V. (eds.) International Conference on E-Business (ICE-B 2008), pp. 235–240. IEEE (2008)

13. Sokol, D.K., Hettige, S.: Poor handwriting remains a significant problem in medicine. Journal of the Royal Society of Medicine 99(12), 645–646 (2006)

14. Gartner: Market Share: Mobile Communication Devices by Region and Country, 3Q11, http://www.gartner.com/resId=1847315 (last access: February 19, 2012)

15. Wang, F., Ren, X.S.: Empirical Evaluation for Finger Input Properties In Multi-touch Interaction. Assoc Computing Machinery, New York (2009)

16. Holzinger, A., Geierhofer, R., Searle, G.: Biometrical Signatures in Practice: A challenge for improving Human-Computer Interaction in Clinical Workflows. In: Heinecke, A.M., Paul, H. (eds.) Mensch & Computer: Mensch und Computer im Strukturwandel, Oldenbourg, pp. 339–347 (2006)

17. Lee, S.W.: Advances in Handwriting Recogntion. Series in Machine Perception and Artificial Intelligence (last access)

18. Holzinger, A., Schlögl, M., Peischl, B., Debevc, M.: Preferences of Handwriting Recognition on Mobile Information Systems in Medicine: Improving handwriting algorithm on the basis of real-life usability research (Best Paper Award). In: ICE-B 2010 - ICETE The International Joint Conference on e-Business and Telecommunications, pp. 120–123 (2010)

19. Holzman, T.G.: Computer-human interface solutions for emergency medical care. Interactions 6(3), 13–24 (1999)

20. Anantharaman, V., Han, L.S.: Hospital and emergency ambulance link: using IT to enhance emergency pre-hospital care. International Journal of Medical Informatics 61(2-3), 147–161 (2001)

21. Baumgart, D.C.: Personal digital assistants in health care: experienced clinicians in the palm of your hand? The Lancet 366(9492), 1210–1222 (2005)

22. Chittaro, L., Zuliani, F., Carchietti, E.: Mobile Devices in Emergency Medical Services: User Evaluation of a PDA-Based Interface for Ambulance Run Reporting. In: Löffler, J., Klann, M. (eds.) Mobile Response 2007. LNCS, vol. 4458, pp. 19–28. Springer, Heidelberg (2007)

23. Holzinger, A., Errath, M.: Mobile computer Web-application design in medicine: some research based guidelines. Universal Access in the Information Society International Journal 6(1), 31–41 (2007)

24. Holzinger, A., Basic, L., Peischl, B., Debevc, M.: Handwriting Recognition on Mobile Devices: State of the art technology, usability and business analysis. In: Proceedings of the 8th International Conference on Electronic Business and Telecommunications, INSTICC, pp. 219–227 (2011)

25. Klann, M., Malizia, A., Chittaro, L., Cuevas, I.A., Levialdi, S.: HCI for emergencies. In: CHI 2008 Extended Abstracts on Human Factors in Computing Systems, pp. 3945–3948 (2008)

26. Lewis, J.R.: Hfes, Input rates and user preference for three small-screen input methods: Standard keyboard, predictive keyboard, and handwriting. In: Proceedings of the Human Factors and Ergonomics Society 43rd Annual Meeting. Human Factors and Ergonomics Soc., vol. 1 and 2, pp. 425–428 (1999)

27. Haller, G., Haller, D.M., Courvoisier, D.S., Lovis, C.: Handheld vs. Laptop Computers for Electronic Data Collection in Clinical Research: A Crossover Randomized Trial. Journal of the American Medical Informatics Association 16(5), 651–659 (2009)

28. Perwej, Y., Chaturvedi, A.: Machine recognition of Hand written Characters using neural networks. International Journal of Computer Applications 14(2), 6–9 (2011)

29. Plotz, T., Fink, G.A.: Markov models for offline handwriting recognition: a survey. International Journal on Document Analysis and Recognition 12(4), 269–298 (2009)

30. Graves, A., Schmidhuber, J.: Offline Handwriting Recognition with Multidimensional Recurrent Neural Networks, http://www.idsia.ch/~juergen/nips2009.pdf (last access: February 17, 2011)

31. Sulong, G., Rehman, A., Saba, T.: Improved Offline Connected Script Recognition Based on Hybrid Strategy. International Journal of Engineering Science and Technology 2(6), 1603–1611 (2010)

32. Liu, Z., Cai, J., Buse, R.: Handwriting Recognition: Soft Computing and Probabilistic Approaches. Springer, New York (2003)

33. Dzulkifli, M., Muhammad, F., Razib, O.: On-Line Cursive Handwriting Recognition: A Survey of Methods and Performance. In: The 4th International Conference on Computer Science and Information Technology, CSIT 2006 (2006)

34. Plamondon, R., Srihari, S.N.: On-Line and Off-Line Handwriting Recognition: A Comprehensive Survey. IEEE Transactions on Pattern Analysis and Machine Intelligence 22(1), 63–84 (2000)

35. Shu, H.: On-Line Handwriting Recognition Using Hidden Markov Models, http://dspace.mit.edu/bitstream/handle/1721.1/42603/37145316.pdf (last access: February 18, 2011)

36. Zafar, M.F., Mohamad, D., Othman, R.M.: On-line Handwritten Character Recognition: An Implementation of Counterpropagation Neural Net. Journal of the Academy of Science, Engineering and Technology 10, 232–237 (2005), http://www.waset.org/journals/waset/v10/v10-44.pdf

37. Zafar, M.F., Mohamad, D., Othman, R.: Neural Nets for On-line Isolated Handwritten Character Recognition: A Comparative Study. In: The IEEE International Conference on Engineering of Intelligent Systems, ICEIS 2006 (2006)

38. Gowan, W.: Optical Character Recognition using Fuzzy Logic, http://www.freescale.com/files/microcontrollers/doc/app_note/AN1220_D.pdf (last access: February 18, 2011)

39. Gader, P.D., Keller, J.M., Krishnapuram, R., Chiang, J.H., Mohamed, M.A.: Neural and fuzzy methods in handwriting recognition. Computer 30(2), 79–86 (1997)

40. Phatware: Calligrapher SDK 6.0 Developer's Manual (2008)

41. Pittman, J.A.: Handwriting Recognition: Tablet PC Text Input. IEEE Computer 40(9), 49–54 (2007)

42. Willis, N.: CellWriter: Open source handwriting recognition for Linux, http://www.linux.com/archive/feed/120867 (last access: February 18, 2011)

43. VisionObjects: MyScript Stylus, http://www.visionobjects.com/handwriting_recognition/DS_MyScript_Stylus_3.0.pdf (last access: February 15, 2011)

44. Castellucci, S.J., MacKenzie, I.S.: Acm: Graffiti vs. Unistrokes: An Empirical Comparison. Assoc Computing Machinery, New York (2008)

45. Sears, A., Arora, R.: Data entry for mobile devices: an empirical comparison of novice performance with Jot and Graffiti. Interacting with Computers 14(5), 413–433 (2002)

46. Holzinger, A.: Finger Instead of Mouse: Touch Screens as a Means of Enhancing Universal Access. In: Carbonell, N., Stephanidis, C. (eds.) UI4ALL 2002. LNCS, vol. 2615, pp. 387–397. Springer, Heidelberg (2003)

47. Neisser, U., Weene, P.: A note on human recognition of hand-printed characters. Information and Control 3, 191–196 (1960)

48. Kwon, S., Lee, D., Chung, M.K.: Effect of key size and activation area on the performance of a regional error correction method in a touch-screen QWERTY keyboard. International Journal of Industrial Ergonomics 39(5), 888–893 (2009)

49. Koskinen, E., Kaaresoja, T., Laitinen, P.: Feel-good touch: finding the most pleasant tactile feedback for a mobile touch screen button. In: Proceedings of the 10th International Conference on Multimodal Interfaces, pp. 297–304 (2008)

Application of Metamorphic Testing
to a Case Study in Web Services Compositions

Carmen Castro-Cabrera and Inmaculada Medina-Bulo

Department of Computer Languages and Systems, University of Cádiz, Cádiz, Spain
{maricarmen.decastro,inmaculada.medina}@uca.es
http://www.uca.es

Abstract. Web services compositions are being widely adopted by developers, therefore the economic impact of WS-BPEL service compositions has increased, and deeper insight on how to test them effectively is required. In fact, new software testing techniques are being developed nowadays, specially those related with applications to Web Services, because of transactions through Internet. Languages for composing web services, such as the OASIS WS-BPEL 2.0 standard, open a new field for large-scale programming and they present a challenge for traditional quality assurance. Metamorphic Testing has proved useful to test and improve the quality of traditional imperative programs. This paper presents a proposal to use Metamorphic Testing to WS-BPEL compositions and provides a component diagram and an implementation approach as well as a case study with promising results.

1 Introduction

Web services are having a strong impact in our society because of the increasing number of Internet transactions and the new ways of conceiving and using web applications dealing with them.

The Web Services Business Process Execution Language (WS-BPEL), [19] allows us to develop new Web Services (WS) by modeling more complex business processes on top of preexisting WS. This evolution of business processes has produced the development of specific software to satisfy this demand. However, this development has not come with an advance in testing for this kind of software. In addition, the economic impact of WS-BPEL service compositions has increased [14], and deeper insight on how to test them effectively is therefore required. We present a proposal to apply MT to WS-BPEL compositions.

MT [7] is a software testing technique using *metamorphic relations* (MR). MR are existing or expected relations defined on a set of inputs and their corresponding outputs for multiple executions of a function under test. The underlying concept is simple and its automation is not difficult. In fact, it has proved successful in testing and improving the quality of traditional imperative programs [27].

Regarding the cost effectiveness of MT, Zhang [25] conducted an experiment where the fault detection capabilities and time cost of MT were compared to the standard assertion checking method. Results show that MT has the potential to detect more faults

M.S. Obaidat, J.L. Sevillano, and J. Filipe (Eds.): ICETE 2011, CCIS 314, pp. 168–181, 2012.

than the assertion checking method. In addition, Chan and his collaborators have re-searched their applications to different areas. The most related to this paper are the application of MT to service-oriented software [6,5].

This paper discusses how to use MT to test WS compositions in WS-BPEL. Al-though MT has not been previously applied to this area, promising results have been obtained in a number of different applications. A component diagram for a testing framework implementing this approach is included and an implementation approach as well as case studies with promising results are showed.

The structure of the rest of the paper is as follows: Section 2 outlines the main con-cepts about service compositions and MT. Section 3.1 presents some techniques that are being applied with success to testing WS compositions. In the following Section 3.2, some applications of MT to different areas are reviewed. Section 4 presents our initial proposal, its main steps, a component diagram for applying MT to WS-BPEL compo-sitions as well as working in advance. Finally, Section 5 presents some conclusions and future research lines.

2   Preliminaries

Next, we introduce the main concepts about service compositions in WS-BPEL and MT.

2.1   Web Services Compositions

This paper focuses in WS compositions, specially when they are implemented using WS-BPEL. WS-BPEL is a programming language based in XML that is used to gener-ate business processes from preexisting services. The resulting business process can be then reused as a WS in higher level compositions. A WS-BPEL composition contains four sections:

1. Declarations of the relationships to the external partners. These include both the client that has invoked the business process and the external partners whose services are required to complete the request of the client.
2. Declarations of the variables used by the process and their types. Variables are used for storing both the messages received and sent from the business process and the intermediate results required by the internal logic of the composition.
3. Declarations of handlers for various situations, such as fault, compensation or event handlers.
4. Description of the business process behavior.

The major building blocks in WS-BPEL are the *activities*. Activities may have both *attributes* and a set of *containers*. These containers can also include elements with their own attributes. Here is an example:

```
<flow>   ← Structured activity
 <links>   ← Container
  <link name="checkFl-BookFl"/>   ← Element
```

```
</links>
<invoke name="checkFlight" ... >  ← Basic activity
 <sources>  ← Container
  <source linkName="checkFl-BookFl"/>  ← Element
 </sources>
</invoke>
<invoke name="checkHotel" ... />
<invoke name="checkRentCar" ... />
<invoke name="bookFlight"  ← Attribute ...>
 <targets>  ← Container
  <target linkName="checkFl-BookFl" />
 </targets>
</invoke>
</flow>
```

WS-BPEL provides concurrency and synchronization primitives. For instance, the flow activity runs a set of activities in parallel. Synchronization constraints between activities can be defined. In the above example, the flow activity invokes three WS in parallel: checkFlight, checkHotel, and checkRentCar. There is another WS, bookFlight, that will only be invoked if checkFlight is completed. Activities are synchronized by linking them: the target activity of every link will only be executed if the source activity of the link has been completed successfully.

2.2   Metamorphic Testing

Software testing is a key activity in any software development project. Fault detection and correction are key activities to ensure program reliability. For this reason, a number of software testing techniques have been developed following different approaches [3,18].

One of the main challenges for most testing techniques is the *oracle problem*. Because of its nature, some programs are inherently difficult to test. For example, the output can be difficult to verify because the precise result is not known *a priori*,[1] or because the size of the output makes it unfeasible to apply standard techniques. In these cases, we should use a different approach to help with the verification and validation process.

Traditionally, human testers have been used to check the results manually, though it is clear that this is both expensive and error-prone. An alternative is to develop a simpler program implementing the same functional requirements that the original program, sacrificing efficiency and other non-functional requirements. However, this is out of the question for complex systems and reduces the problem to the correctness of the simpler program. Any mechanism for checking whether a program under test behaves correctly for any given input is called an *oracle*. As we have argued, there are practical situations where oracles can be unavailable or too expensive to apply. MT has been proposed to alleviate the oracle problem [7,8].

MT relies on the notion of *metamorphic relation* (MR). In [2], they are defined as "existing or expected relations over a series of distinct inputs and their corresponding results for multiple evaluations of a target function". When the implementation is correct, program inputs and outputs are expected to satisfy some necessary properties that

---

[1] Partial knowledge or properties of the result can, indeed, be available.

are relevant for the underlying algorithms. These properties are traditionally known as *assertions*. In this sense, a MR is a kind of assertion.

However, a MR should provide a way of generating new test cases from given ones. In order to illustrate this, let us consider a sorting program *sort* that sorts an input list of integers producing a list with the same integers in ascending order. For example, when the list $l_1 = \langle 4, 7, 2 \rangle$ is used, the expected result of $sort(l_1)$ is $\langle 2, 4, 7 \rangle$. Then, if we use the permutation $l_2 = perm(l_1, \langle (1, 2) \rangle) = \langle 7, 4, 2 \rangle$ as the *follow-up test case*, the expected result is the same. In other words, $sort(l_1) = sort(l_2)$, obviously because any permutation of a list has the same ordered list. Therefore, we could formalize this property, MR_1, as follows:

$$MR_1 \equiv (\exists x \ l_2 = perm(l_1, x)) \rightarrow sort(l_2) = sort(l_1)$$

where l_1 is the original input, l_2 is a follow-up test case (a permutation of l_1 in this particular case) and *perm* is the function applying a permutation to a list (just one swap in the example; the first and the second elements). If the metamorphic property is not satisfied then the program is faulty.

Please, notice that *perm* is the test generation function associated to MR_1. It receives an input list (the given test case) and a permutation (a list of index pairs), and produces a new list (the follow-up test case). Test case generation can be automated as in traditional techniques. For example, replacing the second parameter of *perm* by a random permutation we would obtain the equivalent to traditional random testing for this example. Of course, a single MR is generally insufficient. In the above example, we could not detect certain faults just with MR_1, as correctness for sorting implies permutation preservation (the resulting list must be a permutation of the original) and an order constraint (it must be sorted). On the other hand, a MR is usually devised by an expert in the application domain.

Summing up, MT is a testing technique using MR [5]. It begins with an initial test suite, which is produced with any test case selection strategy, and a set of MR. Once the program is executed on the test suite, errors are fixed until a *successful test suite* (i.e., consisting of non-failing test cases) is obtained. Then, MR are used to generate follow-up test cases. These test cases form the *follow-up test suite* and the process is iterated until the specified test criteria are met.

3 Related Work

In this section, we describe some related papers and tools and techniques applied to test web services compositions.

3.1 Testing Web Services Compositions

There are no so many tools and techniques applied to test web services compositions. We focus in those which are implemented in WS-BPEL, specially the automated ones. Most of them are referred in bibliography to test case generation of those compositions [12,24,26].

There are more complete works including the measure of test case quality and optimizing test case generation through mutation testing. GAmera [21] is a mutation testing framework to WS-BPEL that uses genetic algorithms to reduce the number of mutants required. It classifies mutants as killed (output is different than original composition), alive (output is the same as the original composition against the entire test case set performed), equivalents (output is always the same as the original composition), and erroneous (result in failure of the unfold) [11].

Other testing framework called Takuan [22] is based on dynamic generation of invariants for WS-BPEL compositions. Lastly, a recent work describes different technologies developed in web services and web services testing [4].

3.2   Metamorphic Testing in Some Environments and Programs

The first documented work about MT belongs to Weyuker [23]. In this paper she proposed a new perspective for software testing based on using alternative programs to the original code sharing the same objective to test the original program. However, she only focused on numerical functions and the relations were of equality, such as $(a + b)^2 = a^2 + 2ab + b^2$.

That original notion was later adopted by Chen [7], who defined the term as *Metamorphic Testing* and extended it, including non-numerical functions to be tested and MR but not necessarily equality as previously.

Since then, other works have been written, each one focusing on one or more different aspects of the theory. For example, [27] describes diverse programs to apply MT. The automatization of this technique and where it is applicable are related in [13]. Moreover, a research group from Columbia University has implemented part of the process to apply MT using JML execution environmental [17]. Furthermore, Chen and his colleagues in [10] describe the importance of choosing MR suitable with problem domain and algorithm structure of the program to test. In addition, Chan and his collaborators have different approaches about this subject. Although, the most interesting for us is how to apply MT to SOA software [5,6]. Furthermore, there is other interesting issue based on the analyses of feature models to obtain MR and automate the test data generation [20].

Metamorphic Testing With Numerical Problems. MT may be applied to resolve issues related to oracle problems with partial differential equations where the solution is unknown. A related study case [9] addresses how to successfully apply MT techniques to a thermodynamic problem to obtain certain properties representing MR.

Metamorphic Testing With Non-Numerical Problems. This technique is not limited to numerical problems and may be applied to programs designed to solve non-numerical problems [27]. For example, it has been proven in programs implementing algorithms that solve graph problems, with known properties that may be proven and must be met. MT has also been applied in computer graphics software. Additionally it may be used in testing compilers when it becomes too difficult to prove the equivalence between source and object code. Another approach is to use interactive software where inputs to program are user inputs, instead of data. As example, test cases to testing a browser are HTML files and action sequences like this:

$$EnterURL \rightarrow ClickItem1 \rightarrow$$
$$SelectMenufile \rightarrow SelectOpen...$$

There may be several action sequences for a specific user defined requirement. By relating all inputs to their suitable outputs for every matching action we obtain MR. If we select the appropriate MR set we may apply MT to this kind of software.

Metamorphic Testing With Learning Machine Programs. A group of Columbia University have implemented a framework [16] automating part of the testing process. They have analyzed programs that implement learning machines applications to automate how to obtain properties for this type of software. [16] categorized six types of metamorphic properties that such applications may have. Then implemented a tool called Corduroy to automate the process by allowing developers to specify individual functions of metamorphic properties using the specification language JML; Then these properties could be checked using JML Runtime Assertion Checking [17]. This way they obtain and check MR in order to apply MT.

4 Application of Metamorphic Testing to WS-BPEL

Once the different testing aspects to web services and MT have been analyzed, we propose to apply MT to web services compositions in WS-BPEL and implement it by integrating well-tested open-source systems: ActiveBPEL as the WS-BPEL engine and BPELUnit as the unit test library. ActiveBPEL is a WS-BPEL 2.0 compliant open-source engine. Compared to other engines, it is quite lightweight, reducing the time needed to run a test suite. It is maintained by ActiveVOS [1], which offers commercial products based on it. BPELUnit is a WS-BPEL unit test library [15] which can use any WS-BPEL 2.0 compliant engine. It uses XML files to describe test suites. It can replace external services with mockups providing predefined responses. It is presented firstly our initial approach. Furthermore, current proposed issues are described.

4.1 Our Approach

Our initial approach was based in the two following ideas:

1. The first idea consists of achieving program properties from learning machines software, automating MR selection. This approach is proposed by Murphy and his collaborators in [16,17],
2. The second idea is to specify, design and implement a new web service called *metamorphic service* that wraps the service to test with MR. This approach is proposed by Chan and his colleagues in [5,6]

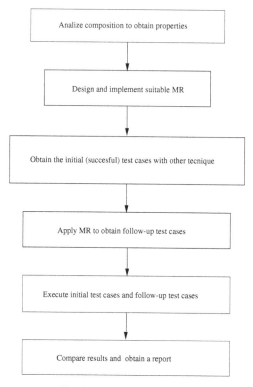

Fig. 1. A component diagram

A generic diagram of our approach is showed in Fig. 1 and it is consists of selecting MR by analyzing the composition to obtain properties. These MRs will allow us to generate follow-up test cases and test if the results satisfy the properties and, therefore, test the original composition. Then, a report with results to be analyzed will be issued. In our proposal is necessary for each composition:

1. Select adequate MR.
2. Generate initial test cases.
3. Get follow-up test cases.
4. Multiple executions of composition.
5. Analyze results.

Next we comment briefly this approach with the classical WS-BPEL example of the *Loan Approval Service* included in the WS-BPEL 2.0 specification [19]. To begin, we have to develop a program to ingest a file containing a BPELUnit Test Suite (BPTS) using templates to generate initial test cases and return other BPTS with follow-up test cases (from initial ones applying MR previously selected). To achieve this, we have followed the next steps:

- Handwrite a BPTS for the original composition using templates.
- Write the data file to generate the initial test cases by the BPTS. It is a CSV file.

- Design MR.
- Implement a program that receives the data file (CSV) and generates a new file (CSV) using the initial BPTS to generate one or more test cases using the MR designed. We have to associate the initial test cases with the new ones.
- Execute the sample composition with the initial and new test cases.
- Analyze and compare the results in both executions.

Another option would be to develop a program to ingest a BPTS (initial test cases written by hand) and return other BPTS once the MR are applied:

- Load BPTS in memory (this would be done by BPELUnit).
- Conver the BPTS in memory using MR.
- Use XMLBeans to save the new BPTS from memory to a file in disk.

We are currently working on the first option of the proposed approach. It includes all the tools and files used to generate initial and follow-up test cases, as well as, MR code implemented besides the original composition.

4.2 Implementation

In order to automate test cases generation, tradicional techniques can be used, although they can be not enough to detect errors.

MT is a testing technique that begins with a previous test suite (initially generated by a different generation strategy), and a MR set. Once program has been executed, we obtain that some test cases detect errors and others not. On one hand, the first group causes the program to be revised and errors corrected. On the other hand, the second group, called *success test cases*, will be selected as input to the architecture that we have designed.

Moreover, MR set is used to generate the *following-up test cases* from that success test suite. These following-up test cases will belong to (initial) test suite for the following iteration and the process will be repeated.

Therefore, once the previous test cases are obtained (by a different generation strategy) to apply MT with success, it is necessary to follow the next steps (see figure 2):

1. Select success test cases. These represent the *initial test cases*.
2. Choose adequate MR taking account problem nature to solve and the algorithm used in the program.
3. Generate following-up test cases applying MR to initial test cases.
4. Execute program with both initial and following-up test cases.
5. Compare results.
6. Improve program correcting errors detected, selecting new test cases and/or new better MR to the following iteration.

4.3 Case Study

In this section the proposal implementation will be applied to an example composition: the *Loan Approval* composition defined in [19]. That composition consists of a client

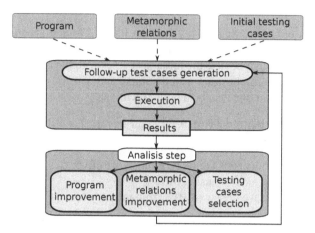

Fig. 2. MT implementation diagram

who requests an amount to a loan bank service. Depending on this amount is less or equal than 10000 euros and assigned risk to the client from an assessor service is low, this service will decide approving the loan or asking to approval service instead. Finally, loan is accepted or not. Composition logic is showing in figure 3.

First step consists in analyzing the composition and the original test cases to design adequate MR to them. Therefore, first of all, an original test cases study and, the design and the implementation of adequate MR to these test cases and the composition must be done.

Next, some examples will be described. From original test cases, new test cases will be obtained by the application of the corresponding MR. It is necessary to take into account that test cases are extended with service answers, namely, it is not only inputs and outputs, but it must be considered the involved service responses.

Firstly, we have to know the elements of a test case:

– *req_amount*, represents the loan amount.
– *ap_reply*, represents approver response.
– *as_reply*, represents assessor response.
– *accepted*, represents the final result, if loan is accepted or not.

We will focus on values that *req_amount*, *ap_reply*, *as_reply* and *accepted* have. Next, how these values are organized in a theoretical test case is showed:

$$(req\_amount, ap\_reply, as\_reply, accepted)$$

– From original test cases, the first one that we are going to consider is:

$$(1500, false, low, true)$$

In this test case, we have an amount (*req_amount*) less than the threshold and, therefore, we enter to the left branch. Assessor is invoked (*as_reply*), and in this case,

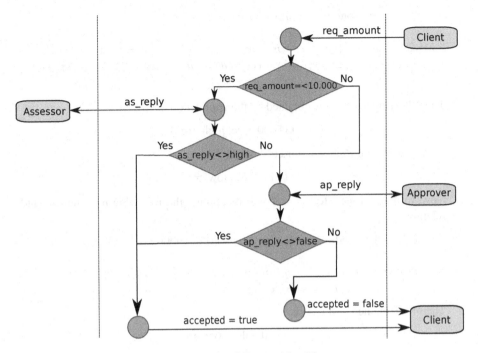

Fig. 3. Loan Approval Composition Diagram

the risk is low. Therefore, the approver response (*ap_reply*) does not influence in the final result, that is positive (*accepted = true*).

Furthermore, to obtain a new test case from the previous one, we will apply the following MR, data with 1 belongs to original test case and data with 2 belongs to a new test case generated as described before:

$$\text{Precondition: } req\_amount_1 * 10 > 10000$$

$$\text{MR1: } req\_amount_2 = req\_amount_1 * 10 \ \wedge \ ap\_reply_2 = not(ap\_reply_1)$$
$$\wedge \ as\_reply_2 = as\_reply_1 \implies accepted_2 = accepted_1 \ \wedge \ ap\_reply_2 = accepted_2$$

The MR1 precondition is that the amount (*req_amount*) multiply by 10 is greater than the threshold. As this test case verifies this precondition, then the following test case is obtained by the application of the MR1:

$$(15000, \text{true}, \text{low}, \text{true})$$

Now, we will analyze a second original test case:

$$(1500, \text{false}, \text{high}, \text{false})$$

To obtain a new test case from this, we apply the following precondition and relation:

Precondition: $req\_amount_1 * 10 > 10000$

MR2: $req\_amount_2 = req\_amount_1 * 10 \land ap\_reply_2 = not(ap\_reply_1)$
$\land as\_reply_2 = as\_reply_1 \implies accepted_2 = not(accepted_1) \land ap\_reply_2 = accepted_2$

The following test case is obtained by the application of MR2:

(15000, true, high, true)

– Finally, it will be studied a third test case:

(150, false, low, true)

Now, to obtain a new test case it will be applied the following precondition and relation:

Precondition: $req\_amount_1 * 10 \leq 10000$

MR3: $req\_amount_2 = req\_amount_1 * 10 \land ap\_reply_2 = ap\_reply_1$
$\land as\_reply_2 = as\_reply_1 \implies accepted_2 = accepted_1$

Therefore, the new test case is:

(1500, false, low, true)

As we mentioned before, this case is the original test case of the first example, so it is possible to get again test cases previously studied.

Automatic Following-Up Test Cases Generation. The previous MR and other ones have been implemented, so that, applying them to the original test cases, we obtain new test cases and improve initial test suite.

As we pointed before, the automatic new test cases generation can result in previously existing test cases. To prevent this, we have developed an application that automatizes the search of new test cases from original ones, including the elimination of previously existing test cases in a BPELUnit format file.

In order to develop the automatic test case generation it has been necessary to study deeply the logic of the composition and the possible properties that can relate the original and the follow-up test cases.

However, that effort is rewarded because the application generates valid new cases, without to have to do it by hand. Indeed, it is possible to generate new test cases from before follow-up test cases, through a new iteration. Consequently, we will obtain a more complete test suite.

Result Evaluation. As a final result of all this process is that new test cases have been generate automatically. In addition, the error detection technique has been improved completing initial test suite. The new test suite now detects existing errors that the initial test suite could not detect. A particular test case is the following:

(1500, true, low, true)

And the follow-up test case generated with MR2:

(15000, false, low, false)

In figure 3 we present the internal logic of the original Loan Approval composition and next we present the corresponding code fragment where the required amount evaluation is checked (*req_amount*):

```
<condition>
  (number(string($processInput.input/ns0:amount)) <= 10000)
</condition>
```

If an error is produced in the composition that consists in adding one more zero to the threshold amount (10000), showing 100000, it will result the following erroneous composition piece:

```
<condition>
  (number(string($processInput.input/ns0:amount)) <= 100000)
</condition>
```

With the original test cases, this error was not detected. Nevertheless, if we focus our attention in the follow-up test case generated where required amount is 15000, it can be checked that the condition does not remain in the original composition. So that, the approver is invoked and the response is depending on him. As in the erroneous composition follows remaining the condition (so that 15000 is less than 100000), the assessor is invoked and, as the risk is low, approves the loan (accept= true). However, it is not match with value (accept=false), therefore the error is detected. That test case is be able to detect an error that its original test case did not detect.

Summing up, in addition to automatically generate an important number of new test cases, some of them have detected new errors, improving the coverage of the test suite. The results can be improved too, implementing new MR that allow to obtain different test cases to those produced with previously existing MR.

5 Conclusions and Future Work

Business processes based in WS-BPEL compositions are rapidly becoming common-place in recent years, so it is important to devote more attention to testing in this context.

Therefore, it is required more innovative and efficient techniques in software testing to WS compositions.

The WS-BPEL programming language is oriented to business processes, and there-fore its peculiarities must be considered. Metamorphic Testing is proven efficient on different applications, and research by several groups continues. Moreover, it is a tech-nique that can be implemented independently of program features to test. Selection of adequate MR is a critical aspect in this technique, therefore, problem knowledge and program structure must be considered.

We have presented a proposal to use Metamorphic Testing to WS-BPEL composi-tions and implement it by integrating well-tested open-source systems. In fact, we have proposed a diagram of a test framework to apply MT to service compositions in WS-BPEL, specifying steps and ways to design it.

Furthermore, a proposal of implementation and a study case with a composition (Loan Approval composition) has been explained. It is included the logical composition diagram and some tests cases. Besides, some Metamorphic Relations have been especified and promising results have been presented in the paper.

Regarding future work, the proposed framework must be formally specified, designed, and implemented, developing every step until the system is completed.

References

1. ActiveVOS: ActiveBPEL WS-BPEL Engine (October 2009),
   http://sourceforge.net/search/?q=ActiveBPEL
2. Andrews, J.H., Briand, L.C., Labiche, Y.: Is mutation an appropriate tool for testing experiments? In: Proceedings of the 27th International Conference on Software Engineering (ICSE 2005), pp. 402–411. ACM Press (2005)
3. Beizer, B.: Software Testing Techniques, 2nd edn. International Thomson Computer Press, 2 sub edn. (June 1990)
4. Bozkurt, M., Harman, M., Hassoun, Y.: TR-10-01: testing web services: A survey. Tech. Rep. TR-10-01, King's College, London (2010)
5. Chan, W.K., Cheung, S.C., Leung, K.R.: A metamorphic testing approach for online testing of service-oriented software applications. International Journal of Web Services Research 4(2), 61–81 (2007)
6. Chan, W.K., Cheung, S., Leung, K.: Towards a metamorphic testing methodology for service-oriented software applications. In: Fifth International Conference on Quality Software (QSIC 2005), pp. 470–476 (2006)
7. Chen, T.Y.: Metamorphic testing: A new approach for generating next test cases. Technical Report HKUST-CS98-01, Department of. Computer Science, Hong Kong University of Science and Technology (1998)
8. Chen, T.Y.: Metamorphic testing: A simple approach to alleviate the oracle problem. In: Proceedings of the 5th IEEE International Symposium on Service Oriented System Engineering. IEEE Computer Society (2010)
9. Chen, T.Y., Feng, J., Tse, T.H.: Metamorphic testing of programs on partial differential equations: A case study. In: Proceedings of the 26th International Computer Software and Applications Conference on Prolonging Software Life: Development and Redevelopment, COMPSAC 2002, pp. 327–333. IEEE Computer Society, Washington, DC (2002), http://portal.acm.org/citation.cfm?id=645984.675903
10. Chen, T.Y., Huang, D.H., Tse, T.H., Zhou, Z.Q.: Case studies on the selection of useful relations in metamorphic testing. In: Proceedings of the 4th Ibero-American Symposium on Software Engineering and Knowledge Engineering (JIISIC 2004), pp. 569–583 (2004)
11. Domínguez-Jiménez, J.J., Estero-Botaro, A., García-Domínguez, A., Medina-Bulo, I.: GAmera: An automatic mutant generation system for WS-BPEL compositions. In: ECOWS 2009: Seventh IEEE European Conference on Web Services, pp. 97–106. IEEE Computer Society, Eindhoven (2009)
12. García-Fanjul, J., Tuya, J., de la Riva, C.: Generación sistemática de pruebas para composiciones de servicios utilizando criterios de suficiencia basados en transiciones. In: JISBD 2007: Actas de las XII Jornadas de Ingeniería del Software y Bases de Datos (2007)
13. Gotlieb, A., Botella, B.: Automated metamorphic testing. In: Annual International on Computer Software and Applications Conference, pp. 34–40 (2003)

14. IDC: Research reports (2008), http://www.idc.com
15. Mayer, P., Lübke, D.: Towards a BPEL unit testing framework. In: TAV-WEB 2006: Proceedings of the 2006 workshop on Testing, Analysis, and Verification of Web Services and Applications, pp. 33–42. ACM, New York (2006)
16. Murphy, C., Kaiser, G., Hu, L., Wu, L.: Properties of machine learning applications for use in metamorphic testing. In: Proc. of the 20th International Conference on Software Engineering and Knowledge Engineering (SEKE), pp. 867–872 (2008)
17. Murphy, C., Shen, K., Kaiser, G.: Using JML runtime assertion checking to automate metamorphic testing in applications without test oracles. In: International Conference on Software Testing Verification and Validation, ICST 2009, pp. 436–445 (2009)
18. Myers, G.J., Sandler, C., Badgett, T., Thomas, T.M.: The Art of Software Testing, 2nd edn. Wiley - Interscience (2004)
19. OASIS: Web Services Business Process Execution Language 2.0 (2007), http://docs.oasis-open.org/wsbpel/2.0/OS/wsbpel-v2.0-OS.html, Organization for the Advancement of Structured Information Standards
20. Segura, S., Hierons, R.M., Benavides, D., Ruiz-Cortes, A.: Automated test data generation on the analyses of feature models: A metamorphic testing approach. In: 2008 International Conference on Software Testing, Verification, and Validation, pp. 35–44 (2010)
21. UCASE Research Group: GAmera home site (2010), http://neptuno.uca.es/~gamera
22. UCASE Research Group: Takuan home site (May 2010), https://neptuno.uca.es/redmine/projects/takuan-website
23. Weyuker, E.: On testing Non-Testable programs. The Computer Journal 25(4), 465–470 (1982), http://dx.doi.org/10.1093/comjnl/25.4.465
24. Yan, J., Li, Z., Yuan, Y., Sun, W., Zhang, J.: BPEL4WS unit testing: Test case generation using a concurrent path analysis approach. In: ISSRE 2006: 17th International Symposium on Software Reliability Engineering, pp. 75–84. IEEE Computer Society, Raleigh (2006)
25. Zhang, Z.Y., Chan, W.K., Tse, T.H., Hu, P.F.: An experimental study to compare the use of metamorphic testing and assertion checking. Journal of Software 20(10), 2637–2654 (2009)
26. Zheng, Y., Zhou, J., Krause, P.: An automatic test case generation framework for web services. Journal of Software 2(3), 64–77 (2007)
27. Zhou, Z.Q., Huang, D.H., Tse, T.H., Yang, Z., Huang, H., Chen, T.Y.: Metamorphic testing and its applications. In: Proceedings of the 8th International Symposium on Future Software Technology (ISFST 2004), Software Engineers Association (2004)

Part III
Optical Communication Systems

Time Stretching of UWB Radio Signals Using a Photonic Analogue-to-Digital Converter System Based on Wavelength Division Multiplexing

Tiago Alves and Adolfo Cartaxo

Group of Research on Optical Fibre Telecommunication Systems (GROFTS),
Instituto de Telecomunicações, Department of Electrical and Computer Engineering,
Instituto Superior Técnico, Technical University of Lisbon, 1049-001 Lisbon, Portugal
{tiago.alves,adolfo.cartaxo}@lx.it.pt
http://www.it.pt

Abstract. A photonic (Ph) analogue-to-digital (ADC) converter architecture using wavelength division multiplexing (WDM) technique is presented. This architecture is proposed as an alternative solution to the time division multiplexing (TDM) Ph-ADC used for ultra wideband radio signals monitoring purposes. The signal at the different points of the WDM Ph-ADC is analyzed in detail and both architectures are compared in terms of implementation complexity, signal-to-noise ratio (SNR) and nonlinear fiber impairments viewpoints.

The main advantage of the WDM Ph-ADC architecture when compared with the TDM Ph-ADC is the possibility of having faster monitoring up-dates of the radio channel due to the higher pulse repetition rate allowed. This is achieved at the expense of system complexity increase. It is also concluded that the SNR of the WDM architecture is worse than in the TDM case and it presents lower tolerance to the fiber nonlinearity.

Keywords: Photonic analogue-to-digital converter, Time stretching, Ultra wideband, Wavelength division multiplexing.

1 Introduction

The photonic (Ph) analogue-to-digital converter (ADC) system was initially proposed as a powerful solution to provide time-stretching/frequency-compression of high frequency signals in order to relax the electrical receivers bandwidth [1–3].

Recently, a multi-channel Ph-ADC system based on time division multiplexing (TDM) technique has been proposed [4–6]. This Ph-ADC system is used to compress the spectrum of ultra-wideband (UWB) radio signals captured from sensor antennas that are strategically located inside home premises. From this compression, spectrum monitoring, fingerprinting and localization of the different UWB transceivers that are being used in a given pico-cell can be performed by digital signal processing (DSP) techniques. The main advantage of such Ph-ADC system is the relaxed requirements of the electronic ADCs (E-ADC) used to monitoring the whole UWB band (from 3.1 until 10.6 GHz). In this work, a Ph-ADC based on the wavelength division multiplexing (WDM) technique is proposed for the first time (to the best of our knowledge). The

M.S. Obaidat, J.L. Sevillano, and J. Filipe (Eds.): ICETE 2011, CCIS 314, pp. 185–199, 2012.

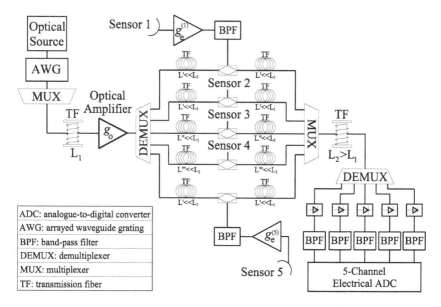

Fig. 1. Schematic diagram of the photonic part of the WDM Ph-ADC architecture

operational limits of the WDM Ph-ADC architecture are analyzed through numerical simulation and discussed in detail. The main advantages/disadvantages of this architecture when compared with the TDM-based architecture are also identified.

2   WDM Ph-ADC Architecture

2.1   System Description

Fig. 1 depicts the setup diagram of the WDM Ph-ADC architecture. The optical source may be implemented using a super continuum (SC) source generating an optical pulsed signal with a flat wideband spectrum. This spectrum is then filtered (for instance, using an arrayed waveguide grating (AWG)) in several slices (as much as the number of sensors used to acquire the electrical signals from the radio interface in a given room scenario), multiplexed and launched into a dispersive spool of fibre in order to stretch the time signal waveforms. After the fibre, the different optical pulsed signals (each one centred at a different optical wavelength) are demultiplexed and used to feed each electro-optic modulator (EOM) that is located in each sensor antenna. The wireless signals acquired in each sensor antenna are then used to modulate the respective optical pulsed signal. It should be highlighted that, with this architecture, the electrical signal snapshots acquired by the different sensors antennas in a given time instant are converted to the optical domain at the same time instant (apart the walk-off between the different wavelengths resulting from the propagation along the first spool of fibre) using optical pulsed signals transmitted at different wavelengths. Instead, in the TDM architecture, only one wavelength is used and the snapshots of the different sensors are transmitted separately in time. The optical pulsed signals are then multiplexed and launched into the second spool of fibre. After achieving the proper time stretching (TS) by adequate adjustment of the dispersion of the first and second spool of fibres, the optical signals carried in the different wavelengths are demultiplexed and the electrical signals snapshots are obtained using positive-intrinsic-negative (PIN) photo-detectors. The detected electrical signals are band-pass filtered (to reduce the low frequency/high power spectrum due to the optical pulsed signal) and applied to the E-ADC card where DSP is accomplished. From the comparison of the WDM with the TDM Ph-ADC architecture presented in [6], the following outcomes are drawn: a wider band optical source is required in the WDM than in the TDM architecture; ii) the WDM architecture may be more expensive than the TDM as it requires additional optical devices as multiplexers (MUXs), demultiplexers (DEMUXs) and PIN photo-detectors, and electrical devices as band-pass filters (BPFs) and electrical amplifiers and iii) the WDM architecture requires a multi-channel E-ADC card as the signals may arrive to the card simultaneously. The main advantage of the WDM architecture over the TDM one is related to the possibility of having a higher pulse frequency rate that enables faster up-dating on the fingerprinting, localization and power levels control of the UWB transceivers used in a given pico-cell.

2.2 Description of the WDM Ph-ADC System Parameters

The analysis of the WDM Ph-ADC architecture is accomplished considering similar parameters to the ones used in [6] for the TDM Ph-ADC architecture. Particularly, it is considered that:

– The arrayed waveguide grating is characterized by a Gaussian transfer function (in order to have optical time pulsed signals with a Gaussian shape) with a -3 dB bandwidth of 1.7 nm.
– The time stretching factor is 3.4 (and consequently the fibre spools lengths are the same as for the TDM solution) in order to meet the time aperture specifications mentioned in [6].
– The electro-optic conversion is performed by conventional Mach-Zehnder modulator biased at the quadrature point.
– The electrical and optical amplifiers present the same noise characteristics to the ones considered in [6].
– A 6-th order band-pass Bessel filter with a -3 dB bandwidth of 13 GHz and with maximum amplitude response at 5.48 GHz is used in each sensor to model the limited bandwidth of the electrical noise and a 6-th order band-pass Bessel filter with a -3 dB bandwidth of 1.4 GHz and with maximum amplitude response at 1.1 GHz is used at the PIN output.
– The transmission over the first and second spools of fibre is linear.

However, the pulse repetition rate used in the WDM architecture is five times higher than the one used in the TDM architecture presented in [6] - 3.23 MHz - as the optical pulses are not multiplexed in time.

3 WDM Ph-ADC Architecture Operation in the Absence of Electrical Signals

The appropriate operation of the WDM Ph-ADC architecture is limited mainly by two parameters: the optical channel spacing used between the different optical transmitted channels and the bandwidth of the MUXs/DEMUXs used to combine/separate those optical channels. In this section, a brief study on the impact of these parameters on the WDM Ph-ADC architecture is accomplished. To simplify the analysis, no electrical signals applied to the EOM are considered.

3.1 Bandwidth of MUXs/DEMUXs

In this work, the absence of (or negligible) time waveform differences between the signals before and after the MUXs/DEMUXs operation is considered as a criterion to identify the most adequate bandwidth for these devices. This criterion is used in order to obtain low distortion induced by the 2 MUXs and 2 DEMUXs chain of the WDM Ph-ADC system on the time waveform. The study is accomplished by taking into account the WDM Ph-ADC system described in section 2 and considering the transmission of only one optical pulsed signal (obtained by proper filtering of the flat spectrum generated by the SC source) in order to avoid inter-channel crosstalk.

Fig. 2 shows the normalized intensity of one optical pulse at the DEMUX (located after the first spool of fibre) input and output for different -3 dB bandwidth values of the DEMUX Gaussian shape. Fig. 2 shows that tight bandwidths decrease the time aperture of the optical pulse. It is also shown that although the optical pulse remains almost unchanged for a bandwidth of 500 GHz, the reduction of the pulse time aperture cannot be neglected anymore for a bandwidth of 300 GHz. For the 400 GHz bandwidth case, a slight reduction of the time aperture is also observed. Nevertheless, this reduction is not much significant and the 400 GHz bandwidth case is preferable (when compared with 500 GHz) as it allows for lower optical channel spacing in the WDM architecture and, consequently, for lower optical bandwidth requirements in the WDM Ph-ADC system. Hence, in this work, the -3 dB bandwidth of the MUXs/DEMUXs used along the optical path is set to 400 GHz.

3.2 Optical Channel Spacing

Due to the very large bandwidth of each optical signal used to "sample" the radio signals captured by the sensors antennas, the walk-off induced by the fibre on each WDM channel may be of special relevance and its impact on the system operation should be carefully analyzed. The study of the influence of the optical channel spacing on the WDM operation is accomplished by considering the Ph-ADC architecture comprising five sensors as depicted in Fig. 1.

Fig. 3 depicts the time waveform and the power spectral density (PSD) of the multiplexed signal at the output of the first spool of fibre considering an optical channel spacing of 600 GHz. Fig. 3(b) shows a zoom of the WDM signal in the time domain. The five pulses presented in Fig. 3(b) are the optical pulses corresponding to each one of

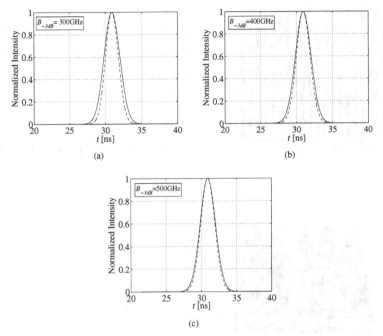

Fig. 2. Normalized intensity of the optical pulses at the DEMUX input (continuous line) and the DEMUX output (dashed line)

the five optical channels used in the WDM Ph-ADC architecture (see the signal spectrum in Fig. 3(c)). They appear separated in time due to the walk-off effect occurred along the first spool of fibre. As the WDM signal is still launched into the second spool of fibre, the impact of the walk-off on the relative delay between the optical channels is still further increased.

Fig. 4(a) depicts the time waveform corresponding to the WDM signal at the output of the second spool of fibre. Fig. 4(b) shows a zoom of Fig. 4(a). Fig. 4 shows that there is a significant overlapping between the different transmitted optical pulses, i. e., the optical pulses of a given signal period that are being transmitted in one optical wavelength are overlapped (partially or totally) in time (but in the adjacent period) with the pulses carried by another wavelength. This is due to the different propagation delays of each optical channel caused by the walk-off effect along the propagation over the first and second spools of fibre. Nevertheless, as the multiplexed signals are being transmitted at different wavelengths, the optical pulses associated with each optical wavelength could still be correctly detected without additional distortion if the demultiplexing operation is performed in such a way that the crosstalk between the optical channels is avoided.

Fig. 5 shows the normalized PSD of the signals obtained at the output of the demultiplexer used in the optical receiver for the sensors corresponding to the channels transmitted at the edges and at the middle of the WDM spectrum. The PSDs of the remaining channels are not shown as they are similar to the one of Fig. 5(b). Fig. 5 shows that, even using a channel spacing of 600 GHz between the WDM channels, there is still a small fraction of the adjacent channels in each demultiplexed signal.

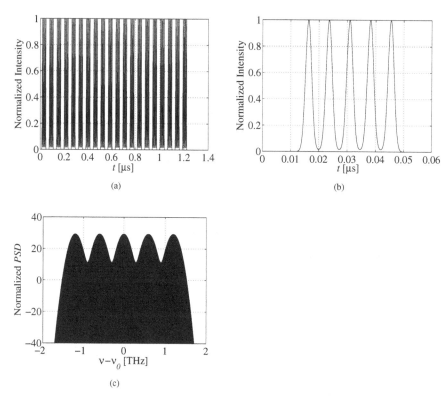

Fig. 3. a) Multiplexed optical pulses at the output of the first spool of fibre. b) Zoom of a). c) PSD of the multiplexed signal represented in a). Results obtained for an optical channel spacing of 600 GHz.

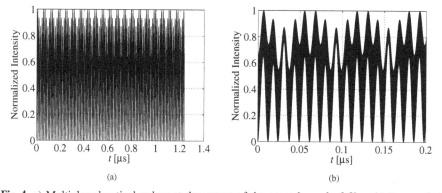

Fig. 4. a) Multiplexed optical pulses at the output of the second spool of fibre. b) Zoom of a). Results obtained for an optical channel spacing of 600 GHz.

This crosstalk power may be of special relevance from the distortion viewpoint. Indeed, as the optical pulses carried by the different wavelengths may be overlapped in time due to the walk-off effect, this crosstalk power due to the adjacent channels that is not completely removed by the demultiplexing operation can lead to two different

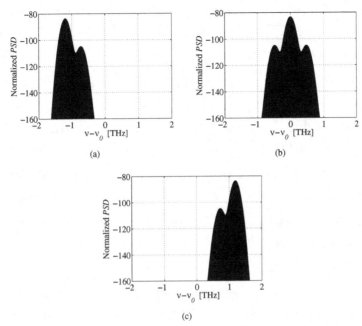

Fig. 5. Normalized PSD of the demultiplexed signal at the PIN input for the sensor corresponding to the channel located at (a) one edge of the spectrum, (b) the middle of the spectrum and (c) on the other edge of the spectrum. Results obtained for an optical channel spacing of 600 GHz.

degradation effects: i) if the pulses carried by the desired wavelength and by the "crosstalk" wavelength are partially (or totally) overlapped in time, then the degradation appears as amplitude distortion and ii) if the pulses carried by the desired wavelength and by the "crosstalk" wavelength are not overlapped, then a fraction of the pulse carried by the "crosstalk" wavelength will appear in a time interval where it is not supposed to be. These conclusions have been drawn considering un-modulated optical pulses, i. e., without considering the electro-optic conversion of the radio signals captured by the sensors antennas. However, it should be stressed that the degradation effects mentioned above will lead to the same consequence when the entire WDM Ph-ADC system is working properly: the current at the output of each photo-detector provides information from the respective sensor (for instance, if the signal from sensor 1 is modulating the optical wavelength 1, the respective detected current provides information from sensor 1) and also information from the sensors that are using the adjacent wavelengths. This effect is not acceptable for adequate Ph-ADC operation as the information provided by each signal is still used by the digital signal processing algorithms and may lead to wrong (or, at least, poor) fingerprinting and localization estimates.

Fig. 6 shows a part of the time waveforms of the signals at the PIN output for the sensors corresponding to the channels located at the edges and at the middle of the spectrum (the remaining time waveforms are similar to the one of Fig. 6(b)).

From the analysis of Fig. 6, it is clear that the received signal corresponding to each optical wavelength presents different peak amplitudes due to the walk-off effect, as identified above.

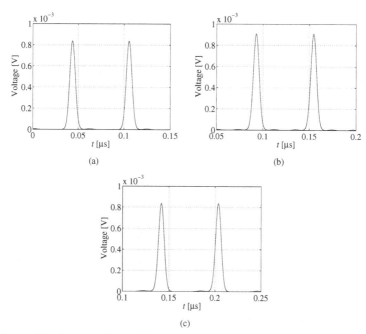

Fig. 6. Zoom of the time waveforms of the signal at the PIN output for the sensor corresponding to the channel located at (a) one edge of the spectrum, (b) the middle of the spectrum and (c) on the other edge of the spectrum. Results obtained for an optical channel spacing of 600 GHz.

Fig. 7 shows results similar to the ones of Fig. 6 but considering an optical channel spacing of 400 GHz rather than 600 GHz. Fig. 7 shows that, when the channel spacing decreases, the crosstalk of the adjacent channels increases and a fraction of power appears around the desired optical pulses due to the optical pulses carried by the adjacent wavelengths. Notice that, although this fraction of power only appears in one side of the pulses presented in Fig. 7(a) and 7(c), it appears in both sides of the pulses shown in Fig. 7(b) (and also in the pulses corresponding to the remaining two channels that are not presented in Fig. 7). This is because the signals depicted in Fig. 7(a) and 7(c) correspond to the channels transmitted at the edges of the WDM spectrum (suffering from the crosstalk induced by only one adjacent optical channel), while the other signals correspond to the channels transmitted at the middle of the WDM spectrum (suffering from the crosstalk induced by two adjacent optical channels). Fig. 7 shows also that the amplitude distortion effect is higher than the one observed in Fig. 6 as the crosstalk power is higher due to the tighter channel spacing used in the results of Fig. 7.

Fig. 8 depicts part of the time waveform obtained at the PIN output for the sensor corresponding to the channel located at the middle of the spectrum, considering an optical channel spacing of 800 GHz. The pulses corresponding to the remaining sensors are not shown as they are identical to the ones of Fig. 8. Fig. 8 shows that there is not any power fraction from adjacent optical pulses falling close to the edges of the desired pulses indicating that the crosstalk due to adjacent channels is negligible. In addition, the comparison with the pulses waveform carried by the other wavelengths showed

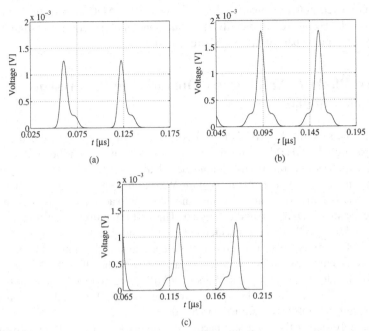

Fig. 7. Zoom of the time waveforms of the signal at the PIN output for the sensor corresponding to the channel located at (a) one edge of the spectrum, (b) the middle of the spectrum and (c) on the other edge of the spectrum. Results obtained for an optical channel spacing of 400 GHz.

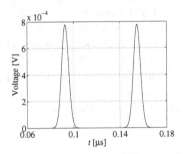

Fig. 8. Zoom of the time waveform of the signal at the PIN output for the sensor corresponding to the channel located at the middle of the spectrum. Results obtained for an optical channel spacing of 800 GHz.

absence of amplitude distortion as the pulses carried from the different wavelengths present similar peak amplitude levels.

Further investigation showed that the absence of signal degradation due to the walk-off effect is only reached for optical channel spacing values of the order of 800 GHz. It should be highlighted that, even with 800 GHz of channel spacing, there is time overlapping between the different pulses that comprise the WDM signal at the 2-*nd* DEMUX input. However, the impact of this effect on the different demultiplexed signals is negligible due to the absence of significant crosstalk power imposed by the adjacent optical channels. Considering this 800 GHz of channel spacing, the entire bandwidth of the multiplexed optical signal used for the WDM Ph-ADC architecture is around 5×800 GHz=4 THz and, consequently, the same bandwidth is required for the devices comprising the optical part of the WDM architecture.

4   WDM Ph-ADC Architecture Operation in the Presence of Electrical Signals

In the previous section, the MUXs/DEMUXs bandwidth (400 GHz) and the optical channel spacing (800 GHz) have been chosen in order to avoid significant degradation of the optical pulses and considering that no electrical signals were modulating the optical carriers. In this section, the operation of the WDM Ph-ADC architecture considering the chosen bandwidth and channel spacing, and taking into account the signals captured by the five sensors is analyzed and discussed. The first three orthogonal frequency division multiplexing (OFDM) ultra wideband (UWB) sub-bands centred at 3.43 GHz, 3.96 GHz and 4.49 GHz are considered as the electrical signals captured by the antennas of the different sensors. The electrical mean power of the OFDM-UWB signals at the input of the electrical sensor amplifiers is -40 dBm and an electrical amplifier gain of 40 dB is used. The gain of the optical amplifier is set 30 dB and the gain of the electrical receiver amplifiers is adjusted to 50 dB.

Fig. 9 and 10 depict the PSD and part of the time waveform of the received time stretched OFDM-UWB snapshots at the output of the BPF used in each branch of the electrical receiver of the WDM Ph-ADC system. Fig. 9 and 10 confirm that time stretching of the signals at the different branches (and that have been transmitted in different optical wavelengths) of the electrical receiver is reached when the WDM architecture is employed. Notice that the OFDM-UWB radio signals centre frequency initially captured by the sensors antenna appears at the output of the WDM Ph-ADC compressed by a factor of 3.4 - the time stretching factor that is being considered. Further investigation showed that the level of the side lobes of the spectrum of the compressed signal in the WDM architecture is similar to the one obtained in the TDM architecture as it is mainly dependent only on the EOM (and the same EOM is used for both WDM and TDM approaches).

5   Discussion on the WDM Ph-ADC Architecture Performance

In this section, the performance comparison between the WDM and TDM Ph-ADC architectures is presented. Particularly, the signal-to-noise ratio (SNR) evaluated from the approach presented in [6] and the degradation due to the fiber nonlinearities are analyzed.

5.1   SNR

In order to compare the SNR of the WDM Ph-ADC architecture with its TDM version, let's consider that the optical peak power of each optical pulsed channel launched into the fiber in the WDM architecture is identical to the one of the TDM architecture and

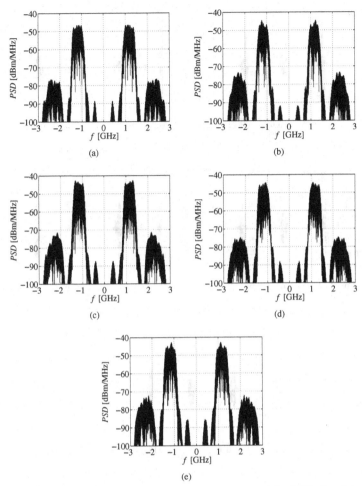

Fig. 9. PSD of the time stretched received signal at the output of the BPF of each branch of the electrical receiver

that the lengths of the two spools of fiber are the same in both architectures. In addition, let's consider also that the propagation in both spools of fiber can be well described as linear transmission. Within these assumptions and taking into account that the photonic structure of the WDM architecture is identical to the one of the TDM architecture, it can be concluded that, if the same electrical and optical gain levels are considered for both architectures, and that the insertion losses imposed by the MUXs/DEMUXs can be neglected, the SNR of the received signal of each branch of the WDM architecture is identical to the SNR obtained for the time stretched signal at the output of the TDM architecture. However, the insertion losses of the MUXs/DEMUXs are usually of the order of a few dB and may impose some changes on the SNR levels obtained in the WDM architecture.

In order to assess the SNR levels obtained by both architectures, the peak SNR [6] was evaluated for three different gain sets and considering ideal MUXs/DEMUXs

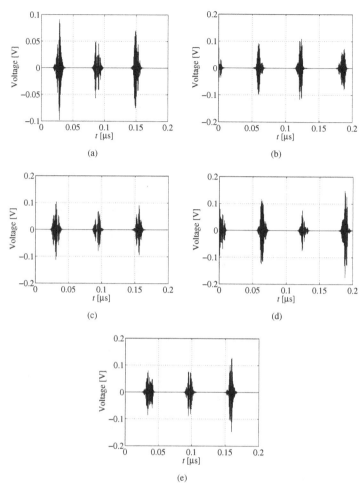

Fig. 10. Time stretched received signal at the output of the BPF of each branch of the electrical receiver

(without insertion losses) and actual MUXs/DEMUXs (with insertion losses of 5 dB). The three gain sets represent situations where the total noise variance is dominantly impaired by the noise introduced by the electrical transmitter, by the optical amplifier or by the electrical receiver. In addition, the optical filter required by the TDM architecture was modeled by a Gaussian shape with a -3 dB bandwidth of 400 GHz (identical to the one of the DEMUXs/MUXs of the WDM architecture) in order to provide a fair comparison between the results. It should be stressed that, in order to have a fair comparison, also the same peak power for each optical pulsed channel launched into the fiber in the WDM architecture and in the TDM architecture has been considered. This means that the insertion losses of the AWG and of the MUX located at the input of the first spool of fiber are not relevant for the analysis.

Table 1 shows the peak SNR levels obtained for three cases: the WDM Ph-ADC considering the absence of MUXs/DEMUXs insertion losses, the WDM Ph-ADC

Table 1. Peak SNR of the TS received signal considering the WDM and TDM Ph-ADC architectures

Peak SNR [dB]	G_e=40 dB G_o=30 dB G_r=50 dB	G_e=20 dB G_o=40 dB G_r=50 dB	G_e=20 dB G_o=20 dB G_r=70 dB
WDM Ph-ADC without MUXs/DEMUXs ins. losses	27	18	13
WDM Ph-ADC with MUXs/DEMUXs ins. losses	17	16	-15
TDM Ph-ADC	27	18	13

considering MUXs/DEMUXs with insertion losses of 5 dB and the TDM Ph-ADC architecture. The results presented in Table 1 confirm that both architectures provide the same SNR performance since the system parameters are identical and MUXs/DEMUXs with negligible insertion losses are considered. However, when actual MUXs/DEMUXs are considered, the peak SNR obtained in the WDM architecture is lower than the one obtained for the TDM case. This is due to the influence of the insertion losses of the MUXs/DEMUXs on the power of the received signal and on the noise variance. In order to clarify this effect, let's analyze separately the influence of the insertion losses on each one of the three different cases of gain sets.

- **Total Noise Variance Dominantly Impaired by the Noise of the Electrical Transmitter (G_e=40 dB, G_o=30 dB, G_r=50 dB).** The total noise variance is reduced due to the insertion losses of the MUX and DEMUXs that are located at the input and at the output of the second spool of fiber, respectively. However, the signal power is further decreased by the insertion losses of the DEMUX located after the optical amplifier. Therefore, the SNR obtained for the WDM architecture is lower than for the TDM.
- **Total Noise Variance Dominantly Impaired by the Noise of the Optical Amplifier (G_e=20 dB, G_o=40 dB, G_r=50 dB).** In this case, the total noise variance and the signal power are reduced by the same levels as the insertion losses of the MUX and DEMUXs of the optical link affect both in a similar way. Hence, the peak SNR obtained for the WDM architecture should be similar to the one achieved in the TDM architecture. However, as the variance due to the ASE noise contribution is reduced due to the insertion losses, the total noise variance may not be any more dominantly impaired by the noise of the optical amplifier. In this case, the peak SNR of the WDM architecture is also reduced as it will fall inside one of the two other cases.
- **Total Noise Variance Dominantly Impaired by the Noise of the Electrical Receiver** (G_e=20 dB, G_o=20 dB, G_r=70 dB). In this situation, the total noise variance is not affected by the insertion losses of the MUX and DEMUXs and thus, the SNR obtained in the WDM architecture is worse than the one achieved in the TDM as the received signal power is lower (when compared with the TDM case) due to the insertion losses.

From the study performed above it is concluded that it is not possible to obtain higher peak SNRs levels in the WDM architecture than the ones obtained for the TDM case.

5.2 Fiber Nonlinearities

In order to perform a fair comparison, let's consider that the optical peak power of each optical pulsed channel of the WDM architecture is identical to the one of the optical pulsed signal used in the TDM architecture and that the pulse repetition rate of the WDM architecture is maximized (in the Ph-ADC application under analysis, it is five times higher than in the TDM case). In this situation, the total optical average power launched into the first spool of fiber is higher in the WDM architecture due to the higher pulse repetition rate. Hence, it is expected that the signals transmitted over the WDM architecture suffer from higher degradation due to the fiber nonlinearities. As the channel spacing is very large and the peak power at the optical source output can exceed 30 dBm, stimulated Raman scattering is very likely the main multi-channel nonlinear impairment. The detailed quantitative assessment of the degradation induced by the fiber nonlinearities of the WDM and TDM Ph-ADC architectures on the TS received signals is out of the scope of this work and will be presented elsewhere.

6 Conclusions

The performance of the WDM Ph-ADC architecture operation has been analyzed. The signal at different points of the Ph-ADC has been presented, the influence of the -3 dB MUXs/DEMUXs bandwidth and of the optical channel spacing on the WDM architecture operation have been assessed, and the WDM architecture has been compared with its TDM counterpart.

It has been shown that the WDM architecture using five sensors and with a channel spacing of 800 GHz provides adequate time stretching of OFDM-UWB radio signals captured from the radio interface. In addition, it has been also shown that the WDM architecture does not allow obtaining better SNR performance than the TDM architecture. It is also expected that the signals transmitted over the WDM architecture suffer from higher nonlinear fiber effects than the TDM architecture.

The -3 dB bandwidth of the MUXs/DEMUXs has been chosen in order to keep the optical pulses shape at the output of those devices almost unchanged when compared with the non-filtered optical pulses. From this study, a Gaussian shape with -3 dB bandwidth of 400 GHz has been used to model the MUXs/DEMUXs. The optical channel spacing between the different optical channels has been chosen in order to have a negligible perturbation on the optical pulses due to the crosstalk induced by the optical pulses carried by the adjacent optical channels. From this study, an optical channel spacing of 800 GHz has been chosen for the WDM architecture.

From the study performed in this work, it has been concluded that the main advantage of the WDM Ph-ADC architecture over its TDM counterpart is the possibility of having higher pulse repetition rate. In the Ph-ADC application considered in this work, this characteristic is of special relevance as it allows for faster wireless signals monitoring. However, this is obtained at the expense of: i) higher number of optical and electrical devices are needed in the WDM than in the TDM architecture and consequently higher implementation costs are required for the WDM case, ii) the signals in the WDM architecture should be less tolerant to nonlinear fiber impairments and iii) the SNR levels obtained in the WDM architecture are worse than the ones reached by the TDM architecture.

Acknowledgements. The work of Tiago Alves was supported by Fundação para a Ciência e a Tecnologia from Portugal under contract SFRH/BD/29871/2006. This work was also supported in part by the EU project UCELLS-FP7-IST-1-216785. The authors would like to thank also to UCELLS' partners by the fruitful discussions about the structure and the parameters of the Ph-ADC system.

References

1. Coppinger, F., Bhushan, A., Jalali, B.: Time magnification of electrical signals using chirped optical pulses. Electronics Letters 34, 399–400 (1998)
2. Clark, T., Kang, J., Esman, R.: Performance of a time- and wavelength-interleaved photonic sampler for analog-digital conversion. Photonics Technology Letters 11, 1168–1170 (1999)
3. Han, Y., Jalali, B.: Photonic time-stretched analogue-to-digital converter: fundamental concepts and pratical considerations. J. Lightwave Technol. 21, 3085–3103 (2003)
4. Llorente, R., Cartaxo, A., Ugen, B., Duplicy, J., Romme, J., Puche, J., Schmertz, D., Lostanlen, Y., Banales, R., Marti, J.: Management of UWB picocell clusters: UCELLS project approach. In: International Conference on Ultra-Wideband, Hannover, Germany, pp. 139–142 (2008)
5. Llorente, R., Morant, M., Puche, J., Alves, T.: Sensing ultra-low-power radio signals by photonic analog-to-digital conversion. In: European Conference on Optical Communications, Vienna, Austria, pp. 1–2 (2009)
6. Alves, T., Cartaxo, A.: SNR approach for performance evaluation of time-stretching photonic analogue to digital converter system. Optics Express 19, 1493–1509 (2011)

Part IV
Security and Cryptography

Spam Filtering through Anomaly Detection

Igor Santos, Carlos Laorden, Xabier Ugarte-Pedrero, Borja Sanz,
and Pablo G. Bringas

S³Lab, DeustoTech - Computing, Deusto Institute of Technology University of Deusto
Avenida de las Universidades 24, 48007 Bilbao, Spain
{isantos,claorden,xabier.ugarte,borja.sanz,
pablo.garcia.bringas}@deusto.es

Abstract. More than 85% of received e-mails are spam. Spam is an important
issue for computer security because it is used to spread other threats such as
computer viruses, worms or phishing. Classic techniques to fight spam, including
simple techniques such as sender blacklisting or the use of e-mail signatures, are
no longer completely reliable. Machine-learning techniques trained using statistical representations of the terms that usually appear in the e-mails are widely used
in the literature. However, these methods demand a time-consuming training step
with labelled data. Dealing with the situation where the availability of labelled
training instances is limited slows down the progress of filtering systems and offers advantages to spammers. In this paper, we present the first spam filtering
method based on anomaly detection that reduces the necessity of labelling spam
messages and only uses the representation of legitimate e-mails. This approach
represents legitimate e-mails as word frequency vectors. Thereby, an email is
classified as spam or legitimate by measuring its deviation to the representation
of these legitimate e-mails. This method achieves high accuracy rates detecting
spam and maintains a low false positive rate, reducing the effort produced by
labelling spam.

Keywords: Computer security, Spam filtering, Anomaly detection, Text classification.

1 Introduction

Electronic mail (e-mail) is a useful communication channel. However, as usually happens with all useful media, it is prone to misuse. In the past decade, spam, or unsolicited
bulk e-mail, has become a significant problem for e-mail users: a huge amount of spam
arrives in people's mailboxes every day. When this paper was written, 87.6% of all e-
mail messages were spam, according to the Spam-o-meter website.[1] Spam not only is
very annoying to every-day e-mail users, but also constitutes an important computer security problem that costs billions of dollars in productivity losses [1]. Moreover, spam
can be used as a medium for phishing (i.e., attacks that seek to acquire sensitive information from end-users) [2] or the spread of malicious software (e.g., computer viruses,
Trojan horses, spyware and Internet worms) [1].

---

[1] http://www.junk-o-meter.com/stats/index.php

M.S. Obaidat, J.L. Sevillano, and J. Filipe (Eds.): ICETE 2011, CCIS 314, pp. 203–216, 2012.
© Springer-Verlag Berlin Heidelberg 2012

Because of the magnitude of the spam problem, several spam filtering systems have been proposed by both the academia and the industry. The simplest methods for junk message filtering are often based on blacklisting or signatures [3].

Blacklisting is a very simple technique that is broadly used in most filtering products. More specifically, these systems filter e-mails from certain senders, whereas whitelisting [4] delivers e-mail from specific senders in order to reduce the number of misclassified legitimate e-mails (also known as 'ham' by the spam community). Another popular approach for these so-called banishing methods is based on DNS blacklisting, in which the host address is checked against a list of networks or servers known to distribute spam [5, 6].

In contrast, signature-based systems create a unique hash value (i.e., a message digest) for each known spam message [7]. The main advantage of this type of methods is that they rarely produce false positives and they are usually very fast to compute. Examples of signature-based spam filtering systems are: Cloudmark[2], a commercial implementation of a signature-based filter that integrates with the e-mail server, and Razor[3], another filtering system that uses a distributed and collaborative approach in order to deliver signatures [3].

However, these simple methods have several shortcomings. First, blacklisting methods have a very high rate of false positives, making them unreliable as a standalone solution [8]. Second, signature-based systems are unable to detect spam until the junk message has been identified, properly registered and documented [3].

In order to find a solution to this problem, the research community has undertaken a huge amount of work. Since machine-learning approaches have succeeded in text categorisation problems [9] and spam filtering can be stated as a text categorisation problem, these techniques have been broadly adopted in spam filtering systems.

Consequently, substantial work has been dedicated to the Naïve Bayes classifier [10], with a high number of studies regarding anti-spam filtering confirming it effective [11–15].

Another broadly embraced machine-learning technique is Support Vector Machine (SVM) [16]. The advantage of SVM is that its accuracy does not degrade even when many features are present [17]. Therefore, such approaches have been adopted to junk mail filtering [18, 19]. Likewise, Decision Trees that classify by means of automatically learned rule-sets (i.e., tests) [20] have also been employed for spam filtering [21].

All of these machine-learning-based spam filtering approaches have been termed as statistical approaches because they rely on an statistical representation of terms within the messages [22]. Machine-learning approaches model e-mail messages using the Vector Space Model (VSM) [23], an algebraic approach for Information Filtering (IF), Information Retrieval (IR), indexing and ranking. This model represents natural language documents in a mathematical manner through vectors in a multidimensional space formed by the words composing the message.

Machine-learning classifiers require a high number of labelled e-mails for each of the classes (i.e., spam and legitimate e-mails). However, it is quite difficult to obtain this amount of labelled data for a real-world problem such as spam filtering issue. To

---

[2] http://www.cloudmark.com
[3] http://razor.sourceforge.net

generate these data, a time-consuming task of analysis is mandatory, and in the process, some spam messages can avoid filtering.

In light of this background, we propose here the first method that applies anomaly detection to spam filtering. This approach is able to determine whether an e-mail is spam or not by comparing word frequency features with a dataset composed only of legitimate e-mails. If the e-mail under inspection presents a considerable deviation to what it is considered as usual (legitimate e-mails), it can be considered spam. This method does not need updated data about spam messages, and thus, it reduces the efforts of labelling messages, working, for instance, only with a user's valid inbox folder.

Summarising, our main findings in this paper are:

- We present an anomaly-based approach for spam filtering.
- We propose different deviation measures to determine whether an e-mail is spam or not.
- We show that labelling efforts can be reduced in the industry, while still maintaining a high rate of accuracy.

The remainder of this paper is organised as follows. Section 2 provides the background regarding the representation of e-mails based on the VSM. Section 3 details our anomaly-based method. Section 4 describes the experiments and presents results. Section 5 discusses the implications of the obtained results and shows its limitations. Finally, Section 6 concludes the paper and outlines avenues for future work.

2 Bag of Words to Represent E-mails

Spam filtering software attempts to accurately classify email massages into 2 main categories: spam or legitimate messages. To this end, we use the information found within the body and subject of an e-mail message and discard every other piece of information (e.g., the sender or time-stamp of the e-mail). To represent messages, we start by removing stop-words [24], which are words devoid of content (e.g., 'a','the','is'). These words do not provide any semantic information and add noise to the model [25].

Afterwards, we represent the e-mails using an Information Retrieval (IR) model. Formally, let an IR model be defined as a 4-tuple $[\mathcal{E}, \mathcal{Q}, \mathcal{F}, R, (q_i, e_j)]$ [26] where:

- $\mathcal{E}$, is a set of representations of e-mail;
- $\mathcal{Q}$, is a set of representations of user queries;
- $\mathcal{F}$, is a framework for modelling e-mails, queries and their relationships;
- $R(q_i, e_j)$ is a ranking function that associates a real number with a query q_i, ($q_i \in \mathcal{Q}$) and an e-mail representation e_j, ($e_j \in \mathcal{E}$). This function is also called a similarity function.

Let $\mathcal{E}$ be a set of text e-mails e, $\{e : \{t_1, t_2, ...t_n\}\}$, each one comprising an n number of t terms. We consider $w_{i,j}$ a weight for term t_i in an e-mail e_j, whereas if $w_{i,j}$ is not present in e, then $w_{i,j} = 0$. Therefore, an e-mail can be represented as a vector, starting from its origin, of index terms $e_j = (w_{1,j}, w_{2,j}, ...w_{n,j})$.

On the basis of this formalisation, we can apply several IR models. Commonly, spam filtering systems use Vector Space Model (VSM). The VSM represents natural language documents in an algebraic fashion by placing the vectors in a multidimensional space. This space is formed by only positive axis intercepts. In addition, documents are represented as a term-by-document matrix, where the $(i, j)^{th}$ element illustrates the association between the ith term and the jth document. This association reflects the occurrence of the ith term in document j. Terms can represent different text units (e.g., a word or phrase) and can also be individually weighted allowing terms to become more or less important within a document or the entire document collection as a whole.

Specifically, we use 'term frequency - inverse document frequency' $(tf - idf)$ [27] to obtain the weight of each word, whereas the weight of the ith word in the jth e-mail, denoted by $weight(i, j)$, is defined by:

$$weight(i, j) = tf_{i,j} \cdot idf_i \tag{1}$$

where the term frequency $tf_{i,j}$ [27] is defined as:

$$tf_{i,j} = \frac{m_{i,j}}{\sum_k m_{k,j}} \tag{2}$$

where $m_{i,j}$ is the number of times the word $t_{i,j}$ appears in an e-mail e, and $\sum_k m_{k,j}$ is the total number of word in the e-mail e.

On the other hand, the inverse document frequency idf_i is defined as:

$$idf_i = \frac{|\mathcal{E}|}{|\mathcal{E} : t_i \in e|} \tag{3}$$

where $|\mathcal{E}|$ is the total number of documents and $|\mathcal{E} : t_i \in e|$ is the number of documents containing the word $t_{i,j}$.

We apply relevance weights to each feature based on Information Gain (IG) [28]:

$$IG(j) = \sum_{v_j \in R} \sum_{C_i} P(v_j, C_i) \cdot \frac{P(v_j, C_i)}{P(v_j) \cdot P(C_i)} \tag{4}$$

where C_i is the i-th class, v_j is the value of the j-th interpretation, $P(v_j, C_i)$ is the probability that the j-th attribute has the value v_j in the class C_i, $P(v_j)$ is the probability that the j-th interpretation has the value v_j in the training data, and $P(C_i)$ is the probability of the training dataset belonging to the class C_i. IG provides a ratio for each feature that measures its importance to consider if a sample is spam or not.

These weights were calculated from two datasets: the LingSpam corpus[4]) composed of 480 spam e-mails and 2,412 legitimate messages and the SpamAssassin corpus[5] composed of 1,896 spam e-mails and 4,150 legitimate spam. These weights are useful to obtain a better distance rating among samples.

---

[4] Available at: http://nlp.cs.aueb.gr/software_and_datasets/ lingspam_public.tar.gz

[5] Available at: http://spamassassin.org/publiccorpus

3   Anomaly Detection Techniques

Anomaly detection models what it is a normal message and every deviation to this model is considered anomalous. Through the word frequency features of the VSM described in the previous section, our method represents legitimate e-mails as points in the feature space. When an e-mail is being inspected our method starts by computing the values of the point in the feature space. This point is then compared with the previously calculated points of the legitimate e-mails.

To this end, distance measures are required. In this study, we have used the following distance measures:

- **Manhattan Distance.** This distance between two points v and u is the sum of the lengths of the projections of the line segment between the two points onto the coordinate axes:

$$d(x, i) = \sum_{i=0}^{n} |x_i - y_i| \qquad (5)$$

  where x is the first point; y is the second point; and x_i and y_i are the ith component of the first and second point, respectively.

- **Euclidean Distance.** This distance is the length of the line segment connecting two points. It is calculated as:

$$d(x, y) = \sum_{i=0}^{n} \sqrt{v_i^2 - u_i^2} \qquad (6)$$

  where x is the first point; y is the second point; and x_i and y_i are the ith component of the first and second point, respectively.

By means of these measures, we are able to compute the deviations between e-mails and the legitimate e-mails. Since we have to compute this measure with the points representing legitimate e-mails, a combination metric is required in order to obtain a final distance value which considers every measure performed. To this end, our system employs 3 simple metrics:

- The mean value calculated from every distance value in the training dataset.
- The lowest distance value from every distance value in the training dataset.
- The highest value of the computed distances from every distance value in the training dataset.

In this way, when our method inspects an e-mail a final distance value is acquired, which will depend on both the distance measure and the combination metric.

4   Experimental Results

In order to validate our proposed method, we used the SpamAssasin public corpus and the Ling Spam Corpus.

Table 1. Comparison of the used dataset. The spam ratio in both datasets does not follow the statistics of the number of spam messages in the real world which is higher of the 85%. SpamAssasin dataset, however, has more real spam and examples of obfuscated mails within it.

Feature	SpamAssasin	Ling Spam
No. Spam Messages	1,896	480
No. of Ham Messages	4,150	2,412
Spam %.	31,36%	16,60%

SpamAssasin corpus contains a total of 6,046 messages, of which 1,896 are spam and 4,150 are legitimate e-mails. To adequate the dataset, we performed a stop word removal based on an external stop-word list.[6] Next, we constructed a file with the resultant vector representations of the e-mails in order to validate our method. We extracted the top 1,000 words using Information Gain [28].

Ling Spam consists of a mixture of both spam and legitimate messages retrieved from the Linguistic list, an e-mail distribution list about linguistics. The dataset was preprocessed by removing HTML tags, separation tokens and duplicate e-mails: only the data of the body and the subject were kept. Ling Spam comprises 2,892 different e-mails, of which 2,412 are legitimate e-mails obtained by downloading digests from the list and 480 are spam e-mails retrieved from one of the authors of the corpus (for a more detailed description of the corpus please refer to [13, 29]). Junk messages represent approximately the 16% of the whole dataset, a rate close to the actual rate [30, 31, 29]. Stop Word Removal [24] and stemming [32] were performed on the e-mails, creating 4 different datasets:

1. **Bare.** In this dataset, the e-mail messages were pre-processed by the removal of HTML tags, separation tokens and duplicate e-mails.
2. **Lemm.** In addition to the removal pre-process step, a stemming phase was performed. Stemming reduces inflected or derived words to their stem, base or root form.
3. **Stop.** For this dataset, a stop word removal task was performed. This process removes all stop words (e.g., common words like 'a' or 'the').
4. **Lemm_stop.** This dataset uses the combination of both stemming and stop-word removal processes.

We used the bare dataset and we performed a stop word removal based on the same stop-word list as for SpamAssasin corpus.

Specifically, we followed the next configuration for the empirical validation:

1. **Cross Validation.** For the SpamAssasin dataset, we performed a 5-fold cross-validation [33] to divide the dataset composed of legitimate e-mails (the normal behaviour) into 5 different divisions of 3,320 e-mails for representing normality and 830 for measuring deviations within legitimate e-mails. In this way, each fold is composed of 3,320 legitimate e-mails that will be used as representation of normality and 2,726 testing e-mails, from which 830 are legitimate e-mails and 1,896 are spam.

---

[6] Available at: http://paginaspersonales.deusto.es/claorden/
resources/EnglishStopWords.txt

With regards to Ling Spam dataset, we also performed a 5-fold cross-validation [33] forming 3 different divisions of 1,930 e-mails and two divisions of 1,929 e-mails for representing normality and other 3 divisions of 482 e-mails and 2 of 483 for measuring deviations within legitimate e-mail. In this way, each fold is composed of 1,930 or 1,929 legitimate e-mails that will be used as representation of normality and 963 or 962 testing e-mails, from which 483 or 482 were legitimate e-mails and 480 were spam. The number of legitimate e-mails varied in the two last folds because the number of legitimate e-mails was not divisible by 5.

2. **Calculating Distances and Combination Rules.** We extracted the aforementioned characteristics and employed the 2 different measures and the 3 different combination rules described in Section 3 to obtain a final measure of deviation for each testing evidence. More accurately, we applied the following distances:
   - Manhattan Distance.
   - Euclidean Distance.

   For the combination rules we have tested the followings:
   - The Mean Value.
   - The Lowest Distance.
   - The Highest Value.

3. **Defining Thresholds.** For each measure and combination rule, we established 10 different thresholds to determine whether an email is spam or not. These thresholds were selected by first establishing the lowest one. This number was the highest possible value with which no spam messages were misclassified. The highest one was selected as the lowest possible value with which no legitimate spam messages were misclassified.

   In this way, the method is configurable in both reducing false positives or false negatives. It is important to define whether it is better to classify spam as legitimate or to classify legitimate as spam. In particular, one may think that it is more important to detect more spam messages than to minimise false positives. However, for commercial reasons, one may think just the opposite: a user can be bothered if their legitimate messages are flagged as spam. To improve these errors, we can apply two techniques: (i) whitelisting and blacklisting or (ii) cost-sensitive learning. White and black lists store a signature of an e-mail in order to be flagged either as spam (blacklisting) or legitimate messages (whitelisting). On the other hand, cost-sensitive learning is a machine-learning technique where one can specify the cost of each error and the classifiers are trained taking into account that consideration [34]. We can adapt cost-sensitive learning for anomaly detection by using cost matrices.

4. **Testing the Method.** To evaluate the results, we measured the most frequently used for spam: precision (Prec.), recall (Rec.) and f-measure (F-meas.). We measured the precision of the spam identification as the number of correctly classified spam e-mails divided by the number of correctly classified spam e-mails and the number of legitimate e-mails misclassified as spam:

$$Precision = \frac{N_{s \to s}}{N_{s \to s} + N_{l \to s}} \quad (7)$$

where $N_{s \to s}$ is the number of correctly classified spam and $N_{l \to s}$ is the number of legitimate e-mails misclassified as spam.

Table 2. Results for different combination rules and distance measures using Spam Assasin corpus. The abbreviation 'Thres'. stands for the chosen threshold. The results in bold are the best for each combination rule and distance measure. Our method is able to detect more than the 90% of the spam messages while maintaining a high precision (a low number of legitimate messages are misclassified). In particular, the best results were obtained with minimum distance combination rule, the Manhattan distance and a 1.32493 of threshold: a 95.40% of precision, a 93.86% of recall and a 94.62% of f-Measure.

Combination	\multicolumn{4}{c}{Manhattan Distance}	\multicolumn{4}{c}{Euclidean Distance}
	Thres.	Prec.	Rec.	F-Meas.	Thres.	Prec.	Rec.	F-Meas.
Mean	1.15978	69.56%	100.0%	82.05%	1.70013	69.64%	100.00%	82.10%
	1.58697	70.55%	99.86%	82.68%	1.91763	76.14%	97.77%	85.61%
	2.01417	79.44%	98.91%	88.11%	2.13512	87.74%	81.04%	84.26%
	2.44136	**91.03%**	**92.85%**	**91.93%**	2.35262	93.56%	56.53%	70.48%
	2.86856	97.01%	76.18%	85.34%	2.57011	94.93%	30.63%	46.32%
	3.29575	98.70%	50.44%	66.76%	2.78761	93.64%	12.57%	22.17%
	3.72295	99.39%	27.62%	43.22%	3.00510	94.44%	6.81%	12.71%
	4.15014	99.22%	14.84%	25.82%	3.22260	95.19%	3.13%	6.07%
	4.57734	99.32%	7.71%	14.31%	3.44009	97.10%	1.41%	2.79%
	5.00453	100.00%	4.55%	8.70%	3.65759	100.00%	0.93%	1.84%
Maximum	3.39114	69.55%	100.00%	82.04%	3.41015	69.67%	100.00%	82.12%
	3.81833	**69.61%**	**99.89%**	**82.05%**	3.55333	72.99%	97.66%	83.54%
	4.24553	69.90%	98.50%	81.77%	3.69652	83.86%	82.23%	83.04%
	4.67272	71.69%	91.74%	80.48%	3.83970	93.57%	55.42%	69.61%
	5.09992	83.51%	67.62%	74.73%	3.98288	95.87%	29.86%	45.54%
	5.52711	94.94%	35.43%	51.61%	4.26925	95.33%	6.46%	12.09%
	5.95431	99.56%	14.48%	25.29%	4.12607	94.76%	12.01%	21.33%
	6.38150	100.00%	5.84%	11.04%	4.41243	95.19%	2.92%	5.67%
	6.80870	100.00%	0.96%	1.90%	4.55562	97.18%	1.46%	2.87%
	6.25298	100.00%	7.49%	13.94%	4.69880	100.00%	1.01%	2.01%
Minimum	0.04335	69.61%	100.00%	0.44679	0.44679	69.76%	100.00%	82.18%
	0.47054	74.51%	99.85%	85.34%	0.76440	70.42%	99.92%	82.62%
	0.89774	87.75%	98.89%	92.99%	1.08201	74.92%	99.78%	85.58%
	1.32493	**95.40%**	**93.86%**	**94.62%**	1.39962	92.10%	94.00%	93.04%
	1.75213	97.91%	79.88%	87.98%	1.71723	98.74%	68.61%	80.96%
	2.17932	98.92%	54.14%	69.98%	2.03484	99.63%	28.54%	44.38%
	2.60652	99.49%	26.88%	42.32%	2.35245	99.65%	6.02%	11.36%
	3.03371	99.91%	11.43%	20.52%	2.67006	98.88%	1.86%	3.64%
	3.46091	100.00%	3.18%	6.15%	2.98767	98.78%	0.85%	1.69%
	3.04013	100.00%	11.31%	20.32%	3.30528	100.00%	0.36%	0.71%

Additionally, we measured the recall of the spam e-mail messages, which is the number of correctly classified spam e-mails divided by the number of correctly classified spam e-mails and the number of spam e-mails misclassified as legitimate:

$$Recall = \frac{N_{s \to s}}{N_{s \to s} + N_{s \to l}} \qquad (8)$$

We also computed the F-measure, which is the harmonic mean of both the precision and recall, simplified as follows:

$$F\text{-}measure = \frac{2N_{m \to m}}{2N_{m \to m} + N_{m \to l} + N_{l \to m}} \qquad (9)$$

Table 2 shows the obtained results for SpamAssasin corpus for the different distances, combination rules and thresholds. The best results were obtained with the Manhattan Distance, the minimum combination rule and a 1.32493 threshold: a 95.40% of precision, a 93.86% of recall and a 94.62% of f-measure. Table 3 shows the obtained results for LingSpam corpus using different distances, combination rules and thresholds. Using

Table 3. Results for different combination rules and distance measures using LingSpam corpus. The abbreviation 'Thres'. means the chosen threshold. The results remarked in bold are the best for each combination rule and distance measure. Using this dataset, our method also can detect more than the 90% of the spam messages whereas maintaining a high precision (a low number of legitimate messages are misclassified). The best results were obtained with the Euclidean Distance, the mean combination rule and 2.59319 as the threshold. In particular, a 92.82% of precision, a 91.58% of recall and a 92.20% of f-measure. These results are a little lower than when using SpamAssasin.

Combination	Manhattan Distance				Euclidean Distance			
	Thres.	Prec.	Rec.	F-Meas.	Thres.	Prec.	Rec.	F-Meas.
Mean	1.86313	49.87%	100.00%	66.56%	1.87061	49.91%	100.00%	66.58%
	2.23637	50.04%	99.79%	66.65%	2.11147	0.50357	99.79%	66.94%
	2.58960	51.02%	97.21%	66.92%	2.35233	68.39%	98.33%	80.67%
	2.95284	56.07%	94.29%	70.32%	**2.59319**	**92.82%**	**91.58%**	**92.20%**
	3.31608	65.86%	84.08%	73.87%	2.83405	97.31%	52.71%	68.38%
	3.67931	**79.18%**	**73.54%**	**76.26%**	3.07490	98.54%	19.75%	32.91%
	4.04255	92.40%	62.29%	74.42%	3.31576	98.33%	7.38%	13.72%
	4.40579	97.89%	52.13%	68.03%	3.55662	98.84%	3.54%	6.84%
	4.76902	99.68%	39.38%	56.45%	3.79748	96.15%	1.04%	2.06%
	5.13226	100.00%	29.88%	46.01%	4.03834	100.00%	0.62%	1.24%
Maximum	3.69053	49.89%	100.00%	66.56%	3.22709	49.93%	100.00%	66.60%
	4.05377	50.08%	99.79%	66.69%	3.41297	50.80%	99.96%	67.37%
	4.41700	51.01%	98.46%	67.21%	3.59886	53.35%	99.33%	69.41%
	4.78024	54.65%	95.00%	69.39%	3.78474	54.89%	96.13%	69.88%
	5.14348	63.06%	85.13%	72.45%	3.97063	59.97%	86.63%	70.87%
	5.50671	**76.23%**	**74.29%**	**75.25%**	**4.15651**	**85.95%**	**79.29%**	**82.49%**
	5.86995	89.49%	61.38%	72.81%	4.34240	97.23%	58.50%	73.05%
	6.23319	99.03%	46.58%	63.36%	4.52828	97.76%	18.17%	30.64%
	6.59642	100.00%	33.08%	49.72%	4.71417	98.08%	6.38%	11.97%
	6.95966	100.00%	20.71%	34.31%	4.90005	100.00%	2.46%	4.80%
Minimum	0.09919	50.29%	100.00%	66.93%	0.69584	50.68%	100.00%	67.26%
	0.46243	51.02%	99.79%	67.52%	1.00615	50.98%	99.79%	67.48%
	0.82566	52.04%	96.88%	67.71%	1.31645	51.95%	99.79%	68.33%
	1.18890	55.16%	94.17%	69.57%	1.62676	59.70%	98.33%	74.30%
	1.55214	58.31%	84.17%	68.89%	**1.93707**	**87.51%**	**93.13%**	**90.23%**
	1.91537	**65.82%**	**74.38%**	**69.84%**	2.24737	97.54%	62.79%	76.40%
	2.27861	74.10%	63.54%	68.42%	2.55768	99.00%	20.67%	34.20%
	2.64185	85.06%	54.79%	66.65%	2.86799	99.42%	7.13%	13.30%
	3.00508	94.66%	43.54%	59.65%	3.17829	96.97%	1.33%	2.63%
	3.84820	100.00%	23.13%	37.56%	3.48860	100.00%	0.29%	0.58%

this dataset, the best configuration was the one performed with the Euclidean Distance, the mean combination rule and 2.59319 as the threshold: the method achieved a 92.82% of precision, a 91.58% of recall and a 92.20% of f-measure.

The fact that the best results were obtained with the minimum distance, which is obviously the most conservative configuration for distance, highlights a possible topic of discussion regarding what should be called anomaly in e-mails. As we aforementioned, currently more than the 85% of the e-mails are spam and, therefore, in terms of normality, receiving a legitimate e-mail is an anomalous.

5   Discussion

The final results show that this method achieves high levels of accuracy. In addition, it can minimise the number of legitimate e-mails that are misclassified and is also able to detect a high number of spam messages. Nevertheless, several points of discussion are important regarding the suitability of the proposed method.

The VSM assumes that every term is independent, which is, at least from the linguistic point of view, not completely true. Despite the fact that e-mails are usually represented as a sequence of words, there are relationships between words on a semantic level that also affect e-mails [35]. Specifically, we can find several linguistic phenomena in natural languages[36]:

- **Synonyms.** Two or more words are interchangeable because of their similar (or identical) meaning (e.g., 'buy' and 'purchase') [37].
- **Hyponyms.** Specific instances of a more general word (e.g., 'spicy' and 'salty' are hyponyms of 'flavour')[38].
- **Metonymy.** The substitution of one word for another with which it is associated (e.g., 'police' instead of 'law enforcement') [39].
- **Homography.** Words with the same orthography but different meaning (e.g., 'bear': 'to support and carry' and 'an animal') [40].
- **Word-groups.** Clusters of words that have semantic meaning when they are grouped (e.g., 'New York City').

Thus, our representation cannot handle the existing linguistic phenomena in natural languages [41]. In fact, attacks exist that evade spam filtering systems through the use of synonyms [42], which our model is not capable of defeating.

As a solution, the *Topic-based Vector Space Model* (TVSM) [41] and the enhanced Topic-based Vector Space Model (eTVSM) [43] have been proposed in the last few years. The TVSM represents documents using a vector-representation where axes are topics rather than terms and, therefore, terms are weighted based upon how strongly related they are to a topic. In contrast, the eTVSM uses an ontology to represent the different relations between terms and, in this way, provides a richer natural language retrieval model that is able to accommodate synonyms, homonyms and other linguistic phenomena [44].

There is also a problem derived from IR and Natural Language Processing (NLP) when dealing with semantics: Word Sense Disambiguation (WSD). A spammer may evade our method by explicitly exchanging the key words of the mail with other polyseme terms and thus avoid detection. WSD is considered necessary in order to accomplish most natural language processing tasks [45]. We propose the study of different WSD techniques (a survey of different WSD techniques can be found in [46]) capable of providing a more semantics-aware spam filtering system. Nevertheless, a semantic approach for spam filtering will have to deal with the semantics of different languages [47] and thus be language-dependant.

Besides, our method has several limitations due to the representation of e-mails. In this way, because most of the spam filtering techniques are based on the frequencies with which terms appear within messages, spammers have started modifying their techniques to evade filters.

For example, Good Word Attack is a method that modifies the term statistics by appending a set of words that are characteristic of legitimate e-mails, thereby bypass spam filters. Nevertheless, we can adopt some of the methods that have been proposed in order to improve spam filtering, such as Multiple Instance Learning (MIL) [48]. MIL divides an instance or a vector in the traditional supervised learning methods into several sub-instances and classifies the original vector based on the sub-instances [49]. Zhou et al. [50] proposed the adoption of multiple instance learning for spam filtering by dividing an e-mail into a bag of multiple segments and classifying it as spam if at least one instance in the corresponding bag was spam.

Another attack, known as tokenisation, works against the feature selection of the message by splitting or modifying key message features, which renders the term-representation as no longer feasible [51].

All of these attacks, which spammers have been adopting, should be taken into account in the construction of future spam-filtering-systems.

In our experiments, we used a dataset that is very small in comparison to the real-world size. As the dataset size grows, the issue of scalability becomes a concern. This problem produces excessive storage requirements, increases time complexity and impairs the general accuracy of the models [52]. To reduce disproportionate storage and time costs, it is necessary to reduce the size of the original training set [53].

To solve this issue, data reduction is normally considered an appropriate preprocessing optimisation technique [54, 55]. This type of techniques have many potential advantages such as reducing measurement, storage and transmission; decreasing training and testing times; confronting the problem of dimensionality to improve prediction performance in terms of speed, accuracy and simplicity; and facilitating data visualisation and understanding [56, 57]. Data reduction can be implemented in two ways. Instance selection (IS) seeks to reduce the number of evidences (i.e., number of rows) in the training set by selecting the most relevant instances or by re-sampling new ones [58]. Feature selection (FS) decreases the number of attributes or features (i.e., columns) in the training set [59].

It is also important to consider efficiency and processing time. Our system compares each e-mail against a big dataset. Despite Euclidean and Manhattan distances are easy to compute, more time-consuming distance measures like Mahalanobis distance will take too much time to process every e-mail under analysis.

6   Concluding Remarks

Spam is a serious computer security issue that is not only annoying for end-users, but also financially damaging and dangerous to computer security because of the possible spread of other threats like malware or phishing. The classic machine-learning-based spam filtering methods, despite their ability to detect spam, have a very time-consuming step of labelling e-mails.

In this paper, we presented a spam filtering system that is inspired in anomaly detection systems. Using this method, we are able to reduce the number of required labelled messages and, therefore, reduce the efforts for the filtering industry. Our experiments show that this approach provides high percentages of spam detection whilst keeping the number of misclassified legitimate messages low. Besides, this method works only with legitimate e-mails and, therefore, it can be trained using the inbox of a user.

Future versions of this spam filtering system will move in five main directions. First, we will focus on attacks against statistical spam filtering systems such as tokenisation or good word attacks. Second, we plan to include the semantics of this method with more linguistic relationships. Third, we will improve the scalability of the anomaly method in order to reduce the number of distance computations required. Fourth, we will study the feasibility of applying Word Sense Disambiguation techniques to this spam filtering method. Finally, we will deeply investigate in what has to be considered an anomaly in the e-mail filtering problem, comparing whether is better to consider spam or legitimate as an anomalous e-mail.

References

1. Bratko, A., Filipič, B., Cormack, G., Lynam, T., Zupan, B.: Spam filtering using statistical data compression models. The Journal of Machine Learning Research 7, 2673–2698 (2006)
2. Jagatic, T., Johnson, N., Jakobsson, M., Menczer, F.: Social phishing. Communications of the ACM 50, 94–100 (2007)
3. Carpinter, J., Hunt, R.: Tightening the net: A review of current and next generation spam filtering tools. Computers & Security 25, 566–578 (2006)
4. Heron, S.: Technologies for spam detection. Network Security, 11–15 (2009)
5. Jung, J., Sit, E.: An empirical study of spam traffic and the use of DNS black lists. In: Proceedings of the 4th ACM SIGCOMM Conference on Internet Measurement, pp. 370–375. ACM, New York (2004)
6. Ramachandran, A., Dagon, D., Feamster, N.: Can DNS-based blacklists keep up with bots. In: Conference on Email and Anti-Spam, Citeseer (2006)
7. Kołcz, A., Chowdhury, A., Alspector, J.: The impact of feature selection on signature-driven spam detection. In: Proceedings of the 1st Conference on Email and Anti-Spam, CEAS 2004 (2004)
8. Mishne, G., Carmel, D., Lempel, R.: Blocking blog spam with language model disagreement. In: Proceedings of the 1st International Workshop on Adversarial Information Retrieval on the Web (AIRWeb), pp. 1–6 (2005)
9. Sebastiani, F.: Machine learning in automated text categorization. ACM Computing Surveys (CSUR) 34, 1–47 (2002)
10. Lewis, D.: Naive (Bayes) at Forty: The Independence Assumption in Information Retrieval. In: Nédellec, C., Rouveirol, C. (eds.) ECML 1998. LNCS, vol. 1398, pp. 4–18. Springer, Heidelberg (1998)
11. Androutsopoulos, I., Paliouras, G., Karkaletsis, V., Sakkis, G., Spyropoulos, C., Stamatopoulos, P.: Learning to filter spam e-mail: A comparison of a naive bayesian and a memory-based approach. In: Proceedings of the Machine Learning and Textual Information Access Workshop of the 4th European Conference on Principles and Practice of Knowledge Discovery in Databases (2000)
12. Schneider, K.: A comparison of event models for Naive Bayes anti-spam e-mail filtering. In: Proceedings of the 10th Conference of the European Chapter of the Association for Computational Linguistics, pp. 307–314 (2003)
13. Androutsopoulos, I., Koutsias, J., Chandrinos, K., Paliouras, G., Spyropoulos, C.: An evaluation of naive bayesian anti-spam filtering. In: Proceedings of the Workshop on Machine Learning in the New Information Age, pp. 9–17 (2000)
14. Androutsopoulos, I., Koutsias, J., Chandrinos, K., Spyropoulos, C.: An experimental comparison of naive Bayesian and keyword-based anti-spam filtering with personal e-mail messages. In: Proceedings of the 23rd Annual International ACM SIGIR Conference on Research and Development in Information Retrieval, pp. 160–167 (2000)

15. Seewald, A.: An evaluation of naive Bayes variants in content-based learning for spam filtering. Intelligent Data Analysis 11, 497–524 (2007)
16. Vapnik, V.: The nature of statistical learning theory. Springer (2000)
17. Drucker, H., Wu, D., Vapnik, V.: Support vector machines for spam categorization. IEEE Transactions on Neural Networks 10, 1048–1054 (1999)
18. Blanzieri, E., Bryl, A.: Instance-based spam filtering using SVM nearest neighbor classifier. In: Proceedings of FLAIRS-20, pp. 441–442 (2007)
19. Sculley, D., Wachman, G.: Relaxed online SVMs for spam filtering. In: Proceedings of the 30th Annual International ACM SIGIR Conference on Research and Development in Information Retrieval, pp. 415–422 (2007)
20. Quinlan, J.: Induction of decision trees. Machine Learning 1, 81–106 (1986)
21. Carreras, X., Márquez, L.: Boosting trees for anti-spam email filtering. In: Proceedings of RANLP-01, 4th International Conference on Recent Advances in Natural Language Processing, Citeseer, pp. 58–64 (2001)
22. Zhang, L., Zhu, J., Yao, T.: An evaluation of statistical spam filtering techniques. ACM Transactions on Asian Language Information Processing (TALIP) 3, 243–269 (2004)
23. Salton, G., Wong, A., Yang, C.: A vector space model for automatic indexing. Communications of the ACM 18, 613–620 (1975)
24. Wilbur, W., Sirotkin, K.: The automatic identification of stop words. Journal of Information Science 18, 45–55 (1992)
25. Salton, G., McGill, M.: Introduction to modern information retrieval. McGraw-Hill, New York (1983)
26. Baeza-Yates, R.A., Ribeiro-Neto, B.: Modern Information Retrieval. Addison-Wesley Longman Publishing Co., Inc., Boston (1999)
27. McGill, M., Salton, G.: Introduction to modern information retrieval. McGraw-Hill (1983)
28. Kent, J.: Information gain and a general measure of correlation. Biometrika 70, 163–173 (1983)
29. Sakkis, G., Androutsopoulos, I., Paliouras, G., Karkaletsis, V., Spyropoulos, C., Stamatopoulos, P.: A memory-based approach to anti-spam filtering for mailing lists. Information Retrieval 6, 49–73 (2003)
30. Cranor, L., LaMacchia, B.: Spam! Communications of the ACM 41, 74–83 (1998)
31. Sahami, M., Dumais, S., Heckerman, D., Horvitz, E.: A Bayesian approach to filtering junk e-mail. In: Learning for Text Categorization: Papers from the 1998 Workshop. AAAI Technical Report WS-98-05, Madison, Wisconsin, vol. 62 (1998)
32. Lovins, J.: Development of a Stemming Algorithm. Mechanical Translation and Computational Linguistics 11, 22–31 (1968)
33. Kohavi, R.: A study of cross-validation and bootstrap for accuracy estimation and model selection. In: International Joint Conference on Artificial Intelligence, vol. 14, pp. 1137–1145 (1995)
34. Elkan, C.: The foundations of cost-sensitive learning. In: Proceedings of the 2001 International Joint Conference on Artificial Intelligence, pp. 973–978 (2001)
35. Cohen, D.: Explaining linguistic phenomena. Halsted Press (1974)
36. Polyvyanyy, A.: Evaluation of a novel information retrieval model: eTVSM. MSc Dissertation (2007)
37. Carnap, R.: Meaning and synonymy in natural languages. Philosophical Studies 6, 33–47 (1955)
38. Cruse, D.: Hyponymy and lexical hierarchies. Archivum Linguisticum 6, 26–31 (1975)
39. Radden, G., Kövecses, Z.: Towards a theory of metonymy. Metonymy in Language and Thought, 17–59 (1999)
40. Ming-Tzu, K., Nation, P.: Word meaning in academic English: Homography in the academic word list. Applied Linguistics 25, 291–314 (2004)

41. Becker, J., Kuropka, D.: Topic-based vector space model. In: Proceedings of the 6th International Conference on Business Information Systems, pp. 7–12 (2003)
42. Karlberger, C., Bayler, G., Kruegel, C., Kirda, E.: Exploiting redundancy in natural language to penetrate bayesian spam filters. In: Proceedings of the 1st USENIX Workshop on Offensive Technologies (WOOT), pp. 1–7. USENIX Association (2007)
43. Kuropka, D.: Modelle zur Repräsentation natürlichsprachlicher Dokumente-Information-Filtering und-Retrieval mit relationalen Datenbanken. Advances in Information Systems and Management Science 10 (2004)
44. Awad, A., Polyvyanyy, A., Weske, M.: Semantic querying of business process models. In: IEEE International Conference on Enterprise Distributed Object Computing Conference (EDOC 2008), pp. 85–94 (2008)
45. Ide, N., Véronis, J.: Introduction to the special issue on word sense disambiguation: the state of the art. Computational Linguistics 24, 2–40 (1998)
46. Navigli, R.: Word sense disambiguation: a survey. ACM Computing Surveys (CSUR) 41, 10 (2009)
47. Bates, M., Weischedel, R.: Challenges in natural language processing. Cambridge Univ. Pr. (1993)
48. Dietterich, T., Lathrop, R., Lozano-Pérez, T.: Solving the multiple instance problem with axis-parallel rectangles. Artificial Intelligence 89, 31–71 (1997)
49. Maron, O., Lozano-Pérez, T.: A framework for multiple-instance learning. In: Advances in Neural Information Processing Systems, pp. 570–576 (1998)
50. Zhou, Y., Jorgensen, Z., Inge, M.: Combating Good Word Attacks on Statistical Spam Filters with Multiple Instance Learning. In: Proceedings of the 19th IEEE International Conference on Tools with Artificial Intelligence, vol. 02, pp. 298–305. IEEE Computer Society (2007)
51. Wittel, G., Wu, S.: On attacking statistical spam filters. In: Proceedings of the 1st Conference on Email and Anti-Spam, CEAS (2004)
52. Cano, J., Herrera, F., Lozano, M.: On the combination of evolutionary algorithms and stratified strategies for training set selection in data mining. Applied Soft Computing Journal 6, 323–332 (2006)
53. Czarnowski, I., Jedrzejowicz, P.: Instance reduction approach to machine learning and multi-database mining. In: Proceedings of the Scientific Session Organized During XXI Fall Meeting of the Polish Information Processing Society, Informatica, pp. 60–71. ANNALES Universitatis Mariae Curie-Skłodowska, Lublin (2006)
54. Pyle, D.: Data preparation for data mining. Morgan Kaufmann (1999)
55. Tsang, E., Yeung, D., Wang, X.: OFFSS: optimal fuzzy-valued feature subset selection. IEEE Transactions on Fuzzy Systems 11, 202–213 (2003)
56. Torkkola, K.: Feature extraction by non parametric mutual information maximization. The Journal of Machine Learning Research 3, 1415–1438 (2003)
57. Dash, M., Liu, H.: Consistency-based search in feature selection. Artificial Intelligence 151, 155–176 (2003)
58. Liu, H., Motoda, H.: Instance selection and construction for data mining. Kluwer Academic Pub. (2001)
59. Liu, H., Motoda, H.: Computational methods of feature selection. Chapman & Hall/CRC (2008)

On the Feasibility of Malware Attacks
in Smartphone Platforms

Alexios Mylonas[*], Stelios Dritsas, Bill Tsoumas, and Dimitris Gritzalis

Information Security and Critical Infrastructure Protection Research Laboratory,
Dept. of Informatics, Athens University of Economics & Business (AUEB),
76 Patission Ave., GR-10434, Athens, Greece
{amylonas,sdritsas,bts,dgrit}@aueb.gr

Abstract. Smartphones are multipurpose devices that host multiple and heterogeneous data. Their user base is constantly increasing and as a result they have
become an attractive target for conducting privacy and security attacks. The attacks' impact increases, when smartphone users tend to use their devices both
for personal and business purposes. Moreover, application development in
smartphone platforms has been simplified, in the platforms developers' effort to
attract more developers and increase its popularity by offering more attractive
applications. In this paper we provide a comparative evaluation of the security
level of well-known smartphone platforms, regarding their protection against
simple malicious applications. We then study the feasibility and easiness of
smartphone malware development by average programmers via an implementation case study. Our study proved that, under certain circumstances, all examined platforms could be used by average developers as privacy attack vector,
harvesting data from the device without the users knowledge and consent.

Keywords: Smartphone, Security Models, Malware, Evaluation Criteria.

1   Introduction

Smartphones are some of the devices that enhance Weiser's vision of ubiquitous computing [30]. Their small size, reduced cost, mobility, connectivity capabilities and
multi-purpose use are some of the reasons for their pervasiveness [10].

Malicious software or malware [1], [3], [15] has also appeared in smartphone platforms [12], but initially their occurrences and severity were limited. Nonetheless, recent reports show that the risk of malicious application execution on smartphones is
severe and contingent [2], [17]. Moreover, smartphones use extends the infrastructure
perimeter of an organization, thus, amplifying the impact and risk of malicious applications [28], especially when users bring their own smartphones in the corporate
premises [22].

Apart from the increasing smartphone sales [10], the annual downloads of smartphone applications from application repositories are also on the rise. According to [9],
the total application downloads - since 2008 when the first application repository, the

---

[*] Corresponding author.

M.S. Obaidat, J.L. Sevillano, and J. Filipe (Eds.): ICETE 2011, CCIS 314, pp. 217–232, 2012.

App Store, was introduced - are bound to exceed 185 billion downloads by the end of 2014. Moreover, popular web applications (Gmail, YouTube, etc.) and social networks (Facebook, Twitter, etc.), are being accessed on smartphones through their corresponding applications, instead of their usual web browser interface. In this context, smartphones often manage a vast amount of user's data, posing a serious privacy threat vector [11], [19]. These data are augmented with smartphone sensor data (i.e., GPS) and data created by daily use (personal or business) making the device a great source of data related with the smartphone owner. This data source if maliciously collected can be used by attackers to increase their revenues (e.g., with blackmail, phishing, surveillance attacks, etc.). Hence, attackers may try to infect smartphones with malicious applications, harvesting smartphone data without the user's knowledge and consent. It should be noted that the growing smartphone use by non-technical and non-security savvy people increases the likelihood of using smartphones as a security and privacy attack vector.

The security model of smartphone platforms has, under these circumstances, two contradicting goals. On the one hand, it must provide mechanisms to protect users from attacks and, on the other hand, it must attract third party developers, since the popularity of a platform depends on the attractiveness of its applications.

The former goal is approached by each smartphone platform under a non-unified and standardized approach and its effectiveness is controversial [5], [6], [21]. For the latter, smartphone platforms provide developers with development friendly environments, which include extensive documentation, programming libraries, and emulators. This development friendliness, nonetheless, may also be used to implement applications that can compromise the security and privacy of smartphone users more effectively.

This paper examines the feasibility and easiness of malware development on smartphones by average programmers that have access to the official tools and programming libraries provided by smartphone platforms. This is achieved through a proof of concept study that aims on evaluating the ease of malware development against users of smartphone devices. Thus, issues such as state of the art attacks that might be performed by sophisticated attackers [16], [27], as well as the relation between malware attacks on smartphones and desktop computing devices, are clearly out of the scope of this paper.

Our work contributes towards this direction by: (a) proposing a set of evaluation criteria, assessing the security level of well-known smartphone platforms (i.e. Android, BlackBerry, Apple iOS, Windows Mobile, Windows Phone), in terms of the development of privacy-attack malware, and, (b) providing a comparative case study analysis where a proof of concept implementation of a location tracking malicious application is attempted in the above-mentioned smartphone platforms.

The paper is organized as follows. Section 2 provides background information about current smartphone operating systems. In section 3 the comparative criteria are introduced, while in section 4 our case study of malware implementation is presented. The paper concludes with section 5.

2   Smartphone Platforms

In this section we discuss the security models and development environments of the surveyed smartphone platforms: (a). Android, (b). BlackBerry, (c). iOS, (d). Windows

Mobile, and (e). Windows Phone. Our analysis focuses on application installation and execution; hence mechanisms that are used for the physical protection of the device (data encryption, anti-theft solutions, etc.) are out of the scope of this paper.

2.1 Android

Android is a Linux based, open source operating system (OS) developed and maintained by Google. It provides a free and publicly available Software Development Kit (SDK) that consists of tools, documentation and emulators necessary for the development of new applications in Java. According to Gartner [10], Android increased its worldwide smartphone sales from 25.3% in the Q3 of 2010 to 52.5% in the Q3 of 2011.

A core element of the Android security model [23] is the *manifest file*. The manifest provides the necessary information to Android for the execution of an application. Security-wise, the manifest file is crucial for the system, since a developer defines within the application permissions, namely: (a) the way the application interacts with the system via access to system API, and (b) the way the system and the other applications interact with the given application's components.

Every application runs in a sandboxed environment without any permission to perform an action that can impact the operating system itself (e.g. crashing), other applications (e.g. disabling an application's components) and the user (e.g. surveillance). Applications request authorization from the user for their permissions during installation. No further permission checks are performed during the applications' execution. Moreover, the user cannot grant a subset of the requested permissions. Hence, the user either accepts all permissions or postpones the installation.

Every Android application has to be digitally signed by its developer. Android's security model then maps the signature of the developer with a unique ID of the application package and enforces signature level permission authorization [23]. Nonetheless, Android's security model does not mandate that a developer certificate must be signed by a trusted certificate authority. As a result, applications are usually signed with self-signed digital certificates; hence, providing only poor source origin and integrity protection. This preserves the anonymity of a potential attacker, since the certificate is not verified by a Trusted Third Party (TTP).

A developer may distribute her application either in the official application repository maintained by Google, the Android Market, or elsewhere. Google does not enforce any restriction in the installation of applications outside its repository (e.g. forums, other markets, etc.). On the other hand, Google developed technologies to remove applications from devices and the Android Market in case they are proven malicious [7]. However, applications enter the Android Market without being tested for malicious behaviour. Thus, an attacker must only use a Google account and pay a small fee for malware distribution in the Android application repository.

2.2 BlackBerry

BlackBerry is an operating system maintained by Research In Motion Inc. (RIM). The OS is executed on BlackBerry smartphones and tablet devices created by RIM.

According to Gartner [10], RIM's device worldwide market share dropped to 11.0% in the Q3 of 2011 from 15.4.% in the Q3 of 2010.

Documentation about the OS details is not provided by RIM. However, RIM provides, through the BlackBerry SDK, the related documentation, tools, API and emulators that are necessary for application development.

The platform's security model [25] enforces restrictions to third party applications trying to access protected APIs, by demanding the signing of the application with a cryptographic key provided by RIM [14]. A developer needs to pay a small fee in order to acquire a valid RIM signing key pair. Yet, this process provides poor source origin and code integrity, without offering any assurance about the validity and/or the security level of the third party application.

BlackBerry maintains an application repository, the App World [25], without restricting application installation from other application repositories. Application distribution in the official repository requires registration for a vendor account. Developers incur a registration cost of $200 for the aforementioned account creation, allowing them to submit 10 applications. For additional submissions an administration fee is required. It should be noted that before application publication in the repository, its code is not examined by BlackBerry for malicious behaviour and, in addition, BlackBerry does not operate a remote application removal mechanism.

2.3   iOS

iOS is a proprietary operating system maintained by Apple. According to [10], Apple's worldwide smartphone market share dropped slightly to 15.0% in the Q3 of 2011 from 16.6% in the Q3 of 2010.

Apple provides, after registration to the company's Dev Center [13], documentation, tools and the necessary API for application development in Objective C programming language. Nevertheless, it should be noted here that this toolset is only compatible with Mac OS X.

The security model of iOS permits only the installation of applications that have been signed by Apple [13] and reside in the official application repository, the App Store. For application distribution in the repository the developers incur an annual cost of $99.

The security model of iOS is not permission based as in Android. Its cornerstone is an application testing mechanism - also referred as 'application vetting' mechanism, which is controlled by Apple. During application submission each application undergoes automatic and manual testing to ensure its functionality consistency, official API use and 'absence' of malicious activity. Nonetheless, the testing process and criteria, which are applied by Apple, are not publicly available.

Once the application is installed to the device the user neither controls nor is prompted when an application accesses most OS' sensitive resources. For few sensitive resources (e.g. location data) the user will be prompted the first time that an application uses the resource and has the ability to revoke application access to the resource in the OS settings. For the rest resources, for instance Internet access, these options are not available. Finally, an in depth analysis of the data that are available to an application in iOS version 3 is provided in [27].

2.4   Windows Mobile

Windows Mobile is a smartphone OS developed and maintained by Microsoft. The OS's worldwide smartphone market share decreased from 7.9% in the Q3 of 2009 to 2.8% in the Q3 of 2010 [8]. Windows Mobile was replaced as the primary Windows smartphone OS in February 2010.

The security model of Windows Mobile [31] depends on the enabled device policy. This policy specifies which applications are allowed to execute, what functionality is accessible to them, how desktop applications interact with the device, and, how a user or an application accesses specific device settings. The enabled policy on a Windows Mobile smartphone is either one-tier access or two-tier access [31]. Due to space limitations this subsection only outlines the details of this security model. A more thorough description is available in the conference paper [20].

According to [26], [31] the default security configuration of Windows Mobile, provides weak security as: (a). it allows the installation of unsigned applications or singed ones with an unknown certificate, hence the platform does not provide any assurance about the application author or its integrity, and, (b). in case (a). the user is prompted to authorize the application execution, hence, in this context, in both access tiers unsigned and unknown code is executed with the user's approval. Furthermore, although the one-tier access does not provide strong security [20], it is the default access tier in some devices [31].

The security model of Windows Mobile includes security mechanisms enabling a Mobile Operator to revoke (i.e. remotely remove or disable) applications running on smartphones [31]. The revocation may concern either (a). a class of applications signed with the same certificate, where the corresponding certificate is being revoked, or (b). a specific application binary, where the hash of a binary is being transferred to the device with transfer mechanisms described in [31].

For application implementation in Windows Mobile 6, Microsoft freely provides the required development toolkit (i.e. SDK, emulator, documentation, etc.). The supported implementation languages (e.g. C#, Visual C++) are compatible with the Compact .NET Framework.

2.5   Windows Phone

Windows Phone is the latest smartphone OS that is maintained by Microsoft. Even though this OS is the descendant of Windows Mobile their differences, especially w.r.t the security model, enables it to be regarded herein as a separate smartphone OS. The market share of the OS is currently very low (1.5% Q3 2011) [10], but in February 2011 a partnership[1] between Nokia and Microsoft was announced where Nokia adopts Windows Phone as its primary smartphone operating system. As a result, this may change the popularity of Windows Phone devices.

Windows Phone provides free and publicly available SDK that consists of tools, documentation and emulators necessary for the implementation of application for the OS using the Silverlight technology.

---

[1] http://www.microsoft.com/presspass/press/2011/ feb11/02-11partnership.mspx

Third party applications in the Windows Phone ecosystem request access to capabilities, which are similar to permissions in Android, so as to acquire access to protected functionality [24]. The capabilities are included in an application's manifest file, are automatically granted at installation and cannot be elevated during execution. Contrarily to Android, users are not prompted to grant access to capabilities during installation time. Nonetheless, users are informed about the capabilities that an application uses via: (a). the application's detail page in the official repository, the Marketplace, (b). an explicit prompt for capabilities that have legal requirements for explicit consent collection, and, (c). the application itself when the location capability is used for the first time. This way, the platform's security model assumes that users *indirectly* accept the capabilities by installing the application. Moreover, this acceptance follows –similarly to Android- an *all-or-nothing* approach, namely users cannot grant a subset of the requested application capabilities.

The security model of Windows Phone permits only the installation of third party applications that are signed by Microsoft and available in the Marketplace. During application submission in the Marketplace each application is tested and the developer is authenticated during registration. During her registration a developer pays an annual registration fee and provides identity information for her authentication. Moreover, Microsoft can use a remote application removal mechanism[2] to 'a posteriori' remove malicious applications from Windows Phone devices, which managed to enter the application repository.

3   Comparative Evaluation Criteria of Smartphone Platforms

A comparative evaluation of smartphone platforms is performed in Section 4, by using a set of evaluation criteria that are elaborated in this section. The proposed criteria concern the development platform and the developer. The platform-based criteria are objective, relying solely on the platform characteristics. Contrarily, the developer-related criteria are subjective, giving details about the development effort and, as a result, depend on the developer's skills and background. The latter, however, are given as an indication on the effort needed to implement a malicious smartphone application. It must be noted that this list of criteria is not exhaustive.

3.1   Development Platform Criteria

In this section we describe the development platform evaluation criteria in relation with their data type.

Development Tools Availability {*Yes, Partial, No*}. Refers to the availability of the necessary tools for application development. The existence of public and free development tools makes the malware development easier and cost effective. The reason for this is that a free emulator reduces the development cost of an attacker, since a device purchase is not necessary. Moreover, the SDK contains all the tools

---

[2] http://news.cnet.com/8301-27076_3-20021791-248.html

(e.g. debuggers, compilers, etc.) that are necessary for the implementation of the malicious application.

Development Friendliness {*Yes, No*}. This Boolean criterion assesses the "developer" friendliness of the programming language that is supported by the smartphone platform. The adoption of a well-known and widely used programming language (e.g. Java) is preferred during any application deployment.

Installation vectors {*Multiple, Restricted*}. This criterion assesses the available installation options for an application on the smartphone device. These installation options include the use of removable media, through the Web, email, etc.

Application Portability {*Yes, No*}. Refers to the ability of a malicious application to execute in different smartphone OS versions. The more compatible an application with different OS versions is, the greater the attack target population becomes.

Application Testing {*Yes, No*}. This criterion refers to the possible application testing procedures, which can be used from application repositories to determine if the application is malicious. These tests usually take place before the application is added in the application repository.

Application Removal {*Yes, No*}. This Boolean criterion refers to the existence of a remote application removal mechanism, commonly referred as 'app kill switch'. An application removal from an application repository and smartphone devices takes place, when evidence is discovered that the application acts in a maliciously way.

Unofficial Repositories {*Yes, No*}. This Boolean criterion refers to whether the security model permits the installation of applications from sources other than the official repository. If the application repository adopts application testing, one option for an attacker is to place the application in alternative sources, e.g. forums.

Distribution Cost {*Yes, No*}. This criterion assesses whether the submission of an application into the application repository incurs costs to a potential attacker.

API Restrictions {*Yes, No*}. This criterion refers to the restrictions imposed by smartphones' OS, in terms of how they control the use of protected API.

Application Signing {*Yes, No*}. This criterion refers to any restrictions imposed by the smartphone OS, w.r.t. the signing of the applications before their installation.

3.2   Developer Criteria

This set of criteria includes the Developer's Background and the Development time. More specifically:

Developer's Background {*Education Level*}. It refers to the developer's knowledge in information security, as well as to her programming skills. We assume that the amount of knowledge a developer possesses in information security and her programming skills, determine the sophistication of the attacks she is able to implement.

Development Time {*Number*}. It is used for determining the development effort that is needed to create the malicious application.

Apparently, the abovementioned criteria are given as an indication for the time and skills needed for the development of an attack by an average-skilled programmer. The evaluation criteria are summarized in Table 1.

Table 1. Proposed evaluation criteria

Table 1. Proposed evaluation criteria

Evaluation Criteria	Type
Development Tools Availability	String {Yes, Partial, No}
Development Friendliness	Boolean
Installation Vectors	String {Multiple, Restricted}
Application Portability	Boolean
Application Testing	Boolean
Application Removal	Boolean
Unofficial Repositories	Boolean
Distribution Cost	Boolean
API Restrictions	Boolean
Application Signing	Boolean
Developer's Background	Education Level
Development Time	Number

4   Case Study of Malware Implementation

This section provides a comparative evaluation of smartphones platforms in terms of malware development and distribution. Our analysis examines the feasibility and easiness of attacks implemented by average developers. Specifically, we examine the implementation feasibility of the simple attack scenario shown in Figure 1.

The evaluation is based on: (a). the proposed qualitative evaluation criteria and (b). a proof of concept malware implementation study, in which the development of a location tracking application is examined. To evaluate the robustness and the security properties of the smartphones platforms, our overall approach focuses on the objective criteria (development platform), while at the same time takes into account the subjective criteria (regarding the developer). At this point it should be stressed that any sophisticated attack conducted by experienced attackers, as well as, publicly available malicious code used by script kiddies are not examined herein. Furthermore, a comparison with malware development in desktop computing is not examined in this paper either. Also, the implementation study assumes that the security models are unmodified, i.e. the smartphones have not been 'jailbroken'.

The attack scenario refers to a location tracking malicious application. The application collects a user's GPS coordinates (i.e. her exact position) and sends them to an attacker. It is assumed that the malicious functionality is included in a free GPS navigation application. The application apart from getting the user's location and presenting it using Google Maps, it also sends the location data to the attacker's server. The described malware is executed, in most cases, without creating any suspicion to a naive smartphone user. This is since the application's functionality requests (i.e. access to device location and Internet access to connect to the Internet) are consistent with the application's expected functionality.

We performed the development case study in our lab using two computers running a Windows XP and a Mac OS Leopard operating system. In the Windows machine we installed the emulators and the SDKs of all smartphone platforms, apart from Apple's iOS that was only compatible with Mac OS X.

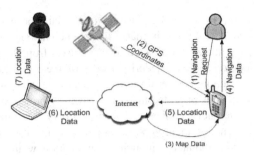

Fig. 1. Case study attack scenario

For the malware implementation we selected two computer science students (one undergraduate and one postgraduate student, respectively) with basic information security background and moderate programming skills. Before the case study the students had successfully completed information security-related courses that are consistent with the Common Body of Knowledge described in [29]. The undergraduate student had completed a course on Information Security Management and the postgraduate had completed the courses Information Security Management, Information System Auditing, Network Security, and Cryptography. Both students were more familiar with the Java programming language, since this was the language used in most implementations during undergraduate and postgraduate projects. The postgraduate student was only involved in the implementation of a smartphone platform only if the undergraduate was unable to implement it.

In the following paragraphs we analyse the results regarding the development and use of this malicious application to the smartphone platforms described in Section 2, namely[3]: Android, BlackBerry, iOS, Windows Mobile and Windows Phone.

4.1   Android Case Study

The malware implementation was successfully developed on Android in one day. The official development toolkit (i.e. SDK and emulator) was used during development. The implementation was aided by: a). the adoption by the platform of a widely used programming language (i.e. Java), and b). the effective documentation of its API. In addition, the same source code successfully compiled and executed in Android versions 2.2 and 2.3; hence the application is considered portable within the Android platform at the time of the writing.

Regarding application distribution an attacker has many options, since Android does not impose any restriction neither on the application source (i.e. originating from an unofficial repository), nor on the installation vector (e.g. removable media, WWW, etc.). A small registration fee is required for application submission in the official repository, but it is inadequate to impede an attacker. Furthermore, application testing

---

[3] The conference paper [20] includes a case study implementation in Symbian. This paper replaces Symbian with Windows Phone, since Nokia (February 2011) decided to use Symbian only in feature phones and Windows Phone 7 in Nokia smartphones.

for malicious behaviour is not taking place if the official repository is selected as the distribution vector. Hence, it is likely that malware such as one described in this case study is currently present and downloaded by naive users from the repository[4].

As mentioned beforehand, the security model of the Android platform imposes some application restrictions concerning the application signing and API control. We argue that these restrictions provide only partial security protection. API requests are authorized by the –often not technical and security savvy- user during application installation. No further checks about application permissions take place after the installation. Hence, it is likely that the malicious application would be granted the requested permissions (i.e. access to location data and the Internet), especially in our case, where the permissions fully match the expected application's functionality. For the latter, the imposed signature can be self-signed by the developer and, as a result, the application's source origin is not verified and unknown. This situation, combined with the fact that an attacker may find valid credit cards numbers in the underground market, could be used to commence elite spoofing attacks. These attack scenarios are out of the scope of this paper. Finally, Google's remote removal mechanism is the only efficient post installation protection mechanism against our case study scenario.

From the above analysis we infer that the likelihood of conducting such an attack on the Android platform is very high.

4.2   Blackberry Case Study

Regarding our malware implementation on BlackBerry platform, the results were again successful. The malware implementation was carried out by the B.Sc. student. RIM's official development toolkit (i.e. SDK and emulator) was used for the implementation. The implementation was not demanding and its duration was one day, due to the adoption by the platform of a widely used programming language (i.e. Java), and the effective API documentation. Furthermore, the same source code successfully compiled and executed in versions 5 and 6 of BlackBerry, therefore the application is considered portable.

The security model of the BlackBerry does not impose any restrictions regarding the application origin. Nevertheless, the application file must be signed to access restricted and sensitive platform APIs. For the signing process the developer incurs a small key acquisition fee. As there is no strong authentication in the key acquisition process, application signing provides only integrity protection and poor source origin.

The cost for the cryptographic keys is considered inadequate to deter an attacker. On the other hand, the cost for the publication is expected to impede an attacker from publishing the application in the RIM's official repository, especially if she is in possession of limited economic resources. The attacker, however, still has the option to submit her malicious application to an unofficial repository.

The security model of BlackBerry does not employ any application testing before adding the application in the official repository. Furthermore, there is no remote

---

[4] The DroidDream incident [4] in the App Market was identified after the submission of our conference paper [20].

application removal mechanism for malicious applications. Hence, if the malware application is submitted in the official repository, then it is very likely to be downloaded and installed in BlackBerry devices by some users.

Conclusively, the development of the malware examined in this scenario is feasi-ble and it demands little development effort. The only impediment is the cost of submitting the application to the official repository.

4.3   iOS Case Study

The malware implementation was successfully completed on iOS by the post graduate student. The implementation lasted 7 days and was tested on emulators running iOS 3 (version 3.1.2) and iOS 4 (version 4.1). The implementation duration was expected a priori to last more than in the other platforms due to no prior experience with Objective C. However, the toolset provided by Apple (i.e. SDK, documentation and emulator) minimized this lack of experience. In Table 2 the relevant criterion was assigned the 'partial' value, since the toolkit is available only to Mac OS X users.

Application installation in devices running iOS is only possible via Apple's App Store. Hence, unofficial application repositories are not available for devices running an unmodified iOS version. As a result, a malware author must submit the application in the official repository. Application submission in the App Store requires a non free registration to Apple's development program. Prior to the application inclusion in the official repository it must be examined and signed by Apple. The details of application testing or 'application vetting' (e.g. automatic static malware analysis, manual inspection, etc.) are not known. The application testing criteria are, also, not publicly available, apart from the automatic rejection of any application that is using not official Apple API. Nonetheless, academic literature has identified the deficiencies of application testing as a proactive mechanism for application repositories [18].

The user has no control on the application's actions after the installation of an application in the device. In addition, the user is not informed when the application uploads data to a remote server. In our case study, the user would only be prompted to permit access to location data the first time the application executes. But, as the application is providing location based services the user is expected to confirm access to location data. Afterwards, the data would be transferred to the attacker's remote server, without the user noticing it.

Apple uses mechanisms allowing the remote deletion of malicious applications from iOS devices and the application repository. As in Android this is a post installation security mechanism, which can be used in case Apple or a user became suspicious of our malicious application.

4.4   Windows Mobile 6 Case Study

The malicious application implementation on a Windows Mobile device was also successfully completed by the student in 2 days. The programming language was C#. The reasons of the implementation effectiveness are the adoption by the platform of a programming language, namely C#, which resembles the programming rationale of Java and the effective API documentation.

The proof of concept malware was implemented for the versions 6.1 and 6.5 of Windows Mobile using the SDK provided by Microsoft. The installation package of the application was not signed. During the implementation the default configuration of the security model was preserved, in essence: (a). unsigned applications would be allowed to run, (b). the user would be prompted to authorize the application execution, and (c). if the application had been authorized by the user it would acquire full access to the OS system services.

The security model of Windows Mobile does not impose restrictions on the installation vector of applications. Hence, applications may be installed on devices even if they are downloaded from a source outside Microsoft's official repository. Hence, the attacker does not have application distribution costs. Furthermore, the application is not being tested for malicious behaviour, since it is not distributed by Microsoft distribution services. Nonetheless, the application removal mechanism, applied by Microsoft, may be used for the automated removal of the implemented malware.

To sum up, the feasibility of our malware attack in Windows Mobile depends on the device configurations regarding the security model, the user authorization at application installation time and the automated application removal security mechanism.

4.5   Windows Phone 7 Case Study

The malware implementation was also successful in Windows Phone and was conducted by the undergraduate student. The implementation duration was one day, due to: a) the student's prior experience with the C# programming language, which was acquired during the implementation in Windows Phone and b) the effective API documentation provided by Microsoft. The official development toolkits (i.e. debuggers, SDK, etc.) were used and the implementation was tested in the version 7.1 of the official Windows Phone emulator. However, the malicious application is not backwards compatible with version 7.0 of Windows Phone [32].

As discussed beforehand the security model of Windows Phone employs different security mechanism decreasing the attacker choices regarding malware distribution. Each application must be signed by Microsoft in order to be installed on a device and it can only reside in the official application repository. As a result, applications cannot be installed from other locations and, hence, the attacker must pay a registration fee and be authenticated in the repository. In addition, the application before being indexed in the application repository, undergoes security testing. Thus - as in iOS - the attacker must circumvent the application testing mechanism in order to spread malware in the official repository, e.g. by encrypting parts of the application.

As in Android, the security model restricts application access to sensitive resources via capabilities. Contrarily to Android this list of capabilities are not prompted for authorization during application installation, but are only indexed in the application's web page in the application repository. As a result, a user has the option to reject application capabilities in an all-or-nothing approach by deciding not to install the application. Finally, the security model of Windows Phone includes a remote 'app kill switch' for a posteriori removal of malicious applications from Windows Phone devices.

4.6   Case Study Overview

The security model of a smartphone operating system has two contradicting goals. On the one hand, it must provide users with security assurance concerning the execution of third-party applications on their devices. On the other hand, it must provide to the developers a secure ecosystem, where consumers are willing to install new applications, and it is easy and efficient to implement new applications.

The proof of concept study demonstrated that, under certain circumstances, the security model of all available smartphone platforms would not counter a location tracking attack. Moreover, it showed that it is possible to easily implement this malicious application on all the examined smartphone platforms. It should be stressed herein that until the writing of this paper, the current antivirus software is inefficient, since: a) as every third party smartphone application, they execute in a sandboxed environment and, thus, are not able to acquire 'root' privileges, e.g. for placing API hooks and b) execute in a resource restrained device.

Our case study implementation was efficiently and effectively completed in all platforms, by using the official development tools, and, it was tested on the official e-mulators. Moreover, the implementation of the malicious applications was conducted by average programmers with the use of the API documentation. Specifically, almost all malware was implemented by the undergraduate student. This fact is a serious indication of how malicious software may evolve in smartphones.

Security testing of applications cannot be avoided only on Apple's iOS and Windows Phone. Furthermore, these were the only platforms having strict application installation requirements, i.e. only via the official application repository.

Among the examined platforms only Windows Mobile allowed, under some security model configurations, the execution of unsigned applications. Yet, the digital signing process in the rest platforms, which were examined, provides different security assurance to a user. The user was found, on the one hand, as not having any control on the API running in the device on some platforms. On the other hand, the user is fully responsible for authorizing application requests for access to sensitive resources in other smartphone platforms. The latter is a major weakness in the security model of these smartphones platforms, since the user's security knowledge and awareness is often insufficient.

Android and Windows Mobile were the only smartphone platforms where an attacker could avoid application distribution costs and only BlackBerry did not use a remote application removal mechanism. Table 2 summarizes our findings.

According to the case study findings, a non-sophisticated attacker would try to avoid iOS and Windows Phone as a privacy and security attack vector, since they are the platforms having the most defensive mechanism in place (i.e. application testing, controlled application installation vectors and remote application removal). Moreover, iOS was also found complex in (malicious) application development. An attacker is expected to prefer one of the rest platforms, especially Android and Windows Mobile, which were found to provide the least protection mechanisms. Nonetheless, it should be stressed that the decision for platform selection, is dependent on whether the attacker is preparing a targeted attack (i.e. against an individual), or not. In the former case the attacker will select the OS running on the individual's device, whereas in the latter case the attacker will chose the platform with the larger user base (i.e. Android during the writing of this paper).

Table 2. Malware scenario implementation overview

Evaluation Criteria	Android	BlackBerry	iOS	Windows Mobile	Windows Phone
SDK & simulator availability	✓	✓	partial	✓	✓
Development Friendliness	✓	✓	✗	✓	✓
Installation Vectors	multiple	multiple	restricted	multiple	restricted
Application Portability	✓	✓	✓	✓	✗
Application Testing	✗	✗	✓	✗	✓
Application Removal	✓	✗	✓	✓	✓
Unofficial Repositories	✓	✓	✗	✓	✗
Distribution Cost	✗	✓	✓	✗	✓
API Restrictions	✓	✓	✗	✗	✓
Application Signing	✓	✓	✓	✗	✓
Developer's Background	B.Sc.	B.Sc.	M.Sc.	B.Sc.	B.Sc.
Development Time	0.5day	1 day	7days	2days	1day

5   Conclusions

Smartphone devices are multi-purpose portable devices enclosing multiple heterogeneous third party applications, which augment the device's functionality. The smartphone security models facilitate mechanisms and processes controlling the installation and execution of third party applications. Even so, the efficiency of the adopted security mechanisms seems to be controversial. Their ability to protect the devices from becoming a privacy attack vector from average developers, such as undergraduate and postgraduate computer science students, is proven to be unclear.

Our paper (a). proposes evaluation criteria assessing the protection from simple smartphone malware, and (b). provides a comparative case study analysis, where a proof of concept implementation of a location tracking malicious application is attempted in well-known smartphone platforms (i.e. Android, BlackBerry, Apple iOS, Windows Mobile, Windows Phone).

Our proof of concept study has proven that, under circumstances, all examined smartphone platforms would not stop average developers from using smartphones as privacy attack vectors, harvesting data from the device without the user's knowledge and consent. It also showed the easiness of malware development by average programmers that have access to the official tools and programming libraries provided by smartphone platforms.

A silver bullet solution against similar attack scenarios is not available. Some of the solutions that can be used to avoid a potential malware outbreak in smartphones are: (a) user awareness, i.e. informing user about the security and privacy risks in smartphone platforms, and (b) providing secure application distribution in smartphone application repositories.

For further work we plan to extend the evaluation criteria and attribute weights to them. We also plan to repeat the case study with more developers to acquire more generalisable results.

Acknowledgements. This work has been partially funded by the European Union (European Social Fund) and Greek national funds through the Operational Program Education and Lifelong Learning of the National Strategic Reference Framework - Research Funding Program: HERACLEITUS II - Investing in Knowledge Society.

References

1. Adleman, L.: An Abstract Theory of Computer Viruses. In: Goldwasser, S. (ed.) CRYPTO 1988. LNCS, vol. 403, pp. 354–374. Springer, Heidelberg (1990)
2. CISCO: Cisco 2011 Annual Security Report. Technical report (2011)
3. Cohen, F.: Computational aspects of computer viruses. Computers & Security 8(4), 297–298 (1989)
4. DroidDream Becomes Android Market Nightmare,
   http://www.pcworld.com/businesscenter/article/221247/droiddr
   eam_becomes_android_market_nightmare.html
5. Egele, M., Kruegel, C., Kirda, E., Vigna, G.: Pios: Detecting privacy leaks in iOS applications. In: Network and Distributed System Security Symposium (2011)
6. Enck, W., Gilbert, P., Chun, G., Cox, P., Jung, J., McDaniel, P., Sheth, N.: Taintdroid: an information-flow tracking system for realtime privacy monitoring on smartphones. In: 9th USENIX Symposium on Operating Systems Design and Implementation (OSDI), pp. 1–6. USENIX Association (2010)
7. Exercising our remote application removal feature, http://android-developers.
   blogspot.com/2010/06/exercising-our-remote-application.html
8. Gartner: Competitive Landscape: Mobile Devices, Worldwide, 3Q10. Technical report (2010)
9. Gartner: Forecast: Mobile Application Stores, Worldwide, 2008-2014. Technical report (2010)
10. Gartner: Market Share: Mobile Communication Devices by Region and Country, 3Q11. Technical report (2011)
11. Hogben, G., Dekker, M.: Smartphones: Information security risks, opportunities and recommendations for users. Technical report, ENISA (December 2010)
12. Hypponen, M.: Malware goes mobile. Scientific American 295(5), 70–77 (2006)
13. iOS Dev Center, http://developer.apple.com/devcenter/ios/
14. Java code signing keys,
    http://us.blackberry.com/developers/javaappdev/codekeys.jsp

15. Kephart, J., White, S.: Directed-graph epidemiological models of computer viruses. In: Symposium on Research in Security and Privacy, pp. 343–359. IEEE Computer Society (1991)

16. Lineberry, A., Richardson, D., Wyatt, T.: These aren't the permissions you 're looking for. Technical report, DEFCON (2010)

17. McAfee:2011 threats predictions. Technical report, McAfee (2010)

18. McDaniel, P., Enck, W.: Not so great expectations: Why application markets haven't failed security. IEEE Security Privacy 8(5), 76–78 (2010)

19. Mobile privacy, http://www.gsmworld.com/our-work/public-policy/mobile_privacy.html

20. Mylonas, A., Dritsas, S., Tsoumas, B., Gritzalis, D.: Smartphone security evaluation: The malware attack case. In: Samarati, P., Lopez, J. (eds.) International Conference of Security and Cryptography (SECRYPT 2011), pp. 25–36. SciTePress (2011)

21. Mylonas, A., Tsoumas, B., Dritsas, S., Gritzalis, D.: A Secure Smartphone Applications Roll-out Scheme. In: Furnell, S., Lambrinoudakis, C., Pernul, G. (eds.) TrustBus 2011. LNCS, vol. 6863, pp. 49–61. Springer, Heidelberg (2011)

22. Nachenberg, C.: A Window Into Mobile Device Security. Technical report, Symantec Security Response (2011)

23. Security and permissions, http://developer.android.com/guide/topics/security/security.html

24. Security for Windows Phone, http://msdn.microsoft.com/en-us/library/ff402533%28v=vs.92%29.aspx

25. Security overview, http://docs.blackberry.com/en/developers/deliverables/21091/Security_overview_1304155_11.jsp

26. Security policy settings, http://msdn.microsoft.com/en-us/library/bb416355.aspx

27. Seriot, N.: iphone privacy. Technical report, Black Hat DC (2010)

28. The security of b2b: Enabling an unbounded enterprise, http://www.forrester.com/rb/Research/security_of_b2b_enabling_unbounded_enterprise/q/id/56670/t/2

29. Theoharidou, M., Gritzalis, D.: Common body of knowledge for information security. IEEE Security & Privacy 5(2), 64–67 (2007)

30. Weiser, M.: The computer for the 21st century. Scientific American 265(3), 94–104 (1991)

31. Windows mobile device security model, http://msdn.microsoft.com/en-us/library/bb416353.aspx

32. Windows Phone OS Application Compatibility, http://msdn.microsoft.com/en-us/library/hh202996%28v=VS.92%29.aspx

Revocation and Tracing Based on Ternary Tree: Towards Optimal Broadcast Encryption Scheme

Kazuhide Fukushima*, Shinsaku Kiyomoto, Yutaka Miyake, and Kouichi Sakurai*

KDDI R&D Laboratories Inc., Saitama, 356–8502, Japan
Faculty of Information Science and Electrical Engineering, Kyushu University,
Fukuoka, 819–0395, Japan

Abstract. This paper proposes a broadcast encryption scheme with traitor tracing based on the ternary tree structure. The subset difference method with ternary tree reduces the communication cost and tracing cost of the original method with the binary tree. However, straightforward expansion of the method ends in failure due to the vulnerability to coalition attacks. Thus, we design a new cover-finding algorithm and label assignment algorithm in order to achieve a coalition-resistant revocation and tracing schemes. Our analysis on efficiency and security shows that our scheme is an improvement of the existing broadcast encryption schemes: complete subtree and subset difference methods.

Keywords: Broadcast encryption, Subset difference method, Traitor tracing, Ternary tree.

1 Introduction

1.1 Background

Digital content broadcasting services have become major in the 3G and beyond 3G mobile market due to advancing of its communication speed. Unauthorized use of the digital content has been a major issue for the mobile services. In digital content distribution, properties should satisfy the following three requirements: 1) only valid user devices that has a valid key can decrypt the broadcasting content, 2) the keys can no longer be used to decrypt the content, if keys in a device are revealed, and 3) invalid users who illegally use keys in a device can be identified. A *broadcast encryption scheme* with a *traitor tracing algorithm* is an essential technique to realize these requirements.

1.2 Previous Work

Broadcast Encryption Scheme. The first scheme is proposed by Berkovits [1]. Fiat et al. [2] formalized the basic definition of a broadcast encryption scheme. Naor et al. [3]

---

* The first and forth authors are partially supported by Strategic Japanese-Indian Cooperative Programme on Multidisciplinary Research Field, which combines Information and Communications Technology with Other Fields by Japan Science and Technology Agency and Department of Science and Technology of the Government of India, en-titled "Analysis of Cryptographic Algorithms and Evaluation on Enhancing Network Security Based on Mathematical Science".

M.S. Obaidat, J.L. Sevillano, and J. Filipe (Eds.): ICETE 2011, CCIS 314, pp. 233–248, 2012.
© Springer-Verlag Berlin Heidelberg 2012

proposed the complete subtree method (the CS method). This scheme uses a tree and devices are assigned to the leaf nodes of the tree. Valid devices are covered by complete subtrees and a key to encrypt the session key is assigned to each subtree. There is one problem associated with the CS method in that the header length increases in proportion to the number of revoked devices. The average header length is given by $O(r \log(n/r))$ for the number of total devices n, the number of revoked devices r. The subset difference method (SD method) is proposed by Naor et al. [3]. This method uses a binary tree to assign labels to devices. A valid device can derive the key to decrypt the message using its labels. The valid devices are covered by subtrees with another subtree covering revoked devices. A key to encrypt the session key is assigned to each subtree. The header lengths in the average and worst case scenarios are given by $2r \log 2$ and $2r - 1$, and each device stores $\log^2 n/2 + \log n/2 + 1$ labels. Many improvements to these SD methods have been proposed. Halevy-Shamir [4], Goodrich et al. [5], Jho et al. [6], Hwang et al. [7] and Attrapadung-Imai [8] proposed schemes based on a pseudo-random number generator. Asano [9], Attrapadung et al. [10] and Gentry-Ramzan [11] proposed a scheme based on the RSA cryptosystem. Jho et al.'s scheme reduces the header length to r/c but increases the storage size in devices to $O(n^c)$ where c is constant. Other schemes reduce the storage size to less than $O(\log^2 n)$ but increase the average header length to greater than $2r \log 2$. Boneh et al. [12] proposed a scheme based on pairing in which the header length and storage size do not depend on r; however, this scheme imposes a heavy computational cost: $O(n)$ on devices.

Group key-management schemes based on the ternary tree have been proposed [13–15]. The CS method can reduce the storage size and tracing cost by using the ternary tree instead of the binary tree. However, the SD method cannot protect against coalition attacks if it is straightforwardly extended to the ternary tree. The construction of a coalition-resistant ternary SD method had been an open problem and we showed a possible solution [16, 17].

Traitor Tracing Scheme.   Chor et al. [18] proposed the first scheme based on combinatorics. This scheme requires $O(k^4 \log n)$ header length and $O(k^2 \log n)$ storage size where k is the allowable number of collaborative traitors. Their other scheme is probabilistic one that requires $O(k^2 \log(n/p))$ header length and $O(k \log(n/p))$ storage size. This scheme can prevent up to k collaborative traitors from producing a pirated decoder with probability $1 - p$. Kurosawa-Desmedt [19] and Boneh-Franklin [20] proposed schemes based on number theory. Then, Kurosawa and Yoshida [21] showed that these schemes are identical. Chabanne et al. [22] and Boneh et al. [23] proposed a scheme based on bilinear maps. The schemes based on number theory and bilinear maps are efficient in terms of the communication overheads and the required storage size of devices; however, they impose heavy computational costs on devices.

1.3   Our Contribution

There exist many improved versions of the CS and SD method providing a traitor tracing. However, no method provide efficient traitor tracing using a feasible header length. The CS method by Naor *et al.* provides an efficient tracing with $t \log n/ \log 2$ computational overhead, but the header length is $r \log(n/r)$, where t is the number of traitors.

Their SD method reduces the header length to $2r \log 2$; however, the traitor tracing requires $t \log n / \log(3/2)$ computation.

This paper proposes a coalition-resistant broadcast encryption scheme; its header length is reduced to $3r \log 2$ and the traitor tracing requires $t \log n / \log 2$ computation that is the same as the computational cost of the CS method. The simulation results show that the proposed method reduces the average header length by up to 15.0 percent of the SD method. However, straightforward optimizations do not work due to the lack of the resistance against coalition attacks; thus, we need new algorithms. We design a new cover-finding algorithm, label assignment algorithm and encryption algorithm in order to achieve a coalition-resistant revocation scheme, and then we evaluate the efficiency of the proposed scheme and prove it is secure against coalition attacks.

The rest of the paper is organized as follows: Section 2 provides the preliminary. We propose the ternary SD (*3SD*) method in Sect. 3. Section 4 analyzes the efficiency and security of the proposed method. We conclude our paper in Sect. 5.

2 Preliminary

Let N be the set of all of the devices, $R(\subset N)$ be the set of revoked devices, and $|N| = n$, $|R| = r$. Broadcast encryption schemes enable the content distribution center to transmit message M to all devices such that any valid devices in $N \backslash R$ can decrypt the message, but none of the coalitions of revoked devices can decrypt it. Keys (or labels to derive keys) are pre-installed on each device and never updated.

The proposed scheme consists of 1) a label assignment algorithm, 2) a cover-finding algorithm, 3) an encryption algorithm, 4) a decryption algorithm, and 5) a tracing algorithm.

Label Assignment Algorithm (by the content distribution center)
> Assign labels to each device. The labels are used to derive a key to decrypt the session key.

Cover-Finding Algorithm (by the content distribution center)
> Find a family of disjoint subsets $\{S_1, S_2, \ldots, S_w\}$ such that $\cup_{t=1}^{w} S_t = N \backslash R$.

Encryption Algorithm (by the content distribution center)
> Derive keys $L_1, \ldots, L_w$ to disjoint subsets $\{S_1, S_2, \ldots, S_w\}$ output by the cover-finding algorithm. Then, encrypt message M with session key K and encrypt K with keys $L_1, \ldots, L_w$.

Decryption Algorithm (by each device $d \in N \backslash R$)
> Find subset S_t to which d belongs. Then, derive key L_t to decrypt K and obtain M.

Tracing Algorithm (by the content distribution center)
> Find traitors who produced a pirated decoder and revoke them.

3 Proposed Scheme

We propose a coalition-resistant ternary subset difference (*3SD*) method. The proposed scheme can reduce the communication cost and storage size in devices, and provide efficient traitor tracing. The *3SD* method can be implemented using encryption functions and one-way functions; that is, the required primitives are the same as the SD method.

3.1 Primitives

The *3SD* method uses the following primitives;

- A symmetric key encryption function $F_K : \{0,1\}^* \rightarrow \{0,1\}^*$ to encrypt message M.
- A symmetric key encryption function $E_L : \{0,1\}^\lambda \rightarrow \{0,1\}^\lambda$ to encrypt session key K.
- One-way functions with pre-image resistance $f_{lbl}, f_{lft}, f_{cnt}, f_{rgt}$ and $f_{kgf} : \{0,1\}^\lambda \rightarrow \{0,1\}^\lambda$. These one-way functions have to be pairwise distinct. Note that one-way functions F_1 and F_2 are pairwise distinct [24] if there is no probabilistic polynomial time adversary that calculates $F_2(x_1)$ from given $F_1(x_1)$, or $F_1(x_2)$ from given $F_2(x_2)$, for any $x_1, x_2 \in \{0,1\}^\lambda$. [1] $f_{lft}, f_{cnt}, f_{rgt}$ and f_{lbl} are used to derive a label $l(u,w)$ from a label $l(u,v)$ or transformed label $f_{lbl}(l(u,v))$, where node w is a child of node v. $l(u,w) = f_{lft}(f_{lbl}(l(u,v)))$ holds for any u, v and w such that w is the left child of v. Similarly, $l(u,w) = f_{cnt}(f_{lbl}(l(u,v)))$ or $l(u,w) = f_{rgt}(f_{lbl}(l(u,v)))$ holds if w is the center or right child of v. f_{kgf} is used to derive a key from a label.

We define the subsets used in the *3SD* method. Then, detailed descriptions of each algorithm is provided in Sect. 3.3.

3.2 Subsets

In the *3SD* method, all the devices in $N \backslash R$ are covered by the collection of disjoint subsets $S_1, \ldots, S_w$. Each subset S_t is in the form of $D_i \backslash D_{j_1}$ or $D_i \backslash (D_{j_1} \cup D_{j_2})$. The former is used in the SD method and denoted by D_{i,j_1}. The latter is a characteristic subset in the *3SD* method and denoted by $D_{i,j_1 \oplus j_2}$. In this subset, all of the devices in D_{j_1} and D_{j_2} are revoked. The nodes j_1 and j_2 must be siblings and the descendants of i. Figure 1 shows these two subsets.

3.3 Revocation Scheme

We describe the detail of the label assigned algorithm, encryption algorithm and decryption algorithm. The encryption algorithm takes the set of revoked devices as input, and the revoked devices cannot decrypt messages. Thus, these algorithms provide a revocation mechanism.

---

[1] Naor et al. [3] constructed three functions using a pseudo random function $G : \{0,1\}^* \rightarrow \{0,1\}^{3\lambda}$. In the SD method, they used $G_L(S), G_M(S),$ and $G_R(S)$ which are the first, second, and third λ bits of $G(S)$, respectively. We can construct the five functions $f_{lbl}, f_{lft}, f_{cnt}, f_{rgt},$ and f_{kgf} based on another pseudo random function $G' : \{0,1\}^* \rightarrow \{0,1\}^{5\lambda}$. Let $G'_i(S)$ be i-th λ bits of $G'(S)$; then, we have $f_{lbl}(S) = G'_1(S), f_{lft}(S) = G'_2(S), f_{cnt}(S) = G'_3(S), f_{rgt}(S) = G'_4(S),$ and $f_{kgf}(S) = G'_5(S)$.

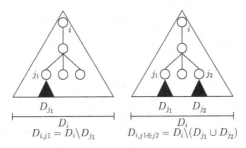

Fig. 1. Subsets in *3SD* method

Label Assignment Algorithm. This algorithm is executed in the content distribution center. Devices are given labels and transformed labels as shown in Figure 2.

Step 1. Construct a ternary tree to manage devices. These devices are assigned to leaf nodes of the tree.

Step 2. Generate random initial labels with λ bits for all of the nodes except for the leaf nodes in the tree. Let the initial label for node u be $l(u, u)$. All of the other labels required in this scheme are derived from these initial labels using one-way functions f_{lft}, f_{cnt}, f_{rgt} and f_{lbl}. Label $l(u, w)$ can be derived as $f_{lft}(f_{lbl}(l(u, v)))$, $f_{cnt}(f_{lbl}(l(u, v)))$, or $f_{rgt}(f_{lbl}(l(u, v)))$ when w is the left, center or right child of v, respectively.

Step 3. Assign labels and transformed labels to devices. The set $Label(u)$ that the device at the node u has is given by

$$Label(u) = \{f_{lbl}(l(v, w))|v \in Path(u), \ w \in LN(u)\}$$
$$\cup \{l(v, w)|v \in Path(u), \ w \in RN(u)\} \cup \{l(all)\}.$$

$Path(u)$ is the set of nodes that are on the path from the root node to u. $LN(u)$ denotes the set of nodes that hang on the left of the $Path(u)$. If $Path(u)$ contains the leftmost node, the rightmost sibling is in $LN(u)$. $RN(u)$ denotes the set of nodes that hang on the right of the $Path(u)$. If $Path(u)$ contains that rightmost node, the leftmost sibling is in $RN(u)$. $l(all)$ is a random label to be used in the special case where there are no revoked devices.

Cover-Finding Algorithm. The cover-finding algorithm takes the set of revoked devices R as the input and outputs the collection of disjoint subsets $\{S_1, \ldots, S_w\}$ that partition $N \backslash R$. Let $ST(R)$ be the tree that consists of leaf nodes that correspond to revoked devices and their ancestor nodes. ϕ denotes the empty set. The output is used for an input parameter of the encryption algorithm. Algorithm 1 shows the details of this algorithm.

The cover-finding algorithm firstly finds the root nodes of eliminating subtrees. If a leaf node in tree T has no sibling (case where $k = 1$) or only one sibling (case where $k = 2$), the algorithm selects these nodes as the root nodes; otherwise (case where k=3), it scans the higher layers. Then, the cover-finding algorithm finds the root

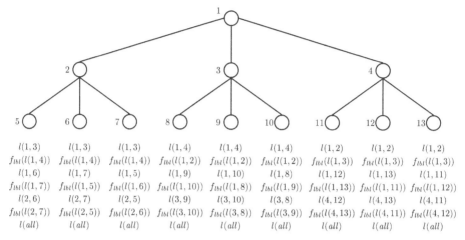

Fig. 2. Assignment of labels in *3SD* method

node of a covering tree. If the parent node of the root nodes of eliminating subtrees has sibling(s), the algorithm selects this node as the root node; otherwise it scans the higher layers. After finding the root node of the covering tree, the algorithm removes all the descendant nodes of it. This algorithm terminates when tree T contains only the root node.

Encryption Algorithm. The encryption algorithm is executed in the content distribution center on message M:

Step 1. Choose session key K and encrypt M with K.
Step 2. Partition all of the valid devices into disjoint subsets $S_1, \ldots, S_w$ using the cover-finding algorithm. Let $L_1, \ldots, L_w$ be the keys associated with these subsets. The key for subset D_{i,j_1} is given by $f_{kgf}(f_{lbl}(l(i, j_1)))$, and the key for subset $D_{i,j_1 \oplus j_2}$ where $right(j_1, j_2)$ is given by $f_{kgf}(l(i, j_1))$. $right(u, v)$ means that v is the immediate right sibling of u. If u is the rightmost node, v is the leftmost sibling. Any two sibling nodes in a ternary tree can be described in the form "$right(u, v)$".
Step 3. Encrypt session key K with keys $L_1, \ldots, L_w$ and send broadcast message

$$\langle [S_1, \ldots, S_w, E_{L_1}(K), \ldots, E_{L_w}(K)], F_K(M) \rangle$$

to all of the devices.

Decryption Algorithm. The decryption algorithm is executed in a device on a received broadcast message:

Step 1. Find subset S_t to which the device belongs. The result is $\perp$ when the device is revoked.
Step 2. Derive key L_t from a label or transformed using one-way functions.
Step 3. Decrypt $E_{L_t}(K)$ using L_t to obtain key K.
Step 4. Decrypt $F_K(M)$ using K to obtain and output message M.

Algorithm 1. Cover-finding algorithm

Require: Input Set of revoked devices R
Ensure: Partition $\{S_1, S_2, \ldots, S_w\}$ such that $\cup_{t=1}^{w} S_t = N \backslash R$
1:   $T \leftarrow ST(R)$
2:   $C \leftarrow \phi$
3: **repeat**
4:     Find leaf nodes $j_1, \ldots, j_k$ that are siblings each other
5:     **if** $k = 3$ **then**
6:       Remove nodes j_1, j_2 and j_3 from T
7:     **else** $\{k = 1 \text{ or } k = 2\}$
8:       $i \leftarrow$ the lowest ancestor node of j_1 (and j_2) that has sibling(s)
9:       **if** there is no such ancestor node **then**
10:         $i \leftarrow$ root
11:       **end if**
12:       **if** $k = 1$ **then**
13:         $C \leftarrow C \cup \{D_{i,j_1}\}$
14:       **else** $\{k = 2\}$
15:         $C \leftarrow C \cup \{D_{i,j_1 \oplus j_2}\}$
16:       **end if**
17:       Remove all of the descendant nodes of i from T
18:     **end if**
19: **until** $T = \{\text{root}\}$
20: **return** C

3.4 Tracing Scheme

We use a global tracing algorithm when we find a pirated decoder. This algorithm outputs the new partition where traitors are eliminated, and this partition is used for further message broadcasting.

Global Tracing Algorithm. The global tracing algorithm takes the current partition as the input and outputs a new partition where traitors are eliminated. We use the subset tracing algorithm to find the subset containing traitors, which is described in the next subsection. Algorithm 2 shows the details of the global tracing algorithm.

This algorithm is based on the divide-and-conquer strategy. Thus, a subset should be split into subsets of approximately the same size in Line 9 in order to improve the efficiency. Figure 3 shows the splitting method for a subset. We consider the following three cases:

i) The root node of the subtree and the root node of an eliminating subtree are adjacent.
ii) The root node of the subtree and the root nodes of two eliminating subtrees are adjacent.
iii) The root node of the subtree and the root node(s) of the eliminating subtree(s) are non-adjacent.

Subset Tracing Algorithm. The subset tracing algorithm takes a partition as the input and outputs a subset containing traitors. The algorithm tests whether the pirated decoder

---

Algorithm 2. Global tracing algorithm

Require: Current partition $\{S_1, S_2, \ldots, S_w\}$
Ensure: New partition where traitors are eliminated
 1: $\mathcal{S} \leftarrow \{S_1, S_2, \ldots, S_w\}$
 2: **loop**
 3:     $S_j \leftarrow subset\ tracing\ algorithm(\mathcal{S})$
 4:     **if** $S_j = \bot$ **then**
 5:         **return** $\mathcal{S}$
 6:     **else if** S_j contains only one device **then**
 7:         $\mathcal{S} \leftarrow \mathcal{S} \backslash \{S_j\}$
 8:     **else**
 9:         Split S_j into two or three subsets: S_{j_1}, S_{j_2} (and S_{j_3} in some cases)
10:         $\mathcal{S} \leftarrow \mathcal{S} \backslash \{S_j\} \cup \{S_{j_1}, S_{j_2}(, S_{j_3})\}$
11:     **end if**
12: **end loop**

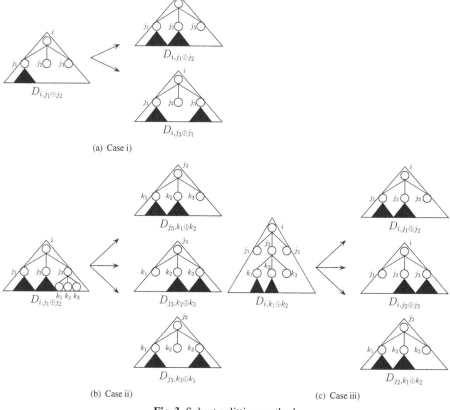

(a) Case i)

(b) Case ii)   (c) Case iii)

Fig. 3. Subset splitting method

Algorithm 3. Subset tracing algorithm

Require: Partition $\{S_1, S_2, \ldots, S_w\}$
Ensure: Subset containing traitors or $\perp$
  1: $\mathcal{S} \leftarrow \{S_1, S_2, \ldots, S_w\}$
  2: $p \leftarrow$ the probability that the pirated decoder can decrypt the message on $\mathcal{S}$
  3: **if** $p <$ threshold **then**
  4:     **return** $\perp$ {There is no subset containing traitors}
  5: **else**
  6:     find S_j such that $|p_j - p_{j-1}| > p/w$
  7:     **return** S_j
  8: **end if**

---

can decrypt the message on the partition with probability p greater than the threshold (i.e., 0.5). If the decoder cannot decrypt the message, the algorithm outputs $\perp$. Otherwise, the algorithm outputs subset S_j such that $|p_j - p_{j-1}| > p/w$ where w is the number of subsets in the partition. We define p_j by the probability that the box decodes the ciphertext

$$\langle [i_1, \ldots, i_w, E_{L_1}(R), \ldots, E_{L_j}(R), E_{L_{j+1}}(K), \ldots, E_{L_w}(K)], F_K(M)\rangle,$$

where R is a random number with the same length as key K. Note that $p_0 = p$, $p_m = 0$; thus, there exists j such that $|p_j - p_{j-1}| > p/w$. The value j can be found efficiently using the binary search algorithm. Algorithm 3 shows the details of the subset tracing algorithm.

4 Analysis

The efficiency and security of the *3SD* method is analyzed in this section.

4.1 Efficiency

We evaluate the *3SD* method from four perspectives:

- Communication cost, i.e., the length of the header that is attached to $F_K(M)$, which can be evaluated by the number of subsets.
- Storage size, which can be evaluated by the number of labels and transformed labels in each device.
- Computational cost, which is imposed on devices to derive the session key.
- Computational cost, which is imposed on the content distribution center to trace traitors.

The header length depends on the location to which revoked devices are assigned, while the storage size and the computational cost are not dependent on this location. Therefore, an analysis of worst and average case scenarios is presented.

Communication Cost. The header length is evaluated in worst and average case scenarios.

Worst Case Analysis. A trivial upper bound of the number of subsets is given by $n/3$. In this case, all of the devices are covered by ternary trees with height 1.

The upper bound in terms of r can be evaluated by the number of chains in the alternative description of the cover-finding algorithm in Naor et al.'s paper [3] (in Sect. 3.2). This alternative description is used to construct chains of nodes in $ST(R)$. In the SD method, each chain is in the form $[u_1, \ldots, u_l]$ and satisfies the following conditions:

- $u_1, \ldots, u_{l-1}$ have an outdegree of 1.
- u_l is either a leaf node or a node with an outdegree of 2.
- The parent of u_1 is either a node with an outdegree of 2 or the root node.

Subset $D_{i,j}$ corresponds to chain $[i, \ldots, j]$. In the *3SD* method, each chain is in the form $[u_1, \ldots, u_l^{(1)}]$ or $[u_1, \ldots, u_{l-1}, u_l^{(1)}; u_l^{(2)}]$ and satisfies the following conditions:

- $u_1, \ldots, u_{l-2}$ have an outdegree of 1 and u_{l-1} has an outdegree of 1 or 2.
- $u_l^{(1)}$ and $u_l^{(2)}$ are leaf nodes or nodes with an outdegree of 3.
- The parent of u_1 is a node with an outdegree of 2 or 3, or the parent is the root node.

Subset D_{i,j_1} corresponds to chain $[i, \ldots, j_1]$ and subset $D_{i,j_1 \oplus j_2}$ corresponds to chain $[i, \ldots, j_1; j_2]$. The head vertex of a chain must be the root node or a child of a node with an outdegree of greater than 1. Thus, a parent node of the head vertices is a branch node of $ST(R)$ (or the head vertex is a root). Let the outdegree of the branch node be b. Then, the number of branch nodes is given by $r/b + r/b^2 + \cdots + 1 = (r-1)/(b-1)$. The number of chains is given by $b(r-1)/(b-1) + 1$ and it takes the maximal value $2r - 1$ for $b = 2$. Thus, the upper bound in terms of r is $2r - 1$.

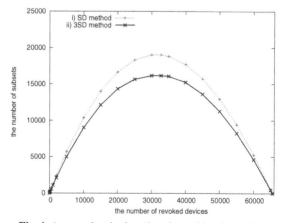

Fig. 4. Average header length estimated by simulation

Average Case Analysis. Naor et al. showed the upper bound of the average header length in the SD method is $2r \log 2$. They evaluated the expected number of subsets by counting the number of chains with an outdegree of 1 that are not *empty*; that is, contain multiple vertices. In the *3SD* method, a chain is *empty* if there is no downstream that has no devices. Thus, a chain is not *empty* if there is downstream without devices. The probability that a chain is not *empty* is calculated as

$$3 \left(\frac{2}{3} \right)^t - 3 \left(\frac{1}{3} \right)^t = \frac{2^t - 1}{3^{t-1}}.$$

The average header length in the *3SD* method is bounded by

$$\sum_{t=1}^{r} \frac{r}{t} \left(\frac{2^t - 1}{3^{t-1}} \right) \leq 3r \log 2.$$

The upper bound in the *3SD* method is larger than that in the SD method based on this evaluation.

Next, we evaluated the average number of subsets in the *3SD* method using a simulation. The total number of devices is 65,536 and the position of revoked devices is randomly determined. We compare the SD method and the *3SD* method. Figure 4 shows the comparison results. We refer the Okuaki et al.'s results [25] to estimate the average number of subsets in the SD method. The subsets number in the *3SD* method is lower than that in the SD method for a large number of revoked devices. The rate of reduction is up to 15.0 percent. Note that this condition is disadvantageous to the *3SD* method with regard to unused nodes.

Storage Size. Each device has $d_T - d$ labels of $l(u, *)$ and $d_T - d$ transformed labels of $f_{lbl}(l(u, *))$ for an ancestor node u at depth d, where $d_T \sim \log_3 n$ is the height of the tree. The label $l(all)$ is needed for the case where there is no revoked key. The number of labels and transformed labels stored in devices is given by;

$$\sum_{d=0}^{\log_3 n} 2(\log_3 n - d) + 1 \sim \frac{\log^2 n}{\log^2 3}.$$

Decryption Cost. We evaluate the computational cost imposed on devices to derive the session key. First, a device finds the subset to which the device belongs. The subset can be found in $O(\log \log n)$ using the techniques for finding table structures in the CS method. And then, the device derives the key. In this process, the device uses a one-way function up to $2 \log_3 n - 1$ times. The total computational cost is bounded by $O(\log \log n) + 2(\log_3 n - 1) = O(\log n)$.

Tracing Cost. We consider the bifurcation value that is the relative size of the largest split subset to the original subset in order to evaluate the efficiency of the global tracing algorithm. Let the number of splits required to identify one of the traitors be x. $N\alpha^x = 1$

holds for the bifurcation number α, and we have $x = -\log n / \log \alpha$. The computational overhead required to trace all of the t traitors is bounded by $-t \log n / \log \alpha$. We can see the relative size of the largest split subset is 1/2, 1/3, and 3/7 in case i), ii), and iii), respectively. Comparing these three cases, the bifurcation value is $1/2$, which o   urs in case i). Thus, our global tracing algorithm requires $t \log n / \log 2$ computational overhead in the worst case scenario.

Our analysis shows that *3SD* methods is an improvement of the CS and SD methods. We summarize the results in Table 1.

Table 1. Comparison between CS, SD, and *3SD* methods

Method	Header Len. (Max.)	Header Len. (U.B. of Ave.)	Stor. Size	Comp. Cost	Tracing Cost
CS (binary)	$O(r \log(n/r))$	N/A	$\log n / \log 2$	$O(\log n)$	$t \log n / \log 2$
CS (ternary)	$O(r \log(n/r))$	N/A	$\log n / \log 3$	$O(\log n)$	$t \log n / \log 3$
SD	$n/2, 2r - 1$	$2r \log 2$	$\log^2 n / 2 \log^2 2$	$O(\log n)$	$t \log n / \log(3/2)$
3SD	$n/3, 2r - 1$	$3r \log 2$	$\log^2 n / \log^2 3$	$O(\log n)$	$t \log n / \log 2$

4.2 Security

The *3SD* method is secure if F_K and E_L are secure encryption algorithms and the label assignment algorithm is coalition resistant. This security result follows by the same argument as Naor et al.'s theorem [3]. Note that the label assignment algorithm is different from that of the SD method. We discuss the coalition resistance of our label assignment algorithm.

First, we define the security conditions of the primitives as follows;

Definition 1. *For any probabilistic polynomial time adversary $\mathcal{A}$, for every message M, random message R_M with length $|M|$ and random session key $K \in \{0,1\}^\lambda$,*

$$|\Pr[\mathcal{A}(F_K(M)) = 1] - \Pr[\mathcal{A}(F_K(R_M)) = 1]| \leq \varepsilon;$$

then, F_K is a secure encryption algorithm with security parameter ε.

Definition 2. *For any probabilistic polynomial time adversary $\mathcal{A}$, for every message x, random message R_x with length $|K|$ and random key $L \in \{0,1\}^\lambda$,*

$$|\Pr[\mathcal{A}(E_L(x)) = 1] - \Pr[\mathcal{A}(E_L(R_x)) = 1]| \leq \varepsilon;$$

then, E_L is a secure encryption algorithm with security parameter ε.

Definition 3. *Assume an adversary $\mathcal{A}$ against the label assignment algorithm and oracle $\mathcal{O}$ for which behaviors are defined below;*

1. *$\mathcal{A}$ determines the set of all of the devices N and the set of revoked devices R and sends them to $\mathcal{O}$.*
2. *$\mathcal{O}$ assigns labels to devices and separates $N \backslash R$ into $S_1, S_2, \ldots, S_w$; then, $\mathcal{O}$ sends $(S_1, S_2, \ldots, S_w)$ to $\mathcal{A}$.*
3. *$\mathcal{A}$ selects t $(1 \leq t \leq w)$ and sends it to $\mathcal{O}$.*

4. $\mathcal{O}$ sends $Label(N\backslash S_t)$, which is the set of labels that all of the devices in $N\backslash S_t$ have, to $\mathcal{A}$.
5. $\mathcal{O}$ derives key L_t, selects random R_{L_t} with length $|L_t|$; then, $\mathcal{O}$ sets $K_0 = L_t$ and $K_1 = R_{L_t}$.
6. $\mathcal{O}$ flips a coin $b \in \{0, 1\}$ and sends K_b to $\mathcal{A}$.

For any probabilistic polynomial time adversary $\mathcal{A}$,

$$|\Pr[\mathcal{A}(L_t, Label(N\backslash S_t)) = 1] - \Pr[\mathcal{A}(R_{L_t}, Label(N\backslash S_t)) = 1]| \le \varepsilon;$$

then, the label assignment algorithm is coalition resistant with security parameter ε.

We now state and prove the main security theorem.

Theorem 1. F_K, E_L are secure encryption algorithms and the label assignment algorithm is coalition resistant with security parameters ε_1, ε_2 and ε_3, respectively. Then, for any probabilistic polynomial time adversary $\mathcal{A}$ with the header of a broadcast message

$$[S_1, \ldots, S_w, E_{L_1}(K), \ldots, E_{L_w}(K)],$$

for every encrypted message $F_K(M)$, encrypted random $F_K(R_M)$ with length M and random key K,

$$|\Pr[\mathcal{A}(F_K(M), [S_1, \ldots, S_w, E_{L_1}(K), \ldots, E_{L_w}(K)]) = 1]$$
$$- \Pr[\mathcal{A}(F_K(R_M), [S_1, \ldots, S_w, E_{L_1}(K), \ldots, E_{L_w}(K)]) = 1]| \le \varepsilon_1 + \frac{2nw}{3}(\varepsilon_2 + 4w\varepsilon_3).$$

Proof. This theorem follows from Theorem 11 of the full version of Naor et al.'s paper [3]. Note that the structure of a broadcast message of the *3SD* method is exactly the same as that of the SD method.

This security theorem assumes the security of the label assignment algorithm. The following lemma shows that our label assignment algorithm can protect against coalition attacks.

Lemma 1. *The label assignment algorithm of the proposed method is coalition resistant.*

Proof. We show that for each subset S_t, a coalition of devices that do not belong to this subset cannot obtain the corresponding key L_t. In the *3SD* method, a subset S_t may be D_{i,j_1} with the revoked subtree rooted at j_1 or $D_{i,j_1 \oplus j_2}$ with the two revoked subtrees rooted at j_1 and j_2.

Case 1: S_t is D_{i,j_1}. In this case, the corresponding key is $L_t = f_{kgf}(f_{lbl}(l(i, j_1)))$, which can be derived by using label $l(i, j_1)$ or transformed label $f_{lbl}(l(i, j_1))$. What needs to be determined is that none of the coalitions of devices in $N\backslash D_i$ and D_{j_1} can obtain the label $l(i, j_1)$ or transformed label $f_{lbl}(l(i, j_1))$.

No coalition of devices in $N\backslash D_i$ can obtain the key. The label $l(i, *)$ can be derived only from the initial label $l(i, i)$ that is generated randomly and independently of other initial labels. Thus, a coalition of these devices in $N \setminus D_i$ cannot obtain labels or transformed labels in the form of $l(i, *)$ and $f_{lbl}(l(i, *))$ since node i is not on the paths from the root node to the leaf nodes where these devices are assigned. Now, we only have to consider that no coalition of devices in D_{j_1} can obtain the key. No device in D_{j_1} has labels or transformed labels in the form of $l(i, j_1)$, $f_{lbl}(l(i, j_1))$, $l(i, u)$ and $f_{lbl}(l(i, u))$, where u is an ancestor node of j_1. Note that the coalition of all of the devices in D_{j_1} can collect all of the labels in the form of $l(i, v)$, where v is a descendant of j_1. However, this coalition cannot derive $l(i, j_1)$ from these labels since it is infeasible to find the inverse of the one-way functions.

Case 2: S_t is $D_{i, j_1 \oplus j_2}$. In this case, the corresponding key is $L_t = f_{kgf}(l(i, j_1))$, which can be derived by using label $l(i, j_1)$. What needs to be determined is that none of the coalitions of devices in $N \setminus D_i$, D_{j_1} and D_{j_2} can obtain label $l(i, j_1)$.

No coalition of devices in $N \setminus D_i$ can obtain the key since none of the coalitions has any labels or transformed labels in the form of $l(i, *)$ and $f_{lbl}(l(i, *))$. Now, we only have to consider that no coalition of devices in D_{j_1} and D_{j_2} can obtain the key. No device in D_{j_1} has labels or transformed labels in the form of $l(i, j_1)$, $l(i, u)$ and $f_{lbl}(l(i, u))$ where u is an ancestor node of j_1. Note that devices in D_{j_2} have the label $f_{lbl}(l(i, j_1))$; however, it is infeasible to derive $l(i, j_1)$ from $f_{lbl}(l(i, j_1))$. The coalition of all of the devices in D_{j_1} and D_{j_2} can collect all of the labels in the form of $l(i, v)$ where v is a descendant of j_1. However, this coalition cannot derive $l(i, j_1)$ from these labels since it is infeasible to find the inverse of the one-way functions.

5   Conclusions

In this paper, we proposed a coalition-resistant ternary subset difference (*3SD*) method and presented quantitative analysis of efficiency and security of the method. This method has the following advantages: 1) both the average header length and storage size imposed are lower than those in the SD method and CS method, 2) the tracing algorithm is more efficient than the SD method and it requires the same computational cost as the CS method.

References

1. Berkovits, S.: How to Broadcast a Secret. In: Davies, D.W. (ed.) EUROCRYPT 1991. LNCS, vol. 547, pp. 535–541. Springer, Heidelberg (1991)
2. Fiat, A., Naor, M.: Broadcast Encryption. In: Stinson, D.R. (ed.) CRYPTO 1993. LNCS, vol. 773, pp. 480–491. Springer, Heidelberg (1994)
3. Naor, D., Naor, M., Lotspiech, J.: Revocation and Tracing Schemes for Stateless Receivers. In: Kilian, J. (ed.) CRYPTO 2001. LNCS, vol. 2139, pp. 41–62. Springer, Heidelberg (2001), eprint.iacr.org/2001/059
4. Halevy, D., Shamir, A.: The LSD Broadcast Encryption Scheme. In: Yung, M. (ed.) CRYPTO 2002. LNCS, vol. 2442, pp. 47–161. Springer, Heidelberg (2002)

5. Goodrich, M.T., Sun, J.Z., Tamassia, R.: Efficient Tree-Based Revocation in Groups of Low-State Devices. In: Franklin, M. (ed.) CRYPTO 2004. LNCS, vol. 3152, pp. 511–527. Springer, Heidelberg (2004)

6. Jho, N.S., Hwang, J.Y., Cheon, J.H., Kim, M.H., Lee, D.H., Yoo, E.S.: One-Way Chain Based Broadcast Encryption Schemes. In: Cramer, R. (ed.) EUROCRYPT 2005. LNCS, vol. 3494, pp. 559–574. Springer, Heidelberg (2005)

7. Hwang, J.Y., Lee, D.H., Lim, J.: Generic Transformation for Scalable Broadcast Encryption Schemes. In: Shoup, V. (ed.) CRYPTO 2005. LNCS, vol. 3621, pp. 276–292. Springer, Heidelberg (2005)

8. Attrapadung, N., Imai, H.: Practical broadcast encryption from graph-theoretic techniques and subset-incremental-chain structure. IEICE Transaction on Fundamental of Electronics, Communications and Computer Sciences, Special Section on Cryptography and Information Security E90-A, 187–203 (2007)

9. Asano, T.: A Revocation Scheme with Minimal Storage at Receivers. In: Zheng, Y. (ed.) ASIACRYPT 2002. LNCS, vol. 2501, pp. 433–450. Springer, Heidelberg (2002)

10. Attrapadung, N., Kobara, K., Imai, H.: Sequential Key Derivation Patterns for Broadcast Encryption and Key Predistribution Schemes. In: Laih, C.-S. (ed.) ASIACRYPT 2003. LNCS, vol. 2894, pp. 374–391. Springer, Heidelberg (2003)

11. Gentry, C., Ramzan, Z.: RSA Accumulator Based Broadcast Encryption. In: Zhang, K., Zheng, Y. (eds.) ISC 2004. LNCS, vol. 3225, pp. 73–86. Springer, Heidelberg (2004)

12. Boneh, D., Gentry, C., Waters, B.: Collusion Resistant Broadcast Encryption with Short Ciphertexts and Private Keys. In: Shoup, V. (ed.) CRYPTO 2005. LNCS, vol. 3621, pp. 258–275. Springer, Heidelberg (2005)

13. Wang, W., Ma, J., Moon, S.: Ternary Tree Based Group Key Management in Dynamic Peer Networks. In: Wang, Y., Cheung, Y.-M., Liu, H. (eds.) CIS 2006. LNCS (LNAI), vol. 4456, pp. 513–522. Springer, Heidelberg (2007)

14. Graham, R.L., Li, M., Yao, F.F.: Optimal tree structures for group key management with batch updates. SIAM J. on Discrete Mathematics 21, 532–547 (2007)

15. Tripathi, S., Biswas, G.P.: Design of efficient ternary-tree based group key agreement protocol for dynamic groups. In: Proc. of First International Conference on Communication Systems and Networks, COMSNET 2009 (2009)

16. Fukushima, K., Kiyomoto, S., Tanaka, T., Sakurai, K.: Ternary Subset Difference Method and Its Quantitative Analysis. In: Chung, K.-I., Sohn, K., Yung, M. (eds.) WISA 2008. LNCS, vol. 5379, pp. 225–239. Springer, Heidelberg (2009)

17. Fukushima, K., Kiyomoto, S., Miyake, Y., Sakurai, K.: Towards optimal revocation and tracing schemes — the power of the ternary tree —. In: Proc. of International Conference on Security and Cryptography (SECRYPT 2011), pp. 37–49 (2011)

18. Chor, B., Fiat, A., Naor, M.: Tracing Traitors. In: Desmedt, Y.G. (ed.) CRYPTO 1994. LNCS, vol. 839, pp. 257–270. Springer, Heidelberg (1994)

19. Kurosawa, K., Desmedt, Y.: Optimum Traitor Tracing and Asymmetric Schemes. In: Nyberg, K. (ed.) EUROCRYPT 1998. LNCS, vol. 1403, pp. 145–157. Springer, Heidelberg (1998)

20. Boneh, D., Franklin, M.: An Efficient Public Key Traitor Scheme (Extended Abstract). In: Wiener, M. (ed.) CRYPTO 1999. LNCS, vol. 1666, pp. 338–353. Springer, Heidelberg (1999)

21. Kurosawa, K., Yoshida, T.: Linear Code Implies Public-Key Traitor Tracing. In: Naccache, D., Paillier, P. (eds.) PKC 2002. LNCS, vol. 2274, pp. 172–187. Springer, Heidelberg (2002)

22. Chabanne, H., Phan, D.H., Pointcheval, D.: Public Traceability in Traitor Tracing Schemes. In: Cramer, R. (ed.) EUROCRYPT 2005. LNCS, vol. 3494, pp. 542–558. Springer, Heidelberg (2005)

23. Boneh, D., Sahai, A., Waters, B.: Fully Collusion Resistant Traitor Tracing with Short Ciphertexts and Private Keys. In: Vaudenay, S. (ed.) EUROCRYPT 2006. LNCS, vol. 4004, pp. 573–592. Springer, Heidelberg (2006)
24. Shin, S., Kobara, K., Imai, H.: A secure network storage system with information privacy. In: Proc. of Western European Workshop on Research in Cryptology (WEWoRC 2005). LNI, vol. P-74, pp. 22–31 (2005)
25. Okuaki, S., Kunihiro, N., Ohta, K.: Estimation of a message length for subset difference method. In: Proc. of Symposium on Cryptography and Information Security (SCIS 2008), vol. 2E1-2 (2008) (in Japanese)

Accelerating Reduction for Enabling Fast Multiplication over Large Binary Fields

Saptarsi Das[1], Ranjani Narayan[2], and Soumitra Kumar Nandy[1]

[1] Indian Institute of Science, Bangalore, India
[2] Morphing Machines Pvt. Ltd, Bangalore, India
sdas@cadl.iisc.ernet.in, nandy@serc.iisc.ernet.in,
ranjani.narayan@morphingmachines.com

Abstract. In this paper we present a hardware-software hybrid technique for modular multiplication over large binary fields. The technique involves application of Karatsuba-Ofman algorithm for polynomial multiplication and a novel technique for reduction. The proposed reduction technique is based on the popular repeated multiplication technique and Barrett reduction. We propose a new design of a parallel polynomial multiplier that serves as a hardware accelerator for large field multiplications. We show that the proposed reduction technique, accelerated using the modified polynomial multiplier, achieves significantly higher performance compared to a purely software technique and other hybrid techniques. We also show that the hybrid accelerated approach to modular field multiplication is significantly faster than the Montgomery algorithm based integrated multiplication approach.

Keywords: Elliptic curve cryptography, Binary fields, Reduction, Polynomial multiplication.

1 Introduction

Proliferation of various kinds of threats has lead to an increased interest in cryptographic solutions for communication equipments. Thus strong cryptography has emerged as an indispensable part of different communication protocols. One of the strongest deterrents against such threats is the class of Elliptic curve cryptography (ECC) algorithms [1,2]. In order to cope with increasing threat levels, the key-length applied to these algorithms is typically very high. In terms of implementation, longer key-length implies operating over finite fields of large order. The two fundamental operations involved in finite field arithmetic are addition and multiplication. Binary fields (finite fields of the form $GF(2^m)$) are especially popular due to the ease of implementation of addition and subtraction (which are equivalent to one another) over them. However, multiplication is a relatively expensive operation. Unlike addition or subtraction, multiplication of two polynomials from a finite field may produce a polynomial whose degree exceeds the order of the finite field. In order to translate such a result to an equivalent canonical form within the order of the finite field, a reduction operation is performed.

ECC algorithms involve several such multiplications. The multiplication operation over large binary fields when implemented in software involves several shift and XOR

M.S. Obaidat, J.L. Sevillano, and J. Filipe (Eds.): ICETE 2011, CCIS 314, pp. 249–263, 2012.

operations. Systems requiring high-performance solutions such as servers, need hardware acceleration since they execute these tasks repeatedly. The task of designing a hardware accelerator for large field multiplication is particularly challenging for the following reasons. The hardware complexity of a polynomial multiplier grows quadratically with the bit-width of the operands. Thus the large order of the binary fields involved in ECC renders the approach of designing hardware polynomial multipliers infeasible beyond a certain limit. In the context of reduction operation, that follows the polynomial multiplication, the situation is even more critical. In case of reduction, both the large order of the binary field and the different possible irreducible polynomials that generate the binary fields influence the hardware complexity of accelerator units. Traditional hardware solutions for reduction [3,4] offer hardware acceleration for a specified set of irreducible polynomials. Supporting all possible irreducible polynomials even upto a specified field order will increase the complexity of the hardware immensely. In order to cope with this, it is necessary to develop hybrid solutions. In a hybrid solution the data-path of the core computations are realized as fast hardware kernels and the control-path to invoke and cascade the hardware kernels is realized using a thin layer of software. The choice of appropriate hardware kernels is extremely important, since the choice determines how flexible the complete solution becomes.

In this paper we investigate the case of large finite field multiplication realized as a hardware-software hybrid solution. In section 2 we discuss the nature of operations involved in finite field multiplication and show that a software-hardware hybrid solution is best suited for flexible multiplication over *any* binary field using *any* irreducible polynomial. We identify the possibility of using a hardware accelerator in the form of a polynomial multiplier for improving the performance of such a hybrid technique. In section 3 we present the design of the proposed polynomial multiplier and compute the improvement in performance achieved through its use. In section 4 we present the experimental results including synthesis results of the proposed polynomial multiplier. We also evaluate the improvement in performance of the proposed hybrid solution, with respect to other techniques presented in literature, over five NIST recommended elliptic curves.

2 Multiplication over Binary Fields: The Basic Operations Involved

In this section we present a brief mathematical background of multiplication operation over binary fields. This is followed by a discussion on two forms of reduction namely, repeated multiplication reduction and Barrett reduction. We show that these two techniques are equivalent. We also discuss about the polynomial multiplication operations involved in reduction.

2.1 Mathematical Background

A binary field is a vector space defined over $GF(2)$. Using polynomial basis, elements of a binary field are represented as polynomials over the base field $GF(2)$ i.e. the degree of the polynomials is determined by the order of the field and the coefficients belong to

$GF(2)$. Multiplication of such elements is governed by the addition and multiplication rules over $GF(2)$. For instance, let us consider two elements $A(x)$ and $B(x)$ belonging to the binary field $GF(2^m)$. These polynomials can be represented as a string of m symbols, where each symbol is 0 or 1. Therefore they are equivalent to two m-bit long binary strings. Equation 1 shows the two polynomials and their product $C(x)$.

$$
\begin{aligned}
A(x) &= \Sigma_{i=0}^{m-1} a_i x^i \\
B(x) &= \Sigma_{i=0}^{m-1} b_i x^i \\
C(x) &= A(x) \times B(x) \\
&= \Sigma_{i=0}^{2m-2} c_i x^i; where \ c_k = \Sigma_{i+j=k} a_i b_j
\end{aligned}
\tag{1}
$$

As is apparent from equation 1, the result $C(x)$ is almost twice as long as the input polynomials. $C(x)$ has an equivalent canonical representation among the set of polynomials of degree $m - 1$. Though, mathematically both the representations are equivalent, efficient utilization of computation resources necessitates conversion from the $2m - 1$-bit representation to the m-bit representation. This conversion often referred to as reduction operation is based on an irreducible polynomial that generates the binary field of interest. The reduction operation is described in equation 2, where $C'(x)$ is the canonical equivalent of the product polynomial $C(x)$ and $P(x)$ is the irreducible polynomial that generates the binary field.

$$
C'(x) \equiv C(x) \ mod \ P(x) \tag{2}
$$

From equation 2 it is clear that the reduced polynomial can be computed by traditional long division technique for polynomials. But this technique is iterative in nature and requires up to $m - 1$ iterations. As mentioned previously, an element of $GF(2^m)$ can be represented as an m-bit wide binary string. Let the word length of a certain machine be w. If $m \leqslant w$, then the number can be represented within a single word. In such a situation, it is feasible to develop a $m \times m$ hardware multiplier and reduction operation can be integrated with the multiplier itself. Such a multiplier requires three inputs to operate, two numbers to be multiplied and an irreducible polynomial for reduction of the product. Equation 3 describes multiplication of $A(x)$ and $B(x)$ belonging to $GF(2^m)$, which is generated by the irreducible polynomial $P(x)$.

$$
\begin{aligned}
C(x) &= (A(x) \times B(x)) \ mod \ P(x) \\
&= (A(x) \times (\Sigma_{i=0}^{m-1} b_i x^i)) \ mod \ P(x) \\
&= \Sigma_{i=0}^{m-1} b_i (A(x) x^i \ mod \ P(x))
\end{aligned}
\tag{3}
$$

Equation 3 describes the operation of a traditional shift-and-add multiplier. Note that, the shifted multiplicands of the form $A(x)x^i$ are reduced at each stage. So the $m - 1$ iterations of the modulo operation are embedded in each stage of the multiplier. Several efficient architectures of finite field multipliers are available in the literature [5], [6], [7].

On the other hand, if $m > w$, the element of the finite field can be represented using $\lceil \frac{m}{w} \rceil$ words. Therefore the direct multiplication-and-reduction approach cannot be applied. Under such circumstances, it becomes imperative to employ a software algorithm to break the m-bit operations into multiple w-bit operations. Two different approaches can be employed for performing such large field multiplications. The first approach is an integrated approach where reduction is performed along with multiplication. One such technique is presented in [8], that involves a binary field analogue of Montgomery multiplication [9].

The second approach is modular multiplication and reduction. In this approach of multiplication of two m-bit polynomials produces a $(2m - 1)$-bit result which is reduced separately. Algorithms such as the Karatsuba-Ofman algorithm (KOA) [10] can be applied iteratively to perform the polynomial multiplications. Extensive studies have been made to prove the superiority of KOA over traditional approaches to multiplication [11]. The $(2m - 1)$-bit result can be reduced by the Repeated Multiplication Reduction (RMR) technique [12,13] or the Barrett Reduction [14]. Note that, in this approach the first step of multiplication refers to polynomial multiplication, not field multiplication. In this paper we will concentrate on this approach of multiplication. In section 2.2 we establish an equivalence between RMR and Barrett reduction.

2.2   Barrett Reduction and the Repeated Multiplication Reduction

The RMR technique and Barrett Reduction [14] technique are the most suitable techniques for flexible reduction. A brief description of the RMR technique is reproduced here from [12]. Let $C_0(x)$ be the product of two polynomials of degree less than m. The degree of $C_0(x)$ is less than $2m - 1$ and it can be split into two parts as shown in equation 4.

$$C_0(x) = C_{h,0}(x)x^m + C_{l,0}(x) \qquad (4)$$

The RMR technique is an iterative technique and the subsequent polynomials are computed by the equation 5.

$$C_{j+1}(x) = C_{h,j}(x)(P(x) - x^m) + C_{l,j}(x)$$
$$until \; C_{h,j+1}(x) = 0 \Leftrightarrow deg(C_{j+1}(x)) \leqslant m - 1 \qquad (5)$$

The RMR technique requires m iterations and each iteration involves multiplication of $C_{h,j}(x)$ with $P(x) - x^m$. This polynomial multiplication can be realized as a set of m left shift operations. However, the most commonly used irreducible polynomials are usually trinomials and pentanomials. This implies, each of the multiplication involves no more than five left shift operations. Moreover $deg(P(x) - x^m) < \frac{m}{2}$. For such classes of polynomials, the RMR technique converges after only two iterations [3]. In [15] the authors have presented an adaptation of the popular Barrett Reduction technique for binary fields.

We reproduce the adaptation of Barrett reduction from [15] to compare with the RMR technique for irreducible polynomials with the following property: $deg(P(x) - x^m) < \frac{m}{2}$. Let us consider the RMR technique first. Let $C_0(x)$ be the product of two polynomials that needs to be reduced. $P(x) = x^m + x^k + \cdots + x^p + 1$ be the irreducible polynomial. Note that, for the RMR technique to converge within two iterations, k should be less than $\frac{m}{2}$. Using equation 5 we reduce the polynomial $C_0(x)$ as shown in equation 6.

$$C_0(x) = C_{h,0}(x)x^m + C_{l,0}(x)$$
$$C_1(x) = C_{h,0}(x)(P(x) - x^m) + C_{l,0}(x)$$
$$= C_{h,1}(x)x^m + C_{l,1}(x)$$
$$where\ C_{h,1}(x) = C_{h,0}(x)(P(x) - x^m)div x^m$$
$$and\ C_{l,1}(x) = C_{h,0}(x)(P(x) - x^m)mod x^m$$
$$+ C_{l,0}(x)$$
$$C_2(x) = C_{h,1}(x)(P(x) - x^m) + C_{l,1}(x)$$

$$(6)$$

Clearly, $deg(C_{h,1}(x)) \leqslant k$ and therefore $deg(C_2(x)) < m$. Now, let us consider the Barrett Reduction technique for the same irreducible polynomial. Barrett Reduction involves computation of three quotients $Q_1(x)$, $Q_2(x)$ and $Q_3(x)$ along with two remainders $R_1(x)$ and $R_2(x)$ as shown in equation 7. The final result is given by the remainder polynomial $R(x)$.

$$Q_1(x) = C_0(x)\ div\ x^m$$
$$= C_{h,0}(x)$$
$$Q_2(x) = Q_1(x)P(x)$$
$$Q_3(x) = Q_2(x)\ div\ x^m$$
$$= C_{h,0}(x)(x^m + x^k + \cdots + x^p + 1)\ div\ x^m$$
$$= C_{h,0}(x) + C_{h,1}(x)$$
$$R_1(x) = C_0(x)\ mod\ x^m$$
$$= C_{l,0}(x)$$
$$R_2(x) = Q_3(x)P(x)\ mod\ x^m$$
$$= Q_3(x)(x^k + \cdots + x^p + 1)\ mod\ x^m$$
$$= C_{h,0}(x)(x^k + \cdots + x^p + 1)mod x^m$$
$$+ C_{h,1}(x)(x^k + \cdots + x^p + 1)mod x^m$$
$$R(x) = R_1(x) + R_2(x)$$
$$= C_{h,1}(x)(P(x) - x^m) + C_{l,1}(x)$$

$$(7)$$

From equations 6 and 7 it is evident that both the techniques are equivalent and both of them require multiplication of m-bit polynomials. Note that, the modulo and division operations in the two techniques translate to partitioning of the polynomials into lower and higher halves and therefore do not require any arithmetic operation. In section 2.3 we present a technique for performing the aforementioned multiplications in order to achieve arbitrary flexibility in reduction.

2.3 Multiplication Operations in Reduction

From equations 6 and 7 we observe that multiplications of the form $C(x)(x^k + \cdots + x^p + 1)$ form the core of the computations. Therefore it is necessary to accelerate these multiplications in order to perform fast reduction. It should also be noted that the only other operations involved in reduction are addition over $GF(2^m)$. Since addition does not require carry propagation, addition of two m-bit polynomials which span more than one word in a w-bit architecture can be realized as $\lceil \frac{m}{w} \rceil$ w-bit XOR operations. Multiplication on the other hand requires multi-word shift and accumulation of results. Consider the two polynomials $C(x)$ and $P'(x)$ of degree m and k respectively. These polynomials can be represented in a w-bit architecture as a collection of m_c and m_p w-bit words respectively. Equation 8 shows the representation.

$$C(x) = \Sigma_{i=0}^{m_c-1} C_i(x) x^{iw} \ where \ m_c = \left\lceil \frac{m}{w} \right\rceil$$

$$P'(x) = \Sigma_{j=0}^{m_p-1} P'_j(x) x^{jw} \ where \ m_p = \left\lceil \frac{k}{w} \right\rceil \tag{8}$$

$C_i(x) x^{iw}$ and $P_j(x) x^{jw}$ denote the i-th and j-th words of the polynomials $C(x)$ and $P'(x)$ respectively. The product of these two polynomials can be computed as follows:

$$\begin{aligned} C'(x) &= C(x)P'(x) \\ &= \Sigma_{j=0}^{m_p-1} C(x) P'_j(x) x^{jw} \\ &= \Sigma_{j=0}^{m_p-1} (\Sigma_{i=0}^{m_c-1} C_i(x) x^{iw} P'_j(x) x^{jw}) \end{aligned} \tag{9}$$

A closer look at equation 9 reveals that computation of $C_i(x)P'_j(x)$ involves computations of the form $C_i(x)x^r$. Each of the individual words like $C'_{i,j}(x)$ (refer to figure 1) in the product of the entire polynomial $C(x)$ and x^r can be computed as follows:

$$C'_{i,j} = (C_i \ll r \mid C_{i-1} \gg (w-r)) \tag{10}$$

The individual words like $C'_{i,j}(x)$ in the product of $C(x)$ and $P'_j(x)$ can be expressed as given by equation 11.

$$C'_{i,j} = \oplus_{r=0}^{w-1} (C_i \ll r \mid C_{i-1} \gg (w-r)) p'_{j,r} \tag{11}$$

Note that, $p'_{j,r} x^r$ denotes the r-th term in the j-th word of the polynomial $P'(x)$ in equation 11. The operations of equation 11 can be repeated for each of the words in $P'(x)$ to compute the final result. Note that the product of $C(x)$ and each of the words in $P'(x)$ is $m_c + 1$ word wide. Henceforward we will refer to products of $C(x)$ with the individual words of $P'(x)$ as "partial products". It should be noted that these $m_c + 1$ word wide partial products need to be aligned to proper word boundaries before they can be added together to produce the final result.

3   A Modified Polynomial Multiplier as a Hardware Accelerator for Reduction

It is clear from the discussion in section 2.3 that the performance of polynomial multiplication kernel critically influences the performance of the entire reduction operation.

Therefore it is obvious that polynomial multiplication kernel is the candidate for acceleration. The simplest way of accelerating a $w \times w$ polynomial multiplication is to introduce a w-bit polynomial multiplier that produces $2w$-bit results. Therefore each word in the input polynomial $C(x)$ produces a pair of words and these pairs need to be added (i.e. XORed) with proper alignment to compute a partial product.

In this section we propose a technique for combining the addition operations with the polynomial multiplications. Instead of considering one word of the polynomial $C(x)$ we focus on one word of the partial product (i.e. $C'_{i,j}(x)$). It is evident from equation 11 that to produce $C'_{i,j}(x)$ two words from the polynomial $C(x)$ and one word from $P'(x)$ are necessary. Thus the intended operation can be described as a $2w \times w$ polynomial multiplication that produces a w-bit result. We design such a $2w \times w$ multiplier and use this in place of a $w \times w$ multiplier. Further, such a multiplier must be capable of operating as a $w \times w$ multiplier, in addition to the $2w \times w$ multiplier mode. We chose the simple parallel multiplier as the base architecture[1]. Let $C_i(x) = \sum_{r=0}^{w-1} c_{i,r} x^r$ and $P'_j(x) = \sum_{r=0}^{w-1} p'_{j,r} x^r$ be the w-bit polynomials that are to be multiplied and $C'_{i,j}(x)$ be the product. The multiplication operation is described in equation 12.

$$C'_{i,j}(x) = \sum_{r=0}^{w-1} c_{i,r} x^r \times \sum_{r=0}^{w-1} p'_{j,r} x^r$$
$$= \sum_{r=0}^{w-1} c'_{i,j,r} x^r + \sum_{r=w}^{2w-2} c'_{i,j,r} x^r \qquad (12)$$
$$where\ c'_{i,j,r} = \sum_{k=0}^{r} c_{i,k} p'_{j,r-k}\ when\ r < w$$
$$= \sum_{k=r-w+1}^{w-1} c_{i,k} p'_{j,r-k}\ when\ r \geq w$$

The $w \times w$ multiplier requires w^2 two-input AND gates and $(w-1)^2$ two input XOR gates. Let t_{AND} and t_{XOR} be the respective gate delays of two-input AND and XOR gates. The critical path gate delay of this multiplier is given by $t_{AND} + \lceil \log_2 w \rceil t_{XOR}$.

$2w \times w$ multiplication is enabled by introducing some additional hardware. As mentioned previously, the modified polynomial multiplier will consume three w-bit inputs. The additional input is the polynomial $C_{i-1}(x) = \sum_{r=0}^{w-1} c_{i-1,r} x^r$. The operation of this multiplier is described in equation 13.

$$c'_{i,j,r} = \sum_{k=0}^{r} c_{i,k} p'_{j,r-k} + \sum_{k=r+1}^{w-1} c_{i-1,k} p'_{j,w-j+r}\ when\ r < w$$
$$= \sum_{k=r-w+1}^{w-1} c_{i,k} p'_{j,r-k}\ when\ r \geq w \qquad (13)$$

We integrated the additional functionality of $2w \times w$ multiplication into the parallel polynomial multiplier by introducing a one-bit control signal. This signal is ANDed with the third operand i.e $C_{i-1}(x)$. When operating in $w \times w$ mode, the mode-select signal is defined as low and the result is product of the two polynomials $C_i(x)$ and $P'_j(x)$. When operating in $2w \times w$ mode, the mode select signal is high and the result is produced in accordance to equation 13. The increase in hardware complexity is $\frac{w(w+1)}{2}$ two input AND gates and $\frac{w(w-1)}{2}$ two input XOR gates. The critical path gate delay is given by $2t_{AND} + \lceil \log_2 w \rceil t_{XOR}$. It can be observed that the critical path of the $2w \times w$

---

[1] Note that, this choice was primarily driven by the necessity of high performance. In principle it is possible to choose a serial polynomial multiplier or a shift-and-add multiplier as the base architecture as well.

multiplier has increased by $t_A ND$ w.r.t the $w \times w$ multiplier. This increase is due to introduction of the additional AND gates for mode selection.

3.1 Performance of the Accelerated Reduction Technique

In this section we compute the improvement in performance of reduction with the modified $2w \times w$ polynomial multiplier as a hardware accelerator. We also show that this technique is arbitrarily flexible in terms of field order and choice of irreducible polynomial. We proceed by first considering the case of multiplication of the $C(x)$ polynomial (all words) with one word of $P'(x)$. This is followed by the analysis of multiplication of $C(x)$ with all words of $P'(x)$.

Multiplying $C(x)$ with One Word of $P'(x)$. From equation 10 it is evident that each m_c-word shift operation corresponding to a single term in the polynomial $P'(x)$ translates to $2m_c$ shift operations and $m_c - 1$ concatenation operations. Note that the concatenations can be conveniently expressed as either bitwise OR operations or bitwise XOR operations. Therefore the total number of logical operations necessary to produce the result of the multi-word multiplication as described in equation 11 is determined by the number of terms (other than 1) present in the word of the irreducible polynomial $P'_j(x)$. Assuming there are p terms present in $P'_j(x)$, the number of logical shifts is $2m_c p$ and the number of concatenation operations is $(m_c - 1)p$. Note that these operations are required to produce the shifted polynomials of the form $C(x)x^r$ for different values of $r < w$. In order to accumulate these shifted polynomials of the form $C(x)x^r$ it is necessary to perform at most $p' - 1$ bitwise XOR operation for each word of the shifted polynomials where p' is total the number of terms present in $P'_j(x)$ (including a 1 if any). Since the shifted polynomials span across $(m_c + 1)$ words, the total number of XORs necessary is $(m_c + 1)(p' - 1)$ to accumulate the shifted polynomials. Thus the total number of basic logic operations necessary to compute $C(x)x^r$ is $2m_c p$ shift operations and $(m_c - 1)p + (m_c + 1)(p' - 1)$ bitwise XORs. Using a modified polynomial multiplier to produce the partial product requires m_c multiplications and $m_c - 1$ XOR operations. Using the proposed multiplier for this operation requires $m_c + 1$ two-word multiplications i.e one extra multiplication for $m_c - 1$ XOR operations. Thus we have reduced the total number of arithmetic and bitwise operations by approximately $4p$ times, when compared to a purely software realization.

Multiplying $C(x)$ with Entire $P'(x)$. So far we have considered multiplication of the polynomial $C(x)$ with one word of the irreducible polynomial $P'(x)$. With the analysis of the previous paragraph as the basis let us compute the number of operations involved in realizing the entire multiplication operation described in equation 9. The number of shift operations involved is determined by the number of terms with *distinct* indices present in the polynomial $P'(x)$. In a w-bit architecture $C(x)x^{tw+r}$ is computed by simply appending t words filled with zeros to the right of $C(x)x^r$. Therefore the terms of $P'(x)$ with indices $tw + r$ are equivalent to one another. Assuming that there are p terms with distinct indices present in the irreducible polynomial, the total number of shift operations necessary is given by $2m_c p$. The number of concatenation operations is $(m_c - 1)p$. However, the total number of XOR operations required for accumulation of these shifted polynomials is determined by the number of terms (with distinct and equivalent indices) present in $P'(x)$. In order to calculate the total number XOR operations for accumulation it is necessary to examine the candidates for accumulation. Let us denote the number of terms present in $P'_j(x)$ by p_j. Therefore the accumulation of the shifted polynomials of the form $C(x)x^r$, produced by these p_j terms require $(p_j - 1)(m_c + 1)$ XOR operations. It should be noted that if $p_j = 0$ for any particular word $P'_j(x)$, no XOR operation is necessary. For simplicity let us assume $p_j > 0$ for all j. The number of XOR operations required to add results produced by different words of the polynomial $P'(x)$ remains unaltered irrespective of whether the hardware multiplier is used or not and is given by $(m_c+1)(m_p-1)$. Total number of basic arithmetic-logic instructions to produce all the polynomials of the form $C(x)P'_j(x)$ is shown in equation 14

$$\#SHIFT = 2m_c p$$
$$\#XOR = (m_c - 1)p + \Sigma_{j=0}^{m_p-1}(m_c + 1)(p_j - 1) + (m_c + 1)(m_p - 1)$$

$$(14)$$

Using the proposed multiplier reduces the number of operation required to perform the same set of operations. Note that, an intelligent sequencing of multiplication operations is necessary to minimize the number of multiplications. Sequencing of multiplication operation can be done by examining the irreducible polynomial. A set of $m_c + 1$ multiplications are necessary to produce a term like $C(x)P'_j(x)$. However, it should be noted that this set of multiplications need to be performed for for each non-zero word of the polynomial $P'(x)$ (in its binary representation). Therefore the maximum number of such multiplications necessary is $(m_c + 1)m_p$. Clearly $(m_c + 1)m_p < 2m_c p + (m_c - 1)p + \Sigma_{j=0}^{m_p-1}(m_c + 1)(p_j - 1)$. Let us take this comparison a little further by making a set of assumptions. Let us assume that on an average p' terms are present in each of the words that constitute the irreducible polynomial. In that case the total number of basic arithmetic-logic operations involved can be simplified to $2m_c p + (m_c + 1)(p' - 1)m_p$. Using a conventional $w \times w$ polynomial multiplier will require $m_c m_p$ multiplications and $(m_c - 1)m_p$ additional XOR operations. Using the proposed multiplier brings down the total number of operations to $(m_c + 1)m_p$. Assuming m_c is large enough so that $m_c \approx m_c + 1$ the reduction in operation count is $\frac{2p}{m_p} + (p' - 1)$ times when compared to a purely software realization and $2\times$ compared to hybrid realization using a conventional polynomial multiplier.

3.2   Karatsuba-Ofman Algorithm for Reduction

It should be noted that the KOA can be applied to perform the large polynomial multiplications needed in reduction. KOA improves performance of large polynomial multiplications by decreasing the number of word-level multiplications, in exchange for some additional XOR operations. [11] provides an extensive survey of complexity of generalised and recursive KOA over finite fields of various orders. We evaluate the performance impact of employing KOA for reduction which is presented in section 4.1. The sparse nature of the irreducible polynomials in NIST curves makes KOA an inefficient choice for reduction.

4   Results

In this section we evaluate the improvement in performance of binary field multiplications over the NIST curves. We primarily concentrate on the reduction operation, since elaborate studies have been made in the literature to establish KOA as the suitable choice for implementing polynomial multiplications. In order to have a unified hardware accelerator for both polynomial multiplication and reduction, basic $w \times w$ multiplication feature is retained in the proposed $2w \times w$ multiplier. Thus we present the hardware cost of the proposed accelerated reduction technique as the increase in hardware complexity with respect to a basic $w \times w$ multiplier. We also compare the performance of the accelerated modular approach towards binary field multiplication with an integrated approach involving Montgomery multiplication.

4.1   Performance Improvement of Reduction over NIST Curves

Each of the NIST curves (listed in table 1) will be referred to henceforth by the value of the exponent of the highest degree term present in the respective irreducible polynomial. For example, $x^{163} + x^7 + x^6 + x^3 + 1$ will be referred to as curve 163. We evaluate the improvement in performance of reduction operation over these curves using two instances of the proposed polynomial multiplier (32-bit and 64-bit). Note that each of the polynomials adhere to the restriction $deg(P(x) - x^m) < \frac{m}{2}$. Therefore only two iterations of polynomial multiplications are sufficient for completion of the reduction operation.

We evaluate the number of operations in each of these iterations. The numbers of operations for the various NIST curves are listed in table 1 (for $w = 32$) and table 2 (for $w = 64$). The columns *Software*, *School-book*, *KOA* and *Proposed* refer to Software based reduction implementation, School-book based reduction implementation, KOA based reduction implementation and the proposed accelerated reduction technique respectively.

Two important observations can be made from the tables 1 and 2. The first observation is regarding the software implementation of reduction. Note that, the number of operations involved in software implementations drop for the trinomials 233 and 409. This is attributed to small number of non-zero terms present in the polynomial $P'(x)$, which leads to smaller number of shift and XOR operations. The second observation is regarding the KOA implementation of reduction. KOA implementation of reduction involves relatively smaller number of $w \times w$ multiplications among the evaluated techniques. However, the number of XOR operations involved in KOA is significantly larger. This is due to the fact that KOA cannot effectively exploit the sparse nature of the polynomial $P'(x)$ to decrease the total number of XORs. For the pentanomials, the general trend indicates that the hybrid techniques are more efficient than the software implementation. A comparison of total number of operations involved in all four techniques over the NIST curves for different values of w is presented in figure 1.

In order to compare the performance of the various implementations, it is necessary to assign cycle counts to each of the operations. It is reasonable to assume Shift and XOR operations execute in 1 clock cycle each. In the case of multiplication, several

Table 1. Comparison of operation-count for reduction for various techniques at $w = 32$

Curve	Software		School-book		KOA		Proposed	
	Shift	XOR	Multiply	XOR	Multiply	XOR	Multiply	XOR
$x^{163} + x^7 + x^6 + x^3 + 1$ (163)	42	42	7	5	7	25	9	0
$x^{233} + x^{74} + 1$ (233)	22	22	22	31	17	60	26	13
$x^{283} + x^{12} + x^7 + x^5 + 1$ (283)	60	60	10	8	10	40	12	0
$x^{409} + x^{87} + 1$ (409)	32	32	32	46	29	153	36	18
$x^{571} + x^{10} + x^5 + x^2 + 1$ (571)	114	114	19	17	19	100	21	0

Table 2. Comparison of operation-count for reduction for various techniques at $w = 64$

Curve	Software		School-book		KOA		Proposed	
	Shift	XOR	Multiply	XOR	Multiply	XOR	Multiply	XOR
163	24	24	4	2	4	8	6	0
233	12	12	12	15	9	32	16	8
283	36	36	6	4	7	25	8	0
409	18	18	18	25	15	68	22	11
571	60	60	10	8	10	40	12	0

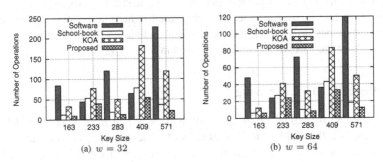

Fig. 1. Comparison of operation-count for various techniques of reduction over NIST curves

possible design points exist: single cycle multipliers to multi-cycle multipliers. In order to determine the number of clock cycles for a multiplication operation, we define $r = \frac{T_m}{T_a}$, where T_m and T_a represent the number cycles taken for multiplication and addition (i.e XOR) respectively. Since we assume $T_a = 1$, it follows that $r = T_m$. Let us consider two different technique involving (M_1, A_1) and (M_2, A_2) operations respectively. M_1 and M_2 represent the number of multiplication operations. A_1 and A_2 represent the number of addition (XOR) operations. To claim that, first technique is faster than the second technique it must be shown that $M_1 T_m + A_1 T_A < M_2 T_m + A_2 T_A$. This condition translates to $r < \frac{A_2 - A_1}{M_1 - M_2}$ or in other words, $T_m < \frac{A_2 - A_1}{M_1 - M_2}$. Therefore, the ratio r which is essentially the number of clock-cycles spent for one multiplication is a threshold beyond which one technique becomes more advantageous than the other. In order to compare the three hybrid techniques, i.e. the traditional school-book technique, KOA based technique and our proposed accelerated technique, we define two such quantities namely $r_{Prop-KOA}$ and $r_{Prop-School}$. For the accelerated technique

Table 3. Table giving the upper-bound on the value of T_m for various NIST curves

Curve	32		64	
	$r_{Prop-School}$	$r_{Prop-KOA}$	$r_{Prop-School}$	$r_{Prop-KOA}$
163	2.5	12.5	1	4
233	4.5	5	1.75	2.1
283	4	20	2	25
409	8	15	3.5	6.9
571	8.5	50	8	40
minimum	2.5	5	1	2.1

to outperform KOA and School-book over a given NIST curve, the condition given in equation 15 needs to be satisfied.

$$T_m < min\{r_{Prop-KOA}, r_{Prop-School}\} \qquad (15)$$

The respective upper-bounds of T_m for all the NIST curves are presented in table 3. As indicated by the data, for 32-bit word-length $T_m < 2.5$ and for 64-bit word-length $T_m < 1$. From this analysis it is clear that, if we synthesise the proposed polynomial multiplier to operate in single cycle, the accelerated reduction technique proposed in this paper will outperform both of the other hybrid techniques for both values of word-length. Details of the hardware synthesis is given in section 4.2.

4.2   Synthesis Results and Timing

We synthesized 32-bit and 64-bit instances of the $w \times w$ and $2w \times w$ polynomial multipliers (where w is the width of the machine word). These multipliers operate in single clock-cycle. The synthesis was performed using Synopsys Design Vision with Faraday 90nm high-speed low-V_t technology library. The area and maximum operating frequency of these multipliers are reported in table 4. As mentioned previously, the critical path delay of the $2w \times w$ multiplier increases by t_{AND} (i.e. the time taken for one 2-input AND operation). The increase has no impact on the maximum operating frequency. The area overhead of the proposed $2w \times w$ multiplier is about 47% for 32-bit and 53% for 64-bit.

From table 4, we observe that the multipliers are capable of producing the result in one clock-cycle while running at 909MHz, i.e. $T_m = 1$. Assuming availability of one multiplier and one bitwise XOR unit, the total number of clock cycles spent in computation is equal to the total number of operations. Therefore figure 1 can be interpreted as performance comparison between the various reduction techniques.

When $w = 32$, for the three pentanomials the accelerated technique is 33.3-71.4% faster than the school-book technique (which is the closest competitor). In this case the accelerated technique is upto $10.85\times$ faster than the software technique and upto $5.67\times$ faster than the KOA technique. For the two trinomials, as discussed previously, the pure software technique is the closest to the accelerated technique in performance. In this case the accelerated technique is 12.8-18.5% faster than pure software technique. For

Table 4. Synthesis Results of the Multipliers

$w = 32$			$w = 64$		
Type of Multiplier	Area in μm^2	Max. Operating Freq. in MHz	Type of Multiplier	Area in μm^2	Max. Operating Freq. in MHz
Polynomial Multiplier	13508	909	Polynomial Multiplier	50934	909
Modified Multiplier	19873	909	Modified Multiplier	78090	909

these trinomials, the accelerated technique is 35.9-44.4% faster than the school-book technique and upto 3.4× faster than the KOA technique.

When $w = 64$, for the pentanomial 163 the accelerated technique is as fast as the school-book technique. For the same curve, the accelerated technique is 8× faster than the software technique and 2× faster than the KOA technique. For the trinomial 233, the accelerated technique is as fast as the software technique. For the same curve, the accelerated technique is 12.5% faster than school-book technique and 70.8% faster than KOA. For the remaining pentanomials (283, 571) the accelerated technique is 25-50% faster than the school-book technique (which is the closest competitor). The accelerated technique is upto 10× faster than software technique and upto 4.2× faster than KOA for these set of curves. For the only remaining trinomial, the pure software technique is the closest to the accelerated technique. In this case the accelerated technique is 9.1% faster. The accelerated technique is about 30.3% faster than school-book and about 4.17× faster than KOA for this curve.

4.3 Performance Comparison of Modular and Integrated Approach for Field Multiplication

Unlike the modular approach for field multiplication discussed thus far, an integrated approach involves use of techniques such as Montgomery multiplication. In [8], the authors have presented a thorough analysis of Montgomery multiplication over binary fields. The Montgomery multiplication technique uses a polynomial multiplier as a hardware accelerator. Therefore the hardware requirement of the Montgomery algorithm based technique is similar to that of school-book technique or KOA based technique.

In our approach, we propose the use of KOA for polynomial multiplication and the accelerated technique for reduction. A comparison of number of operations for these two techniques over different NIST curves is presented in table 5 and figure 2. We achieve 3× better performance at $w = 32$-bit and upto 2.66× better performance at $w = 64$-bit in comparison to the Montgomery algorithm based approach. The poor performance of Montgomery algorithm over NIST curves is attributed to the extra number of polynomial multiplications and its inability in exploiting the sparse nature of the NIST polynomials.

Table 5. Comparison of operation-count for Montgomery Integrated multiplication and our technique over NIST curves

Curve	32				64			
	Montgomery		Proposed		Montgomery		Proposed	
	Multiply	XOR	Multiply	XOR	Multiply	XOR	Multiply	XOR
163	78	144	26	59	21	36	10	15
233	136	256	53	113	64	36	21	40
283	171	324	51	148	55	100	23	46
409	351	676	102	295	105	196	46	107
571	666	1296	138	512	171	324	47	139

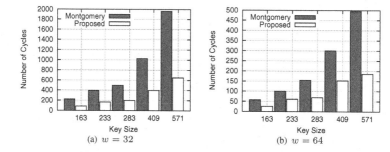

Fig. 2. Comparison of total operation-count for Montgomery Integrated multiplication and our technique over NIST curves

5   Conclusions

Efficient realization of multiplication over binary fields necessitates acceleration of polynomial multiplication and reduction. In this paper we proposed a hardware-software hybrid technique to accelerate both these components. The hardware accelerator used is a modified polynomial multiplier that can perform $2w \times w$ multiplication, where w is length of the machine-word. Synthesis results show that the proposed multiplier occupies about 47% more area when $w = 32$ and 53% more area when $w = 64$, compared to conventional polynomial multipliers of same word-length. Further, the proposed modification has no impact on the frequency of operation. Performance of the proposed accelerated technique for reduction was compared against a pure software approach and two other hybrid approaches, namely Karatsuba-Ofman algorithm based technique and the traditional school-book technique. Compared to the school-book technique, our accelerated technique was found to be upto 44.4% faster when $w = 32$-bit and upto 50% when $w = 64$-bit. Further, we compared performance of the proposed modular field multiplication with Montgomery algorithm based integrated multiplication. The proposed technique is upto $3\times$ faster at $w = 32$-bit and upto $2.66\times$ faster at $w = 64$-bit. The two primary factors contributing to the superior performance of the proposed technique are the use of accelerator for reduction as well as polynomial multiplication and exploitation of the sparse nature of NIST polynomials to reduce number of operations performed.

References

1. Koblitz, N.: Elliptic Curve Cryptosystems. Mathematics of Computation 48, 203–209 (1987)
2. Miller, V.S.: Use of Elliptic Curves in Cryptography. In: Williams, H.C. (ed.) CRYPTO 1985. LNCS, vol. 218, pp. 417–426. Springer, Heidelberg (1986)
3. Batina, L., Bruin-Muurling, G., Örs, S.: Flexible Hardware Design for RSA and Elliptic Curve Cryptosystems. In: Okamoto, T. (ed.) CT-RSA 2004. LNCS, vol. 2964, pp. 250–263. Springer, Heidelberg (2004)
4. Saqib, N.A., Rodriguez-Henriquez, F., Diaz-Pirez, A.: A Parallel Architecture for Fast Computation of Elliptic Curve Scalar Multiplication over $GF(2^m)$. In: International on Parallel and Distributed Processing Symposium, vol. 4, p. 144a (2004)
5. Hinkelmann, H., Zipf, P., Li, J., Liu, G., Glesner, M.: On the Design of Reconfigurable Multipliers for Integer and Galois Field Multiplication. Microprocessors and Microsystems - Embedded Hardware Design 33, 2–12 (2009)
6. Wu, H.: Bit-parallel Finite Field Multiplier and Squarer using Polynomial Basis. IEEE Transactions on Computers 51, 750–758 (2002)
7. Ahlquist, G., Nelson, B., Rice, M.: Optimal Finite Field Multipliers for FPGAs. In: Lysaght, P., Irvine, J., Hartenstein, R.W. (eds.) FPL 1999. LNCS, vol. 1673, pp. 51–61. Springer, Heidelberg (1999)
8. Koç, Ç.K., Acar, T.: Montgomery Multiplication in $GF(2^k)$. Designs, Codes and Cryptography 14, 57–69 (1998)
9. Montgomery, P.: Modular Multiplication Without Trial Division. Mathematics of Computation 44, 519–521 (1985)
10. Karatsuba, A., Ofman, Y.: Multiplication of Multidigit Numbers on Automata. Soviet Physics—Doklady 7, 595–596 (1963)
11. Weimerskirch, A., Paar, C.: Generalizations of the Karatsuba Algorithm for Efficient Implementations. IACR Cryptology ePrint Archive 2006, 224 (2006)
12. Eberle, H., Gura, N., Shantz, S.C., Gupta, V.: A Cryptographic Processor for Arbitrary Elliptic Curves over $GF(2^m)$. Technical report, Mountain View, CA, USA (2003)
13. Satoh, A., Takano, K.: A Scalable Dual-Field Elliptic Curve Cryptographic Processor. IEEE Transactions on Computers 52, 449–460 (2003)
14. Barrett, P.: Implementing the Rivest Shamir and Adleman Public Key Encryption Algorithm on a Standard Digital Signal Processor. In: Odlyzko, A.M. (ed.) CRYPTO 1986. LNCS, vol. 263, pp. 311–323. Springer, Heidelberg (1987)
15. Knežević, M., Sakiyama, K., Fan, J., Verbauwhede, I.: Modular Reduction in $GF(2^n)$ without Pre-computational Phase. In: von zur Gathen, J., Imaña, J.L., Koç, Ç.K. (eds.) WAIFI 2008. LNCS, vol. 5130, pp. 77–87. Springer, Heidelberg (2008)

A Related-Key Attack against Multiple Encryption Based on Fixed Points*

Aslı Bay, Atefeh Mashatan**, and Serge Vaudenay

EPFL, Switzerland
{asli.bay,atefeh.mashatan,serge.vaudenay}@epfl.ch

Abstract. In order to alleviate the burden of short keys, encrypting a multiple times has been proposed. In the multiple encryption mode, there may be encryptions under the same or different keys. There have been several attacks against this encryption mode. When triple encryption is based on two keys, for instance, Merkle and Hellman proposed a subtle meet-in-the-middle attack with a complexity similar to breaking a single encryption, requiring nearly all the codebook. In the case of triple encryption with three keys, Kelsey, Schneier, and Wagner proposed a related-key attack with complexity similar to breaking a single encryption.

In this paper, we propose a new related-key attack against triple encryption which compares to breaking single encryption in the two aforementioned cases. Based on finding fixed points in a decrypt-encrypt sequence, we propose a related-key attack against a two-key triple encryption. Our attack has exactly the same performance as a meet-in-the-middle on double encryption. When considering two keys, it is comparable to the Merkle-Hellman attack, except that uses related keys. And, when considering three keys, it has a higher complexity than the Kelsey-Schneier-Wagner attack, but has the advantage that it can live with known plaintexts.

1 Introduction

A classical security model for symmetric encryption is the key recovery under chosen plaintext or ciphertext attacks. Since ciphers are inevitably broken by generic attacks such as exhaustive search, we use these attacks as reference and hope that their complexity is the minimal cost for breaking the cipher. Indeed, a cipher is secure if there is no attack better than exhaustive search, i.e., if its complexity is lower than 2^ℓ, where ℓ is the key length.

In the 90's, Biham and Knudsen [4,3,10] proposed the notion of related-key attacks in which an adversary can impose to change the secret key following some chosen relation φ. Related-key attacks open a way to new generic attacks such as the ones by Biham [5]. Therefore, exhaustive search may no longer be the reference for assessing the security of a cipher.

---

* This is a full version of [15].

** This author was supported by the National Competence Center in Research on Mobile Information and Communication Systems (NCCR-MICS), a center of the SNF under grant number 5005-67322.

M.S. Obaidat, J.L. Sevillano, and J. Filipe (Eds.): ICETE 2011, CCIS 314, pp. 264–280, 2012.
© Springer-Verlag Berlin Heidelberg 2012

As an example of a related-key attack, Kelsey, Schneier, and Wagner [9] presented an attack against three-key triple encryption which shows that it is not more secure than single encryption.

Notations. In this paper, KP, BKP, CP, and CC denote known plaintexts, broadcast known plaintexts, chosen plaintexts, and chosen ciphertexts, respectively. In the BKP model, the adversary obtains a random plaintext and its encryption under different keys. In addition, RK denotes the related-key model where the adversary either knows or chooses the relation between the unknown keys. On the other hand, d_{KP}, d_{BKP}, and d_{CP}, d_{CC} denote respective data complexities of KP, BKP, CP, and CC attacks and C_K and C_K^{-1} denote block cipher encryption and decryption under K, respectively. Furthermore, $E(X)$ denotes expected value of a random variable X and $\#L$ denotes the cardinality of a set L.

Related Work on Triple-DES. As far as we know, the only related-key attacks against Triple-DES are the generic attack of Biham, the Kelsey-Schneier-Wagner attack, and an attack of Phan [5,9,12]. There are other attacks using no related keys such as attacks based on meet-in-the-middle by Merkle and Hellman, known plaintext variants by Van Oorschot and Wiener, and a nice optimization by Lucks [1,11,13,14]. We use the table of Phan given in Table 1 to compare these attacks with ours [12]. Note that the results are given in sightly different units, that is, our time complexities are measured in terms of triple encryption instead of single encryption; our memory complexities are measured in bits instead of 32-bit words; our number of keys include the target one and not only the related ones. The aforementioned attacks will be discussed in this paper.

Our Contribution. In this paper, we first formalize the various ways to compare the complexity of related-key attacks. Following a full-cost model, an attack is significant if $tm/p < 2^\ell$, where r is the number of related keys, t (resp. m) is the time (resp. memory) complexity, and p is the probability of success. In a more conservative approach, we shall compare $\max(t/p, m)$ with $2^{\ell/2}$. We can also consider comparison in a restricted attack model in order to limit some characteristics such as the number of related keys.

We then present a new attack on triple encryption which is based on the discovery of fixed points for the mapping

$$x \mapsto \mathsf{Enc}_K \circ \mathsf{Enc}_{\varphi(K)}^{-1},$$

for some relation φ. This discovery requires the entire codebook in a *Broadcast Known Plaintext (BKP)* attack for Enc_K and $\mathsf{Enc}_{\varphi(K)}$ which makes our data complexity high. Once we have a (good) fixed point, our attack becomes similar to a standard meet-in-the-middle attack. Hence, it has a pretty low complexity. Finally, we show that our attack has a comparable complexity to the best ones so far. In the two-key case, it becomes the best known-plaintext attack. In the sequel, we discuss the comparison of related-key attacks in different models.

2   Comparing Related-Key Attacks

Given a dedicated attack against a cipher, it is common to compare it with exhaustive search and declare the cipher broken if the attack is more efficient. However, it is unfair

Table 1. Summary of attacks against Triple-DES

| target | data | parameters | | | complexity | |
		memory	time	#keys	$C_{\text{conservative}}$	reference
Two-Key Triple-DES	2 (KP)	2^7	2^{112}	1	2^{112}	exhaustive search
	2^{56} (CP)	2^{62}	2^{56}	2^{56}	2^{62}	[5] (generic)
	2^{56} (KP)	2^{58}	2^{112}	1	2^{112}	[13,14]
	2^{33} (KP)	$2^{91.5}$	2^{86}	2	$2^{91.5}$	[12]
	2^{65} (KP)	2^{72}	2^{56}	2	2^{72}	this paper
	2^{65} (BKP)	2^{63}	2^{56}	2	2^{66}	this paper
	2^{64} (KP)	2^{64}	2^{56}	1	2^{64}	[1] variant
	2^{56} (CP)	2^{63}	2^{56}	1	2^{63}	[1]
Three-Key Triple-DES	3 (KP)	2^8	2^{168}	1	2^{168}	exhaustive search
	2^{84} (CP)	2^{92}	2^{84}	2^{84}	2^{92}	[5] (generic)
	2^{32} (KP)	2^{90}	2^{104}	1	2^{104}	[11]
	3 (CP)	2^{58}	2^{110}	1	2^{110}	[1]
	2^{33} (KP)	2^{35}	2^{86}	2	2^{86}	[12]
	2^{67} (KP)	2^{72}	2^{57}	6	2^{72}	this paper
	2^{67} (BKP)	2^{63}	2^{57}	6	2^{67}	this paper
	2 (BKP)	2^{58}	2^{54}	2	2^{58}	[9]

to do this, since the attack model may already have better generic attacks than exhaustive search. More expilicitly, we should consider other generic attacks in the attack model while comparing the efficiency of the given attack.

As an example, Biham's generic attack [5] applies standard time-memory tradeoffs in the related-key model. His attack consists of collecting $y_i = \text{Enc}_{K_i}(x)$ for a fixed plaintext x and r related keys K_i, $1 \leq i \leq r$. Hence, we use r chosen plaintexts. Then, it builds a dictionary (y_i, i) and runs a multi-target key recovery to find one key K such that $\text{Enc}_K(x)$ is in the dictionary. With t attempts, the probability of success is $p = 1 - (1 - r2^{-\ell})^t \approx 1 - e^{-rt2^{-\ell}}$. The dictionary has size $m = r(\ell + \log r)$ bits. For simplicity, we approximate $m \approx r$. In particular, for $t = r = 2^{\ell/2}$, we have $p \approx 1 - e^{-1} \approx 63\%$, so this is much cheaper than exhaustive search.

The complexity of a related-key attack can be characterized by a multi-dimensional vector consisting of

- the number of related keys r (the number of keys which are involved is r, i.e., $r = 1$ if the attack uses no related keys);
- the data complexity d (e.g., the number of chosen plaintexts), where we may distinguish known plaintexts (KP), broadcast known plaintexts (BKP), chosen plaintexts (CP), and chosen ciphertexts (CC) as they may be subject to different costs in the attack model;
- the time complexity of the adversary t, where we may distinguish the precomputation complexity and the online running time complexity;

- the memory complexity m, which we may further distinguish quick-access, or slow-access memory, read/write memory or read-only memory; and
- the probability of success p.

There are many other possible refinements. We can compare attacks by using the partial ordering p on vectors $(r, d, t, m, 1/p)$, i.e.,

$$(r, d, t, m, p) \leq_p (r', d', t', m', p')$$
$$\Updownarrow$$
$$r \leq r' \text{ and } d \leq d' \text{ and } t \leq t' \text{ and } m \leq m' \text{ and } p \geq p'.$$

When a category such as the data complexity d has a sub-characterization $(d_{KP}, d_{BKP}, d_{CP}, d_{CC})$, then $d \leq d'$ implies another partial ordering on these sub-characteristics.

We can say that an attack is *insignificant* if there is a generic attack with a lower complexity vector. Since it is not always possible to compare two multi-dimensional vectors, whether an attack is significant or not is not always clear. Therefore, it is quite common to extend the partial ordering $\leq_p$ using different models which are discussed below.

Conservative Model. Traditionally, t, m, and p are combined into a "complexity" which is arbitrarily measured by $\max(t/p, m)$. We could equivalently adopt $t/p + m$ since these operations yield the same orders of magnitude.

The idea behind this arbitrary notion is that we can normalize the success probability p by using $1/p$ sessions of the attack. So, t has a factor $1/p$ corresponding to $1/p$ different sessions. Clearly, the running time of every session adds up whereas their memory complexity does not. If we make no special treatment for r and d, we can just extend this simple notion by adding them in the time complexity t (since the adversary must at least read the received data). We can, thus, replace t by $\max(r, d, t)$. This leads us to

$$C_{\text{conservative}}(r, d, t, m, p) = \max\left(\frac{r}{p}, \frac{d}{p}, \frac{t}{p}, m\right).$$

For instance, $2^{\ell/2}$ is the complexity of the Biham attacks [5].[1]

In some cases, there may be a special treatment for r and d though, especially regarding the $1/p$ factor. Actually, the current $1/p$ factor corresponds to the worst case where iterating an attack requires new related keys. In many cases, related keys could just be reused, which means that the total number of related keys may be r instead of r/p. Therefore, we can keep this in mind that the $C_{\text{conservative}}$ formula may not be well adapted to attacks with a probability of success far from 1. We should rather normalize the attack using the most appropriate technique before applying the formula on the normalized attack.

This kind of rule of the thumb is rather convenient because two attacks can always be compared by $C_{\text{conservative}}$: let

$$(r, d, t, m, p) \leq_{\text{conservative}} (r', d', t', m', p')$$
$$\Updownarrow$$
$$C_{\text{conservative}}(r, d, t, m, p) \leq C_{\text{conservative}}(r', d', t', m', p').$$

---

[1] Strictly speaking, we shall have a $1/p$ factor corresponding to $p = 63\%$, but this would give the same order of magnitude and this simple formula aims at comparing orders of magnitude.

This defines a total ordering. An attack is said conservative-significant if it is better than generic ones following the conservative ordering. That is, an attack is conservative-significant if and only if

$$C_{\text{conservative}}(r, d, t, m, p) < 2^{\frac{\ell}{2}}.$$

Limited Related-key Models. Arguably, related keys (or even chosen plaintexts or ciphertexts) are harder to obtain, compared to the time spent in the attack. More explicitly, getting encryption or decryption of the data under different related keys that are chosen by the adversary requires much more work than doing computations in the attack. For instance, an attack with complexity $2^{3\ell/4}$, $r = 1$, and $d = 1$ is declared not significant with $\leq_{\text{conservative}}$ because of the Biham attack [5] with complexity $2^{\ell/2}$, which is a bit unfair. Therefore, we could either go back to some partial ordering or to some attack model restrictions. For example, a common model (when we do not care about related-key attacks) consists of limiting to $r = 1$. A natural model would consist of limiting $r \leq B_r$, for some bound B_r. Finally, we can compare an attack with the best generic one using not more related keys than the attack has. That is, we say that an attack is *conservative-significant in the RK-limited model*, if its conservative complexity is better than the one for all generic attacks using less number of related keys than the attack has. If (r, d, t, m, p) is the complexity vector of the attack, we shall compare $C_{\text{conservative}}(r, d, t, m, p)$ with the one of $(r', r', t', r', 1 - e^{-r't'2^{-\ell}})$ for all t' and $r' \leq r$. Clearly, the minimal complexity is reached for $r' = r$ and $t' = 2^\ell/r'$. So, the attack is conservative-significant in the RK-limited model if

$$C_{\text{conservative}}(r, d, t, m, p) < \frac{2^\ell}{r}.$$

Other Limited Models. We may also consider other limited models. For instance, we can restrict ourselves to attacks using known plaintexts only. All combinations of limitations can be imagined. The relevance of these limited models shall be driven by significance for applications.

Full-cost Model. Wiener [16] introduced the full cost expressed as $\mathcal{O}(t + tm/c + t\sqrt{c\rho^3})$, where c is the number of processors and ρ is the rate of access to the memory of all processors per time unit. (We assume here that parameters are normalized so that we can assume $p = 1$.) Using a single processor and $\rho = 1$, this simplifies to $\mathcal{O}(tm)$. Again, we replace t by $\max(r, d, t)$ to integrate r and d. Therefore, we define the full cost as

$$C_{\text{full}}(r, d, t, m, p) = \max(r, d, t)\frac{m}{p}, \tag{1}$$

and define

$$(r, d, t, m, p) \leq_{\text{full}} (r', d', t', m', p')$$
$$\Updownarrow$$
$$C_{\text{full}}(r, d, t, m, p) \leq C_{\text{full}}(r', d', t', m', p').$$

The total ordering which takes parallelism tricks into account is a bit more complicated. Without using any parallelism trick, Biham's generic attacks have $d = r$, $t = 2^\ell/r$, and

Table 2. Attacks on AES

target	parameters			complexity	significance		reference
	data	memory	time	#keys	$C_{\text{conservative}}$	conservative	RK-limited	
AES-128	1	1	2^{128}	1	2^{128}			exhaustive search
AES-192	1	1	2^{192}	1	2^{192}			exhaustive search
	4	4	2^{190}	4	2^{190}			[5]
	2^{96}	2^{96}	2^{96}	2^{96}	2^{96}			[5]
	2^{123}	2^{152}	2^{176}	4	2^{176}	no	yes	[6]
AES-256	1	1	2^{256}	1	2^{256}			exhaustive search
	4	4	2^{254}	4	2^{254}			[5]
	2^{35}	2^{35}	2^{221}	2^{35}	2^{221}			[5]
	2^{128}	2^{128}	2^{128}	2^{128}	2^{128}			[5]
	2^{131}	2^{65}	2^{131}	2^{35}	2^{131}	no	yes	[7]
	2^{100}	2^{77}	2^{100}	4	2^{100}	yes	yes	[6]

$m = r$. Hence, their full cost is $\max(r^2, 2^\ell)$. Again, this is relevant for $r \leq 2^{\ell/2}$ only and the full cost is 2^ℓ, no matter what the value of r is. In this case, exhaustive search with $r = 2^\ell$ has the same full cost. An attack is full-significant if and only if

$$C_{\text{full}}(r, d, t, m, p) < 2^\ell.$$

As a rule of thumb, we could adopt the simple criterion $tm/p < 2^\ell$.

Note that Equation (1) only gives an upper bound on the full cost which can be pessimistic. For instance, it was shown that meet-in-the-middle [8] with a key of size ℓ_k has a full cost of $2^{4\ell_k/3}$ and may also be reduced to $2^{6\ell_k/5}$ using parallelism [16]. So, the comparison based on full cost shall be done with great care.

As an application, we can look at recent attacks on AES working with $p = 1$. (See Table 2.) As we can see, the Biryukov-Khovratovich attack [6] on AES-192 is only conservative-significant in the RK-limited model, thanks to the low number of related keys, but it is not conservative-significant. The Biryukov-Khovratovich-Nikolić attack [7] on AES-256 is conservative-significant in the RK-limited model, thanks to the low number of related keys, but it is not conservative-significant. The Biryukov-Khovratovich attack [6] on AES-256 is significant for both criteria.

3   Semi-generic Related-Key Attacks against Triple-DES

We propose here a related-key attack against Triple-DES. For the three-key triple encryption case, this attack is semi-generic in the sense that it does not depend on DES, but only on the structure of triple encryption which is used in Triple-DES, that is, the encrypt-decrypt-encrypt structure. For the two-key case, it is generic since it also works for the encrypt-encrypt-encrypt structure. The three-key and the two-key triple encryptions defined by

$$\mathsf{Enc}_{K_1, K_2, K_3} = C_{K_1} \circ C_{K_2}^{-1} \circ C_{K_3}, \text{ and}$$
$$\mathsf{Enc}_{K_1, K_2} = C_{K_1} \circ C_{K_2}^{-1} \circ C_{K_1}.$$

We denote by ℓ_k the length of the K_i subkeys and by ℓ_m the block length. We also consider the two-key triple encryption with the encrypt-encrypt-encrypt structure, i.e., $\text{Enc}'_{K_1, K_2} = C_{K_1} \circ C_{K_2} \circ C_{K_1}$.

3.1 Preliminaries

We will give some necessary background regarding random permutations without providing their proofs due to the space limitation.

Definition 1. *Let π be a permutation over a finite set S. The k-cycles of π is $(c_1, c_2, \ldots, c_k)$ such that $\pi(c_i) = c_{i+1}$ for $i = 1, \ldots, k-1$ and $\pi(c_k) = c_1$.*

For example, when $k = 1$, it is a 1-cycle, i.e., $\pi(c) = c$ and c is also called a *fixed point*. When $k = 2$, it is 2-cycles such that $\pi(c_1) = c_2$ and $\pi(c_2) = c_1$.

Lemma 1. *Let π be a random permutation over a finite set S. The probability of having exactly t k-cycles is $e^{-1/k}/k^t t!$ when the cardinality of S grows to infinity.*

For instance, the probability of having no fixed points is e^{-1} which is computed by substituting $t = 0$ and $k = 1$. On the other hand, given a random permutation, the expected number of fixed points (1-cycles) is 1. Additionally, the expected number of 2-cycles is $1/2$. This is generalized in the following lemma.

Lemma 2. *Let π be a random permutation over a finite set S. The expected number k-cycles tends towards $1/k$ as the cardinality of S grows to infinity.*

3.2 Three-Key Triple Encryption Case

We use the relation $\varphi(K_1, K_2, K_3) = (K_2, K_1, K_3)$. We observe that for $K = (K_1, K_2, K_3)$, we have

$$\text{Enc}_K \circ \text{Enc}_{\varphi(K)}^{-1} = \left(C_{K_1} \circ C_{K_2}^{-1} \right)^2 . \tag{2}$$

The idea of the attack consists of looking for a plaintext x such that $\text{Enc}_K(x) = \text{Enc}_{\varphi(K)}(x)$. By enumerating the codebook we can find one such x with complexity 2^{ℓ_m}. Indeed, this would be a fixed point for the above permutation.

Under heuristic assumptions, the permutation $C_{K_1} \circ C_{K_2}^{-1}$ has a number of fixed points such that $E(a) = 1$ and b number of 2-cycles such that $E(b) = 1/2$. Since, $\left(C_{K_1} \circ C_{K_2}^{-1} \right)^2$ is a composition of $C_{K_1} \circ C_{K_2}^{-1}$ with itself, the a fixed points of $C_{K_1} \circ C_{K_2}^{-1}$ are the fixed points of $\left(C_{K_1} \circ C_{K_2}^{-1} \right)^2$, too. However, the elements of 2-cycles of $C_{K_1} \circ C_{K_2}^{-1}$ become fixed points for $\left(C_{K_1} \circ C_{K_2}^{-1} \right)^2$, as well. So, we have $a + 2b$ fixed points. In the attack, we take advantage of fixed points of $C_{K_1} \circ C_{K_2}^{-1}$. Hence, we call the fixed points of $\left(C_{K_1} \circ C_{K_2}^{-1} \right)^2$ which is also the fixed points of $C_{K_1} \circ C_{K_2}^{-1}$ as *good fixed points* and the elements of 2-cycles of $C_{K_1} \circ C_{K_2}^{-1}$ as *bad fixed points*.

The attack is composed of two parts, namely, the fixed points finding part and the key recovery part. Our attack starts as shown in Fig. 1 or in Fig. 2 depending on the type of

```
 1: select c₁ = 0 and c₂, . . . , cₙ at random
 2: for i = 1 to n do
 3:    set a list Lᵢ to the empty list
 4:    repeat
 5:       get a new BKP x with keys K ⊕ cᵢ and φ(K ⊕ cᵢ)
 6:       let y (resp. z) be the encryption of x under key K ⊕ cᵢ (resp. φ(K ⊕ cᵢ))
 7:       if y = z then
 8:          add y in list Lᵢ
 9:       end if
10:    until all x cover the entire codebook
11: end for
12: set I to the set of all i such that #Lᵢ > 0
```

Fig. 1. Attack on Triple Encryption (First Part — Broadcast Known Plaintext)

```
 1: select c₁ = 0 and c₂, . . . , cₙ at random
 2: for i = 1 to n do
 3:    set a list Lᵢ to the empty list
 4:    dump the entire codebook for key K ⊕ cᵢ (Enc_{K⊕cᵢ}(x) stored at address h(x))
 5:    repeat
 6:       get a new KP x with key φ(K ⊕ cᵢ)
 7:       let z be the encryption of x under key φ(K ⊕ cᵢ)
 8:       let y to the content of cell h(x)
 9:       if y = z then
10:          add y in list Lᵢ
11:       end if
12:    until all x cover the entire codebook
13: end for
14: set I to the set of all i such that #Lᵢ > 0
```

Fig. 2. Attack on Triple Encryption (First Part — Known Plaintext)

the data set (BKP or KP). In the BKP variant, we first determine the relation between related key pairs as $c_1 = 0$ and $c_2, \ldots, c_n$, at random. Then, for each i we have a list L_i of fixed points for $\left(C_{K_1(i)} \circ C_{K_2(i)}^{-1} \right)^2$ by enumerating the codebook. If the cardinality $\#L_i$ of L_i is nonzero, then we keep the index i of L_i in I. Note that, if L_i has an odd number of terms, we ensure that there is at least one fixed point for $C_{K_1(i)} \circ C_{K_2(i)}^{-1}$ in it.

Then, the attack continues as shown in Fig. 3. Starting from the first i in I, we pick every fixed point x from the list L_i and enumerate all ℓ_k-bit keys and find pairs (K_1, K_2) such that $C_{K_1}(x) = C_{K_2}(x)$ with complexity 2^{ℓ_k} using a meet-in-the-middle algorithm. Then, for each remaining j in I, we keep counter c in order to determine whether (K_1, K_2) suggested by the meet-in-the-middle algorithm is right key pair or not. Notice that the correct (K_1, K_2) pair is always suggested if x is a good fixed point. Other pairs are called *wrong pairs*. In order to eliminate wrong pairs, we use the list of other fixed points by checking whether $C_{K_1(j)}(y) = C_{K_2(j)}(y)$ or not, where $K_1(j) = K_1 \oplus c_j$ and $K_2(j) = K_2 \oplus c_j$. If there exists such y, then we increment c by 1. Otherwise, if there is no such y and $\#L_i$ is odd, then we decide that this x

is not a good fixed point. In addition, we make another list R to keep promising key pairs which have nonzero counter, namely, (K_1, K_2, c) and $c \neq 0$. Finally, we make exhaustive search on K_3 with the promising key pairs (K_1, K_2) existing in the list R. If there is no true K_3, we can make several iterations of this method until going through all lists with non-zero cardinality.

Success Probability. Our attack succeeds when there is one related key pair having at least one good fixed point, i.e., $a > 0$. From Lemma 1, for a random permutation, the probability of having no fixed point is e^{-1}. Therefore, the attack fails when there is no good fixed point for each related key pair which happens with probability e^{-n}. Hence, the success probability of the attack is $p = 1 - e^{-n}$.

Complexity Analysis. In order to generate fixed points in Fig. 1, we use $r = 2n$ related keys, $d = n2^{\ell_m+1}$ broadcast known plaintexts, and negligible time and memory. For the known plaintext variant depicted in Fig. 2, data complexity is the same as the BKP variant, but the memory complexity is higher, i.e., $m = \ell_m 2^{\ell_m}$.

The loop in $K_1(i)$ takes $t = 2^{\ell_k}/3$ triple encryptions and $m = (\ell_m + \ell_k)2^{\ell_k}$ bits of memory. The loop in $K_2(i)$ essentially takes $t = 2^{\ell_k}/3$ triple encryptions (the inner loop in the found $K_2(i)$ is negligible).

The loop in (K_1, K_2, c) depends on the size of R. We denote R_n the expected number of remaining wrong keys in R using parameter n. Let $n^* - 1$ be the number of other lists which have an odd number of fixed points. We have $2^{2\ell_k}$ potential pairs, but an equation to satisfy on $n^*\ell_m$ bits to end up in R. So, we have $R_n \approx 2^{2\ell_k - n^*\ell_m}$. We have

$$E(n^*) = 1 + (n-1) \sum_{a \text{ odd}} \frac{e^{-1}}{a!} = 1 + \frac{(n-1)(1 - e^{-2})}{2}, \tag{3}$$

where $\sum_{a \text{ odd}} 1/a! = (e - e^{-1})/2$. Then, we have $E(n^*) \approx 0.4323 \times n + 0.5677$. So, this loop takes $t = (1 + R_n)2^{\ell_k}/3$ triple encryptions for a good fixed point and $t = R_n 2^{\ell_k}/3$ for a bad one. In what follows, we adjust n so that $R_n \approx 0$. Namely, for $n = 6\ell_k/\ell_m$, we have $R_n \approx 2^{-0.4\ell_k - 0.6\ell_m}$ so we can neglect wrong pairs.

The main loop and the x loop iterate until it takes a good fixed point. For each L_i, we have exactly t k-cycles with probability $e^{-1/k}/k^t t!$. Let us assume that the probabilities for $k = 1$ and $k = 2$ are independent. For instance, the best case is $a > 1$ (some good fixed points) and $b = 0$ (no bad fixed points) with probability $e^{-1/2}(1 - e^{-1}) \approx 0.38$. Let N_n (resp. N_n^*) denote the expected number of iterations of the i and x loops (resp. in the case that the attack succeeds). In the case of failure ($a = 0$), we have $2b$ iterations, hence, the expected number of bad fixed point is 1 for each list That is, since there are n lists, the expected number of iterations before the attack fails is n. This happens with probability e^{-n}, therefore, we have

$$N_n^* = \frac{N_n - ne^{-n}}{1 - e^{-n}}.$$

Let (a_i, b_i) be the numbers of 1-cycles and 2-cycles in the lists in I, respectively, where i is at most n. Regarding the first list, for a_1 nonzero good fixed points and $2b_1$ bad

```
 1: sort I in increasing order with first the list of i's with #L_i odd then the remaining ones
 2: while I is not empty do
 3:     pick the first i ∈ I and remove it from I
 4:     for all x in L_i do
 5:         initialize a hash table H and a list R
 6:         for all K_1(i) do
 7:             store (C_{K_1(i)}(x), K_1(i)) in H
 8:         end for
 9:         for all K_2(i) do
10:             for each K_1(i) such that (C_{K_2(i)}(x), K_1(i)) ∈ H do
11:                 compute K_1 and K_2 from K_1(i) and K_2(i) using c_i and set c = 0
12:                 for each j ∈ I do
13:                     compute K_1(j) and K_2(j) from K_1 and K_2 using c_j
14:                     look if there is y ∈ L_j such that C_{K_1(j)}(y) = C_{K_2(j)}(y)
15:                     if there is such y then
16:                         increment c
17:                     end if
18:                     if there is no such y and #L_j is odd then
19:                         exit the j loop and set c to 0
20:                     end if
21:                 end for
22:                 if c ≠ 0, add (K_1, K_2, c) in list R sorted by decreasing c
23:             end for
24:         end for
25:     end for
26:     for each (K_1, K_2, c) ∈ R sorted by c do
27:         for all K_3 do
28:             if (K_1, K_2, K_3) consistent with data then
29:                 yield (K_1, K_2, K_3) and exit
30:             end if
31:         end for
32:     end for
33: end while
34: attack failed
```

Fig. 3. Attack on Three-Key Triple Encryption (Second Part)

ones, the expected number of iterations is

$$N_n(a_1, b_1) = \frac{1}{\binom{a_1+2b_1}{a_1}} \sum_{i=1}^{2b_1+1} i \binom{a_1 + 2b_1 - i}{a_1 - 1},$$

which does not depend on n.

Notice that for $a_1 = 0$, it is $N_n(0, b_1) = 2b_1 + \bar{N}_{n-1}$, where $\bar{N}_{n-1}$ is the expected number of iterations conditioned to that all a_i's are even. This is because, we first consider the lists having odd number of a_i's in the algorithm. Therefore, if $a_1 = 0$, then the remaining lists will contain even number of a_i's. Hence, we will continue searching points in the remaining lists with all bad points of the first list. Furthermore, we have

$$N_n = \sum_{a_1,\,b_1} N_n(a_1, b_1) \Pr[a_1, b_1].$$

Here, we compute the joint probability $\Pr[a_1, b_1]$ as

$$\Pr[a_1, b_1] = \Pr[a_1, b_1 | a_1 \text{ odd}] \Pr[a_1 \text{ odd}] + \Pr[a_1, b_1 | a_1 \text{ even}] \Pr[a_1 \text{ even}].$$

Then, the probability that a_1 is even is computed as

$$\Pr[a_1 \text{ even}] = \Pr[a_1, \dots, a_n \text{ even}] = \left(\sum_i \frac{e^{-1}}{(2i)!} \right)^n = \left(\frac{1 + e^{-2}}{2} \right)^n.$$

We can equivalently write the probability that a_1 is odd as

$$\Pr[a_1 \text{ odd}] = 1 - \Pr[a_1 \text{ even}] = 1 - \left(\frac{1 + e^{-2}}{2} \right)^n.$$

On the other hand, for a_1 odd, we have

$$\Pr[a_1, b_1 | a_1 \text{ odd}] = \frac{\frac{e^{-\frac{3}{2}}}{a_1! 2^{b_1} b_1!}}{\sum_{i \text{ odd}} \frac{e^{-1}}{i!}} = \frac{2}{a_1! 2^{b_1} b_1! (e^{\frac{3}{2}} - e^{-\frac{1}{2}})}.$$

For a_1 even, we get

$$\Pr[a_1, b_1 | a_1 \text{ even}] = \frac{\frac{e^{-\frac{3}{2}}}{a_1! 2^{b_1} b_1!}}{\sum_{i \text{ even}} \frac{e^{-1}}{i!}} = \frac{2}{a_1! 2^{b_1} b_1! (e^{\frac{3}{2}} + e^{-\frac{1}{2}})}.$$

Hence, we get

$$\Pr[a_1, b_1] = \begin{cases} \dfrac{2\left(1 - \left(\frac{1+e^{-2}}{2}\right)^n\right)}{a_1! 2^{b_1} b_1! (e^{\frac{3}{2}} - e^{-\frac{1}{2}})}, & \text{if } a_1 \text{ odd}, \\[4ex] \dfrac{2\left(\frac{1+e^{-2}}{2}\right)^n}{a_1! 2^{b_1} b_1! (e^{\frac{3}{2}} + e^{-\frac{1}{2}})}, & \text{if } a_1 \text{ even}. \end{cases}$$

Now, we compute $\bar{N}_{n-1}$ as

$$\bar{N}_{n-1} = \sum_{\substack{a_1 \text{ even} \\ b_1}} N_{n-1}(a_1, b_1) \Pr[a_1, b_1 | a_1 \text{ even}] = \sum_{\substack{a_1 \text{ even} \\ b_1}} \frac{2 N_{n-1}(a_1, b_1)}{a_1! 2^{b_1} b_1! (e^{\frac{3}{2}} + e^{-\frac{1}{2}})}.$$

Afterwards, N_n by substituting $N_n(0, b_1) = 2b_1 + \bar{N}_{n-1}$ as

$$N_n = \sum_{\substack{a_1=0 \\ b_1}} (2b_1 + \bar{N}_{n-1}) \Pr[0, b_1] + \sum_{\substack{a_1>0 \\ b_1}} N_n(a_1, b_1) \Pr[a_1, b_1].$$

$$= \frac{2(\bar{N}_{n-1}+1)}{(e+e^{-1})}\left(\frac{1+e^{-2}}{2}\right)^n + \sum_{\substack{a_1>0 \text{ even} \\ b_1}} \frac{2N_n(a_1, b_1)}{a_1! 2^{b_1} b_1!(e^{\frac{3}{2}} + e^{-\frac{1}{2}})}\left(\frac{1+e^{-2}}{2}\right)^n$$

$$+ \sum_{\substack{a_1>0 \text{ odd} \\ b_1}} \frac{2N_n(a_1, b_1)}{a_1! 2^{b_1} b_1!(e^{\frac{3}{2}} - e^{-\frac{1}{2}})}\left(1 - \left(\frac{1+e^{-2}}{2}\right)^n\right).$$

We compute some values of $\bar{N}_n$, N_n, and N_n^* in Table 3. As we see from this table, the number of iterations is upper bounded by 2 in any success case. Finally, the total complexity is

$$r = 2n,$$
$$d = n2^{\ell_m+1},$$
$$t = \begin{cases} 2\left(\frac{2}{3}2^{\ell_k} + \frac{1}{2}2^{\ell_k} R_n\right) + \frac{1}{3}2^{\ell_k} & \text{if success, and} \\ n\left(\frac{2}{3}2^{\ell_k} + \frac{1}{2}2^{\ell_k} R_n\right) & \text{if failure,} \end{cases}$$
$$m = \begin{cases} (\ell_m + \ell_k)2^{\ell_k} & \text{for BKP variant, and} \\ \max(\ell_m 2^{\ell_m}, (\ell_m + \ell_k)2^{\ell_k}) & \text{for KP variant,} \end{cases}$$
$$p = 1 - e^{-n}.$$

In general, we suggest $n \approx 6\ell_k/\ell_m$ to get $t = 5 \times 2^{\ell_k}/3$ in a success case.

Table 3. Some values for $\bar{N}_n$, N_n, and N_n^*

n	1	2	3	4	5	6	7	8	9	10	50	100
$\bar{N}_n$	2.613	4.306	1.908	5.403	6.115	6.576	6.874	7.068	7.193	7.275	7.424	7.424
N_n	1.264	1.895	1.908	1.789	1.675	1.593	1.540	1.507	1.488	1.477	1.462	1.462
N_n^*	1.418	1.879	1.851	1.748	1.652	1.582	1.535	1.505	1.487	1.476	1.462	1.462

In the case of DES, we have $\ell_k = 56$ and $\ell_m = 64$. We take $n = 3$ to get $n^* \approx 1.865$ and $R_n \approx 2^{-7.338}$. So, we use $r = 6$ keys. We use $d = 2^{67}$ chosen plaintexts or ciphertexts, or known plaintexts. The time complexity is $t = 2^{57}$ triple encryptions in all cases. The memory complexity is $m = 2^{63}$ bits in the chosen message variant and $m = 2^{72}$ in the known plaintext variant. The key to recover has 168 bits. The attack succeeds with probability $p = 95\%$. Note that this attack is better than the generic related-key attack using tradeoffs. It works in the ideal cipher model. Bellare and Rogaway [2] proved that the best (non-related-key) generic attack in the ideal cipher model would require at least 2^{78} encryptions. This example shows that the result no longer holds in the related-key model.

If we would like to use the triple AES encryption, we obtain different results which are summarized in Table 4.

Table 4. Semi-Generic Attack against Triple Encryption (Chosen Message Variant)

cipher	two-key				three-key			
	DES	AES128	AES192	AES256	DES	AES128	AES192	AES256
key size	116	256	384	512	168	384	576	768
ℓ_k	56	128	192	256	56	128	192	256
ℓ_m	64	128	128	128	64	128	128	128
#keys	2	2	2	2	6	8	14	18
#chosen plaintexts	2^{65}	2^{129}	2^{129}	2^{129}	2^{67}	2^{131}	2^{132}	2^{132}
time complexity	2^{56}	2^{128}	2^{192}	2^{256}	2^{57}	2^{129}	2^{193}	2^{257}
memory complexity	2^{63}	2^{136}	2^{200}	2^{255}	2^{63}	2^{136}	2^{200}	2^{265}
success probability	63%	63%	63%	63%	95%	98%	100%	100%
$C_{\text{conservative}}$	2^{66}	2^{136}	2^{200}	2^{265}	2^{67}	2^{136}	2^{200}	2^{265}

Comparison with the Kelsey-Schneier-Wagner Attack. Kelsey, Schneier, and Wagner presented a related-key attack against three-key triple encryption which has similar performances [9]. It consists in using

$$\varphi(K_1, K_2, K_3) = (K_1 \oplus \Delta, K_2, K_3).$$

Then, $\text{Enc}_K \circ \text{Enc}_{\varphi(K)}^{-1} = C_{K_1} \circ C_{K_1 \oplus \Delta}^{-1}$ which only depends on K_1. Hence, exhaustive search can recover K_1. For DES, this attack has $r = 2$, $d = 2$ (known and chosen plaintexts), $t = 2^{56}$ encryptions, $m = 2^{56}$ bits, and $p = 100\%$. So, it is better than our attack. Contrary to ours, it has no extension to two-key triple encryption. However, this attack extends to the encrypt-encrypt-encrypt triple encryption mode whereas our attack is restricted to the encrypt-decrypt-encrypt construction.

Note that getting $\text{Enc}_K \circ \text{Enc}_{\varphi(K)}^{-1}(y) = z$ on a random y is equivalent to getting $\text{Enc}_K(x) = y$ and $\text{Enc}_{\varphi(K)}(x) = z$ on a random x. So, this attack is in the BKP model.

Comparison with the Phan Attack. In the category of known plaintext attacks, Phan [12] uses

$$\varphi(K_1, K_2, K_3) = (K_1, K_3, K_2)$$

(which is similar to our relation) and a slide attack. It breaks the three-key triple encryption using $r = 2$, $d = 2^{33}$ (known and chosen plaintexts), $t = 2^{88}/3$ triple encryptions, and $m = 2^{38}$ bits. This attack extends to the encrypt-encrypt-encrypt case and to the two-key triple encryption (with a memory complexity inflated to $m = 2^{94.5}$ bits). Our known plaintext attack uses a quite lower time complexity, but a higher number of chosen plaintexts.

3.3   Two-Key Triple Encryption Case

We use the relation $\varphi(K_1, K_2) = (K_2, K_1)$. We observe that for $K = (K_1, K_2)$, we have

$$\text{Enc}_K \circ \text{Enc}_{\varphi(K)}^{-1} = \left(C_{K_1} \circ C_{K_2}^{-1} \right)^3.$$

Fixed points of $\mathrm{Enc}_K \circ \mathrm{Enc}^{-1}_{\varphi(K)}$ are either the fixed points of $C_{K_1} \circ C^{-1}_{K_2}$ or the points in 3-cycles. We just proceed as in the previous attack. The probability to have a fixed points and b cycles of length 3 is $e^{-4/3}/a!3^b b!$ (Lemma 1), and, $E(a) = 1$ and $E(b) = 1/3$ (Lemma 2). The number of values x such that $\left(C_{K_1} \circ C^{-1}_{K_2}\right)^3 (x) = x$ is $a + 3b$. As in the previous attack, a fixed point of $\left(C_{K_1} \circ C^{-1}_{K_2}\right)^3$ is good if it is also a fixed point of $C_{K_1} \circ C^{-1}_{K_2}$. Notice that if the number of fixed points $(a + 3b)$ is not a multiple of 3, then we certainly have a good fixed point.

The final complexity is very similar to the three-key encryption case. The difference is that we no longer need an exhaustive search on K_3 and wrong (K_1, K_2) pairs are discarded by a simple consistency check. We can work with $n = 1$ and $p = 63\%$.

Let a_i and b_i the number of 1-cycle and 3-cycles in the list L_i whose index i is in I. Similar to the previous attack, given a_1 good fixed points and b_1 bad ones of the first list, we have

$$N_n(a_1, b_1) = \frac{1}{\binom{a_1 + 3b_1}{a_1}} \sum_{i=1}^{3b_1 + 1} i \binom{a_1 + 3b_1 - i}{a_1 - 1}.$$

In addition, we observe that $N_n(0, b_1) = 3b_1 + \bar{N}_{n-1}$, where $\bar{N}_{n-1}$ denotes the expected number of iterations conditioned to that all a_i's are multiples of 3. As in the previous attack, we have

$$N_n = \sum_{a_1, b_1} N_n(a_1, b_1) \Pr[a_1, b_1] \quad \text{and} \quad N_n^* = \frac{N_n - ne^{-n}}{1 - e^{-n}},$$

and we write the joint probability $\Pr[a_1, b_1]$ as

$$\Pr[a_1, b_1] = \begin{cases} \dfrac{3\left(1 - \left(\frac{1 + 2e^{-\frac{3}{2}} \cos \frac{\sqrt{3}}{2}}{3}\right)^n\right)}{2a_1! 3^{b_1} b_1! \left(e^{\frac{4}{3}} - e^{-\frac{1}{6}} \cos \frac{\sqrt{3}}{2}\right)}, & \text{if } a_1 \text{ not a multiple of 3,} \\[3ex] e^{-\frac{4}{3}} \dfrac{\left(\frac{1 + 2e^{-\frac{3}{2}} \cos \frac{\sqrt{3}}{2}}{3}\right)^{n-1}}{a_1! 3^{b_1} b_1!}, & \text{if } a_1 \text{ a multiple of 3.} \end{cases}$$

Similarly, we compute $\bar{N}_{n-1}$ as

$$\bar{N}_{n-1} = \sum_{\substack{a_1 \text{ a multiple of 3} \\ b_1}} N_{n-1}(a_1, b_1) \Pr[a_1, b_1 | a_1 \text{ a multiple of 3}].$$

By noticing that $N_{n-1}(0, b_1) = 3b_1 + \bar{N}_{n-2}$, we compute some values of $\bar{N}_n$, N_n, and N_n^* and obtain identical results with the previous attack. Therefore, the complexity of this attack is

$$r = 2n,$$
$$d = n2^{\ell_m+1},$$
$$t = \begin{cases} \frac{4}{3}2^{\ell_k} & \text{if success, and} \\ \frac{2n}{3}2^{\ell_k} & \text{if failure,} \end{cases}$$
$$m = \begin{cases} (\ell_m + \ell_k)2^{\ell_k} & \text{for BKP variant, and} \\ \max(\ell_m 2^{\ell_m}, (\ell_m + \ell_k)2^{\ell_k}) & \text{for KP variant,} \end{cases}$$
$$p = 1 - e^{-n}.$$

While the first part of the algorithm works like in the three-key case with two variants in Fig. 1 and Fig. 2, the second part of the algorithm is shown in Fig. 4.

1: sort I in increasing order with first the list of i's with $\#L_i$ not a multiple of 3 then the remaining ones
2: **while** I is not empty **do**
3:    pick the first $i \in I$ and remove it from I
4:    **for** all x in L_i **do**
5:       initialize a hash table H
6:       **for** all $K_1(i)$ **do**
7:          store $(C_{K_1(i)}(x), K_1(i))$ in H
8:       **end for**
9:       **for** all $K_2(i)$ **do**
10:          **for** each $K_1(i)$ such that $(C_{K_2(i)}(x), K_1(i)) \in H$ **do**
11:             compute K_1 and K_2 from $K_1(i)$ and $K_2(i)$ using c_i
12:             **if** (K_1, K_2, K_1) consistent with data **then**
13:                yield (K_1, K_2, K_1) and exit
14:             **end if**
15:          **end for**
16:       **end for**
17:    **end for**
18: **end while**
19: attack failed

Fig. 4. Attack on Two-Key Triple Encryption (Second Part)

In the case of DES, we take $n = 1$, so $r = 2$. We use $d = 2^{65}$ chosen plaintexts or ciphertexts. The time complexity is $t = 2^{56}$ triple encryptions in all the cases. The memory complexity is $m = 2^{63}$ bits and the key to recover has 112 bits. The known plaintext variant uses $d = 2^{65}$ known plaintexts and the memory complexity becomes $m = 2^{72}$ bits. The attack succeeds with probability $p = 63\%$. Comparison with other attacks is presented in Table 1.

Comparison with the Merkle-Hellman Meet-in-the-middle Attack. Merkle and Hellman proposed to use a simple collision algorithm to find collisions between the list of all $C_{K_2}^{-1}(0)$ and the list of all $C_{K_1}^{-1}(\text{Enc}(C_{K_1}^{-1}(0)))$ [1]. This requires to encrypt all chosen plaintexts $C_{K_1}^{-1}(0)$. A variant with known plaintexts only can be done as follows: first we make a dictionary of all $(C_{K_1}(0), K_1)$ in addition to the dictionary of all

$(C_{K_2}^{-1}(0), K_2)$. Then, every time we receive a plaintext/ciphertext pair (x, y), we look if x is in the first dictionary to find K_1. If it is, we compute $z = C_{K_1}^{-1}(y)$ and get a new element $C_{K_1}^{-1}(\text{Enc}(C_{K_1}^{-1}(0))) = z$. We can look for z in the second dictionary. This doubles the memory complexity and increases the data complexity to essentially the entire codebook.

This attack has lower complexity parameters than ours for the chosen plaintext variant. The known plaintext variants are equivalent (except that we use related keys and the Merkle-Hellman attack does not).

Note that our attack can be extended to the encrypt-encrypt-encrypt case in a way that for $K = (K_1, K_2)$ and the relation $\varphi(K_1, K_2) = (K_2, K_1)$, we have

$$\text{Enc}_K \circ \text{Enc}_{\varphi(K)} = (C_{K_1} \circ C_{K_2})^3,$$

which allows us to attack against two-key triple encryption by using the similar way with the encrypt-decrypt-encrypt case.

4 Conclusions

We presented a new attack on triple encryption which uses related keys. It can use chosen messages or known plaintexts, but requires the entire codebook for related keys. Our attack is the best in the known plaintext attack category in the three-key case. Besides, the best attacks remain the Merkle-Hellman attack [1] in the two-key case and the Kelsey-Schneier-Wagner attack [9] in the three-key case. In addition to the attacks on triple encryption, we formalize the various ways to compare the complexity of related-key attacks and apply it to the recently proposed attacks on AES.

References

1. Merkle, R.C., Hellman, M.E.: On the Security of Multiple Encryption. Commun. ACM 24(7), 465–467 (1981)
2. Bellare, M., Rogaway, P.: The Security of Triple Encryption and a Framework for Code-Based Game-Playing Proofs. In: Vaudenay, S. (ed.) EUROCRYPT 2006. LNCS, vol. 4004, pp. 409–426. Springer, Heidelberg (2006)
3. Biham, E.: New Types of Cryptanalytic Attacks Using Related Keys. J. Cryptology 7(4), 229–246 (1994)
4. Biham, E.: New Types of Cryptanalytic Attacks Using Related Keys. In: Helleseth, T. (ed.) EUROCRYPT 1993. LNCS, vol. 765, pp. 398–409. Springer, Heidelberg (1994)
5. Biham, E.: How to decrypt or even substitute DES-encrypted messages in 2^{28} steps. Inf. Process. Lett. 84(3), 117–124 (2002)
6. Biryukov, A., Khovratovich, D.: Related-Key Cryptanalysis of the Full AES-192 and AES-256. In: Matsui, M. (ed.) ASIACRYPT 2009. LNCS, vol. 5912, pp. 1–18. Springer, Heidelberg (2009)
7. Biryukov, A., Khovratovich, D., Nikolić, I.: Distinguisher and Related-Key Attack on the Full AES-256. In: Halevi, S. (ed.) CRYPTO 2009. LNCS, vol. 5677, pp. 231–249. Springer, Heidelberg (2009)
8. Diffie, W., Hellman, M.E.: Exhaustive Cryptanalysis of the NBS Data Encryption Standard. Computer 10, 74–84 (1977)

9. Kelsey, J., Schneier, B., Wagner, D.: Key-Schedule Cryptanalysis of IDEA, G-DES, GOST, SAFER, and Triple-DES. In: Koblitz, N. (ed.) CRYPTO 1996. LNCS, vol. 1109, pp. 237–251. Springer, Heidelberg (1996)

10. Knudsen, L.R.: Cryptanalysis of LOKI91. In: Zheng, Y., Seberry, J. (eds.) AUSCRYPT 1992. LNCS, vol. 718, pp. 196–208. Springer, Heidelberg (1993)

11. Lucks, S.: Attacking Triple Encryption. In: Vaudenay, S. (ed.) FSE 1998. LNCS, vol. 1372, pp. 239–253. Springer, Heidelberg (1998)

12. Phan, R.C.-W.: Related-Key Attacks on Triple-DES and DESX Variants. In: Okamoto, T. (ed.) CT-RSA 2004. LNCS, vol. 2964, pp. 15–24. Springer, Heidelberg (2004)

13. van Oorschot, P.C., Wiener, M.: A Known-Plaintext Attack on Two-Key Triple Encryption. In: Damgård, I.B. (ed.) EUROCRYPT 1990. LNCS, vol. 473, pp. 318–325. Springer, Heidelberg (1991)

14. van Oorschot, P.C., Wiener, M.J.: Parallel Collision Search with Cryptanalytic Applications. J. Cryptology 12(1), 1–28 (1999)

15. Vaudenay, S.: Related-key Attack against Triple Encryption based on Fixed points. In: Lopez, J., Samarati, P. (eds.) SECRYPT 2011 - Proceedings of the International Conference on Security and Cryptography, SECRYPT is part of ICETE - The International Joint Conference on e-Business and Telecommunications, Seville, Spain, July 18-21, pp. 59–67 (2011)

16. Wiener, M.J.: The Full Cost of Cryptanalytic Attacks. J. Cryptology 17(2), 105–124 (2004)

Byte Slicing `Grøstl`: Improved Intel AES-NI and Vector-Permute Implementations of the SHA-3 Finalist `Grøstl`

Kazumaro Aoki[1,*], Krystian Matusiewicz[2], Günther Roland[3], Yu Sasaki[1], and Martin Schläffer[3]

[1] NTT Corporation, Japan
[2] Intel Technology, Poland
[3] IAIK, Graz University of Technology, Austria
martin.schlaeffer@iaik.tugraz.at

Abstract. `Grøstl` is an AES-based hash function and one of the 5 finalists of the SHA-3 competition. In this work we present high-speed implementations of `Grøstl` for small 8-bit CPUs, and large 64-bit CPUs with the recently introduced Intel AES-NI and AVX instruction sets. Since `Grøstl` does not use the same MDS mixing layer as the AES, a direct application of the AES instructions seems difficult. In contrast to previous findings, our `Grøstl` implementations using the AES instructions are currently by far the fastest known. To achieve optimal performance we parallelize each round of `Grøstl` by taking advantage of the whole bit width of the used processor. This results in the parallel computation of 16 `Grøstl` columns using 128-bit registers, and 32 `Grøstl` columns using 256-bit registers. This way, we get implementations running at 12.2 cylces/byte for `Grøstl`-256 and 18.6 cylces/byte for `Grøstl`-512.

Keywords: Hash function, SHA-3 competition, Grøstl, Software implementation, Byte slicing, Intel AES new instructions, 8-bit AVR.

1 Introduction

In 2007, NIST has initiated the SHA-3 competition [1] to find a new cryptographic hash function standard. 51 interesting hash functions with different design strategies have been accepted for the first round. Many of these SHA-3 candidates are AES-based and might benefit from the Intel AES new instructions set (AES-NI) [2] to speed up their implementations. In [3] those candidates which use the AES round transformation as a main building block have been analyzed and implemented using AES-NI. In that work, the authors claim that algorithms which use a very different MDS mixing matrix (than AES) are too distant from AES and that there is no easy way to benefit from AES-NI.

Since December 2010, `Grøstl`[4] is one of 5 finalists of the SHA-3 competition and uses the same S-box as AES but a very different MDS mixing matrix. In this work we show that it is still possible to efficiently implement `Grøstl` using AES-NI. Moreover, our AES-NI implementation of `Grøstl` is the fastest known implementation of

---

* Parts of this work were done while the author stayed at TU Graz.

M.S. Obaidat, J.L. Sevillano, and J. Filipe (Eds.): ICETE 2011, CCIS 314, pp. 281–295, 2012.
© Springer-Verlag Berlin Heidelberg 2012

Grøstl so far. Furthermore, we present a self-byte sliced implementation strategy which allows to implement Grøstl very efficiently on 8-bit, 128-bit and 256-bit platforms. We achieve very good performance for larger bit widths by optimizing the MDS mixing matrix computation of Grøstl and by computing multiple columns in parallel. The parallel computation of the whole Grøstl round is possible and if parallel AES S-box table lookups (using AES-NI or the vector-permute implementation of [5]) are available.

The paper is organized as follows. In Section 2, we give a short description of Grøstl. In Section 3, we describe requirements and general optimization techniques of our byte sliced implementations. In Section 4, we show how to minimize the computational requirements for MixBytes, the MDS mixing layer of Grøstl. In Section 5, we present the specific details of the 8-bit, 128-bit and 256-bit implementations. Finally, we conclude in Section 6.

2   Description of Grøstl

The hash function Grøstl was designed by Gauravaram et al. as a candidate for the SHA-3 competition [4]. In January 2011, Grøstl has been tweaked for the final round of the competition and we only consider this variant here. It is an iterated hash function with a compression function built from two distinct permutations P and Q, which are based on the same principles as the AES round transformation [6]. Grøstl is a wide pipe design with security proofs for the collision and preimage resistance of the compression function [7]. In the following, we describe the Grøstl hash function and the permutations of Grøstl-256 and Grøstl-512 in more detail.

2.1   The Grøstl Hash Function

The input message M is padded and split into blocks $M_1, M_2, \ldots, M_t$ of ℓ bits with $\ell = 512$ for Grøstl-256 and $\ell = 1024$ for Grøstl-512. The initial value H_0, the intermediate hash values H_i, and the permutations P and Q are of size ℓ as well. The message blocks are processed via the compression function f, which accepts two inputs of size ℓ bits and outputs an ℓ-bit value. The compression function f is defined via the permutations P and Q as follows:

$$f(H, M) = P(H \oplus M) \oplus Q(M) \oplus H.$$

The compression function is iterated with $H_0 = IV$ and $H_i \leftarrow f(H_{i-1}, M_i)$ for $1 \leq i \leq t$. The output H_t of the last call of the compression function is processed by an output transformation g defined as $g(x) = \text{trunc}_n(P(x) \oplus x)$, where n is the output size of the hash function and $\text{trunc}_n(x)$ discards all but the least significant n bits of x. Hence, the digest of the message M is defined as $h(M) = g(H_t)$.

2.2   The Grøstl-256 Permutations

As mentioned above, two permutations P and Q are defined for Grøstl-256. Both permutations operate on a 512-bit state, which can be viewed as an 8×8 matrix of bytes. Each permutation of Grøstl-256 consists of 10 rounds, where the following four AES-like round transformations are applied to the state in the given order:

- AddRoundConstant (AC) XORs a constant to one row of the state for P and to the whole state for Q. The constant changes for every round.
- SubBytes (SB) applies the AES S-box to each byte of the state.
- ShiftBytes (SH) cyclically rotates the bytes of rows to the left by $\{0, 1, 2, 3, 4, 5, 6, 7\}$ positions in P and by $\{1, 3, 5, 7, 0, 2, 4, 6\}$ positions in Q.
- MixBytes (MB) is a linear diffusion layer, which multiplies each column with a constant 8×8 circulant MDS matrix.

MixBytes. As the MixBytes transformation is the most run-time intensive part of Grøstl in our case, we will describe this transformation in more detail here. The MixBytes transformation is a matrix multiplication performed on the state matrix as follows:

$$A \leftarrow B \times A,$$

where A is the state matrix and B is a circulant MDS matrix specified as $B = circ(02, 02, 03, 04, 05, 03, 05, 07)$ or by the following matrix:

$$B = \begin{pmatrix} 02\ 02\ 03\ 04\ 05\ 03\ 05\ 07 \\ 07\ 02\ 02\ 03\ 04\ 05\ 03\ 05 \\ 05\ 07\ 02\ 02\ 03\ 04\ 05\ 03 \\ 03\ 05\ 07\ 02\ 02\ 03\ 04\ 05 \\ 05\ 03\ 05\ 07\ 02\ 02\ 03\ 04 \\ 04\ 05\ 03\ 05\ 07\ 02\ 02\ 03 \\ 03\ 04\ 05\ 03\ 05\ 07\ 02\ 02 \\ 02\ 03\ 04\ 05\ 03\ 05\ 07\ 02 \end{pmatrix}.$$

The multiplication is performed in a finite field $\mathbb{F}_{256}$ defined by the irreducible polynomial $x^8 \oplus x^4 \oplus x^3 \oplus x \oplus 1$ (0x11B). As the multiplication by 2 only consists of a shift and a conditional XOR in binary arithmetic, we will calculate all multiplications by combining multiplications by 2 and additions (XOR), *e.g.* $7 \cdot x = (2 \cdot (2 \cdot x)) \oplus (2 \cdot x) \oplus x$.

For more details on the round transformations we refer to the Grøstl specification [4].

2.3 The Grøstl-512 Permutations

The permutations used in Grøstl-512 are of size $\ell = 1024$ bits and the state is viewed as an 8×16 matrix of bytes. The permutations use the same round transformations as in Grøstl-256 except for ShiftBytes: Since the permutations are larger, the rows are shifted by $\{0, 1, 2, 3, 4, 5, 6, 11\}$ positions to the left in P. In Q the rows are shifted by $\{1, 3, 5, 11, 0, 2, 4, 6\}$ positions to the left. The number of rounds is increased to 14.

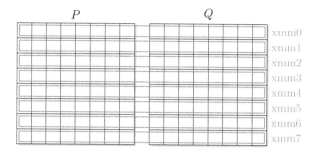

Fig. 1. For the AES-NI implementation, the Grøstl-256 state is stored row-wise in 128-bit xmm registers to compute each column 16 times in parallel

3   Byte Sliced Implementations of Grøstl

In this section, we describe some requirements for the efficient parallel computation of the Grøstl round transformations. Due to the fact that MixBytes applies the same algorithm to every column of the state we can 'byte slice' Grøstl. In other words, we apply the same computations for every byte-wise column of the Grøstl state. On platforms with register sizes larger than 8-bit we can parallelize every transformation by placing several bytes of one row (of the state) inside one register. One column of the state is then distributed over 8 different registers (see Figure 1).

3.1   Transposing the State

Unfortunately, the byte mapping in Grøstl is exactly the opposite of this requirement. The state is mapped to a byte sequence column-wise. Therefore we have to transpose each input state to get bytes of the same row into one register.

Once this realignment is done we can apply the same operations on each column (or byte) stored in the row registers at once. Even ShiftBytes which only reorders the bytes of one row, is easier to implement this way, because no data has to be moved between registers.

3.2   AddRoundConstant

In AddRoundConstant a constant is XORed to the state. This constant is different for P and Q and changes every round. When using large registers, these constants can be precomputed and XORed row-by-row and in parallel to each column of the state.

3.3   SubBytes

In order to improve the performance of the SubBytes layer, we need to compute as many S-box lookups in parallel as possible. In general, there is no easy way to lookup and replace each byte of a register using generic instructions. For this reason the T-table based implementations are currently still the fastest on most platforms.

However, the Intel AES new instructions set (AES-NI) gives us the possibility of 16 parallel S-box lookups within only one instruction (see Section 5). Another approach for parallel AES S-box table lookups is to use small Log tables to efficiently compute the inverse of the AES S-box using the vector-permute (vperm) implementation presented in [5].

3.4 ShiftBytes

ShiftBytes is generally simple to implement on any platform if the state is stored in row ordering. Only byte shufflings, bitshifts and XORs, or addressing different state bytes (or words) is necessary.

3.5 MixBytes

As stated above, MixBytes is the transformation that benefits most from byte slicing. MixBytes is computed using a large number of XORs and multiplications by two in $\mathbb{F}_{256}$. The multiplication in the finite field $\mathbb{F}_{256}$ will be simplified to simple multiplications by two and additions in $\mathbb{F}_{256}$ (XORs).

For the multiplication by two we only need to shift each byte to the left by one bit. To keep the result in $\mathbb{F}_{256}$ we have to observe the carry bit (MSB before the shift operation). If the carry bit is zero the result is already correct (still in $\mathbb{F}_{256}$), if the carry bit is one we have to reduce by the irreducible polynomial (*i.e.* XOR 0x11B).

There are many strategies to reduce the number of XOR computations for MixBytes and we discuss two optimization strategies in detail in Section 4.

4   Optimizing the MixBytes Computation

The MDS matrix multiplication is the most complex operation of Grøstl. Without optimizations all bytes of a column have to be multiplied by $2, 3, 4, 5$ and 7 and then summed up according to the following matrix multiplication:

$$
\begin{bmatrix} b_0 \\ b_1 \\ b_2 \\ b_3 \\ b_4 \\ b_5 \\ b_6 \\ b_7 \end{bmatrix}
=
\begin{bmatrix}
2 & 2 & 3 & 4 & 5 & 3 & 5 & 7 \\
7 & 2 & 2 & 3 & 4 & 5 & 3 & 5 \\
5 & 7 & 2 & 2 & 3 & 4 & 5 & 3 \\
3 & 5 & 7 & 2 & 2 & 3 & 4 & 5 \\
5 & 3 & 5 & 7 & 2 & 2 & 3 & 4 \\
4 & 5 & 3 & 5 & 7 & 2 & 2 & 3 \\
3 & 4 & 5 & 3 & 5 & 7 & 2 & 2 \\
2 & 3 & 4 & 5 & 3 & 5 & 7 & 2
\end{bmatrix}
\cdot
\begin{bmatrix} a_0 \\ a_1 \\ a_2 \\ a_3 \\ a_4 \\ a_5 \\ a_6 \\ a_7 \end{bmatrix}
$$

If we use only multiplications by 2 as described above we can rewrite the same equations with factors of only 2 and 4 as follows (also see Table 1):

$b_0 = a_2 \oplus a_4 \oplus a_5 \oplus a_6 \oplus a_7 \oplus 2a_0 \oplus 2a_1 \oplus 2a_2 \oplus 2a_5 \oplus 2a_7 \oplus 4a_3 \oplus 4a_4 \oplus 4a_6 \oplus 4a_7$

$b_1 = a_0 \oplus a_3 \oplus a_5 \oplus a_6 \oplus a_7 \oplus 2a_0 \oplus 2a_1 \oplus 2a_2 \oplus 2a_3 \oplus 2a_6 \oplus 4a_0 \oplus 4a_4 \oplus 4a_5 \oplus 4a_7$

$b_2 = a_0 \oplus a_1 \oplus a_4 \oplus a_6 \oplus a_7 \oplus 2a_1 \oplus 2a_2 \oplus 2a_3 \oplus 2a_4 \oplus 2a_7 \oplus 4a_0 \oplus 4a_1 \oplus 4a_5 \oplus 4a_6$

$b_3 = a_0 \oplus a_1 \oplus a_2 \oplus a_5 \oplus a_7 \oplus 2a_0 \oplus 2a_2 \oplus 2a_3 \oplus 2a_4 \oplus 2a_5 \oplus 4a_1 \oplus 4a_2 \oplus 4a_6 \oplus 4a_7$

$b_4 = a_0 \oplus a_1 \oplus a_2 \oplus a_3 \oplus a_6 \oplus 2a_1 \oplus 2a_3 \oplus 2a_4 \oplus 2a_5 \oplus 2a_6 \oplus 4a_0 \oplus 4a_2 \oplus 4a_3 \oplus 4a_7$

$$b_5 = a_1 \oplus a_2 \oplus a_3 \oplus a_4 \oplus a_7 \oplus 2a_2 \oplus 2a_4 \oplus 2a_5 \oplus 2a_6 \oplus 2a_7 \oplus 4a_0 \oplus 4a_1 \oplus 4a_3 \oplus 4a_4$$
$$b_6 = a_0 \oplus a_2 \oplus a_3 \oplus a_4 \oplus a_5 \oplus 2a_0 \oplus 2a_3 \oplus 2a_5 \oplus 2a_6 \oplus 2a_7 \oplus 4a_1 \oplus 4a_2 \oplus 4a_4 \oplus 4a_5$$
$$b_7 = a_1 \oplus a_3 \oplus a_4 \oplus a_5 \oplus a_6 \oplus 2a_0 \oplus 2a_1 \oplus 2a_4 \oplus 2a_6 \oplus 2a_7 \oplus 4a_2 \oplus 4a_3 \oplus 4a_5 \oplus 4a_6$$

Table 1. MixBytes computation with multipliers 1, 2 and 4. A "$\bullet$" denotes those inputs (a_i, $2 \cdot a_i$, $4 \cdot a_i$) which are added to get the results b_i. Superscripts denote the order in which the temporary results are computed to result in 58 XORs (1 corresponds to the temporary results of Equation 2).

	a_0			a_1			a_2			a_3			a_4			a_5			a_6			a_7		
	4	2	1	4	2	1	4	2	1	4	2	1	4	2	1	4	2	1	4	2	1	4	2	1
b_0	—	$\bullet^1$	—	—	$\bullet^2$	—	—	$\bullet^1$	$\bullet^9$	$\bullet^d$	—	—	$\bullet^d$	—	$\bullet^2$	—	$\bullet^9$	$\bullet^1$	$\bullet^2$	—	$\bullet^2$	$\bullet^1$	$\bullet^2$	$\bullet^1$
b_1	$\bullet^5$	$\bullet^1$	$\bullet^5$	—	$\bullet^a$	—	—	$\bullet^1$	—	—	$\bullet^5$	$\bullet^b$	$\bullet^d$	—	—	$\bullet^5$	—	$\bullet^1$	—	$\bullet^b$	$\bullet^a$	$\bullet^1$	—	$\bullet^1$
b_2	$\bullet^5$	—	$\bullet^5$	$\bullet^7$	$\bullet^2$	$\bullet^7$	—	$\bullet^c$	—	—	$\bullet^5$	—	—	$\bullet^7$	$\bullet^2$	$\bullet^5$	—	—	$\bullet^2$	—	$\bullet^2$	—	$\bullet^2$	$\bullet^c$
b_3	—	$\bullet^1$	$\bullet^3$	$\bullet^7$	—	$\bullet^7$	$\bullet^3$	$\bullet^1$	$\bullet^3$	—	$\bullet^3$	—	—	$\bullet^7$	—	—	$\bullet^3$	$\bullet^1$	$\bullet^d$	—	—	$\bullet^1$	—	$\bullet^1$
b_4	$\bullet^d$	—	$\bullet^3$	—	$\bullet^a$	$\bullet^4$	$\bullet^3$	—	$\bullet^3$	$\bullet^4$	$\bullet^3$	$\bullet^4$	—	$\bullet^4$	—	—	$\bullet^3$	—	—	$\bullet^4$	$\bullet^a$	$\bullet^d$	—	—
b_5	$\bullet^d$	—	—	$\bullet^6$	—	$\bullet^4$	$\bullet^d$	$\bullet^c$	$\bullet^9$	$\bullet^4$	—	$\bullet^4$	$\bullet^6$	$\bullet^4$	$\bullet^6$	—	$\bullet^9$	—	—	$\bullet^4$	—	—	$\bullet^6$	$\bullet^c$
b_6	—	$\bullet^8$	$\bullet^3$	$\bullet^6$	—	—	$\bullet^3$	—	$\bullet^3$	—	$\bullet^3$	$\bullet^b$	$\bullet^6$	—	$\bullet^6$	$\bullet^8$	$\bullet^3$	$\bullet^8$	—	$\bullet^b$	—	—	$\bullet^6$	—
b_7	—	$\bullet^8$	—	—	$\bullet^2$	$\bullet^4$	—	—	—	$\bullet^4$	—	$\bullet^4$	—	$\bullet^4$	$\bullet^2$	$\bullet^8$	—	$\bullet^8$	$\bullet^2$	$\bullet^4$	$\bullet^2$	—	$\bullet^2$	—

Without optimization, the total number of XORs is $13 \cdot 8 = 104$ and we need 16 multiplications by 2. Note that a multiplication by 2 is usually about 3-5 times more expensive than an XOR operation.

4.1 Minimizing the Number of XORs

In this section, we present optimized MixBytes formulas, which allow to minimize the number of XOR instructions in MixBytes. Using Table 1, we can observe that for each result b_i, many $a_j \oplus a_{j+1}$ terms are needed for each factor of 1, 2 and 4. By computing temporary results t_i, x_i and y_i we get the following optimized MixBytes computation formulas with $i = \{0, \ldots, 7\}$:

$$
\begin{aligned}
t_i &= a_i + a_{i+1} \\
x_i &= t_i + t_{i+3} \\
y_i &= t_i + t_{i+2} + a_{i+6} \\
b_i &= 2 \cdot (2 \cdot x_{i+3} + y_{i+7}) + y_{i+4}
\end{aligned}
\tag{1}
$$

These formulas contain a minimum number of $8 \cdot 2 = 16$ multiplications by 2 and in total, only $8 \cdot 6 = 48$ XOR operations. These formulas are used for the Intel AES-NI implementation in Section 5.1. Note that this variant can also be used to improve Grøstl on the 8-bit platform. However, it is still an open problem to find the smallest number of XORs needed to compute MixBytes of Grøstl.

4.2 Reusing Temporary Results

Another possibility is to compute MixBytes by minimizing the number of XORs and the used registers while keeping the minimum number of 16 multiplications by 2. This strategy is used for the vector-permute implementation in Section 5.2.

Since many terms $(a_i, 2 \cdot a_i, 4 \cdot a_i)$ in the computation are added to more than one result, we can save XORs by computing temporary results (see Table 1). For example, the term

$$t = 2 \cdot a_0 + 2 \cdot a_2 + 1 \cdot a_5 + 4 \cdot a_7 + 1 \cdot a_7 \tag{2}$$

needs to be added to b_0, b_1 and b_3. This has a total cost of $3 \cdot 5 = 15$ XORs using the naive approach. If we first compute the temporary result t and then add t to each of b_0, b_1 and b_3, we can save $15 - (4 + 3) = 8$ XORs.

There are many possibilities to compute temporary results and we used a greedy approach to find a good sequence. In each step of this approach, we try out all possible temporary results and compute the number of XORs we can save. In the first step, the maximum number of XORs we can save is 8. After we remove the already added terms, we continue with the greedy approach until only single terms are left. Using this approach we found a sequence of computing MixBytes which requires 58 XORs and 16 multiplications by two. This sequence is shown by Table 1 and we use superscript numbers to denote the order of computing temporary results.

5   Implementations

In the following we will describe the details of different byteslice implementations of Grøstl. Using 128-bit SSE registers, we can compute 16 columns in parallel using the Intel AES new instruction set (AES-NI) or using the vector-permute (vperm) approach. If AVX registers and instructions are available, we can even compute 32 columns in parallel which is especially useful for Grøstl-512. Additionally, we present an 8-bit AVR implementation which computes only single columns.

5.1   Intel AES-NI

Intel Processors based on the microarchitecture codename Westmere come with a new AES instructions set (AES-NI) [2]. This set consists of six new instructions used for AES encryption and decryption. Next to improving the performance of AES they also provide more security due to their constant-time execution by avoiding cache-based table lookups. Furthermore, all processors with AES-NI come with different versions of SSE which we will also use to improve our implementations. For more information about the instructions used in this document we refer to the Intel Manual [8].

Since Grøstl uses the same S-box as AES we can use AES-NI to improve the performance of Grøstl significantly. The implementation requires the processor to run in 64-bit mode to have access to the 16 128-bit XMM registers. This helps to avoid unnecessary memory accesses that would significantly reduce the performance. These 16 128-bit XMM registers provide enough space for the whole Grøstl state. In the following, we will discuss the main principles of the implementation and important observations.

State Alignment in Registers. For optimal performance, the alignment of the state inside the XMM registers is crucial. We have found that the best solution for Grøstl-256 is to compute P and Q simultaneously and put one row (64-bit) of each state side by side in one 128-bit XMM register. We then need 8 XMM registers to store both states. Thanks to MixBytes having the same MDS matrix for P and Q we can apply an optimized MixBytes algorithm to the whole XMM register and thus, to 16 columns of the state in parallel.

In Grøstl-512 we have 16 columns for each permutation which perfectly fit into 16 XMM registers. Hence, P and Q are computed separately and after each other but the same MixBytes algorithm can still be used 16 times in parallel again.

Transposing the State. To align the column-ordered message to fit the required row-ordering, the message has to be transposed after being loaded. For this purpose we use the PUNPCK instructions. The same has to be done with the IV for the initialization and in reverse order for the last chaining value before truncation. All the intermediate chaining values are kept in the transposed form.

In more detail, the PUNPCK instruction merges two XMM registers into one XMM register by interleaving the high or low bytes/words/doublewords or quadwords of the two source registers [8]. A simple square matrix can be transposed using only PUNPCK instructions [9]. As we initially have two 64-bit columns in each register, and therefore an 8x16 matrix, we also need PSHUFB and MOV instructions to reorder the data correctly.

AddRoundConstant. AC adds a constant to the state matrix. For P a constant is only added to the first row, for Q the constant is added to all rows. Therefore we need 8 128-bit XORs for Grøstl-256 since P and Q share registers. For Grøstl-512 we need 1 XOR for P and 8 for Q.

SubBytes. The Intel AES instructions provide exactly the functionality required for SubBytes of Grøstl since the same AES S-box is used. The last round of the AES encryption applies ShiftRows, SubBytes and AddRoundKey to the state. This functionality is available by the AESENCLAST instruction. Note that AESENCLAST additionally computes the AES ShiftRows transformation which can be combined with ShiftBytes. The following listing shows the parallel computation of 16 AES S-box lookups:

```
aesenclast xmm0, 0x00000000000000000000000000000000
```

ShiftBytes. We can use the PSHUFB instruction (SSSE3) to quickly reorder the bytes in the XMM registers for ShiftBytes. This instruction is even faster than using shift instructions. Note that we need to include the inverse ShiftRows of AES in the PSHUFB instruction to correctly compute ShiftBytes of Grøstl. Two PSHUFB instructions with constant masks can be merged by shuffling the first mask using the second mask:

```
pshufb xmm0, mask1
pshufb xmm0, mask2
```

is equal to:

```
(pshufb mask1, mask2)
pshufb xmm0, mask1
```

where the shuffled mask is again a constant. The new mask (mask1) can be precomputed.

MixBytes. With the new row ordering we can compute 16 columns in parallel in one pass. If AES-NI is available, the first variant of Section 4.1 for the MixBytes computation gives the best overall performance. This variant contains the minimal possible number of 48 XORs and 16 multiplications by two. Furthermore, the computations are also mostly independent. In the following, we first show different implementation variants of the multiplication by 2 which can then be used in the optimized computation of MixBytes.

Multiplication by 2. If SSE is available, the code shown below can be used to calculate the multiplication in parallel. In this example $xmm1$ is multiplied by 2 and $xmm0$ will be lost (paddb is used instead of psllq because of the shorter opcode):

```
movdqa  xmm0, xmm1
psrlw   xmm1, 7
pand    xmm1, 0x01010101010101010101010101010101
pmullw  xmm1, 0x1b1b1b1b1b1b1b1b1b1b1b1b1b1b1b1b
paddb   xmm0, xmm0
pxor    xmm1, xmm0
```

If SSE 4.1 is available we can use the PBLENDVB instruction to slightly speed up the algorithm described above. PBLENDVB merges two XMM registers into one. The source register is selected by the MSB of each byte in a third register. The MSB is also the bit that decides whether or not it is necessary to reduce the byte after shifting. Therefore we can use this instruction to generate a mask to XOR 0x1B where necessary. The multiplication as implemented is shown below where $xmm2$ is multiplied by 2, $xmm0$ and $xmm1$ are lost:

```
movdqa    xmm0, xmm2
pand      xmm2, 0x1b1b1b1b1b1b1b1b1b1b1b1b1b1b1b1b
pxor      xmm1, xmm1
paddb     xmm2, xmm2
pblendvb  xmm1, 0x7f7f7f7f7f7f7f7f7f7f7f7f7f7f7f7f
pxor      xmm2, xmm1
```

We get the fastest implementation using the PCMPGTB instruction. PCMPGTB compares signed bytes. If the MSB is set, the comparison with zero results in 0xFF and in 0x00 otherwise. The multiplication is shown below where xmm1 will be multiplied by 2, xmm0 will be lost and xmm2 has to be all 0x1B.

```
pxor    xmm0, xmm0
pcmpgtb xmm0, xmm1
paddb   xmm1, xmm1
pand    xmm0, xmm2
pxor    xmm1, xmm0
```

If ALU instructions are the bottleneck in the MixBytes implementation, we can also replace some instructions by their memory variant and get for example:

```
movaps  xmm0, 0x00000000000000000000000000000000
pcmpgtb xmm0, xmm1
paddb   xmm1, xmm1
pand    xmm0, 0x1b1b1b1b1b1b1b1b1b1b1b1b1b1b1b1b
pxor    xmm1, xmm0
```

Improving the MixBytes *Computation.* In the following, we consider the whole MixBytes computation according to Equation (1) on 64-bit Intel architectures with SSE2 instructions. In order to closer reflect the constraints of the assembler code, we rewrite the last equation to contain only one type of operation in each pass. This yields the following sequential formulas:

$$
\begin{aligned}
t_i &= a_i \oplus a_{i+1}, \\
y_i &= a_{i+6} \oplus t_i, \\
y_i &= y_i \oplus t_{i+2}, \\
x_i &= t_i \oplus t_{i+3}, \\
z_i &= 02 \cdot x_i, \\
w_i &= z_i \oplus y_{i+4}, \\
v_i &= 02 \cdot w_i, \\
b_i &= v_{i+3} \oplus y_{i+4}.
\end{aligned}
\tag{3}
$$

The main challenge is to minimise the number of register spills when performing the computation in 16 xmm registers and to reorder the instructions in a way to ensuring maximal instruction throughput. The algorithm shown in Table 2 achieves this with only four spills that are not on a critical path and therefore can be masked by other operations.

We start with $a_0, \ldots, a_7$ in registers xmm0, ..., xmm7 and keep building $b_0, \ldots, b_7$ in xmm8, ..., xmm15. The bytewise multiplication by 02 of the content of xmm{i} is done using the PCMPGTB instruction without memory. This requires an extra register xmm{j} as a scratch space and xmm{k} containing the constant reduction value of 1b1b...1b. To get those extra registers, we can temporarily spill xmm8, xmm9 since they hold the values y_4, y_5 which will not be used in a critical path of the computation.

Further Optimizations. For the best overall performance we tried different local optimization techniques. More specifically, we

- tried different variants of the MixBytes computation
- unrolled loops
- used precomputed constants for AddRoundConstant
- analyzed different instruction orders to improve parallel executions in different ALUs (micro-ops)
- used equivalent instructions with smaller opcode where possible
- tried different variants for the multiplication by 2
- used different variants of equivalent LOAD/ STORE or ALU instructions to keep all units busy

While unrolling loops works perfectly for Grøstl-256, we found that unrolling all loops in Grøstl-512 increases the code size to exceed the cache size of the used CPU. This causes an immense drop in performance. Therefore using loops is necessary in this implementation.

Table 2. Improved computation of MixBytes on a 64-bit Intel machine with SSE2 instructions. Each row describes eight operations for $i = 0, \ldots, 7$. Left columns show the content of two banks of registers with updated values shown in bold and the rightmost column describes the performed operation. MUL2(xmma,xmmb,xmmc) doubles the content of xmma using xmmb as scratch and assuming xmmc contains 1b..1b.

xmm0 ... xmm7	xmm8 ... xmm15	operation
$a_0 a_1 \ldots a_7$	—	
$a_0 a_1 \ldots a_7$	$\mathbf{a_2\ a_3} \ldots \mathbf{a_1}$	movdqa xmm$\{i + 8\}$, xmm$\{(i + 2) \bmod 8\}$
$\mathbf{t_0 t_1} \ldots \mathbf{t_7}$	$a_2\ a_3 \ldots a_1$	pxor xmm$\{i\}$, xmm$\{(i + 1) \bmod 8\}$
		pxor xmm$\{i + 8\}$, xmm$\{(i + 4) \bmod 8\}$
$t_0 t_1 \ldots t_7$	$\mathbf{y_4\ y_5} \ldots \mathbf{y_3}$	pxor xmm$\{i + 8\}$, xmm$\{(i + 6) \bmod 8\}$
		spill t_0, t_1, t_2 to memory (used below)
$\mathbf{x_0 x_1} \ldots \mathbf{x_7}$	$y_4\ y_5 \ldots y_3$	pxor xmm$\{i\}$, xmm$\{(i + 3) \bmod 8\}$
	$y_4\ 1b..1b\ y_6 \ldots y_3$	spill xmm8, xmm9 to memory, xmm9← 0x1b...1b
$\mathbf{z_0 z_1} \ldots \mathbf{z_7}$	— $1b..1b\ y_6 \ldots y_3$	MUL2 (xmm$\{i\}$, xmm8, xmm9)
$\mathbf{w_0 w_1} \ldots \mathbf{w_7}$	— $1b..1b\ y_6 \ldots y_3$	pxor xmm$\{i\}$, xmm$\{(i + 8)\}$, y_4, y_5 xored from mem
$\mathbf{v_0 v_1} \ldots \mathbf{v_7}$	— $1b..1b\ y_6 \ldots y_3$	MUL2 (xmm$\{i\}$, xmm8, xmm9)
$v_0 v_1 \ldots v_7$	$\mathbf{y_4\ y_5}\ y_6 \ldots y_3$	reload y_4, y_5 back to xmm8, xmm9
$v_0 v_1 \ldots v_7$	$\mathbf{b_0\ b_1} \ldots \mathbf{b_7}$	pxor xmm$\{i + 8\}$, xmm$\{(i + 3) \bmod 8\}$

5.2 Vperm

Even if no AES-NI are available, we can still implement Grøstl efficiently using a byteslice implementation. Hamburg [5] uses vector permute (vperm) instructions to compute the inversion and affine transformation of the AES S-box in parallel. Grøstl has been first implemented this way in [10]. We have implemented this AES S-box computation and improved the previous results using our optimized MixBytes computations. The resulting implementation needs SSSE3 instructions and thus, also runs on the NIST reference platform.

Again, the state is stored in row-ordering and hence, the input transformation of the message block can be performed as described in Section 5.1. In the following, the computation of SubBytes and MixBytes are somewhat merged. Therefore, we swap the order of AddRoundConstant and ShiftBytes for an easier description.

AddRoundConstant. The AddRoundConstant implementation is implemented using the same instructions as in the AES-NI implementation. However, since the vperm implementation uses a different basis, the constants need to be transformed to this basis as well. The resulting constants can be precomputed and stored in memory. For the specific constants, we refer to the actual vperm implementation of Grøstl.

ShiftBytes. ShiftBytes is computed using single byte shuffle instructions for each row of P and Q. For example, the used rotation constants for the PSHUFB instruction of Grøstl-256 for the first row are given in the following assembly code listing:

```
pshufb xmm0, 0x080f0e0d0c0b0a090706050403020100
```

SubBytes. In the vperm implementation, the inverse in $GF(2^8)$ of the AES S-box is computed using small log tables of the finite field $GF(2^4)$. To efficiently compute these log tables, the 128-bit PSHUFB instruction of SSSE3 is used as a 4-to-8 bit lookup table. For more details, we refer to the original paper [5]. The first vperm implementation has been published by Çalik [10] which served as a reference for our optimized implementation.

Using the vperm implementation, 16 AES S-boxes can be computed in parallel within less than 10 cycles. An additional advantage of this implementation is that we can multiply the resulting outputs by constants in $GF(2^8)$ almost without no additional cost. Hence, the vperm implementation of SubBytes actually returns the values $S(x_i)$, $02 \cdot S(x_i)$ and $04 \cdot S(x_i)$ for each of the 16 input bytes x_i.

MixBytes. Since the multiplication by 02 and 04 of the input bytes to MixBytes are already computed in SubBytes, the formulas resulting in only 48 XORs of Section 4.1 cannot be used. However, we can use the method of Section 4.2 which reuses temporary results once the multiplications have already been performed. The additional 18 XORs of this approach still lead to a more efficient implementation, since we save 5 instructions for each of the 16 multiplications by 02.

5.3 Intel AVX

When AVX instructions are available (starting from Intel Sandy Bridge) we can compute 32 columns of Grøstl in parallel using 256-bit AVX registers. Note that we can only use this full parallelism for Grøstl-512. In this case, we store the state of P and Q in 8 256-bit ymm registers in parallel. Since the AESENCLAST and PSHUFB instructions do not have 256-bit variants, we need two 128-bit instructions in this case. For the computation of Grøstl-256, we use only the lower 128-bits of the AVX registers. However, also Grøstl-256 benefits from AVX, since AVX provides three-operand instructions which slightly reduces the overall number of instructions.

5.4 Intel Benchmarks

The final round version of Grøstl has been benchmarked on an Intel Core i5-2400, Intel Core i7-620LM and Intel Core2 Duo L9400. For comparison, we also show benchmarks of the T-table implementation and the vperm implementation. Note that the resulting vperm implementation is about as fast as the T-table based implementation. The results are shown in Table 3.

5.5 8-bit AVR (ATmega163)

The ATmega163 is an 8-bit microcontroller with 32 8-bit multi-purpose registers, 1024 Bytes of SRAM and 16K of flash memory. The multi-purpose registers can be used to manipulate data. The controller needs 2 cycles to read from and write to the SRAM and 3 cycles to read from flash memory. Six of the 8-bit registers are used as 16-bit address registers X, Y and Z, thus they can usually not be used for computations. For a list of instructions see [11].

Table 3. Speed of the Grøstl AES-NI and vperm implementations in cylces/byte on an Intel Core i5-2400, Intel Core i7-M620 and Intel Core2 Duo L9400 processor

CPU	Version	Grøstl-256	Grøstl-512
Core i5-2400	avx	9.6	20.3
	aesni	9.9	13.8
	vperm	19.1	25.9
	(T-tables)	20.4	31.3
Core i7-M620	aesni	12.2	18.6
	vperm	23.2	32.6
	(T-tables)	24.0	35.9
Core2 Duo L9400	vperm	20.8	29.2
	(T-tables)	20.4	30.3

Because of the limited bit width of the architecture we can only compute one column at once. Therefore the most important part of the 8-bit optimization is minimizing the number of XORs in MixBytes as described above. With 26 available general purpose registers we have just enough space to keep the intermediate values loaded at all times during the computation of one column. All the other columns have to be written back to RAM.

The multiplication in $\mathbb{F}_{256}$ can be implemented with the code shown below, where r0 is multiplied by 2, r1 has to be pre-set to 0x1B and r2 will be lost.

```
LSL   r0         # r0 = r0 << 1
IN    r2 , 0x3F  # r2 = status register
SBRC  r2 , 0     # skip next if no carry
EOR   r0 , r1    # r0 = r0 + 0x1B
```

These instructions will take 4 cycles to process on the selected CPU. As they are executed for every byte of the state it is faster to have a lookup table for the multiplication if enough memory is available.

AddRoundConstant and SubBytes are computed for each byte separately using XORs and table lookups. ShiftBytes is achieved at no cost by simply loading from shifted positions in RAM. For more details on the 8-bit implementation we refer to the full description of the implementation [12]. Note that this implementation can probably be further improved using the MixBytes computation of Section 4.1.

Benchmarks. We have implemented two different versions of the 8-bit implementation with the final round tweak (Grøstl) and three versions without the final round tweak (Grøstl-0) using different amounts of RAM. The versions are compared in Table 4.

Table 4. Speed of three different Grøstl-256 8-bit AVR implementations in cycles/byte on an ATMega163. The last line shows the RAM usage in bytes.

	HighSpeed	Balanced	LowMem
Grøstl	469	530	-
Grøstl-0	456	517	738
RAM	994	226	164

6   Conclusions

In this work we have proposed two optimized algorithms for MixBytes, the MDS mixing layer of Grøstl, which allow to speed up Grøstl on various platforms. Furthermore, byte slicing provides the possibility to parallelize the Grøstl computation if the registers are large enough and parallel AES S-box table lookups are available. This is the case for Intel processors including the new AES instructions set or in general, using the vperm implementation of Hamburg [5].

Both implementations show that Grøstl can be implemented efficiently on very different platforms. The 8-bit implementation will run at 469 cycles per byte on this very limited target hardware. The AES-NI implementation shows that even though Grøstl is very different from AES it can still take advantage of these new instructions. More specifically, our Intel AES-NI implementation of Grøstl is the fastest known implementation so far. Grøstl-256 runs now at less than 10 cycles per byte on an Intel Core i5-2400 or Core i7-620LM, which is about 50% faster than the table-based version on the same CPU.

We have reduced the number of operation needed to compute MixBytes to only 48 XORs with 16 multiplications by 2. Furthermore, we have shown that new CPU features like AVX with 256-bit registers provide another opportunity to increase the performance. Especially in the case of Grøstl-512, we use a byte slice implementation which can compute 32 columns in parallel. Future work includes the optimization of MixBytes for Grøstl-256 to use the full width of AVX registers as well.

Acknowledgements. This work was supported in part by the European Commission through the ICT Programme under Contract ICT-2007-216646 ECRYPT II, by the Austrian Science Fund (FWF), project P21936 and by the IAP Programme P6/26 BCRYPT of the Belgian State (Belgian Science Policy).

References

1. National Institute of Standards and Technology: Cryptographic Hash Project (2007), http://www.nist.gov/hash-competition
2. Gueron, S., Intel Corp.: Intel®Advanced Encryption Standard (AES) Instructions Set (2010), http://software.intel.com/en-us/articles/intel-advanced-encryption-standard-aes-instructions-set/ (retrieved December 21, 2010)
3. Benadjila, R., Billet, O., Gueron, S., Robshaw, M.: The Intel AES Instructions Set and the SHA-3 Candidates (2009), http://crypto.rd.francetelecom.com/ECHO/sha3/AES/ (retrieved December 22, 2010)
4. Gauravaram, P., Knudsen, L.R., Matusiewicz, K., Mendel, F., Rechberger, C., Schläffer, M., Thomsen, S.S.: *Grøstl – a SHA-3 candidate.* Submission to NIST (Round 3) (2011), http://www.groestl.info (retrieved May 03, 2010)
5. Hamburg, M.: Accelerating AES with Vector Permute Instructions. In: Clavier, C., Gaj, K. (eds.) CHES 2009. LNCS, vol. 5747, pp. 18–32. Springer, Heidelberg (2009)
6. National Institute of Standards and Technology: FIPS PUB 197, Advanced Encryption Standard (AES). Federal Information Processing Standards Publication 197, U.S. Department of Commerce (2001)

7. Fouque, P.A., Stern, J., Zimmer, S.: Cryptanalysis of Tweaked Versions of SMASH and Reparation. In: Avanzi, R.M., Keliher, L., Sica, F. (eds.) SAC 2008. LNCS, vol. 5381, pp. 136–150. Springer, Heidelberg (2009)

8. Intel Corp.: Intel®64 and IA-32 Architectures Software Developers Manual (2010), http://www.intel.com/products/processor/manuals/ (retrieved December 21, 2010)

9. Intel Corp.: Using MMX™ Instructions to Transpose a Matrix (1996), ftp://download.intel.com/ids/mmx/MMX_App_Transpose_Matrix.pdf (retrieved July 12, 2011)

10. Çalik, Ç.: Multi-stream and Constant-time SHA-3 Implementations. NIST hash function mailing list (2010), http://www.metu.edu.tr/~ccalik/software.html#sha3 (retrieved May 03, 2010)

11. Atmel: 8-bit AVR Microcontroller with 16K Bytes In-System Programmable Flash. ATmega163 (2003), http://www.atmel.com/dyn/resources/prod_documents/doc1142.pdf (retrieved December 21, 2010)

12. Roland, G.A.: Efficient Implementation of the *Grøstl*-256 Hash Function on an ATmega163 Microcontroller (2009), http://groestl.info (retrieved May 03, 2010)

Attack Interference:
A Path to Defending Security Protocols

Maria-Camilla Fiazza, Michele Peroli, and Luca Viganò

Department of Computer Science, University of Verona, Strada le Grazie 15, Verona, Italy
camilla.fiazza@metropolis.sci.univr.it,
{michele.peroli,luca.vigano}@univr.it

Abstract. Traditionally security protocol analysis relies on a single Dolev-Yao attacker. This type of attacker is so powerful that overall attack power does not change if additional attackers cooperate. In this paper, we take a fundamentally different approach and investigate the case of multiple non-collaborating attackers. We show how non-collaboration between attackers gives rise to interference between ongoing attacks and that it is possible to actively exploit attack interference to mitigate security breaches and provide partial protection to weak protocols.

1 Introduction

1.1 Context

The typical attacker model adopted in security protocol analysis is the one of [12]: the *Dolev-Yao (DY) attacker* can compose, send and intercept messages at will, but, following the perfect cryptography assumption, he cannot break cryptography. The DY attacker is thus in complete control of the network — in fact, he is often formalized as being the network itself. With respect to network abilities, he is actually stronger than any attacker that can be implemented in real-life situations. Hence, if a protocol is proved to be secure under the DY attacker, it will also withstand attacks carried out by less powerful attackers. Aside from deviations from the specification introduced in the implementation phase, the protocol can thus be safely employed in real-life networks, at least in principle.

The standard choice to consider a single DY attacker is motivated by the fact that models with multiple collaborating DY attackers have been shown to be reducible to models with one DY attacker (see, e.g., [8] for a detailed proof, as well as [3,10,18] for general results on the reduction of the number of agents to be considered). Different symbolic models have been recently proposed that consider *multiple attackers* instead of following the usual practice. For instance, [4,17] extend the DY model to account for network topology, transmission delays, and node positions in the analysis of real-world security protocols, in particular for wireless networks. This results in a distributed attacker, or actually multiple distributed attackers, with restricted, but more realistic, communication capabilities than those of the standard DY attacker.

Multiple attackers are also considered in the models of [1,2,5,6], where each protocol participant is allowed to behave maliciously and intercept and forge messages. In fact,

M.S. Obaidat, J.L. Sevillano, and J. Filipe (Eds.): ICETE 2011, CCIS 314, pp. 296–314, 2012.
© Springer-Verlag Berlin Heidelberg 2012

each agent may behave as a DY attacker, without colluding nor sharing knowledge with anyone else. Agents in this model may also carry out *retaliation attacks*, where an attack is followed by a counterattack, and *anticipation attacks*, where an agent's attack is anticipated, before its termination, by another attack by some other agent.

The features of the models of [4,17] and of [1,2,5,6] rule out the applicability of the n-to-1 reducibility result for the DY attacker, as the attackers do not necessarily collaborate, and might actually possess different knowledge to launch their attacks. They might even attack each other. In fact, retaliation and anticipation allow protocols to cope with their own vulnerabilities, rather than eradicating them. This is possible because agents are capable of doing more than just executing the steps prescribed by a protocol: they can decide to anticipate an attack, or to counter-attack by acting even after the end of a protocol run (in which they have been attacked). Still, retaliation may nevertheless be too weak as honest agents can retaliate only *after* an attack has succeeded, and cannot defend the protocol during the attack itself.

1.2 Contributions

In this paper, we take a fundamentally different approach: we show that multiple non-collaborating DY attackers may interfere with each other in such a manner that it is possible to exploit interference to mitigate protocol vulnerabilities, thus providing a form of protection to flawed protocols.

In the approach we propose, instead of looking for attacks and reacting to the existence of one by redesigning the vulnerable protocol, we look for strategies for defending against existing known attacks. We would be performing protocol analysis to identify possible *defenses*, rather than attacks.

To investigate non-cooperation between attackers, we propose a (protocol-independent) model in which: (i) a protocol is run in the presence of multiple attackers, and (ii) attackers potentially have different capabilities, different knowledge and can interfere with each other. This, ultimately, allows us to create a benign attacker for system defense: honest agents can rely on a *network guardian*, an ad-hoc agent whose task is diminishing the frequency with which dishonest agents can succeed in attacking vulnerable protocols. This methodology moves the focus away from an attack-based view of security and towards a defense-based view.

We proceed as follows. In Section 2, we formalize models for the network and the agents, including, in particular, agent attitude, goals, and disposition. We then consider in Section 3 a vulnerable protocol from [7] as a case study and focus on the interactions between attack procedures, interactions which cannot be observed in classical settings. In Section 4, we explain how interference between attacks leads to a methodology that can be used for defending vulnerable protocols against attacks. In Section 5, we conclude by discussing our approach. This paper is a revised version of [13].

2 System Models: Network, Agents, Attitude

2.1 Goals of Modeling and Approach

Network models for security protocol analysis typically either replace the communication channel with a single attacker or build dedicated channels for each attacker (e.g., [3,8,11,14,18]). Traditional modeling strategies are not adequate to describe the non-collaborative scenario under consideration. The main shortcoming is the fact that the ability to spy the communication on a particular channel is hard-wired in the network model and may depend critically on network topology or attacker identity; the result is that an information-sharing mechanism (or a partial prohibition for it) is structurally encoded in the network. We would like, instead, to (i) abstract from positional advantages and focus solely on how attackers interfere *by attacking*; (ii) treat information-sharing (also as a result of spying) as a strategic choice of the agents.

For simplicity, in this paper we restrict our attention to *two* non-collaborative attackers (E_1 and E_2), in addition to the two honest agents A and B and a trusted third-party server S, whose presence is required by the protocol under consideration. In the following, let *Eves*$= \{E_1, E_2\}$ be the *set of attackers* and *Agents*$= \{A, B, E_1, E_2\}$ the *set of all network agents* (honest and dishonest, server excluded). Let X, Y, Z and W be variables varying in *Agents* and E a variable in *Eves*; j takes value in $\{1, 2\}$, whereas $i \in \mathbb{N}$ is reserved for indexing states.

We are aware that, in situations with more than two (dis)honest agents, further types of interactions can arise; however, a full comprehension of the interactions depends on building a clear picture of interference. Such a picture necessarily starts with the elementary interaction between two attackers.

In order to focus on the raw interference between two attackers, both directing their attack towards the same target, it is important for all attackers to have access to the same view of what is taking place with honest agents and possibly different views of what is taking place with the other attacker(s). If attackers do not all have the same information, it is possible to conceive of strategies in which some attackers can be mislead by others on purpose.

If the knowledge[1] available to an attacker affects his view of the system, attacker capabilities and effectiveness can be diversified, without needing to construct asymmetric attackers or hardwire constraints that may hold for some attackers and not for others. We find it relevant that a network model for non-collaborative scenarios — besides reflecting this stance — also support a form of competition for access to messages, especially if attacks rely on erasing messages.

If it is possible in principle to actively interfere with an attack, it should be possible to do so even if all attackers have the same knowledge. However, differentiating attackers with respect to their understanding of the situation — in particular with respect to awareness of other attackers — may bring into focus the conditions, if any, that allow an attacker to interfere with another without being interfered with.

We diversify the activity of our attackers by admitting that attackers may choose to selectively ignore some messages, on the basis of the sender's and receiver's identifiers. This choice reflects actual situations in which attackers pay attention to only a subset of the traffic through a network, focusing on the activity of some agents of interest. In the following, we will use the set $Attend_E$ to model the agents to which attacker E is attentive; the predicate $ofInterest_E(X)$ (see Table 1) models the decisional process

---

[1] Note that we do not attach any epistemic interpretation to the knowledge we consider in this paper. We simply consider the information initially available to the agents, together with the information they acquire during protocol executions.

of attacker E as he considers whether he wishes to augment $Attend_E$ with X, i.e., $ofInterest_E(X)$ implies that X is added into $Attend_E$.

Honest agents are interested in *security properties* (such as authentication or secrecy) being upheld through the use of protocols. Dishonest agents, on the other hand, are interested in changing or negating such properties. The characteristic feature of the attackers we consider is their attitude. In particular, in the case study presented in Section 3, dishonest agents wish to attack the security protocol and are ready, should they encounter unforeseen interference, to take countermeasures with respect to the interference as well. In a sense, each attacker is exclusively focused on attacking the protocol and becomes aware of other attackers through their effect on his success.

Our target is capturing the behavior of *equal-opportunity* dishonest agents that do not cooperate in the classical sense. By equal-opportunity attackers we mean agents that have the same attack power and that may differ with respect to the information content of their knowledge bases. Such differentiation arises out of attentional choices and not out of intrinsic constraints. Strategic and attitude considerations should not be derivable explicitly from the attacker model — rather, they should configure it.

The driving hypothesis of our work is that studying non-collaboration requires a complex notion of attacker, whose full specification involves attentional choices, decisional processes pertaining to the network environment and to other agents, cooperation-related choices and decisional processes pertaining to the attack strategy. To support this type of attacker, we extend the usual notions of protocol and role by introducing a control — a mechanism to regulate the execution of the steps prescribed by the attack trace in accordance with the attacker's strategy. In our model, honest agents perform a controlled execution of the protocol as well, so as to support in-protocol detection of attacks. Honest agents behave according to the protocol's prescription, expect things to go exactly in accordance with the protocol and interpret deviations in terms of the activity of dishonest agents.

2.2   Agent Model

Agent knowledge is characterized in terms of a proprietary dataset. To each X in *Agents*, we associate the dataset D_X, which we assume to be monotonically non-decreasing. Our agents, in particular dishonest agents, collect information but do not forget it. When it is important to highlight that the dataset is to be considered at a particular moment, we will use D_X^i instead.

The network *net* is also formalized through a dataset, which is named D_{net} and indexed in the same manner as D_X^i. A dataset is a simple network model that can be configured to support complex attackers; we believe it can successfully meet all of our modeling requirements for non-collaboration. We postpone to Section 2.3 the discussion of how datasets evolve and how indexing and evolution are related to actions and message transmission.

We adapt the notion of DY attacker [12] to capture a non-collaborative scenario. We show in Table 1 how one such attacker is formalized within our model, writing rules for attacker E with respect to the knowledge base D_E and the network model D_{net}. Let us specify that the rules in Table 1 are transition rules, rather than deduction rules. Taken altogether, they construct a *transition system*, which describes a computation by

Table 1. Dolev-Yao attacker model for non-collaborative scenarios: internal operations (synthesis and analysis of messages), network operations (*spy, inject, erase*) and system configuration (*True-Sender-ID, DecisionalProcess, NetHandler*). *NetHandler* describes the set of attackers who are allowed to spy by applying one of the *spy* rules. We omit the usual rules for conjunction. The rules employed in the case study are marked in boldface.

$$\frac{m_1 \in D_E^i \quad m_2 \in D_E^i}{(m_1, m_2) \in D_E^i} \ \textbf{(Comp)} \qquad \frac{m \in D_E^i \quad k \in D_E^i}{\{m\}_k \in D_E^i} \ \textbf{(Encr)}$$

$$\frac{(m_1, m_2) \in D_E^i}{m_j \in D_E^i \ \text{for} \ j \in \{1, 2\}} \ \textbf{(Proj)} \qquad \frac{\{m\}_k \in D_E^i \quad k^{-1} \in D_E^i}{m \in D_E^i} \ \textbf{(Decr)}$$

$$\frac{< X, m, Y > \in D_{net}^i \quad sender(< X, m, Y >) \in D_E^i \quad Y \in D_E^i \quad \psi}{m \in D_E^{i+1}} \ \textbf{(Restricted-Spy)}$$

$$\frac{< X, m, Y > \in D_{net}^i \quad ofInterest_E(X) \quad Y \in D_E^i \quad \psi}{m \in D_E^{i+1} \wedge sender(< X, m, Y >) \in D_E^{i+1}} \ (Inflow\text{-}Spy)$$

$$\frac{< X, m, Y > \in D_{net}^i \quad sender(< X, m, Y >) \in D_E^i \quad ofInterest_E(Y) \quad \psi}{m \in D_E^{i+1} \wedge Y \in D_E^{i+1}} \ (Outflow\text{-}Spy)$$

$$\text{where } \psi = E \in canSee(< X, m, Y >, i)$$

$$\frac{m \in D_E^i \quad X \in D_E^i \quad Y \in D_E^i}{< E(X), m, Y > \in D_{net}^{i+1}} \ \textbf{(Injection)}$$

$$\frac{< X, m, Y > \in D_{net}^i \quad sender(< X, m, Y >) \in D_E^i}{< X, m, Y > \notin D_{net}^{i+1}} \ \textbf{(Erase)}$$

$$sender(< X, m, Y >) = \begin{cases} E & \text{if there exists } Z \text{ such that } X = E(Z) \\ X & \text{otherwise} \end{cases} \ \textit{(True-sender-ID)}$$

$$ofInterest_E(X) = \begin{cases} true & \text{if } E \text{ decides to pay attention to } X \\ false & \text{otherwise} \end{cases} \ (DecisionalProcess)$$

$$canSee(< X, m, Y >, i) = \{Z \in Eves \mid Z \text{ can spy } < X, m, Y > \text{ on } D_{net}^i\} \ \textit{(NetHandler)}$$

describing the states that are upheld as a result of the transition. We do not intend to carry out in this paper logical inference to identify defenses against attacks; rather, we recognize in the system's evolution what in our eyes corresponds to a defense.

Attackers are legitimate network agents that can *send* and *receive* messages, derive new messages by analyzing (e.g., decomposing) known messages, obtain messages transiting on the network (*spy*) and remove them so that they do not reach their intended receiver (*erase*). Attackers can also partially impersonate other agents, by *injecting* messages under a false identity; we represent impersonification with the notation $E(X)$, where E is the impersonator and X is the identifier of the impersonated agent. This set of abilities describes agents who have control over almost all facets of a communication; their characteristic limitation is that they cannot violate cryptography (we assume perfect cryptography). Note that further rules could be added in Table 1 for other forms of encryption, digital signatures, hashing, creation of nonces and other fresh data, and so on. For conceptual clarity, we explicitly pair an *erase*-rule with the *injection*-rule, to emphasize that an attacker can modify messages (by erasing them and injecting a substitute) or send messages under a false identity (partial impersonification).

The most significant feature concerns spying. Our attackers can employ three different *spy* rules, adapted to formalize the fact that attackers do not pay attention to all of the traffic on the network. The *spy* rules rely on an interpretation for "send" that is modified with respect to the denotational semantics in [9], to reflect the attentional focus of attackers. The default *spy* is the *Restricted-Spy*: only the messages involving known agents in both sender and receiver roles, regardless of hypotheses on their honesty, become part of the attacker's dataset. Note that in our model what matters is the actual sender and not the declared sender (*True-Sender-ID*). This mechanism prevents total impersonification and allows filtering messages on the basis of the agent's attentional choices.

The attentional filter we use is meant as a choice of the agents and not as a constraint to which they are subject; therefore, it must be possible to expand the set of agents of interest. This role is fulfilled by the two exploratory *spy* rules in Table 1, *Inflow-Spy* and *Outflow-Spy*. Attackers have the option of accepting or rejecting the newly discovered identifier X, on the basis of the predicate $ofInterest_E(X)$, which models the decisional process for attention.

Note that an attacker cannot apply any of the *spy* rules to obtain the message m without knowing the identifier of at least one between m's sender and m's intended receiver. By not providing a "generalized spy" rule to waive this requirement, we ensure that $(D_E^0 \cap Agents = \emptyset)$ implies that for all i, $(D_E^i \cap Agents = \emptyset)$. Although E can augment its knowledge base D_E indefinitely — through internal message generation and the synthesis rules *Comp* and *Encr* —, E's network activity is in fact null. One such E is a *dummy attacker*, whose usefulness becomes apparent when considering that proof of reductions for non-collaboration can involve progressively migrating identifiers from an attacker's dataset, until the attacker himself reduces to the dummy attacker.

An attacker's dataset D_E consists of (i) messages that have transited through the network and that have been successfully received, analyzed or spied and (ii) identifiers of the agents to whom the attacker is attentive. The set $Attend_E$ of identifiers of interest to E is further partitioned into three sets: the set H_E of agents believed[2] to be honest, the set A_E of agents believed to be attackers, and the set U_E of agents whose attitude is unknown in E's eyes. Differently from D_{net}, agent datasets do not contain triplets ($\langle sender\text{-}ID, message, receiver\text{-}ID \rangle$), but only messages or identifiers.

Once a new identifier X enters the knowledge base of attacker E, E establishes a belief about the honesty of X and places the identifier in one of the sets H_E, A_E or

---

[2] We do not attach any doxastic interpretation to the beliefs we consider in this paper.

U_E. We do not enter details on how the agents initially build their knowledge base and establish their belief about the attitude of other known agents. In fact, this classification is meant to be dynamic. Agents are on the watch for suspicious messages, which may indicate that an attack is ongoing or may reveal that a certain agent is dishonest. Dynamically adapting their beliefs about the honesty of other agents allows the agents to gather important information during single protocol runs. The agents we wish to consider are *smart*: they always employ the available strategic information.

Attackers do not have automatic access to triplets that relate sender, message and receiver. They must infer this key piece of information on the basis of the identifiers of the agents to which they are attentive, and attempt to relate the identifiers to the messages they spy. Inference is easier if attackers use only the *Restricted-Spy* rule and keep the set $Attend_E$ of known agents small.

2.3   Network Model

All the operations that can change the state of the network dataset D_{net} (*send*, *receive*, *inject* and *erase*) are termed *actions*, whereas we consider *spy* simply as an operation: although it requires interacting with the network, it does not change its state. Messages in transit are inserted in the network dataset D_{net}, where attackers can spy them before they are delivered to their intended receivers. Contextually to delivery, the message is removed from the dataset. Messages transit on the network dataset in the form of triplets of the type $\langle sender\text{-}ID, message, receiver\text{-}ID \rangle$. As a consequence of message delivery or deletion, D_{net} is non-monotonic by construction.

The sequence of actions that takes place during a protocol run is enumerated and used to index the evolution of the network dataset D_{net}; the index of D_{net}^i is shared with all the proprietary datasets D_X^i, whose states are synchronized accordingly. D_{net}^i is the state of the network dataset *after the i-th action*.

Customarily, evolutions are indexed per transition (per rule application), rather than per action. Our chosen indexing strategy reflects three needs: (1) allowing agents to fully analyze newly acquired messages without having to keep track of the number of internal operations performed; (2) supporting a form of competition between attackers for access to the network; (3) supporting a form of concurrency.

Ideally, all attackers act concurrently. However, the state transitions for the network must be well-defined at all times, even if attackers try to perform conflicting actions, such as spying and deleting the same message in transit. To impose a measure of order, we introduce a *network handler* (cf. Figure 1), whose task is to regulate the selection of the next action and implement the dependencies between selected action and knowledge available to each attacker. More specifically, *NetHandler*:

– notifies agents that the state of the network has changed with newly-inserted messages,
– polls agents for their next intended action,
– selects from the set of candidate (requested) actions the one that will be implemented, and
– informs agents of whether the computation they performed to propose an action is a consequence of a message that they did not have access to (rollback).

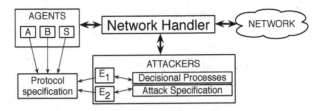

Fig. 1. Network Design for scenarios with non-collaborating attackers: system overview

As soon as the state of the network changes (e.g., as a result of *inject* or *send*), the network handler passes the new triplet to each attacker, who then *simulates* spying and decides on whether to request erasing the message or injecting a new one as a consequence, in accordance with his strategy. The network handler interprets the application of the inject-rule and of the erase-rule as requests and selects the next action from the set of requests. Message deletion, when requested by any attacker, is always successful.

These tasks of the network handler are a necessary component of the system; the network handler, however, can play a larger role, keeping the system evolution in accordance with additional constraints, e.g., modeling information sharing within specific subsets of agents or modeling network topology. Furthermore, a central coordination is needed to implement all the protocol-related operations that cannot be implemented at the agent level, e.g., testing if a given item is a nonce.

The outcome of the process governed by the network handler is described through the function $canSee()$, which returns a subset of *Eves*, highlighting the identifiers of the attackers who can spy "before" the message is erased from D_{net}. The set of agents described by $canSee()$ contains at least the identifier of the attacker whose erase/inject request was served.

If the network handler does not receive any erase-requests or inject-requests, all attentive attackers can acquire the message. If one or more erase-requests are present, the network handler erases the message and confirms success in spying only for a subset of attentive attackers. If an attacker is not in $canSee()$, the prior (simulated) spy is subject to rollback, along with all internal operations that have occurred since the last confirmed action. If no requests are received from attackers, the network handler oversees message delivery or selects actions requested by honest agents.

Although the formulation of $canSee()$ in terms of access time is intuitive, the reason why we favor this mechanism is that time-dependent accessibility is not the only situation it can model. The function can be instantiated to model strategic decision-making and information-sharing, or to capture a particular network topology. In realistic attack scenarios, knowledge of a message that has been erased may depend more on cooperation and information-sharing than on timing. For example, if E_j is sharing information with E_k (but not vice versa), whenever E_j's erase requests are served E_k is automatically in $canSee()$.

The network handler is not an intelligent agent. Specifying its behavior and instantiating the function $canSee()$ corresponds to configuring the particular network environment in which the agents are immersed (i.e., $canSee()$ is a configurable parameter of our model).

Table 2. Representation of operations in Alice&Bob notation

$(i+1)^{\text{th}}$ action	Formalization
$X \to Y \; : \; m$	$m \in D_X^i \quad$ and $\quad Y \in D_X^i$
	$< X, m, Y > \in D_{net}^{i+1} \quad$ and $\quad < X, m, Y > \notin D_{net}^{i+2}$
	$m \notin D_W^{i+2}$, where $W \notin canSee(< X, m, Y >, i+1)$
	$m \in D_Y^{i+2}$
$E(X) \to Y \; : \; m$	$m \in D_E^i \quad$ and $\quad X \in D_E^i \quad$ and $\quad Y \in D_E^i$
	$< E(X), m, Y > \in D_{net}^{i+1} \quad$ and $\quad < E(X), m, Y > \notin D_{net}^{i+2}$
	$m \notin D_W^{i+2}$, where $W \notin canSee(< X, m, Y >, i+1)$
	$m \in D_Y^{i+2}$
$X \to E_I(Y) \; : \; m$	$m \in D_X^i \quad$ and $\quad Y \in D_X^i$
	$< X, m, Y > \in D_{net}^{i+1} \quad$ and $\quad < X, m, Y > \notin D_{net}^{i+2}$
	$m \in D_W^{i+2}$, where $W \in I$ and $I \subseteq canSee(< X, m, Y >, i+1)$

As a result of the network handler and of our chosen indexing strategy, several internal operations can occur in a proprietary dataset between consecutive states, whereas only a single action separates consecutive states of the network dataset. Attackers determine the next state of the network dataset with priority with respect to the actions of honest agents.

In Table 2, we formalize within our model operations in the Alice&Bob notation used in Section 3; we write $E_I(Y)$ to denote the subset of *Eves* who spy message m addressed to Y, at least one of which has requested m to be erased.

With reference to Table 2, note that the $(i+1)^{\text{th}}$ action is requested when the state of the network is D_{net}^i and agent datasets are D_X^i; thus, the sender X must already know in D_X^i both the message m and the identifier of the intended recipient Y. The message correctly transits on D_{net}^{i+1}, immediately after being sent. The $(i+2)^{\text{th}}$ action is either *receive* (first two cases) or *erase* (last case). The availability of m to attackers is conclusively decided after the network handler selects the $(i+2)^{\text{th}}$ action, and thus pertains to D_W^{i+2}.

2.4 Attacker Goals and Disposition

The notion of cooperation between agents can be viewed from at least two perspectives of interest: sharing of information and sharing of success. The notion of attacker cooperation classically employed in protocol analysis encompasses both aspects, as it states the first while assuming that the second holds.

In this paper, we examine attackers that exhibit, with respect to cooperation, the behavior we call *complete non-collaboration*: agents voluntarily abstain from sharing information and do not consider their goals as met if they do not succeed in attacking. The *disposition* of attacker E_1 towards E_2 belongs to one of the following basic

Table 3. The Boyd-Mathuria Example protocol and a masquerading attack against it

BME	Classical Attack
(1) $A \to S : A, B$ (2) $S \to A : \{\!\|k_{AB}\|\!\}_{k_{AS}}, \{\!\|k_{AB}\|\!\}_{k_{BS}}$ (3) $A \to B : \{\!\|k_{AB}\|\!\}_{k_{BS}}$	(1) $A \to E(S) : A, B$ (1') $E(A) \to S : A, E$ (2) $S \to A \quad : \{\!\|k_{AE}\|\!\}_{k_{AS}}, \{\!\|k_{AE}\|\!\}_{k_{ES}}$ (3) $A \to E(B) : \{\!\|k_{AE}\|\!\}_{k_{ES}}$

classes: active collaboration, passive collaboration, competition and conflict.[3] The focus of this paper is on competition — a situation in which the goal is successfully attacking the protocol, regardless of the disposition of other agents. From the perspective of a competitive attacker, other attackers are not of interest per se: they are relevant factors because they are sources of interference. If some interference is detected while carrying out an attack, a competitive attacker will take countermeasures, attempting to negate potentially adverse effects.

Our scenario of interest is composed by a set of two agents that are homogeneous with respect to their (competitive) disposition.

3   A Case Study

A dishonest agent, aware that other independent attackers may be active on the network, will seek to devise suitable novel attacks, so as to grant himself an edge on unsuspecting competitors. As the mechanics of interaction and interference between attackers have not been exhaustively studied in literature yet, it is not known a priori how to systematically derive an attack behavior of this type.

In the following case study, we start from a simple protocol for which a vulnerability is known; we devise for the known ("classical") attack a variant that explicitly considers the possibility of ongoing independent attacks. We describe a possible reasoning for a competitive attacker in the context of the protocol's main features.

The protocol we consider as a case study is a key transport protocol described as an example in [7]; we name it as the Boyd-Mathuria Example (BME), and present it in Table 3 together with a classical attack against it. BME relies on the existence of a trusted third-party server S to generate a session key k_{AB} for agents A and B, where each agent X is assumed to share a symmetric secret key k_{XS} with S.

A is subject to a masquerading attack in which, at the end of a run of BME, A thinks that he shares a session key with the honest agent B, while in fact he shares it with the attacker E. Subsequent communication from A addressed to B is seen by E through the spy-rule and removed with an erase request: E has successfully taken B's place. This attack prevents B from receiving *any* communication from A. Should the two agents have prior agreement that such a communication was to take place, B is in the position

---

[3] In active and passive collaboration there is a common goal to be pursued; the difference lies in choosing a strategy that helps another vs. choosing a strategy that does not hinder another. In conflict scenarios, the primary focus of interest is the attackers, rather than the protocol.

of detecting that something has gone wrong. E can prevent detection by staging a dual man-in-the-middle attack.

If more than one attacker is active during a given protocol run, simultaneous execution of the classical attack could lead to A receiving multiple session keys as a response to his (single) request to the server. This situation clearly indicates to A that an attack is ongoing. A competitive attacker E_1, wishing to prevent this situation from occurring, could try removing from the network all the responses from S to A that do not pertain to his own request. However, the characteristics of the (non-redundant) cryptographic methods employed here do not allow distinguishing $M_1 = \left(\{ \! |k_{AE_1} | \! \}_{k_{AS}}, \{ \! |k_{AE_1} | \! \}_{k_{E_1 S}} \right)$ (to let through) from $M_2 = \left(\{ \! |k_{AE_2} | \! \}_{k_{AS}}, \{ \! |k_{AE_2} | \! \}_{k_{E_2 S}} \right)$ (to block). E_1 can recognize the format of M_1 and M_2 and can successfully decrypt M_1 to recover k_{AE_1}; by decrypting M_2 with the key $k_{E_1 S}$, E_1 can still recover a value, but different from the previous one. Not knowing k_{AE_1} a priori, the attacker is not able to distinguish which of M_1 and M_2 contains the answer to his request for a key with A.

As a consequence, the attacker E_1 is not able to know which messages to remove in order to ensure that A accepts k_{AE_1} as a session key to communicate with B. Competitive attackers cannot rely on step (2) to enforce their attacks at the expense of their competitors; furthermore, the probability of erasing all competing messages (while letting one's own pass) decreases with the number of active attackers. In this situation, it becomes fundamental for a competitive attacker to gain exclusive access to the first message — to gain control over the messages that reach S, as opposed to the messages coming from S.[4]

After spying the initiator's opening message, a competitive attacker E_1 will therefore attempt to mount the classical attack, while keeping watch for other messages that may be interpreted as attack traces. Any transiting message of the type (A, E_m) for which $E_m \in A_{E_1}$ is interpreted as another active attack; E_1 counters by requesting that the message be erased. If E_m is in H_{E_1}, the message may be understood either as a message from A — who would be initiating a parallel session of the protocol to obtain a second session key — or as an indication that E_m has been incorrectly labeled as honest. In the first case, E_1 will let the message through, as he has chosen to target specifically the session key for the communication between A and B; in the second case, he will protect his attack by erasing the message. If E_m is in U_{E_1}, E_1 can choose to either play conservatively and hypothesize the dishonesty of E_m or let the message through and interpret E_m as the culprit in case the current attack fails.

BME is such that at most one attacker E_d can successfully mislead A into accepting the key k_{AE_d} as a session key to communicate with B. Therefore, a successful attack automatically entails exclusivity of success. An attack is successful if it goes undetected by the initiator A. Our honest agents are intelligent and they make use of all information available to perform in-protocol detection of attacks. With respect to BME, a clear indication for A consists in receiving multiple responses from S after a single session key request; if A receives multiple responses, he concludes that there has been

---

[4] Of course, E_1 could guess which message(s) to erase, but he would have the added difficulty of having to decide whether to let the first message pass without knowing how many other messages will transit, if any at all, and how many session keys were requested by A (as opposed to by his competitor(s)).

a security violation and thus does not employ any of the keys so received in his later communications with B. From the attackers' perspective, an ongoing attack can be detected by observing a message of the type (A, X) transiting on the network; however, the attack trace is ambiguous to spying attackers and has to be interpreted on the basis of current beliefs concerning the honesty of X. A last feature of interest is that BME is rather friendly for attacker labeling. Decisional processes can rely on at least some conclusive information on the identity of the agents involved, because identifiers transit in the clear; attackers would have to infer them otherwise.

We examine the outcome of attacks carried out in a non-collaborative environment in six cases, corresponding to different conditions of knowledge and belief for E_1 and E_2. Cases and attack traces are summarized in Table 4. In order to completely specify agent behavior, we posit the following:

1. If an attacker E spies (A, E_m) with $E_m \in H_E$ or $E_m \in U_E$, he will not request that the message be erased. In the latter case, if E's attack fails, E_m is immediately placed in A_E.
2. Both E_1 and E_2 spy the opening message and are interested in attacking the current protocol run; this allows us to leave aside the trivial cases in which only one attacker is active for a given protocol run.
3. Due to space constraints, we detail only the cases in which *canSee* for step (3) yields $\{E_1, E_2\}$.

Case 1: E_1 and E_2 Know each other as Honest. E_1 and E_2 know each other's identifiers (i.e., they are paying attention to each other: $E_1 \in D_{E_2}$ and $E_2 \in D_{E_1}$), but they are both mistaken in that they have labeled the other as honest ($E_1 \in H_{E_2}$ and $E_2 \in H_{E_1}$). E_1 and E_2 are unaware of active competitors and mount the classical attack in steps (1_1) and (1_2). When the attackers spy two requests to the server transiting on the network, they both believe that A wishes to request keys with the honest agents B and E_j.

(1.T1): *S Sends Two Messages before A Can Address a Message to B.* With the messages in steps (2_1) and (2_2), A receives two keys instead of the single key requested. A now knows that at least one attacker is active and abandons the protocol without sending a message to B. The attackers do not spy the message they were hoping for (timeout) and acquire the certainty that at least another active attacker is around. The attackers can employ ad-hoc strategies to search for the mislabeled or unknown attacker. If the attackers are careful to keep track of the messages (A, X) pertaining to a given session, they can make informed guesses as to whom, amongst the known agents, they might have mislabeled.

(1.T2): *A Receives a Reply from S, Answers B and Stops Listening.* A receives the messages he expects and closes the current session before receiving the second response from S. E_1 is successful in his attack, whereas E_2 believes that he has succeeded when he has, in fact, decrypted the wrong key. None of the agents have an opportunity for detection.

(1.T3): *A Receives a Reply from S, Answers B and Keeps Listening.* A replies with the message in step (3), resulting in both E_1 and E_2 believing that they have succeeded. However, after receiving (2_2), A detects the attack and abstains from employing k_{AE_1} in his future communications with B. Thus, even if for different reasons, both attackers

Table 4. Traces for non-collaborative attacks against BME. Traces are exhaustive: E_1 and E_2 have priority over honest agents and S is honest. Arrows: relative order between (1_1) and (1_2) is irrelevant in determining the outcome.

T1: cases 1, 3, 4, 6	T2 and [T3]: cases 1, 3, 4, 6
$\begin{aligned} &(1\ ) \ A \to E_{1,2}(S) : A, B \\ \downarrow &(1_1) \ E_1(A) \to S \quad : A, E_1 \\ \uparrow &(1_2) \ E_2(A) \to S \quad : A, E_2 \\ &(2_1) \ S \to A \qquad\quad : M_1 \\ &(2_2) \ S \to A \qquad\quad : M_2 \end{aligned}$	$\begin{aligned} &(1\ ) \ A \to E_{1,2}(S) \ : A, B \\ \downarrow &(1_1) \ E_1(A) \to S \quad : A, E_1 \\ \uparrow &(1_2) \ E_2(A) \to S \quad : A, E_2 \\ &(2_1) \ S \to A \qquad\quad : M_1 \\ &(3\ ) \ A \to E_{1,2}(B) : \{\!|k_{AE_1}|\!\}_{k_{E_1 S}} \\ &[(2_2) \ S \to A \qquad\quad : M_2\,] \end{aligned}$

T4: case 2	T5: case 5
$\begin{aligned} &(1\ ) \quad A \to E_{1,2}(S) \qquad : A, B \\ \downarrow &(1_1)^+ \ E_1(A) \to E_2(S) : A, E_1 \\ \uparrow &(1_2)^+ \ E_2(A) \to E_1(S) : A, E_2 \end{aligned}$	$\begin{aligned} &(1\ ) \ A \to E_{1,2}(S) \quad : A, B \\ \downarrow &(1_1) \ E_1(A) \to E_2(S) : A, E_1 \\ \uparrow &(1_2) \ E_2(A) \to S \qquad : A, E_2 \\ &(2\ ) \ S \to A \qquad\qquad : M_2 \\ &(3\ ) \ A \to E_{1,2}(B) \qquad : \{\!|k_{AE_2}|\!\}_{k_{E_2 S}} \end{aligned}$

Where: $M_1 = \{\!|k_{AE_1}|\!\}_{k_{AS}}, \{\!|k_{AE_1}|\!\}_{k_{E_1 S}}$, $M_2 = \{\!|k_{AE_2}|\!\}_{k_{AS}}, \{\!|k_{AE_2}|\!\}_{k_{E_2 S}}$

in fact fail. Furthermore, they both continue to hold their mistaken belief that the other attacker is in fact honest.

Case 2: E_1 and E_2 Know each other as Attackers. E_1 and E_2 know each other's identifier ($E_1 \in D_{E_2}$ and $E_2 \in D_{E_1}$) and have correctly understood that the other is behaving as a dishonest agent ($E_1 \in A_{E_2}$ and $E_2 \in A_{E_1}$). Each attacker is aware of the presence of a competitor, which they have correctly labeled. Each attacker is attempting to gain exclusive access to the initial communication towards S and to ensure that only his request reaches S. E_1 and E_2 erase each other's request to S. Within our model, no attacker can be certain that his message has been received by its intended receiver; the attackers may wish to replay step (1_1) and (1_2) if a message of the type $\{\!|k_{AE_j}|\!\}_{k_{AS}}, \{\!|k_{AE_j}|\!\}_{k_{E_j S}}$ is not spied on the network within a reasonable time. This option is marked with $(\cdot)^+$ in Table 4. However, the active presence of the competitor ensures that no message reaches S. A notices that an anomalous situation is occurring, because his request to the server is not being served in a reasonable time. A interprets the situation as a denial-of-service attack and abandons the protocol.

Case 3: E_1 and E_2 are Unaware of each other. E_1 and E_2 are unaware of the other's presence — i.e., they are not paying attention to the other's activity ($E_1 \notin D_{E_2}$ and $E_2 \notin D_{E_1}$). The subcases follow closely those described for case 1 above. The only significant difference concerns detection for trace T1: here the attackers must employ exploratory strategies (*Inflow-Spy* or *Outflow-Spy*), because they failed to spy an additional message of type (A, E_m) transiting on the network. The failure to observe such a message is a strong indicator that the competitor's identifier is unknown. In 2-attacker scenarios this is the only legitimate conclusion, whereas with three or more attackers this situation may also arise from the interplay between erase and spy operations.

Case 4: E_2 Knows E_1 as Honest. Only one out of the two attackers E_1 and E_2 is paying attention to the other and knows his identifier. Here we consider $E_1 \in H_{E_2}$ and $E_2 \notin D_{E_1}$. Regardless of the order in which steps (1_1) and (1_2) occur, the attacker in disadvantage E_1 does not spy the message at step (1_2); E_2 does spy (1_1) but, trusting his judgement on E_1's honesty, does not request it to be erased. As a consequence, similarly to case 1, the traces follow schemes T1, T2 and T3. Significant differences concern detection in T1: E_1 detects the presence of an unknown attacker, whereas E_2 learns of a mislabeled or unknown attacker. The successful attackers in traces T2 and T3 are those whose requests to S are served first; knowledge does not affect the outcome.

Case 5: E_2 knows E_1 as Dishonest. Only one out of the two attackers E_1 and E_2 is paying attention to the other and knows his identifier. Here we consider $E_1 \in A_{E_2}$ and $E_2 \notin D_{E_1}$ Regardless of the order in which steps (1_1) and (1_2) occur, E_1 does not spy the message at step (1_2) and E_2 uses a direct attack against the competitor. E_2 removes E_1's request to the server and remains the only attacker in play, leading A into accepting $k_{A E_2}$ as a session key. E_1 does not have an opportunity to detect the competitor.

Case 6: E_2 Knows E_1, but he is Unsure of E_1's Honesty. Only one out of the two attackers E_1 and E_2 is paying attention to the other and knows his identifier. Here we consider $E_1 \in U_{E_2}$ and $E_2 \notin D_{E_1}$. This case reduces to case 4, with the only difference that E_2 is testing the dishonesty of E_1, instead of believing his honesty. Whenever E_2 realizes that he has failed his attack, he adds E_1 into A_{E_2} and deletes it from U_{E_2}.

General Considerations. In traces T2 and T3, the winning attacker is the one whose request is served first by S. S is an honest agent but it is not constrained to answering requests in the exact order in which they are received. Attackers do not have control over which requests are served first, although this factor determines whether they cannot do better than acquire the wrong key. Attackers realize in-protocol that they have failed only when they cannot spy a response from A, i.e., when they do not acquire any keys. Post-protocol detection, on the other hand, can occur also when an attacker with a wrong key attempts to decrypt the later communications addressed by A to B.

The case study highlights that, if A keeps the session open for a reasonable time after step (3), he can improve his chances of discovering that the key is compromised. This is a simple strategy that is beneficial and does not depend on the particular protocol. Furthermore, when A receives two answers from S in response to his single request, he now has two keys – at least one of which is shared with an attacker. If honest agents are immersed in a retaliatory framework [5,6], such keys can be used to identify attackers, to feed them false information or, in general, to launch well-aimed retaliatory attacks.

4   Defending Protocols

Key exchange protocols are amongst the most used cryptographic protocols. It is a common security practice to establish a secure channel by first exchanging a session key and then using it to authenticate and encrypt the data with symmetric cryptography. The security of all communications occurring during a session rests on the integrity of the key. In this context, it is not important per se that a key has been acquired by an attacker: what matters is whether a compromised key is used. Rather than on preventing the acquisition of a session key from ever occurring, the focus is on detecting that the key has been compromised – so as to prevent an attack from spreading to the entire session traffic.

If a protocol is vulnerable, a single DY attacker will succeed with certainty. However, if attacks to the same protocol are carried out in a more complex network environment, success is not guaranteed. As shown in the case study, in competitive scenarios with equal-opportunity attackers it is not possible for a given attacker to ensure that an attack is successful under all circumstances. The outcome depends on the strategy and knowledge conditions of all active agents, on the visibility of erased messages to other attackers ($canSee \neq \{E_1, E_2\}$) and on the order in which S processes requests. In a sense, the presence of an independent active attacker constrains the success of otherwise sure-fire attacks.

In order to make use of the emergent interference between concurrent attacks, it is necessary to ensure that attacks mounted by a malicious attacker are immersed in a multi-agent scenario. To this end, we construct an additional non-malicious attacker, who carries out attacks against the protocol, discards the "security secret" whenever he acquires it and reasons on the basis of what he can observe, to assist honest agents in detection tasks. In a sense, we are manipulating the *execution environment* of malicious attacks to gain a chance to thwart them.

The presence of a non-malicious agent that behaves as an attacker can be exploited to facilitate detection of attacks against vulnerable protocols. Honest agents should not, in principle, be informed of the specific attack trace to which they are vulnerable. Hence, if honest agents can perform detection at all, it has to be on the basis of flags that are independent of the specific attack trace – and, in general, independent also of the protocol in use. Such flags encode *local* defense criteria and can be as simple as realizing that no answer has arrived within a time considered reasonable or realizing that two (different) answers have been sent in response to a single request.

The basic idea is constructing a network agent that causes protocol-independent flags to be raised – via deliberate interference with ongoing attacks. In addition, one such *guardian agent* is formally an attacker, and can therefore be configured with knowledge of the attack trace(s). The guardian's task can be formulated as raising protocol-independent flags in correspondence to protocol-dependent indicators.

By using such an ad-hoc competitor as defense, it is possible, in some cases, to allow detection of otherwise-undetectable attacks. If no flag is raised for A, the guardian may be the only attacker at work. In this case, no ill-intentioned attacker has successfully concluded an attack; from the standpoint of A, actual security is not affected. In Table 5, we show the effects of introducing a guardian G for BME, configured as the attackers in the case study.

A guardian is a practical solution even when it is not all-powerful: any attack detected by A thanks to the guardian's active presence is an improvement in security. It is not necessary to demand that the guardian monitor all traffic – which is unrealistic at best; on the other hand, all monitored traffic enjoys partial protection.

Table 5. Effects of introducing a guardian G for BME when attacker E is active. G operates according to the same strategy as the attackers in the case study. G's active interference results in A detecting attacks always ($\sqrt{}$), sometimes ($\sim$), always if A commits to listening after step (3) ($^+$). The guardian is progressively more effective the more his beliefs and knowledge reflect the actual set of attackers. G can be effective even when he is not aware of E's presence.

canSee step(3)	Cases 1,3,4,6	Case 2	Case 5: $E \in A_G$	Case 5: $G \in A_E$
$\{E, G\}$	$\sim^+$	$\sqrt{}$	$\sqrt{}$	
$\{G\}$	$\sqrt{}$	$\sqrt{}$	$\sqrt{}$	$\sqrt{}$
$\{E\}$	$\sim^+$	$\sqrt{}$	$\sqrt{}$	

Attacks failing are, by themselves, markers that there are other dishonest agents at work; this fact can be used by the guardian G as a basis for further detection, possibly on behalf of honest agents. Employing guess-and-test strategies can then lead to an understanding of the second attacker's identity; a rudimentary example is the strategy used by our attackers for BME when they spy (A, E_m) and $E_m \in U$. Across multiple iterations of the attack procedure and under different hypotheses concerning (H_G, A_G, U_G), the attacker's identity will eventually be revealed.

In actual scenarios, protocols are implemented through programs in the users' computers. Protocols with vulnerabilities have been in use in the past and it is easy to anticipate that this situation will occur in the future as well. Even some deployments of important protocol standards such as Kerberos or Single-Sign On have been shown to be vulnerable — but only after entering mass-scale use. Vulnerabilities are known to attackers or security engineers well before the awareness that the protocol is flawed reaches the users.

It is very difficult to force users to stop using a protocol as soon as a vulnerability is discovered. The more widespread the protocol, the more difficult it is to ensure that it quickly goes out of use. Two aspects are important: that every user (a) is informed of the new vulnerability and (b) takes action in switching to a secure protocol. Statistics on software upgrades are an unfortunate example of this type of issue.

By designing the user-end software to inform the user of a security failure whenever protocol-independent flags are raised, a guardian can help solve the notification issue as well as raise the likelihood that the user will take action and upgrade. When the weakness in the protocol is understood, it may be a cost-effective investment to design a guardian with an effective interference strategy, so as to facilitate restoring network security.

5   Discussion

The traditional goal of protocol analysis is discovering attacks, to prompt replacing a vulnerable protocol with an improved and more secure one. Reductions are centered on attacks, either to reduce the search space for attacks (e.g., [3,15,16]) or to reduce the number of agents (e.g., [3,10]). In particular, if there exists an attack involving n collaborating attackers, then there exists an "equivalent" attack involving only one. Within this perspective, it is known that n-DY attackers equal in attack power a single DY attacker, and that the same can be said of Machiavelli-type attackers [18]. As a result, an exhaustive search for attacks can be performed in a reduced-complexity model.

With vulnerable protocols, in a single-attacker situation there is no protocol-independent indicator that could be used by honest agents to become aware that security has been compromised. If there is a single attacker, no simple defense is possible and the protocol inevitably fails its security goals. On the other hand, by deploying an additional ad-hoc competitor (the guardian) as defense, in certain conditions we can successfully raise protocol-independent indicators of ongoing attacks and protect the system. Introducing an appropriate guardian procedure as soon as new attacks are discovered can mitigate the consequences of flawed protocols still being in use.

In the case study, we have shown a counterexample to the statement: "if there exists a defense against an attack in a 2-attacker scenario, then there exists an equivalent defense in a 1-attacker scenario". This statement mirrors the classical result on n-to-1 reducibility and the counterexample shows that exhaustive searches for (guardian-based) defenses cannot be carried out in reduced-complexity settings, as they require at least two attackers. Within our proposed approach, the goal of analysis is finding a strategy to defend the system against existing attacks, rather than identifying vulnerabilities to prompt redesigning the protocol. We would be performing protocol analysis to identify possible *defenses*, rather than attacks.

So far, we have formalized a framework for non-collaboration, described the notion of competitive attacker, shown a proof-of-concept result on concurrent attacks giving rise to interference, delineated a novel strategy for defending protocols and presented a proof-of-concept result on the effectiveness of a network guardian configured as a competitive attacker.

We are currently working on realizing an implementation of our framework for non-collaboration. One of the key issues is how to systematically generate competitive attack behaviors, given a vulnerable protocol and a base ("classical") attack. In the case studies we have explored so far, this step was addressed by taking the point of view of an attacker and observing our reasoning. The ability to construct competitive attack behaviors rests on our intuitive understanding of key features in both the protocol and the attack, as well as on our ability to reason at a high level of abstraction to anticipate the consequences of an action.

Along with the possibility of pursuing defenses for vulnerable protocols, non-collaboration and attack interference also call for a small revolution in system modeling and, especially, in the way we conceptualize of protocols and protocol security. Interference highlights that protocols have a dynamic aspect and that, when multiple agents interact under a given protocol P, P exhibits features that we would expect to find associated to the notion of environment.

From our point of view, a protocol does not only specify the behavior of honest agents in terms of a sequence of message exchanges: it also norms the possible interactions that can occur under such specification. Under this light, a protocol defines a "world" in which interactions matter and so do agents' choices.

It is quite natural to look towards robotics and AI for mature tools, which we plan to recruit to open the path towards appropriate abstractions on protocol properties. Some properties of "protocol runs in execution", such as exclusivity of attacker success, are currently unexplored in security protocol analysis. Abstraction on protocol properties of interest in non-collaborative scenarios can serve as the conceptual basis for a qualitative but rigorous analysis of a given protocol and possibly even serve as a basis for protocol design.

We advocate that the security of protocols should not be evaluated only as to whether the target security property is preserved under an attack, but also according to how much scope protocols provide for honest agents to defend themselves. This stance is related to security in depth: even if attackers succeed in bypassing the protocol's security mechanism (i.e., an attack exists), there might be other mechanisms to put in play to preserve the security property, such as deploying a network guardian.

Acknowledgements. The work presented in this paper was partially supported by the FP7-ICT-2009-5 Project no. 257876, "SPaCIoS: Secure Provision and Consumption in the Internet of Services" (www.spacios.eu). We thank Davide Guardini for his constructive comments.

References

1. Arsac, W., Bella, G., Chantry, X., Compagna, L.: Validating Security Protocols under the General Attacker. In: Degano, P., Viganò, L. (eds.) ARSPA-WITS 2009. LNCS, vol. 5511, pp. 34–51. Springer, Heidelberg (2009)
2. Arsac, W., Bella, G., Chantry, X., Compagna, L.: Multi-attacker protocol validation. Journal of Automated Reasoning 46(3), 353–388 (2011)
3. Basin, D., Caleiro, C., Ramos, J., Viganò, L.: Distributed temporal logic for the analysis of security protocol models. Theoretical Computer Science 412(31), 4007–4043 (2011)
4. Basin, D., Capkun, S., Schaller, P., Schmidt, B.: Let's Get Physical: Models and Methods for Real-World Security Protocols. In: Berghofer, S., Nipkow, T., Urban, C., Wenzel, M. (eds.) TPHOLs 2009. LNCS, vol. 5674, pp. 1–22. Springer, Heidelberg (2009)
5. Bella, G., Bistarelli, S., Massacci, F.: A Protocol's Life After Attacks.. In: Christianson, B., Crispo, B., Malcolm, J.A., Roe, M. (eds.) Security Protocols 2003. LNCS, vol. 3364, pp. 3–10. Springer, Heidelberg (2005)
6. Bella, G., Bistarelli, S., Massacci, F.: Retaliation against protocol attacks. Journal of Information Assurance and Security 3, 313–325 (2008)
7. Boyd, C., Mathuria, A.: Protocols for Authentication and Key Establishment. Springer (2003)
8. Caleiro, C., Viganò, L., Basin, D.: Metareasoning about security protocols using distributed temporal logic. Electronic Notes in Theoretical Computer Science 125(1), 67–89 (2005)
9. Caleiro, C., Viganò, L., Basin, D.: On the Semantics of Alice & Bob Specifications of Security Protocols. Theoretical Computer Science 367(1-2), 88–122 (2006)
10. Comon-Lundh, H., Cortier, V.: Security Properties: Two Agents Are Sufficient. In: Degano, P. (ed.) ESOP 2003. LNCS, vol. 2618, pp. 99–113. Springer, Heidelberg (2003)
11. Dilloway, C., Lowe, G.: On the specification of secure channels. In: Proceedings of WITS 2007 (2007)
12. Dolev, D., Yao, A.C.: On the security of public key protocols. IEEE Trans. Inform. Theory 29(2), 198–208 (1983)

13. Fiazza, M.-C., Peroli, M., Viganò, L.: Attack Interference in Non-Collaborative Scenarios for Security Protocol Analysis. In: Proceedings of SECRYPT 2011, pp. 144–156. SciTePress (2011)
14. Kamil, A., Lowe, G.: Specifying and Modelling Secure Channels in Strand Spaces. In: Degano, P., Guttman, J.D. (eds.) FAST 2009. LNCS, vol. 5983, pp. 233–247. Springer, Heidelberg (2010)
15. Millen, J.K., Denker, G.: Capsl and mucapsl. Journal of Telecommunications and Information Technology 4, 16–27 (2002)
16. Mödersheim, S., Viganò, L., Basin, D.A.: Constraint differentiation: Search-space reduction for the constraint-based analysis of security protocols. Journal of Computer Security 18(4), 575–618 (2010)
17. Schaller, P., Schmidt, B., Basin, D., Capkun, S.: Modeling and verifying physical properties of security protocols for wireless networks. In: Proceedings of CSF, vol. 22. IEEE Computer Society (2009)
18. Syverson, P., Meadows, C., Cervesato, I.: Dolev-Yao is no better than Machiavelli. In: Proceedings of WITS 2000, pp. 87–92 (2000)

A Framework for Dynamic Optimization of Security and Performances

Antonio Vincenzo Taddeo, Luis Germán García Morales, and Alberto Ferrante

ALaRI, Faculty of Informatics, Università della Svizzera Italiana,
via G. Buffi 13, Lugano, Switzerland
{antonio.taddeo,luis.german.garcia.morales,
alberto.ferrante}@usi.ch
http://www.alari.ch

Abstract. Implementing security solutions in embedded systems is challenging due to their intrinsic limitations on performances as well as on available energy. Furthermore, traditional security solutions, designed by assuming static environments, do not provide the ability to tail security to the current operational conditions of the system. Thus, the efficiency and the applicability of security solutions to embedded dynamic applications, such as the ones often used in wireless sensor networks, are often limited.

In this paper we introduce a solution to this problem by proposing a framework in which *gradual adaptation* of security is provided: the system is able to adjust security and workload settings depending on the current operating conditions. The adaptation is performed moving through adjacent configurations. In this paper we discuss the policies that can be used to control the adaptations and we present the results obtained when implementing a case study on Sun SPOT nodes. The results show that the use of the framework increases the energy efficiency of the network nodes. Furthermore, they show the effects of different adaptation policies on the behavior of nodes.

Keywords: Gradual adaptation, Framework, Performances, Workload, Security, Adaptation, Self-adaptivity.

1 Introduction

Wireless Sensor Networks (WSN) are composed of a large number of nodes that are usually able to perform some measures through suitable sensors, process the gathered data, and send information to other nodes of the network. A number of more powerful devices are also usually in the network with the goal of collecting the data produced by the other nodes. Nodes are placed in the environment that they have to sense and, therefore, they are resource-constrained being limited in terms of area, memory, computation capabilities, and power. Power consumption is always among the most important constraints for WSN nodes [1]; power sources can, in some cases, be recharged by means of local power generators (e.g., small solar panels). Though, the batteries might require to last, even for long times, without being recharged.

M.S. Obaidat, J.L. Sevillano, and J. Filipe (Eds.): ICETE 2011, CCIS 314, pp. 315–329, 2012.

An important factor that influences design and performance of WSNs is communication security. In particular, security services such as authentication, confidentiality, and availability are critical for sensor networks operating in hostile environments and, at the same time, handling sensitive data. Designing a secure system in these conditions is challenging [2]: traditional security solutions are designed by using ad-hoc approaches which offer specific protection against certain attacks (e.g., countermeasures against denial of service attacks). However, they rely on the assumption that the operative environment is well-known and quite static as well. Moreover, some of these technologies have not been specifically developed for embedded systems; in many cases, their adoption in the pervasive world would be impossible due, for example, to high hardware resources requirements [3].

Typically, when designing secure systems the worst case scenario is considered: the system has to guarantee adequate protection against the strongest possible security attacks. By following this philosophy, security in WSN is typically based on an "on-off" approach: either security is totally ignored or it is enabled with the strongest algorithms available, with a corresponding high consumption of resources. This is generally in contrast with the requirements of a resource-constrained devices such as mobility, flexibility, real-time configuration, open and dynamic operative environment [4,5].

The problem of optimizing resources used for security, yet providing an adequate level of protection, is a hot topic at the moment [2]. In particular, the trade-off between energy and performance requirements of security algorithms is of utmost relevance for embedded systems [6]. As discussed above, each adopted security solution should be a good compromise among factors that are conflicting in nature such as, for example, power consumption and performances. This optimization is a complex task, especially when performed run-time [7,8].

In this paper we concentrate on systems that are able to change their configurations at run-time. In particular, we propose a run-time mechanism to deal with the optimization of security and of system workload in accordance both with application security requirements and with system dynamic energy constraints. Our work is based on the "Adequate Protection Principle" [9] which states that security should be adequately applied to a given context. We implemented such principle by adopting a *gradual adaptation* of application security and of system workload: security is adapted by moving between adjacent configurations that are compatible with application requirements. System workload can be reduced by modifying task periodicity or by suspending some of them.

In WSNs composed of nodes that can be recharged (e.g., by using local generators such as solar cells), our solution increases WSN nodes lifetime in between recharges. Different strategies are used to favor either security or system workload. The strategy to be used and the way in which it will be applied depends on specific node energy conditions and applicative scenario. The solution proposed in this paper has been implemented on Sun SPOT nodes [10].

In Section 2 we discuss a number of relevant related works; in Section 3 we introduce our framework and in Section 4 we describe a number of adaptation policies that we propose; in 5 we introduce the energy models used by the framework. In Section 6 we discuss a case study and we show the results obtained when applying the framework on a sensor network based on Sun SPOT nodes.

2   Related Work

The principle of *gradual adaptation* described in this paper can recall the graceful degradation techniques used in fault tolerant systems; in this kind of systems, in fact, performance may be degraded to keep the system operational even in presence of faults [11,12]. Typically this approach does not address the optimization of security.

The challenge of selecting the best set of cryptographic algorithms that optimizes the trade-off between resource requirements and security provided has been tackled in many works. Techniques to minimize the energy consumed by secure wireless sessions have been proposed in [13]. The authors investigated the selection of encryption algorithms and of key exchange protocols. However, they did not provide explicitly a run-time self-adaptation mechanism; instead, they shown techniques to minimize energy consumption by matching block sizes of message compression algorithms with data cache sizes. In [6] a battery power optimizer for wireless networks has been presented. Authors have performed experiments to model the relationship between power consumption and security of cryptographic algorithms. Such information have been used to formulate a knapsack problem and to find the optimal level of vulnerability by changing the number of rounds in cryptographic algorithms. In contrast with our work, neither application requirements nor the possibility of managing changes in cryptographic algorithms were considered. In [7] the authors describe a self-adaptive security framework at protocol level. The mechanism proposed provides the ability to select the optimal set of security protocols with the best security/performance ratio depending on the malicious level of a node neighbors. However, their adaptation is not triggered by an energy consumption constraint, rather on intrusion detection and peer trust evaluation. On the other hand, their systematic approach to security evaluation can be replicated in our framework in order to better define each security level.

Adaptation of cryptographic primitives is instead presented in [14], where the basic idea is to change the AES cryptography key length according to the confidentiality level required by the user. The matching between confidentiality level and key length is done statically and is not changeable at run-time. Moreover, they mainly lead to improve the overall system performances in terms of encryption rate rather than energy consumption.

In [15] an approach for gradual adaptation is described; the system considered is a sensor node that may be used in multimedia applications. In this paper we propose a more complete and dynamic framework for gradual adaptation of security along with a set of policies for the system. This includes, as explained in the following of this paper: adaptation of sample period for periodic tasks; dynamic energy budget computation; dynamic monitoring period; adaptation decisions policies specified for each task by means of its requirements.

3   The Framework

In this section we describe our framework for gradual adaptation. This framework has been designed for extending battery lifetime in WSN nodes, yet respecting the constraints fixed by the application designers.

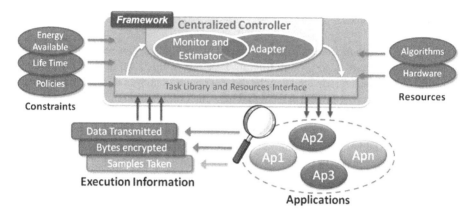

Fig. 1. The framework

Our framework contains a number of software components that monitor the execution of the tasks in the nodes, decides the possible adaptations on system configuration, and applies them. The current node conditions and the *policies* – directives and constraints previously defined by system and application designers – are used to decide when an adaptation is necessary and how it should be performed. Adaptations consist in changing task parameters such as level of security, execution period, and execution state. The purpose of the framework is to set the best security configuration, and, at the same time, extend the battery life. Figure 1 shows a general scheme for the framework with its main blocks.

The framework is composed of two main blocks: the centralized controller and the task library.

3.1 Centralized Controller

The centralized controller monitors the system behavior periodically and performs suitable downgrades or upgrades on the task parameters with the goal of meeting the battery lifetime defined by system designers. The controller computes the energy available in each monitoring period by considering the energy remaining in the battery and the lifetime constraint. This amount of energy is called *Energy Budget*. When the energy consumption is higher than the energy budget, the controller downgrades the parameters (security, execution period, or execution status) of some tasks to reduce energy consumption. In the same way, when the energy consumption is lower than the energy budget, the controller upgrades the parameters of tasks to bring them closer to their ideal configuration. The parameters to be changed for each task are determined by the controller depending on the policies defined by application designers. These policies are called *Tasks Policies*. The tasks are selected for adaptation based on a node-level policy named *Framework Policy* and on a task energy estimator. The estimator monitors the execution of tasks and it provides the energy figures of each one of them. Policies are discussed in Section 4.

3.2 The Task Library and Resources Interface

The task library and resources interface provides the ability to install applications and to define their policies. Furthermore, this library is used to determine the energy spent by tasks during their execution.

The task library is composed of a collection of methods and properties. The tasks are created by extending one of the objects provided in this library. The designer, while extending these objects, needs to specify the kind of task to be created (periodic or non periodic) and the required policies.

Additionally, the framework provides a resource interface that makes easy the access to the different software and hardware resources (e.g. security algorithms). This interface is composed of a collection of functions named "intermediate functions". They are in charge of calling the real resources and also collecting the execution behavior of every resource with the intention of estimating the energy spent by each one. This information collected and the resource model are used by the estimator when the monitoring process is being performed.

3.3 Security Services

Security can be provided through suitable services called *security services*. These services can be of different kinds such as, for example, encryption/decryption, authentication, and access control. In this work we only consider encryption algorithms as possible security services. Authentication algorithms could be considered as well without any change in the framework. Other services are not relevant in the application field considered in this work.

We divided the encryption algorithms considered in three groups, depending on their level of security. These algorithms are defined to have a high, medium, or low level of security based on their resistance to known attacks: the higher the number of combinations to be tried for breaking the algorithm, the higher its security. Inside each group a sorting is performed based on the energy consumption measured while encrypting/decrypting each byte for each algorithm.

Each task has a range of security levels defined by the application programmers. At the beginning of the execution, the framework assigns to the task the best security algorithm available and compatible with this range. When a downgrade on security is required for the considered task another security algorithm might be selected. Some degradations are *intra-level* (i.e., a new, less energy hungry, security algorithm is selected, but the algorithm belongs to the same security level), while some others are *inter-level* (i.e., the new security algorithm may belong to a different security level). The same applies for security upgrades.

4 Policies

In the framework different decisions are taken about security and performances adaptations. These decisions are governed by policies that describe what can be done for each task (i.e., if and how its security and performance can be modified) and how the framework should work (i.e., which are the adaptations to be performed, in which order, and with which speed). Policies for the tasks are named *Task Policies*; policies that govern the framework are called *Framework Policies*.

Table 1. Task policy

Parameter	Description
Security	Kind of degradation that can be applied to security. The options available are: – no degradation; – intra-level degradations only; – intra and inter level degradations; optionally the range of security levels accepted can be specified.
Period	Range of periods accepted by the task.
Execution status	Sets if the task accepts temporarily suspensions.
Task priority	Sets the priority of the task (High, Medium, and Low) with respect to adaptations.
Adaptation order	Specifies the order in which the adaptations are made. There are five different options available: – *Auto*: the framework has the freedom to decide which parameters to downgrade. – *First security, then the others*: the framework downgrades security first; when it is no longer possible to downgrade security, the period is downgraded; as a last option, if the other parameters are no longer degradable the task is suspended. – *First period, then the others*: this policy is similar to the previous one, but the period is adapted first. – *Suspend only*: whenever an adaptation is required, the task is suspended without considering the security and the period. – *None*: no degradation is performed on the task.

4.1   Task Policy Parameters

The task policies allow designers to specify how security and performance can be changed for each running task. More specifically, the elements that can be altered by the framework are related to the desired level of security, the execution period (for periodic tasks), and the execution status (i.e., the possibility to suspend tasks or not). Therefore, each policy contains 5 parameters as shown in Table 1.

4.2   Framework Policies

The framework requires proper rules to govern the adaptations and to monitor the execution of tasks and their energy consumption. The rules should provide both information on the tasks that should be considered for degradation and on how to monitor them. The parameters that compose framework policies are listed below:

- **Task Selection.** This parameter tells the framework which are the tasks that should be considered for degradation. We consider four different options:
  - *Most-Energy-Demanding Tasks.* Energy consumed by each task is estimated at runtime. The tasks with highest energy demand are considered.
  - *Least-Degraded Tasks.* The tasks that are in lowest levels of degradation (i.e., the ones that are closer to their optimal performances) are considered.
  - *Lowest-Priority First.* Degradation is first performed on tasks with the lowest priority level (low); degradations are done on tasks with increasing priority levels if necessary.
  - *Last-Recently-Started Tasks.* The tasks that have been started more recently are degraded.
- **Adaptation Speed.** This parameter specifies the percentage or the maximum number of tasks to be adapted in each control period, regardless the adaptation policy considered. This parameter contributes significantly to the speed of adaptation.

The *monitoring period* used by the self-adaptation mechanism has to be defined properly: a too short monitoring interval can lead to excessive energy and computational overhead on the system; a too long monitoring interval can lead, instead, to far from optimal timing on the adaptation of tasks, thus decreasing the effectiveness of the self-adaptation mechanism. A correct trade off between these two parameters should be found to obtain both efficiency and effectiveness of the self-adaptation mechanism. To this end, the framework allows the designer to specify a range of values for the monitoring period. At run-time, the self-adaptation mechanism starts with the minimum monitoring period. If no adaptations occur, the monitoring period is increased in the specified range. When adaptations are necessary, the monitoring period is decreased to allow a more frequent analysis of system conditions. The range to be used for the monitoring period should be determined by the designer at design-time by considering the characteristics of the running tasks and the applicative scenario. For example, the minimum monitoring period could coincide with the minimum period among all the periodic tasks.

5 Energy Estimation

In our framework the run-time monitoring of energy consumption is performed through a piece of software named *energy estimator*. The aim of the estimator is twofold: on the one hand, to estimate the energy consumption of each task; on the other hand, to compute the *energy budget* associated with each monitoring interval. These pieces of data are used by the framework to perform the related adaptations.

5.1 Energy Consumption Models

In each node we can consider two different types of energy consumptions: static and dynamic. Static energy is the energy that is necessary to provide the basic node functionalities. This energy cannot be changed for a given node and operating system. Dynamic energy is the one used to execute tasks. Our framework tries to optimize the dynamic energy.

Energy consumption of tasks is estimated through a model that includes the most significant contributions to energy consumption. We considered the following contributions to task energy consumption:

- Radio, $E_{radio}(b)$: the energy required by the radio module to transmit a certain amount of bytes b.
- Sensors, $E_{sensor}(n_s)$: energy consumption required to acquire n_s samples in the observation period.
- Encryption/decryption, $E_{algo}(b)$.

When no task is being executed the node can be switched to one of the low-power modes. In this case the energy consumption becomes $E_{mode}(t)$.

The energy consumption of cryptographic algorithms are estimated by considering the following contributions: the energy spent for initializing the algorithm key, E_{init}; and the energy per byte consumed to processing a block of 16 bytes, E_{block}.

$$E_{alg}(b) = E_{init} + E_{block} * b = \tag{1}$$
$$= E_{init} + (E_{padding} + E_{call} + E_{enc}) * b \tag{2}$$

where b is the number of blocks. Moreover, E_{block} can be further divided into the energy spent for: padding, $E_{padding}$; function calling, E_{call}; encryption, E_{enc}.

All the aforementioned models (excluding E_{mode}) refer to the dynamic energy consumption.

The energy consumed by each task can be estimated as the sum of the different contributions mentioned above. Similarly, the total energy consumption of the system within an observation period can be estimated as the sum of the energy consumption of all tasks running on the system and the energy spent in the current power mode (if enabled).

All of the aforementioned power consumptions are estimated by using linear models (see Table 2 for a complete model description). Using a linear equation for modeling the energy consumption of a security algorithm has been proved to be quite accurate [5,4]. Instead, linear equations might not be as accurate for other parts of the energy consumption. Such models, in fact, are technology-dependent and have to be characterized according to the particular node technology considered. Our framework relies on an energy consumption model to take decisions on adaptations and the accuracy of the model can influence the efficiency of the adaptation mechanism. Though, different energy consumption models can be easily inserted in the framework without any change in the adaptation logic.

5.2   Energy Budget Computation

For each monitoring interval, the framework computes the total energy consumption based on real consumption. The framework, then, evaluates if the measured energy consumption is compatible with the desired system lifetime. When the energy consumption is evaluated to be too high, the system must gradually reduce it during the successive monitoring intervals. To evaluate if the energy consumption is compatible with the desired battery lifetime, the framework compares it with the reference discharge curve specified by the system designer. An example of a discharge curve is shown in Figure 2. According to this figure, in the monitoring intervals I_1 and I_2, the current energy consumed (continuous line) is lower then the reference one (dashed line). Thus, the system does not need any adaptation. Starting from interval I_3, the current energy consumption becomes higher than the desired one; in this case adaptations are necessary to lower the energy consumption.

In this work, we define the *energy budget* as the amount of energy that can be consumed in a given monitoring interval according to the reference curve and the real energy consumed in previous monitoring intervals. The energy budget is compared with the current overall energy consumption; the result of this comparison drives the adaptations performed by the framework.

If a linear reference discharge curve is considered, the energy budget can be computed as follows. Considering Figure 2, the reference curve is given by:

$$\bar{E}(t) = \frac{minEC - maxEC}{t_{lifetime}} * t + maxEC \qquad (3)$$

Thus, the reference consumption in a given interval [j,j+1] is:

$$\tilde{E}_{[j,j+1]} = \bar{E}(t_j) - \bar{E}(t_{j+1}) \qquad (4)$$

Therefore, the energy budget E_{budget} can be computed as:

$$E_{budget,[j,j+1]} = \tilde{E}_{[j,j+1]} + E_{prev,[j-1,j]} \qquad (5)$$

where $E_{prev,[j-1,j]}$ is the energy budget not consumed in the previous interval. When the energy consumed in the previous interval is higher than the associated energy budget, E_{prev} becomes negative value to take into account this extra energy consumption. Note that, the framework allows the designer to specify his custom discharge model and corresponding computation of the energy budget keeping the validity of self-adaptation approach here proposed.

6   Case Study

Our framework has been implemented and tested in a real WSN. In this section we describe this implementation and the results obtained by running a number of experiments on this WSN. The goal of the experiments was both to measure the overhead introduced by the framework and to evaluate the effects of different policies on energy consumption and on performances.

6.1   Scenario

The network is based on the Sun SPOT (Sun Small Programmable Object Technology) nodes [10]. Sun SPOTs are small wireless devices, compliant with the IEEE 802.15.4 standard and running the Squawk Java Virtual Machine (VM) without any underlying OS. The VM acts as both operating system and software layer to provide high portability and fast prototyping capabilities. The Sun SPOTs platform is designed to be a flexible, capable of hosting widely differing application modules. From the hardware

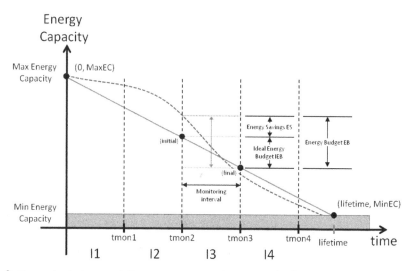

Fig. 2. Energy budget computation: parameters and conceptual scheme. Dashed-line is the real energy consumption; continuous-line represents the reference discharge curve.

point of view, Sun SPOT nodes are equipped with: a 32 bit ARM920T working at 180 MHz; 512K RAM/4M Flash Memory; 2.4GHz IEEE 815.4 radio with integrated antenna; 720 mAh as maximum battery capacity. By default, these devices are equipped with an accelerometer, a temperature, and a light sensor. Sun SPOT nodes may use two different low power modes: *shallow sleep* and *deep sleep* mode.

Concerning security suites, Sun SPOTs support the TLS/SSL protocol with several cryptographic algorithms: AES with 128, 192, and 256 bit keys and RC4 with 40 and 128 bit keys.

The applications in this scenario are classified in three groups according to the different sensors (light, temperature, or acceleration) that they use. Each group contains three tasks, each one performing one of the following operations:

1. Obtaining data from the environment periodically (short period).
2. Encrypting and transmitting the measures previously collected periodically (large period).
3. Detecting possible alarm conditions in the environment (e.g. fire condition). As soon as an alarm is detected, a picture of the environment is taken and transmitted, in an encrypted form, to the other nodes in the network. Since the SunSPOT does not have a camera to take pictures, this functionality is emulated by taking several samples using the respective sensor (temperature).

Different tasks have been implemented as different threads.

6.2 Profiling and Modeling

To determine the parameters of the energy models of Section 5, we profiled the different elements of our nodes. The average values obtained are shown in Table 2. Static energy consumption has been measured to be about 44% of the total energy consumption.

Table 2. Value of parameters for energy consumption models described in Section 5. To model each resource energy consumption a linear model ($y = a + bx$) has been considered.

RESOURCES	a	b
Shallow sleep mode	$E_{sm,on/off} = 0$ [mAh]	$E_{status} = 8.13E - 3$ [mAh/s]
Deep sleep mode	$E_{dm,on/off} = 8.22E - 3$ [mAh]	$E_{status} = 5.27E - 6$ [mAh/s]
Radio	$E_{r,on/off} = 6.40E - 5$ [mAh]	$E_{process} = 5.60E - 7$ [mAh/bytes]
Temp. sensor	$E_{ts,on/off} = 0$ [mAh]	$E_{sample} = 1.41E - 6$ [mAh/sample]
Light sensor	$E_{ls,on/off} = 0$ [mAh]	$E_{sample} = 1.36E - 6$ [mAh/sample]
Accel. sensor	$E_{as,on/off} = 0$ [mAh]	$E_{sample} = 4.34E - 6$ [mAh/sample]

Table 3. Values of factors in Eq. 2.

Factor	AES-256	AES-192	AES-128	RC4-128	RC4-40
E_{init} [mAh]	1.39E-5	1.28E-5	1.14E-5	2.25E-5	2.26E-5
$E_{padding}$ [mAh/16B]	9.40E-8	2.77E-7	3.27E-7	1.27E-7	9.40E-8
E_{call} [mAh/16B]	4.55E-7	2.13E-7	3.89E-7	4.29E-7	3.44E-7
$E_{processing}$ [mAh/16B]	9.89E-6	8.65E-6	7.37E-6	1.57E-6	1.59E-6

The cryptographic algorithms available in the TLS implementation of SunSPOTs have been also profiled to determine their energy consumptions and the execution times. By using these information we could order the algorithms as explained in Section 3.3. The algorithms have been grouped in three security levels as follows:

- *High*: AES-256, AES-192;
- *Medium*: AES-128, RC4-128;
- *Low*: RC4-40.

6.3 Results

Two different sets of experiments have been performed to evaluate the framework overhead and the effects produced by applying different policy combinations.

Framework Overhead. The monitoring and adaptation activities performed by the framework introduce an overhead in the system in terms of time and energy. In order to measure this overhead, we measured the energy consumed both when the framework was completely disabled and when the framework was enabled. In both cases we considered tasks programmed to always perform the same actions and to make use of all system resources (sensors, security algorithms, and the radio). In order to study the overhead scalability, measurements have been collected by repeating the experiment with increasing number of tasks.

When the framework was enabled the following additional conditions applied:

- The framework was forced to downgrade all the tasks running over the system in every monitoring interval (worst case scenario assumption).
- The framework was forced to adapt all the available parameters (e.g., security, period and execution state).

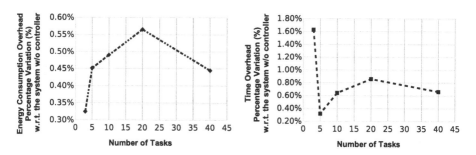

Fig. 3. Framework energy consumption (left) and execution time (right) overheads, with respect to the system w/o the framework

- The framework applied fake adaptations over the tasks. In this way both task and framework performance are kept constant along the experiment execution.

In Figure 3 the energy consumption and the execution time overhead are shown. The overhead introduced by enabling the framework increases when the number of tasks in the system is increased. In terms of energy the overhead ranges from 0.3% to 0.6%. These two values correspond to 3 and 30 tasks in the system, respectively. In terms of time the overhead ranges from 0.3% to 1.6%. We can conclude that the overhead introduced by the framework is almost negligible in terms of energy and very small in terms of time. The overhead is highly compensated by the added system flexibility.

Effects of Different Policies. The purpose of this set of experiments was to verify the effects of the different combinations of policies on the execution of tasks and on battery life. In these experiments we considered a node equipped with three sensors, each one associated with three tasks. Each of these tasks had different task policies corresponding to different settings for security, period, and execution status. To simulate the most demanding conditions for the framework, we anyway specified policies providing a high degree of flexibility.

We considered 6 different experiments in which all the different policies described in Section 4, except the *Last-Recently-Started* tasks, are combined.

The policies used in these experiments are listed in Table 4. The adaptation speed refers to the percentage of tasks that can be adapted in the set of candidates: *fast* corresponds to 70% of possible candidates; *slow* corresponds to 20%. A desired system lifetime constraint has been set to 12 hours. Note that, the system without the adaptation framework (case #0) is not able to meet such a lifetime constraint; the same happens in cases #4 and #5; in all the remaining cases the desired battery lifetime is met.

In Table 4 is also reported the percentage of energy saved both with respect to the reference system, case #0 (indicated with *Rel. Energy Saving*), and with respect to the system life time constraint (indicated with *Abs Energy Saving*). In average, our saves about 8.8% of energy with respect to the case #0, even in the cases where is not able to meet the system lifetime constraint. Instead, considering the absolute energy saving, the average gain for using our framework is not too high. However, this is perfect predictable

Table 4. Different combinations of policies used in the experiments and energy saving w.r.t. the case #0 (*Rel. Energy*) and with respect to the lifetime constraint (*Abs Energy*)

CRITERION	Framework disabled	most energy dem.		lowest priority		least degraded	
CASE #	0	1	2	3	4	5	6
ADAPTATION SPEED	–	fast	slow	fast	slow	fast	slow
LIFETIME MEET	N	Y	Y	Y	N	N	Y
REL ENERGY SAVING [%]	rif.	10.8	9.2	8.9	7.4	8.3	8.4
ABS ENERGY SAVING [%]	-5.5	2.6	0.8	0.5	-1.5	-0.1	1.4

since the framework's goal is to meet such a constraint following a linear discharge and not to save as much energy as possible. When the lifetime constraint is not meet, our framework still requires less energy (i.e., maximum 1.5%) than the case #0.

In order to compare the different cases, we considered the impact of each policy in terms of degradation level reached by all the tasks within the observation time frame. Figure 4(a) shows the percentage of time (computed over the total simulation time) in which each task has been degraded to some degree (e.g., degradations of security, workload, or execution status). Generally, our self-adaptation mechanism keeps tasks in one of their possible degradation levels for a period that spans from 10% to 48% of the total time.

As expected, the cases with a *low* adaptation speed show fewer degradations compared to others. *Most-Energy-Demanding* and *Least-Degraded* criteria show a similar behavior from the number of degradation stand point.

Figures 4(b), 4(c) and 4(d) show details about how the degradation of security has been performed for each task according to different adaptation policies. Values are the percentage of total time in which a task has been in a given degradation level. In general our framework was able to meet the system lifetime constraint even by using optimal or almost optimal settings for the tasks in most of the time. The *Most-Energy-Demanding* criterion provides the best results concerning energy consumption. Though, this is achieved by heavily degrading security of most energy demanding tasks. The *Least-Degraded* criterion provides best balance in terms of saved energy and degradation level of tasks: in this case the optimization of energy consumption is obtained by distributing a low level of degradation on all tasks.

The aforementioned results also provide some guidelines for the choice of different adaptation policies. The *Most-Energy-Demanding* policy is suitable when energy is the most important constraint. This policy, in fact, tends to limit the energy consumption of the most power-hungry tasks, even by heavily limiting their performances. The *Least-Degraded*, instead, is the policy with the lowest influence on task performances. Therefore, it is suitable when energy consumption should be limited, but performances remain the most important requirement. The *Last-Recently-Started* tasks policy instructs the system to perform adaptations on the tasks started more recently, supposedly the ones that are "additional" (i.e., not the basic ones that had been started at system boot). An

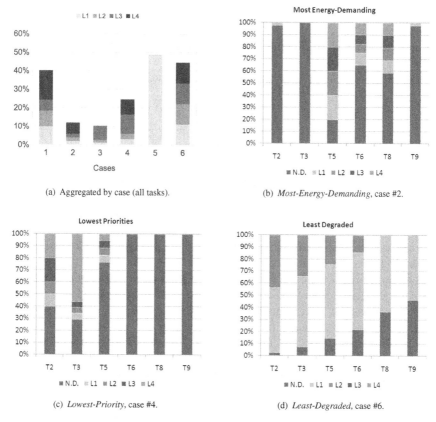

(a) Aggregated by case (all tasks).

(b) *Most-Energy-Demanding*, case #2.

(c) *Lowest-Priority*, case #4.

(d) *Least-Degraded*, case #6.

Fig. 4. Percentage of time in every security degradation level per task. In Figures 4(b), 4(c) and 4(d) only tasks that support security degradation are shown.

adaptation policy based on task priorities (*Lowest-Priority*) gives the programmers flexibility, but it is also complex to design.

7   Conclusions and Future Work

In this paper we discussed a framework for gradual adaptation of security and of system workload. The framework tunes the execution of tasks and their security settings runtime with the goal of optimizing the trade-off among performances, security, and energy consumption. Different policies for controlling the framework along with a model for energy consumption estimation have been also proposed in the paper. The framework has been tested on a real system along with the policies.

Although the framework introduces a small, but inevitable, energy and time overhead, it also allows the nodes to meet battery lifetime constraints, yet providing an adequate level of security to tasks.

Future work includes the extension of our framework to support smarter parameters for upgrade policies. Learning mechanisms may be introduced to further optimize the gradual adaptation mechanism.

References

1. Mura, M.: Ultra-low power optimizations for the ieee 802.15.4 networking protocol. In: Proceedings of MASS (2007)
2. Ravi, S., Raghunathan, A., Kocher, P., Hattangady, S.: Security in embedded systems: Design challenges. Trans. on Embedded Computing Sys. 3, 461–491 (2004)
3. Ferrante, A., Piuri, V., Owen, J.: IPSec Hardware Resource Requirements Evaluation. In: NGI 2005, Rome, Italy. EuroNGI (2005)
4. Keeratiwintakorn, P., Krishnamurthy, P.: Energy efficient security services for limited wireless devices. In: Proc. 1st International Symposium on Wireless Pervasive Computing, pp. 1–6 (2006)
5. Grossschädl, J., Szekely, A., Tillich, S.: The energy cost of cryptographic key establishment in wireless sensor networks. In: ASIACCS 2007: Proceedings of the 2nd ACM Symposium on Information, Computer and Communications Security, pp. 380–382. ACM, New York (2007)
6. Chandramouli, R., Bapatla, S., Subbalakshmi, K.P., Uma, R.N.: Battery power-aware encryption. ACM Trans. Inf. Syst. Secur. 9, 162–180 (2006)
7. Chigan, C., Li, L., Ye, Y.: Resource-aware self-adaptive security provisioning in mobile ad hoc networks. In: 2005 IEEE Wireless Communications and Networking Conference, vol. 4, pp. 2118–2124 (2005)
8. Lighfoot, L., Ren, J., Li, T.: An energy efficient link-layer security protocol for wireless sensor networks. In: 2007 IEEE International Conference on Electro/Information Technology, pp. 233–238 (2007)
9. Pfleeger, C.P., Pfleeger, S.L.: Security in Computing, 4th edn. Prentice Hall PTR (2006)
10. Microsystems, S.: Sun Small Programmable Object Technology (2008)
11. Herlihy, M., Wing, J.: Specifying graceful degradation. IEEE Transactions on Parallel and Distributed Systems 2, 93–104 (1991)
12. Li, J., Song, Y., Simonot-Lion, F.: Providing real-time applications with graceful degradation of qos and fault tolerance according to (m, k) -firm model. IEEE Transactions on Industrial Informatics 2, 112–119 (2006)
13. Karri, R., Mishra, P.: Minimizing energy consumption of secure wireless session with qos constraints. In: Proc. IEEE International Conference on Communications, ICC 2002, vol. 4, pp. 2053–2057 (2002)
14. El-Hennawy, M.E., Dakroury, Y.H., Kouta, M.M., El-Gendy, M.M.: An adaptive security/performance encryption system. In: Proc. International Conference on Electrical, Electronic and Computer Engineering, ICEEC 2004, pp. 245–248 (2004)
15. Taddeo, A.V., Micconi, L., Ferrante, A.: Gradual adaptation of security for sensor networks. In: IEEE WoWMoM 2010: Proceedings of the IEEE International Symposium on a World of Wireless Mobile and Multimedia Networks, Montreal, Canada (2010)

Broadcast Authentication in a Low Speed Controller Area Network

Bogdan Groza and Pal-Stefan Murvay

Department of Automatics and Applied Informatics,
Politehnica University of Timisoara, Romania
bogdan.groza@aut.upt.ro, stefan.murvay@gmail.com

Abstract. Controller Area Network (CAN) is a communication bus that has no cryptographic protection against malicious adversaries. Once isolated, the environments in which CAN operates are now opened to intruders and assuring broadcast authentication becomes a concern. To achieve this, public key primitives are not a solution because of the computational constraints, but symmetric primitives can be used with time synchronization at the cost of additional delays. Here we study several trade-offs on computational speed, memory and bandwidth having the main intention to depict the lower bounds on the efficiency of such protocols. For this purpose we use a wide spread controller from Freescale located somewhat on the edge of the market capable of low speed, fault tolerant CAN communication. To further improve the computations we also make use of the XGATE co-processor available on the S12X derivative. The performance of both hash functions and block ciphers is examined for efficient construction of the key chains.

Keywords: Authentication, Broadcast, Controller area network.

1 Introduction and Related Work

Controller Area Network or simply CAN is a communication bus initially developed by BOSCH to be used by controller units in vehicular systems [1]. The initial specifications are now superseded by ISO 11898 [2] while its area of application also extended outside vehicles to automation applications in general. Although high performance buses were developed in the last decade, such as FlexRay, because of its efficiency and reduced cost CAN is still the most commonly used communication bus in automotives today.

Traditionally, in control systems in general and in automotives in particular, reliability was a main concern but only with respect to natural phenomenons (electromagnetic disturbances, thermal noise, etc.) or accidents of various causes but not in front of Dolev-Yao adversaries. Thus CAN has very efficient mechanisms to deal with errors and to recover afterwards. In fact, the probability of an undetected error on CAN is extremely low, informally one undetected error occurs at about one thousand years for each vehicle that operates eight hours a day with an error each 0.7s. For the interested reader, an in-depth study of the performance of CAN error detection mechanism was done by Charzinski in [3].

However, in the last decade, industrial control systems and automotives become opened to malicious adversaries as well and a significant part of the security community

M.S. Obaidat, J.L. Sevillano, and J. Filipe (Eds.): ICETE 2011, CCIS 314, pp. 330–344, 2012.

focused on this kind of issues. A recent comprehensive book for security and in particular cryptographic security in automotives is [4] but a high amount of papers were published since then.

In this context, of malicious adversaries that can manipulate messages over the network, CAN does not have intrinsic support for any kind of security. Indeed, such kind of security is not needed if one sees CAN as operating in a secure perimeter. But, it is very likely that soon CAN like networks will operate in environments that are opened for intruders. Recent research showed current automobiles to be unexpectedly vulnerable to external adversaries [5] and it is likely that many other environments in which CAN operates are not completely isolated from the outside world. Security in front of such adversaries can be achieved by implementing this at the application level. In fact such improvements happened in the past, for example when deterministic delays were needed on the CAN bus with the development of Time Triggered CAN [6]. Still, to best of our knowledge there is no implementation available to assure authenticity in CAN networks. Thus, the main intention of this paper is to develop a higher layer implementation and to study several trade-offs to increase its efficiency. We analyze this both at a theoretical level by introducing the corresponding formalism and by designing an efficient protocol and at a practical level by following an efficient implementation. This is done on S12X microcontrollers from Freescale, a family of microcontrollers commonly used in the automotive industry, with the use of the XGATE co-processor available on S12X derivatives to speed up cryptographic functions.

As for the cryptographic mechanism that can be employed for this purpose, public-key cryptography is not the solution because of both the computational and communication overhead. As messages are short in CAN networks, usually fitting in the 64 bits of data carried by one CAN frame, using a public-key primitive such as the RSA will require thousands of bits and cause a significant overhead. Elliptic curves will significantly reduce the size of the messages, but still the computational overhead is too much to assure small authentication delays. While the computational overhead can be alleviated by dedicated circuits, such as ASICs and FPGAs, this will largely increase the cost of components, an issue that is largely avoided by manufacturers.

In contrast, symmetric primitives were efficiently employed for authentication in constrained environments such as sensor networks [7], [8], [9]. Due to the broadcast nature of CAN, protocols similar in nature to the well known TESLA protocol [10], [11] can be used in this context as well. There is an extensive bibliography related to the TESLA protocol. Its history can be traced back to Lamport's scheme which uses one-way chains to authenticate users over an insecure network [12]. The work of Bergadano et al. [13] proposes several variants of one-way chain based protocols, with or without time synchronization. Previous work which inspired this family of protocols is the Guy Fawkes protocol from [14]. The context which is more related to our setting here is that of the application of such protocols in sensor networks. In particular, several trade-offs for sensor networks were studied by Liu and Ning in [8], [9] and several variants of the protocols are presented by Perrig as well in [10], [11].

In the case of the industrial controllers, some of the constraints are similar. For example, computational power is also low and, although high speed microcontrollers are also available on the market, low speed microcontrollers are preferred to reduce costs. But while low computational power gives some similarities, other constraints are different. For example, energy consumption is a relevant issue in sensor networks, but usually for control units inside a car this is not a main concern since they do not strongly rely on small batteries. On the other side, a different constraint here, that is not so prevalent in sensor networks, is the size of the message which is limited to 64 bits on a CAN frame. Indeed, larger messages can be split in smaller messages but the overhead inflicted by the structure of the CAN frame is around 50%. This becomes prevalent in the case of one-way chain based protocols, where hash-functions are used to compute the chain elements and thus to send an element of the chain will require at least two exchanged messages (assuming the simplest hash function outputs 128 bits). To this, one will need to add the message authentication code as well, which again requires at least two exchanged messages, etc. Thus, at least four CAN frames are needed to transmit just the security elements of one frame of useful information. Still, the most critical part, in automotive communication and control systems in general, where this protocol is mostly used, are the authentication delays, i.e., how fast a packet can be deemed as authentic. For this purpose, the most relevant constraint to which we want to give a positive answer is the authentication delay. In particular we must assure that a node, if the bus is not taken by a higher priority message, is able to transmit the message and the message can be checked for authenticity as soon as possible. This condition is initially limited by the computational power, but as checking for authenticity can happen only as soon as the disclosure delay expires and the next element of the chain is committed, this also depends on the structure of the chain which is determined by the amount of memory, and also on the bandwidth. Using too large chains means too much time in the initialization stage and large amounts of memory, while too short chains means either high authentication delays or too frequent re-initializations, etc. Depicting an optimum in this context is not straight forward and we study this in detail in what follows. In particular, we used in our scheme several levels of one way chain. While three levels of one-way chains were reported to be closed to optimal in sensor networks, due to memory constraints and to reduce initialization in some situations we used more levels. This is because of both the time horizon of the protocol and of the duration of the disclosure interval. In sensor networks the disclosure interval was in the order of tens or hundreds of milliseconds, while here, to increase communication speed we want to reduce this as much as possible. Of course, we are finally limited by the bus speed at 128 kbps and by the synchronization error, which in fault-tolerant CAN will not allow us to drop the disclosure delay under several milliseconds. Practical examples are given in the experimental results section.

The paper is organized as follows. Section 2 gives an overview of the protocol, starting from several details of the CAN protocol to the examination of the influence of chain lengths, structure and timings on performance. In section 3 we present experimental results concerning the implementation of the proposed protocol on S12X microcontrollers. This includes experimental results for the implementation of cryptographic primitives on the XGATE co-processor. Section 4 holds the conclusions of our paper.

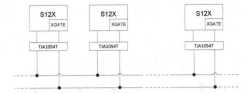

Fig. 1. Fault tolerant CAN bus topology with S12X controllers and TJA1054 transceivers

2   The Protocol

From an upper view the design paradigm is the following. Memory, computational speed and bandwidth give bounds on the length of the chains that can be used and the number of levels. This, along with the synchronization error, further bounds the authentication delay, as messages cannot be authenticated faster than the disclosure delays. Further, to improve on the delays, we allocate equidistant timings in order to avoid a non-uniform load on the CAN bus. Indeed, since initialization packets must have the highest priority, if timings are non-uniform, there will be periods when more chains need to be initialized and thus the bus will be heavily loaded by initialization packets. Before getting to the description of the protocol we briefly enumerate in what follows some relevant aspects of the CAN bus.

2.1   Short Description of the CAN Protocol

We are not interested here in typical aspects of the protocol such as error detection, synchronization, etc., so we will not mention them. CAN bus has a broadcast nature. Nodes are connected by a two wire bus topology, as shown in Figure 1, and access to the bus is gained with priority based on a message identifier which forms the first part of a frame. This identifier has 29 bits in extended frames and 11 bits in standard frames. The structure of the CAN frame consists in the arbitration field (the identifier), 6 bit control field, 0-64 bits of data, 15 bit CRC and a 2 bit acknowledgement. Additionally 1 bit marks the start of frame and 7 bits mark its end. Few words on arbitration are in order. The way of arbitrating is by judging the winner based on the state of a particular bit, namely recessive bits (value 1) are overwritten by dominant bits (value 0). So, if the case, all nodes can start to write a message at the same moment on the bus, but, whenever a node writes a recessive bit and reads a dominant one it means that it lost the arbitration and will stop, otherwise it can continue. After each 6 consecutive bits of identical values a stuffing bit of different value is added. The body of a message can have at most 8 bytes and is followed by a 15 bit CRC. In the worst case a frame can have 154 bits out of which only 64 bits are of actual useful information. Thus, the overhead is high from the basic design of the protocol, in the worst case exceeding 50%. But this is needed to achieve reliability as mentioned before. Two kinds of CAN nodes are commonly available on the market: fault tolerant low-speed nodes which operate at 128kbps and high-speed nodes that work up to 1Mbps.

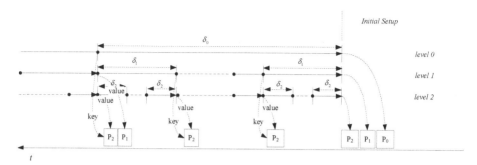

Fig. 2. Basic structure of the key chains and packets as they are dropped on the bus

2.2 Overview of the Authentication Protocol

We use time synchronization and multiple levels of one-way chains in order to authenticate the broadcast from a particular node. The generic structure of the key chains is depicted in Figure 2. Packets arriving on the communication bus are depicted as well, the dotted lines from an element of the chain to the packet denotes that the element was used as a key, and for the re-initialization packets in particular one element of the key chain was also used as a message. Packet P_i is sent to initialize a chain from level i. In what follows we will use the following notations:

- L - number of chain levels,
- $\lambda_i, i = 0..L$ - length of the chain on level i,
- $\delta_i, i = 0..L$ - disclosure delay on level i,
- B - bus speed, normalized to packets per second (one packet can carry one key),
- M - available memory (measured in elements of the key chain that can be stored),
- S - computational speed (number of keys that can be computed per second),
- T - time horizon of the protocol,
- t - time as integer value, a subscript indicates particular details.

Based on these notations in the next section we discuss the optimal allocation of the broadcast parameters.

In principle we need two distinct protocols: an initialization protocol and a broadcast protocol. The role of the initialization protocol is to allow each unit to commit its initialization values and to achieve time synchronization with other participants. This part of the protocol can rely on more expensive operations required by public-key cryptography. In this stage we consider that each principal will authenticate itself by using a public key certificate that is signed by a trusted authority. Initial authentication based on public-key infrastructure is important to assure composability. This ensures that different components, from potentially different manufacturers, can be assembled in one system and is a common demand of the market today. For example, in a different context (that of communication alone), the latest state-of-the-art protocol, FlexRay, has communication segments that are preallocated such that different components from different providers can be bind into a system. Thus we require that each node must store the public key of a trusted authority. The initialization protocol must also ensure time synchronization. This is done with respect to a central node, which will play the role of a communication master. As usual, synchronization between two nodes is loose and it requires a handshake and counting the round trip time until it is below a tolerance margin. This is usually achieved in two protocol steps as follows: $A \to B : N_A; B \to A : Sig_B(t_B, N_A)$. Here N_A denotes a nonce generated by principal A and t_B denotes the current time at principal B when sending its response. However, in our scenario a digital signature costs tens, or hundreds milliseconds, which will result in a high tolerance margin that will further require an even larger disclosure delay. Because of this, instead of a digital signature we will use a message authentication code which is several orders of magnitudes faster, in particular in our experiments the round-trip-time was less than 2 milliseconds. Afterwards, the round trip time ϵ_{AB} becomes the synchronization error. If the nonce was sent by A at time t_0 and now A's clock points to t_1 then A knows that the time on B side is in the interval $[t_B+t_1-t_0, t_B+t_1-t_0+\epsilon_{AB}]$. Further, the initialization values for the chains can be shared between each node and the central node who can broadcast them to all communication participants. We will not insist on details of the initialization protocol which is done in the initial phase with no constraints.

2.3 Optimal Allocation of Key Chain Lengths and Levels

For brevity we consider a homogeneous network with nodes that have equal computational abilities, thus the same computational delays and lengths for the chains can be handled by all of them. Otherwise, the protocol can be scaled according to the computational abilities of each client, but we want to keep the model as simple as possible.

To formalize the optimal allocation of chain lengths and levels, different to previous work, we use a tolerance relation to define the lengths of the chains and the disclosure delays at each level. The tolerance relation is formed by vectors which are defined as initialization values for each communication participant.

Definition 1. We say that a set of pairs $< \lambda_i, \delta_i >$ forms tolerance relation with respect to memory, computational speed, bandwidth and time, denoted as $< \Lambda, \Delta >_{M,S,B,T}$ if the following constraints hold:

$$\sum_{i=0,L} \lambda_i = \lambda_0 + \lambda_1 + ... + \lambda_L \leq M \tag{1}$$

$$\lambda_0 + (\lambda_0 + 1) \cdot \lambda_1 + (\lambda_0 + 1) \cdot (\lambda_1 + 1) \cdot \lambda_2 + ... \tag{2}$$

$$+ (\lambda_0 + 1)...(\lambda_{L-1} + 1)\lambda_L = \sum_{i=0,L} \lambda_i \prod_{j=0}^{i-1} (\lambda_j + 1) = \prod_{i=0}^{L} (\lambda_i + 1) - 1 \leq B \cdot T$$

$$\lambda_0 + (\lambda_0 + 1) \cdot \lambda_1 + (\lambda_0 + 1) \cdot (\lambda_1 + 1) \cdot \lambda_2 + ... \tag{3}$$

$$+ (\lambda_0 + 1)...(\lambda_{L-1} + 1)\lambda_L - \lambda_0 - ... - \lambda_L = \prod_{i=0}^{L} (\lambda_i + 1) - 1 - \sum_{i=0}^{L} \lambda_i \leq S \cdot T$$

Relation (1) gives the memory bound, i.e., the sum of the lengths of the chains cannot exceed the total memory. Relation (2) and (3) are bounds on bandwidth and computational time, i.e., the total number of elements of the one-way chain cannot exceed the available bandwidth for transmission and cannot require more computational time than available over protocol lifetime T. Values $\lambda_0, \lambda_1, ..., \lambda_L$ are subtracted from relation (2) to get (3) since the first key chain on each level is computed in the initialization stage. Indeed, relations (2) and (3) can be further refined for the disclosure delays on all up to the last level since the re-initialization of each chain should be done in the disclosure delay of the previous level. We introduced this definition to keep our presentation formal, but it is obvious that defining good tolerance relations is a matter of good engineering.

Remark 1. Relations (2), (3) correspond to the case when all chains are committed in the initialization stage and each element from each level commits a new chain from all levels below. This can be modified to the case when only the keys on the first level are committed in the initialization stage and further each element on each level commits a new chain only on the first level below. This will give cleaner tolerance relations: $\sum_{i=1,L} \prod_{j=0,i} \lambda_j = \lambda_0 \cdot \lambda_1 + ... + \lambda_0 \cdot \lambda_1 \cdot ... \cdot \lambda_L \leq S \cdot T$ and $\sum_{i=0,L} \prod_{j=0,i} \lambda_j = \lambda_0 + \lambda_0 \cdot \lambda_1 + ... + \lambda_0 \cdot \lambda_1 \cdot ... \cdot \lambda_L \leq B \cdot T$. While in this way the number of commitments will be constant 1, the lifetime of the protocol will be reduced as fewer chains are committed. Otherwise, the number of commitments increases, but at most to the number of levels (usually 3 or 4) which should be easily supported on the bus. This appears to be preferable since it improves the protocol lifetime.

Remark 2. The general relation between chain lengths and disclosure delays will now be the following: $\delta_i = \delta_{i-1}/(\lambda_i + 1), i > 0$. Intuitively, this also means that it must be feasible to compute and send λ_i chain elements in time δ_{i-1}. Thus λ_i can also be defined as a function of δ_{i-1} considering the computational power of the device.

Remark 3. Given a tolerance relation $< \Lambda, \Delta >_{M,S,B,T}$ with respect to time, space and bandwidth the disclosure delay and the computational overhead have an inverse variation. Thus: the minimal disclosure delay is achieved if chains are of equal size, i.e., $\lambda_i = M/L$, while the minimal computational and communication overhead is achieved if upper level chains are smaller, i.e., $\lambda_0 < \lambda_1 < ... < \lambda_L$. This is intuitively since the product of two values whose sum is fixed is maximal if the two values are equal and minimal if one of the values is 1. For example, assume $x + y = z$ then $\forall k \geq 1, z/2 \cdot z/2 > (z/2 - k) \cdot (z/2 + k) = z^2/4 - k^2$. Now, to achieve the minimum delay, the product of the chain lengths $\lambda_0 \cdot \lambda_1 \cdot ... \cdot \lambda_L$ must be maximal. If we split this product exactly into the half left and half right terms, assuming an even number of terms which is wlog, then the maximum product is achieved if: the left and right terms are maximal and equal, and so on. To achieve minimal bandwidth and computational requirements we need $\lambda_0 \cdot \lambda_1 + ... + \lambda_0 \cdot \lambda_1 \cdot ... \cdot \lambda_L$ to be minimal. This can be written as $\lambda_0 \cdot (\lambda_1 + ... + \lambda_1 \cdot ... \cdot \lambda_L)$ and as right term cannot be equal to 1 the left term must be in order to minimize the product and so on. Thus, the optimum choice of lengths with respect to delays, is to have all chains of equal size. For the purpose of generality, as well as for the fact that in practice small variations between chain lengths may occur when the amount of available memory is not directly divisible with the number of levels, we will keep the following exposition for the case when chains are of arbitrary sizes.

2.4 Optimal Allocation of Timings

By optimal allocation of the key disclosure time we want to achieve minimal delays for sending messages and authenticating them. Of course, the authentication delay is bounded by the disclosure delay, i.e., packets cannot be authenticated sooner than the disclosure delay from the last level. This bound was already fixed by the tolerance relation. However, the straight forward mechanism suggested in Figure 2, in which chains are re-initialized successively, causes more overhead at the disclosure time of keys from upper layer chains (since at this time all chains from lower levels need to be re-initialized as well). To overcome this, we define a procedure which we call *equidistant timing* by which all packets are disclosed at periods of time separated by equal delays. More, we will use chains from upper levels to authenticate information packets as well and not only forthcoming key chains. Thus, we will normalize the disclosure time to:

$$\delta_{norm} = \frac{T}{\prod_{i=0}^{L} (\lambda_i + 1) - 1} \qquad (4)$$

This relation comes from the assumption that each tip of a chain is committed by a MAC code but once it is not released until the precise time when it can be already used for authentication. If the tip of the chain is also sent with the MAC code, then the denominator will be $\prod_{i=0}^{L} \lambda_i - 1$. In the forthcoming scheme, keys on all levels are released at δ_{norm} intervals. Of course, if we use relation (4), δ_{norm} is equal to δ_L but we prefer to use this notation to avoid confusion with a generic scheme in which this may not happen, i.e., not all keys are released at δ_{norm} but only the keys from the chain on level L.

In what follows we need to establish three things: i) which is the disclosure time for a particular key k (Definition 4), ii) given a particular time t which key must be disclosed, or which is the last key that was disclosed upon t (Remark 4) and iii) given a particular packet, containing authentication information, what condition must be met on the receiver's side to deem this packet as on-time (Definition 5).

To determine all these, the easiest way to decide is by writing the time with respect to the vectors of the tolerance relation which is established by the next definition.

Definition 2. Given a discrete time value t by $t_{<\Lambda,\Delta>} = < t_0 ... t_L >$ we denote the decomposition of t with respect to the lengths of the chains $(\lambda_0, \lambda_1, ..., \lambda_L)$ and normalized time (δ_{norm}) as a basis. In this way, each element from $t_{<\Lambda,\Delta>}$ gives the last element that was released on the corresponding level. That is, given $t' = t \bmod \delta_{norm}$ we write:

$$t = t_0 \cdot (\lambda_1 + 1) \cdot ... \cdot (\lambda_L + 1) \cdot \delta_{norm} + ... + t_{L-1} \cdot (\lambda_L + 1) \cdot \delta_{norm} + t_0 \cdot \delta_{norm} + t'$$

$$= \delta_{norm} \cdot \sum_{i=0..L} t_i \cdot \prod_{j=i+1..L} (\lambda_j + 1) + t' \qquad (5)$$

Sender's Perspective. For the moment we consider the case of a single sender. Let t_{start} denote the time at which the broadcast was started and assume that it is started by the communication master which is also responsible for time synchronization. Thus t_{start} is the exact time at which the broadcast started (no drifts for the sender).

Definition 3. Let $\tau_{\text{left}} = \tau_0\tau_1...\tau_{i-1}$ denote a vector of i positive integers such that each element on position i is less or equal to λ_i. Given a tolerance relation $< \Lambda, \Delta >_{M,S,B,T}$, an indexed key K_τ is a key entailed by a vector τ. An indexed key chain $\mathcal{K}_{<\Lambda,\Delta>}$ is a collection of indexed keys, derived as follows: having a fixed fresh seed K_{master}, a key derivation process $\mathcal{KD}$ and a one-way function $\mathcal{F}$, then $\forall i \in [0, L], \tau_i \in [1, \lambda_i]$, given $K_{\tau_{\text{left}}|0|\overline{0}} = \mathcal{KD}(K_{\text{master}}, \tau_{\text{left}})$:

$$K_{\tau_{\text{left}}|\tau_i|\overline{0}} = \mathcal{F}(K_{\tau_{\text{left}}|\tau_i+1|\overline{0}}) \tag{6}$$

Definition 4. Let $\mathcal{DT}(K_\tau)$ denote the disclosure time of the indexed key K_τ. Given a broadcast started at t_{start} the disclosure time of this key is:

$$\mathcal{DT}(K_\tau) = t_{start} + \delta_{norm} \cdot \sum_{i=0..L} \tau_i \cdot \prod_{j=i+1..L} (\lambda_j + 1) \tag{7}$$

Definition 4 allows the creation of chains with the structure from Figure 2 while definition 5 allows keys to be released at equal time intervals δ_{norm}.

Remark 4. The key released by the sender at time $t_{current}$ given a broadcast started at t_{start} is $K_{t_{<\Lambda,\Delta>}}$ where $t = t_{current} - t_{start}$. This means that the key is from level l, where l is the first non-zero index from right to left and the position of the key on the key chain from level l is t_l.

Reinitialization Packets and Efficiency. To avoid a non-uniform bus load, as discussed previously, re-initialization packets will be dropped *equidistantly* in the δ_{norm} intervals. Otherwise, packets carrying data must be delayed until all re-initialization packets are sent. This is because re-initialization packets must have priority on the bus, otherwise the protocol will succumb an will require a new initialization stage which is even more expensive. Thus we can also use as an efficiency criteria the maximum delay until a new CAN frame can be send. For the basic scheme the maximum delay fluctuates with the number of initialization packets. This delay can be easily established for the basic scheme. Let $z_i(x)$ denote the number of consecutive zeros in vector x starting from the rightmost position. At discrete time value t, given $t_{<\Lambda,\Delta>}$ the delay until the next packet can be sent is:

$$delay = \max[0, z((t - t_{start})_{<\Lambda,\Delta>})] \tag{8}$$

Indeed, the number of consecutive zeros at the end of the time value denotes how many chains need to be initialized at that particular time. This value becomes constant for the equidistant scheme and data packets are delayed by at most one packet.

To complete the view on efficiency, we should also define the overhead induced by the authentication mechanism. The overhead has two distinct components, the *authentication overhead* which is the overhead inflicted by the authentication keys that are released on the bus, and the *re-initialization overhead* which is the overhead inflicted by the re-initialization material, i.e., MAC codes that commit the key chains. Indeed, to this one may want to add the overhead induced by the message authentication codes, MACs, associated to each data packet that is send over the bus. We will not take this

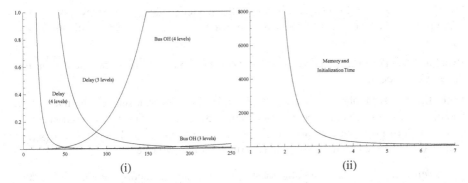

Fig. 3. Delay and overhead variation with chain length (i) and memory, initialization time and re-initialization packets variation with number of levels (ii)

into account because this is application dependent, not protocol dependent, indeed in some applications the size of the data packets can be small, and thus adding a MAC to each data packet will greatly increase the overhead. In other applications it may be the reverse, and data packets can be large while the MAC will not significantly increase the overhead. Based on these we can also define the total overhead inflicted by the protocol.

Remark 5. Given a tolerance relation $< \Lambda, \Delta >_{M,S,B,T}$ the authentication and re-initialization overheads and the bus load induced by the protocol is: $OH_{auth} = B^{-1} \cdot \prod_{i=0}^{L} (\lambda_i + 1) - 1$ (as given in relation (2), the right term of the product covers all key released on the bus), $OH_{reinit} = B^{-1} \cdot \sum_{i=1}^{L} (\prod_{j=0}^{i-1} (\lambda_j + 1) - 1)$ (the right term of the product gives al the key chains that are committed on the bus) and $OH_{total} = OH_{auth} + OH_{reinit}$.

One may note that if the authentication delay is bigger the overhead also becomes lower since fewer elements of the chain are sent. Also, the re-initialization overhead increases with the number of levels. We give concrete examples for these in the experimental results.

Figure 3 shows the influence of chain length on bus overhead and disclosure delays. Plots are given for three and four levels of key chains. We note that the delays drop rapidly by increasing the number of levels, but in the same manner the overhead increases (at 100% the bus is locked and communication halted). Figure 3 shows the variation of memory requirements with the number of chain levels, which is the same as the initialization time. All plots are taken for a time range of 24 hours, the delay is fixed to 5 ms.

Receiver's Perspective. We consider the case of a sender S with synchronization error ϵ_S and a receiver $\mathcal{R}$ with synchronization error $\epsilon_\mathcal{R}$. Now we define the security condition that must be met by all packets that contain authentication information, i.e., MAC codes, produced with an indexed key K_τ.

Definition 5. Given synchronization errors ϵ_S and $\epsilon_\mathcal{R}$ for sender and receiver, an authentication packet indexed by τ must discarded unless:

$$\mathcal{T}_{rec}(P) \le \mathcal{DT}(\tau) + \epsilon_S + \epsilon_\mathcal{R} \qquad (9)$$

Here $\mathcal{T}_{rec}(P)$ denotes the estimated time on the sender's side computed by the receiver when packet P arrives. If the sender is also responsible for time synchronization then $\epsilon_{\mathcal{S}} = 0$.

Protocol Description. We can now summarize previous notions in one definition for the entire protocol.

Definition 6. Given tolerance relation $< \Lambda, \Delta >_{M,S,B,T}$, an indexed key chain $\mathcal{K}_{<\Lambda,\Delta>}$ and the two roles sender and receiver denoted by $\mathcal{S}, \mathcal{R}$ each with synchronization errors $\epsilon_{\mathcal{S}}, \epsilon_{\mathcal{R}}$ with respect to a common clock, protocol Broadcast$[\mathcal{S}, \mathcal{R}, < \Lambda, \Delta >_{M,S,B,T}, \mathcal{K}_{<\Lambda,\Delta>}]$ is formed by the following two rules for the two roles:

1. $\mathcal{S}$ sends K_τ at $\mathcal{DT}(K_\tau)$ and the message M and its corresponding $MAC(K_\tau, M)$ in any empty time-slot with the condition that $MAC(K_\tau, M)$ is released no latter than $\mathcal{DT}(K_\tau) + \xi$,
2. $\mathcal{R}$ discards all $MAC(K_\tau, M)$ received later than $\mathcal{DT}(K_\tau) + \epsilon_{\mathcal{S}} + \epsilon_{\mathcal{R}}$ and deems authentic all other messages for which $MAC(K_\tau, M)$ can be verified with an authentic key. A key $K_{\tau_{left}|\tau_i|\overline{0}}$ is authentic only if $K_{\tau_{left}|\tau_i|\overline{0}} = \mathcal{F}(K_{\tau_{left}|\tau_i+1|\overline{0}})$ and $K_{\tau_{left}|\tau_i|\overline{0}}$ is a previously received/computed authentic key.

Here ξ denotes a tolerance margin until the sender can send a MAC with a particular key. Indeed, sending MACs too close to the disclosure time may be useless because the receiver may have to discard them if the security condition cannot be met. Thus ξ must be fixed as initial parameter for the protocol and it must hold that $\epsilon_{\mathcal{S}} + \epsilon_{\mathcal{R}} << \xi$. In time interval $[\mathcal{DT}(K_\tau), \mathcal{DT}(K_\tau) + \xi]$ the sender can safely disclose any kind of data packet, but not MACs.

Broadcast$[\mathcal{S}, \mathcal{R}, < \Lambda, \Delta >_{M,S,B,T}, \mathcal{K}_{<\Lambda,\Delta>}]$ is a secure broadcast authentication protocol. The security of this family of protocols is well established, the informal argument is that the adversary cannot construct $MAC(K_i, M)$, until K_i is released. As function $\mathcal{F}$ is one-way he cannot derive K_i from $\mathcal{F}(K_i)$ and by the time K_i is released any MAC with K_i that is further received will be discarded. Formal proofs for such protocols can be found in [11], [13].

2.5   The Case of Multiple Senders

The case of k senders can now be easily derived from the previous formalism. To preserve the *equidistant* time schedule we use the nominal disclosure time δ_{norm} and divide it by the number of senders k. Let us define the next sender delay as:

$$\delta_{next} = \frac{\delta_{norm}}{k} \tag{10}$$

Definition 7. Let $\mathcal{DT}(K_\tau)$ denote the disclosure time of an indexed key by the by the kth sender. Given a broadcast started at t_{start} we have:

$$\mathcal{DT}(K_\tau, k) = \mathcal{DT}(K_\tau) + k \cdot \delta_{next} \tag{11}$$

The security conditions which has to be verified by receivers must also add the $k \cdot \delta_{next}$ term to the disclosure time of the k-th sender.

3 Application Setting and Experimental Results

As stated, for the implementation of the previously described protocol, we used a Freescale 16-bit automotive grade microcontroller (MC9S12XDT512) from the S12X family on SofTec Microsystems ZK-S12-B development board. One special feature of this family is the presence of an incorporated co-processor called XGATE which can be used to increase the microcontroller's data throughput [15]. We made use of this module to increase the efficiency of our implementation by assigning it the task of computing the underlying cryptographic functions.

The S12X microcontrollers used in our experiments have 512kbytes of FLASH memory and 20kbytes of RAM. Both FLASH and RAM memories are banked as a consequence of the 16 bits wide address bus which is not sufficient to access all memory locations. Thus, a total of 8kbytes of RAM space can be used for continuous allocation while the rest of the RAM can be accessed in 4kbyte windows. The amount of RAM memory that can be used for storing key chains is relevant as it determines the maximum number of chain levels and their lengths.

The maximum bus frequency that can be set using the PLL module is, according to the data-sheet, 40MHz. We configured the PLL for frequencies beyond this specified value and were able to go up to speeds of 80MHz. After assessing that the behaviour of the microcontroller at this overclocked frequency is normal we used it in our tests and compared the results with the ones obtained for 40MHz.

The on-chip CAN module implements version 2.0A/B of the CAN protocol and supports a programmable bit-rate up to 1 Mbps. A limitation for the maximum achievable CAN speed comes from the on board low speed fault tolerant transceiver which can only run at speeds up to 125kbaud.

3.1 XGATE Module

The XGATE module has a built in RISC core with instructions for data transfers, bit manipulations and basic arithmetic operations. The RISC core can access the internal memories and peripherals of the microcontroller without blocking them from the main S12X CPU. The S12X CPU always has priority when the two CPUs access the same resource at the same time. To assure data consistency, the access priority can be controlled by using the hardware semaphores available on the microcontroller.

Interrupts can be routed to the XGATE module in order to decrease the interrupt load of the main S12X CPU. Additionally, up to 8 software triggered channels can be used by the S12X CPU to request software execution on XGATE.

In order to obtain the maximum XGATE CPU speed, the code can be executed from RAM. Because RAM is a volatile memory, XGATE code is being stored into the FLASH memory and copied into RAM after each reset. Having a better RAM access speed and a speed-optimized instruction set, a typical function can run up to 4.5 times faster on XGATE than on the S12X CPU [16]. Because it was designed for quick execution of small code requested by interrupts, the flash memory available for storing XGATE code is limited. For controllers in the S12XD family this limit is 30 kbytes.

3.2 Implementation Details

To decrease the communication overhead that could be introduced by computing cryptographic primitives we assigned this task to the XGATE module. In order to evaluate the computational performance of the microcontroller we measured the execution speed of three hash functions: MD5, SHA1 and SHA-256. Measurements were done on S12X and XGATE for different input lengths using both the maximum specified frequency and the overclocked frequency. The measurements presented in tables 1 and 2 show that on average the hash functions were performed approximately 2.12 times faster on XGATE than on S12X. The overclocking also increases the speed with a factor of 2.

Table 1. Performance of S12X in computing MD5, SHA-1 and SHA-256

| Length | Execution time MD5 | | Execution time SHA1 | | Execution time SHA-256 | |
(bytes)	@ 40MHz	@ 80MHz	@ 40MHz	@ 80MHz	@ 40MHz	@ 80MHz
0	$732\mu s$	$371\mu s$	$2.285ms$	$1.144ms$	$5.51ms$	$2.755ms$
1	$736\mu s$	$373\mu s$	$2.290ms$	$1.146ms$	$5.52ms$	$2.760ms$
3	$737\mu s$	$373\mu s$	$2.290ms$	$1.146ms$	$5.52ms$	$2.760ms$
14	$738\mu s$	$374\mu s$	$2.290ms$	$1.148ms$	$5.50ms$	$2.755ms$
26	$739\mu s$	$374.5\mu s$	$2.295ms$	$1.148ms$	$5.49ms$	$2.750ms$
62	$1414\mu s$	$717\mu s$	$4.510ms$	$2.255ms$	$10.86ms$	$5.44ms$
90	$1374\mu s$	$697\mu s$	$4.470ms$	$2.235ms$	$10.80ms$	$5.40ms$

Table 2. Performance of XGATE in computing MD5, SHA-1 and SHA-256

| Length | Execution time MD5 | | Execution time SHA1 | | Execution time SHA-256 | |
(bytes)	@ 40MHz	@ 80MHz	@ 40MHz	@ 80MHz	@ 40MHz	@ 80MHz
0	$312.5\mu s$	$156.2\mu s$	$1.000ms$	$500\mu s$	$3.155ms$	$1.578ms$
1	$314.5\mu s$	$157.4\mu s$	$1.002ms$	$501\mu s$	$3.155ms$	$1.580ms$
3	$314.5\mu s$	$157.2\mu s$	$1.002ms$	$502\mu s$	$3.155ms$	$1.580ms$
14	$316.0\mu s$	$158\mu s$	$1.004ms$	$502\mu s$	$3.150ms$	$1.578ms$
26	$317.5\mu s$	$158.9\mu s$	$1.004ms$	$503\mu s$	$3.145ms$	$1.578ms$
62	$605\mu s$	$303\mu s$	$1.976ms$	$988\mu s$	$6.24ms$	$3.125ms$
90	$592\mu s$	$296.5\mu s$	$1.962ms$	$982\mu s$	$6.22ms$	$3.115ms$

We chose MD5 for building the one-way chains which are needed by the protocol. Due to the small disclosure delay we consider that using MD5 is safe for our scenario. Each chain element will thus be a 128 bit value which is used to perform an HMAC over the message that has be sent at a certain point in time.

One other possible method of building one-way chains is to use block ciphers as hash functions. This can be done by always encrypting a fixed value (e.g. 0) using the previously generated value as the encryption key: $k_i \leftarrow Enc(k_{i-1}; 0)$. Table 3 shows the performance obtained by S12X in computing some known block ciphers.

All cryptographic computations are done on the XGATE module following a software request. For passing data between the two processing units, a common memory area is used. Each time a hash needs to be computed, the S12X writes the input data in the common memory area and makes a software request to the XGATE module. While

Table 3. Performance of S12X in computing symmetric primitives @ 80MHz

Primitive name	Block size	Key size	Rounds	Execution time
Anubis	16 bytes	16 bytes	12	$916\mu s$
Blowfish	8 bytes	16 bytes	16	$25.2ms$
Cast5	8 bytes	16 bytes	16	$321\mu s$
Kasumi	8 bytes	16 bytes	8	$129.4\mu s$
Skipjack	8 bytes	10 bytes	32	$116.2\mu s$
Xtea	8 bytes	16 bytes	32	$233.5\mu s$

the hash is being computed on the XGATE side, the main CPU is free to execute other tasks such as, receiving messages or sending messages that have been already built. The XGATE module can signal the end of the function execution by issuing an interrupt to the S12X CPU.

After protocol implementation, the total RAM memory left for storing key chains can hold 1216 elements (16 bytes each). Having this upper limit for M, L and λ have to be determined for best performances based on the bus speed and the desired disclosure delay. If we consider packets of 16 bytes in size the measured bus speed for sending packets is 578 packets/second (one packet each $1.730ms$).

For example, if we decide to use three levels to assure authentication over a period of one day with a speed of 578 packets/second, we would have 233 elements on each level and the key disclosure time δ would be 6.8ms. The bus overhead for this situation is 25,2% and the time needed to initialize the key chains is approximately 700ms. Increasing the number of levels to 5 leads to chains of 26 elements so less memory is necessary and the time needed for initialization is reduced to 131ms. The cost of these improvements is a bus overhead of 26.9%. The bus load grows exponentially with the increase in the number of levels used while the disclosure delay depends on the transmission speed and the total communication duration. The duration of the communication also affects the number of elements on each level which is upper bounded to M/L ($1216/L$ in our setting).

4   Conclusions

A protocol for assuring broadcast authenticity on the CAN bus was provided. By this research we hope that we give a first analysis on the feasibility of such a solution in low speed CAN. We studied different trade-offs in order to depict the optimal choice of parameters. In particular we concluded that the main limitation is the bus speed (limited to 128kbps in fault-tolerant CAN), followed by memory and last by computational power. This is also due to the performance of the XGATE co-processor which is about two times faster than the regular S12 processor. In some cases, to reduce memory consumption and to shorten the initialization time, chains with more than three levels were also efficient. The theoretical estimations are entailed by experimental results on the S12X processor, a commonly used automotive grade microcontroller. Current and future work includes extending the results on high end microcontrollers capable of high speed CAN communication.

Acknowledgements. This work was supported by CNCSIS-UEFISCDI project number PNII-IDEI 940/2008 and by the strategic grant POSDRU 107/1.5/S/77265, inside POSDRU Romania 2007-2013 co-financed by the European Social Fund - Investing in People.

References

1. ISO: CAN Specification Version 2.0. Robert BOSCH GmbH (1991)
2. ISO: ISO 11898-1. Road vehicles - Controller area network (CAN) - Part 1: Controller area network data link layer and medium access control. International Organization for Standardization (2003)
3. Charzinski, J.: Performance of the error detection mechanisms in can. In: Proceedings of the 1st International CAN Conference, pp. 20–29 (1994)
4. Lemke, K., Paar, C., Wolf, M.: Embedded Security in Cars Securing Current and Future Automotive IT Applications. Springer (2006)
5. Koscher, K., Czeskis, A., Roesner, F., Patel, S., Kohno, T., Checkoway, S., McCoy, D., Kantor, B., Anderson, D., Shacham, H., Savage, S.: Experimental security analysis of a modern automobile. In: IEEE Symposium on Security and Privacy (SP), pp. 447–462 (2010)
6. ISO: ISO 11898-4. Road vehicles - Controller area network (CAN) - Part 4: Time triggered communication. International Organization for Standardization (2004)
7. Perrig, A., Canetti, R., Song, D., Tygar, J.D.: SPINS: Security protocols for sensor networks. In: Seventh Annual ACM International Conference on Mobile Computing and Networks (MobiCom 2001), pp. 189–199 (2001)
8. Liu, D., Ning, P.: Efficient distribution of key chain commitments for broadcast authentication in distributed sensor networks. In: Proc. of the 10th Annual Network and Distributed System Security Symposium, pp. 263–276 (2003)
9. Liu, D., Ning, P.: Multilevel μtesla: Broadcast authentication for distributed sensor networks. ACM Trans. Embed. Comput. Syst. 3, 800–836 (2004)
10. Perrig, A., Canetti, R., Tygar, J., Song, D.X.: Efficient authentication and signing of multicast streams over lossy channels. In: IEEE Symposium on Security and Privacy, pp. 56–73 (2000)
11. Perrig, A., Canetti, R., Song, D., Tygar, J.D.: Efficient and secure source authentication for multicast. Network and Distributed System Security Symposium, NDSS 2001, 35–46 (2001)
12. Lamport, L.: Password authentication with insecure communication. Commun. ACM 24, 770–772 (1981)
13. Bergadano, F., Cavagnino, D., Crispo, B.: Individual authentication in multiparty communications. Computers & Security 21, 719–735 (2002)
14. Anderson, R., Bergadano, F., Crispo, B., Lee, J.H., Manifavas, C., Needham, R.: A new family of authentication protocols. SIGOPS Oper. Syst. Rev. 32, 9–20 (1998)
15. Freescale: MC9S12XDP512 Data Sheet, Rev. 2.21 (October 2009)
16. Mitchell, R.: Tutorial: Introducing the XGATE Module to Consumer and Industrial Application Developers, Freescale (March 2004)

Part V
Signal Processing
and Multimedia Applications

Efficiently Managing Multimedia Hierarchical Data with the WINDSURF Library*

Ilaria Bartolini, Marco Patella, and Guido Stromei

DEIS, Università di Bologna, Italy
{i.bartolini,marco.patella,guido.stromei}@unibo.it

Abstract. Complex multimedia data are at the heart of several modern applications, such as image/video retrieval and the comparison of collection of documents. Frequently, such complex data are modeled as hierarchical objects that consist of different components, like videos including shots, images including visually coherent regions, and so on. When such complex objects are to be compared, for example, for assessing their mutual similarity, this is usually done by recursively comparing component elements. However, due to such complexity, it is often hard to efficiently perform a number of tasks, like processing of queries or understanding the impact of different alternatives available for the definition of similarity between objects. In this article, we propose a unified model for the representation of complex multimedia data, introducing the WINDSURF software library, with the goal of allowing a seamless management of such data. The library provides a framework for evaluating the performance of alternative query processing algorithms for efficient retrieval of multimedia data. Important features of the WINDSURF library are its generality, flexibility, and extensibility. These are guaranteed by the appropriate instantiation of the different templates included in the library: in this way, each user can realize her particular retrieval model of need.

1 Introduction

Despite their ubiquitous and prominent role in nowadays life, Multimedia (MM) information still present a variety of challenges for their effective and efficient retrieval. Among these, the extraction of content and its subsequent indexing represent two of the most analyzed areas of research. However, the inherently complex nature of some multimedia data (like videos, images, web pages, and so on) makes it hard to exploit out-of-the-box solutions that were devised for simpler scenarios (e.g., textual documents). Indeed, in many MM cases the classical information retrieval (IR) models cannot be applied without either oversimplifying the type of queries that can be issued by an user or completely giving up efficiency or effectiveness. An example, that arises in several MM scenarios, is that of MM documents that are composed of several component *elements*. Requesting documents that are relevant to a given query document Q entails retrieving elements that are relevant to Q elements, and then somewhat combining the results at the document level. This *hierarchical* structure of documents is general enough to be able to model

---

* This work was partially supported by the CoOPERARE MIUR Project.

M.S. Obaidat, J.L. Sevillano, and J. Filipe (Eds.): ICETE 2011, CCIS 314, pp. 347–361, 2012.

different MM IR applications, but poses some peculiar challenges due to its very nature: for example, how are document elements compared to query elements? how the relevance of elements is aggregated in order to assess the relevance of whole documents? is indexing of whole documents a possible choice? in case, is it a better choice than indexing elements? Above questions recur whenever the hierarchical model is applied for the retrieval of MM documents; however, answers cannot be given independently from the application at hand, since each particular scenario presents its peculiarities. When enhancing differences among applications, we should however note that several affinities are still present and that solutions proposed for a particular scenario could be applied to other similar scenarios as well, provided that the underlying model is the same.

In this paper, we present the WINDSURF library for management of MM hierarchical data, with the goal of providing a general, flexible, and extensible software framework for analyzing the impact on performance of the different aspects included in its retrieval model. In particular, the library presents an emphasis on query processing techniques, offering different index-based algorithms for the efficient resolution of similarity retrieval queries, where documents are requested whose content is (in some sense) *similar* to that of the query. Indeed, it turns out that algorithms included in the WINDSURF library have a wide range of applicability and can therefore be helpful for a variety of scenarios. We expect the library to be particularly useful to those researchers that have to analyze how different alternatives in the representation/comparison of elements/documents interact in providing different effectiveness/efficiency performances, without the burden of defining ex-novo algorithms for retrieving query results. We also note that processing of similarity queries may not be the main goal of the application at hand, rather it could be just a component of a more complex system: as an example, TRECVID 2011 (http://trecvid.nist.gov/) includes several tasks calling for efficient retrieval of similar video shots. For instance, the semantic indexing (SIN) task involves the automatic tagging of video segments in order to perform filtering, categorization, browsing, and search (this is commonly performed by associating the same tags to shots sharing similar visual/audio content [4]); the content-based copy detection (CCD) task, on the other hand, aims to automatically detect copies of video segments, which clearly can be based on the retrieval of similar video content.

We first precisely define the hierarchical retrieval model of WINDSURF (Section 2), by also presenting real-world examples of its use, and provide a general view of the library (Section 3), including its query processing algorithms (Section 4). Then (Section 5), we show how the library can be customized so as to behave according to the requirements of the particular application at hand and we provide examples of use of the library in the Region-Based Image Retrieval (RBIR) scenario (Section 6): this was the original application scenario of the library and also justifies its name (WINDSURF standing for Wavelet-based INDexing of imageS Using Region Fragmentation [1]). Finally, we draw our conclusions, by also highlighting future directions of research (Section 7).

2   The WINDSURF Retrieval Model

The retrieval model of WINDSURF is as follows: we have a database $\mathcal{D}$ of N documents, $\mathcal{D} = \{D^1, \ldots, D^N\}$, where each document D is composed of n_D *elements*,

$D = \{R_1, \ldots, R_{n_D}\}$. Each element R is described by way of *features* that represent, in an appropriate way, the content of R. Given a query document $Q = \{Q_1, \ldots, Q_n\}$ composed of n elements, and an element distance function δ, that measures the dissimilarity of a given pair of elements (using their features), we want to determine the set of *best* documents in $\mathcal{D}$ with respect to Q.

The above formulation of the problem is sufficiently general to encompass different retrieval paradigms, each having a different way of specifying which documents are to be considered "best" for the query at hand: this can be demonstrated by applying the WINDSURF retrieval model to some real world examples.

Example 1. Our first example deals with the comparisons of web sites. In this case, each element R is a web page contained in a web site D and we want to discover whether a new web site Q is similar to some existing web sites in our database $\mathcal{D}$. Comparison between web pages is performed by taking into account contained keywords, e.g., by using the vector space model [18], so that features extracted from each page include keywords using $tf \times idf$ values after stopping & stemming (see Figure 1).

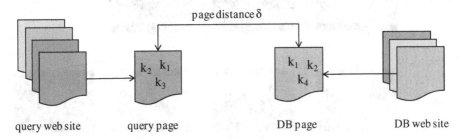

Fig. 1. Comparing web sites

Example 2. In RBIR, the $\mathcal{D}$ database consists in still images that are segmented into regions, where pixels included in a single region R share the same visual content (e.g., color & texture). Image regions are compared according to their visual features and we want to retrieve images that are similar in content to a user-specified query image Q (see Figure 2).

Example 3. As a third example, we consider the comparison of videos based on similarity, where each video D is first segmented into shots, i.e., sequences of video frames that are coherent in their visual content. Then, each shot R is represented by a single key frame (this can be either the first frame of the shot, or the middle one, or the medoid of shot frames), so that shots can be compared by means of a simple image similarity function. Finally, we can compare whole videos by aggregating the similarities between shots (see Figure 3). Note that different applications (like duplicate video detection) might impose different constraints on the "matching" of video shots, e.g., requesting that only shots of similar length can be coupled or that shots that are shown in very different moments cannot be matched; clearly, this has an impact on the computation of similarity between videos, thus a researcher might be interested in investigating the effect of such constraints on the result of a query requesting for, say, the 5 videos most similar to a given query video Q.

region distance δ

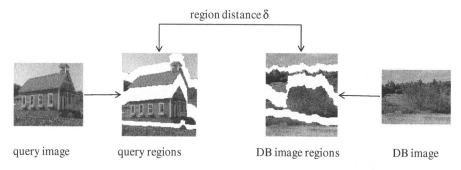

query image   query regions   DB image regions   DB image

Fig. 2. Comparing segmented images in Region-based Image Retrieval

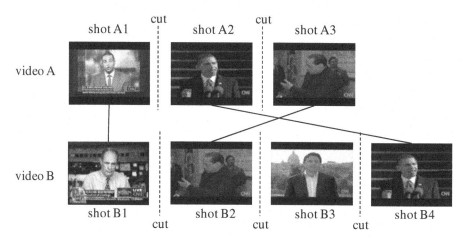

Fig. 3. Comparison of videos based on video shots

For the rest of the paper, we will assume as given the way documents are divided into elements (e.g., the image segmentation algorithm in Example 2, or the shot segmentation of videos in Example 3), the features used to represent such elements, and the (element) distance function δ, being understood that similar elements will have a low δ value: our focus here is to demonstrate how different retrieval models can be enclosed by the WINDSURF model, thus proving its generality.

Another important factor to be considered is the definition of the query result, i.e., how the best documents wrt Q are specified. Indeed, different applications typically have different ways of assessing the similarity between documents, given the similarities between component elements. In WINDSURF, two different retrieval modalities are supported: quantitative (k-NN) and qualitative (Skyline).

– In the k Nearest Neighbor (k-NN) quantitative model [14], similarity between documents is numerically assessed by way of a document distance function d that combines together the single element distances into an overall value. Consequently, document D^a is considered better than D^b for the query Q iff $d\left(Q, D^a\right) < d\left(Q, D^b\right)$ holds and the query result consists of the k DB documents closest to the query.

– As an alternative to the quantitative model, the qualitative (Skyline) model does not rely on the specification of a numerical value, according to which DB documents can be sorted for decreasing values of similarity wrt to the query, rather document D^a is considered better than D^b for the query Q iff D^a does no worse than D^b on all query elements and there exists at least one query element on which D^a is strictly better than D^b. This necessarily includes those documents that would be the best alternative according to some specific document distance function [8].

Regarding k-NN queries, it has to be noted that, usually, the computation of the document distance d is obtained by combining three basic ingredients:

1. the element distance δ,
2. the set of constraints that specify how the component elements of the query Q have to be matched to the component elements of another (database) document D, and
3. the aggregation function that combines distance values between matched elements into an overall document distance value (e.g., a simple average of distance values between matched elements).

Often, the overall document distance is computed by aggregating scores of the best possible matching, i.e., the one that minimizes the overall document distance; in this case, the computation of d also includes the resolution of an optimization problem in the space of possible matchings between elements of Q and elements of D. We finally note that the result of any query depends on the combination of all three ingredients, so that changing one of them might lead to completely different results. As we will show later, the characteristics of the overall document distance also determine which algorithms can be used to efficiently solve the k-NN query.

As to the Skyline retrieval model, our definition of domination among documents follows the one described in [3] for the case of segmented images. Intuitively, the concept of domination is defined for tuples, while here we are considering sets of elements; thus, the dominance criterion needs to be properly extended to deal with this additional complexity in the structure of objects to be compared. For this purpose, each document can be defined as the set of possible matchings of its elements with query elements, each matching being a tuple of distance values between a query element Q_i and its matched element of D, R_j. The domination between matchings can be then straightforwardly defined. Finally, domination between documents is built on top of the concept of domination between matchings, stating that a document D^a dominates another document D^b wrt the query Q iff for each matching of D^b there exists a matching of D^a that dominates it.

2.1 Alternative Retrieval Models

Albeit the WINDSURF retrieval model is sufficiently general to encompass the characteristics of several multimedia scenarios, see [10] for a recent example, it is interesting to note its analogies with other different models. For example, the *Bag of Words* (BoW) model for computer vision [7] represents images as sets of *patches* (these are similar to elements in WINDSURF). Then, all patches included in any DB image are converted into *codewords*, where each codeword is representative of several patches. This produces a *codebook* and each image can be described as the set of codewords representing its patches. In this way, the retrieval models used for textual documents [18] can be directly applied for images, since the codebook is equivalent to a dictionary. The difficult part here is the generation of the codebook (how many codewords? how to compare patches?).

We also note that our k-NN retrieval model also includes those cases where the image distance d also considers *global* characteristics; for example, this is the case when the particular d to be used for a given query is *learned* by exploiting side information [19,10].

3   Overview of the WINDSURF Library

The WINDSURF library is written in Java and is released under the "QPL" license, being freely available at URI http://www-db.deis.unibo.it/Windsurf/ for education and research purposes only. It consists of five main packages, each focusing on a section of the main architecture.

Document: the Document package includes the definition of classes modelling documents, elements, and features. It also contains the specification of the element distance δ and (possibly) of the document distance d.

FeatureExtractor: the FeatureExtractor is the component in charge of extracting the features from a given document. This is performed in two steps: first the document is decomposed into elements (segmentation), then features are computed for each element (extraction).

QueryProcessor: the QueryProcessor (QP) is the component that solves queries over document features. It contains algorithms for the efficient resolution of both k-NN and Skyline queries, by exploiting the presence of indices built on document features. In case indices are not available, the package also incorporates sequential algorithms for solving queries.

FeatureManager: the FeatureManager (FM) is the component in charge of storing/retrieving the document features from the DB, providing an abstraction from the underlying used DBMS. In order to achieve an efficient management of features, these can be saved into a relational DBMS (in particular, the WINDSURF library includes code for using the MySQL[1] RDBMS).

IndexManager: the IndexManager (IM) package contains classes managing the feature indices. These can be exploited by the QP for the efficient resolution of queries over the features (see Section 4). WINDSURF supports indices built on top of both elements and documents: as we will see in the following, this allows the definition of alternative query processing algorithms. In particular, an implementation of the M-tree index [6] is included.[2]

Figure 4 provides an abstract view of how packages of the library cooperate during the insertion and the retrieval phase. When a new document is to be added to the document

---

[1] http://www.mysql.com/

[2] For efficiency reasons, the implementation of M-tree is written in C++.

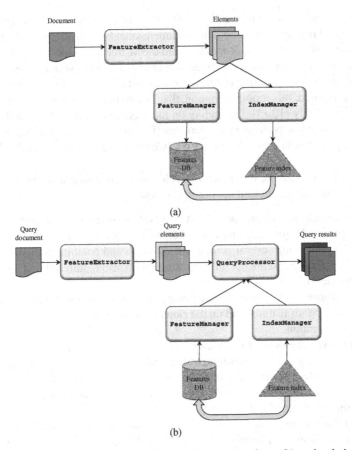

Fig. 4. Data flow in the WINDSURF library: (a) insertion phase, (b) retrieval phase

database (Figure 4 (a)), it is first processed by the `FeatureExtractor` package which breaks it into component elements and extracts elements' features. These are then forwarded to the FM and IM components that store the features in the features DB and the features index, respectively. On the other hand, at query time (Figure 4 (b)) features extracted by the `FeatureExtractor` are fed into the QP component, whose algorithms exploit the Feature and Index managers in order to pick query results out.

4   Query Processing Algorithms

Our main goal in designing the WINDSURF library was the performance comparison of different algorithms for the retrieval of complex documents, in terms of both efficiency and effectiveness. In this view, the core of the library consists of the QP component, that presents alternative algorithms for the resolution of queries. Regarding efficiency, QP algorithms might exploit indices built on features in order to avoid a full sequential evaluation, a non viable solution for large document DBs. Our arguments will be developed independently of the specific index; rather, we will refer to a generic *distance-based* index, i.e., any index that relies on the computation of distances to return back objects. Distance-based indices include both multi-dimensional [9] and metric [5] indices, relevant examples of which are the R-tree [11] and the M-tree [6], respectively. To be useful for our purposes, distance-based indices should also provide a sorted access interface, i.e., to output data in increasing order of distance with respect to the object with which the index is queried: this is quite common, thanks also to the existence of algorithms of general applicability [12,13]. Depending on the used algorithm, indices in the WIND-SURF library might be built on either elements (for which the element distance δ is used for indexing purposes) or whole documents (where indexing is based on the document distance d).

In order to evaluate the efficiency of each query processing algorithm, all classes provide statistics about relevant operations, including:

Document distances: the number of distance evaluations among documents (only relevant for k-NN queries); this is considered a costly operation, since it typically involves comparing several component elements and combining them in order to produce the overall score (as said, the latter might also require solving an optimization problem).

Element distances: the number of distance evaluations among elements; depending on the number of features and on the element distance function δ, this too might be a costly operation.

Sorted accesses: the number of accesses to the underlying element index; as we will show, some algorithms exploit an index built on document elements, that is used to sort DB elements in order of increasing distance values with respect to query elements. A sorted access returns a single DB element and requires the index to perform some computations.

Document dominations: the number of comparisons among documents in order to see whether a document dominates another one (Skyline queries only); again, this is a costly operation since it might require comparing several matchings.

Time: the overall time needed to solve a single query; this can be also detailed by considering the time needed for retrieving features from the DB, accessing the underlying indices, computing document distances, or comparing documents for domination.

The QP includes efficient algorithms for the efficient resolution of both k-NN and Skyline queries [3]. Each algorithm will be described here in general terms, by specifying under which hypotheses it is able to correctly solve a query.

SEQ. This sequential k-NN algorithm (`QueryProcessor.SF.QuerySFSequential` class) retrieves all documents in $\mathcal{D}$ and compares them with Q, by using the document distance d. Only the k best documents, i.e., the ones having the lowest d values, are kept and returned as the query result. No specific requirement on d or δ is needed, since the algorithm simply follows the definition of k-NN query.

k-NN-set. This index-based k-NN algorithm (`QueryProcessor.SF.kNNset.kNNset` class) exploits an element index $\mathcal{T}_R$ to reduce the number of document and element distances to be computed [3]. The k-NN-set algorithm iteratively alternates sorted accesses to the index $\mathcal{T}_R$ to retrieve DB elements with random accesses that compute a document distance $d(Q, D)$ between the query and the document whose element has been retrieved by the last sorted access. In this case, document distances are computed only during the random access phase, while element distances can be computed within the index and during each random access (since distances between all elements of both Q and of D might be required to compute $d(Q, D)$).

The algorithm applies to any document distance function d that can be bounded from below, i.e., for those d such that if, for document $D = \{R_1, \ldots, R_{n_D}\}$ and query $Q = \{Q_1, \ldots, Q_n\}$, it is $\delta(Qi, Rj) \geq \theta_i, \forall i, j$, then a function T exists such that $d(Q, D) \geq T(\theta_i)$. This is required to guarantee correctness of the provided result: it means that, for a document D^a whose all elements are "closer" to query elements than all those of another document D^b, it is also $d(Q, D^a) \leq d(Q, D^b)$. Indeed, since the underlying index $\mathcal{T}_R$ provides DB elements in order of increasing distance to query elements (sorted access), the algorithm cannot terminate until it is guaranteed that no document yet to be seen in a sorted access is closer to Q than the best k documents seen so far.

k-NN-imgIdx. This k-NN algorithm (`QueryProcessor.SF.ImgIdx.QuerySFIndex` class) exploits a document index $\mathcal{T}_D$. Since, for hypothesis, $\mathcal{T}_D$ supports sorted accesses, the k-NN-imgIdx algorithm simply performs k of such accesses to return the query result. We note here that multi-dimensional access methods cannot be used to index whole documents, because a document is a set (and not a vector) of elements, thus metric indices are needed for this purpose. It then follows that the distance d used to compare documents should be a metric.

Sky-set. This is the only index-based Skyline algorithm included in the WINDSURF library (`QueryProcessor.Skyline.Skyset.Skyset` class) and uses an element index $\mathcal{T}_R$ [3] (the Skyline retrieval model cannot be supported by document indices, because a document distance function is not defined in this case). Similar to the k-NN-set algorithm, Sky-set resorts to sorted and random accesses; the main difference with k-NN-set is that, after each sorted access, no document distance is computed, rather the newly accessed document D is compared for domination with documents in the current solution, possibly leading to drop some current results or D itself. The correctness of Sky-set follows from the very definition of domination among documents and the use of a threshold tuple $\underline{\theta}$. In fact, unseen documents will only contain elements whose distance values are higher than those included in $\underline{\theta}$: it follows that any document D which is not dominated by $\underline{\theta}$ cannot be dominated by any unseen document, thus it can be output as a Skyline result. We finally note that, although our definition of the result of a Skyline query only include undominated documents, Sky-set is able to iteratively return results in layers [2]: according to this definition, documents in a layer are not dominated by any document, except by documents in previous layers (for each document D in layer i and for all $j < i$, it exists at least a document D' in layer j that dominates D).

5   Customizing the Library

The WINDSURF library includes abstract and general classes able to represent any application following the retrieval model described in Section 2. As stated in the introduction, one of the basic features of the library is its generality and ability of being customized to cover a broad range of application scenarios. In this section we first detail how a user of the WINDSURF library can instantiate classes so as to implement her specific needs, then describe some possible customizations.

In order to correctly exploit the library, a user has to follow five basic steps:

1. Extending the `Document` and `Element` classes within the `Document` package. For this, the user has to specify the format of features that represents documents and document elements. In particular, the element distance δ is modelled by the `distance` method in the `Element` class, while the document distance d is (possibly) implemented by the `distance` method in the `Document` class.
2. Implementing classes in the `FeatureExtractor` package for analyzing documents, in order to break them into their component elements and extract their features.
3. Writing classes in the `FeatureManager` and `IndexManager` packages for storing/retrieving document/element features to/from the underlying DBMS and indices.
4. Building the DB and the indices containing documents and elements. This is performed by way of the `insert` method within the `FeatureManager` and `IndexManager` classes, that save features of a single `Document` within the DB/index, according to the insertion logic depicted in Figure 4 (a).
5. Querying the DB (possibly exploiting indices) by creating an instance of the `Query` class within the `QueryProcessor` package. Such object (which is built using a single `Document`) could be used in conjunction with any of the algorithms listed in Section 4, see Figure 4 (b).

Although the previously listed steps are the only ones required for the basic use of the library, advanced users may require additional, more sophisticated, customizations. Most commonly, these will affect classes in the following packages.

FeatureManager and IndexManager packages: The library already includes generic code for using the MySQL DBMS and the M-tree [6] index (a template-based C++ library itself), but other implementations of the generic abstract classes for features management are possible. It is worth noting that, as stated in Section 4, separate index structures should be provided for the management of documents *and* elements, and that such indices should support the sorted access interface: this is required by the k-NN-set and the Sky-set algorithms, but also allows the retrieval of documents/elements using k-NN or range queries [21].

QueryProcessor package: This package contains the implementations of algorithms described in Section 4, but also allows the specification of other aspects of document retrieval using either the k-NN or the Skyline model. Particularly important is the `QueryProcessor.SF` sub-package, containing the implementation of several alternatives for the computation of the document distance d via the use of *scoring functions*. The library already implements four of such functions, that will be detailed in the following.

Earth's Mover Distance (EMD): using the EMD scoring function [17], elements of the documents to be compared are matched in a many-to-many modality. The "amount" of matching of any element is limited to the "size" of such element (for example, in the case of image regions, this equals the fraction of image pixels included in the region at hand); the average of best-matched elements is used as the aggregation function, thus defining an optimization problem that corresponds to the well-known transportation problem, which can be solved in $O(n^3 \log n)$ time. It is easily proved that a document distance d defined in this way is a metric and can be bounded from below, thus it could be exploited by algorithms described in Section 4.

IRM: the IRM scoring function used by the SIMPLIcity RBIR system [20] is based on a greedy algorithm (with complexity $O(n^2 \log n)$) that obeys the same constraints and uses the same aggregation function (i.e., the average) as EMD. Consequently, the document distance computed by IRM is never lower than the one of EMD: this also implies that IRM can be also bounded from below (although with a looser bound wrt the one for EMD) but it does not satisfy the metric postulates.

$1 - 1$ **Assignment:** in this case, which is the one originally exploited by the WINDSURF RBIR system [1], each element of a document can be only matched to at most one element of the other document, and vice versa. Then a "biased" average is used to aggregate distance values of matched elements, so as to appropriately penalize documents that do not match all the query elements. This defines an assignment problem, which can be solved using the Hungarian Algorithm in $O(n^3)$ time [16]. Again, it is easy to see that this document distance can be bounded from below but is not a metric.

Greedy $1 - 1$: this last scoring function is computed by way of a greedy algorithm (whose complexity is $O(n^2)$) for the assignment problem. The corresponding document distance is thus never lower than the one computed using the previous function, is also bounded from below, but is not a metric.

In case the number of document elements, n, is high, above algorithms would be limited by their super-linear complexity. In such cases, it is likely that the user would specify alternative (approximate) algorithms, e.g., the pyramid match algorithm detailed in [10].

6   Use Cases

In this section, we demonstrate how the use of the WINDSURF library classes can be helpful in performing complex tasks over documents that comply with the WINDSURF model. The case study we consider here is that of a researcher investigating the impact of the different alternatives offered by the WINDSURF RBIR system (see Example 2). In particular, she is interested in the efficiency and the effectiveness of the query models available in the library as applied to the WINDSURF image features, which are detailed in [1]. Following the five steps enumerated in Section 5, the user has to first implement classes in the following packages (note that the library already includes such code):

Document package: features for each image region (element) include color/texture characteristics that are represented by way of a 36-dimensional vector; the region distance δ implements the Bhattacharyya metric distance [15], while the image distance d implements all the alternatives included in Section 5, see [3].

FeatureExtractor package: a Haar-Wavelet filter is applied to each image (document) and pixels of the filtered image are then clustered together using a K-means algorithm; so-obtained clusters correspond to image region, whose features are extracted from visual characteristics of included pixels.

FeatureManager and IndexManager packages: classes are included for storing/retrieving image/region features to/from the MySQL DBMS and the M-tree index.

We include here the results of some experiments performed on a real image dataset consisting of about 15,000 color images (corresponding to about 63,000 regions) extracted from the IMSI collection (http://www.imsisoft.com).

As a first demonstration of use of the library, we compare the effectiveness of the Bhattacharyya region distance with respect to a simpler Euclidean (L_2) distance for establishing the similarity between region features: this is easily done by simply redefining the δ distance within the Document package. Figure 5 shows that the use of the Bhattacharyya distance is justified by its far superior accuracy with respect to the Euclidean distance, in spite of its higher cost (almost doubling the time needed to compute the L_2 metric). Although we only present here results for k-NN queries, experiments for Skyline queries (not included here for the sake of brevity) confirm the trend exhibited by Figure 5. Again, we note that this result can be obtained by simply redefining the distance method of the Element class within the Document package.

As another proof of usability of the library, we compared the effectiveness of the document distances described in Section 5. To this end, the k-NN-set algorithm was repeatedly executed with the different d distances. We obtained the results shown in Figure 6. It can be seen that all image distances behave almost the same, with the remarkable exception of the Greedy $1 - 1$ alternative, whose accuracy is very low for the first retrieved results. This result, which has been obtained with no cost, since all alternatives are already available within the library, may suggest that a choice between the first three alternatives should be based on efficiency considerations only.

Finally, we show a result of the performance comparison for the three index-based algorithms described in Section 4: Figure 7 compares the efficiency of k-NN-set (using both the EMD and the $1 - 1$ document distance), k-NN-imgIdx (using EMD), and Sky-set according to 4 different performance metrics, as described in Section 4. It is worth noting that k-NN-imgIdx performs the worst among considered algorithms: this might sound strange at first, since only k sorted accesses to the document index are needed and no computation is done outside of the index itself, but this is not enough to compensate

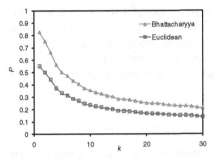

Fig. 5. Effectiveness of different element distance functions for the RBIR case: Precision (P) as a function of the number of retrieved documents (k)

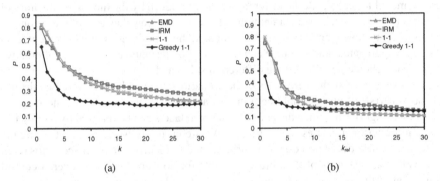

(a)   (b)

Fig. 6. Effectiveness of different document distance functions for the RBIR case: Precision (P) as a function of (a) retrieved documents (k) and (b) relevant retrieved documents (k_{rel})

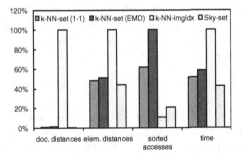

Fig. 7. Efficiency of the query processing index-based algorithms: k-NN-set using the EMD and the $1 - 1$ document distances, k-NN-imgIdx using EMD and Sky-set (graphs are normalized to the maximum values so as to emphasize relative performance)

for the very high number of document distances that are computed within the index.[3] Again, the library classes already contain the code for obtaining this important result, demonstrating that, when dealing with complex documents, a simplistic approach is not always the best one, and several alternatives should be taken into account to find out the best combination of efficiency and effectiveness.

7   Conclusions

We have presented the WINDSURF library for the management of complex (hierarchical) multimedia data, with the goal of providing tools for their efficient retrieval. The library was designed with the aim of generality and extensibility, so as to be applicable to a wide range of multimedia scenarios that fit its similarity-based retrieval model. Due to the inherent complexity of multimedia data, we designed the WINDSURF retrieval model to include all the different facets introduced by the hierarchical nature of the data (for example, how documents are characterized, how they are split into component elements, how elements are to be compared, how similarities at the element level are to be aggregated, and so on). Such facets can be instantiated in several alternative ways (each choice possibly giving different results) and an user may want to compare the performance of such alternatives in the scenario at her hand: we believe that the use of the WINDSURF library could help in abstracting away the details of generic query processing algorithms, since the above-mentioned facets can be realized by simply implementing abstract classes of the library. We are currently working in extending the library with new query processing algorithms and to incorporate other scenarios (e.g., videos [4]) as instances of the library available for downloading. Moreover, a current limitation of the WINDSURF retrieval model is that elements of a document are all of a same type: we plan to extend the model to consider elements of different types, so that only elements of the same type can be compared. For example, if we consider a multimedia document composed of textual sections and images, it makes sense to only compare text with text and images with images. Another important application of this concept is the use of cross-domain information to improve the retrieval of a given type of content, for example, exploiting surrounding text and/or links existing to other documents (à la PageRank) to boost image/video retrieval.

References

1. Ardizzoni, S., Bartolini, I., Patella, M.: Windsurf: Region-based image retrieval using wavelets. In: IWOSS 1999, Florence, Italy, pp. 167–173 (September 1999)
2. Bartolini, I., Ciaccia, P., Oria, V., Özsu, T.: Flexible integration of multimedia sub-queries with qualitative preferences. Multimedia Tools and Applications 33(3), 275–300 (2007)

---

[3] We note here that k-NN-set computes document distances outside of the index, only for those documents that are retrieved under sorted access. On the other hand, Sky-set does not compute *any* document distance, but has nonetheless to compare documents for domination: in Figure 7 each of such comparisons is computed as a document distance, in order to compare algorithms on a fair basis.

3. Bartolini, I., Ciaccia, P., Patella, M.: Query processing issues in region-based image databases. Knowledge and Information Systems 25(2), 389–420 (2010)
4. Bartolini, I., Patella, M., Romani, C.: SHIATSU: Semantic-Based Hierarchical Automatic Tagging of Videos by Segmentation using Cuts. In: AIEMPro 2010, Florence, Italy (September 2010)
5. Chávez, E., Navarro, G., Baeza-Yates, R., Marroquín, J.L.: Proximity searching in metric spaces. ACM Computing Surveys 33(3), 273–321 (2001)
6. Ciaccia, P., Patella, M., Zezula, P.: M-tree: An efficient access method for similarity search in metric spaces. In: VLDB 1997, Athens, Greece, pp. 426–435 (August 1997)
7. Fei-Fei, L., Fergus, R., Torralba, A.: Recognizing and learning object categories. In: CVPR 2007 Short Course, Minneapolis, MN (June 2007)
8. Fishburn, P.: Preference structures and their numerical representations. Theoretical Computer Science 217(2), 359–383 (1999)
9. Gaede, V., Günther, O.: Multidimensional access methods. ACM Computing Surveys 30(2), 170–231 (1998)
10. Grauman, K.: Efficiently searching for similar images. Communications of the ACM 53(6), 84–94 (2010)
11. Guttman, A.: R-trees: A dynamic index structure for spatial searching. In: SIGMOD 1984, Boston, MA, pp. 47–57 (June 1984)
12. Hjaltason, G.R., Samet, H.: Distance browsing in spatial databases. ACM TODS 24(2), 265–318 (1999)
13. Hjaltason, G.R., Samet, H.: Index-driven similarity search in metric spaces. ACM TODS 28(4), 517–580 (2003)
14. Ilyas, I.F., Beskales, G., Soliman, M.A.: A survey of top-k query processing techniques in relational database systems. ACM Computing Surveys 40(4) (October 2008)
15. Kailath, T.: The divergence and Bhattacharyya distance measures in signal selection. IEEE Transactions on Communication Technology 15(1), 52–60 (1967)
16. Kuhn, H.W.: The hungarian method for the assignment problem. Naval Research Logistic Quarterly 2, 83–97 (1955)
17. Rubner, Y., Tomasi, C.: Perceptual Metrics for Image Database Navigation. Kluwer, Boston (2000)
18. Salton, G.: Automatic Text Processing: The Transformation, Analysis, and Retrieval of Information by Computer. Addison-Wesley, Reading (1989)
19. Wu, L., Hoi, S.C.H., Jin, R., Zhu, J., Yu, N.: Distance metric learning from uncertain side information with application to automated photo tagging. In: ACM MM 2009, Vancouver, Canada, pp. 135–144 (October 2009)
20. Wang, J.Z., Li, J., Wiederhold, G.: SIMPLIcity: Semantics-sensitive Integrated Matching for Picture LIbraries. IEEE TPAMI 23(9), 947–963 (2001)
21. Zezula, P., Amato, G., Dohnal, V., Batko, M.: Similarity Search - The Metric Space Approach, Advances in Database Systems, vol. 32. Springer (2006)

A Method of Real-Time Non-uniform Speech Stretching

Adam Kupryjanow and Andrzej Czyzewski

Multimedia Systems Department, Gdansk University of Technology
Narutowicza 11/12, Gdansk, Poland
{adamq,andcz}@sound.eti.pg.gda.pl

Abstract. Developed method of real-time non-uniform speech stretching is presented. The proposed solution is based on the well-known SOLA algorithm (Synchronous Overlap and Add). Non-uniform time-scale modification is achieved by the adjustment of time scaling factor values in accordance with the signal content. Dependently on the speech unit (vowels/consonants), instantaneous rate of speech (ROS), and speech signal presence, values of the scaling factor are selected. This provides as low as possible difference in the duration of the input and output signal and high naturalness and quality of the modified speech. In the experimental part of the paper accuracy of the proposed ROS estimator is examined. Quality of the speech stretched using the proposed method is assessed in the subjective tests.

Keywords: Time-scale Modification, Voice Detection, Vowels Detection, Rate of Speech Estimation.

1   Introduction

Time-scale modification algorithms have been widely investigated by many researchers over last 25 years. Mainly this issue was considered in terms of maximizing the quality of synthesized speech [8], reduction of computational complexity or its adaptation for real-time signal processing [10]. In this work the main stress was put on design and evaluation of the algorithm which will be able to stretch the speech signal in a real-time, whilst preserving the general synchronization of the original and modified signal. Synchronization is obtained here by the reduction of redundant information in the input signal i.e. shortening of silence and vowels prolongation intervals, stretching vowels and consonants with a different stretching factors and adjusting stretching factor value according to the actual ROS (Rate of Speech).

The proposed algorithm, named Non-Uniform Real-Time Speech Modification algorithm (NU-RTSM), was designed to improve the perception of speech by people with the hearing resolution deficit. It was shown in Tallal's work that the reduction of the speech speed improves its intelligibility [12]. Authors of this paper had proposed the idea of the real-time speech stretching using mobile devices (e.g. Smartphone). Results of that work were described in the conference paper [3]. Some improvements of that algorithm are proposed, i.e. usage of non-uniform time-scaling, in this paper.

As it was shown by Demol [1], non-uniform time-scaling algorithm can improve the quality of processed signal. The assumption of his work was based on the idea that every unit of speech such as: vowels, consonants, plosives, phones transitions and

M.S. Obaidat, J.L. Sevillano, and J. Filipe (Eds.): ICETE 2011, CCIS 314, pp. 362–373, 2012.

silence should be time-scaled using different scaling factors. Differences between factors were implicated by the prosody rules. Realization of that algorithm is impossible in real-time conditions, because of the problem with the synchronization of the input and output signal (there is no mechanism for the reduction of redundant signal content). In this paper such a mechanism is proposed and examined.

Owing to the structure of the algorithm, it could be implemented on the mobile phone, but because of the legal limitations the processing of the incoming speech stream may be prohibited. Despite the limitations, the modification of the speech could be implemented on the telephone service provider severs or locally on the mobile device working in off-line mode.

2   Algorithm Description

In Fig. 1, a block diagram of the NU-RTSM algorithm is presented. The algorithm provides a combination of voice activity detection, vowels detection, rate of speech estimation and time-scale modification algorithms.

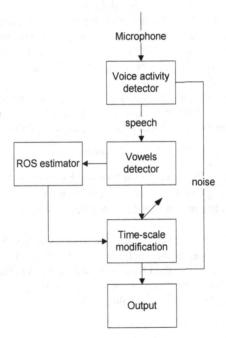

Fig. 1. NU-RTSM block diagram

Signal processing is performed in time frames in the following order:

1. Voice activity detector examines speech presence,

2. For noisy components frame synchronization procedure is performed; if the output signal is not synchronized with the input then noise sample frames are not sent to the output,

3. Speech sample frames are tested in order to find vowels,

4. Information about vowels locations is used by the ROS estimator to determine the speech rate,

5. Speech frames are stretched up with different stretching factors.

All algorithms presented in this section were designed and customized to work in a real-time. The input signal for all of them was captured by the headset microphone.

2.1   Voice Activity Detector

Voice activity detection is performed at the beginning of the analysis. The algorithm is designed as a typical VoIP voice detector. Detection of the voice is done in the time frames with a length of 46 ms. For every signal frame spectral energy, defined by Eq. 1, is determined and compared with the energy threshold Eth:

$$E = \frac{\sum_{k=1}^{K} A(k)^2}{K} \tag{1}$$

where E represents energy of the frame, $A(k)$ is the k-th spectral line of the input's signal magnitude spectrum and K is the total number of spectrum lines. Energy threshold is obtained at the beginning of the processing, by calculating the mean value of the energy determined for the first 20 frames of the signal. It is assumed that at the beginning of the analysis only noise is recorded by the microphone. Frame is marked as speech if its energy exceeds the Eth value.

Threshold value is adjusted to the current noise variations using the two-stage adaptation procedure. First stage is done every time when the frame was marked as noise. For that situation Eth is updated using the following formula (Eq. 2):

$$Enth = C((1 - p) \cdot Eth + p \cdot E) \tag{2}$$

where $Enth$ is the new value of energy threshold, Eth is the previous value of energy threshold, E is the energy of the current frame, C is correction factor, and p is the variable which determines how much the new value of the noise energy will influence the value of $Enth$.

The task of the second stage is to fit p value to the actual background noise energy fluctuations. If the variation of the vector that contains last 10 energies, used in the first stage of adaptation, is low, then the energy for the current frame should have low impact on Eth adaptation. Therefore, p value is set to 0.2. Otherwise, impact of the current energy should be high, so the p value is set to 0.1.

2.2   Vowels Detector

Vowels detection algorithm is based on the assumption that all vowels amplitude spectra are consistent. To quantify this similarity parameter called PVD (peak-valley difference) is used [14]. Initially PVD was introduced for the robust voice activity detection. It is defined by the following formula (Eq. 3):

$$PVD(VM, A) = \frac{\sum_{k=0}^{N-1}(A(k) \cdot VM(k))}{\sum_{k=0}^{N-1}VM(k)} - \frac{\sum_{k=0}^{N-1}(A(k) \cdot (1-VM(k)))}{\sum_{k=0}^{N-1}(1-VM(k))} \tag{3}$$

where $PVD(VM, A)$ is the value of peak-valley difference for one frame of the input signal, $A(k)$ is the value of the k-th spectral line of the input's signal magnitude spectrum and $VM(k)$ is the value of the k-th value in the vowel model vector.

VM is created in the training stage on the basis of the average magnitude spectra calculated for the pre-recorded vowels. The model consists of the binary values, where 1 is placed in the position of the peak in the average magnitude spectrum and 0 for all other positions. When the magnitude spectrum of the input signal is highly correlated with the vowels spectra, PVD value is high. Therefore, for the vowels PVD takes higher values than for consonants or silence parts.

Vowels detection is executed only for speech frames. Algorithm is based on time frames with the duration of 23 ms. Each signal frame is windowed using triangular window defined as:

$$\omega(n) = \begin{cases} \dfrac{2n}{L}, & 1 \le n \le \dfrac{L+1}{2} \\ \dfrac{2(L-n+1)}{L}, & \dfrac{L}{2}+1 \le n \le L \end{cases} \tag{4}$$

where L- is the size of the window and n - is the sample number. This type of window ensures a higher accuracy of vowels detection than other shapes.

Vowel detection requires the initialization step which is performed in parallel to the initialization of the voice activity detection algorithm. In this step the threshold for the PVD is calculated as the mean value of first 40 frames of the signal according to the formula (Eq. 5):

$$Pth = C \frac{\sum_{n=1}^{N} PVD(n)}{N} \tag{5}$$

where Pth- is initial value of the threshold, $PVD(n)$ -is the value of peak-valley difference for the n-th signal frame, N - is number of frames that were used for initial threshold calculation, C - is correction factor. The correction factor was selected experimentally and was set to 1.1.

For every signal frame PVD value is determined and smoothed by calculating the average of last three values. The signal frame is marked as a vowel when: the value of the smoothed PVD is higher than Pth threshold and it has a local maximum in the PVD curve or its value is higher than 75 % of the value of the last local maximum. If the value is lower than Pth then the decision of voice activity detector is corrected and frame is marked as silence. For other situations frame is assigned to the consonant class.

In the real-time analysis assumptions presented above are tested in the following manner:

1. if the PVD for the frame $n-1$ is greater than for frames n and $n-2$, where n is the number of the current analysis frame, and greater than Pth threshold, then frame $n-2$ is marked as vowel and information about peak detection in $n-1$ frame is saved,

2. if the condition 1 is not fulfilled, the second condition is checked, namely: if the information about peak presence is up to date and *PVD* value for the frame *n*-2 is greater than 75 % of that peak, then frame *n*-2 is marked as vowel,

3. if conditions 1 and 2 are not fulfilled and *PVD* value for the frame *n*-2 is lower than *Pth*, then decision obtained using voice detector is corrected and frame is marked as noise (information about peak presence is canceled),

4. otherwise frame *n*-2 is marked as consonant and information about peak presence is canceled.

An example of the vowels detection in real-time conditions is presented in Fig 2.

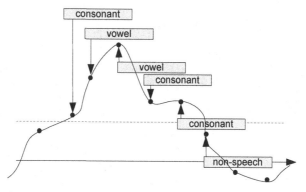

Fig. 2. Vowels detection in real-time. Grey boxes represent analysis frames, dotted line represents *Pth* value.

Despite the fact that a simple voice activity detection algorithm was used, false positive errors appearing during the classification, have no impact on the vowel detection algorithm. It is achieved owing to the third step of the vowel detection algorithm, where all misclassified noise frames are detected and removed from the analysis.

2.3   ROS Estimation

ROS is a useful parameter in many speech processing systems. For the most part it is used in the automatic speech recognition (ASR). In the ASR many speech parameters are highly related to ROS. Hence, ROS is used to adjust the HMM model for different speech rates [9].

In the literature several definitions of ROS can be found. All of them require speech signal segmentation. For example Narayanan defines ROS as a number of syllables per second (SPS). In other works ROS is defined inter alia as: phones per second (PPS) [6], vowels per second (VPS) [11], phones per second normalized to the probability of the specific phone duration [15], word duration normalized to the probability of its duration [16]. Some measures, like those proposed by the Zheng et al., required the ASR or the transcription of the utterances. Therefore, for real-time unknown input signal, ROS estimation could be done only by statistical analysis. In this work, as ROS definition, the VPS parameter is used, as the derivate of SPS measure. Therefore, ROS is defined as (Eq. 6):

$$ROS(n) = \frac{N_{vowels}}{\Delta t} \qquad (6)$$

For every signal frame ROS estimation is performed using the knowledge about the frame content, which is provided by vowels and voice activity detectors. Therefore, ROS value is updated for every 23 ms (length of the vowel detector analysis frame). Instantaneous ROS value is calculated as the mean number of vowels in the last 2 s of speech signal. Period of the time for the averaging was chosen experimentally in such a way that local ROS changes could be captured.

The highest ROS value that could be measured by this method equals 21 vowels/s, provided that all vowels and consonants durations are equal to 23 ms. It is worth mentioning that the instantaneous value of ROS is updated only when the current frame does not contain silence or prolongation of the vowel. At the beginning of the algorithm work, to eliminate the situation when the ROS values increase from zero to some value, initial ROS value is set to 5.16 vowels/s.

During the analysis instantaneous ROS value is used to assign, to the current utterance, one of speech rates categories, high or low. This division is obtained using the ROS threshold value (*ROSth*). *ROSth* was determined during the analysis of the mean ROS values of the speech rates recorded for 8 persons. Each person read five different phrases with three speech rates: high, medium and low. Results of the ROS statistics were presented in Tab. 1.

Table 1. Mean value and standard deviation of ROS calculated for the different speech rates

speech rate	low	medium	high
μ(ROS)[vowels/s]	4.80	5.17	5.52
σ(ROS)[vowels/s]	0.76	0.75	0.79

It can be seen that, because of the high value of the standard deviation (nearly 0.76 for all classes) and as a consequence of the low distance between the neighboring classes, only two classes could be separated linearly using the instantaneous ROS value. On the basis of the statistics, the ROS value was set to 5.16 vowels/s. The threshold was calculated according to the equation (7):

$$ROS_{th} = \frac{\mu(ROS)_{low} + \mu(ROS)_{high}}{2} \qquad (7)$$

where $\mu(ROS)_{low}$ is the mean value of ROS for the low rate speech and $\mu(ROS)_{high}$ is the mean value of ROS for the high rate speech.

In Sec. 3 the accuracy of speech rate class recognition as well as its applicability to the non-uniform speech stretching are investigated.

2.4   Time-Scale Modification Algorithm Selection

Many algorithms dedicated for speech time-scaling can be found in literature. All of them are based on the overlap-and-add technique. Most of the known algorithms were not optimized for real-time signal processing. Therefore, for real-time speech stretching only a few methods could be used. The best quality of time-scaled speech is achieved for complex methods that combine precise speech signal analysis such as speech periodicity judgment and adjustment of the analysis and synthesis frame sizes to the current part of the signal [8]. The algorithms, for instance PSOLA (Pitch Synchronous Overlap and Add) or WSOLA (Waveform Similarity Based Overlap and Add) produce high quality modified signals [2,13], but require changing analysis shift sizes (WSOLA) or synthesis (PSOLA) frame sizes according to the current speech content.

It was shown that those algorithms could be used for real-time signal processing [5, 13] but for the non-uniform time-scale modification variable sizes of analysis time shift or synthesis frame would add complexity to the detection algorithms (voice activity detection, vowels detection). For this reason, NU-RTSM algorithm is based on the SOLA algorithm (Synchronous Overlap-and-Add) which in the fundamental form uses constant values of the analysis/synthesis frame sizes and analysis/synthesis time shift [10] as well ensures quality of the processed speech nearly as good as for the other methods [4, 13].

2.5   SOLA Based Non-uniform Time-Scale Modification Algorithm

To achieve a high quality of the stretched speech, analysis/synthesis frame size and analysis time shift should be selected properly i.e. frame length L should cover at least one period of the lowest speech component and in the synthesis stage, for all used scaling factors $\alpha(t)$, overlap size should be at least $L/3$ length. For the designed algorithm L value was set to 46 ms and analysis time shift Sa to 11.5 ms.

The synthesis time shift Ss is dependent on the current value of the scaling factor $\alpha(t)$. The scaling factor is defined as:

$$\alpha(t) = \frac{Ss}{Sa} \tag{8}$$

Synchronization between two synthesized overlapped frames is obtained by calculating the highest similarity point which is determined by the maximum of the cross-correlation function calculated for the overlapped parts of successive frames.

To reduce the duration of the stretched speech and to improve the quality of the modified signal, the scaling factor is changed for different speech content. For both speech rates (low and high) vowels are stretched up with the designed scale factor value ($\alpha(t)=\alpha_d$, being the value that is specified for the processing), and noise is not modified ($\alpha(t)=1$) or removed from the signal dependently on the input/output synchronization state. For the low rate speech consonants are stretched up with the factor lower than α_d and equal to $\alpha(t)=0.8\cdot\alpha_d$, and for the high rate speech consonants are not stretched ($\alpha(t)=1$). As it was shown in the third Sec. of this paper, the quality of speech preserved with the proposed method is better than the quality achieved with typical uniform SOLA algorithm.

3   Experiments

The evaluation of the proposed algorithms was presented in this section. All algorithms were implemented in Matlab in such a way that the real-time signal processing was simulated. Sampling frequency of processed signals was set to 22.05 kHz.

3.1   Rate of Speech Estimation

The proposed method of real-time ROS estimation was tested in two experiments. In the first one 80 recordings of 8 persons (1 woman, 7 men) were used. Each person spoke five different phrases with 2 different speech rates: low, and high. Tab. 2 presents the accuracy of the speech rate detection. It can be seen that for the slow speech rate nearly 73 % of frames were recognized correctly and for the high rate speech 66 %. The main errors are connected to the fact that the rate of speech in the recording was not ideally constant.

In Fig. 3 waveforms corresponding to the recorded male high rate speech with the detected vowels and estimated speech rate are presented. It can be observed that the main error occurs at the beginning of the ROS extraction. It is connected to the fact that the ROS algorithm assumes that the most probable is low speech rate as a typical speech rate of every person (it is assumed in the ROS initialization phase). The second type of error can be seen after the prolongation of the vowel. It is connected to the fact that the current value of ROS is highly related to the historical data, so ROS estimation needs several new frames to enable following high variations of the instantaneous ROS.

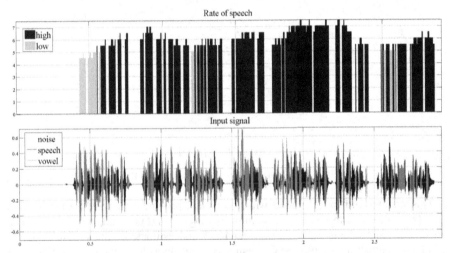

Fig. 3. Speech rate recognition for high rate male speech

In the second experiment 120 recordings were used. Those recordings were obtained by the extension of database used in the first experiment with the 40 utterances. Extra sentences were spoken with the medium rate (5 sentences per speaker, 8 speakers). The ROS estimation algorithm was tested in order to find the relation between the real value of the ROS and the estimated one. Real value of the ROS was calculated for every utterance based on the duration of the speech in the recording and the number of vowels in the sentence. Number of vowels was calculated from the transcription. One extra rule was added, namely neighboring vowels within one word were count as one vowel. This restriction allows counting only vowels related to the syllable nuclei. Therefore, strategy used during the calculation of the real ROS is consistent with the approach used in the vowel detection algorithm. In Fig. 4 relation between the real ROS and estimated one was presented. Value of the estimated ROS of the sentence was obtained as the average value of the instantaneous ROS values estimated for the sentence. It can be observed that there is high correlation between the real rates and estimated ones. Pearson's correlation coefficient calculated for those data sets was equal to 0.741.

Table 2. Percentage number of frames marked as low/high rate speech, calculated for female and male speech expressed with low and high rate

Speech rate	low rate speech recording	high rate speech recording
low	**72.67**	34,15
high	27.32	**65.84**

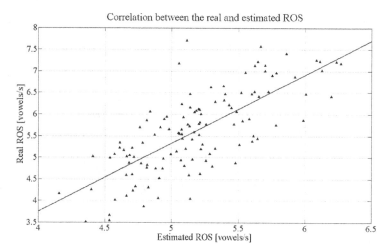

Fig. 4. Relation between real and estimated ROS

This result could be compared with the results presented by the Morgan [7] and Pfau [11] who have tested their algorithm for English and German, respectively. The correlation coefficients between the real ROS and estimated values were equal to 0.671 for English and 0.796 for German, but their algorithms were not operating in the real-time as the algorithm presented in this paper. Consequently, the results presented here, should be appropriate to be adopted in the proposed non-uniform speech stretched method.

3.2   Time-Scaled Speech Assessment

Quality of NU-RTSM algorithm was assessed in subjective tests performed for 19 healthy persons (2 women, 17 men). Each person had to assess the quality of the speech stretched using the typical SOLA algorithm implementation and the proposed NU-RTSM algorithm. Two values of the stretching factors were chosen: 1.9 and 2.1. Four recordings were used during the experiment: two spoken with the low rate, and two with the high rate. Both of them were spoken by a woman and a man. In all recordings the same phrase was uttered.

Three parameters were rated during tests: signal quality, speech naturalness and speech intelligibility. The assessment was made using the following scale: 1- very poor, 2- poor, 3-medium, 4-good, 5-very good. In Figs. 5-7 histograms of the speech stretching assessment are presented. It can be seen that for both speech rates, as well as for all parameter values, histograms that represent NU-RTSM assessment have higher placed gravity centers than for the SOLA algorithm. For the high rate speech this difference becomes more significant.

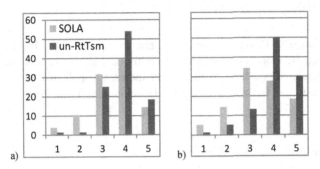

Fig. 5. Signal quality assessment for different speech rates: a) low, b) high

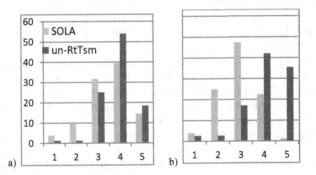

Fig. 6. Speech naturalness assessment for different speech rates: a) low, b) high

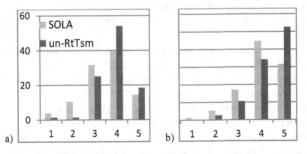

Fig. 7. Speech intelligibility assessment for different speech rates: a) low, b) high

4   Conclusions

The proposed Non-Uniform Speech Real-Time Speech Modification algorithm ensures high quality of the stretched speech. Subjective tests have shown that naturalness and intelligibility of the processed speech is higher than in case of a typical uniform signal stretching. In the future implementation of the algorithm real-time mode should be enabled on a mobile device. Moreover, speech perception tests for the people with hearing time-resolution problems should be made in order to verify modification usability.

Acknowledgements. Research funded within the project No. POIG.01.03.01-22-017/08, entitled "Elaboration of a series of multimodal interfaces and their implementation to educational, medical, security and industrial applications". The project is subsidized from the European Regional Development Fund by the Polish State bud-get".

References

1. Demol, M., Verhelst, W., Struye, K., Verhoeve, P.: Efficient Non-Uniform Time-Scaling of Speech with WSOLA. In: Speech and Computers, SPECOM (2005)
2. Grofit, S., Lavner, Y.: Time-Scale Modification of Audio Signals Using Enhanced WSOLA with Management of Transients. IEEE Trans. on Audio, Speech, and Language Processing 16(1) (2008)
3. Kupryjanow, A., Czyzewski, A.: Real-time speech-rate modification experiments. Audio Engineering Society Convention Paper, Preprint No. 8052, London (2010)
4. Kupryjanow, A., Czyzewski, A.: Time-scale modification of speech signals for supporting hearing impaired schoolchildren. In: Proc. of the International Conference NTAV/SPA, New Trends in Audio and Video, Signal Processing: Algorithms, Architectures, Arrangements and Applications, Poznan, pp. 159–162 (2009)
5. Le Beux, S., Doval, B., d'Alessandro, C.: Issues and solutions related to real-time TD-PSOLA implementation. Audio Engineering Society Convention Paper, Preprint No. 8085 (2010)
6. Mirghafori, N., Fosler, E., Morgan, N.: Towards Robustness to Fast Speech in ASR. In: Proc. ICASSP 1996, pp. I335–I338 (1996)
7. Morgan, N., Fosler-Lussier, E.: Combining multiple estimators of speaking rate. In: ICASSP, Seattle (1998)
8. Moulines, E., Laroche, J.: Non-parametric techniques for pitch-scale and time-scale modification of speech. Speech Communication 16(2), 175–205 (1995)
9. Narayanan, S., Wang, D.: Speech rate estimation via temporal correlation andselected sub-band correlation. In: ICASSP (2005)
10. Pesce, F.: Realtime-stretching of speech signals. In: DAFX, Italy (2000)
11. Pfau, T., Ruske, G.: Estimating the speaking rate by vowel detection. In: ICASSP 1998, Seattle (1998)
12. Tallal, P., et al.: Language Comprehension in Language-Learning Impaired Children Improved with acoustically modified speech. Science 271 (1996)

13. Verhelst, W., Roelands, M.: An overlap-add technique based on waveform similarity (WSOLA) for high quality time-scale modification of speech. In: IEEE International Conference on Acoustics, Speech, and Signal Processing, ICASSP 1993 (1993)
14. Yoo, I.C., Yook, D.: Robust Voice Activity Detection Using the Spectral Peaks of Vowel Sounds. ETRI Journal 31(4), s. 451–s. 453 (2009)
15. Zheng, J., Franco, H., Stolcke, A.: Rate of Speech Modeling for Large Vocabulary Conversational Speech Recognition (2000)
16. Zheng, J., Franco, H., Weng, F., Sankar, A., Bratt, H.: Word-level rate-of-speech modeling using rate-specificphones and pronunciations. In: Proc. IEEE Int. Conf. Acoust. Speech Signal Process., Istanbul, vol. 3, pp. 1775–1778 (2000)

Decoding of LDPC-Based 2D-Barcodes Using a 2D-Hidden-Markov-Model

Wolfgang Proß[1,2], Franz Quint[1], and Marius Otesteanu[2]

[1] Faculty of Electrical Engineering and Information Technology
University of Applied Sciences Karlsruhe, Moltkestr. 30, 76131 Karlsruhe, Germany
[2] Faculty of Electronics and Telecommunications, Politehnica University of Timişoara
Bd. Vasile Parvan 2, 300223 Timişoara, Romania
{wolfgang.pross, franz.quint}@hs-karlsruhe.de,
marius.otesteanu@etc.upt.ro

Abstract. This paper deals with the decoding of a new 2D-barcode that is based on Low-Density Parity-Check (LDPC) codes and Data Matrix Codes (DMC). To include typical damages that occur in industrial environment we chose a Markov-modulated Gaussian-channel (MMGC) model to represent everything in between the embossing and the camera-based acquisition of a LDPC-based DMC. For the decoding of LDPC codes with a MMGC the performance of Estimation-Decoding (ED), that adds a Hidden-Markov-Model (HMM) to the standard Belief-Propagate (BP)-decoder, is analyzed. We prove the advantage of ED in combination with a reestimation of the HMM's transition probabilities. With respect to our application a decoding algorithm called ED2D-algorithm is developed that includes ED, a 2-dimensional HMM (2D-HMM) and a reestimation of the 2D-HMM's transition probabilities. In a following evaluation the results of the ED-performance analysis are confirmed and a superior decoding behavior of our LDPC-based DMC decoded with the ED2D-decoder compared to the original Reed-Solomon-based version is shown.

Keywords: Data matrix code, LDPC code, Estimation-Decoding, 2D-Hidden-Markov-Model.

1 Introduction

In 1952 the first barcode system was patented by J. N. Woodland and B. Silver [17]. Today one dimensional barcodes are more and more replaced by their two dimensional (2D) successors. They offer a high information-density as well as an integrated error-correction capability in most cases. One of the most successful 2D-barcodes is the *Data Matrix Code* (DMC) which is internationally standardized in [9]. A DMC is formed by the three major components shown in Figure 1. The finder-pattern is comprised of the solid border and the broken border. The L-shaped solid border helps in locating the DMC whereas the alternating pattern of the broken border allows to determine the DMC's size. The data region contains the encoded information. Thereby a binary one is represented by a black squared module and a binary zero by a white squared module. This is only true if the DMC is printed black on a white surface. When used in industrial

M.S. Obaidat, J.L. Sevillano, and J. Filipe (Eds.): ICETE 2011, CCIS 314, pp. 374–387, 2012.

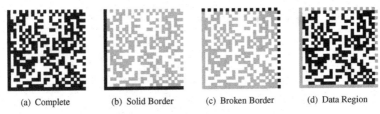

(a) Complete   (b) Solid Border   (c) Broken Border   (d) Data Region

Fig. 1. Three major parts of a DMC

environment the codes get stamped, milled and laser-etched on different kinds of material. Furthermore there are different kinds of interferences that may disturb the barcode. Thereby decoding is much more challenging.

2   LDPC-Based DMC

Considering the application in industrial environment, a 2D-barcode based on *Low-Density-Parity-Check* (LDPC) codes was developed. The outer appearance of our barcode is similar to that of the DMC since the finder-pattern that surrounds a DMC has been adopted.

PEG-LDPC Codes. The information is encoded in our barcode by use of a regular PEG-LDPC code unlike the standard DMC that is based on Reed-Solomon (RS) codes. The first introduction of LDPC codes has already been in 1962 by Gallager [5]. Since the rediscovery of LDPC codes by MacKay and Neal in 1995 [12], many further developments have been published, making LDPC codes a serious competitor to RS codes and the more recent Turbo codes for many fields of application. One important contribution was the introduction of the *Progressive-Edge-Growth* (PEG) construction of the LDPC codes underlying Parity-Check-Matrix [7] that made LDPC codes attractive for short block length applications as well. A single LDPC codeword is used to fill the data region of the DMC because it is well known that the decoding performance of LDPC codes increases with the codeword-length.

Symbol-Placement. The procedure of placing the LDPC codeword's symbols within the available grid of the DMC's data region is done with respect to typical interferences that may occur in industrial environment. The probability that damages caused by dirt, rust, scratches, unequal illumination etc. affect a contiguous part of the DMC is very high. Considering this, the symbol-nodes connected to the same check-node in the LDPC code's *Tanner graph* [15] are placed as far as possible from each other in the data region under the constraint of the limited area occupied by the code. This way each check-node is affected by the fewest possible number of disturbed symbol-nodes. The placement procedure is based on an optimization process and is explained in detail in [13]. As an example, Figure 2 depicts the symbol-placement of three symbol-nodes connected to the same check-node.

Image-Processing. For the localization of the DMC, the already known standard procedures are applied. In contrast to the RS code used by the original DMC, the LDPC decoder uses soft-decisions (SDs) as an input. For the computation of these SDs a

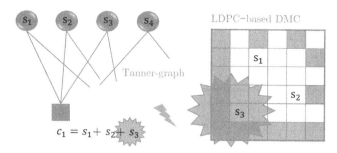

Fig. 2. Symbol placement

correlation coefficient r_{ij} is calculated for each module in row i and column j of the DMC as follows:

$$r_{ij} = \frac{\sum_{k=1}^{h} \sum_{l=1}^{v} (x_{kl}^{ij} - \bar{x}^{ij})(y_{kl} - \bar{y})}{\sqrt{\sum_{k=1}^{h} \sum_{l=1}^{v} (x_{kl}^{ij} - \bar{x}^{ij})^2 \sum_{k=1}^{h} \sum_{l=1}^{v} (y_{kl} - \bar{y})^2}} \tag{1}$$

k and l are the indices for the h horizontal and v vertical pixels in each module respectively. Considering one module in row i and column j of the DMC, x_{kl}^{ij} denotes one pixel in row k and column l of the module. y_{kl} stands for one pixel in the reference module. The reference module is generated based on an averaging of all modules that belong to the DMC's finder-pattern and represent a binary one. $\bar{y}$ and $\bar{x}^{ij}$ are the means of all the pixels referring to the reference module and the module in row i and column j of the DMC, respectively.

3   Design of the Decoder

The choice of an appropriate channel-model is essential for the decoding success of the new designed LDPC-based DMC. The channel-model has a high impact on:

1. The design of the employed LDPC code;
2. The computation of the SDs passed to the LDPC decoder;
3. The decoding procedure.

Therefore one has to study the DMC environment and carefully choose an appropriate channel-model to represent everything in between the embossing and the capturing of a DMC.

3.1   Channel-Model in Absence of Damages

In order to describe the distribution of the correlation-coefficients computed by equation (1), one has to find an appropriate channel-model. The correlation-coefficients are separated into two data-sets referring to one-modules and zero-modules respectively. Then one has to choose a Probability-Density-Function (PDF) for each of the two data-sets that together describe the channel.

The distribution is affected by the embossing-technique, the material, the camera-based system and of course strongly by the damages. However, we first consider the case without damages. Thus various pictures of DMCs milled on different types of material like aluminum, copper, steel, brass and different colored plastic have been analyzed. Thereby several cutting depths have been considered as well. Dependent on the material, the acquisition of the codes was done in a bright or a dark field. This can be seen in the two examples in Figure 3. In Figure 3(a) the DMC was milled on a plate of steel and the illumination setting caused the cavities to reflect the light directly into the camera's lens. Opposed to that the surface reflects the light into the camera in Figure 3(b) where the DMC was milled into a white plate of plastic.

The test of the null hypotheses that the one-samples and the zero-samples belong to a Gaussian distribution was done based on a 5% Shapiro-Wilk (SW) test as well as a 5% Anderson-Darling (AD) test. Only in a few cases the null hypotheses have not been rejected. Furthermore this was only true for the zero-modules. Because of that, another analysis was done by use of the Johnson distribution [10] [11] that provides a system of curves with the flexibility of covering a wide variety of shapes. Although the fitting to lots of different shaped samples works very good, the Gaussian approximation was chosen in the context of DMCs. The reason for that is explained using the example of Figure 3(b) and the corresponding histograms shown in Figure 4. Figure 4(a) shows the histogram of the zero-modules and the one-modules of the DMC under the situation of correct labeling of the modules. According to the employed SW-test and the AD-test the zero-modules belong to a Gaussian-distribution whereas the hypothesis for a Gaussian distribution of the one-modules has been rejected. Thus the histogram of the zero-modules on the left side in Figure 4(a) has been approximated by a Gaussian curve whereas the curve on the right side stems from a Johnson fitting to the histogram of the one-modules. It is well seen that the two histograms as well as their fitted curves overlap each other.

In contrast to the above, the codeword is not known when considering a common decoding-process of a DMC. For the purpose of estimating the PDF of the two types of modules we provisionally separate the modules into two classes by applying a threshold to the correlation coefficients. The only difference between Figure 4(b) and Figure 4(c) is that the fitting curve to the histogram of the one-modules in Figure 4(b) is obtained by a Johnson fitting whereas the approximation in Figure 4(c) has been done by using a Gaussian fitting. The zero-samples have been approximated by a Gaussian-PDF in both cases as the hypothesis-test has been successful. As seen in Figure 4(b), the approximation of the histogram with the Johnson PDF leads to an overfitting. This suggest a good confidence for correlation values just below the tentative threshold to belong to zero-modules. In reality, this is not the case since the histograms of the two classes heavily overlap. The suggested high confidence leads to large log-likelihood ratios (LLRs) which are used in the subsequent decoding algorithm. In this case the advantage of soft-decoding is lost. Furthermore, when calculating the LLRs based on a Gaussian approximation, the histogram-skewness that in many cases is responsible for the failure of the hypothesis test, does not have a critical effect.

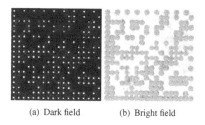

(a) Dark field   (b) Bright field

Fig. 3. DMC milled on a) steel b) white plastic

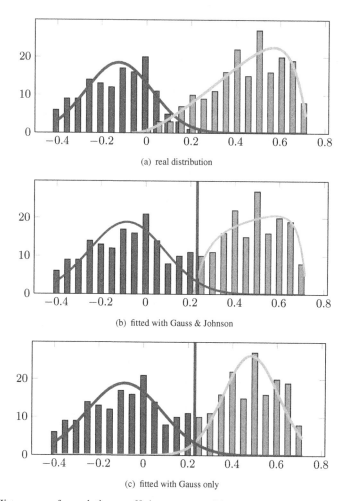

(a) real distribution

(b) fitted with Gauss & Johnson

(c) fitted with Gauss only

Fig. 4. Histograms of correlation-coefficients separated into one-modules and zero-modules

3.2   Channel-Model for Damaged DMCs

The situation changes a lot when taking possible damages into account. In industrial environment, these are typically blots, scratches, dirt and rust as well as effects caused

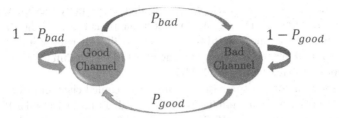

Fig. 5. Channel-model based on a two-state hidden-markov model

by unequal illumination or soiled camera-lenses. This leads to a change of the gray-value distributions. In most cases one can observe a stretching of the histograms that refer to ones and zeros respectively. Because of that a two-state Markov-channel is utilized that includes possible effects caused by damages. The resulting channel-model can be seen in Figure 5. The two states of the Hidden-Markov Model (HMM) represent the following two sub-channels:

Good Channel. This sub-channel is an Additive White Gaussian Noise (AWGN) channel as described in Section 3.1. This channel does not consider the above mentioned damages and thus is referred to as good channel.

Bad Channel. The second sub-channel is denoted as bad channel and takes damages into account. It turns out to be an AWGN channel as well, but with larger variances compared to the good channel.

Thus the whole model represents a channel with memory whose behavior is dependent on the current underlying channel state. Moreover it is a Markov-modulated Gaussian channel (MMGC) since it can be described as a memoryless AWGN channel parameterized by the noise variances. The probabilities for a transition from the good to the bad sub-channel and vice versa are denoted as P_{bad} and P_{good} respectively.

3.3 Estimation-Decoding

The random-like connection of symbol-nodes with check-nodes in a LDPC-code's Tanner graph can be interpreted as a build in interleaver. In traditional approaches channel interleavers are used to obtain a channel which is assumed to be memoryless. However, it has been shown [3] [6] [14] [16] that significant improvement is obtained by use of an Estimation-Decoding (ED) algorithm that takes the channel's memory into account.

The ED-algorithm is based on the so called Markov-LDPC factor graph which comprises two subgraphs, namely the LDPC code's Tanner-graph and a Markov chain. On the Markov-subgraph a state-estimation is computed by use of the Forward-Backward algorithm that is similar to the BCJR-algorithm [1]. This algorithm is bit-wise connected with the Belief-Propagation (BP) algorithm [5] on the LDPC-subgraph to form the ED-algorithm.

The computation of the state-estimations using the Forward-Backward algorithm is based on the four transition-probabilities depicted in Figure 5. The authors in [3] and [14] assumed the transition-probabilities to be known which is not always the case. To prevent from state-estimations based on mismatched transition-probabilities one can start with initial values for P_{bad} and P_{good} and then continually reestimate P_{bad} and P_{good} during the iterative ED-process. This reestimation is based on the Baum-Welch method [2] and was introduced in [6] for the Gilbert-Elliot channel. With respect to the channel-model for damaged DMCs we extended the ED-algorithm by the reestimation of the transition-probabilities for the MMGC.

Figure 6 shows a comparison based on different detailed channel-information provided to the decoder. A simulation has been done with a rate 0.61 regular PEG-LDPC code of length $n = 576$ and a MMGC with $P_{bad} = 0.3$ and $P_{good} = 0.6$. The standard-deviation σ_{bad} of the AWGNC representing the bad subchannel was $\sigma_{bad} = 5 * \sigma_{good}$ and thus greater than σ_{good} refering to the good subchannel. Instead of the BP-algorithm we used the Min-Sum (MS) approximation [8] to operate on the LDPC-subgraph. In order to evaluate the decoding performance we computed the Word-Error-Ratio (WER) dependent on the average E_b/N_0-values (ratio of energy per information-bit to the spectral noise density). A total of 100 decoding iterations have been performed for each of the four decoding variants in Figure 6. Furthermore a minimum of 100 word errors was ensured for each E_b/N_0-value. The simulation based on the *MS*-Decoder in Figure 6 excluded the Markov-chain and thus the state-estimation, which means that the decoder assumed the dataword to stem from an AWGNC. The curve labeled with *EDf* refers to an ED-Decoder that estimated the states (the appropriate subchannels that distorted the received bits) but based on false transition-probabilities $P_{bad}^f = 0.05$ and $P_{good}^f = 0.95$. Due to that mismatch between $P_{bad} = 0.3$ and $P_{good} = 0.6$, used for the MMGC in the simulation and the transition-probabilities used during the decoding-process, the decoding performance decreases compared to the *MS*-decoder. In our application we don't know the correct P_{bad} and P_{good} and thus the curve labeled with *EDc* is depicted just for comparison-purposes. In this simulation the ED-decoder operated based on the correct transition-probabilities. When applying our extended ED-algorithm including the reestimation of P_{bad} and P_{good} (labeled with *EDEPf*), the decoding performance is nearly as good as when knowing the correct transition-probabilities. This is due to the fact that the reestimated transition-probabilities converged after only a few decoding-iterations very close to the correct values, especially for higher E_b/N_0-values. This can be seen in Figure 7.

3.4   ED2D-Algorithm

So far ED of LDPC codes has only been applied to time dependent and thus one-dimensional systems. Considering the application of Estimation-Decoding on DMCs the one-dimensional timescale turns into a geometry of two dimensions. This leads to a replacement of one Markov-chain by several Markov-chains. In our Estimation-Decoding in two dimensions (ED2D), we assign a sub-Markov-chain to each row and each column of the DMC's data region as depicted in the example in Figure 8. This way the state-estimation referring to a single module is based on a horizontal Markov-chain and a vertical Markov-chain. The complete 2D-Markov-LDPC factor graph that the ED2D-algorithm is based on is depicted in Figure 9 and the messages of one sector are shown in Figure 10. For clarity purposes only the messages for the horizontal Markov-chain are depicted. r and c are the indices for the rows and columns of the 2D-Markov-subgraph. The check-nodes c and the symbol-nodes x are part of the

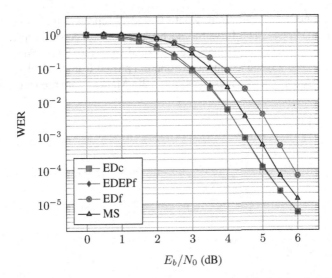

Fig. 6. Comparison of 4 decoder variants based on different detailed channel information provided to the decoder

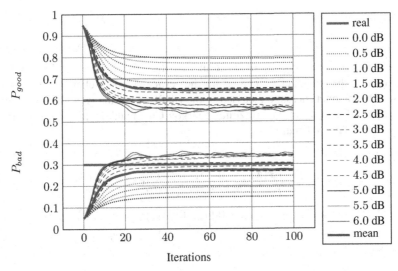

Fig. 7. Reestimation of P_{good} and P_{bad} during the EDEPf decoding procedure for several E_b/N_0 (dB) values

LDPC-subgraph whereas the state-nodes s and the channel-nodes (black squares) belong to the Markov-subgraph. The soft-decisions (SDs), that the ED2D-algorithm receives from our image-processing part (Section 2) are denoted by y. The noise added to the binary value of a DMC-module in row r and column c is assumed to stem either from the good sub-channel or the bad sub-channel of the MMGC which is dependent on the state that the state-node $s_{r,c}$ is estimated to be in. $\mathcal{S} = \{G, B\}$ is the set of states a state-node $s_{r,c}$ can be in, where G and B represent the good and the bad sub-channel respectively. The forward and backward messages are represented by α and β respectively. The channel-message ζ is send from the 2D-Markov-subgraph to the LDPC-subgraph. χ is the extrinsic information passed from the LPDC-subgraph to the 2D-Markov-subgraph. The messages of the 2D-Markov-subgraph are computed as follows.

Forward-message α:

$$
\begin{aligned}
\alpha^h_{r,c+1}(s_{r,c+1}) = &\sum_{s_{r,c} \in S} Pr(s_{r,c+1} \mid s_{r,c})\alpha^h_{r,c}(s_{r,c}) \\
&\cdot \sum_{x_{r,c} \in \{0,1\}} Pr(x_{r,c} \mid \chi_{r,c})Pr(y_{r,c} \mid x_{r,c}, s_{r,c})
\end{aligned}
\tag{2}
$$

Backward-message β:

$$
\begin{aligned}
\beta^h_{r,c}(s_{r,c}) = &\sum_{s_{r,c+1} \in S} Pr(s_{r,c+1} \mid s_{r,c})\beta^h_{r,c+1}(s_{r,c+1}) \\
&\cdot \sum_{x_{r,c} \in \{0,1\}} Pr(x_{r,c} \mid \chi_{r,c})Pr(y_{r,c} \mid x_{r,c}, s_{r,c})
\end{aligned}
\tag{3}
$$

where $Pr(s_{r,c+1} \mid s_{r,c})$ is one of the four transition probabilities of Figure 5. The computation of the messages α^v and β^v for the vertical Markov-chains of Figure 8 are likewise. The channel-message ζ passed to the LDPC-subgraph is computed based on the messages α^h and β^h of the horizontal Markov-Chain and the messages α^v and β^v of the vertical Markov-Chain:

$$
\begin{aligned}
\zeta_{r,c} = &\log \frac{Pr(x_{r,c} = 0 \mid \alpha^h_{r,c}(s_{r,c})\beta^h_{r,c+1}(s_{r,c+1}))}{Pr(x_{r,c} = 1 \mid \alpha^h_{r,c}(s_{r,c})\beta^h_{r,c+1}(s_{r,c+1}))} \\
&+ \log \frac{Pr(x_{r,c} = 0 \mid \alpha^v_{r,c}(s_{r,c})\beta^v_{r+1,c}(s_{r+1,c}))}{Pr(x_{r,c} = 1 \mid \alpha^v_{r,c}(s_{r,c})\beta^v_{r+1,c}(s_{r+1,c}))}
\end{aligned}
\tag{4}
$$

with

$$
\begin{aligned}
Pr(x_{r,c} = 0 \mid &\alpha^h_{r,c}(s_{r,c}), \beta^h_{r,c+1}(s_{r,c+1})) = \\
&\sum_{s_{r,c} \in S} \sum_{s_{r,c+1} \in S} Pr(y_{r,c} \mid x_{r,c} = 0, s_{r,c}) \\
&\cdot Pr(s_{r,c+1} \mid s_{r,c})\alpha^h_{r,c}(s_{r,c})\beta^h_{r,c+1}(s_{r,c+1})
\end{aligned}
\tag{5}
$$

h and v refer to horizontal and vertical rows respectively. Concerning the application of the ED2D-algorithm in the context of DMCs, the DMC's finder-pattern offers another advantage next to the original purpose. Since the values of the finder-pattern are

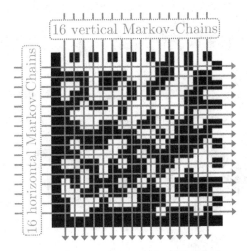

Fig. 8. 2D-Hidden-Markov-Model

always known, the corresponding messages χ do not change during the iterative ED2D-decoding so that

$$Pr(x_{r,c} \mid \chi_{r,c}) = \begin{cases} 0 & , x_{r,c} = 0 \\ 1 & , x_{r,c} = 1 \end{cases} \qquad \forall x_{r,c} \in \mathcal{F}_1 \tag{6a}$$

and

$$Pr(x_{r,c} \mid \chi_{r,c}) = \begin{cases} 1 & , x_{r,c} = 0 \\ 0 & , x_{r,c} = 1 \end{cases} \qquad \forall x_{r,c} \in \mathcal{F}_0 \tag{6b}$$

with $\mathcal{F}_1 =\{$one-modules of the finder-pattern$\}$ and $\mathcal{F}_0 =\{$zero-modules of the finder-pattern$\}$. The channel-message ζ and the extrinsic message χ represent the interface from the 2D-Markov-subgraph to the LDPC codes Tanner-graph on which the messages are computed based on a common BP-algorithm [5] or an approximation of it like the MS-algorithm [8].

4   Implementation and Evaluation

The ED2D-algorithm has been tested based on a DMC of size 26×26. The data has been encoded with a rate 0.61 regular PEG-LDPC code of length $n = 576$. The finder-pattern that surrounds the 24×24 sized data region and the code rate referring to the DMC size have been chosen conforming to standard [9]. The 576 bits of the LDPC codeword have been placed in the data region using the optimization technique described in section 2.

For comparison purposes the new designed LDPC-based DMC and the original RS-based version have been milled one next to the other on three different kinds of material. For both versions, the information to be encoded, the DMC-size and the code rate have been chosen identically. In addition, the conditions of the following acquisition and image processing were exactly the same for all DMC-pairs. To include possible damages,

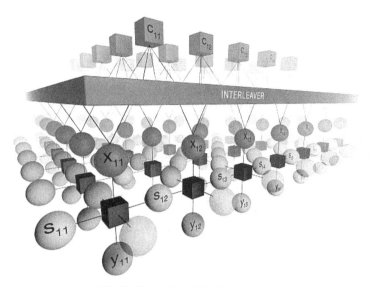

Fig. 9. 2D-Markov-LDPC factor graph

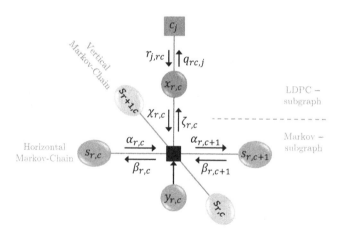

Fig. 10. Local messages in the 2D-Markov-LDPC factor graph

a simulation of water drops and oil drops was integrated. The simulation ensured that both versions of the DMC were interfered with identical damages. For this test plates of brass, aluminum and gray plastic have been used. For the evaluation we established an automated process and interfered each DMC-pair with 10000 randomly generated oil drop simulations and 10000 water drop simulations. Table 1 shows some examples of the damage-simulation. The disturbed LDPC-based DMCs have then been decoded with the Min-Sum (MS)-algorithm and our ED2D-algorithm. In [8] the authors proved that the performance of the MS-decoder is very close to the conventional BP-decoder if used with a correction factor. The correction factor is determined as described in [4]. The constant c was thereby set to $c = 0.39$. For the decoding of the original DMC we

Table 1. Examples for DMC-pairs milled on the same plate and interfered with identical blob simulations

| Material | Water drops | | Oil drops | |
	LDPC	RS	LDPC	RS
Brass				
Aluminum				
Plastic				

Table 2. Comparison results of the LDPC-based DMC decoded with the MS-decoder as well as our ED2D-algorithm and the standard RS-based DMC. The rightmost column represents the gain of the LDPC-based DMC decoded with our ED2D-algorithm compared to the RS-based DMC.

| | | | MS | | ED2D | | RS | | Gain |
Material	Interference	Decodings	Successes	%	Successes	%	Successes	%	%
Brass	Water	3556	2957	83	3448	97	3301	93	4
Alu	Water	6107	5118	84	6036	99	5719	94	5
	Oil	6864	3382	49	4793	70	4281	62	7
	Total	12971	8500	66	10829	83	10000	77	6
Plastic	Water	7830	6349	81	7658	98	7144	91	7
	Oil	9715	2724	28	6548	67	3306	34	33
	Total	17545	9073	52	14206	81	10450	60	21
Total	Water	17493	14424	82	17142	98	16164	92	6
	Oil	16579	6106	37	11341	68	7587	46	23
	Total	34072	20530	60	28483	84	23751	70	14

used the RS-decoder as described in the standard [9]. The results of the comparison can be seen in Table 2. The number of decodings in the column *Decodings* differs from 10000 since all cases, in which the first hard decision of both DMC-versions resulted in zero bit errors, were not considered. For brass the oil drop disturbances are not mentioned since they did not affect the DMCs (captured in a dark field) too much so that all versions could be successfully decoded. Opposed to that the oil drop simulations made it difficult for the following decoders in the case of DMCs milled in gray plastic and captured in a bright field.

The decoding of LDPC-based DMCs using the MS-decoder succeeded in 60% of the cases and thus does not yield in an improvement compared to the RS-based DMCs where 70% could be decoded successfullly. The situation completely changes when considering the ED2D-algorithm that we propose for the decoding of LDPC-based DMCs. In this case a total of 84% succeeded in decoding which is an improvement of 14% compared to the standard version.

5   Conclusions

For the decoding of LDPC-based DMCs an algorithm called ED2D-algorithm was established. This decoding-algorithm is an extension of the one-dimensional ED-algorithm. ED2D-decoding is based on a two-dimensional Hidden-Markov-Model (2D-HMM) that has been constructed in order to include possible damages into the underlying channel-model. In addition a reestimation of the 2D-HMM's transition probabilities is integrated in the iterative ED2D-decoding procedure. Two types of damages that are typical in industrial environment were simulated. Based on the damage-simulation an automated evaluation showed a superior decoding behavior of our LDPC-based DMCs decoded with the ED2D-algorithm compared to the standard RS-based DMC.

Acknowledgements. This work is part of the project MERSES and has been supported by the European Union through its European regional development fund (ERDF) and by the German state Baden-Württemberg.

References

1. Bahl, L.R., Cocke, J., Jelinek, F., Raviv, J.: Optimal decoding of linear codes for minimizing symbol error rate. IEEE Trans. Inform. Theory 20(2), 284–287 (1974)
2. Baum, L.E., Petrie, T., Soules, G., Weiss, N.: A maximization technique occurring in the statistical analysis of probabilistic functions of markov chains. The Annals of Mathematical Statistics 41(1), 164–171 (1970)
3. Eckford, A.W.: Low-density parity-check codes for Gilbert-Elliott and Markov-modulated channels. Ph.D. thesis, University of Toronto (2004)
4. Eleftheriou, E., Mittelholzer, T., Dholakia, A.: Reduced-complexity decoding algorithm for low-density parity-check codes. Electronics Letters 37(2), 102–104 (2001)
5. Gallager, R.G.: Low density parity check codes. IRE Trans. on Information Theory 1, 21–28 (1962)
6. Garcia-Frias, J.: Decoding of low-density parity-check codes over finite-state binary markov channels. IEEE Transactions on Communications 52(11), 1841 (2004)

7. Hu, X.Y., Eleftheriou, E., Arnold, D.M.: Regular and irregular progressive edge-growth tanner graphs. IEEE Transactions on Information Theory 51(1), 386–398 (2005)
8. Hu, X.Y., Eleftheriou, E., Arnold, D.M., Dholakia, A. (eds.): Efficient implementations of the sum-product algorithm for decoding LDPC codes, vol. 2 (2002)
9. ISO/IEC: Information technology — international symbology specification — data matrix (2000)
10. Johnson, N.L.: Systems of frequency curves generated by methods of translation. Biometrika 36(1-2), 149 (1949)
11. Johnson, N.L., Kotz, S., Balakrishnan, N.: Continuous univariate distributions. A Wiley-Interscience Publication, 2nd edn. Wiley, New York (1994)
12. MacKay, D., Neal, R.: Good codes based on very sparse matrices. In: Cryptography and Coding, pp. 100–111 (1995)
13. Proß, W., Quint, F., Otesteanu, M.: Using peg-ldpc codes for object identification. In: 2010 9th Electronics and Telecommunications (ISETC), pp. 361–364 (2010)
14. Ratzer, E.A. (ed.): Low-density parity-check codes on Markov channels. In: Proceedings of 2nd IMA Conference on Mathematics and Communications, Lancaster, UK (2002)
15. Tanner, R.M.: A recursive approach to low complexity codes. IEEE Transactions on Information Theory 27, 533–547 (1981)
16. Wadayama, T. (ed.): An iterative decoding algorithm of low density parity check codes for hidden Markov noise channels. In: Proceedings of International Symposium on Information Theory and Its Applications, Honolulu, Hawaii, USA (2000)
17. Woodland, J.N., Silver, B.: Classifying apparatus and method (1949)

A Comparative Evaluation of Gaussian Multiscale Aggregation for Hand Biometrics

Alberto de-Santos-Sierra, Carmen Sánchez-Ávila,
Javier Guerra-Casanova, and Gonzalo Bailador-del-Pozo

Group of Biometrics, Biosignals and Security, Centro de Domótica Integral
Technical University of Madrid, Madrid, Spain
{alberto,csa,jguerra,gbailador}@cedint.upm.es

Abstract. The process of segmentation consists of dividing the image in regions with similar characteristics. In other words, segmentation is the partitioning of digital images into several regions, according to a given criteria [6]. In addition, applying biometrics to daily scenarios involves difficult and challenging requirements in terms of software and hardware. On the contrary, current biometric techniques are also being adapted to present-day devices, like mobile phones, laptops and the like, which are considered to be unconstrained and contact-less. In fact, achieving a combination of both necessities is one of the most difficult problems at present in biometrics. Segmentation in these kind of environments require special effort and attention, since although there exist an obvious difficulty in providing accurate segmentation to these scenarios, the constraints in terms of software and hardware are important and affect the segmentation performance. Therefore, this paper presents a segmentation algorithm able to provide suitable solutions in terms of precision for hand biometric recognition, considering a wide range of backgrounds like carpets, glass, grass, mud, pavement, plastic, tiles or wood. Results highlight that segmentation accuracy is carried out with high rates of precision (F-measure$\geq 88\%$), presenting competitive time results when compared to state-of-the-art segmentation algorithms time performance. Finally, the accuracy of the proposed method is compared to the performance of Normalized Cuts in terms of segmentation accuracy and time performance.

1 Introduction

Biometrics based on hand recognition have received an increasing attention in latter years due to their huge applicability in daily scenarios and the relation between user acceptance and identification/verification rates [8,9].

In addition, hand biometrics system requirements are easily met with a standard camera and hardware processor, so that these systems can be easily adapted to devices like PC, mobile phones and the like.

This paper presents a segmentation method for isolating hand from background in real environments oriented to mobile devices. However, biometrics systems in general strongly rely on the environment conditions such as illumination, background, proximity to sensor and so forth, and therefore, applying biometrics to mobile devices requires to solve more demanding problems in terms of segmentation and invariance to changes in feature extraction with less resources.

M.S. Obaidat, J.L. Sevillano, and J. Filipe (Eds.): ICETE 2011, CCIS 314, pp. 388–399, 2012.

The proposed method is based on Gaussian Multiscale Aggregation (GMA) [11], gathering those pixels with similar characteristics under a same cluster, providing a hierarchichal structure along scales to find a proper segmentation where segments correspond to objects within image.

Segmentation involves a database to properly evaluate to what extent the method can isolate objects within an image. In order to assess the proposed method with real scenarios, a synthetic database has been collected with a total of 408000 images, containing samples with different backgrounds like soil, skins/fur, carpets, walls, grass and the like, corresponding to those possible scenarios where hand images can be taken.

The layout of this paper remains as follows: First of all, a literature review is presented under Section 2. The proposed approach is described in Section 3, together with the database used to test and evaluate the algorithm (Section 4) and the evaluation criteria (Section 5). Finally, results in Section 6 and conclusions in Section 7 will end this paper.

2   Literature Review

Segmentation problem has been cope with from different mathematical approaches with a wide number of different applications [7,18].

Concretely, one approach which has experienced a great development in recent years is based on multiscale aggregation [15]. This procedure is based on processing the image according to a set of mathematical operations, so that pixels with similar properties are gathered in a same segment. The main characteristic of this approach relies on repeating this procedure through subsequent scales, in which the number of pixels is reduced for each scale, due to former aggregation [15]. Moreover, recent results obtained by these algorithms have shown improvements when compared to other methods [1], like the Normalized Cuts [17] and Mean-Shift method [3].

Multiscale aggregation methods gather a wide range of algorithms involving different mathematical operations applied to pixels in image.

In fact, several approaches have been proposed based on Segmentation by Weighted Aggregation (SWA [15]), providing accurate results by means of similarities between intensities of neighboring pixels [13], measurements of texture differences and boundary integrity [14], more complicated operations, such as Gradient Orientations Histograms (GOH [12]), or more straightforward grouping methods based on the intensity contrast between two segments boundary and each segment inner [4].

3   Gaussian Multiscale Aggregation

Let define an image I as a graph $\mathcal{G} = (\mathcal{V}, \mathcal{E}, \mathcal{W})$ were $\mathcal{V}$ represents nodes in graph corresponding to pixels in image, $\mathcal{E}$ stands for the edges connecting pairs of previous nodes $\mathcal{V}$ and $\mathcal{W}$ the weight of previous edges, measuring the similarity between two nodes (pixels) in $\mathcal{V}$.

The idea is to divide graph $\mathcal{G}$ into two subgraphs $\mathcal{G} = \mathcal{G}_h \cup \mathcal{G}_b$, so that subgraph $\mathcal{G}_h$ contains pixels corresponding to hand and the subgraph $\mathcal{G}_b$ gathers pixels corresponding to background. In addition, nodes in V contains two parameters: intensity (represented by μ) and deviation (represented by σ). This intensity corresponds in the first scale to the intensity in terms of grayscale images [5], and to average intensities in subsequent scales. However, despite of existing deviation intensity value in subsequent scales, this parameter lacks of sense within first scale. The deviation in first scale will be set based on their neighbourhood of each pixel, which is a 4-neighbourhood structure for the first scale. These two parameters are gathered into a single function $\phi_{v_i}^{[s]}(\mu_{v_i}^{[s]}, \sigma_{v_i}^{[s]})$ representing the degree of being similar to node v_i, where s represents the scale. For simplicity sake, $\phi_{v_i}^{[s]}(\mu_{v_i}^{[s]}, \sigma_{v_i}^{[s]}) = \phi_{v_i}^{[s]}$, to avoid and excessive complicated notation.

Thus, similarity functions leads to the concept of likelihood between nodes in connecting edges, providing a definition of weights within graph $\mathcal{G}$.

Given a graph $\mathcal{G} = (\mathcal{V}, \mathcal{E})$, the similarity among pair of nodes is provided by means of weights $\mathcal{W}$, which are defined for each scale s as:

$$\mathcal{W}_{i,j}^{[s]} = \int_\alpha \sqrt{\phi_{v_i}^{[s]} \phi_{v_j}^{[s]}} d\alpha \tag{1}$$

where $v_i, v_j \in \mathcal{V}, \forall i, j$ and $\phi_{v_i}^{[s]}, \phi_{v_j}^{[s]}$ represent the similarity function for nodes v_i and v_j, respectively. In addition, α stands for the selected colour space, which in this paper corresponds to the a layer of the CIELAB (CIE 1976 L*,a*,b*) colour space, due to its ability to describe all visible colors by the human eye [6].

Figure 1 represents two functions $\phi^{[s]}$ associated to a pair of nodes v_i and v_j, showing the weight associated to their similarity (striped region). The higher the similarity between both nodes, the bigger the striped region.

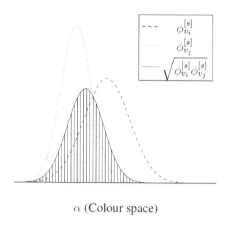

α (Colour space)

Fig. 1. Visual representation of two functions $\phi^{[s]}$ and the weighted $\mathcal{W}_{i,j}^{[s]}$ associated (striped region)

Therefore, graph $\mathcal{G} = (\mathcal{V}, \mathcal{E}, \mathcal{W})$ contains not only structural information on a given scale s but also relational details about the similarity of each node neighbourhood.

Furthermore, $\mathcal{W}_{i,j}$ can be regarded as the weight associated to edge $e_{i,j}$, so that $\mathcal{W}_{i,j} = \mathcal{W}(e_{i,j})$. Notice that weights are not defined for each pair of nodes in $\mathcal{V}$, but only for those pairs of nodes with correspondence in edge set $\mathcal{E}$.

Some properties can be extracted from the definition of $W_{i,j} \in W$ as the similarity between two nodes v_i and v_j, then $W_{i,j}$ satisfies $\forall i, j$:

1. $W_{i,j} \geq 0$
2. $W_{i,j} = W_{j,i}$
3. $W_{i,j} = 1 \leftrightarrow \phi_i = \phi_j$

Property (1) results from the definition given by Equation 1, since the integration of two non-negative functions provides a non-negative result. Similarly, property (2) is derived from the commutative product of a function product. Property (3) indicates that maximum value of weight is obtained if and only if nodes v_i and v_j have the same similarity distribution.

These former properties stand for each scale s, although for the sake of simplicity this index was not included on previous notation.

Furthermore, each node $v_i \in V$ contains also information on the location within the image in terms of positions, which will be useful in posterior scale aggregation steps.

On the other hand, the essence of this algorithm relies on aggregation, which consists of grouping and clustering those similar nodes/segments in subgraphs, according to some criteria along scales.

The proposed method bases the aggregation procedure on the weights in W, given the fact that, those pairs of nodes/subgraphs with higher weights are more similar than those with lower weights, and therefore, those former pairs deserve to be aggregated under a same segment/subgraph. Thus, a function must be defined to provide some order in set W, so that posterior subgraphs in subsequent scales contain nodes with high weights and, therefore, high similarity.

Let Ω be an ordering function, which orders edges in $\mathcal{E}$ according to W, as follows:

$$\Omega : \mathcal{E} \mapsto \mathbb{R} \tag{2}$$
$$e \mapsto \Omega(e)$$

so that if $W_{i,j} = W(e_{i,j}) \geq W_{i,k} = W(e_{i,k})$, then $\Omega(e_{i,j}) \geq \Omega(e_{i,k})$.

In other words, let $e = \{e_1, \ldots, e_m\}$ be a set of edges. If Ω is applied to previous set e, then it is satisfied that $\Omega(e)_i \geq \Omega(e)_j$, with $i \leq j$, $\forall i, j$, being $\Omega(e)_i$ the ith element in the ordered set $\Omega(e)$. Concretely, Ω_W represent the weight set W after Ω is applied.

Once the concept of ordering function is introduced, the algorithm aggregates pair of nodes based on this former weight ordering, ensuring that the dispersion of each segment remains bounded. This aggregation criteria is represented by the Equation 3:

$$\delta_{i,j} = \begin{cases} 1, & \sigma_{i,j} \leq \sqrt{\sigma_i \sigma_j} \\ 0, & \text{otherwise} \end{cases} \tag{3}$$

where $\sigma_{i,j}$ represent the dispersion of aggregating nodes v_i and v_j. Despite of selecting the geometric mean as the comparison criteria in previous equation, other methods are possible such as arithmetic mean, generalized mean or harmonic mean. The selection of geometric mean was carried out based on experimental results.

Once pairs of nodes have been ordered and an aggregation criteria have been stated, the Gaussian Multiscale Algorithm aggregates pair of nodes with previous criteria

(Equation 4), considering the fact that $\mathcal{G}_{v_i}^{[s]}$ represents the n-th graph in scale s, so that $v_i \in \mathcal{G}_n^{[s]}$.

$$\left(\mathcal{G}_{v_i}^{[s]}, \mathcal{G}_{v_j}^{[s]}\right) =$$

$$\begin{cases} \left(\mathcal{G}_p^{[s]}\delta_{\sigma_{i,j}} + \mathcal{G}_{p+1}^{[s]}\bar{\delta}_{\sigma_{i,j}}, \mathcal{G}_p^{[s]}\right) & \not\exists n/v_i \in \mathcal{G}_n^{[s]}, \not\exists m/v_j \in \mathcal{G}_m^{[s]} \\ \left(\mathcal{G}_n^{[s]}, \mathcal{G}_n^{[s]}\delta_{\sigma_{i,j}} + \mathcal{G}_p^{[s]}\bar{\delta}_{\sigma_{i,j}}\right) & v_i \in \mathcal{G}_n^{[s]}, \not\exists m/v_j \in \mathcal{G}_m^{[s]} \\ \left(\mathcal{G}_m^{[s]}\delta_{\sigma_{i,j}} + \mathcal{G}_p^{[s]}\bar{\delta}_{\sigma_{i,j}}, \mathcal{G}_m^{[s]}\right) & v_j \in \mathcal{G}_m^{[s]}, \not\exists n/v_i \in \mathcal{G}_n^{[s]} \\ \left(\mathcal{G}_n^{[s]}, \mathcal{G}_m^{[s]}\right) & v_i \in \mathcal{G}_n^{[s]}, v_j \in \mathcal{G}_m^{[s]} \end{cases} \quad (4)$$

In other words, GMA approach aggregates a pair of nodes in scale s under the same existing segment when at least one of both is already assigned to a segment. In case none has previously assigned to any segment, a new segment is provided. In all previous cases, aggregation is carried out as long as $\delta_{i,j}$ holds, otherwise, different segments are assigned to previous pair of nodes.

In addition, the number of assigned graphs in scale s is given by p, whose description is provided in Equation 5, which depends on $\bar{\delta}_{i,j} = 1 - \delta_{i,j}$ as follows:

$$p = p + \bar{\delta}_{i,j} + \xi_{i,j} \quad (5)$$

where function $\xi_{i,j}$ is defined as

$$\xi_{i,j} = \begin{cases} \bar{\delta}_{i,j}, & \not\exists n, m, \in \mathbb{N}, m \neq n, v_i \in \mathcal{G}_n^{[s]}, v_j \in \mathcal{G}_m^{[s]} \\ 0, & \text{otherwise} \end{cases} \quad (6)$$

This assignment is done for each value in the ordered set $\Omega_{\mathcal{W}}$, until whether every element in $\Omega_{\mathcal{W}}$ is evaluated or every node in $\mathcal{V}$ is assigned a segment in subsequent scale.

Gaussian Multiscale Aggregation assures that every node in scale $s - 1$ is assigned a segment/subgraph in scale s.

After aggregation, nodes in scale s are gathered into p subgraphs, with $p < N^{[s]}$, being $N^{[s]}$ the number of nodes in scale s. Each subgraph contains a set of nodes, whose number is unknown a priori. These subgraphs must be compared in subsequent scales, and thus the similarity function in subgraphs is defined in Equation 7.

Consequently, let $\mathcal{G}_n^{[s+1]}$ be the nth aggregated graph in scale $s + 1$, which gathers a set of m subgraphs $\{\mathcal{G}_1^{[s]}, \ldots, \mathcal{G}_m^{[s]}\}$ in scale s. Then the similarity function for graph $\mathcal{G}_n^{[s+1]}$, namely $\phi_{\mathcal{G}_n^{[s+1]}}$ is defined as

$$\phi_{\mathcal{G}_n^{[s+1]}} = \frac{\sum_{i=1}^m \phi_{\mathcal{G}_i^{[s]}}}{\int_\alpha \sum_{i=1}^m \phi_{\mathcal{G}_i^{[s]}} d\alpha} \quad (7)$$

Notice that the definition of the similarity functions $\phi_{\mathcal{G}_n^{[s+1]}}$ has sense also for individual nodes in $\mathcal{V}$, considering nodes as graphs of one element. This is essential during the aggregation in first scale, where graphs gathers nodes instead of subgraphs. In this case, function $\phi^{[0]}$ is represented by a gaussian function of mean and deviation corresponding to the average and dispersion intensity of their neighbour nodes, as stated before.

Therefore, similarity functions can be completely defined as in Equation 8

$$\phi_{\mathcal{G}^{[s+1]}} = \begin{cases} \mathcal{N}(\mu, \sigma) & s = 0 \\ \dfrac{\sum_{i=1}^{m} \phi_{\mathcal{G}_i^{[s]}}}{\int_\alpha \sum_{i=1}^{m} \phi_{\mathcal{G}_i^{[s]}} \, d\alpha} & s > 0 \end{cases} \tag{8}$$

where $\mathcal{N}(\mu, \sigma)$ stands for the gaussian distribution given an average μ and a σ, both of them corresponding to their respective neighbour properties. For clarity sake, first scale ($s = 0$) is obtained based on nodes $v \in \mathcal{V}$ and subsequent scales are obtained by gathering subgraphs.

Concerning location, the position of subgraphs is obtained by averaging the position of the nodes contained on each subgraph. This is essential in order to provide a neighbourhood structure, since after aggregation every scale s collects a scatter set of subgraphs. This structure is given by means of Delaunay triangulation.

A Delaunay graph for a set $S = \{p_1, \dots, p_n\}$ of points in the plane has the set S as its vertices. Two vertices p_i and p_j are joined by a straight-line (representing an edge) if and only if the Voronoi regions $V(p_i)$ and $V(p_j)$ share an edge. In addition, for a set of points in $\mathbb{R}^2$, knowing the locations of the endpoints permits a solution in $O(n \log n)$ time. Therefore, Delaunay triangulation is a suitable method to provide a neighbourhood structure to previous aggregated subgraphs.

This operation represents the final step in the loop, since at this moment, there exist a new subgraph $\mathcal{G}^{[s+1]} = \bigcup_k \mathcal{G}_k^{[s+1]}$ at scale $s + 1$ where each $\mathcal{G}_k^{[s+1]}$ represents a node, and edges $\mathcal{E}^{[s+1]}$ are provided by Delaunay triangulation, and weights $\mathcal{W}^{[s+1]}$ are obtained based on Equations 1 and 8.

The whole loop is repeated until only two subgraphs remain, as stated at the begining of this section. However, due to the constraints provided to aggregate (Equation 9), the method could not aggregate more segments, without achieving the goal of dividing image into two subgraphs. Therefore, Equation 3 is in practice relaxed and stated as follows in Equation 9:

$$\sigma_{i,j}^{[s+1]} \le \sqrt{\sigma_i^{[s]} \sigma_j^{[s]}} + k^{[s]} \tag{9}$$

being $k^{[s]}$ a factor able to avoid aggregation method from being stuck in the loop. This factor can be dynamically increased or decreased, according to previous method necessities. However, this value is initially set to $k^{[s]} = 0.01$, for each scale s. The capability of $k^{[s]}$ to adapt the necessities of the algorithm remains as future work.

The computational cost of this algorithm is quasi-linear with the number of pixels, since each scale gathers nodes in the sense that nodes in subsequent scales are reduced by (in practice) a three times factor. Therefore, time to process the first scale (which contains the highest number of nodes) is greater than the rest of times to process subsequent scales, and the total time is approximately comparable to two times the processing time to aggregate first scale. This statement will be supported within the results Section 6.

4   Database

With the aim of evaluating the segmentation method a synthetic database has been created, gathering different hand positions, rotation degrees and environments, being possible to assess to what extent the segmentation algorithm can satisfactory perform a hand isolation from background on real scenarios.

Many different backgrounds are considered so that all possible scenarios are selected, containing textures from carpets, fabric, glass, grass, mud, different objects, paper, parquet, pavement, plastic, skin and fur, sky, soil, stones, tiles, tree, wall and wood. In addition, five different samples from every texture were collected to provide a more realistic evaluation scenario.

Initially, hands were taken with a blue-coloured background, so that hand can be easily extracted, being this prior segmentation result considered as ground-truth for posterior segmentation evaluation. This database contains a total of 120 individuals, with their both hands and 20 acquisitions per hand. Some acquisition examples of this database can be seen in Figure 2.

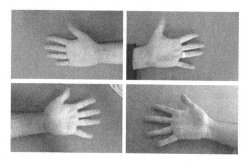

Fig. 2. Samples of first database, with blue-coloured background. Synthetic database is based on this database, considering different backgrounds. In addition, the segmentation result of this database, will be considered as ground truth in a posterior evaluation.

Hand is then isolated and superposed to former backgrounds, carrying out an opening morphological operation (with a disk structural element of radius 5) for colour images [5] to avoid possible edges separating hand and underlying texture, ensuring a more realistic image.

For each image, a total of 5×17 (five images and 17 textures) images are created. Therefore, second database collects a total of $120 \times 2 \times 20 \times 5 \times 17 = 408000$ images (120 individuals, two hands, 20 acquisitions per hand, five images and 17 textures) to properly evaluate segmentation on real scenarios. A visual example of this database is provided in Figure 3.

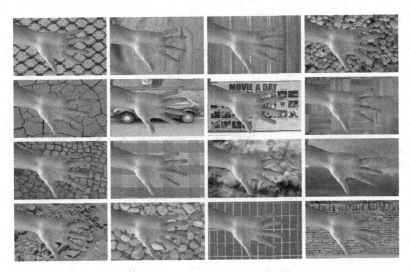

Fig. 3. Samples from the synthetic database in different backgrounds for a given acquisition taken from the first database

5 Evaluation Criteria

The proposed segmentation algorithm must be evaluated according to criteria able to assess to what extent the algorithm is able to isolate hand from background. There exist several methods to evaluate segmentation in literature [2,19,10], but most of them consider several manual/human segmentations carried out by different individuals.

The presented evaluation criteria is based on a ground-truth segmentation, automatically obtained, but on the contrary, very reliable since the background is very easily distinguishable from hand (Figure 2). Therefore, the proposed method is based on F-Factor, [1], defined as follows:

$$F = \frac{2RP}{R + P} \qquad (10)$$

where P (Precision, Confidence) stands for the number of true positives (true segmentation, i.e. classify a hand pixel as hand) in relation to the number of true positives and false negatives (false hand segmentation), and R (Recall, Sensitivity) represents the number of true positives in relation to the number of true positives and false positives (false background segmentation, i.e. consider background as hand). F-Factor is within $[0, 1]$ interval, so that 0 states a bad segmentation, while on the contrary 1 represents the best segmentation result.

In addition, a very important aspect of segmentation algorithm regards the required time to perform the aim of isolating objects on an image. This time depends strongly on the image size, the computer where experiments take place and the implementation, among other characteristics.

These former criteria will permit to assess to what extent the proposed algorithm meet their goals in an adequate time.

6   Results

Under this section, results are presented according to evaluation criteria presented in previous Section 5.

First of all, segmentation is evaluated in terms of performance, considering F-Factor (Equation 10) as the main criterion. The obtained results are summerized in Table 1.

Table 1. Segmentation evaluation by means of F-measure in database GB2S with 17 different background textures, together with the corresponding standard deviation. In addition, the results for NCut are also provided for comparison.

Texture	Proposed, $F(\%)$	NC, $F(\%)$
Carpets	92.1±0.1	65.1±0.3
Paper	91.3±0.1	72.8±0.4
Stones	91.2±0.1	71.5±0.3
Fabric	88.4±0.3	60.1±0.2
Parquet	88.3±0.2	62.3±0.3
Tiles	90.1±0.2	68.7±0.2
Glass	94.1±0.1	71.4±0.1
Pavement	88.9±0.2	63.7±0.2
Tree	96.0±0.2	67.2±0.1
Grass	93.3±0.2	65.3±0.2
Skin and Fur	95.3±0.3	71.8±0.3
Wall	94.1±0.1	62.3±0.2
Mud	89.5±0.2	60.1±0.2
Sky	96.1±0.1	71.3±0.1
Wood	93.5±0.1	73.5±0.1
Objects	92.0±0.1	61.6±0.3
Soil	89.0±0.2	59.7±0.2

In addition, accuracy can be also visually evaluated. Figure 4 presents a comparative frame for segmentation evaluation, comparing the results obtained with Normalized Cuts and the proposed method. Reader can compare the obtained results (columns 4-6) to the ground-truth (column 2). The results obtained by the proposed approach conserve more precisely the shape of the hand even in scenarios with similar textures like parquet (row 5) or wood (last row).

Secondly, concerning computational cost, Table 2 presents the segmentation time in relation to the number of pixels of the images. This temporal evaluation was carried out in a PC computer @2.4 GHz Intel Core 2 Duo with 4GB 1067 MHz DDR3 of memory, considering that the proposed method was completely implemented in MATLAB.

The results provided in Table 2 shows that the proposed algorithm is faster than the compared approaches. In addition, the proposed method can segment images of higher sizes, but NCut cannot handle higher sizes images without running out of memory.

A more refined implementation remains as future work. Nonetheless, this temporal result is very competitive if compared to previous approaches in literature, [2,1].

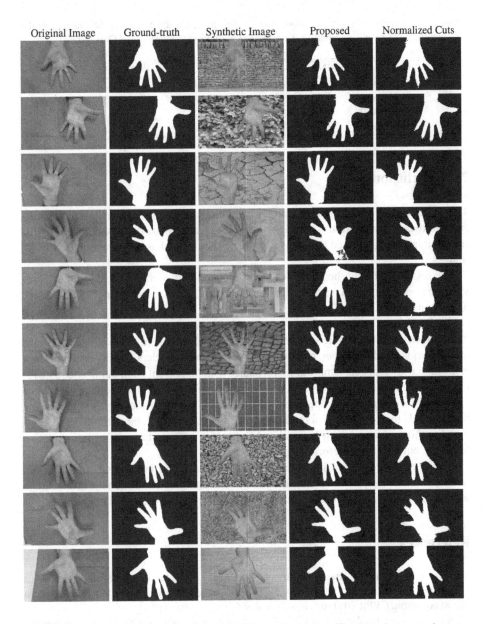

Fig. 4. A comparative study of results provided by segmentation algorithm in comparison to ground-truth. First column gathers examples from first database, together with their segmentation on second column, considered as ground truth. Third column presents synthetic images based on first column images, providing on the fourth column the final segmentation result. Last column presents the segmentation result provided by Normalized Cuts [16], respectively.

Table 2. Relation between time performance (in seconds), the dimension of the image, and the size in number of pixels, comparing the proposed method with Normalized Cuts (NCut)

Image Dimensions	Number of Pixels	Proposed (seconds)	NCut (seconds)
600x800	480000	30.1	321.7
450x600	270000	19.8	129.5
300x400	120000	9.4	25.1
150x200	30000	3.1	7.2

7   Conclusions

This paper has presented an approach for hand biometric segmentation based on gaussian multiscale aggregation. This method is able to isolate hand from background in different situations, simulated by an own synthetic public database, with a total of 408000 images.

The results highlight the fact that hand is isolated with a competitive accuracy, providing a good result for a posterior feature extraction, independently on the background of the hand image.

Applications of this method are very suitable for mobile applications, since hand mobile biometrics must be able to identify individuals everywhere, without no constrains on the background. However, more efforts must be done to adapt this approach for mobile biometrics, since its temporal performance is far at present from being adequate for real-time applications. In addition, the time performance is still low (18 seconds), when compared to other similar approaches in literature, and considering the challenging backgrounds to segment. Concretely, the results obtained are competitive when compared to those obtained with Normalized Cuts [16], not only in terms of segmentation accuracy, but also time performance.

Future work regards an improvement and refinement in implementation, together with a mobile orientation, so that mobile hand biometrics could benefit of a reliable segmentation algorithm, and therefore, increase their identification accuracy.

References

1. Alpert, S., Galun, M., Basri, R., Brandt, A.: Image segmentation by probabilistic bottom-up aggregation and cue integration. In: IEEE Conference on Computer Vision and Pattern Recognition, CVPR 2007, pp. 1–8 (June 2007)
2. Chen, S., Cao, L., Wang, Y., Liu, J., Tang, X.: Image segmentation by map-ml estimations. IEEE Transactions on Image Processing 19(9), 2254–2264 (2010)
3. Comaniciu, D., Meer, P., Member, S.: Mean shift: A robust approach toward feature space analysis. IEEE Transactions on Pattern Analysis and Machine Intelligence 24, 603–619 (2002)
4. Felzenszwalb, P.F., Huttenlocher, D.P.: Efficient graph-based image segmentation. International Journal of Computer Vision 59 (2004)
5. Gonzalez, R.C., Woods, R.E.: Digital Image Processing. Addison-Wesley Longman Publishing Co., Inc., Boston (1992)

6. Gonzalez, R.C., Woods, R.E.: Digital Image Processing, 3rd edn. Prentice-Hall, Inc., Upper Saddle River (2006)
7. Kang, W.X., Yang, Q.Q., Liang, R.P.: The comparative research on image segmentation algorithms. In: ETCS 2009: Proceedings of the 2009 First International Workshop on Education Technology and Computer Science, pp. 703–707. IEEE Computer Society, Washington, DC (2009)
8. Kukula, E., Elliott, S.: Implementation of hand geometry at purdue university's recreational center: an analysis of user perspectives and system performance. In: 39th Annual 2005 International Carnahan Conference on Security Technology, CCST 2005, November 14, pp. 83–88 (2005)
9. Kukula, E., Elliott, S.: Implementation of hand geometry: an analysis of user perspectives and system performance. IEEE Aerospace and Electronic Systems Magazine 21(3), 3–9 (2006)
10. Meilă, M.: Comparing clusterings: an axiomatic view. In: Proceedings of the 22nd International Conference on Machine Learning, ICML 2005, pp. 577–584. ACM, New York (2005), http://doi.acm.org/10.1145/1102351.1102424
11. García-Casarrubios Muñoz, Á., Sánchez Ávila, C., de Santos Sierra, A., Guerra Casanova, J.: A Mobile-Oriented Hand Segmentation Algorithm Based on Fuzzy Multiscale Aggregation. In: Bebis, G., Boyle, R., Parvin, B., Koracin, D., Chung, R., Hammoud, R., Hussain, M., Kar-Han, T., Crawfis, R., Thalmann, D., Kao, D., Avila, L. (eds.) ISVC 2010, Part I. LNCS, vol. 6453, pp. 479–488. Springer, Heidelberg (2010)
12. Rory Tait Neilson, B. N., McDonald, S.: Image segmentation by weighted aggregation with gradient orientation histograms. Southern African Telecommunication Networks and Applications Conference, SATNAC (2007)
13. Sharon, E., Brandt, A., Basri, R.: Fast multiscale image segmentation. In: Proceedings of IEEE Conference on Computer Vision and Pattern Recognition, vol. 1, pp. 70–77 (2000)
14. Sharon, E., Brandt, A., Basri, R.: Segmentation and boundary detection using multiscale intensity measurements. In: Proceedings of the IEEE Computer Society Conference on Computer Vision and Pattern Recognition, CVPR 2001, vol. 1, pp. I–469 – I–476 (2001)
15. Sharon, E., Galun, M., Sharon, D., Basri, R., Brandt, A.: Hierarchy and adaptivity in segmenting visual scenes. Macmillan Publishing Ltd. (2006)
16. Shi, J., Malik, J.: Normalized cuts and image segmentation. IEEE Transactions on Pattern Analysis and Machine Intelligence 22(8), 888–905 (2000)
17. Shi, J., Malik, J.: Normalized cuts and image segmentation. IEEE Transactions on Pattern Analysis and Machine Intelligence 22, 888–905 (2000)
18. Shirakawa, S., Nagao, T.: Evolutionary image segmentation based on multiobjective clustering. In: CEC 2009: Proceedings of the Eleventh Conference on Congress on Evolutionary Computation, pp. 2466–2473. IEEE Press, Piscataway (2009)
19. Unnikrishnan, R., Pantofaru, C., Hebert, M.: Toward objective evaluation of image segmentation algorithms. IEEE Trans. Pattern Anal. Mach. Intell. 29, 929–944 (2007), http://dx.doi.org/10.1109/TPAMI.2007.1046

Touching Character Segmentation Method
of Archaic Lanna Script

Sakkayaphop Pravesjit and Arit Thammano

Computational Intelligence Laboratory Faculty of Information Technology,
King Mongkut's Institute of Technology Ladkrabang, Bangkok, 10520, Thailand
sakkayaphop.pr@up.ac.th, arit@it.kmitl.ac.th

Abstract. In general, character recognition consists of four stages: image preprocessing, segmentation, feature extraction, and classification. Character segmentation is one of the most important and difficult tasks in character recognition. Incorrectly segmented characters are not likely to be correctly recognized. Touching characters, which always arises when handwritten characters are being segmented, makes the task even more difficult. Therefore, this paper emphasizes the interest to the segmentation of touching and overlapping characters. This paper proposes two new techniques which are shown to dramatically improve the segmentation accuracy. The first proposed technique emphasizes on converting a greyscale image to a binary image while the second proposed technique emphasizes on the process of character segmentation itself. In the proposed character segmentation process, the bounding box analysis is initially employed to segment the document image into images of isolated characters and images of touching characters. The thinning algorithm is applied to extract the skeleton of the touching characters. Next, the skeleton of the touching characters is separated into several pieces. Finally, the separated pieces of the touching characters are put back to reconstruct two isolated characters. The proposed algorithm achieves an accuracy of 89.26%.

Keywords: Character segmentation, Touching character, Dissection method, Archaic script.

1 Introduction

Lanna language was used in the 13th to 18th centuries in the Kingdom of Lanna. However, after the kingdom had been annexed by Siam (as Thailand was called until 1939) in 1774, Lanna script became obsolete and was replaced with Thai script. Few people nowadays know how to read or write this language. Lanna manuscripts were typically written about the people's ways of life, believes, laws, folklore, herbal medicine ingredients, history, astrological knowledge, and other general knowledge. Lanna manuscripts were generally inscribed on palm leaves (Figure 1), or on the surface of stones. As time goes by, these ancient documents have been decayed, damaged, destroyed, or lost. Termites, insects, and general decay have left these old manuscripts in poor condition (Figure 2). In order to preserve valuable historical information

M.S. Obaidat, J.L. Sevillano, and J. Filipe (Eds.): ICETE 2011, CCIS 314, pp. 400–408, 2012.
© Springer-Verlag Berlin Heidelberg 2012

Fig. 1. Palm leaf manuscripts

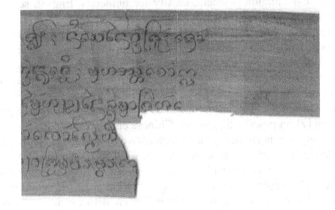

Fig. 2. Example of Lanna script

inscribed on these documents, computerized systems must be put to use in order to translate the inscribed script into the current Thai script.

Touching and overlapping of characters is the first problem encountered when attempting to recognize the handwritten Lanna characters. Touching of characters can emerge when two or more adjacent characters are written too close; therefore, some parts of characters are connected [6]. There are many kinds of touching characters commonly found in the written documents (Figure 3). This is because characters of each language have different styles and characteristics. Therefore, the types of touching characters vary from language to language, which in turn require different methods for segmenting the touching characters in each language. For example, the handwritten cursive characters shown in Figure 3(a) are a type of touching characters typically found in English handwritten manuscripts but not in Lanna manuscripts. Only the types shown in Figures 3(b), 3(c), and 3(d) can be found in Lanna manuscripts. The purpose of this research is to separate the touching or overlapping Lanna characters, which have not been effectively solved using any other character segmentation methods.

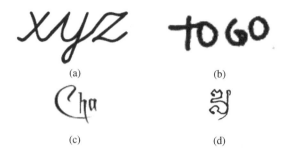

(a)   (b)

(c)   (d)

Fig. 3. Four types of touching characters

Character segmentation is a process that seeks to decompose a sequence of characters into individual symbols. There have been substantial researches undertaken to solve character segmentation problem, mostly for numerals, English script, Chinese script, Arabic script, and Bangla script. Segmentation strategies can be divided into three main categories [2]; [5]: dissection methods, recognition-based methods, and holistic methods. Dissection methods decompose the image into a sequence of sub-images using general features, e.g., character height and width [4]. Recognition-based methods search the image for components that match classes in its alphabet. Holistic methods seek to recognize entire words as a whole, thus avoiding the need to segment the image into characters. Among the methods proposed for character segmentation, Tseng and Chen [7] proposed a three-stage Chinese character segmentation algorithm. Firstly, a bounding box is created around each stroke of a Chinese character. Secondly, the knowledge-based merging operations are used to merge the stroke bounding boxes together. Finally, a dynamic programming is used to find the optimal segmentation boundaries. The experimental results show that the proposed algorithm is a very effective segmentation algorithm. It works well even with touching and/or overlapping characters. Xiao and Leedham [8] proposed a novel approach to English cursive script segmentation. In the proposed approach, connected components are split into sub-components based on their face-up or face-down background regions. Then the over-segmented sub-components are merged into characters according to the knowledge of character structures are their joining characteristics. Bhowmik, Roy, and Roy [1] proposed a segmentation scheme for handwritten Bangla words. The authors use the analysis of directional chaincode and the positional information to extract the features from the image, then employ multilayer perceptron neural network to determine the segmentation points. The authors also point out that their segmentation result can be significantly improved if their proposed technique is combined with the recognition process in a holistic system.

This study focuses mainly on the dissection methods. Projection analysis, connected component processing, and bounding box analysis are three widely used dissection methods [3]. While projection analysis is very effective for segmenting good quality machine printed manuscripts [2], it has limited success when segmenting handwritten manuscripts. Connected component processing and bounding box analysis usually offer an efficient way to segment handwritten manuscripts. However, they might lead to incorrect segmentation when dealing with touching characters as shown in Figure 4.

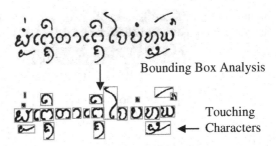

Fig. 4. Segmentation results by bounding box analysis

In this paper, the new dissection algorithm is proposed to segment touching Lanna characters. The performance of the proposed algorithm is measured by the ability of the proposed algorithm to correctly segment 6 different handwritten Lanna manuscripts.

Following this introduction, section 2 briefly describes the general process of the proposed character segmentation process. Section 3 explains the proposed character segmentation algorithm. In section 4, the experimental results are presented and discussed. Finally, section 5 is the conclusion.

2   Methodology

The process of this Lanna character segmentation has been divided into five steps:

Step 1:   Scan a manuscript and convert it into a binary image. This step consists of two parts: the conversion of an RGB image to a greyscale image and the conversion of a greyscale image to a binary image. In this paper, the new method in converting a greyscale image to a binary image is introduced. This conversion method employs the concepts of the multithresholding method and Otsu's method. Let $T = \{T_1, T_2, ..., T_k, ..., T_{J-1}\}$ be a set of threshold values, where $T_1 < T_2 < ... < T_k < ...< T_{J-1}$. T_t is a threshold value obtained by Otsu's method. T_t is used to separate T into two groups: the group of T_k which is less than T_t and the group of T_k which is greater than T_t. Then determine T_{min}, T_{max} and T_{new} by using the equations (1), (2) and (3). Finally, the resulting binary image is obtained by applying the equation (4) to every pixel in the image.

Step 2:   Use the bounding box analysis to segment the entire manuscript image into subimages. Since the bounding box analysis is only effective in segmenting nontouching characters, the obtained subimages therefore consist of both images of isolated characters and images of touching characters.

Step 3:   Detect touching characters by looking at the aspect ratio (width/height) of each subimage. From the facts that (1) touching characters commonly have an aspect ratio larger than single isolated characters and (2) the aspect ratio of Lanna isolated characters is typically smaller than 3/2, therefore, if the aspect ratio of the subimage is larger than 3/2, it will be identified as the touching characters.

Step 4:   Use the thinning algorithm to reduce the thickness of the character image to its skeleton, which is then sent to the segmentation engine.

Step 5: Employ the proposed character segmentation algorithm to decompose the touching characters into individual characters.

$$T_{min} = \underset{\forall T_k : T_k < T_t}{\arg\min} \ [T_t - T_k] \tag{1}$$

$$T_{max} = \underset{\forall T_k : T_k > T_t}{\arg\max} \ [T_t - T_k] \tag{2}$$

$$T_{new} = \begin{cases} \dfrac{T_t + T_{max}}{2} & \text{if } T_{max} < [T_t + (T_t \times 0.05)] \\[2mm] \dfrac{T_{min} + T_{max}}{2} & \text{if } T_{max} > [T_t + (T_t \times 0.05)] \end{cases} \tag{3}$$

$$I_T(x,y) = \begin{cases} 1 & \text{if } I(x,y) \geq T_{new} \\ 0 & \text{if } I(x,y) < T_{new} \end{cases} \tag{4}$$

3   The Proposed Character Segmentation Algorithm

A description of the proposed segmentation algorithm is given below.

A. Search the touching characters image for end points and junction points. Then, adopting the junction points as the partition points, break up the touching characters into several pieces. From each end point, start tracing the contour of touching characters until the nearest junction point is reached. Then, extract such contour from the touching characters. For example, in Figure 5, four end points and two junction points are found. By using the above mentioned technique, the touching characters are broken into 5 contours as shown in Figure 6. Out of the five contours, four contains both a junction point and an end point while one contains two junction points (with no end point on the contour). The contour which contains no end point is a part of the touching characters where two characters touch each other.

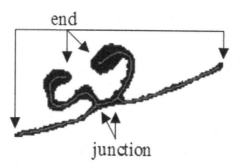

Fig. 5. Example of touching characters

B. For each extracted contour, translate the contour so that the junction point coincides with the origin (where x and y axes intersect).

$$T\begin{bmatrix} C_{ix} \\ C_{iy} \end{bmatrix} = \begin{bmatrix} C_{ix} \\ C_{iy} \end{bmatrix} - \begin{bmatrix} J_{ix} \\ J_{iy} \end{bmatrix} \qquad (5)$$

Where: T is the translation operator.

C_{ix} and C_{iy} are x and y coordinate of the ith contour.

J_{ix} and J_{iy} are the x and y coordinate of the junction point of the ith contour.

C. At the origin, create the reference unit vectors along the x axis ((1, 0) and (-1, 0)) and along the y axis ((0, 1) and (0, -1)).

Fig. 6. Five contours of the example touching characters

D For each translated contour, create a vector V_1 that starts at the origin and ends one pixel away from the starting point. Then, determine an angle between the vector V_1 and the x axis in a clockwise direction by using the following equation:

$$\theta_n = \cos^{-1} \frac{U \cdot V_n}{\|U\| \|V_n\|} \qquad (6)$$

Where: U is a unit vector along the x axis.

V_n is the nth vector along the translated contour i.

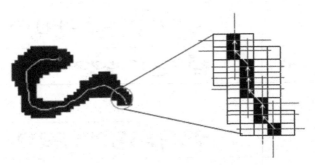

Fig. 7. Illustration of step D

Next, sequentially create the vectors V_2, V_3, ..., V_n, ..., V_N. However this time instead of starting the vector at the origin, start the vector V_n at the point where the vector V_{n-1} ends. For example, the starting point of the vector V_2 is the ending point of the vector V_1. After each vector V_n is created, determine the clockwise angle of the vector V_n relative to the x axis. If the angle of three consecutive vectors is the same, stop the creation of further vectors.

D. Use the linear regression method to calculate the equation of the best-fit line for a series of points, starting at the origin and ending at the ending point of the third consecutive vector. Calculate the angle of the line from the overlapping contour line and assign it to represent the angle of the whole contour.

$$y = a + bx \tag{7}$$

$$b = \frac{\sum (x - \bar{x})(y - \bar{y})}{\sum (x - \bar{x})^2} \tag{8}$$

$$a = y - bx \tag{9}$$

E. After obtaining the angles of all contours, compare the angle of each contour to that of other contours. According to the characteristic of Lanna characters whose trajectories typically do not abruptly change the direction, group the closest match, angle wise, together. Finally, the contours within the same group are combined to form each isolated character.

4 Experimental Results

In this study, the images of Lanna characters used in testing the performance of the proposed algorithm were obtained from 6 manuscripts. Samples of the tested manuscripts are shown in Figure 8. Each manuscript is written by a different handwriting script. Four pages from each manuscript were scanned and processed using steps 1 through 5 outlined in section 2. In the scanned pages, a total of 121 touching characters were found. All of them only consist of two characters. Similar to other languages, touching characters of three or more components are very uncommon in Lanna manuscripts.

Manuscript 1	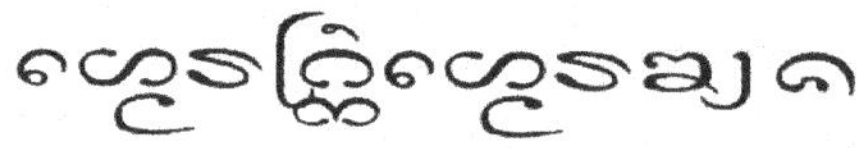
Manuscript 2	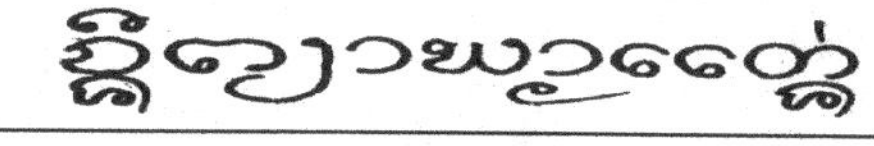
Manuscript 3	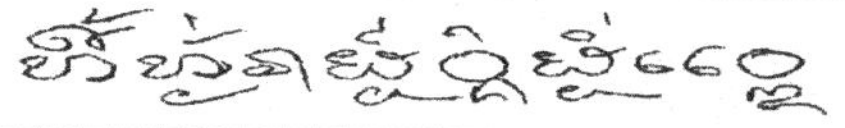
Manuscript 4	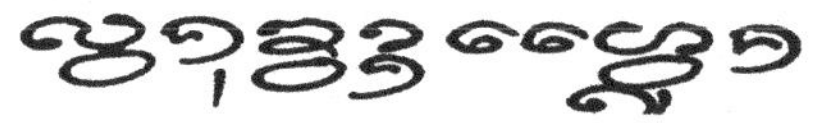
Manuscript 5	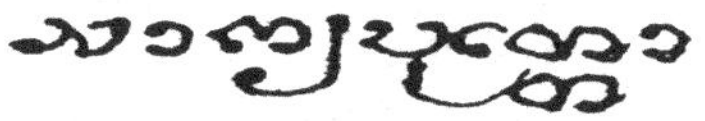
Manuscript 6	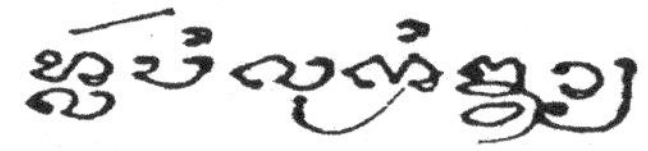

Fig. 8. Samples of the tested manuscripts

Of the 121 touching character images, 89.26% were correctly segmented with the proposed algorithm. Figures 9 and 10 show some of correctly and incorrectly segmented Lanna characters.

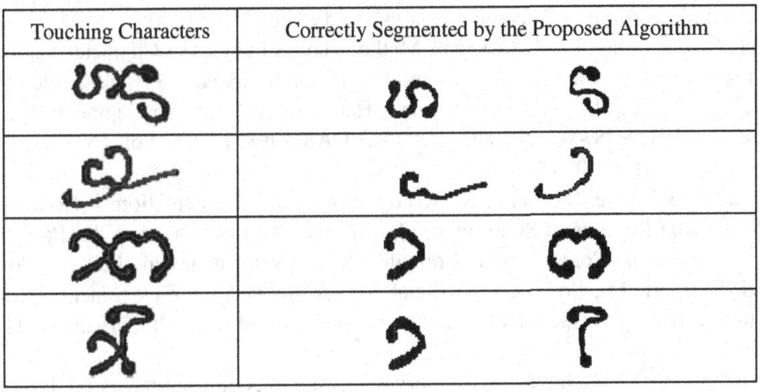

Touching Characters	Correctly Segmented by the Proposed Algorithm

Fig. 9. Samples of correctly segmented characters

Touching Characters	Incorrectly Segmented by the Proposed Algorithm	Expected Segmentation Results

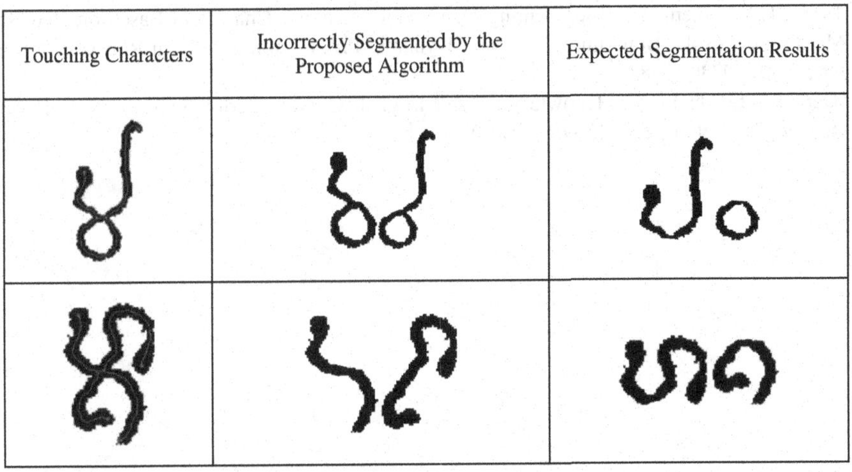

Fig. 10. Samples of incorrectly segmented characters

5   Conclusions

A new segmentation algorithm for the archaic Lanna characters is proposed in this paper. To segment real world documents, segmentation of touching characters is a major problem we have to deal with. With the use of the characteristic of Lanna characters, the touching characters is separated into several pieces, then the separated pieces of the touching characters are put back to reconstruct two isolated characters. From the experimental results, it is clear that the proposed algorithm is quite capable of segmenting touching Lanna characters.

References

1. Bhowmik, T.K., Roy, A., Roy, U.: Character Segmentation for Handwritten Bangla Words Using Artificial Neural Network. In: Proceedings of the International Workshop on Neural Networks and Learning in Document Analysis and Recognition (2005)
2. Casey, R.G., Lecolinet, E.: A Survey of Methods and Strategies in Character Segmentation. IEEE Transactions on Pattern Analysis and Machine Intelligence 18(7), 690–706 (1996)
3. Chen, J.-L., Wu, C.-H., Lee, H.-J.: Chinese Handwritten Character Segmentation in Form Documents. In: Lee, S.-W., Nakano, Y. (eds.) DAS 1998. LNCS, vol. 1655, pp. 348–362. Springer, Heidelberg (1999)
4. Hoang, T.V., Tabbone, S., Pham, N.: Recognition-based Segmentation of Nom Characters from Body Text Regions of Stele Images Using Area Voronoi Diagram. In: Proceedings of the 13th International Conference on Computer Analysis of Images and Patterns (2009)
5. Marinai, S., Gori, M., Soda, G.: Artificial Neural Networks for Document Analysis and Recognition. IEEE Transactions on Pattern Analysis and Machine Intelligence 27(1), 23–35 (2005)
6. Soba, T., Sulong, G., Rehman, A.: A Survey on Methods and Strategies on Touched Characters Segmentation. International Journal of Research and Reviews in Computer Science 1(2), 103–114 (2010)
7. Tseng, L.Y., Chen, R.C.: Segmenting Handwritten Chinese Characters Based on Heuristic Merging of Stroke Bounding Boxes and Dynamic Programming. Pattern Recognition Letter 19, 963–973 (1998)
8. Xiao, X., Leedham, G.: Knowledge-based English Cursive Script Segmentation. Pattern Recognition Letters 21, 945–954 (2000)

Small and Large Vocabulary Speech Recognition of MP3 Data under Real-Word Conditions: Experimental Study

Petr Pollak and Michal Borsky*

Faculty of Electrical Engineering, Czech Technical University in Prague,
Technicka 2, 166 27 Prague, Czech Republic
{pollak,borskmic}@fel.cvut.cz

Abstract. This paper presents the study of speech recognition accuracy both for small and large vocabulary task with respect to different levels of MP3 compression of processed data. The motivation behind the work was to evaluate the usage of ASR system for off-line automatic transcription of recordings collected from standard present MP3 devices under different levels of background noise and channel distortion. Although MP3 may not be an optimal compression algorithm, the performed experiments have prooved that it does not distort speech signal significantly for higher compression rates. Realized experiments showed also that the accuracy of speech recognition (both small- and large-vocabulary) decreased very slowly for the bit-rate of 24 kbps and higher. However, slightly different setup of speech feature computation is necessary for MP3 speech data, mainly PLP features give significantly better results in comparison to MFCC.

Keywords: Speech recognition, Small vocabulary, Large vocabulary, LVCSR, MPEG compression, MP3, Noise robustness.

1 Introduction

Automated speech recognition (ASR) represents a field which is nowadays more present in everyday human life in growing number of applications as in voice operated control of consumer devices, automated information services, or general conversion of uttered speech into text record. The systems for automatic transcription of speech to text are currently well developed for all important world languages. It is possible to meet today dictation software for standard PC enabling users to input texts into documents without using the keyboard, e.g. Dragon dictate, or for mobile devices, e.g. [1]. Further, the transcription of broadcast news is currently a very important task solved by many research teams [2], [3]. Probably the most popular is the transcription of news, but there are also other applications such as automated subtitling of TV programmes, e.g. parliament meetings [4] or sportscasts [5]. Special attention is also paid to the transcription and indexing of large audio archives enabling better search within them in the future [6], [7].

When audio records are transcribed on-line, e.g. the above-mentioned subtitling of TV programmes, ASR systems work with full quality input signal. On the other hand,

---

* This research was supported by grant GAČR 102/08/0707 "Speech Recognition under Real-World Conditions".

M.S. Obaidat, J.L. Sevillano, and J. Filipe (Eds.): ICETE 2011, CCIS 314, pp. 409–419, 2012.

when they work off-line, recordings can be saved in formats of different quality and typically, MP3 format (more precisely MPEG Layer III) represents one of the most frequently used formats for the saving of sound files in compressed form [8], [9]. It is well known that this format uses psychoacoustic models reducing the precision of components less audible to human hearing so it makes it possible to decrease the size of the sound file to 10% while CD quality is preserved. Although this format has been developed especially for saving the music, it is standardly used also in simple dictation devices or mobile phones enabling recording and saving audio speech files. Some works in MP3 speech data recognition have been already done. The recognition of spontaneous speech from large oral history archives published in [7] used signals saved in MP3 format but rather high bit-rate (128 kbps) was used in this case. In [10] the study of automatic transcription of compressed broadcast audio with different bit-rates was done. The comparison of various compression schemes was realized in this study, however, the quality of the signal was rather better.

This paper is an extension of experimental study published at the conference SIGMAP 2012 [11]. Commonly with previously presented results for small-vocabulary task, accuracy analysis of basic Large Vocabulary Continuous Speech Recognition (LVCSR) with respect to different quality of compressed data is additionally presented within this paper. As current ASR systems need to work accurately under real conditions, often under presence of additive background noise or channel distortion, the analysis is performed on signals from different channels with different signal quality depending mainly on the position of the microphone used. Standard features used most commonly in ASR systems have typically modified versions increasing their robustness in real environment [12], [13], [14]. But these methods are designed usually for uncompressed data, so our study focuses mainly on the analysis of the information loss in compressed speech signals when varying levels of additive noise and channel distortion appear in speech signal. The results of this study are supposed to be helpful for further application of automated speech recognition from MP3 speech files.

2   MP3 Speech Recognition

Within this study, the behavior of both small and large vocabulary recognition tasks are analyzed. When we want to analyze mainly the sensitivity of ASR system to loss of information after MP3 compression and without a further dependency on complex blocks such as statistic language model, it is convenient to use much simpler small vocabulary digit recognizer for this purpose in the first step. Finally, complex LVCSR system is used for selected cases as a confirmation of previously obtained results within simpler recognition task.

2.1   Speech Compression Scheme

MP3 compression was developed for the compression of music audio files [9], [8] and it is known that it gives slightly worse results for speech signal. The masking and attenuation of some frequency components can yield to a suppression of a phone at the beginning or at the end of the word, sometimes inter-word pause shortening can appear.

Less naturalness of decoded utterance is then the main effect of this fact and consequently, the accuracy of speech recognition can decrease too. Algorithms, which have been designed and optimized for speech signal, are represented mainly by G.729 [15], AMR [16], or Speex [17]. These encoders are based typically on CELP algorithm, but they are used rather in telecommunications and they do not appear so frequently in standard audio devices.

Consequently, although speech signals can be compressed in a better way, our attention was paid just to MP3 compression in this study because the long-term goal of our work was mainly in off-line mode of ASR operation on compressed speech data from wide-spread audio consumer devices. The study was realized with signals from the database SPEECON recorded in real environment with full-precision PCM coding. The MP3 compression was then simulated by successive encoding and decoding of signals from SPEECON database using publicly available software LAME [18] which made it possible to simulate also different levels of MP3 compression bit-rate.

2.2 Speech Recognition Setup

Current ASR systems are usually based on Hidden Markov Models (HMM). HMM based recognizer consists typically of 3 principal function modules: feature extraction (parameterization), acoustic modelling, and decoding (see block scheme in Fig 1). Generally known principles of HMM based recognizer are not explained in this paper, as they are known or can be found in many sources, e.g. in [19], [20], and others. Only a brief description of our ASR setups, which is relevant for the next parts of this paper, is presented.

Feature Vector

Concerning the parameterization, two sets of features are most standardly used in ASR systems: *Mel-Frequency Cepstral Coefficients* (MFCC) and *Perceptually based Linear Predictive cepstral coefficients* (PLP). All our experiments were carried out just with these two feature sets. Both of them use their own non-linear filter-bank which in both cases models the perceptual properties of human auditory system, for more detail see [19], [20], [21], or [22]. Finally, feature setup can be summarized in the following points:

- 12 cepstral coefficients plus logarithm of frame energy form vector of static features,
- 1st and 2nd derivatives of static parameters are added,
- settings of short-time analysis originates from typically used values, i.e. 16-32 ms for frame length and 8-16 ms for frame period.

Acoustic Modelling

Acoustic modelling in our study was slightly different for mentioned two tasks, according to requirements of small and large vocabulary system respectively.

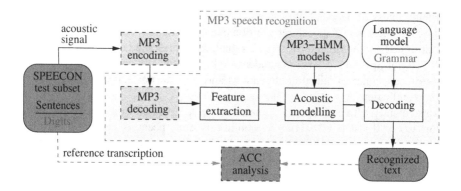

Fig. 1. Block scheme of experimental setup for HMM-based ASR testing

– *small vocabulary digit recognizer*
This system was based on simpler monophone HMM models, i.e. phones modelled without any context to neighboring phones. Finally, HMM models of 44 Czech monophones with 3 emitting states were used as the simplest sub-word acoustic models in ASR. As used phone models were context independent, their higher variability was modelled by 32 mixtures of Gaussian emitting function of HMM models and 3 streams were also used for modelling of static, dynamic and acceleration features respectively.

– *large vocabulary continuous speech recognizer*
This system was based on cross-word triphone HMM models, i.e. phones modelled with left and right context to neighboring phones. Finally, all HMM models had again 3 emitting states, triphone variability was modelled by 16 mixtures of Gaussian emitting function and all (static, dynamic and acceleration) features were processed in 1 stream.

Language Modelling
Language modelling is principally different for small and large vocabulary system, i.e.

– *grammar in small vocabulary digit recognizer*
Connected digit ASR uses simple grammar in the phase of decoding. On the other hand, though just basic digits from 0 to 9 can appear in the utterance, the number of digits in the utterance can vary and they can be pronounced with or without pauses and with possible repetitions. Finally, it means that our digit recognizer should be sufficiently general for our experiments and we can assume that it simulates well operating mode of target practical application, see Fig 1.

– *statistical language model in LVCSR*
Our LVCSR system works with the simplest statistical language models (bigram) and moderate size of vocabulary (240k words). Such simple setup enables off-line processing with tools from the HTK Toolkit [20]. Language model (LM) were created from SYN2006PUB 5-gram corpus from Czech National Corpus (CNC) [23],

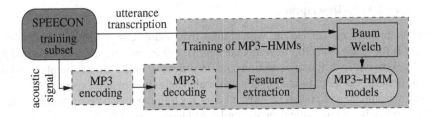

Fig. 2. Block scheme of HMM-based acoustic model training

[24]. More details about the creation of this LM and its performance in LVCSR under standard conditions (using full-precision PCM data) can be found in [25].

2.3   Training of Speech Recognizer

Training of HMM models, which are composed of Gaussian emitting functions representing probability distribution of a feature in given state and from probabilities of transitions between particular states, is performed on the basis of iterative embedded training procedure from large training data (Baum-Welch algorithm). The size of the training database containing speech signals with precisely annotated content must guarantee sufficient appearance of each acoustic element. The training procedure, which has been based on Czech SPEECON data in our case, is illustratively represented by block scheme in Fig. 2, more details can be found in [20] or [19].

Our acoustic models (monophone- and triphone-based described above in the section 2.2) were trained iteratively with flat start for each parameterization and also for many operating conditions. As training data had to match these conditions, we have finally obtained comprehensive set of HMM models for particular channels, for different bit-rates in MP3 encoding, and for selected feature vector used.

2.4   Implementation Tools

The training of acoustic HMM models, small vocabulary ASR and also LVCSR, were realized by tools from publicly available HTK Toolkit [20] which is often used worldwide for the realization of HMM based recognition. For readers without detail knowledge of the HTK Toolkit, typical and core tools of the HTK Toolkit are *HCopy* as parameterization tool, *HERest* as the tool for the training by Baum-Welch algorithm, or *HVite* as Viterbi based word recognizer for digit recognizer and finally *HDecode* tool for cross-word triphone-based LVCSR decoding.

The computation of PLP cepstral coefficients was performed by *CtuCopy* tool [12] and [26], providing some extensions to *HCopy* from the standard set of HTK Toolkit.

3   Experiments

Experiments described in this part comprise the core contribution of this study, which is mainly in the analysis of ASR performance for MP3 compressed speech data under different real-word conditions.

3.1   Speech Data Description

All experiments were carried out with signals from Adult Czech SPEECON database [27]. It is the database (DB) of sentences, digits, command, names, etc. recorded by 580 speakers under different conditions, i.e. in offices or home environment, at public places, or in the car. For this study, only well-balanced subset of adult speaker data from office environment were used, i.e. 90% of data for training and 10% for testing (digits or sentences). It contains signals with similar and not so strong background noise.

Speech data in SPEECON DB are raw 16 bit linear PCM sound files sampled by 16 kHz sampling frequency. These signals were then encoded into MP3 sound files with different bit-rates. The MP3 compression was simulated by successive encoding and decoding by the above-mentioned *lame* software encoder/decoder [18].

Although only data from one environment were used in our experiments, the influence of additive noise and channel distortion could be analyzed, because signals in SPEECON DB were recorded in 4 channels which differed in microphone type and its position, see [28]. Following Tab. 1 describes the properties of particular channels. Although different types and quality of microphones were used, it was mainly the distance from the speaker's mouth that played the key role in the quality of recorded speech signal. Finally, signals from close talk head-set channel CS0 are then almost without any additive noise and reasonable channel distortion appears only in signals from channels CS2 and CS3. These data can simulate well real MP3 recordings made by standard devices in various environments.

Table 1. Description of channels recorded in SPEECON database

Channel ID	Microphone type	Distance	Additive noise	Channel distortion
CS0	head-set	2 cm	-	-
CS1	hands-free	10 cm	+	-
CS2	middle-talk	0.5-1 m	++	+
CS3	far-talk	3 m	+++	++

3.2   Recognition Accuracy

The accuracy (ACC) of a recognizer was measured standardly on the basis of errors on word level. It was defined according to [20] as

$$ACC = \frac{N - D - S - I}{N} \cdot 100 \quad [\%], \qquad (1)$$

where N is the total number of words in the testing set while D, S, and I are numbers of word deletions, substitutions, and insertions respectively. The following sections describe in details obtained results.

3.3   Analysis of Optimum Segmentation for MP3 Speech Data

Within the first experiment, the influence of short-time analysis setup on target accuracy of MP3 recognition was analyzed. In accordance with phonetically based assumptions as well as default settings used in [20], the optimum length of the frame for short-time acoustic analysis is 25 ms with the period of 10 ms for uncompressed speech data, while for MP3 compressed data the segmentation with frame length 32 ms and frame period 16 ms gives the best results for both studied feature sets.

The reasons for this effect lie in the first modules of both feature extraction algorithms which realize short-time Fourier analysis followed by non-linear filter banks computing perceptually based power spectra. Due to the decrease of short-time frame length, frequency resolution of Discrete Fourier Transform decreases too and consequently the masking and deletions of some frequency components within the MP3 compression scheme increase the estimation error of power spectrum at the output of the filter bank.

The results of this experiment for both MFCC and PLP features are in Tab 2. MP3 compression was realized with bit-rate of 160 kbps and results are presented for the CS0 channel. It can be supposed that this error at the output of filter bank increases for shorter frame length also when uncompressed speech signal is more corrupted by additive noise, which is the case of channels CS1, CS2, and CS3.

Abbreviations used in the following tables describe the feature extraction used, e.g. MFCC_3216 means MFCC features computed from 32 ms long frame with the period of 16 ms.

Table 2. ASR accuracy (ACC) dependence on varying segmentation for WAV or MP3 signals: (a) MFCC features, (b) PLP features

(a)

Features	WAV	MP3
MFCC_1608	95.55	54.39
MFCC_2510	96.89	76.31
MFCC_3216	95.22	93.21

(b)

Features	WAV	MP3
PLP_1608	95.11	72.64
PLP_2510	96.33	81.76
PLP_3216	95.11	93.10

Table 3. Digit ASR accuracy for varying MP3 bit-rate: (a) MFCC features, (b) PLP features

(a)

MP3 bit-rate	CS0	CS1	CS2	CS3
WAV	95.22	92.44	89.54	61.18
160 kbps	93.21	83.31	42.83	30.03
64 kbps	93.21	84.43	43.60	31.59
48 kbps	93.33	85.54	43.83	32.26
40 kbps	93.33	86.43	43.94	31.59
32 kbps	89.77	88.54	44.75	33.48
24 kbps	89.32	37.71	38.71	27.92
8 kbps	21.02	16.35	12.57	6.90

(b)

MP3 bit-rate	CS0	CS1	CS2	CS3
WAV	95.11	89.43	88.88	64.63
160 kbps	93.10	82.09	78.75	27.36
40 kbps	92.66	87.32	83.09	28.48
24 kbps	92.32	88.21	80.09	28.70
8 kbps	62.40	36.15	24.25	11.01

3.4   Results of MP3 Digit ASR

Within the second experiment, the influence of digit recognition accuracy in particular channels on different MP3 bit-rates was analyzed. All these experiments were realized

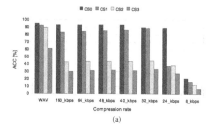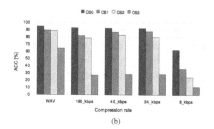

Fig. 3. ASR accuracy (ACC) dependence on varying MP3 bit-rate for all channels: (a) MFCC features, (b) PLP features

with optimum segmentation parameters, i.e. 32 ms frame length and 16 ms frame period. Achieved results are presented numerically in the following tables and for quick illustrative overview also in figures showing the same data in graphical form.

Tab. 3(a) and Fig. 3(a) present results obtained with mel-frequency cepstral coefficients. Looking at the results achieved for CS0 channel, we can see that for rather high quality signal the MP3 compression has just minimum effect for bit-rate of 24 kbps and higher. For other channels the trend is always similar but the absolute values of the achieved ACC are lower according to our assumptions. We can also see that for channels CS2 and CS3, containing higher level of background noise and stronger channel distortion, the ACC falls rapidly already for rather high bit-rates of MP3 compression. Such results disable in principle the recognition of MP3 data collected under similar conditions. On the other hand it must be mentioned that all experiments in this study were carried out with basic feature setup, i.e. no algorithm for additive noise suppression or channel normalization was used.

Tab. 3(b) and Fig. 3(b) show similar results for the recognition with perceptually based linear predictive cepstral coefficients. The same trends have been observed again, so in the end the experiments were realized just with 4 different bit-rates. In comparison with MFCC, better performance can be observed for PLP for channels CS1 and CS2. Especially the results for channel CS2 represent acceptable values of ACC for MP3 compressed data for the bit-rate of 24 kbps and higher (80.09% as for MFCC it was 38.71%) which is similar to the high quality CS0 channel. In principle it allows the practical usage of ASR of MP3 compressed data collected by middle-distance microphone, e.g. it can be the case of MP3 recorder placed on the table.

Finally, we computed sizes of compressed data so we could compare the level of compression (in percent) with the achieved accuracy of speech recognition. These results are shown in Fig. 4 where we can observe minimum decrease of ASR accuracy for 20% compression of sound file and higher. Strong downfall appears as far as beyond 10% compression. These results were obtained for MFCC features and the high quality CS0 channel.

3.5   Results of MP3 LVCSR

Finally, the experiments with LVCSR were performed. As it was mentioned above, these experiments were realized using the tool HDecode from the HTK Toolkit. As this

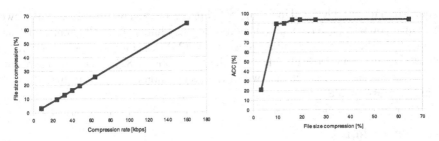

Fig. 4. Dependence of file size reduction and ASR accuracy on varying MP3 bit-rate (MFCC features and channel CS0)

tool is not working in the real-time, we used mentioned very basic setup of LVCSR (bigram LM and dictionary of 240 kwords). Nevertheless, the real-time factor for this setup ranged from 5 to 10 for signals with higher quality. When we started working with MP3 data with high compression level (8kbps) the accuracy began falling down rapidly and the real-time factor increased strongly due to bad acoustic models.

Table 4. LVCSR accuracy for varying MP3 bit-rate for MFCC (a) and PLP (b) features

<table>
<tr><td colspan="3" align="center">(a)</td><td colspan="3" align="center">(b)</td></tr>
<tr><td>MP3 bit-rate</td><td>CS0</td><td>CS1</td><td>MP3 bit-rate</td><td>CS0</td><td>CS1</td></tr>
<tr><td>WAV, see [25]</td><td>67.82</td><td>-</td><td>160 kbps</td><td>65.26</td><td>55.13</td></tr>
<tr><td>160 kbps</td><td>61.87</td><td>46.63</td><td>40 kbps</td><td>65.10</td><td>54.60</td></tr>
<tr><td>40 kbps</td><td>59.09</td><td>46.51</td><td>24 kbps</td><td>60.81</td><td>48.67</td></tr>
<tr><td>24 kbps</td><td>49.57</td><td>4.67</td><td>8 kbps</td><td>10.91</td><td>2.69</td></tr>
<tr><td>8 kbps</td><td>1.43</td><td>1.27</td><td></td><td></td><td></td></tr>
</table>

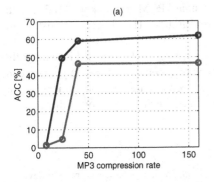
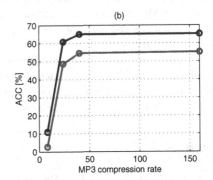

Fig. 5. LVCSR accuracy dependence on varying MP3 bit-rate for channels CS0 (blue line) and CS1 (green line): (a) MFCC features, (b) PLP features

For LVCSR tests we worked only with data from channels CS0 and CS1, i.e. channels with the most typical quality of signals used in LVCSR. Also only compression rates of 160, 40, 24, and 8 kbps were used (160 kbps can be assumed very close to full-precision data). The results were very similar to digit recognition task and they are summarized in the table 4 and in the figure 5. Finally, the accuracy is significantly lower in comparison with digit recognition but it is given by limits of used dictionary size and bigram LM. The reference accuracy presented in [25] was computed with more precise acoustic models and for MFCC features the value was 67.82%. Very similar results, around 65%, can be achieved also with MP3 recognition using PLP features from 40 kbps compression rate.

4   Conclusions

The analysis of speech recognition using MP3 compressed audio data was done. The achieved results confirmed acceptable accuracy of speech recognition of MP3 compressed speech data when reasonable compression rate is used. The most important contributions can be summarized in the following points.

- ACC decreases rapidly for shorter frame length of short-time features when MP3 speech is recognized. It is affected by perceptual masking in MP3 compression scheme and decreasing of short-time Fourier analysis frequency resolution used in computation of MFCC and PLP features. It means that the usage of longer short-time frame for Fourier analysis is necessary.
- Generally, the loss of accuracy is very small from bit-rate of 24 kbps. It was proved both with small vocabulary and large vocabulary recognition task. The size of compressed data for 24 kbps is just 10% of full precision linear PCM and ACC decreased for digit recognition by 6% for MFCC and 3% for PLP features. For LVCSR the difference in accuracy between results for signals with very high compression rate 160 kbps and low 24 kbps was approximately 11% for MFCC and only 5% for PLP.
- The results are worse for noisy channels where 50% decrease of ACC can be observed for MFCC features, comparing the standard PCM and 24 kbps MP3 speech signal from desktop microphone for digit recognition. This decrease is just about 8% for PLP features.
- Realized experiments proved that MP3 compressed speech files used in standardly available consumer devices such as MP3 players, recorders, or mobile phones, can be used for off-line automatic conversion of speech into text without critical loss of accuracy. PLP features seem to be preferable for speech recognition in this case.

References

1. Nouza, J., Červa, P., Ždánský, J.: Very large vocabulary voice dictation for mobile devices. In: Proc. of Interspeech 2009, Brighton, UK, pp. 995–998 (2009)
2. Chen, S.S., Eide, E., Gales, M.J.F., Gopinath, R.A., Kanvesky, D., Olsen, P.: Automatic transcription of broadcast news. Speech Communication 37(1-2), 69–87 (2002)
3. Gauvain, J.-L., Lamel, L., Adda, G.: The LIMSI broadcast news transcription system. Speech Communication 37(1-2), 89–108 (2002)
4. Vaněk, J., Psutka, J.: Gender-dependent acoustic models fusion developed for automatic subtitling of parliament meetings broadcasted by the Czech TV. In: Proc. of Text, Speech and Dialog, Brno, pp. 431–438. Czech Republic (2010)

5. Psutka, J., Psutka, J., Ircing, P., Hoidekr, J.: Recognition of spontaneously pronounced TV ice-hockey commentary. In: Proc. of ISCA & IEEE Workshop on Spontaneous Speech Processing and Recognition, Tokyo, pp. 83–86 (2003)
6. Makhoul, J., Kubala, F., Leek, T., Liu, D., Nguyen, L., Schwartz, R., Srivastava, A.: Speech and language technologies for audio indexing and retrieval. Proc. of the IEEE 88(8), 1338–1353 (2000)
7. Byrne, W., Doermann, D., Franz, M., Gustman, S., Hajič, J., Oard, D., Pichney, M., Psutka, J., Ramabhadran, B., Soergel, D., Ward, T., Zhu, W.J.: Automatic recognition of spontaneous speech for access to multilingual oral history archives. IEEE Trans. on Speech and Audio Processing 12(4), 420–435 (2004)
8. Bouvigne, G.: MP3 standard. Homepage (2007), http://www.mp3-tech.org
9. Brandenburg, K., Popp, H.: An introduction to MPEG layer 3. EBU Technical Review (June 2000)
10. Barras, C., Lamel, L., Gauvain, J.L.: Automatic transcription of compressed broadcast audio. In: Proc. of the IEEE International Conference on Acoustics, Speech, and Signal Processing, Salt Lake City, USA, pp. 265–268 (2001)
11. Pollak, P., Behunek, M.: Accuracy of MP3 speech recognition under real-world conditions. Experimental study. In: Proc. of SIGMAP 2011 - International Conference on Signal Processing and Multimedia Applications, Seville, Spain, vol. 1, pp. 5–10 (July 2011)
12. Fousek, P., Pollák, P.: Additive noise and channel distortion-robust parameterization tool. performance evaluation on Aurora 2 & 3. In: Proc. of Eurospeech 2003, Geneve, Switzerland (2003)
13. Bořil, H., Fousek, P., Pollák, P.: Data-driven design of front-end filter bank for Lombard speech recognition. In: Proc. of ICSLP 2006, Pittsburgh, USA (2006)
14. Rajnoha, J., Pollák, P.: ASR systems in noisy environment: Analysis and solutions for increasing noise robustness. Radioengineering 20(1), 74–84 (2011)
15. ITU-T: International Telecommunication Union Recommendation G.729, coding of speech at 8 kbit/s using conjugate-structure algebraic-code-excited linear prediction(CS-ACELP) (2007), http://www.itu.int/ITU-T
16. ETSI: Digital cellular telecommunications system (Phase 2+) (GSM). Test sequences for the Adaptive Multi-Rate (AMR) speech codec (2007), http://www.etsi.org
17. Valin, J.M.: The speex codec manual. version 1.2 beta 3 (2007), http://www.speex.org
18. Cheng, M., et. al.: LAME MP3 encoder 3.99 alpha 10 (2008), http://www.free-codecs.com
19. Huang, X., Acero, A., Hon, H.-W.: Spoken Language Processing. Prentice-Hall (2001)
20. Young, S., et al.: The HTK Book, Version 3.4.1, Cambridge (2009)
21. Psutka, J., Müller, L., Psutka, J.V.: Comparison of MFCC and PLP parameterization in the speaker independent continuous speech recognition task. In: Proc. of Eurospeech 2001, Aalborg, Denmark (2001)
22. Hermansky, H.: Perceptual linear predictive (PLP) analysis of speech. Journal of the Acoustical Society of America 87(4), 1738–1752 (1990)
23. Institute of the Czech National Corpus: Homepage (2010) http://www.korpus.cz.
24. Institute of the Czech National Corpus: SYN2006PUB - corpus of newspapers and magazines from 1989-2004 (2006), http://ucnk.ff.cuni.cz/english/syn2006pub.php
25. Prochazka, V., Pollak, P., Zdansky, J., Nouza, J.: Performance of Czech speech recognition with language models created from public resources. Radioengineering 20(4), 1002–1008 (2011)
26. Fousek, P.: CtuCopy-Universal feature extractor and speech enhancer (2006), http://noel.feld.cvut.cz/speechlab
27. ELRA: Czech SPEECON database. Catalog No. S0298 (2009), http://www.elra.info
28. Pollák, P., Černocký, J.: Czech SPEECON adult database. Technical report (April 2004)

Weight Based Fast Mode Decision for H.264/AVC Video Coding Standard

Amrita Ganguly and Anil Mahanta

Department of Electronics and Electrical Engineering
Indian Institute of Technology Guwahati, Assam, India
{a.ganguly,anilm}@iitg.ernet.in
http://www.iitg.ernet.in

Abstract. H.264/AVC video coding standard outperforms former standards in terms of coding efficiency but at the expense of higher computation complexity. Of all the encoding elements in H.264/AVC, inter prediction is computationally most intensive and thus adds to the computational burden for the encoder. In this paper, we propose a fast inter prediction algorithm for JVT video coding standard H.264/AVC. All images have certain characteristics that are inherent to them. Natural videos have many homogeneous regions. In video sequences, there are stationary regions between frames and regions with moderate to complex motion. From an in-depth analysis of the full search algorithm in which properties of each macroblock (MB) are studied in details, a method is proposed where each MB is given a weight depending upon its characteristics. The motion content and the homogeneity parameters of each MB is determined prior to the ME process. The MBs correlation with neighboring MBs in respect of predicted motion vectors (MV) and encoding modes are studied. Weights are assigned for these parameters and the final mode is selected based upon these weights. We propose a Weight Based Fast Mode Decision (WBFMD) process where we define four weights for each MB based on its motion content, homogeneity, value of the predicted MV and the encoding modes of the neighboring MBs. Smaller weights are assigned when these parameters have low values indicating a simple MB whereas larger weights are assigned when these parameters have high value indicating a more complex MB. The average video encoding time reduction in the proposed method is 70% compared to the JVT benchmark JM12.4 while maintaining similar PSNR and bit rate. Experimental results for various test sequences at different resolutions are presented to show the effectiveness of the proposed method.

Keywords: H.264/AVC, Inter prediction, Motion estimation, Weighted prediction.

1 Introduction

The H.264/AVC is the latest video coding standard developed by Joint Video Group (JVT) of ITU-T Video Coding Experts Group (VCEG) and ISO/IEC MPEG Video Group [1]. It offers better compression efficiency and greater flexibility in compressing, transmitting and storing video. There are many advanced techniques that significantly improve the performance of the H.264/AVC video coding standard but at the

M.S. Obaidat, J.L. Sevillano, and J. Filipe (Eds.): ICETE 2011, CCIS 314, pp. 420–431, 2012.
© Springer-Verlag Berlin Heidelberg 2012

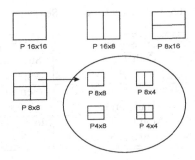

Fig. 1. Inter prediction block sizes for a MB

cost of higher computational overhead. The efficient inter prediction using the variable block size motion estimation (ME) and compensation increase the coding complexity. H.264/AVC permits the use of different block sizes, 16×16 pixels called a macroblock (MB) down to 4×4 pixels.

The H.264/AVC standard supports both intra and inter prediction processes. In the inter prediction process, there are seven block sizes P_{16x16}, P_{16x8}, P_{8x16}, P_{8x8}, P_{8x4}, P_{4x8} and P_{4x4} that are used by H.264 besides the SKIP and the INTRA modes [3], [2]. The block sizes are shown in Fig.1. For each MB, all the modes are tried and one which gives the least rate distortion (RD) cost is selected for encoding. The computation of the RD cost requires the availability of the reconstructed image and the actual bit count. This necessitates that the encoding and decoding processes are completed for every mode. Thus the computational requirements for the mode selection process is very high.

Several approaches have been proposed to reduce the complexity and time for the inter mode decision [4–14]. In [5] adaptive MB selection is used for mode decision. In [7] the fast motion estimation is based on the successive elimination algorithm (SEA) using sum norms to find the best estimate of the motion vectors and to implement efficient calculations for variable blocks. In [13] edge histogram parameters have been used for fast inter mode decision. In this paper, the characteristics of a MB is first analyzed based on the stationarity, homogeneity, predicted motion vectors (MV) and the encoding modes of neighboring MBs. All these parameters are first determined for each MB. Weights are then assigned to these MBs depending upon the values of these four parameters. The decision on the final encoding mode for the MB is taken based upon the weights of all these parameters. The proposed method gives a simple model for arriving directly at the encoding mode without performing rigorous ME. Results show that the proposed method speeds up the encoding process by 70% when compared to the JM12.4 software with negligible loss in quality and coding efficiency.

The paper is organized as follows. The next section introduces the proposed fast mode decision algorithm. Section 3 illustrate the results. The conclusions are drawn in Section 4.

2   Proposed Fast Decision Algorithm

In real video sequences the distribution of modes is not uniform among the MBs [3].

Table 1. Different Classes of Sequences

Type	CIF Sequence	QCIF Sequence
Class A	News, Mother and daughter Container, Hallmonitor	Suzie, Claire Missamerica
ClassB	Foreman, Coastguard Harbour, Ice	Foreman, Silent Crew
Class C	Mobile, Flower Tempete, Stefan	Mobile, Football Soccer

It depends upon the characteristics of the video sequences. Regions with homogenous motion, smooth motion of moving background and static background use larger block size motion compensation. For regions with high detail and complex motion, smaller block sizes to represent motion gives better coding efficiency. Changes between video frames may be caused by object motion, camera motion, uncovered regions and lighting variations. The neighboring video frames have large similarities between them. ME and compensation attempts to reduce the temporal redundancy by exploiting these similarities. Natural video sequences contain many regions with homogeneous motion that result in a large number of MBs being encoded with larger block sizes. The block size is also dependent on the QP. For large value of QP, more MBs tend to be encoded with larger block sizes. Since video sequences have different motion complexity, the sequences have been divided into three different classes: Class A having low and simple motion, Class B with medium to high motion and Class C with high and complex motion as given in Table 1.

2.1 Determination of Motion Content in a MB

Stationarity refers to the stillness between consecutive frames in the temporal direction. Regions having similar motion in consecutive frames are also considered temporally stationary. The MBs which are temporally stationary usually get encoded in the SKIP or in the P_{16x16} mode whereas MBs with large motion get encoded with smaller block sizes.

Figure 2 shows the difference frame formed by subtracting frame 10 from frame 11 of the Mother and Daughter (MaD) sequence. Regions which have little or no motion have zero or low frame difference residual values represented by the grey regions and are encoded with larger block sizes. The light and dark grey areas correspond to the positive and the negative differences representing higher motion activity and hence use smaller block sizes. The frame difference residue block R_{DF} is first obtained by subtracting the MB in the previous frame (MB_P) from the collocated MB in the current frame (MB_C).

$$R_{DF}(i,j) = MB_C(i,j) - MB_P(i,j), \quad i,j = 1,\ldots,16 \tag{1}$$

After performing full search on different classes of sequences, the MBs which are encoded in the SKIP mode and the corresponding residues in R_{DF} are studied at different QPs . Table 2 shows the distribution of these residues whose values are below a certain

Fig. 2. Difference image of frame 10 and 11 of Mother and Daughter sequence

Table 2. Relation between Residues per MB and SKIP mode

Type	QP	% of residues per MB in R_{DF} with residues					
		0	$\geq$1 and <2	$\geq$2 and <3	$\geq$3 and <4	$\geq$4 and <5	$\geq$5
	16	29.25	39.45	23.76	4.15	2.15	1.20
Class A	24	28.44	36.31	20.12	9.16	4.36	1.61
	36	24.77	34.35	20.16	10.11	5.74	4.87
	16	29.46	38.32	21.15	5.74	3.14	2.19
Class B	24	28.79	31.53	19.80	13.58	1.01	5.29
	36	19.81	34.71	18.13	9.09	3.95	13.31
	16	28.56	38.36	24.79	5.21	1.66	1.42
Class C	24	31.51	39.74	18.06	6.83	2.67	1.19
	36	30.34	25.96	15.15	7.65	12.42	8.48

quantity for different QP values (16, 24 and 36). The entries in the table are the percentage of residues averaged over all MBs in SKIP mode for the sequences of a particular class. Here we further show that more than 90 % of the values of the residues in R_{DF} for the skipped MBs are below 3 for low QPs.

From the analysis of the values in R_{DF}, we observe that at low values of QP, a MB encoded in SKIP mode has very low values of residuals in the corresponding R_{DF}. As QP increases, MBs in the SKIP mode have larger values of residuals in R_{DF}. Usually when MBs are encoded in SKIP mode, a large number of residuals in R_{DF} have values that are below 3 (Table 2). MBs having large motion have high valued residuals in R_{DF}. From Table 2, we note that the residuals (for QP values upto 24) of MBs encoded in the SKIP mode have more than 90% residuals with absolute values that are usually below 3. In the WBFMD algorithm, this variation in the value of the residuals with the QP for each mode is taken into consideration while assigning the weights. For each MB a weight is assigned depending upon the QP and the values of the residuals in R_{DF}. MBs with low values of residuals are given lower weights indicating a region with little motion whereas MBs with large values of residuals are assigned higher weights indicating high to complex motion. Thus a threshold TH_{24} for the residuals is taken for QP values upto 24 and TH_{24} is taken equal to 2. For higher values of QP, the threshold is defined as

$$\text{TH}_{\text{QP}} = \begin{cases} \text{TH}_{24} & \text{if QP} \leq 24 \\ \text{floor}[\frac{1}{4}(\text{QP} - 24) + \text{TH}_{24}] & \text{if QP} > 24 \,, \end{cases} \tag{2}$$

Hence with the increase in QP the threshold also increases. For each MB, let there be N residues in R_{DF} that are below the TH_{QP}. We define a residual ratio 'R' for each MB as the fraction of the residues 'N' in R_{DF} that are below the TH_{QP} to the total number of residues in R_{DF}.

$$R = \frac{\text{Number of Residues in } R_{\text{DF}} \text{ below } \text{TH}_{\text{QP}}}{\text{Total number of residues in } R_{\text{DF}}} = \frac{N}{256}.$$

A difference frame weight DF_{wt} is assigned to each MB based on the value of R and is given in Table 3 below.

Table 3. Difference Frame Weights DF_{wt}

R range	> 0.9	0.8-0.9	0.7-0.8	0.6-0.7	< 0.6
DF_{wt}	0	1	2	3	4

Larger values of DF_{wt} indicate a MB with higher motion content. Lower weights are assigned for MBs which have larger number of residuals below the threshold.

2.2   Determination of Homogeneity in a MB

Natural videos have many homogeneous regions. Homogeneous regions have similar spatial properties. A homogeneous region is defined by a common unifying character- istic throughout the whole area: there are no abrupt changes in the gray levels in the image. These regions in most cases get encoded with larger block sizes. Regions with more complex texture get encoded with smaller block sizes. If the homogeneity of a MB is detected early, then a decision on the possible encoding modes can be taken. There exist many techniques for detecting homogenous regions. In this work, the detection of homogeneous region is based on the edge information in the frame as video objects have strong edges. Homogeneous regions will have low values of the edge amplitude.

Sobel Operators are used to obtain the edge information. Each pixel in the block will be associated with an edge vector containing edge direction and amplitude. An edge vector $D_{i,j} = \{dx_{i,j}, dy_{i,j}\}$ is defined where

$$dx_{i,j} = p_{i-1,j+1} + 2 \times p_{i,j+1} + p_{i+1,j+1} - p_{i-1,j-1} - 2 \times p_{i,j-1} - p_{i+1,j-1} \tag{3}$$
$$dy_{i,j} = p_{i+1,j-1} + 2 \times p_{i+1,j} + p_{i+1,j+1} - p_{i-1,j-1} - 2 \times p_{i-1,j} - p_{i-1,j+1} \tag{4}$$

Here $dx_{i,j}$ and $dy_{i,j}$ are the differences in the vertical and the horizontal directions. The amplitude of the edge vector is computed as

$$Amp(D_{i,j}) = |dx_{i,j}| + |dy_{i,j}| \,. \tag{5}$$

Next, the sum of the edge amplitudes ($S_{Amp(N)}$) for a MB is considered, where

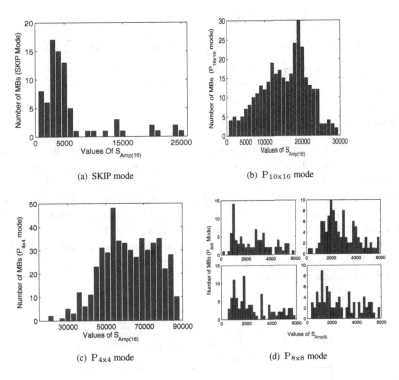

(a) SKIP mode

(b) P_{16x16} mode

(c) P_{4x4} mode

(d) P_{8x8} mode

Fig. 3. Distribution of number of MBs in different encoding modes with $S_{Amp(N)}$ for Mobile Sequence

$$S_{Amp(N)} \triangleq \sum_{i=1,j=1}^{N,N} abs(Amp(D_{i,j})), \quad N = 16, \tag{6}$$

Homogeneous regions have low values of edge amplitude. Thus $S_{Amp(N)}$ will have low values for such regions. If $S_{Amp(N)}$ is below a certain threshold (T_{th}) it is designated as a homogenous block otherwise it is nonhomogeneous. The decision is taken as follows:

$$Decision = \begin{cases} Homogeneous, & if & S_{Amp(N)} < T_{th(N)} \\ Non - homogeneous, & otherwise \end{cases}$$

The number of MBs in different modes was plotted against the value of $S_{Amp(N)}$ (N=16) and is shown in Figure 3 for the Mobile sequence. It clearly shows that for the SKIP mode the value of $S_{Amp(16)}$ is below 5000. For large block sizes, $S_{Amp(16)}$ is generally below 30000. For smaller block sizes, this value is significantly large.

In WBFMD algorithm, weights are assigned based on the values of $S_{Amp(16)}$ which are obtained from the study of the histogram characteristics for different sequences. Depending upon these statistics the weights assigned are given in Table 4. Lower weight is given for the MB if $S_{Amp(16)}$ is low and higher weight for larger values of $S_{Amp(16)}$.

Table 4. Homogeneous MB Weights Hom_{wt}

$S_{Amp(16)}$ Range	< 5000	5001-15000	15001-20000	20001-25000	> 25000
Hom_{wt}	0	1	2	3	4

2.3 Determination of Predicted MV

In H.264/AVC the predicted MVs (pmv) for a MB are obtained from the MVs of the neighboring MBs [3]. Motion vectors for neighboring partitions are often highly correlated. Thus the calculated pmvs give a good indication of the degree of possible motion in the MB. Higher pmvs indicate the possibility of higher motion for the MB and vice versa. In WBFMD algorithm, a pmv weight (pmv_{wt}) is introduced where weights are assigned for an MB depending upon the pmv for the MB. For low values of pmvs smaller weights are assigned and for higher values larger weights are assigned. This is given in Table 5 where pmv_x and pmv_y respectively are predicted MVs in in the horizontal and vertical directions.

Table 5. Predicted MV Weights pmv_{wt}

max $|pmv_x|$ or max $|pmv_y|$ or both	0	1-2	3-4	5	> 5
pmv_{wt}	0	1	2	3	4

2.4 Determination of Predicted Mode from Neighboring Modes

It is observed that the encoding modes of the neighboring MBs are often correlated. Referring to Figure 4(a), let C be the current MB and A, B and D be the neighboring MBs that have already been encoded. Let the encoding modes of A, B and D be A_{MODE}, B_{MODE} and D_{MODE} which take values assigned corresponding to the modes as given in Table in Figure 4(b). The following relation is used to determine the likely mode for C from the modes of A,B anc D:

$$Neigh_{MODE} = median\{A_{MODE}, B_{MODE}, D_{MODE}\}$$

Depending upon the value of $Neigh_{MODE}$ for a MB, a neighboring mode weight (NM_{wt}) is defined. If $Neigh_{MODE}$ for the MB indicate large block size partition then smaller weight is assigned to NM_{wt} and higher weight is assigned if block partition is small. The NM_{wt} for the MB is as given in the Table 6.

Table 6. Neighboring Mode Weights NM_{wt}

$Neigh_{MODE}$	SKIP	P_{16x16}	P_{16x8} P_{8x16}	P_{8x8} P_{8x4}, P_{4x8}	P_{4x4} INTRA
NM_{wt}	0	1	2	3	4

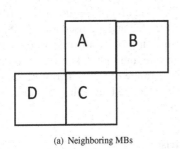

Mode	Value Assigned
SKIP	0
P16x16	1
P16x8	2
P8x16	3
P8x8	4
P8x4	5
P4x8	6
P4x4	7
INTRA	8

(a) Neighboring MBs   (b) Values assigned

Fig. 4. Neighboring MBs: C is the current MB and Values Assigned for different Modes

2.5 Overall WBFMD Algorithm

In WBFMD algorithm, for each MB, the four different weights are first determined and a total weight $Total_{wt}$ is defined for each MB as

$$Total_{wt} = [\,DF_{wt}\; Hom_{wt}\; pmv_{wt}\; NM_{wt}\,]$$

- If at least three weights in $Total_{wt}$ are same and is equal to say x (where x=0,1,2,3,4) then $Final_{wt}=x$
- If any two weights in $Total_{wt}$ are equal, then
  $Final_{wt}=$ceil (median ($Total_{wt}$))
- If all the weights in $Total_{wt}$ are unequal, then
  $Final_{wt}=$max($Total_{wt}$)

Based on this value of $Final_{wt}$, the decision on the encoding mode is taken. A low value of $Final_{wt}$ for a MB suggest that the MB is homogeneous with little motion and will be encoded with larger block sizes. A high value of $Final_{wt}$ indicate higher motion and complexity and will be encoded using smaller block sizes. The mode selection for each MB based on the value of the $Final_{wt}$ is given in Table 7.

Table 7. Final Encoding Modes for MBs

$Final_{wt}$	0	1	2	3	4
Mode	SKIP	P_{16x16}	P_{16x8} P_{8x16}	P_{8x8} P_{8x4},P_{4x8}	P_{4x4} INTRA

3 Results and Discussions

This section compares the results of the proposed algorithm with the previously reported Wu. *et al.*'s algorithm [13]. Results are presented as improvements over the standard H.264/AVC benchmark JM12.4. The experiments were carried out using some common video sequences of different classes at the CIF and QCIF resolution. The configuration used is the baseline profile, motion search range of ±16, sequence type IPPP and one reference frame. Only the first frame is intra coded and QP used are 24, 28, 32 and 36 as per the recommended simulation conditions in [16]. Comparisons are made in terms of distortion and percentage differences in rate and time taken for encoding. To evaluate the average encoding performance over a range of QPs, the differences in PSNR (ΔPSNR) in dB and bitrate (ΔRate (%)) are calculated according to numerical averages between RD curves as given by Bjontegaard [15].

3.1 Distortion and Compression Ratio Comparisons

Table 8 lists the performance of the proposed algorithm in comparison to JM12.4 implementation and Wu *et al.*'s algorithm [13]. The results are arranged for different classes

Table 8. Performance Comparison For Different Sequences

Class	Sequence	Performance Comparison					
		Proposed			Wu *et al.*'s [13]		
		ΔPSNR	ΔRate (%)	ΔT (%)	ΔPSNR	ΔRate (%)	ΔT (%)
CIF Class A	News	-0.05	2.29	88.42	0.02	2.01	39.23
	MaD	0.02	2.86	81.38	0.01	0.85	43.21
	Container	0.01	1.32	60.33	0.05	1.55	46.18
	Hall	0.09	0.40	76.84	0.06	0.90	34.67
Class B	Foreman	0.08	0.82	72.79	0.07	1.22	34.90
	Coastguard	-0.05	0.66	65.07	0.05	0.54	26.30
	Ice	0.05	3.14	85.17	0.07	1.29	45.68
	Harbour	0.06	1.88	65.37	0.05	1.10	21.56
Class C	Flower	0.08	0.19	76.43	0.05	2.98	36.85
	Stefan	0.08	1.59	70.59	0.02	1.46	32.25
	Tempete	0.02	0.82	71.88	0.09	1.02	27.21
	Mobile	0.04	1.88	62.41	0.09	1.69	12.35
	Average	**0.03**	**1.48**	**73.05**	**0.05**	**1.38**	**33.36**
QCIF Class A	Claire	-0.01	-2.81	90.69	-0.01	-0.95	47.35
	MissAmerica	-0.07	-1.40	89.87	0.02	0.91	48.23
	Suzie	0.04	1.21	77.73	0.05	0.49	42.91
Class B	Foreman	0.08	1.04	67.73	0.04	1.29	30.25
	Silent	0.03	2.40	82.46	0.09	0.79	42.62
	Crew	0.08	2.17	63.86	0.05	1.65	19.64
Class C	Football	0.10	1.50	65.30	0.05	1.86	32.42
	Mobile	0.14	1.62	28.09	0.07	1.50	15.32
	Soccer	0.04	1.17	63.67	0.03	3.03	20.19
	Average	**0.04**	**0.76**	**69.93**	**0.04**	**1.17**	**33.21**

MaD: Mother and Daughter.

ΔPSNR(+/-): picture quality loss/gain measured in dB.

ΔRate(+/-): bitrate increase/decrease measured as a %.

ΔT(+/-): encoding time saving/loss measured as a %.

of sequences. Class A sequences have simple motion, Class B sequences have medium to high motion and Class C sequences have high to complex motion. The trend in the results shows that for the sequences, there is only a marginal loss in the PSNR performance. There is an average 0.03 dB loss in PSNR in the proposed method. Also the average bitrate increase is 1.5%. The results demonstrate the effectiveness of the proposed algorithm.

3.2 Comparison with JM12.4 Modes

Table 9 shows the percentage of MBs that are encoded (using the proposed method) in the same mode as the JM12.4 for different QP. The results show that the proposed method is effective as it has been able to maintain the same final encoding modes as the JM12.4 to a large extent.

Table 9. % of MBs encoded in the same mode w.r.t FME

Sequence (CIF)	Quantization Parameter			
	24	28	32	36
News	82.10	75.12	84.12	86.01
MaD	66.12	87.86	89.6	90.66
Container	76.50	86.01	89.30	89.15
Hall	59.11	68.69	72.45	83.33
Foreman	46.11	58.71	64.90	76.23
Coastguard	62.33	67.83	78.84	79.47
Ice	67.42	73.99	71.97	72.98
Harbour	46.21	52.66	55.08	63.33
Flower	69.70	70.71	69.44	72.14
Stefan	22.73	57.32	66.31	68.99
Tempete	52.27	59.75	68.23	70.43
Mobile	29.80	34.34	49.39	66.19

3.3 Computational Speedup

Table 8 shows the percentage reduction in encoding time $\Delta T(\%)$ for sequences of different classes. The time saving obtained depends upon the type of sequence. An increased saving is noted for Class A sequences where for some sequences 90% time saving is noted whereas time saving obtained for Class C sequences is comparatively low. This is due to the fact that Class A sequences have low motion complexity and hence a large number of MBs get encoded with larger block sizes. The saving in time is achieved as the decision on the final mode for encoding is taken prior to the ME and for each MB at the most only three modes are searched. However, for all sequences, the proposed algorithm exhibits a good computational saving regardless of the QP setting.

4 Conclusions

In this paper, an improved mode decision algorithm for H.264/AVC video coding standard has been proposed based on the weights assigned for different characteristics of the

MB. Stationarity based weights are obtained from frame difference residuals. Homogeneity based weights are obtained from edge histograms parameters. The pmv weight and the neighboring mode weights are obtained from the correlation the the MB with neighboring MBs. Results of simulations carried out on different sequences demonstrate that there is very little degradation of the PSNR and the bitrate performance in the proposed algorithm despite a large saving in encoding time and computation. The average encoding time saving is around 70%. The proposed method achieves almost the same coding performance in terms of picture quality and compression ratio as that of the H.264/AVC standard and improves on Wu *et al.*'s [13] algorithm. Hence, for a variety of sequences with varying motion activities, the proposed algorithm gives a consistent performance on encoding time reduction, computational saving and coding efficiency.

References

1. Joint Video Team of ITU-T and ISO/IEC JTC 1, Draft ITU-T Recommendation and Final Draft International Standard of Joint Video Specification (ITU-T Rec. H.264— ISO/IEC 14496-10 AVC), document JVT-G050r1 (2003)
2. Wiegand, T., Sullivan, G.J., Bjontegaard, G., Luthra, A.: Overview of the H.264/AVC Video Coding Standard. IEEE Trans. on Circuits and System for Video Technology 13, 560–576 (2003)
3. Richardson, I.E.G.: H.264 and MPEG-4 Video Compression: Video Coding for Next-generation Multimedia. John Wiley and Sons (2003)
4. Jing, X., ChauSmith, L.F.: Fast approach for H.264 inter mode decision. Electronics Letters 40, 1050–1052 (2004)
5. Kim, D., Kim, J.-H., Jeong, J.: Adaptive Macroblock Mode Selection for Reducing the Encoder Complexity in H.264. In: Blanc-Talon, J., Philips, W., Popescu, D., Scheunders, P. (eds.) ACIVS 2006. LNCS, vol. 4179, pp. 396–405. Springer, Heidelberg (2006)
6. Kim, G.Y., Moon, Y.H., Kim, J.H.: An Early Detection of All-Zero DCT Block in H.264. ICIP 13, 453–456 (2004)
7. Lee, Y.-L., Lee, Y.-K., Park, H.: A Fast Motion Vector Search Algorithm for Variable Blocks. In: Blanc-Talon, J., Philips, W., Popescu, D., Scheunders, P. (eds.) ACIVS 2006. LNCS, vol. 4179, pp. 311–322. Springer, Heidelberg (2006)
8. Liu, Z., Shen, L., Zhang, Z.: An Efficient Intermode Decision Algorithm Based on Motion Homogeneity for H.264/AVC. IEEE Trans. on Circuits and System for Video Technology. 19, 28–132 (2009)
9. Park, I., Capson, D.W.: Improved Inter Mode Decision Based on Residue in H.264/AVC. In: International Conference on Multimedia and Expo., pp. 709–712 (2008)
10. Shen, L., Liu, Z., Zhang, Z., Shi, X.: Fast Inter Mode Decisions Using Spatial Property of Motion Field. IEEE Trans. on Multimedia. 10, 1208–1214 (2008)
11. Wang, H., Kwong, S., Kok, C.: An Efficient Mode Decision Algorithm for H.264/AVC Encoding Optimization. IEEE Trans. on Multimedia 9, 882–888 (2007)
12. Ganguly, A., Mahanta, A.: Fast Mode Decision Algorithm for H.264/AVC Intra Prediction. IEEE Region 10 Conference,TENCON, Singapore (2009)

13. Wu, D., Pan, F., Lim, K.P., Wu, S., Li, Z.G., Lin, X., Rahardja, S., Ko, C.C.: Fast Inter-mode Decision in H.264/AVC Video Coding. IEEE Trans. on Circuits and System for Video Technology 15, 953–958 (2005)
14. Zeng, H., Cai, C., Ma, K.: Fast Mode Decision for H.264/AVC Based on Macroblock Motion Activity. IEEE Trans. on Circuits and System for Video Technology 19, 1–11 (2009)
15. Bjontegaard, G.: Calculation of average PSNR difference between RD-curves. ITU-T VCEG, Doc. VCEG-M33. 1–2 (2001)
16. Sullivan, G., Bjontegaard, G.: Recommended Simulation Common Conditions for H.26L Coding Efficiency Experiments on Low-Resolution Progressive-Scan Source Material. ITU-T VCEG, Doc. VCEG-N81, 1–3 (2001)

Investigation and Improved Configuration Settings for H.264 CGS/MGS Quality Scalable Coding

Shih-Hsuan Yang and Wei-Lune Tang

Department of Computer Science and Information Engineering,
National Taipei University of Technology, 1, Sec. 3, Chung-Hsiao E. Rd., Taipei, Taiwan
shyang@ntut.edu.tw, allen08312002@hotmail.com

Abstract. The H.264/AVC scalable video coding (SVC) includes three kinds of video scalability, namely spatial scalability, temporal scalability, and quality scalability. Two options of quality scalability, CGS and MGS, may be used in combinations to achieve various quality layers. Using the CGS alone may incur high encoding complexity. Although the use of MGS may degrade the coding efficiency, it provides higher adaptation flexibility and reduces the coding complexity. In this paper, we investigate the CGS/MGS configurations that lead to good performance. From extensive experiments using the JSVM reference software, we suggest that MGS should be carefully employed. Although MGS always reduces the encoding complexity as compared to using CGS alone, its rate-distortion performance is unstable. Some configurations may cause an unexpected PSNR decrease with an increased bit rate. We investigate the reason and resolve the anomaly by a new CGS/MGS configuration scheme that restricts motion estimation to larger matching blocks.

Keywords: Scalable video coding (SVC), Rate-distortion optimization, Coding complexity, H.264/AVC.

1 Introduction

Video is used in diversified situations. The same video content may be delivered in different and variable transmission conditions (such as bandwidth), rendered in various terminal devices (with different resolution and computational capability), and served for different needs. Adaptation of the same video content to every specific purpose is awkward and inefficient. Scalable video coding (SVC), which allows once-encoded content to be utilized in flexible ways, is a remedy for using video in the heterogeneous environments [1].

Video scalability refers to the capability of reconstructing lower-quality video from partial bit streams. An SVC signal is encoded at the highest quality (resolution, frame rate) with appropriate packetization, and then can be decoded from partial streams for a specific rate or quality or complexity requirement. There are three common categories of scalability in video: spatial (resolution), temporal (frame rate), and quality (fidelity). The major expenses of SVC, as compared to state-of-the-art non-scalable single-layer video coding, are the gap in compression efficiency and increased encoder and decoder complexity.

M.S. Obaidat, J.L. Sevillano, and J. Filipe (Eds.): ICETE 2011, CCIS 314, pp. 432–445, 2012.
© Springer-Verlag Berlin Heidelberg 2012

The H.264 standard [2], also known as MPEG-4 AVC (Advanced Video Coding), has been dominating the emerging video applications including digital TV, mobile video, video streaming, and Blu-ray discs. Among the various efforts toward improving the coding efficiency, the most distinguished feature of H.264 is the adaptive coding mode decision. Flexible block sizes ranging from 16×16 to 4×4 can be used in motion estimation (ME) that finds the best match in the reference frames. There are two categories of coding modes, macroblock types (M types) and sub-macroblock types. The M-type partitioning includes matching areas of 16×16, 16×8, 8×16, or 8×8 luma samples and corresponding chroma samples. The sub-macroblock partitioning is activated if the 8×8 partitioning produces the lowest rate-distortion cost among the four M types. An additional syntax element is then used to specify each 8×8 partition for its further division into regions of 8×4, 4×8, or 4×4 luma samples.

The wide adoption and versatility of H.264/AVC leads to the inclusion of scalability tools in its latest extension [2][3]. There are two options for H.264 quality scalability, CGS (coarse-grain quality scalable coding) and MGS (medium-grain quality scalability). For CGS, a refinement of texture information is achieved by re-quantizing the texture signal with a smaller quantization step size (i.e., QP). Interlayer prediction may be employed to increase compression efficiency of CGS. The number of available CGS quality layers is restricted to the number of selected QPs. MGS is proposed to increase the flexibility of bit stream adaptation with possibly better coding efficiency. MGS provides the capability to distribute the CGS enhancement layer transform coefficients into more layers. Grouping information of the transform coefficients is signaled in the slice headers, and thus, a CGS layer can be partitioned into several MGS sub-layers and separately packetized. Pulipaka et al. [4] conducted statistical analyses of SVC, including the rate distortion and rate variability distortion performances. Görkemli et al. [5] compared MGS fragmentation configurations of SVC, including the slice mode and extraction methods.

In this paper, we examine the various H.264 CGS/MGS configurations that achieve multiple quality layers using the official reference software JSVM (Joint Scalable Video Model) [6]. Throughout the comprehensive experiments, unusual rate-distortion behavior for some configurations of SVC options was discovered. It is generally believed that an enhanced quality layer (with more received bits) shall improve the video quality. However, we find that adding an MGS sub-layer in some cases may conversely decrease the PSNR. We thus analyze and investigate this anomaly, which leads to an improved configuration scheme. The rest of this paper is organized as follows. In Section 2, we briefly review the H.264 SVC techniques, particularly CGS and MGS. Experiments on H.264 quality scalability with various JSVM CGS/MGS configurations are given in Section 3, which demonstrates the aforementioned oddity. An investigation to the abnormal rate-distortion behavior is also conducted. An improved CGS/MGS configuration scheme is proposed in Section 4. By restricting motion estimation to blocks larger than or equal to 8×8, the anomaly can be avoided along with better rate-distortion performance and lower encoding complexity. The conclusion is given in Section 5.

2   H.264 Scalable Video Coding

H.264 includes two layers in structure: video coding layer (VCL) and network abstraction layer (NAL). Based on the core coding tools of the non-scalable H.264 specification, the SVC extension adds new syntax for scalability [2][3]. The representation of the video source with a particular spatio-temporal resolution and fidelity is referred to as an SVC layer. Each scalable layer is identified by a layer identifier. In JSVM, three classes of identifiers, T, D, and Q, are used to indicate the layers of temporal scalability, spatial scalability, and quality scalability, respectively. A constrained decoder can retrieve the necessary NAL units from an H.264 scalable bit stream to obtain a video of reduced frame rate, resolution, or fidelity. The first coding layer with identifier equal to 0 is called the base layer, which is coded in the same way as non-scalable H.264 image sequences. To increase coding efficiency, encoding the other enhancement layers may employ data of another layer with a smaller layer identifier.

Temporal scalability provides coded bit streams of different frame rates. The temporal scalability of H.264 SVC is typically structured in hierarchical B-pictures. In this case, each added temporal enhancement layer doubles the frame rate. These dyadic enhancement layer pictures are coded as B-pictures that use the nearest temporally available pictures as reference pictures. The set of pictures from one temporal base layer to the next is referred to as a group of pictures (GOP). It is found from experiments that the GOP size of 8 or 16 usually achieves the best rate-distortion performance [3]. Note that the GOP size also determines the total number of temporal layers, i.e., the number of temporal layers = $(\log_2 \text{GOPsize}) + 1$.

Each layer of H.264 spatial scalability corresponds to a specific spatial resolution. In addition to the basic coding tools of non-scalable H.264, each spatial enhancement layer may employ the so-called interlayer prediction, which employs the correlation from the lower layer (resolution). There are three prediction modes of interlayer coding: interlayer intra prediction, interlayer motion prediction, and interlayer residual prediction. Accordingly, the up-sampled reconstructed intra signal, the macroblock partitioning and the associated motion vectors, or the up-sampled residual derived from the colocated blocks in the reference layer, are used as prediction signals. The interlayer prediction shall compete with the intra-layer temporal prediction for determining the best prediction mode.

Quality scalable layers, which are the main concern of this paper, have identical spatio-temporal resolution but different fidelity levels. H.264 offers two options for quality scalability, CGS (coarse-grain quality scalable coding) and MGS (medium-grain quality scalability). An enhancement layer of CGS is obtained by requantizing the (residual) texture signal with a smaller quantization step size (i.e., quantization parameter, QP). CGS incorporates the interlayer prediction mechanisms very similar to those used in spatial scalability, but with the same picture sizes for the base and enhancement layers. Besides, the up-sampling operations and the interlayer deblocking for intra-coded reference layer macroblocks are omitted. Also, the interlayer intra and interlayer residual predictions are directly performed in the transform domain. SVC supports up to 8 CGS layers but the interlayer prediction is constrained to at most three CGS layers including the required base layer. Usually, a significant difference in QP, which corresponds to largely deviated bit rates, is expected in order to achieve good RD performance [3][4]. In Fig. 1, 4-layer CGS and 8-layer CGS are

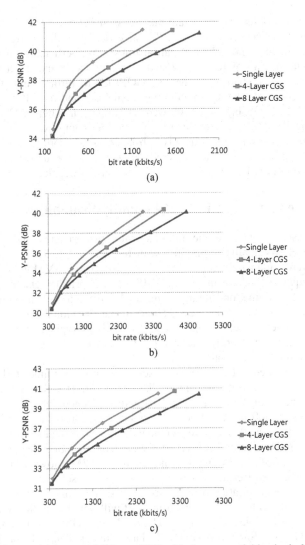

Fig. 1. Comparisons of 4-layer and 8-layer CGS with the non-scalable single-layer coding, (a) Foreman, (b) Mobile, (c) Tempete. 4-layer CGS: QP = 36-28-24-20, 8-layer CGS: QP = 36-32-30-28-26-24-22-20. The single layer is individually coded for each QP (36-28-24-20) with non-scalable H.264 coding. Simulation is based on JSVM 9.19.9, and the results with JSVM 9.19.13 show little difference.

compared with the non-scalable single-layer H.264 coding. More notable PSNR losses are observed for 8-layer CGS, as expected.

MGS is proposed in SVC to increase the adaptation flexibility, improve the coding efficiency, and reduce the coding complexity. A CGS layer that corresponds to a certain QP can be partitioned into several MGS sub-layers and distributed over different NAL units. An MGS sub-layer corresponds to a group of transform coefficients of 4x4 blocks in the zigzag order. The first and the last scan index for transform coefficients are signaled in the slice headers. Thus, the slice data (and the corresponding NAL units) may only include the indicated partial transform coefficients for a certain QP. The MGS sub-layers can more flexibly switch in any access unit in contrast that the CGS layers can only be changed in the next GOP. JSVM further limits the total number of rate points not exceeding 16, counting both CGS and the MGS quality layers. Note that at most 8 CGS layers are allowed and a large number of CGS layers may incur significant PSNR degradation and high encoding complexity. Therefore, it may be preferable to incorporate MGS quality sub-layers inside some CGS layers if more rate points (say more than 4) are desired. However, some unusual rate-distortion performance is observed for some MGS configurations, as detailed in the next section.

3 Observed Anomaly in H.264 Quality Scalability

We comprehensively evaluate the rate-distortion performance and computational complexity for H.264 quality scalability, with focuses on CGS/MGS configurations. Experiments were conducted with JSVM 9.19.9 (2010) and JSVM 9.19.13 (2011) [6], on nine test sequences shown in Fig. 2. In JSVM, the primary encoding parameters are specified in the Main Configuration File (main.cfg), and the encoding parameters associated with each CGS layer are specified in the individual Layer Configuration File (layer$x$.cfg, where x denotes the dependency_id). A typical Main Configuration File and a typical Layer Configuration File are shown in Table 1. We list only the parameters important to our evaluations.

The GOPsize is fixed to be 16. We thus set the number of frames to be encoded as a multiple of 16 plus 1, to its maximum. (The extra one is added for accomplishing the reference pictures of the hierarchical B structure.) Hence, 289 frames are used for image sequences of 300 frames. EncodeKeyPictures controls the drift of prediction. The value set to 1 means that pictures with MGS ($Q > 0$) refinement are coded as key pictures. Only minor variation is observed if we use another EncodeKeyPictures value and the global rate-distortion trend does not change. JSVM allows at most three CGS layers if we set CgsSnrRefinement = 0. Therefore, we set CgsSnrRefinement = 1 (MGS) along with appropriate LayerCfgs to generate more than three quality layers. It is also found that the value of CgsSnrRefinement will not change the coding results if no more than three CGS layers are used. Thus, 3-layer CGS (CgsSnrRefinement = 0) and 3-layer MGS (CgsSnrRefinement = 1) have almost identical rate-distortion results. The parameter NumLayers specifies the total number of spatial/CGS layers. (Recall that CGS is regarded as a special case of spatial scalability.)

In a Layer Configuration File that corresponds to a specific QP, the parameter MGSVectorMode specifies whether MGS is used, i.e., whether the transform coefficients of the CGS layer are split into several MGS quality layers according to MGSVectorX. The parameter MGSVectorX specifies the number of transform coefficients in the Xth MGS sub-layer. The position of the transform coefficients is scanned in the zigzag order.

In the following, we present the simulation results for 4 quality layers and 8 rate points on three sequences Foreman, Tempete, and Flower. Throughout this paper, all the simulation is conducted on a personal computer with an Inter Core 2 Quad CPU (2.33 GHz) and 4GB RAM. The results for 4 quality layers are shown in Fig. 3. Three SVC configurations are examined: (i) 4-layer CGS, QP = 36-28-24-20; (ii) 3-layer CGS, QP = 36-28-20(4-12); (iii) 2-layer CGS, QP = 36-20(4-4-8).

Fig. 2. Test sequences, (a) Foreman (289), (b) Mobile (289), (c) Tempete (257), (d) City (289), (e) Bus (145), (f) Flower (241), (g) Soccer (289), (h) Football (257), (i) Harbour (257). The number in the parentheses indicates the number of frames to be encoded for simulation.

Table 1. Encoding parameters

(a) main.cfg

Parameter	Value	Remarks
FrameRate	30.0	
FramesToBeEncoded	-	number of frames
GOPSize	16	
CgsSnrRefinement	1	1: MGS; 0: CGS
EncodeKeyPictures	1	
MGSControl	2	ME+MC with EL, closing prediction loop at lowest and highest rate point
SearchMode	4	FastSearch
SearchRange	32	In full pels
NumLayers	4	CGS layers
LayerCfg	layer0-3.cfg	Layer configuration file

(b) layer3.cfg

Parameter	Value	Meaning
SourceWidth	352	Input frame width
SourceHeight	288	Input frame height
InterLayerPred	2	Interlayer Prediction (0: no, 1: yes, 2:adaptive)
MGSVectorMode	1	MGS vector usage selection
MGSVector0	4	Specifies 0th position of the vector
MGSVector1	4	Specifies 1st position of the vector
MGSVector2	8	Specifies 2nd position of the vector
QP	20	Quantization parameters

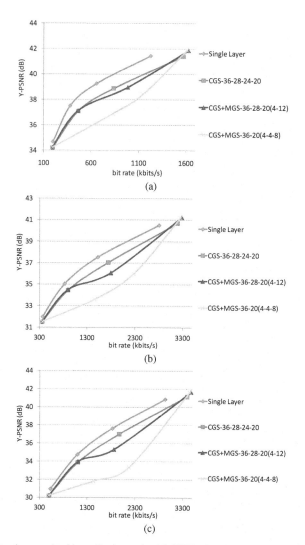

Fig. 3. Rate-distortion results (4 quality layers) with JSVM 9.19.13, (a) Foreman, (b) Tempete, (c) Flower

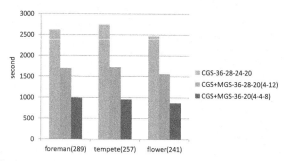

Fig. 4. Encoding time comparison (4 quality layers) with JSVM 9.19.13

A number in parentheses after a QP value denotes the MGSVector. Therefore, Configuration (ii), 36-28-20(4-12), indicates that 2 MGS sub-layers exist for the CGS layer with QP = 20 and these two sub-layers consist of 4 and 12 transform coefficients, respectively. As shown in Fig. 3, the inserted MGS sub-layers degrade PSNR performance. However, incorporating MGS significantly reduces the encoding time as compared to using CGS alone, as shown in Fig. 4. On the other hand, whether MGS is used has little effect on the decoding time. Although the results are shown only for three test sequences, the results for the other sequences generally exhibit similar behaviors.

The rate-distortion results for 8 quality layers are shown in Fig. 5 (with JSVM 9.19.9). Three SVC configurations are examined: (i) 8-layer CGS, QP = 36-32-30-28-26-24-22-20; (ii) 4-layer CGS, QP = 36-32-26(4-4-8)-20(4-4-8); (iii) 3-layer CGS, QP = 36-28(4-4-8)-20(2-4-5-5). Adding MGS sub-layers outperforms the pure CGS layers in most rate points for most test sequences. The inefficiency of CGS attributes to the decreasing interlayer correlation with dense QP settings. However, the first MGS sub-layer for QP = 20 may exhibit an unusual PSNR drop for some test sequences (Mobile, Tempete, Bus, Flower) with JSVM 9.19.9! A decreased PSNR is observed with more received bits, and then the rate-distortion plots gradually go back to their normal values. This anomaly becomes less significant in JSVM 9.19.13, but is not fully resolved as shown in Fig. 6. The encoding time comparison is shown in Fig. 7, which again confirms the time savings of MGS.

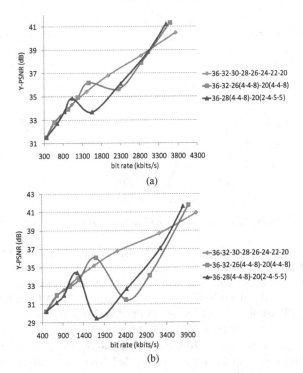

Fig. 5. Rate-distortion results (8 quality layers) with JSVM 9.19.9, (a) Tempete, (b) Flower

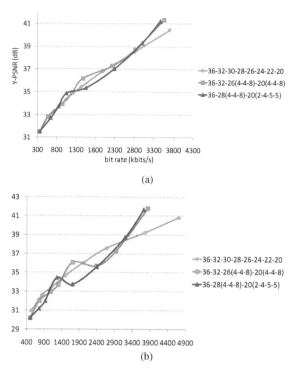

(a)

(b)

Fig. 6. Rate-distortion results (8 quality layers) with JSVM 9.19.13, (a) Tempete, (b) Flower

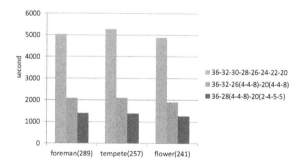

Fig. 7. Encoding time comparison (8 rate points) with JSVM 9.19.13

Further performance evaluations for JSVM 9.19.9 and JSVM 9.19.13 are shown in Fig. 8 for the Flower sequence, which yields the severest PSNR drop. We have explored the differences between these two versions, and found that the code is in fact the same. However, the default settings of two parameters, **BiPred8x8Disable** and **MCBlocksLT8x8Disable** are different. **BiPred8x8Disable** specifies whether the bidirectional prediction (bi-prediction) is disabled for sub-macroblock partitions (blocks smaller than 8×8). **MCBlocksLT8x8Disable** specifies whether motion-compensated blocks smaller than 8×8 are disabled. The values of these two parameters can be assigned at each Layer Configuration File. They are all set to 0 (enabling bi-prediction and motion compensation for sub-macroblock partitions) in JSVM 9.19.9. In JSVM9.19.13, however, these two parameters will be changed to 1 for encoding an MGS layer of a key picture (the last picture of a GOP) if the MGS layer is not the highest MGS layer. Further investigation on this issue reveals that the rate-distortion anomaly is strongly related to the fall-back of interlayer prediction, which implies that interlayer prediction fails to function. It is found that fall-back occurs at the last pictures of GOPs for some sub-macroblock partitions, and prediction error becomes significant when fall-back happens. We calculate the percentages of using sub-macroblock partitions and the occurrence of fall-back, and the results are summarized in Table 2, which substantiates the correlation between the fall-back and rate-distortion anomaly.

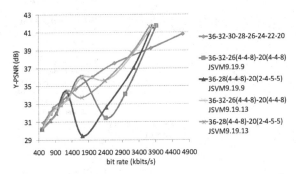

Fig. 8. Comparison JSVM 9.19.9 and JSVM 9.19.13 of the Flower sequence

Table 2. Percentages of small blocks and fall-back (in the last pictures of GOPs)

Test sequence	Rate-distortion anomaly	Percentage of sub-macroblock partitions (4x8, 8x4, 4x4) in ME	Percentage of fall-back
Football	No	1.35%	0.06%
Soccer	No	1.26%	0.14%
Foreman	No	4.00%	0.43%
Bus	Marginal	5.98%	0.73%
City	Marginal	14.33%	2.25%
Harbour	Marginal	15.51%	2.96%
Mobile	Yes	22.52%	6.83%
Tempete	Yes	26.21%	9.47%
Flower	Yes	25.46%	10.77%

4   Proposed Configuration Settings

Although sub-macroblock partitioning produces better prediction, it may cause fall-back and damage the compression performance. From experiments we found that disabling sub-macroblock partitioning (called 8x8disable in the following) by setting BiPred8x8Disable and MCBlocksLT8x8Disable to 1 can prevent the fall-backs to happen. Furthermore, such setting generally causes no or little rate-distortion penalty. In Fig. 9, six SVC configurations are examined: (i) 8-layer CGS, QP = 36-32-30-28-26-24-22-20; (ii) 4-layer CGS, QP = 36-32-26(4-4-8)-20(4-4-8) without 8x8disable (JSVM 9.19.13); (iii) 4-layer CGS, QP = 36-32-26(4-4-8)-20(4-4-8), 8x8disable at the first CGS layer; (iv) 4-layer CGS, QP = 36-32-26(4-4-8)-20(4-4-8), 8x8disable at the first two CGS layers; (v) 4-layer CGS, QP = 36-32-26(4-4-8)-20(4-4-8), 8x8disable at first three CGS layers; (vi) 4-layer CGS, QP = 36-32-26(4-4-8)-20(4-4-8), 8x8disable at all the four CGS layers. The results show that adopting 8x8disable defeats the CGS alone (case (i)) and JSVM 9.19.13 (case (ii)). The encoding time comparison is shown in Fig. 10. Disabling sub-macroblock partitioning also notably reduces the encoding time. The decoding time comparison is shown in Fig. 11. Decoding is far (at least fifty times) less complicated than encoding. It is observed that the difference in time consumption for different CGS layers and options is negligible.

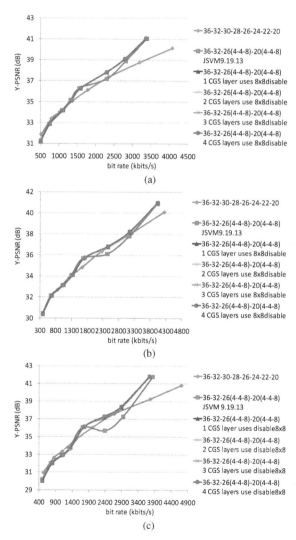

Fig. 9. Comparing 8x8disable (disabling sub-macroblock partitioning) with CGS alone and JSVM 9.19.13 for their rate-distortion performance, (a) Bus, (b) Mobile, (c) Flower

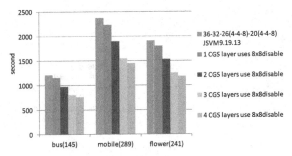

Fig. 10. Encoding time comparison, JSVM 9.19.13 vs. 8x8disable (disabling sub-macroblock partitioning) with different number of CGS layers

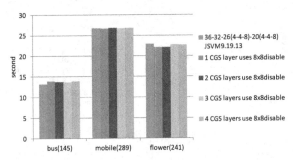

Fig. 11. Decoding time comparison, JSVM 9.19.13 vs. 8x8disable (disabling sub-macroblock partitioning) with different number of CGS layers

Table 3. Encoding time comparison (8 quality layers) for JSVM 9.19.9, JSVM 9.19.13, and the proposed configuration

Sequence	Encoding Time for CGS Alone (100%)	Encoding Time Percentage Relative to CGS Alone		
		JSVM 9.19.9	JSVM 9.19.13	Proposed Configuration
foreman(289)	5035.93s	41.37%	41.45%	26.43%
mobile(289)	6194.74s	38.33%	38.31%	23.33%
tempete(257)	5271.87s	39.85%	39.79%	24.11%
city(289)	4752.01s	41.34%	41.39%	24.94%
bus(145)	3037.60s	39.73%	39.85%	24.98%
flower(241)	4884.99s	38.97%	39.04%	24.32%
soccer(289)	5403.41s	41.63%	41.69%	25.76%
football(257)	5725.79s	40.30%	40.37%	25.05%
harbour(257)	6201.01s	39.16%	39.33%	24.19%
Average		**40.08%**	**40.14%**	**24.79%**

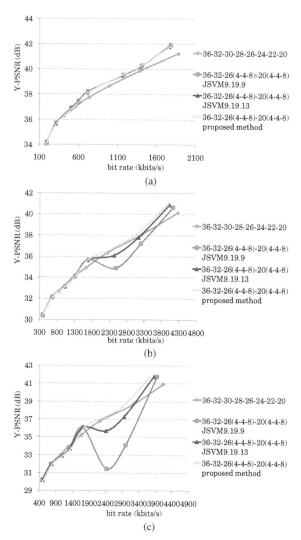

Fig. 12. Rate-distortion comparison JSVM 9.19.9, JSVM 9.19.13, and proposed configuration, (a) Foreman, (b) Mobile, (c) Flower

It is found that the MGS abnormality occurs only when the number of quality layers is more than 6. Therefore, we propose a configuration scheme by adaptively setting the two parameters **MCBlocksLT8x8Disable** and **BiPred8x8Disable**. If the number of quality layer is less than or equal to the threshold, **MCBlocksLT8x8Disable** and **BiPred8x8Disable** will be set to 0 (enabling sub-macroblock partitioning) at all layer configurations. If the number of quality layer is larger than the threshold, **MCBlocksLT8x8Disable** and **BiPred8x8Disable** are set to 1 at all layer configurations. The rate-distortion comparisons among JSVM 9.19.9, JSVM 9.19.13, and the proposed configuration are shown in Fig. 12. For sequences with normal rate-distortion behavior (such as Foreman, Soccer and Football), the proposed configuration achieves slightly better performance. For sequences with abnormal rate-distortion behavior (such as Mobile, Tempete, and Flower) the proposed configuration exhibits a significant PSNR edge. The proposed configuration outperforms method JSVM 9.19.13 by 1.61 dB at the sixth quality layer for the Flower sequence. The encoding time comparison is shown in Table 3, which substantiates the superiority of the proposed configuration. The proposed configuration is approximately 50 percent faster than JSVM 9.19.13.

5   Conclusions

The effects of CGS/MGS configurations of H.264 SVC are investigated in this paper. For four or fewer quality layers, CGS coding alone gives better coding performance despite of its high encoding complexity. For more quality layers, adding MGS sub-layers to the existing CGS layers may give better rate-distortion performance with reduced coding complexity. However, it is observed that some CGS/MGS configurations in the reference software may cause an unexpected PSNR drop for an enhanced quality layer. This abnormal behavior results from the malfunctioning of the interlayer prediction for sub-macroblock partitioning. Although this anomaly is relieved in the newer version of reference software (JSVM 9.19.13), it is not fully resolved. We propose a new configuration scheme that disables motion estimation and motion compensation with sub-macroblock partitioning when the number of quality layers is more than six. The proposed configuration achieves better rate-distortion performance with reduced encoding complexity.

Acknowledgements. This work was supported in part by the National Science Council, Taiwan (R.O.China), under the Grant NSC 100-2219-E-027-002.

References

1. Ohm, J.-R.: Advances in Scalable Video Coding. Proceedings of the IEEE 93, 42–54 (2005)
2. ITU-T Rec. H.264 (MPEG-4 AVC), Fifth Edition (including SVC and MVC extensions) (2009)
3. Schwarz, H., Marpe, D.: Overview of the Scalable Video Coding Extension of the H.264/AVC Standard. IEEE Trans. Circuits Syst. Video Technol. 17, 1102–1103 (2007)
4. Pulipaka, A., Seeling, P., Reisslein, M., Karam, L.J.: Overview and Traffic Characterization of Coarse-Grain Quality Scalable (CGS) H.264 SVC Encoded Video. In: Consumer Communications and Networking Conference, pp. 1–5 (2010)
5. Görkemli, B., Şadi, Y., Tekalp, A.M.: Effects of MGS Fragmentation, Slice Mode and Extraction Strategies on the Performance of SVC with Medium-Grained Scalability. In: IEEE International Conference on Image Processing, pp. 4201–4204 (2010)
6. JSVM Software Manual, Version 9.19.9 and Version 9.19.13 (2010/2011)

Part VI
Wireless Information Networks and Systems

Downlink Multiuser MIMO-OFDM Systems

Sebastian Aust[1], Andreas Ahrens[1], Francisco Cano-Broncano[2],
and César Benavente-Peces[2]

[1] Hochschule Wismar, University of Technology, Business and Design
Department of Electrical Engineering and Computer Science
Communications Signal Processing Group, Philipp-Müller-Straße 14, 23966 Wismar, Germany
[2] Universidad Politécnica de Madrid, E.U.I.T de Telecomunicación
Ctra. Valencia. km. 7, 28031 Madrid, Spain
aust.seba@googlemail.com, andreas.ahrens@hs-wismar.de
http://www.hs-wismar.de
fcbroncano@gpss.euitt.upm.es, cesar.benavente@upm.es
http://www.upm.es

Abstract. Multiple input multiple output (MIMO) techniques for wireless communication systems have attracted in the last years huge research activity due to the possibility of improving the link performance by increasing the channel capacity and decreasing the bit-error rate (BER). Due to the strongly increasing demand in high-data rate transmission systems, frequency non-selective MIMO links have reached a state of maturity and frequency selective MIMO links are in the focus of interest. In this field, the combination of MIMO transmission and OFDM (orthogonal frequency division multiplexing) can be considered as an essential part of fulfilling the requirements of future generations of wireless systems. However, single-user scenarios have reached a state of maturity. By contrast multiple users' scenarios require substantial further research, where in comparison to ZF (zero-forcing) multiuser transmission techniques, the individual user's channel characteristics are taken into consideration in this contribution. Furthermore, the use of multiple antennas both at the transmit and the receive front-ends introduces a correlation effect between the antennas due to their proximity producing interference. In consequence, the BER increases and the channel capacity decreases. The goal of the present contribution is to analyze the system performance under different spatial antennas distributions for Multiuser MIMO-OFDM systems in correlated and non-correlated fading channels. The performed joint optimization of the number of activated MIMO layers and the number of transmitted bits per subcarrier along with the appropriate allocation of the transmit power shows that not necessarily all user-specific MIMO layers per subcarrier have to be activated in order to minimize the overall BER under the constraint of a given fixed data throughput.

Keywords: Multiple-Input Multiple-Output System, Orthogonal Frequency Division Multiplexing, Singular-value Decomposition, Bit Allocation, Power Allocation, Wireless Transmission.

1 Introduction

Multicarrier transmission represents a suitable method for the digital signal transmission over linear distorting channels [1,2,3]. The available transmission bandwidth is

M.S. Obaidat, J.L. Sevillano, and J. Filipe (Eds.): ICETE 2011, CCIS 314, pp. 449–463, 2012.

decomposed into a number of narrowband channels in which data streams are transmitted with reduced speed. However, in order to comply with the demand on increasing available data rates in particular in wireless technologies, systems with multiple transmit and receive antennas, also called MIMO (multiple-input multiple-output) systems, have become indispensable and can be considered as an essential part of increasing both the achievable capacity and integrity of future generations of wireless systems [4,5,6]. Therein, the MIMO term refers to a technique which takes advantage of the spatial dimension of the underlying wireless channel by using multiple antennas at both the transmit (Tx) and the receive (Rx) side transmitting different data streams through each antenna at the same time and the same frequency. Multiple transmitting and receiving antennas are capable to reduce the error probability and increase the communication channel capacity without any bandwidth extensions.

MIMO systems have emerged as a promising technique to achieve high transmission capacities in wireless communication systems. MIMO systems feature a stronger dependency with the propagation channel conditions than single input single output (SISO) systems present; however MIMO systems are capable to reduce the bit-error probability and increase the communication channel capacity by exploiting received multipath signals without increasing neither the required transmitted power nor the signal bandwidth.

With the increasing desire for high-data rate communication, frequency non-selective MIMO links have reached a state of maturity. By contrast, frequency selective MIMO links require substantial further research. Spatial-temporal vector coding (STVC) introduced by RALEIGH seems to be an appropriate candidate for broadband transmission channels. Unfortunately, such solutions appear to be highly complex [7,8]. Therefore, complexity-reduced solutions are of great interest, where multicarrier transmission such as OFDM (orthogonal frequency division multiplexing) combined with multiple transmit and receive antennas seems to be a promising solution to reduce the complexity significantly. The combination of MIMO transmission and OFDM, as investigated in this work, can be considered as an essential part of fulfilling the requirements of future generations of wireless systems. However, single-user scenarios have reached a state of maturity. By contrast multiple users' scenarios in frequency-selective channel conditions require substantial further research [9,10].

Against this background, in this paper a SVD-assisted multiuser MIMO-ODFM scheme is investigated, where multiuser interferences as well as multi-antenna interferences are perfectly eliminated on each subcarrier. Instead of treating all users' channels jointly as in ZF (zero-forcing) multiuser transmission techniques, the investigated solutions take the individual users' channel characteristics into account [10]. The novel contribution of this paper is that we demonstrate the benefits of amalgamating a suitable choice of activated MIMO layers and number of bits per subcarrier under the constraint of a given fixed data throughput.

The remaining part of this paper is organized as follows: Section 2 introduces the subcarrier-specific MIMO-OFDM system model, while the proposed optimization objects are discussed in section 3. The associated performance results are presented and interpreted in section 4. Finally, section 5 provides some concluding remarks.

2   MIMO-OFDM System Model

In this section a subcarrier-specific MIMO-OFDM system model for both single-user and multi-user scenarios is developed where the arising subcarrier-specific interferences are perfectly eliminated. The system model considered in this work consists of a single base station (BS) supporting K mobile stations (MSs). The BS is equipped with n_T transmit antennas, while the kth (with $k = 1, \ldots, K$) MS has $n_{R\,k}$ receive antennas, i. e. the total number of receive antennas including all K MSs is given by $n_R = \sum_{k=1}^{K} n_{R\,k}$.

In order to combat the effects of the frequency selective MIMO channel, OFDM is used as transmission technique [11,1]. Together with a sufficient guard interval length, interferences between the subcarriers can be avoided and only symbols that are transmitted over the different antennas at same subcarrier can interfere each other. Thus, the arising multi-antenna and multiuser interferences between the different data streams, transmitted over the same subcarrier, require appropriate subcarrier-specific signal processing strategies [12].

2.1   Single-User System

Considering a single-user MIMO link ($K = 1$) composed of n_T transmit and n_R receive antennas, the obtained (n_R, n_T)-MIMO-OFDM system transmits an N-point IFFT (N subchannels) modulated data signal over every transmit antenna. The subcarrier-specific system is modelled by

$$\mathbf{u}^{(\kappa)} = \mathbf{H}^{(\kappa)} \cdot \mathbf{c}^{(\kappa)} + \mathbf{n}^{(\kappa)} \ . \tag{1}$$

In (1), the ($n_T \times 1$) vector $\mathbf{c}^{(\kappa)}$ contains the complex input symbols transmitted over the κth subcarrier on each input. Applying OFDM with a sufficient guard interval length, the ($n_R \times n_T$) matrix $\mathbf{H}^{(\kappa)}$ in (1) results in

$$\mathbf{H}^{(\kappa)} = \begin{bmatrix} h_{1\,1}^{(\kappa)} & \cdots & h_{1\,n_T}^{(\kappa)} \\ \vdots & \ddots & \vdots \\ h_{n_R\,1}^{(\kappa)} & \cdots & h_{n_R\,n_T}^{(\kappa)} \end{bmatrix} \ , \tag{2}$$

with the elements $h_{\nu\,\mu}^{(\kappa)}$ describing the couplings of the data symbols on the subchannel κ. The elements can be ascertained calculating the FFT of the channel impulse response from transmitter μ to receiver ν. Finally, $\mathbf{u}^{(\kappa)}$ describes the ($n_R \times 1$) received vector and $\mathbf{n}^{(\kappa)}$ is the ($n_R \times 1$) vector of the Additive, White Gaussian Noise (AWGN) having a variance of U_R^2 for both the real and imaginary parts.

The subcarrier-specific interference, introduced by the non-diagonal matrix $\mathbf{H}^{(\kappa)}$, requires appropriate signal processing strategies. A popular technique is based on the singular-value decomposition (SVD) of the matrix $\mathbf{H}^{(\kappa)}$, which can be written as

$$\mathbf{H}^{(\kappa)} = \mathbf{U}^{(\kappa)} \cdot \mathbf{V}^{(\kappa)} \cdot \mathbf{D}^{(\kappa)\,\mathrm{H}} \ , \tag{3}$$

where $\mathbf{U}^{(\kappa)}$ and $\mathbf{D}^{(\kappa)\,\mathrm{H}}$ are unitary matrices and $\mathbf{V}^{(\kappa)}$ is a real-valued diagonal matrix of the positive square roots of the eigenvalues of the matrix $\mathbf{H}^{(\kappa)\,\mathrm{H}} \mathbf{H}^{(\kappa)}$ sorted in descending order. The transpose and conjugate transpose (Hermitian) of $\mathbf{D}^{(\kappa)}$ are denoted by $\mathbf{D}^{(\kappa)\,T}$ and $\mathbf{D}^{(\kappa)\,H}$, respectively. Using $\mathbf{D}^{(\kappa)}$ as preprocessing matrix at the transmitter side and $\mathbf{U}^{(\kappa)\,H}$ as postprocessing matrix at the receiver side, the overall transmission relationship results in

$$\mathbf{y}^{(\kappa)} = \mathbf{U}^{(\kappa)\,H} \left(\mathbf{H}^{(\kappa)} \cdot \mathbf{D}^{(\kappa)} \cdot \mathbf{c}^{(\kappa)} + \mathbf{n}^{(\kappa)} \right)$$
$$= \mathbf{V}^{(\kappa)} \cdot \mathbf{c}^{(\kappa)} + \mathbf{w}^{(\kappa)} \ . \tag{4}$$

Thereby, as $\mathbf{D}^{(\kappa)}$ and $\mathbf{U}^{(\kappa)\,H}$ are unitary matrices, neither the transmit power nor the noise power is enhanced.

As a consequence of the processing in (4), the subcarrier-specific channel matrix $\mathbf{H}^{(\kappa)}$ is transformed into independent, non-interfering layers having unequal gains. The resulting subcarrier-specific layer-based MIMO-OFDM system model is highlighted in Fig. 1.

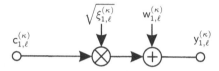

Fig. 1. Resulting subcarrier-specific layer-based single-user MIMO-OFDM system model

The data symbol $c_{1,\ell}^{(\kappa)}$ to be transmitted over the layer ℓ at the subcarrier κ (with $\ell = 1, 2, \ldots, \min(n_T, n_R)$ and $\kappa = 1, 2, \ldots, N$) is weighted by the layer-specific factor $\sqrt{\xi_{1,\ell}^{(\kappa)}}$, corresponding to the positive square root of the eigenvalue in $\mathbf{V}^{(\kappa)}$, and together with the additive noise term $w_{1,\ell}^{(\kappa)}$ the received data $y_{1,\ell}^{(\kappa)}$ results in

$$y_{1,\ell}^{(\kappa)} = \sqrt{\xi_{1,\ell}^{(\kappa)}} \cdot c_{1,\ell}^{(\kappa)} + w_{1,\ell}^{(\kappa)} \ . \tag{5}$$

Therein, the number of easily separable layers per subcarrier L is limited by the minimum numbers of antennas at both sides, the transmitter as well as the receiver side, i. e.,

$$L \leq \min(n_T, n_R) \ . \tag{6}$$

However, it is worth noting that with the aid of powerful non-linear near Maximum Likelihood (ML) sphere decoders it is possible to separate $n_R > n_T$ number of layers [13].

2.2 Multi-user System

Now, the subcarrier-specific single-user MIMO-OFDM system model ($K = 1$) is extended by considering a single base station (BS) supporting K mobile stations (MSs). The $(n_{R\,k} \times 1)$ user specific symbol vector $\mathbf{c}_k^{(\kappa)}$ to be transmitted by the BS over the subcarrier κ is given by

$$\mathbf{c}_k^{(\kappa)} = \left(c_{k,1}^{(\kappa)}, c_{k,2}^{(\kappa)}, \ldots, c_{k,n_{R\,k}}^{(\kappa)} \right)^T \ . \tag{7}$$

The vector $\mathbf{c}_k^{(\kappa)}$ is preprocessed before its transmission by multiplying it with the $(n_T \times n_{R\,k})$ subcarrier-specific DL preprocessing matrix $\mathbf{R}_k^{(\kappa)}$ and results in the $(n_T \times 1)$ user-specific transmit vector

$$\mathbf{s}_k^{(\kappa)} = \mathbf{R}_k^{(\kappa)}\,\mathbf{c}_k^{(\kappa)} \ . \tag{8}$$

After subcarrier-specific DL transmitter preprocessing, the n_T-component signal $\mathbf{s}^{(\kappa)}$ transmitted by the BS specific antennas over the subcarrier κ to the K MSs results in

$$\mathbf{s}^{(\kappa)} = \sum_{k=1}^{K} \mathbf{s}_k^{(\kappa)} = \mathbf{R}^{(\kappa)}\,\mathbf{c}^{(\kappa)} \ , \tag{9}$$

with the $(n_T \times n_R)$ preprocessing matrix

$$\mathbf{R}^{(\kappa)} = \left(\mathbf{R}_1^{(\kappa)}, \mathbf{R}_2^{(\kappa)}, \ldots, \mathbf{R}_K^{(\kappa)} \right) \ . \tag{10}$$

In (9), the overall $(n_R \times 1)$ transmitted DL data vector $\mathbf{c}^{(\kappa)}$ combines all K DL transmit vectors $\mathbf{c}_k^{(\kappa)}$ (with $k = 1, 2, \ldots, K$) and is given by

$$\mathbf{c}^{(\kappa)} = \left(\mathbf{c}_1^{(\kappa)\,\mathrm{T}}, \mathbf{c}_2^{(\kappa)\,\mathrm{T}}, \ldots, \mathbf{c}_K^{(\kappa)\,\mathrm{T}} \right)^{\mathrm{T}} \ . \tag{11}$$

At the receiver side, the $(n_{R\,k} \times 1)$ vector $\mathbf{u}_k^{(\kappa)}$ of the kth MS is given by

$$\mathbf{u}_k^{(\kappa)} = \mathbf{H}_k^{(\kappa)}\,\mathbf{s}^{(\kappa)} + \mathbf{n}_k^{(\kappa)} = \mathbf{H}_k^{(\kappa)}\,\mathbf{R}^{(\kappa)}\,\mathbf{c}^{(\kappa)} + \mathbf{n}_k^{(\kappa)} \ . \tag{12}$$

and can be expressed by

$$\mathbf{u}_k^{(\kappa)} = \mathbf{H}_k^{(\kappa)}\,\mathbf{R}_k^{(\kappa)}\,\mathbf{c}_k^{(\kappa)} + \sum_{i=1, i \neq k}^{K} \mathbf{H}_k^{(\kappa)}\,\mathbf{R}_i^{(\kappa)}\,\mathbf{c}_i^{(\kappa)} + \mathbf{n}_k^{(\kappa)} \ , \tag{13}$$

where the MSs received signals at the subcarrier κ (with $\kappa = 1, 2, \ldots, N$) experience both multi-user and multi-antenna interferences. In (12), the $(n_{R\,k} \times n_T)$ subcarrier-specific channel matrix $\mathbf{H}_k^{(\kappa)}$ connects the n_T BS specific transmit antennas with the $n_{R\,k}$ receive antennas of the kth MS.

The subcarrier-specific interference, which is introduced by the off-diagonal elements of the channel matrix $\mathbf{H}_k^{(\kappa)}$, requires appropriate signal processing strategies. A popular technique is based on the SVD of the system matrix $\mathbf{H}_k^{(\kappa)}$. Upon carrying out the SVD of $\mathbf{H}_k^{(\kappa)}$ with $n_T \geq n_R$ and assuming that the rank of the matrix $\mathbf{H}_k^{(\kappa)}$ equals $n_{R\,k}$, i.e., $\mathrm{rank}(\mathbf{H}_k^{(\kappa)}) = n_{R\,k}$, we get

$$\mathbf{H}_k^{(\kappa)} = \mathbf{U}_k^{(\kappa)} \cdot \mathbf{V}_k^{(\kappa)} \cdot \mathbf{D}_k^{(\kappa)\,\mathrm{H}} \ , \tag{14}$$

with the $(n_{R\,k} \times n_{R\,k})$ unitary matrix $\mathbf{U}_k^{(\kappa)}$ and the $(n_T \times n_T)$ unitary matrix $\mathbf{D}_k^{(\kappa)\,\mathrm{H}}$, respectively. The $(n_{R\,k} \times n_T)$ diagonal matrix $\mathbf{V}_k^{(\kappa)}$ can be decomposed into a

$(n_{R\,k} \times n_{R\,k})$ matrix $\mathbf{V}_{k\,u}^{(\kappa)}$ containing the non-zero square roots of the eigenvalues of $\mathbf{H}_k^{(\kappa)\,H} \mathbf{H}_k^{(\kappa)}$, i.e.,

$$
\mathbf{V}_{k\,u}^{(\kappa)} =
\begin{bmatrix}
\sqrt{\xi_{k,1}^{(\kappa)}} & 0 & \cdots & 0 \\
0 & \sqrt{\xi_{k,2}^{(\kappa)}} & \ddots & \vdots \\
\vdots & \ddots & \ddots & \vdots \\
0 & 0 & \cdots & \sqrt{\xi_{k,n_{R\,k}}^{(\kappa)}}
\end{bmatrix} ,
\tag{15}
$$

and a $(n_{R\,k} \times (n_T - n_{R\,k}))$ zero-matrix $\mathbf{V}_{k\,n}^{(\kappa)}$ according to

$$
\mathbf{V}_k^{(\kappa)} = \left(\mathbf{V}_{k\,u}^{(\kappa)} \ \mathbf{V}_{k\,n}^{(\kappa)} \right) = \left(\mathbf{V}_{k\,u}^{(\kappa)} \ \mathbf{0} \right) .
\tag{16}
$$

Additionally, the $(n_T \times n_T)$ unitary matrix $\mathbf{D}_k^{(\kappa)}$ can be decomposed into a $(n_T \times n_{R\,k})$ matrix $\mathbf{D}_{k\,u}^{(\kappa)}$ constituted by the eigenvectors corresponding to the non-zero eigenvalues of $\mathbf{H}_k^{(\kappa)\,H} \mathbf{H}_k^{(\kappa)}$ and a $(n_T \times (n_T - n_{R\,k}))$ matrix $\mathbf{D}_{k\,n}^{(\kappa)}$ constituted by the eigenvectors corresponding to the zero eigenvalues of $\mathbf{H}_k^{(\kappa)\,H} \mathbf{H}_k^{(\kappa)}$. The decomposition of the matrix $\mathbf{D}_k^{(\kappa)\,H}$ results in

$$
\mathbf{D}_k^{(\kappa)\,H} = \begin{pmatrix} \mathbf{D}_{k\,u}^{(\kappa)\,H} \\ \mathbf{D}_{k\,n}^{(\kappa)\,H} \end{pmatrix} .
\tag{17}
$$

Finally, the subcarrier-specific downlink received signal $\mathbf{u}_k^{(\kappa)}$ of the kth MS may be expressed as

$$
\mathbf{u}_k^{(\kappa)} = \mathbf{U}_k^{(\kappa)} \mathbf{V}_{k\,u}^{(\kappa)} \mathbf{D}_{k\,u}^{(\kappa)\,H} \mathbf{R}^{(\kappa)} \mathbf{c}^{(\kappa)} + \mathbf{n}_k^{(\kappa)} ,
\tag{18}
$$

with the vector $\mathbf{n}_k^{(\kappa)}$ of the Additive, White Gaussian Noise (AWGN). Taking all MSs received DL signals $\mathbf{u}_k^{(\kappa)}$ into account, the $(n_R \times 1)$ receive vector results in

$$
\mathbf{u}^{(\kappa)} = \left(\mathbf{u}_1^{(\kappa)\,T}, \mathbf{u}_2^{(\kappa)\,T}, \ldots, \mathbf{u}_K^{(\kappa)\,T} \right)^T .
\tag{19}
$$

The overall DL signal vector $\mathbf{u}^{(\kappa)}$ including the received signals of all K MSs can be expressed by

$$
\mathbf{u}^{(\kappa)} = \mathbf{U}^{(\kappa)} \mathbf{V}_u^{(\kappa)} \mathbf{D}_u^{(\kappa)\,H} \mathbf{R}^{(\kappa)} \mathbf{c}^{(\kappa)} + \mathbf{n}^{(\kappa)} ,
\tag{20}
$$

with the overall $(n_R \times 1)$ noise vector

$$
\mathbf{n}^{(\kappa)} = \left(\mathbf{n}_1^{(\kappa)\,T}, \mathbf{n}_2^{(\kappa)\,T}, \ldots, \mathbf{n}_K^{(\kappa)\,T} \right)^T ,
\tag{21}
$$

the $(n_R \times n_R)$ block diagonal matrix $\mathbf{U}^{(\kappa)}$

$$
\mathbf{U}^{(\kappa)} =
\begin{bmatrix}
\mathbf{U}_1^{(\kappa)} & \mathbf{0} & \cdots & \mathbf{0} \\
\mathbf{0} & \mathbf{U}_2^{(\kappa)} & \ddots & \vdots \\
\vdots & \ddots & \ddots & \vdots \\
\mathbf{0} & \mathbf{0} & \cdots & \mathbf{U}_K^{(\kappa)}
\end{bmatrix} ,
\tag{22}
$$

the $(n_R \times n_R)$ block diagonal matrix $\mathbf{V}_u^{(\kappa)}$

$$\mathbf{V}_u^{(\kappa)} = \begin{bmatrix} \mathbf{V}_{1u}^{(\kappa)} & \mathbf{0} & \cdots & \mathbf{0} \\ \mathbf{0} & \mathbf{V}_{2u}^{(\kappa)} & \ddots & \vdots \\ \vdots & \ddots & \ddots & \vdots \\ \mathbf{0} & \mathbf{0} & \cdots & \mathbf{V}_{Ku}^{(\kappa)} \end{bmatrix} , \tag{23}$$

and the $(n_T \times n_R)$ matrix $\mathbf{D}_u^{(\kappa)}$ which is given by

$$\mathbf{D}_u^{(\kappa)} = \left(\mathbf{D}_{1u}^{(\kappa)}, \mathbf{D}_{2u}^{(\kappa)}, \ldots, \mathbf{D}_{Ku}^{(\kappa)} \right) . \tag{24}$$

In order to suppress the DL multiuser interferences (MUI) at the subcarrier κ perfectly, the DL preprocessing matrix $\mathbf{R}^{(\kappa)}$ has to be designed to satisfy the following condition

$$\mathbf{D}_u^{(\kappa)\,H} \mathbf{R}^{(\kappa)} = \mathbf{P}^{(\kappa)} , \tag{25}$$

with the real-valued $(n_R \times n_R)$ diagonal matrix $\mathbf{P}^{(\kappa)}$ taking the transmit-power constraint into account. In order to satisfy (25), $\mathbf{R}^{(\kappa)}$ can be defined as follows

$$\mathbf{R}^{(\kappa)} = \mathbf{D}_u^{(\kappa)} \left(\mathbf{D}_u^{(\kappa)\,H} \mathbf{D}_u^{(\kappa)} \right)^{-1} \mathbf{P}^{(\kappa)} . \tag{26}$$

Taking the ZF design criterion for the DL preprocessing matrix into account, the matrix $\mathbf{P}^{(\kappa)}$ simplifies to an $(n_R \times n_R)$ diagonal matrix, i.e. $\mathbf{P}^{(\kappa)} = \sqrt{\beta^{(\kappa)}}\, \mathbf{I}_{n_R \times n_R}$, with the parameter $\sqrt{\beta^{(\kappa)}}$ describing the transmit-power constraint. When taking the DL preprocessing matrix, defined in (26), into account, the overall subcarrier-specific received vector of all K MSs, defined in (20), can be simplified to

$$\mathbf{u}^{(\kappa)} = \mathbf{U}^{(\kappa)} \mathbf{V}_u^{(\kappa)} \mathbf{P}^{(\kappa)} \mathbf{c}^{(\kappa)} + \mathbf{n}^{(\kappa)} . \tag{27}$$

Therein, the $(n_R \times n_R)$ block diagonal matrix $\mathbf{P}^{(\kappa)}$ is given by

$$\mathbf{P}^{(\kappa)} = \begin{bmatrix} \mathbf{P}_1^{(\kappa)} & \mathbf{0} & \cdots & \mathbf{0} \\ \mathbf{0} & \mathbf{P}_2^{(\kappa)} & \ddots & \vdots \\ \vdots & \ddots & \ddots & \vdots \\ \mathbf{0} & \mathbf{0} & \cdots & \mathbf{P}_K^{(\kappa)} \end{bmatrix} . \tag{28}$$

In (27), the user-specific $(n_{R\,k} \times 1)$ vector $\mathbf{u}_k^{(\kappa)}$ can be expressed as

$$\mathbf{u}_k^{(\kappa)} = \mathbf{U}_k^{(\kappa)} \mathbf{V}_{ku}^{(\kappa)} \mathbf{P}_k^{(\kappa)} \mathbf{c}_k^{(\kappa)} + \mathbf{n}_k^{(\kappa)} , \tag{29}$$

with the user-specific $(n_{R\,k} \times n_{R\,k})$ power allocation matrix

$$\mathbf{P}_k^{(\kappa)} = \begin{bmatrix} \sqrt{p_{k,1}^{(\kappa)}} & 0 & \cdots & 0 \\ 0 & \sqrt{p_{k,2}^{(\kappa)}} & \ddots & \vdots \\ \vdots & \ddots & \ddots & \vdots \\ 0 & 0 & \cdots & \sqrt{p_{k,n_{R\,k}}^{(\kappa)}} \end{bmatrix} . \tag{30}$$

As long as the transmit power is uniformly distributed over the number of activated MIMO layers per subcarrier, the matrix $\mathbf{P}_k^{(\kappa)}$ simplifies to

$$\mathbf{P}_k^{(\kappa)} = \sqrt{\beta^{(\kappa)}}\,\mathbf{I}_{n_{\mathrm{R}\,k} \times n_{\mathrm{R}\,k}}\ . \tag{31}$$

After postprocessing of the received signal vectors $\mathbf{u}_k^{(\kappa)}$ with the corresponding unitary matrix $\mathbf{U}_k^{(\kappa)\,\mathrm{H}}$, the user-specific decision variables at the subcarrier κ result with $\mathbf{U}_k^{(\kappa)\,\mathrm{H}}\mathbf{n}_k^{(\kappa)} = \mathbf{w}_k^{(\kappa)}$ in

$$\mathbf{y}_k^{(\kappa)} = \mathbf{U}_k^{(\kappa)\,\mathrm{H}}\,\mathbf{u}_k^{(\kappa)} = \mathbf{V}_{k\,\mathrm{u}}^{(\kappa)}\,\mathbf{P}_k^{(\kappa)}\,\mathbf{c}_k^{(\kappa)} + \mathbf{w}_k^{(\kappa)}\ , \tag{32}$$

or alternatively for the whole system with $\mathbf{U}^{(\kappa)\,\mathrm{H}}\mathbf{n}^{(\kappa)} = \mathbf{w}^{(\kappa)}$ in

$$\mathbf{y}^{(\kappa)} = \mathbf{U}^{(\kappa)\,\mathrm{H}}\,\mathbf{u}^{(\kappa)} = \mathbf{V}_{\mathrm{u}}^{(\kappa)}\,\mathbf{P}^{(\kappa)}\,\mathbf{c}^{(\kappa)} + \mathbf{w}^{(\kappa)}\ , \tag{33}$$

where subcarrier-specific interferences between the different antenna data streams as well as MUI imposed by the other users are avoided. The resulting resulting layer-specific multiuser SVD-based MIMO-OFDM system model is depicted in Fig. 2.

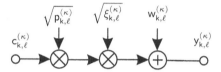

Fig. 2. Resulting kth user system model per MIMO layer ℓ (with $\ell = 1, 2, \ldots, n_{\mathrm{R}\,k}$) on subcarrier κ (with $\kappa = 1, 2, \ldots, N$)

3   Optimization Objectives

In general, the user-specific quality of data transmission can be informally assessed by using the signal-to-noise ratio (SNR) at the detector's input defined by the half vertical eye opening and the noise power per quadrature component according to

$$\varrho = \frac{(\text{Half vertical eye opening})^2}{\text{Noise Power}} = \frac{(U_{\mathrm{A}})^2}{(U_{\mathrm{R}})^2}\ , \tag{34}$$

which is often used as a quality parameter [14,9]. The relationship between the signal-to-noise ratio $\varrho = U_{\mathrm{A}}^2/U_{\mathrm{R}}^2$ and the bit-error probability evaluated for AWGN channels and M-ary Quadrature Amplitude Modulation (QAM) is given by [15]

$$P_{\mathrm{BER}} = \frac{2}{\log_2(M)}\left(1 - \frac{1}{\sqrt{M}}\right)\mathrm{erfc}\left(\sqrt{\frac{\varrho}{2}}\right)\ . \tag{35}$$

When applying the proposed system structure for the kth user, depicted in Fig. 2, the applied signal processing leads to different eye openings $U_{\mathrm{A}\,k\,\ell}^{(\kappa)}$ per activated MIMO layer ℓ (with $\ell = 1, 2, \ldots, L$ and $L \leq n_{\mathrm{R}\,k}$ describing the number of activated user-specific MIMO layers) and per subcarrier κ (with $\kappa = 1, 2, \ldots, N$) according to

$$U_{\mathrm{A}\,k\,\ell}^{(\kappa)} = \sqrt{p_{k,\ell}^{(\kappa)}} \cdot \sqrt{\xi_{k,\ell}^{(\kappa)}} \cdot U_{\mathrm{s}\,k\,\ell}^{(\kappa)} , \tag{36}$$

where $U_{\mathrm{s}\,k\,\ell}^{(\kappa)}$ denotes the kth user and κth subcarrier specific half-level transmit amplitude assuming M_ℓ-ary QAM, $\sqrt{\xi_{k,\ell}^{(\kappa)}}$ represents the corresponding subcarrier-specific positive square roots of the eigenvalues of the matrix $\mathbf{H}_k^{(\kappa)\,\mathrm{H}}\,\mathbf{H}_k^{(\kappa)}$ and $\sqrt{p_{k,\ell}^{(\kappa)}}$ represents the corresponding power allocation weighting parameters (Fig. 2). Together with the noise power per quadrature component, introduced by the additive, white Gaussian noise (AWGN) vector $\mathbf{U}_k^{(\kappa)\,\mathrm{H}}\,\mathbf{n}_k^{(\kappa)} = \mathbf{w}_k^{(\kappa)}$ in (32), the kth user-specific SNR per MIMO layer ℓ and subcarrier κ becomes

$$\varrho_{k\,\ell}^{(\kappa)} = \frac{\left(U_{\mathrm{A}\,k\,\ell}^{(\kappa)}\right)^2}{U_{\mathrm{R}}^2} . \tag{37}$$

Realizing a parallel transmission over L MIMO layers and taking all N subcarriers into account, the overall mean user-specific transmit power becomes $P_{\mathrm{s}\,k} = \sum_{\kappa=1}^{N}\sum_{\ell=1}^{L} P_{\mathrm{s}\,k\,\ell}^{(\kappa)}$. Considering QAM constellations, the average user-specific transmit power $P_{\mathrm{s}\,k\,\ell}^{(\kappa)}$ per MIMO layer ℓ and subcarrier κ may be expressed as [15]

$$P_{\mathrm{s}\,k\,\ell}^{(\kappa)} = \frac{2}{3}\left(U_{\mathrm{s}\,k\,\ell}^{(\kappa)}\right)^2 (M_{k\,\ell}^{(\kappa)} - 1) . \tag{38}$$

Combining (37) and (38) together with (36), the layer-specific SNR at the subcarrier κ results in

$$\varrho_{k\,\ell}^{(\kappa)} = p_{k,\ell}^{(\kappa)}\,\xi_{k,\ell}^{(\kappa)}\,\frac{3}{2\,(M_{k\,\ell}^{(\kappa)} - 1)}\,\frac{P_{\mathrm{s}\,k\,\ell}^{(\kappa)}}{U_{\mathrm{R}}^2} . \tag{39}$$

Assuming that the user-specific transmit power is uniformly distributed over the number of activated MIMO layers and subcarriers, the quality on each subcarrier is affected by both, the choice of the QAM-constellation sizes per layer and the layer-specific weighting factors [12]. In order to transmit at a fixed data rate while maintaining the best possible integrity, i. e., bit-error rate, an appropriate number of user-specific MIMO layers has to be used, which depends on the specific transmission mode, as detailed in Table 1 for the exemplarily investigated two-user system ($n_{\mathrm{R}\,k} = 4$ (with $k = 1,2), K = 2, n_{\mathrm{R}} = n_{\mathrm{T}} = 8$). An optimized adaptive scheme would now use the particular transmission modes on each subcarrier, e. g., by using bit auction procedures, that results in the lowest BER for each MIMO-OFDM data vector [16]. However, this would lead to a high signaling overhead. Therefore, in order to avoid signalling overhead, fixed transmission modes are used in this contribution regardless of the channel quality.

4 Results

In this contribution the efficiency of fixed user-specific transmission modes on each subcarrier is studied regardless of the channel quality. Assuming predefined transmission modes, a fixed data rate can be guaranteed. In order to obtain numerical results for

Table 1. Investigated user-specific transmission modes per subcarrier

throughput	layer 1	layer 2	layer 3	layer 4
8 bit/s/Hz	256	0	0	0
8 bit/s/Hz	64	4	0	0
8 bit/s/Hz	**16**	**16**	**0**	**0**
8 bit/s/Hz	**16**	**4**	**4**	**0**
8 bit/s/Hz	4	4	4	4

the analyzed subcarrier-specific signal processing strategies, a two-path channel model is investigated under time-variant conditions between any given transmit and receive antenna combination. The exemplary impulse response between the μth transmit and νth receive antenna as a function of the multicarrier symbol duration T_s is given by

$$g_k^{(\nu\,\mu)}(t,\tau) = g_{k,0}(t) \cdot \delta(\tau) + g_{k,1}(t) \cdot \delta(\tau - 3/2\,T_s) \;, \qquad (40)$$

whereby the time-variant behaviour is described by $g_{k,0}(t)$ and $g_{k,1}(t)$, respectively. It is assumed that the path amplitudes have the same averaged power and undergo a Rayleigh distribution [17]. Furthermore, a block fading channel model is applied, i. e., the channel is assumed to be time invariant for the duration of one MIMO-OFDM data vector including a guard interval length of $T_g = T_s/2$. The number of subcarrier of the investigated OFDM system was exemplarily chosen to be $N = 4$.

4.1   Single-User System

Considering a single-user MIMO-OFDM link ($K = 1$) composed of $n_T = 4$ transmit and $n_R = 4$ receive antennas, the corresponding calculated BER curves are depicted in Fig. 3 for the different subcarrier-specific QAM constellation sizes and MIMO configurations of Table 1, when transmitting at a fixed bandwidth efficiency of 8 bit/s/Hz per subcarrier. Assuming a uniform distribution of the transmit power over the number of activated MIMO layers per subcarrier, it still turns out that not all subcarrier-specific MIMO layers have to be activated in order to achieve the best system performance.

However, the lowest BERs can only be achieved by using bit auction procedures leading to a high signalling overhead [16]. Analyzing the probability of choosing subcarrier-specific transmission modes by using optimal bitloading, as highlighted in [12], it turns out that only an appropriate number of subcarrier-specific MIMO layers has to be activated to reach the best results, e. g., the $(16, 4, 4, 0)$ QAM configuration. Therefore, the results, obtained by using bit auction procedures, justify the choice of fixed subcarrier-specific transmission modes regardless of the channel quality as investigated in this contribution. Further improvements can be achieved by taking power allocation into account[18,19,20].

4.2   Antennas' Spatial Distribution

Spatial multiplexing is a method to reach the theoretical maximum channel capacity with a reasonable implementation complexity. Spatial multiplexing achieves the best

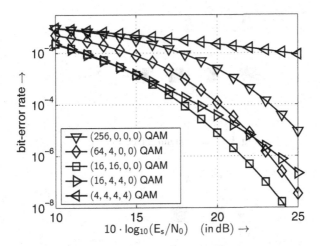

Fig. 3. BER when using the transmission modes introduced in Tab. 1 and transmitting 8 bit/s/Hz per subcarrier

performance in rich-scattering channels in which the paths suffer from uncorrelated fading. In many cases correlations between the transmit antennas as well as between the receive antennas can't be neglected. There are several methods to model and characterize the antenna signals correlation effects on the MIMO channel model in the Rayleigh flat-fading channel case. In this work it is assumed that the correlation among receive antennas is independent of the correlation between transmit antennas. The way to include the antenna signal correlation effect on the MIMO channel is described in [21,22].

In this section, we additionally analyze and simulate two different antennas spatial distributions (linear and non-linear uniform antennas distributions) for a MIMO system composed of $n_T = 4$ transmit and $n_R = 4$ receive antennas (single-user MIMO link, $K = 1$). The goal is showing the high dependency of both separation and distribution on the correlation degree and the impact of antennas correlation on the communication link performance. In the case of linear spatial distribution it is considered that the antennas are linearly distributed and equally spaced where this spacing is set to Δ_t and Δ_r (given in wavelength units) at the transmitter and receiver side, respectively. Fig. 4 represents the antennas' spatial distribution. In the second case of study a non-linear antenna array distribution with equal distance between adjacent elements is assumed. We have imposed in this exemplarily case that the chosen distribution is a square with one antenna at each corner. Again, the implemented MIMO system contains $n_T = 4$ transmit and $n_R = 4$ receive antennas (single-user MIMO link, $K = 1$). Fig. 5 shows the geometrical disposition of the antennas to be evaluated.

Taking the correlated MIMO channel instead of the uncorrelated one into consideration, we observe that the influence of the layer with the largest weighting factor increases.

Decreasing the distance between the receive antennas increases the correlation effect. Fig. 7 highlights the resulting BER for some exemplarily transmission modes (from those in Tab. 1) when diminishing the antennas spacing with respect to the previous

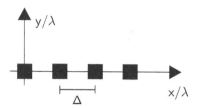

Fig. 4. Linear Antennas Distribution

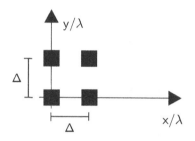

Fig. 5. Non-linear Antennas Distribution

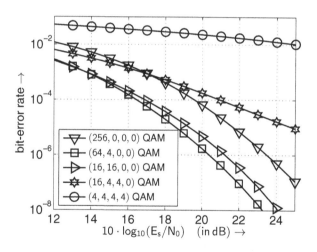

Fig. 6. BER when using the transmission modes introduced in Tab. 1 and transmitting 8 bit/s/Hz over correlated frequency non-selective channels (linear distribution of both the transmit and receive antennas with $\Delta_t = 10$ and $\Delta_r = 4$).

cases. In comparison with the results in Fig. 6 it is concluded that the shorter the distance between receive antennas the larger the BER and finally the link performance. Furthermore, continuing with the reasoning described above it is concluded that not all MIMO layers must be activated in order to obtain the best results. Concerning the

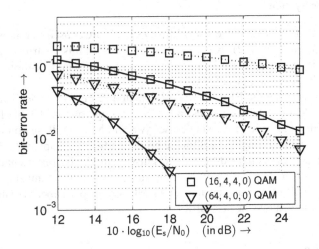

Fig. 7. BER with linear antenna distribution (solid line) and with non-linear antenna distribution (dotted line) when using the transmission modes introduced in Tab. 1 and transmitting 8 bit/s/Hz over correlated frequency non-selective channels ($\Delta_t = 10$ and $\Delta_r = 0{,}1$).

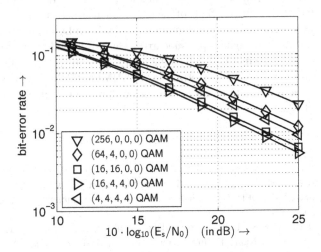

Fig. 8. User-specific BERs when using the transmission modes introduced in Table 1 and transmitting 8 bit/s/Hz per subcarrier

relation between the best performing transmission modes and the probability distribution function of the singular values, the high dependency of the transmission mode with the largest singular value can be remarked. This dependency increases with the correlation degree, the larger the correlation the higher the dependency. In consequence, as the correlation becomes stronger, the probability to use a lower number of layers increases.

4.3 Multi-user System

The parameters of the analyzed two-users MIMO system are chosen as follows: $P_{s\,k} = 1\,\text{V}^2$, $n_{R\,k} = 4$ (with $k = 1, 2$), $K = 2$, $n_R = n_T = 8$. In this contribution a power with the dimension $(\text{voltage})^2$ (in V^2) is used. At a real constant resistor this value is proportional to the physical power (in W).

The obtained user-specific BER curves are depicted in Fig. 8 for the different sub-carrier-specific QAM constellation sizes and MIMO configurations of Table 1 and confirm the obtained results within the single-user system ($K = 1$). Based on the higher total subcarrier-specific throughput within the given bandwidth compared to the single-user system, the gap between the different transmission modes becomes smaller.

Assuming a uniform distribution of the transmit power over the number of activated MIMO layers, it still turns out that not all MIMO layers per subcarrier have to be activated in order to achieve the best BERs.

5   Conclusions

In this paper, the DL performance of a multiuser MIMO-OFDM system is investigated theoretically and by software simulation. Frequency selective MIMO channels are considered and conditions to eliminate multiuser and multi-antenna interferences on each subcarrier are established using the SVD of the individual user subcarrier-specific channel matrix. Furthermore, bit allocation in multiuser MIMO-OFDM systems was investigated for constant data throughput per subcarrier. Here, it turned out that the choice of the number of bits per symbol as well as the number of activated MIMO layers per subcarrier substantially affects the performance of a MIMO-OFDM system, suggesting that not all user-specific MIMO layers per subcarrier have to be activated in order to achieve the best BERs.

References

1. Bingham, J.A.C.: ADSL, VDSL, and Multicarrier Modulation. Wiley, New York (2000)
2. van Nee, R., Prasad, R.: OFDM for Wireless Multimedia Communications. Artech House, Boston and London (2000)
3. Hwang, T.J., Hwang, H.S., Balik, H.K.: Adaptive OFDM with Channel Predictor over Frequency-Selective and Rapid Fading Channel. In: Personal, Indoor and Mobile Radio Communications (PIMRC), Bejing (China), September 7-10, pp. 859–863 (2010)
4. Zheng, L., Tse, D.N.T.: Diversity and Multiplexing: A Fundamental Tradeoff in Multiple-Antenna Channels. IEEE Transactions on Information Theory 49(5), 1073–1096 (2003)
5. Kühn, V.: Wireless Communications over MIMO Channels – Applications to CDMA and Multiple Antenna Systems. Wiley, Chichester (2006)
6. Zhou, Z., Vucetic, B., Dohler, M., Li, Y.: MIMO Systems with Adaptive Modulation. IEEE Transactions on Vehicular Technology 54(5), 1073–1096 (2005)
7. Raleigh, G.G., Cioffi, J.M.: Spatio-Temporal Coding for Wireless Communication. IEEE Transactions on Communications 46(3), 357–366 (1998)
8. Raleigh, G.G., Jones, V.K.: Multivariate Modulation and Coding for Wireless Communication. IEEE Journal on Selected Areas in Communications 17(5), 851–866 (1999)

9. Ahrens, A., Benavente-Peces, C.: Modulation-Mode and Power Assignment for SVD-assisted and Iteratively Detected Downlink Multiuser MIMO Systems. In: International Conference on Wireless Information Networks and Systems (WINSYS), Athens (Greece), July 26-28, pp. 107–114 (2010)

10. Liu, W., Yang, L.L., Hanzo, L.: SVD Assisted Joint Transmitter and Receiver Design for the Downlink of MIMO Systems. In: IEEE 68th Vehicular Technology Conference (VTC), Calgary, pp. 1–5 (2008)

11. Bahai, A.R.S., Saltzberg, B.R.: Multi-Carrier Digital Communications – Theory and Applications of OFDM. Kluwer Academic/Plenum Publishers, Dordrecht, New York (1999)

12. Aust, S., Ahrens, A., Benavente-Peces, C.: Modulation-Mode Assignment in SVD-aided Downlink Multiuser MIMO-OFDM Systems. International Journal of Electronics and Telecommunications (JET) 57(4), 459–464 (2011)

13. Hanzo, L., Keller, T.: OFDM and MC-CDMA. Wiley, New York (2006)

14. Ahrens, A., Lange, C.: Modulation-Mode and Power Assignment in SVD-equalized MIMO Systems. Facta Universitatis (Series Electronics and Energetics) 21(2), 167–181 (2008)

15. Proakis, J. G.: Digital Communications. McGraw-Hill, Boston (2000)

16. Wong, C.Y., Cheng, R.S., Letaief, K.B., Murch, R.D.: Multiuser OFDM with Adaptive Subcarrier, Bit, and Power Allocation. IEEE Journal on Selected Areas in Communications 17(10), 1747–1758 (1999)

17. Pätzold, M.: Mobile Fading Channels. Wiley, Chichester (2002)

18. Krongold, B.S., Ramchandran, K., Jones, D.L.: Computationally Efficient Optimal Power Allocation Algorithms for Multicarrier Communications Systems. IEEE Transactions on Communications 48(1), 23–27 (2000)

19. Jang, J., Lee, K.B.: Transmit Power Adaptation for Multiuser OFDM Systems. IEEE Journal on Selected Areas in Communications 21(2), 171–178 (2003)

20. Park, C.S., Lee, K.B.: Transmit Power Allocation for BER Performance Improvement in Multicarrier Systems. IEEE Transactions on Communications 52(10), 1658–1663 (2004)

21. Durgin, G.D., Rappaport, T.S.: Effects of Multipath Angular Spread on the Spatial Cross-Correlation of Received Voltage Envelopes. In: IEEE Vehicular Technology Conference (VTC), Houston, Texas, USA, May 16-20, pp. 996–1000 (1999)

22. Zelst, A. V., Hammerschmidt, J. S.: A Single Coefficient Spatial Correlation Model for Multiple-Input Multiple-Output (MIMO) Radio Channels. In: 27th General Assembly of the International Union of Radio Science, Maastricht, August 02 (2002)

Experience in Deploying a Wireless Sensor Network in a Vineyard

José A. Gay-Fernandez and Iñigo Cuiñas

Universidade de Vigo, Dept. Teoría do Sinal e Comunicacións
Maxwell, s/n, 36310 Vigo, Spain
{jagfernandez,inhigo}@uvigo.es

Abstract. The experience in deploying and maintaining a wireless sensor network in a vineyard is presented in this chapter. The first problem to be solved is the lack of propagation models for radio propagation in vegetation environments when applying a peer to peer network design. So, the first task was to carry out measurement campaign that allows the definition of propagation models. Once the model is defined, the distances between adjacent networks could be estimated and then the network could be planned. Different problems appeared after deploying the network, and some of them are reported and analysed in the chapter. Finally some sensor data are presented as well.

Keywords: Propagation, Power Decay Factor, Wireless Sensor Network, Vineyard, Node, Sensor, Humidity, Temperature.

1 Introduction

The use of wireless sensor networks is nowadays in an exponential growing. Initially, these wireless networks were intended for indoor use, like home automation and industrial control [1] or medical applications [2]. But many other applications that were not considered at the beginnings are nowadays coming to light: outdoor networks and, especially, sensor/actuator networks in rural areas, forests and plantations. The research results provided by this work consider this later environment.

A wireless sensor network is intended to be deployed in a vineyard, and the maximum distance between installed nodes is necessary to be previously estimated. Thus, some propagation studies have been conducted in order to analyze the behavior of such specific radio channel at the frequency band assigned to these wireless networks: 2.4 GHz. Propagation studies in rural environments and plantations have to take into account the presence of vegetation in the propagation channel. Although there are several research works related to propagation at such condition [3,4] and also an International Telecommunication Union - Radiocommunication Sector recommendation [5], most of them are focused on classical master-slave (or base station to mobile terminal) configuration, where the base has a prominent height over the coverage area.

M.S. Obaidat, J.L. Sevillano, and J. Filipe (Eds.): ICETE 2011, CCIS 314, pp. 464–476, 2012.

However, the proposed sensor application is proposed to be deployed in terms of peer to peer collaborative networks where both, the transmitter and the receiver are at similar heights. And there is a lack in the scientific knowledge for radio propagation with such configuration [6].

Some previous work related to the deployment of a wireless sensor network (WSN) in a forest has been checked. In [7], the authors showed the importance of these WSN in the forest fire propagation analysis, but a radio propagation study appears to be needed in order to optimize the deployment of these WSN. Other reports [8] inform about the deployment of a WSN in order to analyze the forest fire propagation, but no study was done regarding the radio propagation conditions in these wooded environments.

The principal aim of this chapter is to provide a model to estimate the propagation behavior in vegetation environments, and to present the results obtained in an actual wireless network deployment in a vineyard, installed using this model.

Firstly, a propagation analysis is built, in order to compute the maximum distances between nodes. Then, the environment where the WSN were deployed is presented and after that, the main elements of the WSN are showed. The following section indicates the way the network has been installed, as well as the lessons learned during its deployment and maintenance. Results regarding sensor data and network behavior are presented in the fifth section. Finally, some conclusions are presented to close this paper.

2   Propagation Modeling

Before installing the wireless sensor network, it is necessary to study the maximum distance between consecutive nodes. There are some propagation studies in rural environments at 2.4 GHz, as [9], which presents a study on the propagation in mature forest at 2.4 GHz. Furthermore, the main parameters to take into account when deploying a wireless sensor network are shown in [10]. Thus, since wireless sensor nodes were going to be deployed at a mean height of 3 meters over the ground, and the vineyard grew up to 2 m, the propagation environment seems to be quite different from the ones presented at [9].

Since the propagation analysis could not be performed in a vineyard due to the advanced status of the vineyard harvest, two measurement campaigns were deployed into grasslands and scrublands, in order to obtain a general propagation equation for the vineyard environment by extrapolating data from these two different ambiences.

2.1   Measurement Campaign

A separate transmitter and receiver configuration has been used during both measurement campaigns. Thus, large distances between transmitter and receiver could be accomplished in order to check how the signal strength attenuation with distance is.

The transmitter equipment consisted of a signal generator Rohde-Schwarz SMR, which fed an omnidirectional wide band antenna, Electrometrics EM-6865. A portable spectrum analyser Rohde-Schwarz FSH-6 is used at the receiver system with an omnidirectional antenna, similar to the transmitter end.

The data was collected around two different radials at each environment. Each radial consists of 25 points and 150 meters at the grassland environment, and 16 points and 32 meters at the scrubland one. The number of power samples gathered at grass and scrub lands is 301 and 3010 respectively.

Three different heights were analysed for the transmitting and receiving antennas: 0.9, 1.2 and 1.6 meters. Both antennas were placed at the same height in our analysis, in order to simulate the best conditions for a peer to peer propagation.

2.2   Propagation Model

903 power samples per frequency were collected at each one of the 50 points under measure at the grassland environment. The power samples per frequency at each point were 9030 at the scrubland environment, because there was a high time-variance of the received power.

The objective of the data processing is the analysis of the results by means of a regression to know how the power decays with distance. The attenuation of the received power seems to fit a linear equation of the form:

$$P = P_0 - n \cdot 10 \cdot \log_{10}(d) \tag{1}$$

where d is the distance between transmitter and receiver in meters, P_0 is the received power, in dBm, at 1 meter from the transmitter, P is received power, in dBm too, at a distance d from the transmitter and n is a factor that shows the rhythm of the power decay with distance.

However, the performance of meadow environments suggests that the best option is the use of a double linear regression, with two sections depending on the distance to the transmitter, as defined in (2) and (3), where each one of the regression sections fits an equation similar to that mentioned above. In these two equations, d_{break} indicates the distance where both linear equations converge; P_{0x} is the received power, expressed in dBm, at 1 meter from the transmitter for the "x" regression; and n_x represents the power decay factor for the "x" regression, where "x" could be 1 or 2.

$$P = P_{01} - n_1 \bullet 10 \bullet \log_{10}(d) \; ; \; d < d_{break} \tag{2}$$

$$P = P_{02} - n_2 \bullet 10 \bullet \log_{10}(d) \; ; \; d > d_{break} \tag{3}$$

This situation could be explained because the presence of high vegetation could cut significantly the first Fresnel ellipsoid in the radio link between transmitter and receiver at some larger distances. Thus, at shorter distances the conditions could be considered line of sight, but the conditions are obstructed line of sight at distances approximately similar to the shoulder at the power decay curve.

When the previously explained regression fitting is applied to the collected samples, data from Tables 1 and 2 are obtained for grassland and scrubland respectively. These tables show the attenuation factors "n_1" and "n_2", obtained for the first and second regression section respectively; the mean error produced with this estimation; and the cut-off point (d_{break}) of the two regressions.

Table 1. Grassland regression data

H(m)	n_1	n_2	Error[dB]	d_{break} [m]
0.90	1.75	4.13	1.47	22
1.20	2.07	3.55	1.20	37
1.60	2.04	3.61	1.70	85

Table 2. Scrubland regression data

H(m)	n_1	n_2	Error[dB]	d_{break} [m]
0.90	2.63	4.63	2.61	13
1.20	2.20	5.18	1.23	13
1.60	1.88	5.58	1.60	13

Errors show in tables 1 and 2 represent the mean error that would be obtained when trying to predict the received power at a distance d from the transmitter with each one of the propagation equations.

Thus, results show a mean fitting error under 1.7 dB for each one of the three antenna height configurations under analysis at the grassland environment. This appears to indicate a quite high linearity of the regarded power samples. Furthermore, the higher the antennas are placed, the larger cut-off distances. As the first propagation piece of each equation shows much lower attenuation factors than the second piece, placing antennas as higher as possible seems to be the best choice, in order to get the best free space propagation conditions.

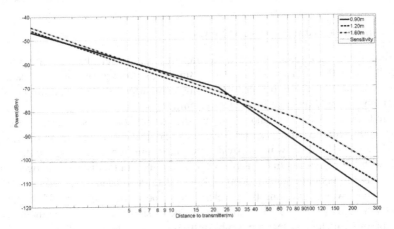

Fig. 1. Propagation equations in grasslands

Figures 1 and 2 show the equation fitting results at both environments. All the power values that are shown in the figures have been normalized to a transmission power of 0 dBm, in order to easily use with another transmitting power value.

The other environment under study, scrublands, appears to show more complicated propagation behaviour. Due to the high height vegetation in this environment, both antennas, transmitting and receiving, were surrounded by foliage, for the three antenna heights under study, and therefore, propagation models and results are very similar regardless the antenna height. For instance, the cut-off point is the same for the three antenna height and the power decay factors are very close. The main difference between these models seems to be related to the mean errors obtained in the regression process, which reach up to 2.61 dB for the lower antenna height.

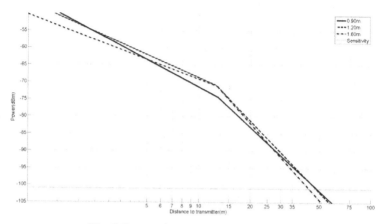

Fig. 2. Propagation equations in scrublands

Free space propagation conditions are not very common in vegetation environments for large distances between transmitter and receiver. Thus, this study addresses the problematic of determining the maximum distance between nodes.

2.3   Estimated Distance between Nodes

According to the eko node datasheet, the transmission power of these wireless nodes is +3 dBm and their sensitivity is -101 dBm. Thus, taking into account data from tables I and II and these power values, an estimation of the maximum distance between nodes could be done for both environments.

As indicated, figures 1 and 2 show the regression lines obtained for both environments with the aid of data from Tables 1 and 2. Furthermore, these figures show a dotted line at -101 dBm which provides the maximum range coverage at the point it crosses with the regression lines. Table 3 shows the maximum distances between nodes for each environment and antenna height. These data have been extracted from Figures 1 and 2. Thus, when deploying the wireless sensor network, nodes should be deployed with a maximum distance of 250 m if there is line of sight (LoS) between them and at a maximum of 48 meters if there are scrubs or trees between them.

Table 3. Maximum distances between nodes

H(m)	Grassland	Scrubland
0.90	123 m	48 m
1.20	162 m	48 m
160	254 m	44 m

The antenna heights considered for grasslands and scrublands campaign could represent the vineyard situation. There, the antennas would be higher over the ground, but the distance to the canopies would be similar to the distance to the ground at the commented measurements.

3   Environment

The selected environment to deploy this wireless sensor network is a vineyard located in a mountain side from Ribadavia, in Ourense, Spain. This vineyard is property of a large winery company founded on the appellation region "Ribeiro", in Galicia. This area is a very traditional wine producer, with more than two thousand years of history, documented since Greek and Roman eras.

This terrain is located in an exclusive area just in front of a water reservoir. The proximity of such amount of water causes high humidity in the surrounding terrains, and because of this, and the high mean temperature, the risk of suffering a plague in the vineyard rise up to values extremely high. So, the interest in controlling the ambient parameters is also high. Besides, different grape varieties are planted at various sections of the terrain. These are the main reasons for which this environment has been selected for this pilot experience.

4   Equipment

The Crossbow Eko pro series kit was the selected equipment for the wireless sensor network (WSN) deployment. This kit is a wireless agricultural and environmental sensing system for precision agriculture, microclimate studies and environmental research. Figure 3 depicts the main components of this WSN kit.

The Eko system can be enhanced with various sensors such as soil moisture, ambient humidity and temperature, leaf wetness, soil water content and solar radiation. All of them are going to be used in the deployment under analysis.

The main components of the WSN are showed in figure 4. There are the eko nodes, an Eko base station, and several sensors plugged into each eko node. The following sections describe each item in detail and the way they are interconnected.

4.1   Wireless Sensor Nodes

The eko nodes (Figure 3 in yellow) are a fully integrated, outdoor, solar-powered wireless sensing device that allows users to deploy a multi-point monitoring solution that provides real-time data from their environment. These nodes are capable of an outdoor range up to 2 miles depending on the environment and node hardware configuration chosen.

Each eko node can accommodate up to 4 different sensors. These nodes integrate a Memsic's IRIS processor radio board and antenna, powered by rechargeable batteries and a solar cell.

Six of these nodes were deployed in this test, each one with four different sensors plugged in.

Fig. 3. Eko pro series kit

4.2   Sensors

Crossbow manual [11] contains the main features of the sensors installed in this pilot. The number of each kind of sensor in the WSN has been fixed according to the requirements of the vineyard owner. All of the nodes plugged temperature and humidity sensors, as well as leaf wetness. One of them was equipped by a meteorological station. Other installed sensors are focused on measuring solar radiation, or soil water content.

4.3   Gateway and Base Station

The eko base station (Figure 3 in black and grey) consists of three components: the eko base radio, the eko gateway and the eko view application.

The eko gateway is an embedded sensor network gateway device. It provides an Ethernet connection where a PC can be connected to view or copy all the WSN collected data.

The eko base radio is a fully integrated packaged that provides the connection between the nodes, sensors and Gateway. The base radio integrates another IRIS processor/radio board, antenna and USB interface board. This interface is used for data transfer between the base radio and the gateway. The eko view application has not been used for this pilot, since data cannot be visualized at the gateway location.

4.4   WSN Architecture

Sensor data gathered with the aid of the WSN is going to be locally stored in a PC. Both the computer and the gateway are going to be installed in a hut to get power supply for the equipment during the pilot duration.

The data stored in the local PC should be transmitted to a remote server at the University of Vigo. Thus, all the sensor data could be available in real time outside the vineyard. A GPRS modem is needed to achieve this data transmission, since there is no line of sight between the hut location and the winery building.

Figure 4 depicts the main schema of the whole system.

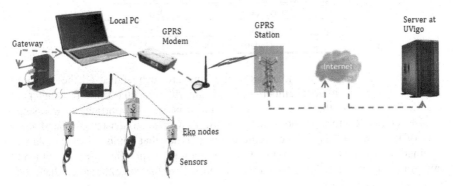

Fig. 4. System architecture

Figure 5 shows the transmission system, composed by the eko base station and a TC-65 GPRS modem from Siemens. This modem is connected to the laptop by a RS232-serial interface.

5   Network Deployment

5.1   Nodes Location

Up to 6 eko nodes have been deployed inside the vineyard. Each one with four different sensors plugged in. The distribution of the nodes along the vineyard has been done so each one was located in a sector planted with different variety of grape, according to the vineyards owner. Thus, the correspondence between node location and varietal at its terrain sector is shown in table 4. This table depicts also the estimated distances to the base station.

Fig. 5. Transmission system

Table 4. Node location and environment

Node	Grape variety	Distance to BS (m)
1	Godello	165
2	Albariño	345
3	Treixadura	80
4	Treixadura	200
5	Loureira	295
6	Godello	105

According to the recommendations of the vineyard technicians, all the eko nodes are able to measure ambient temperature and humidity, and the same parameters for the soil. Furthermore, the leaf wetness appears to be quite important, so this sensor has been connected to each node too. The interest of such sensor is related to the utility of its provided data in the prediction of plagues that could affect the plants: a combination of leaf wetness and direct solar radiation, in specific doses, could lead to some grape or vine illness. Solar radiation and soil water content sensors have been also equally distributed within the WSN.

5.2   Network Behavior

Table 5 shows the final network configuration and behavior according to the data gathered during December 2010. The second column presents the following node in the path towards the base station. These nodes are usually called "father" node. The third column indicates the distance between one node and its father. The last column shows the received signal strength indicator (RSSI) in dBm between a node and its father. These values depict that almost all the radio links between one node and its father are strong. The only one with some problems is the link between nodes 3 and 6. This link seems to have very low signal strength probably because there is a small terrain elevation between these nodes.

Figure 6 shows the architecture of the WSN deployment in the vineyard. Nodes are identified by an orange circle with the node number identification inside. Base station is represented by a blue circle. Black arrows show the main links of the network. Furthermore, if any of the nodes falls down, the network is able to auto-reconfigure by itself. For instance, in figure 6, if node 1 falls down, node 2 may communicate to the base station by node 6 directly, although the link quality probably would be worse.

Table 5. Network configuration and behavior

Node	Father	Distance (m)	RSSI (dBm)
1	3	88.5	-77.5<P<-74.5
2	1	80	-77.5<P<-74.5
3	6	110	-86.5<P<-83.5
4	Base	156	-77.5<P<-74.5
5	4	150	-77.5<P<-74.5
6	Base	40	-77.5<P<-74.5

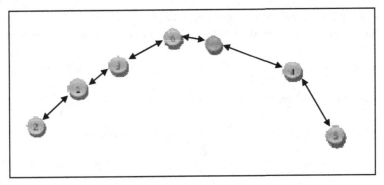

Fig. 6. WSN architecture

5.3   Learned Lessons

After the tests carried out during the network deployment, various lessons have been learned for future deployments, regarding base station and nodes locations and characteristics.

The base station should be in a clear zone, with the major line of sight to all the area to be covered. Thus, the range coverage will be as large as possible. Furthermore, the height of the base station antenna should be quite larger than the rest of the devices, in order to get line of sight with the higher number of nodes. Using an omnidirectional high gain antenna would be advisable with the purpose of increasing the range of coverage of the base station.

Nodes should be located always in line of sight with the following one and the predecessor. So if there are some foliage and vegetation blocking the line of sight to those devices, nodes should be placed in a higher position in order to improve the network behavior.

Nodes should be located according to the maximum ranges of coverage estimated in Table 3. On the one hand, when nodes were in line of sight situation, grassland values should be taken as an upper limit of the range of coverage. On the other hand, when nodes were in obstructed lien of sight due to foliage and vegetation, scrubland values should be used as the upper limits.

6   Results

Figures 7 to 10 present different data gathered by the sensors of the eko nodes.

For instance, Figure 7 shows the evolution of the ambient and soil temperature, in °C, during December, 2010. According to this data, the mean ambient temperature was 6.28°C with a standard deviation of 4.67°C, while the soil mean temperature was 7.26°C with a standard deviation of only 2.63°C.

Figure 8 represents the ambient humidity of node 1 during the same month. These data reveals that the mean ambient humidity is around 90% with a standard deviation of 10%.

Figure 9 depicts the soil water content present at the node 1 location. Peaks at day 7 and 10 indicate they were rainy days, followed by a 12 days period almost without rain.

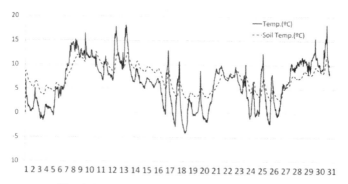

Fig. 7. Ambient and soil temperature (°C) Node 2

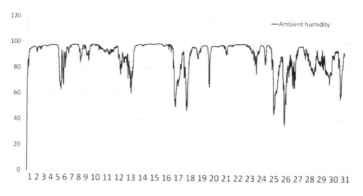

Fig. 8. Ambient humidity (%) Node 1

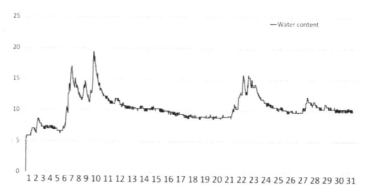

Fig. 9. Soil water content (%) Node 1

Other sensor data shows, for example, solar radiation, in Watts per square meter, present at each node location. (Figure 10).

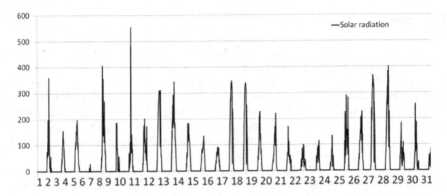

Fig. 10. Solar radiation (W/m2) Node 1

7   Conclusions

A complete measurement campaign was developed to model the propagation channel of the links among elements of a wireless sensor network. This propagation model has been used for planning an actual installation in a vineyard close to Ribadavia, in Galicia. The Eko technology, from Memsic, has been selected for this deployment. Up to 6 eko nodes were set up into the vineyard, to cover an area of approximately 6 km².

Four different sensors have been plugged into each eko node, to collect different ambient and soil parameters, like humidity, temperature, solar radiation, water content, etc.

With the aid of these sensor data, vineyard owners could, for instance, predict the appearance of a plague in their terrains or optimize the terrain irrigation. Furthermore, the time between chemical treatment applications in the vineyard could be extended. This last improvement may allow farmers to save a lot of money in material and labor, and reduce the amount of products applied to the vineyard, and so that, to the environment

The experience in deploying such a WSN had a return of investment in terms of learned lessons on some good practices. Thus, we could recommend the installation of the base station in an open and clear area, with line of sight to the nodes and placing the antenna as high as possible. The nodes should be placed looking for maintain line of sight conditions among the larger number of neighbors as possible, and respecting the maximum coverage ranges computed by the proposed propagation model.

Acknowledgements. This work has been supported by the Autonomic Government of Galicia (Xunta de Galicia), Spain, under Project PGIDIT 08MRU045322PR and by European Union under project "RFID from Farm to Fork" (CIP-Pilot actions grant number 250444).

The authors would also like to acknowledge Mr. Manuel Leites, who helped during the deployment.

References

1. Egan, D.: The emergence of ZigBee in Building Automation and Industrial Controls. Computing & Control Engineering Journal 16(2), 14–19 (2005)
2. Timmons, N.F., Scanlon, W.G.: Analysis of the performance of IEEE 802.15.4 for medical sensor body area networking. In: First Annual IEEE Communications Society Conference on Sensor and Ad Hoc Communications and Networks, pp. 16–24. IEEE SECON (2004)
3. LaGrone, A., Chapman, C.: Some propagation characteristics of high UHF signals in the immediate vicinity of trees. Transactions on Antennas and Propagation, IRE 9(5), 487–491 (1961)
4. Richter, J., Caldeirinha, R.F.S., Al-Nuaimi, M.O., Seville, A., Rogers, N.C., Savage, N.: A generic narrowband model for radiowave propagation through vegetation. In: Vehicular Technology Conference, vol. 1, pp. 39–43 (2005)
5. International Telecommunications Union-Radiocommunication Section (ITU-R): Attenuation in Vegetation-ITU-R Recomm. 833-6 (2007)
6. Hashemi, H.: Propagation Channel Modeling for Ad hoc Networks. In: European Microwave Week (2008)
7. Nükhet, S., Haldun, A.: The Importance of Using Wireless Sensor Networks for Forest Fire Sensing and Detection in Turkey. In: 5th IATS 2009, Karabuk, Turkey (2009)
8. Hefeeda, M., Bagheri, M.: Wireless Sensor Networks for Early Detection of Forest Fires. In: IEEE International Conference on Mobile Adhoc and Sensor Systems, pp. 1–6. IEEE MASS (2007)
9. Cuinas, I., Gay-Fernandez, J.A., Alejos, A., Sanchez, M.: A comparison of radioelectric propagation in mature forests at wireless network frequency bands. In: European Conference on Antennas and Propagation, EuCAP, pp. 1–5 (2010)
10. Gay-Fernandez, J.A., Garcia Sanchez, M., Cuiñas, I., Alejos, A.V., Sánchez, J.G., Miranda-Sierra, J.L.: Propagation Analysis and Deployment of a Wireless Sensor Network in a Forest. In: Progress In Electromagnetics Research, PIER, vol. 106, pp. 121–145 (2010)
11. Crossbow Technology, Inc.: Eko PRO Series Users Manual, Rev. C. (2010)

Experimental Detection and Synchronisation Validation for a TR-UWB System Based on the Time Delayed Sampling and CorreleHtion Scheme

Jorge A. Pardiñas-Mir, Muriel Muller, Roger Lamberti, and Claude Gimenes

Institut Telecom, Telecom SudParis, 9, rue Charles Fourier, 91011 Evry, France
{Jorge.Pardinas,Muriel.Muller,Roger.Lamberti}@it-sudparis.eu,
claudemonique.gimenes@orange.fr
http://www.telecom-sudparis.eu

Abstract. The detection and synchronization experimental validation of the "Time Delayed Sampling and Correlation" (TDSC) detection scheme for transmitted reference ultra-wideband signals (TR-UWB) is presented. This structure has been proposed to achieve a UWB system with low cost, low complexity and low power consumption for medium to low data rate applications which includes ranging for localization purposes. The scheme is implemented in CMOS technology and a test platform has been designed. Detection of TR-UWB signals and the principle of the proposed synchronization process have been done successfully in both a direct cable connection as well in a wireless system with a real channel. In both cases they were used in the sub GHz band (group 1) and also in the low band UWB signals. Further work and experimental results are also shown for a distance measurement strategy, based on the time of arrival (TOA) using the TDSC scheme.

Keywords: Ultra-wideband, TR-UWB, CMOS, TDSC, Time of arrival, TOA, Ranging, Indoor localization.

1 Introduction

Research and industrial work related to the use of the ultra-wideband (UWB) signals has increased in the last years since the new regulations on the subject were adopted by the U.S. Federal Communications Commission [1], leading to the definition of many standards [2], [3] and encouraged new applications [4], [5]. The Time Delayed Sampling and Correlation (TDSC) detection scheme is an alternative for pseudo-coherent receivers based on transmitted reference UWB (TR-UWB) signals, [6].The development of such device that presents low complexity, low power consumption and low-cost is the main goal at low-data rate communication applications. This scheme has been implemented in 0.35 μm CMOS technology, which design and first validation tests are presented in [7] and [8], while its theoretical study is explained in [9]. Work has also been done for developing a ranging strategy for positioning purposes based on the TDSC detection scheme considering that UWB signals are well suited for this application because of its time resolution [10].

M.S. Obaidat, J.L. Sevillano, and J. Filipe (Eds.): ICETE 2011, CCIS 314, pp. 477–491, 2012.
© Springer-Verlag Berlin Heidelberg 2012

This paper presents first, the results of the experimental validation of the TDSC scheme using the CMOS circuit, secondly, the development of a test platform to continue its study and finally, the work on a ranging strategy based on the time of arrival (TOA) estimation of TR-UWB signals. The TDSC detection method and the integrated circuit that implements it are described briefly in section 2. A synchronization process proposed for a receiver that uses the TDSC detection is explained in section 3. Section 4 presents the platform developed for testing the circuit and the detection scheme as well as the test configurations, while section 5 shows the results. Finally, section 6 describes the TOA measurement proposed strategy and some simulation and experimental results.

2   Time Delayed Sampling and Correlation Detection

2.1   The TDSC Detection Method

The TDSC method is based on the use of a UWB signal with a transmitted reference which is called a TR-UWB signal. In its simplest way this signal uses a pair of pulses, called doublet $d(t)$,(1) conforming to the FCC spectrum mask for each symbol transmitted with a period of T_S seconds: a reference pulse $g_1(t)$ and an information pulse $g_2(t)$ delayed by T_D seconds from the reference and modulated by the information bits b_k, (2).

$$d(t) = g_1(t) + g_2(t) \tag{1}$$

$$g_1(t) = p(t) \qquad g_2(t) = b_k p(t - T_D) \tag{2}$$

In the case of synchronization or ranging related symbols, $g_2(t)$ is not modulated, $b_k = 1$, carrying the same pulse shape as that of $g_1(t)$ but delayed by T_D seconds. The structure of a TR-UWB symbol can be seen in figure 1, with a length of T_S, for the case where a BPSK modulation is used. An information packet is transmitted by a series of M symbols (3).

$$d_s(t) = \sum_{m=0}^{M-1} d(t - mT_S) \tag{3}$$

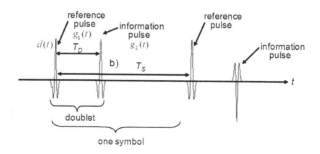

Fig. 1. Symbol structure of a TR-UWB signal

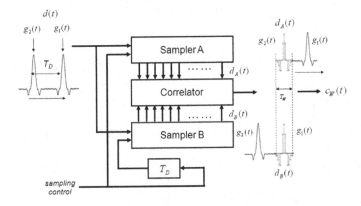

Fig. 2. TR-UWB detection scheme and samplers that substitute the analog delay line

In the wireless multipath propagation environment the received signal $d_r(t)$, (4), corresponds to the sum of many replicas of the transmitted signal plus the added noise $n(t)$, where each multipath component is a scaled and delayed version of the original pulse [11], as represented by the impulse response in (5). α_i and τ_i are the gain and the delay of the ith component respectively. When $i = 1$ then $\tau_i = \tau_{TOA}$, which represents the time of arrival of the first component or direct path.

$$d_r(t) = d_s(t) * h(t) + n(t) \qquad (4)$$

$$h(t) = \sum_{i=1}^{N} \alpha_i \delta(t - \tau_i) \qquad (5)$$

The detection of the TR-UWB signal is made through a correlation receiver which correlates the information pulse with the transmitted reference that has been delayed in time, as it can be seen at the modified block diagram of such a receiver in figure 2 where the effects of channel and noise have been omitted for ease of illustration.

At the instant t_0 the received signal $d(t)$ is delayed by T_D, so at the time of detection, $t_0(t) + T_D$, the reference pulse of the delayed doublet, $g_1(t)$ from $d(t - T_D)$, coincides at the input of the correlator with the information pulse of the not delayed doublet, $g_2(t)$ from $d(t)$. The correlator evaluates these signals at t_0 for a duration T_W, (6). For the case of the BPSK modulation a positive value would mean an information pulse in phase, while a negative value would mean an information in opposition.

$$c_W(t_0) = \int_{t_0}^{t_0+T_W} d(t)\, d(t - T_D) dt \qquad (6)$$

In this type of detector the delay line must have a wide frequency response, highly linear phase, very good impedance matching and highly stable delay, which is difficult to integrate. The TDSC detection scheme substitutes the wide band analog delay line by a pair of samplers controlled digitally with a delay corresponding to T_D, which are shown in figure 2. In this way both pulses $g_1(t)$ and $g_2(t)$ are sampled and available at

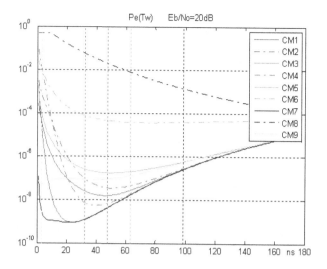

Fig. 3. Error bit probability vs correlation window time T_W

the same time inside the two registers. The discrete value at the output of the correlator can be expressed as (7)

$$c_{W0} = \sum_{n=0}^{N_W-1} d(t_0 + nT_e)\, d(t_0 + nT_e + T_D) \qquad (7)$$

where $T_e = 1/f_e$ is the sampling period of the samplers and $N_W = T_W/T_e$ is the number of samples per register. T_W is also known as the length of the correlation window. This operation can be expressed in terms of the effects of channel and noise, using (4) and (5), as the addition of a meaningful signal plus noise. Here, E_b is the bit energy (doublet), N_0 is the noise power and u_{cw} is a variable that depends on the characteristics of the channel and the correlation time T_W. This allows to express the bit error probability, considering a BPSK modulation, as in (8)

$$P = Q\left(\sqrt{\frac{2u_{cw}E_b}{N_0\left(1 + \frac{N_W N_0}{u_{cw}E_b 4}\right)}}\right) \qquad (8)$$

A statistical model for u_{cw}, based on the IEEE channels [11], has been developed (9), from which some values of the bit error probability have been calculated and presented in figure 3 as a function of the length of the correlation time T_W.

$$u_{cw}(T_W) = \frac{p_1 T_W{}^3 + p_2 T_W{}^2 + p_3 T_W + p_4}{T_W{}^3 + q_1 T_W{}^2 + q_2 T_W + q_3}, \qquad \forall\, T_W > 0 \qquad (9)$$

From here it is seen that it exists an optimal correlation time which produces, for each channel, a minimal bit error rate. At the same time, the technology used for the TDSC

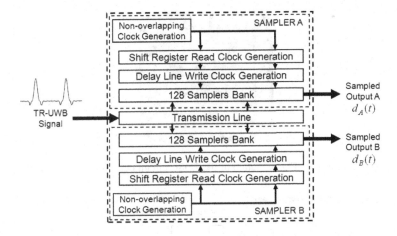

Fig. 4. Block diagram of the TDSC prototype circuit

circuit implementation imposes a bandwidth that depends upon the number of cells of the samplers, so the value of the correlation time T_W is a compromise between these two factors. Details of statistical studies and simulations to evaluate the performance and the optimal correlator size for the TDSC detection scheme are presented in [12]. A prototype circuit following some of the previous results was designed and implemented in 0.35 μm CMOS technology, [8]. The most important details of this prototype are explained in the next section in order to better understand the experimental validation results and further development presented in this paper.

2.2 CMOS Implementation

The block diagram of the prototype circuit that implements the TDSC detection scheme is shown in figure 4. It includes the two samplers described in the previous section, designed using nMOS transmission gates (TG), each one including a register with a length of 128 cells. The high speed sample clock generation circuit uses as its basis an analogically-adjustable edge triggered asynchronous delay line which allows multi-gigahertz sampling frequencies as high as 7.5 GHz. A coplanar wave guide (CPW) is used for guiding the RF signal, [13].

The sampling and recording of each TR-UWB pulse into the TDSC chip registers is made through the digital delayed sampling control, figure 2. At the maximum sampling frequency of the chip, around 7.5 GHz, each register corresponds to a 17 ns length window (T_W), while for the minimum frequency, around 1.7 GHz, they acquire 75 ns. In figure 5 it is shown the packaged circuit of the TDSC receiver circuit, whose chip dimensions are L=3.5 mm and W=1.7 mm.

3   Synchronization Process

The goal of the synchronization process is to find a time reference into the symbol for sampling the pulses at the maximum S/N that gives the best symbol detection. The

Fig. 5. Picture of the TDSC circuit chip

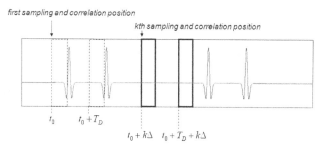

Fig. 6. Time shift $k\,\Delta$ between sampling and correlation windows

technique used here for the TDSC detection method is based on [9]. The synchronization process searches a pair of T_W length windows which produces the maximum correlation value among all the other windows pairs along the symbol. This happens when the received reference and information pulses are located in these windows.

The process starts by sampling the sliding correlation at an arbitrary reference point t_0. The sampled signal waveforms are saved in registers A and B and they are correlated according to (7). This operation is repeated at different positions t_k along the symbol,(10) and (11), each of them separated by a time shift Δ. $K = T_S/\Delta$ is the number of needed correlations for the whole symbol. The maximum value c_{Wk} corresponds to the instant $t_{k_{max}}$,(12), where the pulses are present into the registers, meaning that the receiver is synchronized. The process is shown in figure 6 for the first sampling and correlation position, followed by a Δ-shifted new one.

$$c_{Wk} = \sum_{n=0}^{N_W-1} d(t_0 + k\Delta + nT_e)\, d(t_0 + k\Delta + nT_e + T_D). \tag{10}$$

$$c_{Wk} = \begin{bmatrix} c_{W0}, c_{W1}, \cdots, c_{Wk}, \ldots, c_{W(K-1)} \end{bmatrix} \qquad k = 0, 1, 2, \ldots, K - 1 \tag{11}$$

$$t_{k_{max}} = t_0 + \Delta \, \arg\max_{k} [c_{Wk}] \tag{12}$$

Due to the stationarity of the channel, i.e. the coherence time, the detector can then correctly acquire the transmitted pulses in subsequent symbols at instants t_{det_k}, (13).

$$t_{det_k} = t_{k_{max}} + k\, T_S \tag{13}$$

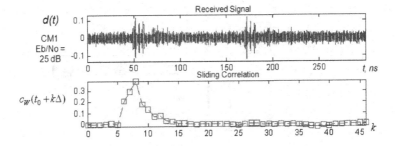

Fig. 7. Sliding correlation after the swept of the equivalent of one complete symbol

Figure 7 shows one example of the simulations made to test the synchronization procedure using channel CM1 of the IEEE channel model proposed in [11]. Here the sliding correlation is shown along only one symbol. In this example the maximum value is obtained for $k = 8$, which means that the doublet is located 8Δ seconds after the starting reference time t_0.

As it has been shown, the synchronization procedure is based on the localization of the maximum of the sliding correlation. Once the system is synchronized it can start to detect the incoming information. In the next section we validate the detection of the pulses of the TR-UWB signal using the TDSC circuit with different configurations.

4   Evaluation Tests Framework

This section presents the tests carried out to validate the detection method using real signals acquired through the TDSC CMOS prototype. First, the structure of the test cards is described, in order to show the conditions under which the validation was done. Second, it is explained the different configurations used for the tests and finally the experimental results are presented.

4.1   Test Cards

In order to make in-deep tests of the TDSC IC and evaluate the synchronization and data detection, a transmitter card and a receiver card were designed. The transmitter is based on a DS89C450 microcontroller, a step recovery diode (SRD) and a short-circuited transmission line. This circuit is an implementation based on [14], where the short-circuited line is used in parallel to the output of the diode to generate a short pulse produced by the difference between the output pulse of the diode and the reflected, reversed and delayed pulse from the short-circuited line. Thanks to this transmitter, TR-UWB signals are generated in a simple way independently of other equipment. It is also possible to control the time between the pulses that could be as short as 140 ns and can be incremented in 33 ns steps. The receiver card is also based on the DS89C450 microcontroller, figure 8, which sends the start control signals to the TDSC circuit to sample and write into the registers the pulses of the incoming TR-UWB signal. The outputs of the registers are fed to an analog to digital converter (ADC) and sent to a

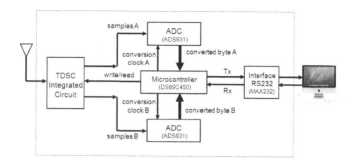

Fig. 8. Block diagram of the receiver test card

computer where the correlation is done by means of a MATLAB program. This let us to be able to better analyse and acquire the needed data to validate the method.

4.2 Cable Connected and Wireless Test Configurations

The tests were run using two kinds of TR-UWB signals: a baseband signal, whose bandwidth extends to around 1 GHz, and a frequency translated signal centred at 4 GHz. A mixer was employed to easily translate the baseband signal in frequency for the tests at 4 GHz. It was used both a wired channel, with the transmitter and the receiver connected directly by a cable, and a real wireless channel.

5   Experimental Results

5.1 Transmitted Signal

The transmitted TR-UWB signal comprised pulses with a length of around 1 ns, a T_D spacing time of 366 ns and a symbol period of 2.66 μs. The waveform reaches a maximum amplitude of 1.16 volts as shown in figure 9. The power spectral density of the signal, measured directly at the output of the transmitter, showed that the bandwidth at the power level of -43 dBm reaches a value of around 1.1 GHz. The sampling frequency

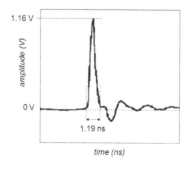

Fig. 9. Waveform of the transmitter output pulse

of the TDSC circuit used during the tests was estimated to be 7.5 GHz according to the measurement procedure proposed in [8].

To allow the MATLAB program to automatically manage the reception process, it was necessary to previously manually calibrate it. This was achieved for each test case, identifying an adequate threshold value of the correlation to distinguish between the presence and absence of pulses in the received signal. In this way the test system was able to continually receive and detect the symbols in a reproducible way. Some examples of the received signals are presented in the following subsection.

5.2 Configuration with Cable Connection

Figure 10 shows an example of a result corresponding to the direct connection between the transmitter and the receiver with the signal translated at 4 GHz. The first and the second waveforms are the contents of registers A and B respectively when a pulse is present, while the last waveform is the result of a cross-correlation between them. The value shown as Corr. Max is the maximum value of this cross-correlation, it corresponds to the term c_{W0} maximum when the pulses are present, as it was explained in section 2.2 and defined in (7). The amplitude of the signals is normalized and the correlation value threshold of around 0.2 was successfully found and fixed to detect the pulses.

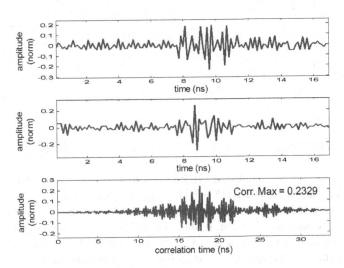

Fig. 10. Results with a 4 GHz signal directly connected to the receiver

5.3 Configuration with Wireless Channel

In the case of tests using an indoor wireless channel, both line-of-sight (LOS) and non line-of sight (NLOS) conditions were considered. Figure 11.a shows the results for the transmission of a baseband signal from a distance of one meter from the receiver. In this case the correlation value threshold was fixed between 0.14 and 0.135 with good results. In order to allow comparison between the maximum correlation values, we also

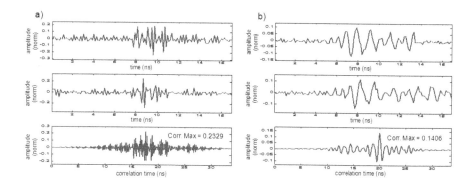

Fig. 11. Results with a) a baseband signal transmitted at 100 cm with line of sight (LOS). b) a baseband signal transmitted at 40 cms. with non-line-of-sight (NLOS)

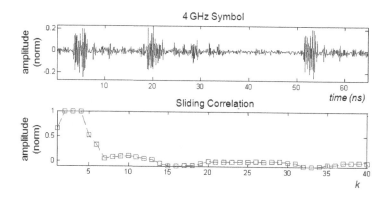

Fig. 12. Sliding correlation simulation obtained with real signals at 4 GHz

made tests without signals and with symbols carrying only one of the doublet pulses. Detailed results are presented in [15] which are synthesized in Table 1.

Finally, figure 11.b shows the waveform results in NLOS conditions, for a baseband signal, with a separation of 40 cm. In this case the pulses were successfully detected with a correlation threshold value around 0.06. As expected, in the case of the NLOS test, the amplitude of the received signal is smaller than that obtained in the LOS test, as well as the value of the cross correlation. In any case, the pulses were successfully detected.

After this validation phase a test was made combining simulation and real acquired signals. Real acquired pulses were used in a simulated symbol to compute the sliding correlation to evaluate the synchronization process. We did that for a baseband signal as well for a 4 GHz signal symbol, shown in figure 12. It both cases the maximum value of the sliding correlation was clearly found, which means that the position for a correct detection was identified and so the detector is synchronized.

These results show that the proposed detection method can successfully detect TR-UWB signals through the TDSC CMOS prototype. Good detection results were

Table 1. Synthesis of tests results

Signal	Connection	Threshold	Corr. Max.
Baseband LOS	Cable	3.5	4.21
Baseband LOS	Wireless 40 cm	0.19	0.217
Baseband LOS	Wireless 1 m	0.12	0.14
4 GHz LOS	Cable	0.19	0.232
4 GHz LOS	Wireless 40 cm	0.10	0.152
Baseband NLOS	Wireless 40 cm	0.025	0.0747
Baseband NLOS	Wireless 40 cm	0.025	0.0623
No pulses	Wireless 40 cm	0.19	0.009
Only one pulse	Wireless 40 cm	0.19	0.022

obtained for different indoor environments and distances and the synchronization process was positively validated.

6   Distance Measurement with the TDSC Scheme

The previous results allowed us to continue studying the TDSC scheme applied to the measurement of the distance for localization purposes. In this section we will described briefly some advances made in particular for the measurement of the time of arrival (TOA), including the simulation and experimental results of a TOA estimation proposed strategy.

6.1   TOA Measurement

The base for computing a distance for positioning purposes is the measurement of the time of flight (t_{TOF}) of the signal propagating from one device to the other at a velocity V_p, where $d = V_p\, t_{TOF}$. When the time of depart, t_d, is known it's only the time of arrival, t_a, at the receiver which must be estimated under the wireless indoor environment. It is known that in the case of statistical estimation based on the ideal signal model for the time of arrival, (14), the minimum value of the variance that the estimator could achieve is given by its Cramer-Rao Lower Bound (CRLB). As this value is inversely proportional to the bandwidth of the signal, (15), it shows that ultra wideband signals are specially well suited for positioning systems, [4].

$$r(t) = \alpha s(t - \tau) + n(t) \tag{14}$$

$$Var[\hat{\tau}] > \frac{1}{2\beta SNR} \tag{15}$$

Figure 13 shows as example the minimum standard deviation for TOA estimation using two UWB signals of different bandwidth: 500 MHz and 1 GHz. The first signal presents a deviation of 1.34 cm at 14 dB and 0.67 cm at 20 dB, while for the 1 GHz bandwidth signal its deviation is 0.67 cm at 14 dB and 0.33 cm at 20 dB, illustrating the high precision potential of UWB signals for TOA measurement. As discussed before and expressed in (4) and (5), the propagation characteristics of UWB signals produce at the

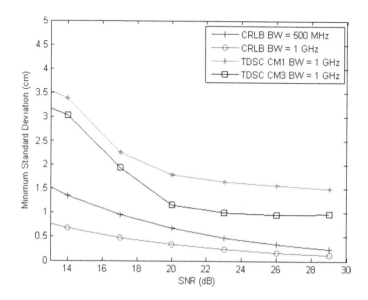

Fig. 13. Simulated minimum standard deviation according to the Cramer-Rao lower bound

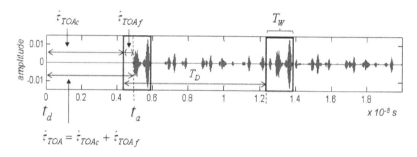

Fig. 14. a) Transmitted signal at time t_d. b) Received signal at time t_a

receiver the addition of pulses coming from different paths and with different attenuations, all of them originated from the transmitted pulse. The result is a multipath signal, as the one shown in figure 14, where the first peak, whose time of arrival corresponds to the real time of flight, is generally not the peak with the highest amplitude, making harder its detection.

6.2   TOA Estimation Proposed Solution

The proposed solution estimates the time of arrival $\hat{\tau}_{TOA}$ searching for the first path as the one that produces a high rate of change of the values of the sliding correlation. It doesn't matter if the first path isn't the one with the largest amplitude, it will produce an important change in the correlation values. This solution is applied in a two-step basis in order to achieve a high resolution related to the relative high sampling frequency of the TDSC circuit. First, a coarse estimate searches along the received symbol for a T_W length block that contains the first path, corresponding to the reference pulse of the doublet, as seen in figure 14. Then this received reference and its corresponding information blocks, starting at $\hat{\tau}_{TOA_c}$ and at $\hat{\tau}_{TOA_c} + T_D$ respectively, are saved into the TDSC registers. Secondly, the fine estimate searches for instant $\hat{\tau}_{TOA_f}$ corresponding to the beginning of the pulse into the saved blocks. The addition of the coarse time and the fine time gives the final estimates: $\hat{\tau}_{TOA} = \hat{\tau}_{TOA_c} + \hat{\tau}_{TOA_f}$.

The rate of change of the sliding correlation is evaluated through its first derivative (16) and a threshold γ defined from the maximum value of the correlation, (17). The position of the first value of the derivative greater than the threshold is chosen as the time estimate in both coarse and fines estimates, (18) and (19).

$$\Delta c_{Wk} = c_{Wk} - c_{W(k-1)} \tag{16}$$

$$\gamma = a_1 \left[max \left[\Delta c_{Wk} \right] \right] \tag{17}$$

$$\hat{k} = f_2 \left[\Delta c_{Wk} \geq \gamma \right] \tag{18}$$

$$\hat{\tau}_{TOA} = \hat{k}\Delta \tag{19}$$

In the case of the coarse estimate, the sliding correlation and its derivative are computed for the whole symbol in the same way as for the synchronization process: K points shifted by Δ. In this case Δ defines the precision to identify a position to find the first path, which doesn't need to be very accurate, it's enough to make the pulse fall inside the T_W window. The value of Δ depends upon the speed of the controller of the receiver to generate the control signals to the samplers.

In the fine estimate case the sliding correlation is computed only on the T_W length blocks found by the coarse estimate at positions $\hat{\tau}_{TOA_c}$ and at $\hat{\tau}_{TOA_c} + T_D$. Here, K_f points are produced from T_{Wf} length correlation windows shifted by Δ_f, with $K_f = T_W/\Delta_f$. Δ_f can also be expressed in terms of the sampling period of the frequency of the TDSC circuit as $\Delta_f = N_{Df}T_e$. At its highest sampling frequency of 7.5 GHz, Δ_f can be as small as 0.133 ns, which corresponds to an equivalent distance measurement of around 4 cm.

6.3   TOA Estimation Simulations and Experimental Results

The proposed TOA estimation strategy was simulated using the IEEE 802.15.4a channels CM1 (residential), and CM3 (office) for the LOS case and also channels CM2 (residential) and CM4 (office) for the NLOS case, with a 1 GHz bandwidth signal. Figure 13 illustrates, additionally to the CRLBs early discussed, the minimum standard deviation obtained for the CM1 and CM3 cases. For the first one, some of the values obtained are 3.37 cm at a SNR value of 14 dB and 1.78 cm at 20 dB, while for CM3 there were 3 cm at 14 dB and 1.16 cm at 20 dB. This last value corresponds to 3.5 times that of the corresponding CRLB case.

A set of wireless tests was carried out using the test cards. A distance was estimated for each different separation set between the transmitter and the receiver according to the fine step strategy, supposing that the first step has already found the correct block

Table 2. Estimation results

Distance (cm)	Estimated distance (cm)	Error (σ) (cm)	Error (%)
80	86.74	6.74	8.42
90	95.08	5.08	5.65
100	100.52	0.52	0.52
110	107.50	-2.50	-2.27
120	120.00	0.00	0.00

at $\hat{\tau}_{TOA_c}$. In such a case it was necessary to fix a reference distance in place of the coarse time and compute the TOA by comparing the measurement to the reference; we chose the 120 cm distance as reference. The results are shown in Table 2, where the errors change from 0.5 to 8.4% as the distance from the reference increases. Each distance was computed as the mean of 50 consecutive measures. More simulation and experimental results are presented in [16]

These results show that, in general, the proposed TOA estimation strategy has a consistent performance with the simulations. These results bring us valuable information in order to improve our system and make a better approach to the TOA estimation remaining as a practical and simple solution, requiring a low computational complexity.

7 Conclusions

This paper has presented experimental results that validate the TDSC detection scheme using real TR-UWB signals. Through this work we also improve the knowledge of the TDSC performance regarding the T_D implementation, frequency response, signal detection through indoor wireless channel and synchronization. The analog TR-UWB signals were acquired from a directed connection as well through an indoor wireless channel to a distance as long as 1 meter as first step of experimentation. It was demonstrated that the use of the TDSC integrated circuit, as the receiving device, allows the detection of such signals through different environment or frequency condition (BB or 4 GHz), including line-of-sight as well as non-light-of-sight conditions. That validates also the generation of a precise delay T_D in order to detect TR-UWB signals. We also showed the results of a feasible solution to the measurement of the TOA, based on a TDSC receiver, with a potential good performance with a low computational complexity.

References

1. Federal Communications Commission. Revision of part 15 of the commissions rules regarding ultra-wideband transmission systems. Technical report (2002)
2. IEEE standard for information technology - telecommunications and information exchange between systems - local and metropolitan area networks - specific requirement part 15.4: Wireless medium access control (mac) and physical layer (phy) specifications for low-rate wireless personal area networks (wpans) (2007)
3. Ecma International. High rate ultra wideband phy and mac standard (December 2008)

4. Gezici, S.: A survey on wireless position estimation. Wireless Personal Communications 44, 263–282 (2008), doi:10.1007/s11277-007-9375-z
5. Jofre, L., Broquetas, A., Romeu, J., Blanch, S., Toda, A.P., Fabregas, X., Cardama, A.: Uwb tomographic radar imaging of penetrable and impenetrable objects. Proceedings of the IEEE 97(2), 451–464 (2009)
6. D'Amico, A.A., Mengali, U., Taponecco, L.: Ranging algorithm for the ieee 802.15.4a standard, pp. 285–289 (September 2009)
7. Hirata-Flores, F.I., Muller, M., Ni, Y., Gimenes, C.: Cmos implementation of a tr-uwb receiver based on time delayed sampling and correlation method, pp. 1–5 (June 2008)
8. Hirata-Flores, F.: CMOS Prototype for a TDSC-UWB Receiver Based on TR Detection Scheme. PhD thesis, Telecom SudParis (2008)
9. Saber, C., Lamberti, R., Gimenes, C.: Synchronization solution for the tdsc-uwb detection method. In: Sobh, T., Elleithy, K., Mahmood, A., Karim, M.A. (eds.) Novel Algorithms and Techniques In Telecommunications, Automation and Industrial Electronics, pp. 311–316. Springer, Netherlands (2008)
10. Gezici, S., Tian, Z., Giannakis, G.B., Kobayashi, H., Molisch, A.F., Poor, H.V., Sahinoglu, Z.: Localization via ultra-wideband radios: a look at positioning aspects for future sensor networks. IEEE Signal Processing Magazine 22(4), 70–84 (2005)
11. Molisch, A.F., Cassioli, D., Chong, C.-C., Emami, S., Fort, A., Kannan, B., Karedal, J., Kunisch, J., Schantz, H.G., Siwiak, K., Win, M.Z.: A comprehensive standardized model for ultrawideband propagation channels. IEEE Transactions on Antennas and Propagation 54(11), 3151–3166 (2006)
12. Saber, C.: Ultra Large Bande Radio par Impulsions. Contributions à la Dèfinition du Rècepteur TDSC. Relation à la filière technologique. PhD thesis, Telecom SudParis (2008)
13. Muller, M., Hirata-Flores, F., Ni, Y., Lamberti, R., Saber, C.: Fully cmos low power low complexity detection method for tr-uwb. In: 6th Edition of IEEE Faible Tension Faible Consommation, FTFC 2007, Paris (2007)
14. Lee, J.S., Nguyen, C., Scullion, T.: New uniplanar subnanosecond monocycle pulse generator and transformer for time-domain microwave applications. IEEE Transactions on Microwave Theory and Techniques 49(6), 1126–1129 (2001)
15. Pardiñas-Mir, J.A., Muller, M., Lamberti, R., Gimenes, C.: Experimental Validation for TR-UWB Systems - By Time Delayed Sampling & Correlation (TDSC). In: Proc. WINSYS, pp. 87–94 (2011)
16. Pardiñas-Mir, J.A., Lamberti, R., Muller, M., Gimenes, C.: An Experimental Approach to a Low-Complexity Two-Step TOA Measurement for TR-UWB Signals. In: 2012 IEEE International Conference on Communications (ICC) (June 2012)

Link Adaptation in Ad Hoc Networks Based on Interference Minimization

Fredrick Awuor[1], Karim Djouani[1], Kimutai Kimeli[2], and Dorothy Rambim[3]

[1] Dept. of Electrical Engineering, French South African Technical Institute - FSATI
Tshwane University of Technology, Private Bag X680, Pretoria 0001, South Africa
[2] Chepkoilel University College, Box 1125, Eldoret 30100, Kenya
[3] Moi University, P.O. Box 3900, Eldoret 30100, Kenya

Abstract. This paper proposes a link adaptation algorithm (LAA) for ad hoc networks based on coupled interference minimization whereby network interference is dynamically controlled by adjusting the transmit power. Such adjustment exploits link status and hence, users are aware of channel conditions as they determine the data rates. Users are encouraged to maximize utilities of others as they maximize their own due to forced cooperation resulting from the pricing/costing effect attached to transmit power choices. This is equivalent to super-modular game, thus, network utility maximisation (NUM) problem is formulated and analysed using such tool.

Keywords: Interference minimization, Data rates, Transmit power, Network Utility Maximization (NUM), Ad Hoc Network, Cost (penalty).

1 Introduction

Due to the success that has been achieved by the cellular revolution, attention has been drifted to realising reliable communications without relying on a fixed infrastructure which has lead to development of wireless networks (WNs) to support user mobility (mobile ad hoc networks - MANET). Designing data transmission mechanisms for WN is, however, a challenge since such mechanisms must effectively convey the information using an unreliable physical channel within a highly dynamic connected set of nodes without the support of any infrastructure. Moreover, such mechanisms should jointly optimise throughput, minimise delay and energy dissipation in the network without sacrificing fairness, robustness and quality of service (QoS). Nevertheless, the aforementioned set of design goals is a collection of contradicting metrics, implying that trade-offs are required to attain them. Since WN is a dynamic and a distributed entity, which is inherently a chaotic system [1], its optimal control need to be dynamic and adaptive. This global optimal solution can be achieved by continuously monitoring the entire network status, which is not realisable, or at least not scalable, due to absence of centralised controller. A distributive control is therefore essential to address this problem. However, such a distributive approach needs to enhance efficient and fair distribution of network resources e.g. bandwidth and energy and be able to quickly adapt to network dynamics e.g. variations in traffic, node density and mobility [2].

M.S. Obaidat, J.L. Sevillano, and J. Filipe (Eds.): ICETE 2011, CCIS 314, pp. 492–502, 2012.
© Springer-Verlag Berlin Heidelberg 2012

Energy efficiency is one of the key issues in wireless ad hoc networks since most mobile devices are battery operated that have finite lifespan. An effective way to achieve energy efficiency is to reduce the transmission power whenever possible. However, in a multi-rate enabled network, reducing transmission power may result in reduced transmission rate (assuming that the bit error rate (BER) has to be below a certain threshold). Hence, power control and rate adaptation need to be jointly considered [3]. This is essential to support services that require high data rates and helps to maximize the throughput or minimise the transmission delay for real-time applications. The key idea is to allow a wireless station, based on the link quality between itself and the receiver, to select the most energy-efficient transmission strategy, which consists of transmission rate, transmit power and/or data payload length. Link adaptation is an effective strategy in nature to achieve the ideal modulation to be selected depending upon signal quality at the terminals in wireless networks. Consequently, transmission performance can be improved by optimising the operation of link adaptation in cooperative wireless networks therein adjusting the rate-changing parameters based on physical layer measurement [4].

In heterogeneous wireless network where network resources are limited, users adopt selfish behaviours (and compete) to maximise their individual utilities at the expense of others [5]. Accordingly, users get prompted to transmit at maximum power levels which leads to abnormal interference in the network even in situations where the same transmissions could have been sustained at lower transmit power. Consequently, network performance gets degraded leading to low throughputs, lack of spatial reuse and loss of connectivity among others. The aim of this study is to develop efficient and dynamic link adaptation algorithm to optimise data rate and power efficiency performance in ad hoc networks, thus reducing users' interferences. By applying coupled interference NUM concept, a distributive link adaptation algorithm is designed. Controlled transmit power assist in the prolonging of the lifespan of batteries of the communicating devices. An optimal reduction in transmit power levels leads to increase in network capacity: Due to the shared nature of wireless channel, any transmission causes interference in its surrounding region. A reduction in the transmission range leads to a reduction in the interference range. With an optimal reduction in the interference range, such that there are not too many shorter paths in a single source destination path, there is bound to be an increase in spatial reuse and this leads to an increase in capacity. This is because nodes will be able to communicate simultaneously as long as they are not within the interference range of the other [6]. In addition, this prolongs the lifespan of the network. Adaptive power and rate adaptation also optimising network utility (local and global) performance since users adapt their transmission parameter based on the time variant link conditions.

Link adaptation through interference minimisation proposed in this work aims at establishing the optimal transmission power and data rates that maximises network performance therein attaining the optimal solution to this contradicting objective. The network users are therefore able to transmit at optimal power and data rates wherein the network resources are efficiently and fairly shared.

The reminder of this paper is organized as follows: Section II reviews related works; Section III gives the problem formulation and the analysis of the proposed algorithm. Simulation test and results are presented in Section IV while Section V concludes this paper.

2 Related Work

Performing link adaptation involves estimating channel condition and selecting feasible data rate out of the multiple available transmission rates taking into account interference minimisation strategy[2][4]. Often, performing link adaptation relies on feedback from the receiver. In this approach the channel quality is estimated using the SNR, the received signal strength, or packet error rate measurements to determine transmit rate or power level to be used in subsequent transmissions. This information is then sent back to the transmitter over a feedback channel[8]. Unfortunately, the 802.11 MAC standards do not provide any logical means for the receiver to inform the transmitter about the link quality or the transmission rate to be used. Since performing link adaptation on a feedback channel requires modification of the 802.11 standard, "Ready-To-Send/Clear-To-Send" (RTS/CTS) has been proposed[8]. The RTS/ CTS protocol is defined in the 802.11 standard to combat the well-known "hidden" terminal problem. Before sending a data frame, a transmitting station makes a reservation for the wireless channel by sending a short RTS frame. The receiving station replies with a CTS frame. The transmitting station proceeds with the transmission of the data frame after having received the CTS frame. All other stations in the vicinity of the transmitter and the receiver that have received these two frames will defer their own transmissions until the end of the reservation. Thus, the RTS/CTS protocol can be exploited to exchange link adaptation parameters such as rate and packet size, or interference margins and transmit power levels. Alternatively, link adaptation can be achieved by measuring the received signal strength and derive the transmit parameters from that measurement[9]. The transmit power level can also be included in the packets, such as in the method described in[10], where a combined rate and power adaptation for 802.11a WLANs operating under the Point Coordination Function (PCF) is employed. The information about the transmit power level is included in the MAC frame that is sent by the Point Controller (PC) which allows the receiver of the frame to estimate the path loss between itself and the PC and to determine the best rate power pair to be used for future transmissions. A similar method is defined in [10] for the 802.11 Distributed Coordination Function (DCF). It uses the RTS/CTS frames sent at full power prior to any data transmission to estimate the path loss. The wireless stations (WSTAs) determine the best power rate combination from a table indexed by the packet length, the path loss condition and the retry counters of the DCF procedure. However, the table entries are calculated off-line which may not reflect the adaptive environment in the channel condition. As noted in [8] most of these algorithms described so far require either a modification of the 802.11 standard or cooperation of peer stations, e.g. when making use of the RTS/CTS procedure. These drawbacks can be addressed by utilizing information available at the transmitter to determine the transmission parameters. In addition, such an approach will reduce the number of signalling messages.

Network performance is often modelled as NUM where the utility function represents performance or satisfaction of the independent users (while the optimal total utility represents maximum system performance i.e. the global optimality [3]). Much research effort has been put in the design of distributed algorithms for NUM. The main ingredient to obtain distributed algorithms is the decomposition techniques i.e., primal and dual decomposition approaches. An explicit discussion on decomposition is available in[11].

Due to the distributed and heterogeneous nature of the modern networks, it is often challenging to design distributed algorithms that can achieve the global optimal NUM solution. The difficulty in distributed algorithm design often lies in the coupling nature of the NUM problem. Nonetheless, energy minimisation and throughput maximisation in ad hoc requires a distributive approach since there is no centralised infrastructure or AP. The majority of the utility problem formulations considered in the literature concern uncoupled utilities where the local variables corresponding to one node do not directly affect the utilities of the other nodes. However, systems with competition or cooperation do not satisfy this assumption and the utilities are indeed coupled. For instance, cooperation between nodes is required in WN since these nodes form clusters and the utility obtained by each node depends on the rate allocated to other nodes within the cluster, hence their utilities are functions of the SINRs that are dependent on the transmit powers of other users[12]. The key idea to tackle coupled utilities is to introduce auxiliary variables and additional equality constraints, thus transferring the coupling in the objective function to coupling in the constraints, which can be decoupled by dual decomposition and solved by introducing additional consistency pricing. It is reasonable to assume that if two nodes have their individual utilities dependent on each other's local variables, then there is need for some communication channels in which they can locally exchange pricing messages[11].

Motivated by aforementioned properties of ad hoc networks and need to mitigate interference in such networks, we propose a link adaptation algorithm based on interference mitigation where user's utility functions are coupled. In the proposed approach, coupled interference NUM problem formulated optimizes network performance by allowing users to determine transmit power and data rates based on their local observations (i.e., channel condition). Therefore, a user's choice of data rate is a function of link dynamics and coupled interference that is controlled by attaching cost function to users' transmission power choices. This obligates users to transmit at the least power that can sustain the intended transmission. Moreover, network users are obliged to cooperate thus maximizing both their local and global network utility.

3 System Model

3.1 Problem Formulation

Consider an ad hoc network with N users where users autonomously adapt their transmission data rate and power based on their own preferences and target utility (goal). Assuming user $i \in N$ communicates to $j \in N$ on single hop, such that all other nodes in the network are able to hear each other's transmissions and therefore can actively interfere with on going transmission. Define transmission power p and data rate r choices for user i as $p_i \in p$ and $r_i \in r$ such that $p_{min} \leq p_i \leq p_{max}$ and $r_{min} \leq r_i \leq r_{max}$. The link ij is normally a subject to path loss, shadowing and multi path fading dynamics estimated as $p_j = h_{ij}p_i$ where h_{ij} is the channel gain (path loss), p_i is i's transmit power while p_j is the received power at j [2].

We formulate interference minimization NUM problem where users determine transmit power to optimize their utilities based on local observations as in (1) given that every user $i \in N$'s utility function $u_i(\gamma_i(p))$ is concave, differentiable and increasing function of the received SINR [13][11].

$$\max \sum_{i \in I} u_i(\gamma_i(p)) \tag{1}$$

where $\gamma_i(p)$ is SINR on link ij given by $\gamma_{ij} = \frac{h_{ij}p_i}{\sum_{k \neq i,j} h_{kj}p_k + \eta_o}$. In this expression, $\sum_{k \neq i,j} h_{kj}p_k$ is the sum of interference power I_{ij} at j due to transmissions of other network users other than the intended transmitter i while η_o is the thermal noise.

Due to existence of mutual interference, network users have coupled utility function that depends on both the user's local decision and that of other network users. Hence, we derive the NUM problem that attains global optimality from (1) as follows:

$$\max_{\{p:p_i \in p \forall i\}} \sum_{i=1}^{N} u_i(\gamma_i(p)) \tag{2}$$

Since $U_i(.)$ in (2) is concave in γ_i, we adopt reverse-engineering based on KKT conditions to solve the coupled objective function (2)[12][13][14]. Such approach localizes the NUM function (2) and uses limited message passing to inform users of their neighbour's utility choices.

3.2 Interference Minimization

Define a power profile p such that $p \in \{p_i; p_{-i}\}$, power profile of user i as p_i and power profile for user i's opponents as p_{-i} i.e., $p_{-i} = (p_1, ..., p_{i-1}, p_{i+1}, ..., p_I)$. The NUM can be modelled as a power control game $G = [N, \{p_i\}, \{u_i\}]$ where all the players, selects transmit power p_i that maximize their utilities u_i given that $u_i(i)$ represents user i's reward (satisfaction). Then $i \in N$ maximizes its response (utility) as follows ([14][15]).

$$\beta_n(p_{-i}) = \arg\max_{p_i \in p} u_i(\gamma_i(p_i, p_{-i})) \tag{3}$$

In this expression, $u_i(\gamma_i(p_i, p_{-i}))$ is strictly increasing with p_i Assuming that p_{-i} is fixed.

In case of a non cooperative game where users selfishly choose transmit power to maximize their utilities without considering other networks users' utilities, then a fixed point $p = p^*$ defined in

$$u_i\left(\gamma_i\left(p_i^*; p_{-i}^*\right)\right) \geq u_i\left(\gamma_i\left(p_i^{'}; p_{-i}^*\right)\right)$$

is the best operating point, Nash Equilibrium (NE)[17][18] where $p' \in p$ is any power chosen by i other than p^* in view of the fact that each user's reward $u_i(\gamma_i(p_i, p_{-i}))$ is strictly increasing with p_i for fixed p_{-i} [13][19][20]. Since pricing has effect of discouraging users' selfish behaviours but promoting cooperation, introduce penalty (cost) function to users' choices would improve the NE in the this expression.

If the reward (utility) is defined as $f_i(\gamma_i)$ in (4), then users will be prompted to minimize the cost c in (4) attached to power choice p_i.

$$u_i(p_i, p_{-i}) = f_i(\gamma_i) - cp_i \tag{4}$$

Considering (4) as cost function penalized on user i for generating interference to other network users, i has to minimize the cost to maximize its utility. Since c depends on h_{ij} and network factor ε_j, (4) can be expressed as surplus function defined in (5) where $u_i(p_i, p_{-i}) = u_i(\gamma_i(p_i; p_{-i}))$ (i.e. expressing $u_i(p_i, p_{-i})$ as a function of γ_i) [12][13].

$$S_i(p_i; p_{-i}, \varepsilon_{-i}) = u_i(\gamma_i(p_i; p_{-i})) - p_i \sum_{j \neq i} \varepsilon_j h_{ij} \tag{5}$$

Lemma 1 (KKT Conditions) [12]: For any local optimal p^* of problem (2), there exist unique lagrange multipliers $\mu_{1,u}^*, ..., \mu_{N,u}^*$ and $\mu_{1,g}^*, ..., \mu_{N,g}^*$ such that for all $i \in N$,

$$\frac{\partial u_i(\gamma_i(p^*))}{\partial p_i} + \sum_{k \neq i} \frac{\partial u_k(\gamma_k(p^*))}{\partial p_k} = \mu_{i,u}^* - \mu_{i,g}^* \tag{6}$$

where

$$\mu_{i,u}^*(p_i^* - p_i^{\max}) = 0, \mu_{i,g}^*(p_i^{\min} - p_i^*) = 0, \mu_{i,u}^*, \mu_{i,g}^* \geq 0 \tag{7}$$

The KKT set of problem (2) need to contain all solutions that satisfy conditions (6) and (7) for all $i \in I$ [13]. We therefore need to design a distributed algorithm that converges to KKT set.

Let

$$\varepsilon_j(p_j, p_{-j}) = -\frac{\partial u_j(\gamma_j(p_j, p_{-j}))}{\partial I_j(p_{-j})} \tag{8}$$

$I_j(p_{-j})$ is locally measured total interference at user j given by $\sum_{i \neq j} p_i h_{ij}$. Notably, the cost function $\varepsilon_j(p_j, p_{-j})$ is always non-negative and represents user j's marginal increase in utility per unit decrease in total interference. Using (8), condition (6) can be expressed as

$$\frac{\partial u_i(\gamma_i(p^*))}{\partial p_i} \sum_{k \neq i} \varepsilon_j(p_j^*, p_{-j}^*) h_{ik} = \mu_{i,u}^* - \mu_{i,g}^* \tag{9}$$

The reward is the product of the user's transmission power p and weighted sum of other users' prices defined in (5). The notation ε_{-j} is equal to the cost c in (4) and defines the penalty inflicted on network users for generating interference to user i, hence (9) is a necessary and sufficient optimality condition for the problem in which user i chooses transmit power $p_i \in p$ to maximize the surplus function

$$S_i(p_{-i}, \varepsilon_{-i}) =$$

$$\min\left(\max\left(p_{\min}, \frac{p_i}{\gamma_i(p)}\left(\frac{p_i}{\gamma_i(p)}\left(\sum_{k \neq i} \varepsilon_i h_{ik}\right)\right)\right), p_{\max}\right) \tag{10}$$

where

$$\varepsilon_i(p) = \frac{\partial u_i(\gamma_i(p))}{\partial \gamma_i(p)} \frac{(\gamma_i(p))^2}{\beta p_i h_{ij}} \tag{11}$$

In the above expression, β is the spreading factor while $\frac{\partial u_i(\omega_i)}{\partial \omega_i}$ is given by $\frac{u_i(\omega_i^t) - u_i(\omega_i^{t-1})}{\omega_i^t - \omega_i^{t-1}}$ [4].

At an instance of time t, network users announce their cost in reference to (11) and adjust their transmit power taking into account network dynamics according to (10). The chosen power is constrained to (9) and as a result, an optimal localized distributive power algorithm with costing constraints is derived where the surplus function (10) and cost function (11) are derived from (5) and (8) respectively.

3.3   Rate Adaptation

Employing the SINR derived from the distributive pricing interference minimization in subsection B, we can determine the best constellation size for modulation that is supported by the SINR (i.e.) in (10) and (11). Using Shannon theory of communication ([22]) we can deduce the following:

$$M = 1 + \left(\frac{-\vartheta_1}{ln - \vartheta_2 BER)} \right) SINR$$

where BER is the bit error rate while ϑ_1 and ϑ_2 are modulation type dependent constants.

Let $\delta = \frac{-\vartheta_1}{\ln(\vartheta_2 BER)}$, then data rate r_i for transmit power p_i between transmitter i and receiver j is a function of $\gamma_i(p_i)$ given as $M = 1 + \delta\gamma_i(p_i)$ i.e.,

$$r_i = \frac{1}{T} \log_2 (1 + \delta\gamma_i(p_i)) \approx r = \frac{1}{T} \log_2 (\delta\gamma_i(p_i)) \tag{12}$$

where $\delta SINR \gg 1$ while $\frac{1}{T}$ is the bandwidth of the channel used for data transmission. When the signal level is much higher than the interference level or when the spreading gain is large, then r_i lies within $r_{\min} \leq r_i \leq r_{\max}$.

3.4   Convergence and Optimality

Lemma 2 [19]: Let $X \subseteq \mathbb{R}$ and $T \subset \mathbb{R}^k$ for some k, a partial ordered set with the usual vector order. Let $f : X \times T \to \mathbb{R}$ be a twice continuously differential function. Then, the following statements are equivalent: (i) The function f has increasing differences in (x,t), (ii) For all $t' \geq t$ and $x \in X$, we have $\frac{\partial f(x,t')}{\partial x} \geq \frac{\partial f(x,t)}{\partial x}$ and, (iii) For all $x \in X, t \in T$ and all $i=1,2,...,k$, we have $\frac{\partial^2 f(x,t)}{\partial x \partial t_i} \geq 0$.

Theorem 1 Define $X \subseteq \mathbb{R}$ as a compact set and T as some partially ordered set. Assume that the function $f : X \times T \to \mathbb{R}$ is upper semi-continuous in x for all $t \in T$ and has increasing differences in (x, t). Define $x(t) = \arg\max_{x \in X} f(x, t)$. Then, we have: for all $t \in T$, $x(t)$ is non-empty and has a greatest and least element, denoted by $\overline{x}(t)$ and $\underline{x}(t)$ respectively and, for all $t' \geq t$, $\overline{x}(t') \geq \overline{x}(t)$ and $\underline{x}(t') \geq \underline{x}(t)$ [19][20].

From *lemma 2* and *theorem 1*, every user's utility function $u_i(p_i, p_{-i})$ has increasing differences in (p_i, p_{-i}) given that $\frac{-\gamma_i f_i''(\gamma_i)}{f_i'(\gamma_i)} \geq 1, \forall \gamma_i \geq 0$ hence the convergence.

Definition 1 [19]: Super modular games have the following properties: (i) Pure strategy NE exists, (ii) The largest and smallest strategies are compatible with iterated strict dominance nationalization, correlated equilibrium, and NE are the same and, (iii) If a super modular game has a unique NE, it is dominance solvable (and lots of learning and adjustment rules converge to it, e.g., optimal (best) response dynamics.

Assume $(I, (p), (u_i))$ is a super modular game. Then $\beta_i(p_{-i})$ in (3) has a greatest and least element, denoted by $\overline{\beta}_i(p_{-i})$ and $\underline{\beta}_i(p_{-i})$, and if $p'_{-i} \geq p_{-i}$ then $\overline{\beta}_i(p'_{-i}) \geq \overline{\beta}_i(p_{-i})$ and $\underline{\beta}_{-i}(p'_{-i}) \geq \underline{\beta}_{-i}(p_{-i})$ [19][22].

This implies that each player's best response is increasing in the actions of other players. The set of strategies that survive iterated strict dominance (i.e., iterated elimination of strictly dominated strategies) has greatest and least elements $\overline{p}$ and $\underline{p}$, which are both pure strategy in NE. Since (3) satisfies all the conditions of a super modular game, the solution derived from (3) is optimal. Comprehensive definition and formulation of super-modular game theory can be found in [1][2][5].

We further analyse the optimality and uniqueness of LAA solution using super-modular game theory as follows:

By LAA, the derived solution is unique and optimal if the power vector $p = [p_{\min}, ..., p_{\max}]$ exist for all the transmissions. In such a solution, an iterative power control algorithm $p(q + 1) = I(p(q))$ is optimal if $\forall p \geq 0$, the following properties are observed [2][17] i.e. (i) Positivity: $I(p) \geq 0$ and (ii) Monotonicity: if $p \geq p'$, then $I(p) \geq I(p')$ where $I(p)$ is the interference function.

Preposition 1: If LAA is optimal on $[\underline{p_i}, \overline{p_i}]$ $\forall i$, the interference function is defined as $I(p) = [I_1(p), I_2(p), ..., I_n(p),]$ where $p = [p_{\min}, ..., p_{\max}]$ and $I_i(p) = \gamma_i(p)$, then the following properties can deduced from γ_{ij} defined in (1).

The positivity is ensured since background noise $\eta_0 > 0$ and therefore $I(p) > 0$.

The monotonicity is guaranteed as well: $I(p) = \gamma_i(p_i) = \frac{SINR_i}{\psi_i}$ where $\psi_i = h_{ii}\left(\sum_{j=1, j \neq i}^{K} h_{ij}p_j + \eta_0\right)$, we get $\psi_i(p) \leq \psi_i(p^*)$ for $p \leq p^*$. Since $\gamma_i(p_i)$ increases with increase in p_i on $[\underline{p_i}, \overline{p_i}]$ $\forall i$, $I(p)$ is increasing with p_i. Therefore, for a fixed price coefficient ε_{-i}, $I(p^*) \geq I(p)$.

3.5 LAA Algorithm

1. At time $t = 0$, set the initial transmit power and interference cost to random non-negative value.

2. Determine data rate according to (12)
3. For $t = 1 : end\_of\_communication$
   (a) Update and advertise interference cost according to (11)
   (b) Update transmit power according to (10)
   (c) Determine data rate according to (12)

4   Simulation Test and Results

Simulation is performed in MATLAB considering simulation parameters in table 1 where only transmitter Tx and receiver Rx are assumed to transmit while other network users are actively interfering. It is further summed that all transmissions are successful. We compare the performance of LAA to both IEEE 802.11a and adaptive auto response power and rate control algorithm proposed by [23].

Table 1. Simulation Parameters

Parameter	Values
Thermal noise	$-96dB$
Simulation area	$20m$ by $20m$
Radio propagation model	Free space
Number of nodes	32
Number of transmissions	50
P_{max}	$10dBm$
P_{min}	$1dBm$
Spreading factor, β	5
Initial cost	0.1
Utility function, $u_i(\gamma_i)$	$log(\gamma_i)$
Channel bandwidth	$20MHz$
Speed of mobility	$10kmps$
Interval of mobility	After 2 transmission

It is observed that LAA achieves high data rates at minimal transmission power (thus minimal interference) in all the runs compared to both 802.11 and LP. 802.11 records better SINR performance than LAA since 802.11 scheme employs maximum allowable power throughout the transmission with no much attention to link dynamics. However, in LAA, transmit power is adjusted depending on the network channel status.

Moreover, users are restricted from using high transmit powers (unless deemed necessary) as this would result to high interference cost and thus lowers the user's utility. As a result, minimal power level that can sustain the connectivity and ensures correct delivery of data frames is always chosen. Further, 802.11 has constant SINR throughout the transmission process due to its fixed single power choice. The power level that LAA settles on is apparently the most optimal power that maximizes both local and global utility based on the network conditions. 802.11 has no effect of reducing interference in the network thus users are at will to use feasible transmit power to maximize their utility without consideration to other users' utilities. After few iterations, LAA converges to NE transmit power where interference cost function is always minimized while reward function (data rate) is maximized hence improving network performance.

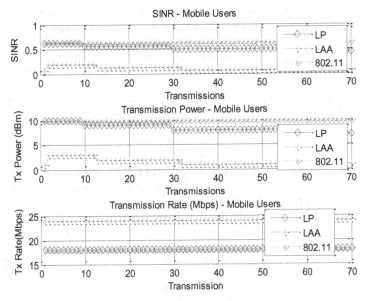

Fig. 1. Mobile Users

5   Conclusions

This paper proposes link adaptation algorithm for ad hoc networks based on penalty/pricing effect. Transmit power choices of users in the network are dynamically adjusted to minimize network interference. Such dynamic adjustments exploit the locally available network link conditions and interference cost penalties attached to that transmit power choice. Therefore the users are conversant with the link conditions as they determine data rates. In effect, users maximize utility of other users as they maximize their own utilities due to the inevitable cooperation thereby improving collective network performance (utility). Extension of this work may consider cross layering optimization to incorporate packet routing in the model.

References

1. Tavli, B.: Protocol architectures for energy efficient real-time data communications in mobile ad hoc networks, Ph.D. dissertation, Electrical and Computer Engineering, University of Rochester, New York (2005)
2. Olwal, T.O., et al.: Interference-aware power control for Multi-Radio Multi-Channel wireless mesh networks. In: AFRICON 2009, pp. 1–6 (2009)
3. Wang, K., et al.: Distributed cooperative rate adaptation for energy efficiency in IEEE 802.11-based multi-hop networks. In: The Third International Conference on Quality of Service in Heterogeneous Wired/Wireless Networks, QShine 2006 (2006)
4. Djouani, K., et al.: An Effective link adaptation method in cooperative wireless networks. In: Asia-Pacific Services Computing Conference, APSCC 2008, pp. 914–919. IEEE (2008)
5. Yahya, A., et al.: Energy-aware architecture for multi-rate ad hoc networks. Egyptian Informatics Journal 11, 6 (2010)

6. Aron, F.O.: Energy efficient topology control algorithm for wireless mesh networks, Master thesis, Electrical Engineering, Electrical Engineering, Tshwane University of Technology, Pretoria (2008)

7. Mahmood, H., Comaniciu, C.: A cross-layer game theoretic solution for interference mitigation in wireless ad hoc networks. In: Military Communications Conference, MILCOM 2006, pp. 1–7. IEEE (2006)

8. Jelitto, J., et al.: Power and rate adaptation in ieee 802.11a wireless LANs. In: The 57th IEEE Semiannual on Vehicular Technology Conference, VTC 2003, vol. 1, pp. 413–417 (Spring 2003)

9. Wu, S., et al.: A multi-channel mac protocol with power control for multi-hop mobile ad hoc networks. Computer Journal 45, 101–110 (2002)

10. Qiao, D., et al.: Energy-efficient pcf operation of IEEE 802.11a wireless LAN. In: Twenty-First Annual Joint Conference of the IEEE Computer and Communications Societies, INFO-COM 2002, vol. 2, pp. 580–589 (2002)

11. Palomar, D.P., Mung, C.: A tutorial on decomposition methods for network utility maximization. IEEE Journal on Selected Areas in Communications 24, 1439–1451 (2006)

12. Huang, J.: Wireless resource allocation: auctions, games and optimization, Doctor of Phylosophy, Electrical and Computer Engineering, Northwestern University, Evanston, Ilinois (2005)

13. Huang, J., et al.: Distributed interference compensation for wireless networks. IEEE Journal on Selected Areas in Communications 24, 1074–1084 (2006)

14. Chee Wei, T., et al.: Distributed optimization of coupled systems with applications to network utility maximization. Presented at the Acoustics, Speech and Signal Processing, ICASSP 2006 Proceedings (2006)

15. Bacci, G., Luise, M.: A noncooperative approach to joint rate and power control for infrastructure wireless networks Presented at the IEEE (2009)

16. Han, X., et al.: Joint rate control and power control in wireless ad hoc networks with QoS requirements. Presented at the Fourth International Conference on Networked Computing and Advanced Information Management (2008)

17. Wang, L., et al.: Joint rate and power adaptation for wireless local area networks in generalized Nakagami fading channels. IEEE Transactions on Vehicular Technology, 1375–1386 (2009)

18. Luo, J., et al.: Engineering wireless mesh networks: joint scheduling, routing, power control, and rate adaptation, Presented at the IEEE/ACM Transactions on Networking (2010)

19. Ozdaglar, A.: 6.254 Game theory with engineering applications, spring, ed: Massachusetts Institute of Technology: MIT OpenCourseWare (2010), http://ocw.mit.edu

20. Lu, S., et al.: Joint power and rate control in Ad Hoc networks using a supermodular game approach. In: Military Communications Conference, MILCOM 2006, pp. 1–7. IEEE (2006)

21. Yu-Chee, T., et al.: A Multi-channel MAC protocol with power control for multi-hop Mobile Ad Hoc Networks. Presented at the 2001 International Conference on Distributed Computing Systems Workshop (2001)

22. Peng, G., et al.: Non-cooperative power control game for adaptive modulation and coding. The Journal of China Universities of Posts and Telecommunications 17, 31–37 (2010)

23. Chevillat, P., et al.: Dynamic data rate and transmit power adjustment in IEEE 802.11 wireless LANs. International Journal of Wireless Information Networks 12 (2005)

Unidirectional Traffic Flow to Protect Wireless Sensor Networks against Byzantine Attacks

Björn Stelte

Universität der Bundeswehr München, Werner-Heisenberg-Weg 39,
85577 Neubiberg, Germany
bjoern.stelte@unibw.de
http://www.unibw.de/bjoern.stelte

Abstract. Due to its cheap costs and data processing ability it is expected that sensor networks will be widely used for monitoring environments. But it is also well known that Wireless Sensor Networks (WSNs) are vulnerable to many different kind of attacks. Especially insider attacks are very harmful and is not easy to defend a wireless sensor network against such attacks, because it is much easier to perform insider attacks in WSNs than in classical computer network. Securing WSNs with traditional cryptographic is not sufficient because available resources are limited and nodes have no hardware tampering protection. In this paper, we propose a concept of a cluster-based sensor network with cluster heads equipped with data diodes. These data diodes will defeat malicious code spreading and build a containment of the degree of attack damage. The presented cluster head nodes are build based on a low-voltage FPGA chip. The benefits of the partitioning of the network in clusters are shown next to the usage of the Byzantine Generals' Problem to detect node tampering. Through a smart positioning of nodes of different clusters, compromised and misbehaving nodes will be limited in their harmful impact on the network.

Keywords: Wireless sensor network, FPGA, Data diode, Insider attack, Byzantine attack.

1 Introduction

A Wireless Sensor Network (WSN) consists of several autonomous sensor nodes. A sensor node is a small device that can react on changes in the monitored environment. Each device is equipped with at least one sensor used to monitor physical or environmental conditions. Therefore, WSNs can be used to cooperatively monitor large environments such as critical infrastructures in gas and oil industries [10] or even a battlefield in military scenarios. The challenge of using WSN lies in its hard constraints on resources such as energy, computational power, and memory. Sensor nodes have to be cheap and small in size. Thus, physical protection (tamper protection) is unavailable, but security in WSN is very important aspect in such scenarios. So far critical WSN security issues have not been solved [10]. One of the most critical issues is known as Byzantine Attack in which a fraction of nodes are tampered. Several kind of Byzantine Attacks are known such as black hole, flood rushing, wormhole, and replayed routing information

M.S. Obaidat, J.L. Sevillano, and J. Filipe (Eds.): ICETE 2011, CCIS 314, pp. 503–518, 2012.

[3]. These attacks work perfectly under the assumption that devices or a set of devices can be captured by attackers and afterward compromised to obtain control over parts of the net or to prevent the network from fulfilling its task. Protection against this kind of insider attacks is hard to guarantee. E.g. authentication and data integrity mechanisms will not provide protection against insider attacks [10], because these mechanisms can not force a sensor node to behave according to the protocol. Awerbuch et al. define in [3] a Byzantine Attack as any attack that involves the leaking of authentication secrets so that an adversarial device is indistinguishable from a legitimate one.

Making one single node secure is nearly impossible due to the available computational power and memory as well as cost constraints. But it is possible to improve the security of the whole WSN by using redundancy and incorporate voting. Therefore, we will show in this paper how to improve security of a WSN and not how to protect a single node.

In our scenario the WSN is divided into clusters. Each cluster consists of a small number of nodes controlled by a cluster head. Cluster head nodes are gateway nodes for the controlled sensor nodes in the cluster. A data diode (also called security gateway) implemented in the cluster head node will only allow to transfer data from the sensor to the sink over the cluster head / gateway node. A transfer from one sensor node to a sensor node in another cluster will be effectively prevented. This prevention is useful to thwart spreading of malicious code which is needed for inside attacks.

We will show in this paper that it is possible to thwart Byzantine Attacks on WSNs by data diodes implemented in cluster head nodes. Note, we are not talking about sensor-actor networks, our WSN consists of sensor-only nodes which monitor an environment and report detected events regularly. Therefore, in our scenario we assume that only uni-directional transport protocols will be used in the network. This assumption is suitable for most sensor application scenarios.

The paper is structured as follows. In Section 2 related research is presented. Insider attacks on sensor nodes are shown in Section 3. A concept of a data diode enabled sensor node is presented in Section 4, followed by implementation details of our proof-of-concept in Section 5. Finally, Section 6 concludes the paper.

2   Related Work

To the best of the authors' knowledge, work proposed in the fields of object tracking and surveillance do not provide solutions for security problems induced by a malicious inside attacker in the WSN. A group of German researchers (Dudek et al.) have build a WSN prototype with the scope on a border control scenario. The work was financed by the german Federal Office for Information Security (BSI) and finished in 2010. Dudek et al. have presented their ideas of the FleGSens project in several publications like [6]. They used in their project the Dolev-Yao attacker model with WSN-specific avenues: the attacker may destroy nodes he has physical access to; the memory of nodes may be read-out and thus access to the cryptographic secrets stored there is gained; nodes may be even reprogram with malicious code. The FleGSens network consists of two kind of nodes, gateway nodes and sensor nodes. Gateways nodes have a permanent connection to the network authority and permanent power supply. Only sensor nodes may be compromised in their model and the network can cope with up to 5% of compromised nodes in total. A security protocol was defined to detect node failures. This is possible because nodes in the FleGSens network are positioned on a defined grid. Every nodes has the same distance to its neighbors. The detection protocol is based on a heartbeat mechanism. The FleGSens network does not need cluster heads because of its assumption to have placed nodes on a grid, which is unrealistic for most real-world scenarios. The work has shown that a limited amount of compromised nodes is acceptable when the degree of damage can be hold under a certain limit.

Deng et al. have shown security issues in cluster-based WSNs [5]. A WSN is vulnerable against a variety of threats that can lead to the failure of the cluster head, which represents a central point of failure. First, multi-path routing to multiple destination base stations was analyzed as a strategy to provide tolerance against individual attacks on cluster nodes or sensor node compromises. Second, confusion of address and identification fields in packet headers via hashing functions was explored as a technique to help disguise the location of the cluster head from eavesdroppers. Third, relocation of the cluster node in the network topology was studied as a means of enhancing resiliency and mitigating the scope of damage. The work shows that some attacks on the cluster head can be prevented but insider attacks, such as the presented Byzantine Attack, are not preventable by these counter-measurements.

In the next section we will briefly describe cyber attacks on WSNs and their relation to the Byzantine Generals' Problem.

3   WSN Cyber Security Attacks

How to secure WSNs against attacks is one of the top challenges today [16]. Especially in military scenarios the security of a network is critical since a disruption can lead to loss of live. Authenticated network devices (here sensor nodes) can be easily captured by the enemy forces and analyzed afterward. The risk of loosing devices in a chaotic battlefield environment is extremely high [3].

3.1   Byzantine Attack and the Generals' Problem

The WSN is typically deployed and managed by one authority. Network devices such as sensor nodes are seen as honest and cooperative entities and the authority has the control over all devices deployed in the environment. Only the authority has the right to access the network. All tries to illegally access and control the network can be classified in external and internal attacks [10]. An external attack is launched by a malicious node outside of the logical network. The node maybe only virtual if the attacker uses a laptop class based attack. The impact of external attacks is often limited, an internal attacks is more harmful than an external attack. An internal attacker has obtained authorization to access the network. Therefore, the misbehaving node is seen as a legitimate network device but it is under the control of the attacker. Two opportunities are available for an internal attacker, deploying malicious nodes that can pass the authentication process or by hijacking network devices such as sensor nodes.

One of these internal attacks is known as Byzantine Attack in which a set of authenticated sensor nodes are tampered. The goal of the Byzantine Attack is to disturb the communication of nodes in a WSN without regard to its own resource consumption. Therefore, it is assumed that authenticated nodes are under the control of the attacker. Authentication and integrity are the holy grail to protect used network protocols, e.g. by TinySec [8] etc., since they guarantee that only authenticated nodes can send legal data packets. However, it can not be given any guarantee about the legitimacy of actions taken by already authenticated nodes [3].

3.2 Byzantine Generals' Problem

The name Byzantine Attack is based on the Byzantine Generals' Problem which is a generalized version of the famous Two Armies Problem [7][2]. The Byzantine Generals' Problem was first introduced by Lamport et al. in [9] and is well known in the community. The goal of a Byzantine protocol is to find a collective and trustworthy decision.

The problem describes a decision problem where one Commander in Chief and $n-1$ generals communicate with each other. The communication between two persons is handled over a synchronous and non error-prone communication channel. The commander informs his generals his decision to attack or to retreat. The action is successful only if all generals carry out the instruction of the commander. In this scenario it is possible that at least one person (general or commander) tries to tamper. The goal of a Byzantine protocol is to let the honest generals come to a collective decision (under the assumption that the commander is honest).

Two examples will show the Byzantine Generals' Problem:

- Three honest generals and one betrayer
  - commander communicates his generals the decision
  - each general transmits the received decision to the other generals
  - each general will attack when the majority of the generals and the commander are for it
- Two honest generals and one betrayer
  - Case 1: Commander is dishonest: one general receives attack message and the other general receives a retreat message
  - Case 2: Commander is honest: one general is dishonest and tries to threat
  - in both cases the honest general(s) can not verify the received decision

Lamport et al. have formulated the thesis that for n persons with k betrayers there is a communication protocol that leads to a common decision if and only if $n \geq 3k + 1$. The proof of this thesis can be found at [9].

The Byzantine Attack problem is based on the Byzantine Generals Problem, such as Byzantine nodes try to disturb the network communication and confuse the network authority by let the WSN behave in a malicious manner. The functionality of the network will be disturbed and monitored events are not communicated to the authority or even wrong information are provided. There are four Byzantine Attack occurrences, namely Black Hole Attack, Flood Rushing Attack, Wormhole Attack, and Replayed Routing Information Attack. In the following we will describe these four attacks.

3.3 Black Hole Attack

A black hole attack is defined as an internal attack where an authenticated node stops forwarding data packets. The node will not stop completely its network association. The misbehaving note will still participate in the routing protocol correctly. To extend the impact on the network, the node will try to influence the routing protocol in such a way that more and more data packets are transported over a path where the misbehaving node is a part of. The Black Hole Attack prevents communication where it is selected as part of the message path. Detection of one or more malicious nodes acting as a Black Hole is very difficult because nodes are only equipped with unreliable wireless transmitters. Neither neighbor nodes nor the network authority can easily decide if packet loss arises due to problems with the communication channel (radio) or due to an active Black Hole Attack.

3.4 Flood Rushing Attack

A flood technique is often used in WSN routing protocols, e.g. to exchange neighborhood discovery messages. When an arbitrary node of the network tries to disturb the legitimate flood in its propagation phase and replaces the flood message with its own chosen values, we name this kind of attack Flood Rushing Attack. It can be seen as a kind of race between these two message floods. Normally, routing protocols use a flood duplication detection mechanism. Therefore, the routing protocol will drop all flood messages after it has received a flood messages, regardless if the flood messages was the legitimate one or not. When attacker can successfully propagate enough adversarial flood messages, the routing process will be disturbed if not even completely stopped. For the authority it is impossible to react afterward, since all routes to its sensor nodes are disturbed sustainable.

3.5 Wormhole Attack

If one sensor node is prone to get compromised, it is possible that more than one node is overtaken by an attacker. In order to gain additional advantages it is reasonable that these node form a low latency link between each other over which an attacker replays sniffed network messages. A Wormhole Attack is characterized by malicious nodes which eavesdrop data packets and tunnel them through the network to other malicious nodes to replay the packets. Such attack can obviously disturb the routing protocol by manipulating the neighbor discovery phase. A Wormhole Attack needs a tunnel between the corresponding nodes, this could be a covert channel (steganography) or more a classic tunnel created with a packet encapsulation technique. In an extended version the Wormhole Attack is used to increase the probability of being selected as part of a route by sending a route request message over the wormhole link and can afterward drop all data packets of this link in order to harmfully disturb the network communication. When many compromised nodes form a overlay network, it is even easier for the attacker to manipulate the routing process. By tunneling packets through such an overlay network the attacker can choose routing information in such a way that all misbehaving nodes appear as neighbors.

3.6   Replayed Routing Information Attack

A routing protocol can be attacked directly if it is possible to spoof, alter, or replay routing information. Even if cryptography is used to protect those messages, a replay of even encrypted routing information is still possible. The encryption will only protect information from being altered or spoofed. The attack is harmful if it is possible to create routing loops, extend and short certain source routes, generating fake errors, or even increasing end-to-end latency.

The presented Byzantine Attack occurrences work under the assumption that all nodes in the network can communicate with each other (even per multi-hop) and that every node is vulnerable against internal attacks. In the next section we will show our concept of a data diode followed by a description why this data diode will prevent the presented Byzantine Attack.

3.7   Byzantine Attacks on ZigBee Devices

Among the latest events of the wireless revolution, the fast-growing of ZigBee as a standard for WSNs is certainly one of these. ZigBee and IEEE 802.15.4 had been proving in the last years that they can achieve the results that WiFi had achieved for high bit-rate wireless LANs and some large reliable deployments are now in place implementing ad-hoc WSN in critical applications, like environment monitoring, asset tracking, and also military scenarios [4]. Currently all relevant WSN nodes, like MicaZ, IRIS, TelosB, etc., use ZigBee-conform transceivers to communicate with each other. The ZigBee standard for short-range wireless networking is targeted mainly for battery-powered applications where low costs and low power consumption are main requirements. Technically the ZigBee standard is based on IEEE802.15.4 PHY/MAC standard. The IEEE802.15.4 MAC layer implements several features which are used by the ZigBee protocol in network and application layers. The security services are one of these features. The underlying IEEE802.15.4 protocol sets the encryption algorithm to use when transmitted data should be cyphered. However, IEEE802.15.4 does not specify the key management or what kind of authentication policies have to be applied. These issues are treated in the upper layers which are managed by protocols such as ZigBee. The ZigBee standard implements two extra security layers on top of the IEEE802.15.4 protocol, namely the Network and the Application security layer.

IEEE802.15.4 defines security policies for data confidentiality, data authenticity, and replay protection.

Nevertheless these security policies will not efficiently prevent attackers to jam the association process or to execute a replay message attack. The following ZigBee security problems are well known:

- **Weak Integrity Protection on AES-CTR.** Integrity protection is based on a simple CRC calculation. It is possible to change the payload and then recalculate the new CRC and it is possible to forge messages to begin confidentially attacks.
- **DoS Attack on AES-CTR.** As sequential freshness mode is used a unique forged packet with the frame counter and key sequential counter set to the maximum value will stop the receiving of any other frame from this address.

- **Non Effective Packet Replay Protection.** IEEE802.15.4/ZigBee has only meager replay protection (4-octet frame counter).
- **Device Association Requests are send in Clear.** ZigBee does not use a challenge-response process nor signatures to at least secure the association process basically.
- **More and more Functionality is done by Hardware (ZigBee Transceiver).** Software is flexible, hardware not. A bug in the hardware implementation cannot be easily corrected.
- **CCMP known Plaintext Recovery.** ZigBee has problems with CCMP as a stream cipher and IV reuse as any stream cipher has potential IV reuse issues.
- **By default NO security** The application controls the security required, ACK packets are always send in clear, other packets can optionally use encryption or integrity checks.
- **IEEE802.15.4 MAC Layer Attacks.**
  - Guaranteed Time Slot (GTS) attack [14]
  - back-off interval manipulation (DCF) [11]
  - ACK attack [18]
  - PANId conflict attack [13]
  - ... and more [12].

Joshua Wright has developed a framework attacking ZigBee and IEEE802.15.4 networks, called KillerBee[17]. This framework simplifies sniffing and injecting network traffic, next to packet decoding and manipulation. So far two *AVR RZ Raven* USB sticks are needed to physically attack a deployed ZigBee network. The framework provides a modified firmware for the USB ZigBee transceiver sticks. Once uploaded to the sticks the user has full control over the USB stick, and can sniff and send injected ZigBee packets. The framework includes the following tools (as proposed by Joshua Wright in [17]) and assumes that sophisticating security features are not activated:

- **zbassocflood:** Repeatedly associate to the target PANId in an effort to cause the device to crash from too many connected stations.
- **zbconvert:** Convert a packet capture from libpcap to Daintree SNA format, or vice-versa.
- **zbdsniff:** Captures ZigBee traffic, looking for NWK frames and over-the-air key provisioning. When a key is found, zbdsniff prints the key to stdout.
- **zbdump:** A tcpdump-like took to capture IEEE 802.15.4 frames to a libpcap or Daintree SNA packet capture file. Does not display real-time stats like tcpdump when not writing to a file.
- **zbfind:** A GTK GUI application for tracking the location of an IEEE802.15.4 transmitter by measuring RSSI. Zbfind can be passive in discovery (only listen for packets) or it can be active by sending Beacon Request frames and recording the responses from ZigBee routers and coordinators.
- **zbgoodfind:** Implements a key search function using an encrypted packet capture and memory dump from a legitimate ZigBee or IEEE 802.15.4 device. This tool accompanies Travis Goodspeed's GoodFET hardware attack tool, or other binary data that could contain encryption key information such as bus sniffing with legacy chips (such as the CC2420).

- **zbid:** Identifies available interfaces that can be used by KillerBee and associated tools.
- **zbreplay:** Implements a replay attack, reading from a specified Daintree DCF or libpcap packet capture file, retransmitting the frames. ACK frames are not retransmitted.
- **zbstumbler:** Active ZigBee and IEEE 802.15.4 network discovery tool. Zbstumbler sends beacon request frames out while channel hopping, recording and displaying summarized information about discovered devices.

Two of these tools are of certain interest, *zbassocflood* and *zbreplay*. Joining a ZigBee network is possible by two ways: MAC association and network (NWK) rejoin. The later is possible if a node already knows the correct and actual NWK crypto key. Therefore, only nodes who have disassociate themselves once and now try to rejoin the network can use these mode. Nodes trying to join a network for the first time have to use the association method as shown in Figure 1. The coordinator send periodically beacon messages which a device receives and internally decides if it wants to join the network or not. A joining device send an *Association Request* Message to the Coordinator (Short-Address: 0x0000) and waits on an acknowledgment. In a second message the joining device transmits a *Data Request* command to the coordinator. Also this transmission is acknowledged by the coordinator. In the next phase the Coordinator sends an *Association Response* message to the device, which the device answers by a acknowledgment message with the sequence-number of the *Association Response*. The *Association Response* message includes a short address for the device to use while associated to the ZigBee network. Since all the associated frames are sent in the clear, the MAC association procedure is vulnerable to packet manipulation. The KillerBee framework *zbassocflood* uses exactly this vulnerable. Therefore, the tool produces randomized MAC addresses and starts to associate non-existent devices. Since every associated device gets an unique short address (16 Bit) the amount of available address is limited and the KillerBee tool can very quickly simulate a huge amount of joining devices. A ZigBee transceiver has to hold a kind of address resolution table for conversion of short and long (MAC) ZigBee addresses. A coordinator can control up to 2^{16} devices (address space of short local addresses). So a transceiver willing to cope with 2^{16} addresses has to store an address resolution table of $16 * 2^{16}Bit + 64 * 2^{16}Bit$ (640 kByte) size. This amount does not seam to be huge but a typical microcontroller on a sensor node does not have 640 kByte free memory nor has the transceiver such an amount of memory. By the way, a normal ZigBee stack is about 120 kByte size in total. So a KillerBee association flooding attack could be - depended on the transceiver implementation - harmful even if not the whole address space is blocked.

The second tool called *zbreplay* attacks the IEEE802.15.4 protocol by re-sending former sniffed packets. As Joshua Wright mentions the attack is somewhat comparable to the well known ARP attacks of former days [17]. The given example shows how successful and harmful such an attack could be is if one considers: replaying a message actuating water control valve to open one degree several times. IEEE802.15.4 specifies frame counters and at least in ZigBee-Pro transceivers have freshness checking (time-based protection) build-in. The problem is that replay protection can be turned on or off, the application developer has to explicit turn this feature on to activate the

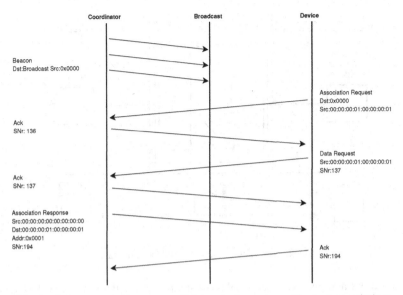

Fig. 1. ZigBee association process: Joining device and coordinator transmissions

build-in replay protection mechanism. Many WSN applications are build with optimization in mind, especially concerning power consumption. Therefore, often developers try to reduce lines of code and also the amount of additional used features to a minimum.

Tools of the KillerBee framework can be used to start Byzantine Attacks such as Wormhole and Flood Rushing. Manipulated routing data packets can be published in the ZigBee network by the *zbreplay* tool. Therefore, more sophisticating attacks like a Black Hole Attack and a Routing Information Attack are also possible.

4   Concept of a Data Diode

In a secure area network with different security levels, reliable unidirectional data transfer is needed. In such scenarios a so called security gateway is often used to guarantee that confidential data from a secure network is never transferred to the network with the lower classification. Connections between networks with a different security classification are also called red-black transitions. The red network has a lower classification than the black network. Data can be only transferred from the red network to the black network. So, the data diode builds a secure one-way data path.

The hearth of our security gateway is a data diode. The data diode will separate the two networks with different classification. Several commercial data diode for classical IP networks are available, such as FoxDataDiode and GeNUGate. These gateways enable reliable real-time transmission of information from one network to the other in a unidirectional mode only. Assurance for some of these products have been provided by NATO (secret) and Common Criteria EAL7+. The idea is now to build a data diode for WSN in order to thwart parts of the network against Byzantine Attacks.

In our scenario cluster head nodes will be equipped with a data diode. Therefore, our cluster head node needs a second radio transmitter and a second micro-controller.

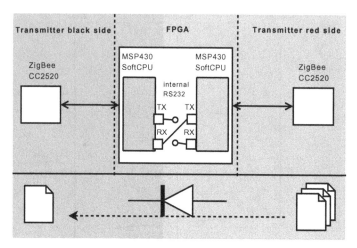

Fig. 2. Overview of the data diode architecture

One transmitter and one micro-controller is used for one of the two networks (red and black). The red network consists of sensor nodes and the first part of the cluster head node and the classified black network consists only of the second part of the cluster heads surplus the sink node towards the network authority.

Our data diode architecture consists of two micro-controllers and a half-open serial interface between these two devices as shown in Figure 2. One transmitter and one micro-controller is used for one of the two networks (red and black). Due to power requirements and security reasons we have implemented the data diode within a low-power FPGA. The implementation on a FPGA guarantees that bypassing the devices is not easily possible, since the connection is wired inside the FPGA chip. This can be seen as a kind of light tamper protection. In Section 5 we will describe some details how we have implemented the node. In the following we would like to present the benefits of our concept and why the data diode is a solution to solve the Byzantine Attack problem.

As described before, four occurrences of the Byzantine Attack are known, Black Hole Attack, Flood Rushing Attack, Wormhole Attack, and Replayed Routing Information Attack. We contend that a data diode implemented in cluster heads will pretend the network for those attacks or at least reduce the degree of damage. Figure 3 shows the partitioning of the network in clusters. Therefore, the concept of a cluster based sensor-only network is used. Nodes within the cluster belong to the red network and the classified black network only consists of cluster head nodes. Every cluster has one cluster head equipped with a data diode implementation. The cluster head node is available within the cluster and the cluster head nodes can communicate with each other and to the sink node towards the network authority.

4.1   Black Hole Attack

A Black Hole Attack tries to drop as much as possible data packets of a communication. Therefore, at least one sensor node has to be compromised and claims to act as a forwarding device. In our scenario the WSN is portioned in smaller clusters. Thus, if an

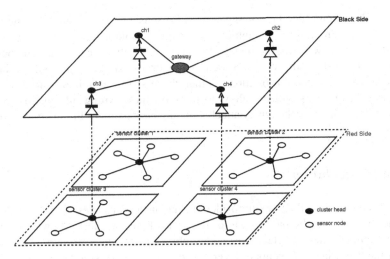

Fig. 3. High-layer graph of a typical sensor network

attack successfully implements a black hole on a sensor node only a certain part of the network - the cluster - will be affected. The data diode on the cluster head will prevent a spread of further manipulated routing information to other parts of the WSN (other clusters). Therefore, our concept can curtail the Black Hole Attack.

4.2 Flood Rushing Attack

In a Flood Rushing Attack an ambitious attacker tries to send manipulated routing information. Like the Black Hole Attack scenario, our concept will prevent a spread of these wrong routing data packets on neighbored sensor nodes in close-by clusters.

4.3 Wormhole Attack

For the Wormhole Attack an attacker tries to build a tunnel between two captured nodes. There are two possible attack scenarios, a tunnel within the cluster or a tunnel between two sensor nodes of different clusters. A tunnel between two sensor nodes of the same cluster is possible but because of the limited cluster area not very harmful. Malicious information send through the tunnel will only affect the routing within the cluster. A more harmful situation occurs if an attacker can build a tunnel between two nodes of different clusters. In this case the attacker can spread manipulated routing information and thus consequently stop any network transmission. The data diode will prevent such an attack by preventing any data exchange between sensor nodes in different clusters. A tunnel can not been established and therefore an extended Wormhole Attack on the complete WSN is defeated.

4.4 Replayed Routing Information Attack

An attacker may sniff data packets with routing information and replay these packets on a later point in time. Because the size of a cluster is very limited the replay message will not have a huge impact on the routing table of the sensor nodes within the cluster. Even if the attacker can harmfully manipulate the routing table in such a way that packets get lost, the nodes will rebuild the legally routing table after the regular neighborhood discovery phase (depended on the chosen routing protocol). The attack will not be able to spread wrong routing information to other clusters. The data diode implemented in the cluster head nodes will not allow to transport these wrong information to other sensor nodes. Therefore the replay attack will only have a timely-limited impact on one cluster.

5   Implementation

So far we have only talked about insider attacks on sensor nodes. If the attacker will be able to overcome the partitioning of the network, the whole WSN will be in danger. In contrast to the simple sensor nodes, cluster head nodes are part of the cluster and of the upper layer. This upper layer called byzantine decision layer consists of all cluster head nodes and the data sink. Our concept of data diodes successfully prevents any communication between nodes of different clusters. This case enables not only to prevent some insider attack but also to build a more secure WSN. If the attacker would be able to control a cluster head, he could also start an insider attack on the upper layer and therefore send manipulated information to the data sink.

To detect such an attack and secondly to avoid manipulation concerning the event transmission, we will use the Byzantine Generals' Problem to form a protocol for fault tolerance. Therefore, we build clusters of sensor nodes which overlap and communicate with their own cluster encryption key. The overlapping clusters will guarentee that a monitored event will be transmitted to a sink node over different paths. Even if one cluster head tries to betray, the sink will get the legally event message from different clusters. Although, other cluster heads can detect the betraying cluster, inform the network authority, and finally isolate the malicious cluster head. Figure 4 shows our concept exemplary for a WSN with four clusters.

Concerning the Byzantine Generals' Problem we need at least $3k + 1$ clusters to overcome k betrayers. We will further assume that at most one node behaves malicious, so we need four clusters with four cluster head nodes in our scenario. All sensor nodes of the WSN are placed randomly in the environment. The decision which node belongs to which cluster is also decided in a random behavior with the exception that the disposition is in some degree balanced. This means that each cluster monitors approximately the same environment and event reports are send on different independent paths to the data sink. Therefore, the density of nodes deployed in the environment will be upgraded, and the safeness of the whole system is improved. As described before the data sink will receive for each monitored event four messages and can decide by a Byzantine majority decision if the reported message is trustworthy, and if one cluster is infected by an internal attacker. In this concept only the data sink (gateway node) needs tamper protection, which reduces the costs for a trustworthy WSN significantly.

To show that it is possible to securely implement a data diode on a cluster head, we have started to build a prototype. This prototype consists mainly of three devices:

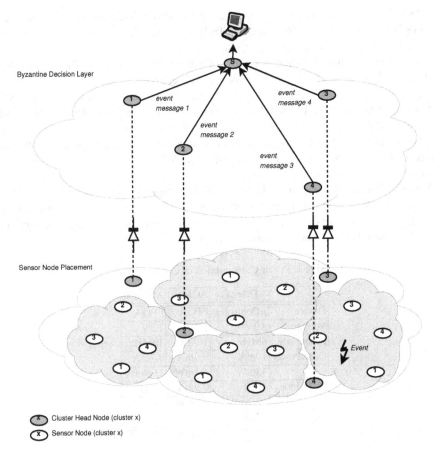

Fig. 4. Sensor node placement and Byzantine Layer

- A Texas Instruments CC2520 ZigBee Transmitter chip for the red network (cluster nodes).
- A Texas Instruments CC2520 ZigBee Transmitter chip for the black network (decision layer).
- A Actel IGLOO AGL600 flash-FPGA holding two Soft-Cores and the data diode.

We haven chosen a FPGA instead of two μcontrollers in order to have more flexibility in the design and to secure the data diode against a simple tampering by bridging the μcontrollers. As described in [15], it is possible to use flash-based low-power FPGA instead of μcontrollers on WSN nodes. It was shown that a typical TinyOS application can run on a OpenMSP430 Soft-Core μcontroller within the FPGA without modification of the operating system. Therefore, we have extended this work to implement two Soft-Cores on the low-power FPGA and connect these two embedded μcontroller by the data diode.

Several Soft-Cores for FPGAs are already available, e.g. CoreMP7 from Actel, OpenMSP430 from OPENCORES.ORG, etc. For our implementation we have chosen the OpenMSP430 Soft-Core which operates like a MSP430 μcontroller. The famous TinyOS WSN operating system supports MSP430 μcontrollers, therefore we can program and use the Soft-Core for our purpose.

Figure 1 shows the schematic overview of our cluster head node. The μcontroller on the red side is connected to one ZigBee transmitter and the μcontroller on the black side used the other ZigBee transmitter. Each side can be seen as an autonomy WSN node with a different task. The red μcontroller will control the cluster sensor nodes and forward event messages to the black side. The black μcontroller will wait on forwarded event messages and send them to the data sink. In a second step the black μcontroller will receive event messages of other cluster head nodes and tries to verify the messages based on the Byzantine Generals' Problem.

Table 1 shows the aggregation of the power consumption comparison. It shows that the Actel FPGA has a dominant power advantage over a typically μcontroller used for WSN nodes [1]. So, we can use the FPGA without risking huge power consumption. Our FPGA-based cluster node is usable in real-world scenarios.

Table 1. Power Consumption of Cluster CPUs

	ATMega	AGL030	AGL600
Device	μController	FPGA	FPGA
Voltage	3.3V	1.2V	1.2V
Frequency	8MHz	10Mhz	10MHz
Core Power	10mA	0.9mA	9.7mA
	33mW	1.1mW	11.6mW
Idle Mode	4mA	0.9mA	9.7mA
	13.2mW	1.1mW	11.6mW
Sleep Mode	15μA	4μA	28μA
	49μW	4.8μW	33.6μW

Our VHDL implementation needs after the synthesis 11478 tiles (84%) on the AGL600 FPGA [1]. With this parameters the Actel power calculator can estimate a power calculation under typical conditions. The resulting calculation for a OpenMSP430 implementation shows that a active total power of 9,05 mW, about 0,229 mW in flash freeze mode, and about 0,024 mW in sleep mode is expected for two Soft-Core implementations on one FPGA chip.

As mentioned before, a RS-232 data diode is used to allow one-way data flow from the serial line of one μcontroller to the other one. The idea is to protect the μcontroller on the black side from potential threats posed by insecure nodes on the red side. As with any serial communication, source and destination system have to use the same data rate, number of bits-per-character, and parity setting. In our implementation we have used a data rate of 9600 baud. This is also the maximum supported data rate of the Open-MSP430 μcontroller. The channel between the controller is a non-loose one, because both controllers are implemented on the same FPGA chip. So the maximum data rate of 9600 baud is reliable in our configuration. Communication exchange between the controllers is affected by short messages encoded by an ASCII character set. Therefore, we set a bits-per-character value of seven. A parity bit is not necessary having a non-loss and reliable channel, but could be used to prevent data lose do to internal timing issues. Because the data diode does not support the usage of a reverse channel, parity could be used. Odd parity has slight advantages for 7-bit data communication and should be used in this case.

The two implemented μcontrollers are internally connected by a serial line interface. This interface has a RX and a TX connection point on each side. In our FPGA implementation only the black side RX and the red side TX connection point are wired, forming a unidirectional channel. The software implementation on both side use this serial line interface for a unidirectional communication. Because the serial interfaces are implemented with the FPGA data lose can be neglected and acknowledgment messages are not necessary. The serial interface on the black side has a buffer, which once filled with a message rises an interrupt. Therefore, the application on the black μcontroller can act as a simple message forwarder by forwarding message out of the serial interface buffer to the data sink over a broadcast channel of the ZigBee-based Byzantine Layer network.

6   Conclusions

This position paper shows our idea of how to build a trustworthy sensor-only network. Therefore, we have first partitioned the network in clusters of the same size and secondly implemented a dual μcontroller cluster head node with a data diode. A smart positioning of sensor nodes of each cluster enables us to detect events occurred in the monitored environment on different cluster sensor nodes and thus reports of the same event are transported redundant over independent paths to the network authority. We have used the Byzantine Generals' Problem as base to verify that the received event messages are trustworthy. To overcome certain harmfully insider attacks, we have implemented a data diode on the cluster head. Therefore, the cluster head acts as a unidirectional security gateway between sensor nodes in different clusters and the data sink. To the best of our knowledge this is the first publications presenting the idea of a data diode for WSN. The present approach is suitable for sensor-only networks.

References

1. ACTEL Corporation: IGLOO AGL0600 Datasheet,
   http://www.actel.com/documents/IGLOO_DS.pdf
2. Akkoyunlu, E.A., Ekanadham, K., Huber, R.V.: Some constraints and tradeoffs in the design of network communications. In: Proceedings of the Fifth ACM Symposium on Operating Systems Principles, SOSP 1975, pp. 67–74. ACM, New York (1975),
   http://doi.acm.org/10.1145/800213.806523
3. Awerbuch, B., Curtmola, R., Holmer, D., Nita-rotaru, C., Rubens, H.: Mitigating Byzantine Attacks in ad hoc Wireless Networks (2004), http://citeseerx.ist.psu.edu/viewdoc/summary?doi=?doi=10.1.1.3.6309
4. Carcelle, X., Heil, B., Chatellier, C., Pailler, P.: Next WSN applications using ZigBee. In: 1st IEEE Home Networking Conference, Paris - France (December 2007)
5. Deng, K., Han, R., Mishra, S.: Enhancing Base Station Security in Wireless Sensor Networks. Technical Report CU-CS-951-03 (2003)

6. Dudek, D., Haas, C., Kuntz, A., Zitterbart, M., Krüger, D., Rothenpieler, P., Pfisterer, D., Fischer, S.: A Wireless Sensor Network for Border Surveillance. In: Proceedings ACM SenS., ACM Sensys, Berkeley (2009), http://doc.tm.uka.de/2009/FleGSens-A-Wireless-Sensor-Network-for-Border-Surveillance.pdf

7. Gmytrasiewicz, P.J., Durfee, E.H.: Decision-theoretic recursive modeling and the coordinated attack problem. In: Proceedings of the First International Conference on Artificial Intelligence Planning Systems, pp. 88–95. Morgan Kaufmann Publishers Inc., San Francisco (1992), http://portal.acm.org/citation.cfm?id=139492.139503

8. Karlof, C., Sastry, N., Wagner, D.: TinySec: a link layer security architecture for wireless sensor networks. In: SenSys 2004: Proceedings of the 2nd International Conference on Embedded Networked Sensor Systems, pp. 162–175. ACM Press, New York (2004), http://dx.doi.org/10.1145/1031495.1031515

9. Lamport, L., Shostak, R., Pease, M.: The Byzantine Generals Problem. ACM Transactions on Programming Languages and Systems 4, 382–401 (1982)

10. Radmand, P., Talevski, A., Petersen, S., Carlsen, S.: Taxonomy of Wireless Sensor Network Cyber Security Attacks in the Oil and Gas Industries. In: International Conference on Advanced Information Networking and Applications, pp. 949–957 (2010)

11. Radosavac, S., Cárdenas, A.A., Baras, J.S., Moustakides, G.V.: Detecting IEEE 802.11 MAC layer misbehavior in ad hoc networks: Robust strategies against individual and colluding attackers. J. Comput. Secur. 15(1), 103–128 (2007)

12. Raymond, D.R., Midkiff, S.F.: Denial-of-Service in Wireless Sensor Networks: Attacks and Defenses. IEEE Pervasive Computing 7, 74–81 (2008)

13. Sokullu, R., Korkmaz, I., Dagdeviren, O., Mitseva, A., Prasad, N.: An Investigation on IEEE 802.15.4MAC Layer Attacks. In: Proceedings of 8th International Symposium on Wireless Personal Multimedia Communications (WPMC 2005), Aalborg, Denmark (September 2007)

14. Sokullu, R., Dagdeviren, O., Korkmaz, I.: On the IEEE 802.15.4 MAC Layer Attacks: GTS Attack. In: International Conference on Sensor Technologies and Applications, pp. 673–678 (2008)

15. Stelte, B.: Toward development of high secure sensor network nodes using an FPGA-based architecture. In: Proceedings of the 6th International Wireless Communications and Mobile Computing Conference, pp. 539–543. ACM Press, New York (2010), http://doi.acm.org/10.1145/1815396.1815521

16. Winkler, M., Tuchs, K.D., Hughes, K., Barclay, G.: Theoretical and Practical aspects of military wireless sensor networks. Journal of Telecommunications and Information Technology, 37–45 (2008)

17. Wright, J.: Killerbee:Practical Zigbee Exploitation Framework. In: Toorcon11 (October 2009)

18. Xiao, Y., Sethi, S., Chen, H., Sun, B.: Security services and enhancements in the IEEE 802.15.4 wireless sensor networks. Proceedings of IEEE GLOBECOM 3 (2005)

Successive Interference Cancellation for Multi-user MIMO-OFDM Ad-Hoc Networks: A Performance-Complexity Tradeoff

Nikolaos I. Miridakis and Dimitrios D. Vergados

Department of Informatics, University of Piraeus,
80 Karaoli and Dimitriou St., GR-185 34, Piraeus, Greece
{nikozm,vergados}@unipi.gr

Abstract. In this paper, we consider a multi-user ad-hoc framework which is established on a Multiple Input-Multiple Output Orthogonal Frequency Division Multiplexing (MIMO-OFDM) infrastructure. The reception is accomplished by utilizing the Successive Interference Cancellation (SIC) approach. Particularly, we emphasize on the performance-complexity tradeoff of SIC by implementing two well-known equalizers, namely Zero-Forcing (ZF) and Minimum Mean Squared Error (MMSE). Our main objective is the provision of the system robustness in terms of the error resilience and the computational complexity efficiency. Thereby, a novel hybrid-SIC is proposed, which jointly performs either ZF-SIC or MMSE-SIC according to the instantaneous channel statistics, on an OFDM subcarrier basis. Furthermore, a complexity analysis is provided whereas upper and lower complexity bounds for the proposed scheme are also derived. Finally, the analysis is accompanied with detailed Bit-Error-Rate (BER) numerical results, which along with the corresponding complexity results, demonstrate the usefulness of the proposed scheme.

Keywords: Multiple-Input Multiple-Output Orthogonal Frequency Division Multiplexing (MIMO-OFDM), Hybrid Successive Interference Cancellation (Hybrid SIC), Performance-Computational tradeoff, Multi-user networks.

1 Introduction

Wireless ad hoc networks form a collection of autonomous nodes that communicate in a distributed manner without relying on a pre-established infrastructure or on a centralized control unit. One approach for improving the link robustness and the system capacity of an ad hoc network is through the establishment of Multiple-Input Multiple-Output Orthogonal Frequency Division Multiplexing (MIMO-OFDM) adaptation. OFDM is proposed as one of the key technologies for modulation and signal propagation. Recently, most of the research activity has focused on its multiuser access method, namely orthogonal frequency division multiple access (OFDMA), since it provides high data rates and reliable links in multiuser environments. On the other hand, MIMO technologies hold the premise of achieving significant performance improvement and capacity enhancement in such systems. Moreover, MIMO fading channels can be explored to provide either *spatial diversity* gain (SD) in order to enhance the system robustness,

M.S. Obaidat, J.L. Sevillano, and J. Filipe (Eds.): ICETE 2011, CCIS 314, pp. 519–533, 2012.

or *spatial multiplexing* gain (SM) to the scope of the system capacity increase and the transmission gain. Due to the complementary benefits of MIMO and OFDM, the real-ization of MIMO-OFDM systems is, therefore, of a great importance [1], [2] to ensure both the effectiveness and the reliability of future service demands in modern wireless ad hoc networks.

Nevertheless, the interference effect represents a major efficiency inhibitor while induces a typical upper bound to the performance of such networks. Successive inter-ference cancellation (SIC) represents quite an effective methodology, which tends to counteract the later limitation. The equalization methodology used in conjunction with the SIC-based reception, determines both the reliability of SIC, in terms of the bit-error-rate (BER) performance, and the overall computational complexity of the process. The maximum likelihood (ML) criterion is the most optimal yet most demanding equaliza-tion technique, in terms of the BER performance and the computational complexity, respectively. In fact, the computational burden of an ML equalizer is found to be over-whelmed for most practical applications [3]. Hence, most of the research community has rather focused on suboptimal equalization techniques, based on either zero forcing (ZF) or minimum mean squared error (MMSE) detection. Generally, in a noisy envi-ronment, MMSE-SIC is less susceptible to errors than ZF-SIC at the cost of a higher computational complexity and vice versa [4].

In principle, SIC-based reception can provide efficiency enhancement in MIMO ad hoc networks [5], since it accomplishes significant capacity and throughput improve-ment. Both ZF-SIC and MMSE-SIC can sufficiently reduce the outage probability [6], especially under SM regimes [7]. Along with the later optimization trend, the re-searchers have focused on the reliability and the robustness of such networks, which represents another fundamental issue for the provisioning of the overall system effi-ciency. However, the robustness and, hence, the reduction of the BER probability of SIC-based reception in such networks have not studied in the appropriate depth so far.

In general, most of the researchers have focused on advanced signal processing tech-niques to enhance the accuracy of SIC and/or to enhance the overall complexity of the process [8]-[10]. On the other hand, some researchers moved towards another direc-tion by adopting hybrid SIC schemes based on joint equalization strategies, in order to appropriately balance the tradeoff between the BER performance and the computa-tional complexity. As an indicative example, a hybrid ZF-ML-SIC [11] has previously been proposed in order to enhance this tradeoff, by adopting a partial ML. The use of the demanding ML, however, burdens the overall computational cost and this gets more emphatic as the number of the transmit/receive antennas increases. Furthermore, a hybrid ZF-MMSE-SIC [12] has been proposed for coded (or spread) MIMO-OFDM (MIMO-OFCDM) systems. In such systems, each symbol is spread in several subcar-riers while the spreading range depends on a predefined spreading gain. Hence, there is no applicable solution for symbol isolation and, therefore, for detection on a sub-carrier basis. In [12], all symbols are carried out by ZF-SIC in the spatial domain and by MMSE-SIC in the frequency domain, afterwards. This approach, however, increases enormously the complexity of the process in order to suppress the BER probability, whereas a power adaptation user profile for each user was not considered.

We focus, in this paper, on the performance of SIC for *uncoded* MIMO-OFDM ad hoc networks and, more specifically, we propose a joint detection methodology based on ZF and MMSE equalization. Upon a signal decoding, the decision statistic, which determines whether a symbol will be carried out by a ZF-SIC or by an MMSE-SIC, exclusively, depends on a threshold. The value of the threshold is defined on an OFDM frame (or block) basis by taking into account statistics from the received information on each subcarrier. Each ad hoc user/node is assigned a unique power profile depending on its location with respect to (w.r.t.) the receiver and to the other transmitting nodes' locations at a given time instance. Our main objective, here, is the establishment of an appropriate tradeoff between the BER performance and the computational complexity of the proposed hybrid SIC. Moreover, in this study we focus on multiuser MIMO-OFDM ad hoc networks where all the nodes transmit using QPSK modulation schemes. For the best of our knowledge, joint SIC-based detection schemes have never been studied for ad hoc MIMO-OFDM networks, whereas a hybrid ZF-MMSE-SIC reception methodology has never been proposed for uncoded MIMO implementations at large.

The rest of this paper is organized as follows. In Section 2, the system model is presented. In Section 3, the conventional ZF-SIC and MMSE-SIC are reviewed while typical BER expressions are provided. In Section 4, the proposed scheme is analytically described whereas certain BER probabilities are explicitly obtained. In Section 5, a performance evaluation of the proposed scheme is presented with respect to the computational complexity and the BER performance, followed by concluding remarks provided in Section 6.

2 System Model

We consider a MIMO-OFDM system consisting of N_C subcarriers with N_T and $N_R (\geq N_T)$ transmit and receive antennas, respectively. Let $N_U(t)$ denote the number of transmitting users, transmitting at a certain time instance t, to a receiving node. In this paper, we focus on an uncoded OFDMA system, where data symbols from a reference user are not modulated on all the subcarriers, but different users have assigned different subcarriers. Commonly, the carrier assignment for OFDM schemes is based on clustered, random or interleaved subcarrier allocation. As the optimization of the carrier assignment and/or reassignment is out of the scope of this paper we, therefore, assume a generic subcarrier allocation scheme, in which all the subcarriers have uniformly distributed among the transmitting nodes.

2.1 Notations

The notations used throughout this paper are the following: Vectors and matrices are represented by lowercase bold typeface and uppercase bold typeface letters, respectively. $\mathbf{A}_{\alpha, b}$ denotes the (α, b)-th element of $\mathbf{A}$. $E\{.\}$ stands for the statistical mean. A complex Gaussian random variable with mean m and variance σ^2 is expressed as $G(m, \sigma^2)$. Superscripts $(.)^T$ and $(.)^H$ denote the transposition and the conjugate (or Hermitian) transposition, respectively. $\mathbf{I}_N$ stands for the $N \times N$ identity matrix, $\lfloor . \rfloor$ represents the floor function and $\|.\|$ denotes the norm of a vector/matrix. The real and imaginary parts of a complex number x are denoted, respectively, as $\Re(x)$ and $\Im(x)$. Finally, $arg(x) = angle\ tan(\Im(x)/Re(x))$.

2.2   Network Architecture and Power Decay Profile

We consider a wireless ad hoc network consisting of $M \geq N_U$ nodes (or users), which are randomly placed in a squared plain $\mathbf{R}^2$. Arbitrary transmitter-receiver pairs are generated at a given time instance t, according to a homogeneous Poisson Point Process (HPPP), since it represents a common method for traffic generation in such networks [5]-[7]. However, the transmitter-receiver assignment of the M nodes remains fixed for a certain time interval Δt, which equals to an OFDM frame duration. Focusing on the system robustness and the reception accuracy, we consider a fixed location of the receiver in the center of the plain, which represents the 'worst-case scenario' in a dense ad hoc network, by increasing the diversity of potential transmitters [13]. In other words, considering the later condition, we obtain the maximum density at a receiver, caused by the remaining transmitting nodes and, thus, we may have the highest BER probability in a MIMO-OFDM environment. Then, we define the network architecture consisting of all the active users for an OFDM frame duration, as a directed acyclic graph, denoted as $\Omega_{|\Delta t} = (N_U, N_E)$, where N_E denotes the physical links directed from all the transmitters to the origin, which is the location of the receiver.

Typically, in ad hoc networks two power allocation schemes are used, namely uniform or linear power allocation [14]. In case of a uniform power allocation, all the nodes use a common power profile for their transmissions. In case of the linear power allocation, the transmit power is proportional to d_u^α, where d_u denotes the Euclidean distance from the u-th transmitting node to the receiving node and α the path loss exponent. In our research, we consider the linear power allocation scheme, since the power variation in every subcarrier enhances the performance of SIC-based reception, in general. More specifically, we propose a linear power allocation with adaptation to fairness scheme in order to counteract the peak-to-average-power ratio (PAPR), which represents one of the most essential weaknesses of the OFDM transmissions. Consequently, when the u-th node intends to transmit to the receiver, we define the transmit power level at all the transmit antennas of the u-th node as

$$P_u = R\,d_u^\alpha \sum_{m \neq u,r} d_u^{-\alpha}, \tag{1}$$

where R is a constant, playing the role of a normalization factor, which is predetermined by the network manufacturer according to the quality-of-service (QoS) requirements of the respective users. In order to achieve the maximum capacity, the transmitted signal power needs to be equally distributed over all the transmit antennas of each node, yielding to $P_u\,\mathbf{I}_{N_T}$ for the u-th user[1] [2]. Moreover, the proposed model considers only path

---

[1] In case we have a uniform network topology, all the nodes transmit to an equal power P, yielding to $P\mathbf{I}_{N_T}$ for all the transmit antennas of all the nodes. Assuming that P is unit-valued, this yields to $P = \mathbf{I}_{N_T}$, which is a simplified condition. However, in this paper, we focus in a generic framework in terms of the nodes' topology, including both uniform and random topologies, to address more realistic network scenarios.

loss effects in terms of propagation attenuation and ignores additional channel effects, such as fast fading [15].

2.3   Transmitter

First, the information data stream of the u-th user, where $0 \leq u \leq N_U - 1$, is bit-by-bit mapped to QPSK symbols $s_l^u(t)$ with $l \in \{0, 1, ..., K_u - 1\}$ and K_u denotes the number of subcarriers assigned to the user u, i.e. $K_u(t) = \lfloor (N_C - 1 + N_U(t) - u)/N_U(t) \rfloor$, which is a subset of the available subcarriers[2]. Then, a Serial-to-Parallel (S/P) conversion occurs and the data block of the u-th user $\mathbf{s}_u(t) \equiv [s_0^u(t), s_1^u(t), ..., s_{K_u-1}^u(t)]^T$ is transformed into a block of N_C symbols $\mathbf{\check{x}}_u(t) \equiv [x_0^u(t), x_1^u(t), ..., x_{N_U-1}^u(t)]^T$, whose indices correspond to the assigned subcarriers of the u-th user, whereas zeroes are inserted in correspondence to the other subcarriers. After taking an Inverse Fast Fourier transformation (IFFT), the transmitted discrete time signal vector can be obtained as

$$\mathbf{x}_u(t) = \mathbf{F}_{N_C}^H \mathbf{\check{x}}_u(t), \tag{2}$$

where $\mathbf{F}_{N_C}$ denotes the N_C-point FFT matrix. In order to avoid Inter-Carrier Interference (ICI) and Inter-Symbol Interference (ISI) caused in multipath environments, a cyclic prefix (CP) is appended to each OFDM symbol. Then, the OFDM symbols are appropriately parceled out to all the given N_T antennas of each user[3] and every symbol is assigned a unique spatial signature and the appropriate signal power (which is further analyzed in section 3) before the transmission.

2.4   Channel

In OFDM systems, the frequency selectivity of the channel becomes flat to all the given subcarriers. We, therefore, define the MIMO-OFDM $N_R \times N_T$ channel matrix of the u-th user $\mathbf{H}_u$, where $\|\mathbf{H}_u\|^2 = \mathbf{H}_u^T \mathbf{H}_u$. Apparently, the j-th column of $\mathbf{H}_u$ represents the channel from the j-th transmit antenna of the u-th user to all the receive antennas of the receiver node. Since, in an ideal rich scattering environment the entries of $\mathbf{H}_u$ are mutually uncorrelated [16], the amplitude of each n-th entry is modeled as an independent and identically distributed (i.i.d.) random Rayleigh channel component as $G(0, 1)$. We assume a slowly varying channel, i.e. $\mathbf{H}_u$ remain constant over an OFDM frame duration, but may vary from one frame duration to another. Hence, without loss of generality and for notational simplicity, we drop indices t and u in the rest of this paper, assuming generic user cases and compact OFDM frame transmissions.

2.5   Receiver

The overall signal is superimposed within an OFDM frame at the receiver, which plays the role of a sink node. After the CP removal, the receiver conventionally performs fast

---

[2] If N_C is a multiple of N_U each user has assigned the same number of subcarriers ($K_u(t) = N_C/N_U(t)\forall u$).

[3] We assume in this paper, for simplicity sake, that $K_u = bN_T, b \in \mathbf{N}^+$.

Fourier transform (FFT) at each subcarrier, which yields to the actual received signal expressed as

$$\mathbf{y}_n = \mathbf{H}_n \mathbf{P}_n \mathbf{x}_n + \mathbf{w}_n, \tag{3}$$

where $\mathbf{y}_n = [y_0^n + y_1^n + ... + y_{N_R-1}^n]^T$ and $\mathbf{x}_n = [x_0^n + x_1^n + ... + x_{N_T-1}^n]^T$ represent the received and the transmit signal vector, respectively, at the n-th subcarrier. The transmission power of each user associated with the n-th subcarrier represents a diagonal matrix which is expressed as $\mathbf{P}_n = diag\{\sqrt{P_1}, \sqrt{P_2}, ..., \sqrt{P_{N_T}}\}$, where $\sqrt{P_j}$ denotes the transmission power of the j-th transmit antenna at the n-th subcarrier. Also, the $\mathbf{w}_n = [w_0^n + w_1^n + ... + w_{N_R-1}^n]^T$ is a zero-mean complex AWGN vector with covariance matrix given as

$$\Phi_w = E\{\mathbf{w}_n \mathbf{w}_n^H\} = \sigma_w^2 \mathbf{I}_{N_R}, \tag{4}$$

where σ_w^2 represents the noise variance introduced by the communication channel.

Finally, we provide a compact input-output relation between all the OFDM subcarriers at all the transmit and receive antennas of all the network transmitting nodes, which is expressed as

$$\underline{\mathbf{Y}} = \sum_{u=0}^{N_U-1} \sum_{k=0}^{K_u-1} \mathbf{H}_k \mathbf{P}_k \mathbf{x}_k + \mathbf{w}_k = \sum_{n=0}^{N_C-1} \mathbf{H}_n \mathbf{P}_n \mathbf{x}_n + \mathbf{w}_n = \underline{\mathbf{H}} \cdot \underline{\mathbf{P}} \cdot \underline{\mathbf{X}} + \underline{\mathbf{W}}, \tag{5}$$

where $\underline{\mathbf{Y}} = [\mathbf{y}_0^T, \mathbf{y}_1^T, ..., \mathbf{y}_{N_C-1}^T]^T$, $\underline{\mathbf{X}} = [\mathbf{x}_0^T, \mathbf{x}_1^T, ..., \mathbf{x}_{N_C-1}^T]^T$, $\underline{\mathbf{P}} = [\mathbf{P}_0^T, \mathbf{P}_1^T, ..., \mathbf{P}_{N_C-1}^T]^T$, $\underline{\mathbf{W}} = [\mathbf{w}_0^T, \mathbf{w}_1^T, ..., \mathbf{w}_{N_C-1}^T]^T$ and $\underline{\mathbf{H}} = [\mathbf{H}_0^T, \mathbf{H}_1^T, ..., \mathbf{H}_{N_C-1}^T]^T$. Note that $\underline{\mathbf{H}}$ is a multi-block diagonal matrix, assuming that both ISI and ICI which are caused mainly due to time or frequency offsets, are perfectly compensated by an appropriate CP length.

3   Conventional SIC Strategies

The conventional SIC for MIMO infrastructures was first introduced in [17] and later modified w.r.t. an adaptable transmit power allocation scheme in [18]. This approach (also known in the bibliography as V-BLAST), relies on a successive symbol isolation and then detection, based on a *hard* decision policy[4], followed by an appropriate channel nulling operation. This process recurs for N_T iterations whereas at each SIC stage the channel relaxes in terms of the Multiple Access Interference (MAI), in the space domain. The channel nulling and, thus, the interference relaxation performance depend mostly on the equalization technique used throughout the reception process.

The conventional MIMO-SIC-OFDM [17], properly adapted for OFDM transmissions, is presented in Table 1. In the given Table, the SIC-based reception is carried out under either ZF or MMSE equalization, with adaptation to the transmit power allocation [19] and the N_C multiple parallel transmissions. The overall SIC process at a reference

---

[4] In general, soft decision policies are more effective in terms of BER performance, but they present significant complexity augmentation in comparison to the hard ones. Hence, we focus only on hard estimates.

Table 1. The conventional ZF-SIC and MMSE-SIC for MIMO-OFDM systems

$Initialization:$	
$for\ n = 0, 1, ..., N_C - 1$	(a)
$for\ i = 0, 1, ..., N_T - 1$	(b)
$\mathbf{y}_1 = \mathbf{y}$	(c)
$\mathbf{G}_1 = \begin{cases} (\mathbf{HP})^+ = \mathbf{P}^{-1}\mathbf{H}^+, & in\ case\ of\ ZF - SIC \\ ((\mathbf{HP})^H(\mathbf{HP}) + \sigma_w^2\mathbf{I}_{N_T})^{-1}(\mathbf{HP})^H, & in\ case\ of\ MMSE - SIC \end{cases}$	(d)
$k_1 = \begin{cases} arg\ min_j \left\| \langle \mathbf{HP}^+ \rangle_j \right\|^2, & in\ case\ of\ ZF - SIC \\ arg\ max_j \dfrac{\left|(\mathbf{G}_1\mathbf{HP})_{jj}\right|^2}{\sigma_w^2 \left\|\langle \mathbf{G}_1 \rangle_j\right\|^2 + \sum_{l \neq j}\left|(\mathbf{G}_1\mathbf{HP})_{jl}\right|^2}, & in\ case\ of\ MMSE - SIC \end{cases}$	(e)
$Recursion:$	
$\mathbf{w}_{k_i} = \langle \mathbf{G}_i \rangle_{k_i}$	(f)
$z_{k_i} = \mathbf{w}_{k_i}\mathbf{y}_i$	(g)
$\widehat{x}_{k_i} = \mathbf{Q}(z_{k_i})$	(h)
$\mathbf{y}_{i+1} = \mathbf{y}_i - \widehat{x}_{k_i}[[\mathbf{HP}]]_{k_i}$	(i)
$\mathbf{G}_{i+1} = \begin{cases} ([[\mathbf{HP}]]_{\overline{k}_i})^+ = \mathbf{P}^{-1}[[\mathbf{H}]]_{\overline{k}_i}^+, & in\ case\ of\ ZF - SIC \\ (([[\mathbf{HP}]]_{\overline{k}_i})^H([[\mathbf{HP}]]_{\overline{k}_i}) + \sigma_w^2\,[[\mathbf{I}_{N_T}]]_{\overline{k}_i})^{-1}([[\mathbf{HP}]]_{\overline{k}_i})^H, & in\ case\ of\ MMSE - SIC \end{cases}$	(j)
$k_{i+1} = \begin{cases} arg\ min_{j \notin \{k_1,k_2,...,k_i\}} \left\| \langle ([[\mathbf{HP}]]_{\overline{k}_i})^+ \rangle_j \right\|^2, & in\ case\ of\ ZF - SIC \\ arg\ max_{j \notin \{k_1,k_2,...,k_i\}} \dfrac{\left|(\mathbf{G}_{i+1}[[\mathbf{HP}]]_{\overline{k}_i})_{jj}\right|^2}{\sigma_w^2 \left\|\langle \mathbf{G}_{i+1} \rangle_j\right\|^2 + \sum_{l \neq j}\left|(\mathbf{G}_{i+1}[[\mathbf{HP}]]_{\overline{k}_i})_{jl}\right|^2}, & in\ case\ of\ MMSE - SIC \end{cases}$	(k)
$i \leftarrow i + 1$	(l)
$n \leftarrow n + 1$	(m)

receiver is implemented over N_T steps in all the system subcarriers, yielding to a total number of $N_C N_T$ iterations.

Note that $(.)^+$ denotes the Moore-Penrose pseudoinverse, i.e. $\mathbf{H}^+ = (\mathbf{H}^H\mathbf{H})^{-1}\mathbf{H}^H$, $\langle . \rangle_j$ is the j-th row of a matrix, $[[.]]_{\overline{k}_i}$ is the deflated version of a matrix whose $k_1, k_2, ...,$ k_i-th columns have been zeroed, $\mathbf{Q}(.)$ denotes the slicing operator associated with the current modulation scheme and $\widehat{x}_{k_i}$ represents the hard estimate of x_{k_i} on the k_i-th detection layer. In case of the MMSE detection, $\mathbf{G} = (\mathbf{HP})^H((\mathbf{HP})(\mathbf{HP})^H + \sigma_w^2\mathbf{I}_{N_R})^{-1} = ((\mathbf{HP})(\mathbf{HP})^H + \sigma_w^2\mathbf{I}_{N_T})^{-1}\mathbf{HP})^H$. In this paper, we focus on the latter equality of the MMSE expression as it leads to lower computational complexity for $N_T \leq N_R$ [20].

In general, ordered SIC (OSIC) outperforms the facilitated SIC under random or serial ordering in terms of BER performance, at the expense of higher complexity. In case of ZF-SIC, the ordering is implemented according to a descending norm basis at each OSIC step between all the remaining uncancelled transmitting symbols of each node, as shown in Table 1 (*step e*). In Table 1 (*step f*), the decision statistic at each detection layer is based on the sequence order $\{k_1, k2, ..., k_{N_T}\}$, which in turn determines the overall BER performance. Thus, the error covariance matrix on the n-th subcarrier is obtained as

$$\Phi_n^{ZF} = \sigma_w^2((\mathbf{HP})_n^H(\mathbf{HP})_n)^{-1}, \tag{6}$$

Consequently, the Signal-to-Noise Ratio (SNR) at the l-th detection layer on the n-th subcarrier is given as [21]

$$\rho_n^{l,ZF} = \frac{1}{\Phi_{n_{l,l}}^{ZF}}, \tag{7}$$

yielding to a BER probability given as

$$Pe_{n,l}^{ZF} = Q\left(\sqrt{\rho_n^{l,ZF}}\right),$$ (8)

where $Q(.)$ is the Gaussian Q-function.

In case of the MMSE-SIC, the symbol detection at each SIC step is determined according to a descending order of the Signal-to-Interference-plus-Noise Ratio (SINR) between all the remaining uncancelled layers. For the MMSE-SIC case, the error covariance matrix on the n-th subcarrier is obtained as

$$\Phi_n^{MMSE} = \sigma_w^2((\mathbf{HP})_n^H(\mathbf{HP})_n + \sigma_w^2\mathbf{I}_{N_T})^{-1},$$ (9)

and the SINR at the l-th detection layer on the n-th subcarrier is given as

$$\rho_n^{l,MMSE} = \frac{1}{\Phi_{n_{l,l}}^{MMSE} - 1},$$ (10)

yielding to a BER probability given as

$$Pe_{n,l}^{MMSE} = Q\left(\sqrt{\rho_n^{l,MMSE}}\right).$$ (11)

4   The Proposed Hybrid SIC

On MIMO-OFDM infrastructures, in case of ZF-SIC, the ZF equalization leads to noise enhancement because the pseudoinverse channel matrix is not always added destructively and, hence, it could result to the potentially colored additive noise at the receiver. Moreover, the diversity gain provided by the multiple receive antenna array for the interference suppression is eliminated along with the channel matrix coefficients by exploiting the ZF equalizer in MIMO channels, which correspondingly results in a lower overall diversity order [22]. In fact, the selected stream for detection at the first SIC step has a diversity gain of N_R, while the stream at the last SIC step has a diversity gain of $N_R - N_T + 1$, which is a rather undesirable condition.

On the contrary, in case of MMSE-SIC, the interference is not totally removed. The imperfect interference cancellation is, however, compensated by providing a higher diversity performance in the decoding process. Moreover, MMSE does not enhance the noise coefficients in comparison to the respective ZF equalization, whereas the higher diversity order tenet is found to be beneficial, especially in low SINR regions [23]. It is, then, straightforward that a conventional equalization methodology based on MMSE detection results to a lower BER probability in comparison to the one based on ZF detection. Nevertheless, the higher computational cost is a fundamental prerequisite for the enhanced BER performance. Hence, the selection of the appropriate equalizer is still debatable, depending mostly on the users' QoS requirements and/or the network manufacturer. The complexity analysis for ZF-SIC and MMSE-SIC in a MIMO-OFDM ad hoc network is presented in Section 5.A.

Taking into account the benefits and the drawbacks of the abovementioned equalizers, we propose a novel framework for MIMO-OFDM ad hoc networks, which is based on a hybrid detection-switching technique, associated with the conventional SIC method. Since we are focusing on a QPSK modulation, the signal is demodulated as two independent BPSK signals in quadrature, thereby only the real or the imaginary symbol part is captured in each branch. The detection criterion is tightly determined on a *priori* basis at each OFDM frame according to a threshold value. In this content and while the transmitting symbols are independent of each other, we introduce a threshold S, representing the mean amplitude of the overall received signal [24], which is expressed as

$$S = \beta \left(\frac{1}{N_C N_R} \left(\Re \left(|(\underline{\mathbf{Y}}|) + \Im \left(|(\underline{\mathbf{Y}}|) \right) \right) \right) = \beta \left(\frac{1}{N_C N_R} \sum_{n=0}^{N_C-1} \left(\Re \left(|\mathbf{y}_n| \right) + \Im \left(|\mathbf{y}_n| \right) \right) \right)$$

$$= \beta \left(\frac{1}{N_C N_R} \sum_{n=0}^{N_C-1} \sum_{j=0}^{N_R-1} \left(\Re \left(|y_n^j| \right) + \Im \left(|y_n^j| \right) \right) \right) \tag{12}$$

where β is a constant which plays the role of a tuning parameter.

In order to maintain, and particularly to enhance the accuracy of the proposed hybrid SIC, the signals with the highest SINR are chosen to be cancelled first by using ZF detection, since the spatial degrees of freedom are still high enough at the first SIC steps. Subsequently, the weaker signals are decoded and cancelled by using MMSE detection, sacrificing computational cost in order to enhance the BER performance. Therefore, upon a signal reception y_n^j, the decision statistic is determined by using ZF detection if both $\Re |y_n^j| \geq S$ and $\Im |y_n^j| \geq S$ or by using MMSE detection if $\Re |y_n^j| < S$ and/or $\Im |y_n^j| < S$. Moreover, switching the more reliable signals to ZF-SIC and the less reliable ones to MMSE-SIC, we also balance the overall complexity of the process. Under this regime, we set the accuracy of the reception process upon a *reliability* classification basis. Furthermore, an appropriate balance on the tradeoff between the performance efficiency and the complexity reduction, depending always on the S value, is accomplished. In Table 2, the proposed hybrid-SIC is presented in detail.

In the proposed scheme, the BER probability Pe_{k_i} w.r.t. S, at each detection layer k_i is obtained as

$$Pe_{k_i|S} = \begin{cases} Q \left(\sqrt{\rho_n^{k_i,ZF}} \right), & if \ [Table \, 2 - step \, d] \ holds \, true. \\ Q \left(\sqrt{\rho_n^{k_i,MMSE}} \right), & otherwise. \end{cases} \tag{13}$$

Since all the transmitting symbols are independent of each other, the overall BER probability can be calculated as the statistical mean of the BER probability for every OFDM symbol, expressed as

$$\widetilde{Pe} = \frac{1}{N_C N_T} \sum_{n=1}^{N_C} \sum_{i=1}^{N_T} \left(Pe_{k_i|S} \right). \tag{14}$$

Table 2. The proposed hybrid detection-switching SIC for MIMO-OFDM networks

$for\ n = 0, 1, ..., N_C - 1$	(a)
$for\ c = 0, 1, ..., N_R - 1$	(b)
$for\ i = 0, 1, ..., N_T - 1$	(c)
$if\ \left\{ \Re\left(\left\|\langle \mathbf{y}\rangle_c\right\|\right) \geq S\ and\ \Im\left(\left\|\langle \mathbf{y}\rangle_c\right\|\right) \geq S\right\}\ then$	(d)
$\mathbf{G}_1 = (\mathbf{HP})^+ = \mathbf{P}^{-1}\mathbf{H}^+$	(e)
$k_i = arg\ min_j \left\|\langle \mathbf{HP}^+\rangle_j\right\|^2$	(f)
$\mathbf{w}_{k_i} = \langle \mathbf{G}_i\rangle_{k_i}$	(g)
$z_{k_i} = \mathbf{w}_{k_i}\mathbf{y}_i$	(h)
$\hat{x}_{ki} = Q(z_{k_i})$	(i)
$\mathbf{y}_{i+1} = \mathbf{y}_i - \hat{x}_{k_i}\left[[\mathbf{HP}]\right]_{k_i}$	(j)
$\mathbf{G}_{i+1} = \left(\left[[\mathbf{HP}]\right]_{\bar{k}_i}\right)^+ = \mathbf{P}^{-1}\left[[\mathbf{H}]\right]_{\bar{k}_i}^+$	(k)
$k_{i+1} = arg\ min_{j \notin \{k_1, k_2, ..., k_i\}} \left\|\left\langle \left(\left[[\mathbf{HP}]\right]_{\bar{k}_i}\right)^+\right\rangle_j\right\|^2$	(l)
$i \leftarrow i + 1\ (when\ i \leftarrow N_T\ then\ go\ to\ (13z))$	(m)
$elseif\ \left\{ \Re\left(\langle \mathbf{y}\rangle_c\right)\ and/or\ Im\left(\langle \mathbf{y}\rangle_c\right) \in (-S, S)\right\}\ and\ while\ \{c < N_R - 1\}\ then$	(n)
$c \leftarrow c + 1$	(o)
$else\ \left\{ \Re\left(\langle \mathbf{y}\rangle_{N_R-1}\right)\ and/or\ \Im\left(\langle \mathbf{y}\rangle_{N_R-1}\right) \in (-S, S)\right\}\ then$	(p)
$\acute{\mathbf{G}}_1 = \left((\mathbf{HP})^H(\mathbf{HP}) + \sigma_w^2\mathbf{I}_{N_T}\right)^{-1}(\mathbf{HP})^H$	(q)
$\acute{k}_1 = arg\ max_j \dfrac{\left\|(\mathbf{G}_1\mathbf{HP})_{jj}\right\|^2}{\sigma_w^2\left\|\langle \mathbf{G}_1\rangle_j\right\|^2 + \sum_{l \neq j}\left\|(\mathbf{G}_1\mathbf{HP})_{jl}\right\|^2}$	(r)
$\mathbf{w}_{\acute{k}_i} = \langle \mathbf{G}_i\rangle_{\acute{k}_i}$	(s)
$z_{\acute{k}_i} = \mathbf{w}_{\acute{k}_i}\mathbf{y}_i$	(t)
$\hat{x}_{\acute{k}i} = Q(z_{\acute{k}_i})$	(u)
$\mathbf{y}_{i+1} = \mathbf{y}_i - \hat{x}_{\acute{k}_i}\left[[\mathbf{HP}]\right]_{\acute{k}_i}$	(v)
$\acute{\mathbf{G}}_{i+1} = \left(\left(\left[[\mathbf{HP}]\right]_{\acute{k}_i}\right)^H\left(\left[[\mathbf{HP}]\right]_{\acute{k}_i}\right) + \sigma_w^2\left[[\mathbf{I}_{N_T}]\right]_{\acute{k}_i}\right)^{-1}\left(\left[[\mathbf{HP}]\right]_{\acute{k}_i}\right)^H$	(w)
$\acute{k}_{i+1} = arg\ max_{j \notin \{k_1, k_2, ..., k_i\}} \dfrac{\left\|\left(\mathbf{G}_{i+1}\left[[\mathbf{HP}]\right]_{\acute{k}_i}\right)_{jj}\right\|^2}{\sigma_w^2\left\|\langle \mathbf{G}_{i+1}\rangle_j\right\|^2 + \sum_{l \neq j}\left\|\left(\mathbf{G}_{i+1}\left[[\mathbf{HP}]\right]_{\acute{k}_i}\right)_{jl}\right\|^2}$	(x)
$i \leftarrow i + 1$	(y)
$n \leftarrow n + 1$	(w)

5 Performance Evaluation

In this section, we provide a performance analysis focusing on the computational complexity and the BER performance of the proposed scheme, which represent the main aspects in this paper.

5.1 Complexity Analysis

We provide computational complexity upper and lower bounds of the proposed scheme and we also present a cross-analysis demonstration between this scheme and the quite complex MMSE-SIC, in a MIMO-OFDM environment. The computational complexity has been evaluated w.r.t. the number of the expected floating point operations (flops). Since both the transmit and the receive signals as well as the channel matrix coefficients are complex-valued, all the appropriate operations including multiplications, additions and divisions, are conducted upon complex values. In the rest of the paper, when we discuss computational complexity we refer to the complex operations (COs) including only complex multiplications (CMs) and complex additions (CAs). We count each complex CA as two flops and each complex CM as six flops [20], [25] in order to evaluate the overall computational complexity of the proposed scheme.

From the property of Hermitian matrices, only the half of the complexity can be obtained in comparison to the complexity of computing a general matrix of the same size. Typically, the main computational burden is obtained by the number of CMs. Computing $\mathbf{H}^H\mathbf{H}$ requires $N_R N_T^2 - 1/2N_T^2 + 1/2N_T$ CMs, while $3/2N_T^3 + (N_R + 1)N_T^2 + 1/2N_T$ CMs are needed in order to calculate $(\mathbf{H}^H\mathbf{H} + \sigma^2\mathbf{I}_{N_T})^{-1}\mathbf{H}^H$, assuming that the real-valued $\sigma^2\mathbf{I}_{N_T}$ is *priori* estimated at the receiver. However, the exact number of COs for a matrix inversion event may vary, depending mostly on how the channel coefficients are handled. Several elimination approaches (e.g. Gauss-Jordan elimination) or advanced signal processing techniques based on matrix decomposition methods (e.g. QR or LDL^H decomposition), result to potentially different computational burden at the cost of either BER performance or hardware gain. We, hence, approximate the complexity of the channel inversion, w.r.t. the CAs, CMs and COs, as $O(N_T^3)$. In case of a SIC reception, the channel inversion procedure is suppressed due to the channel nulling operation at each SIC step. Thus, the computational burden at the i-th SIC step is obtained as $O((N_T - i)^3)$.

The lower complexity bound of the proposed scheme can be obtained as $\beta \to 0$, where all transmitting symbols at all the OFDM subcarriers are carried out by a ZF-SIC reception. Therefore, the total number of COs are obtained as

$$CO_{\beta \to 0} = \sum_{i=0}^{N_C-1} (2N_R N_T^2 + 2N_R N_T - 2iN_R - 4iN_R N_T + 2i^2 N_R + N_T + N_R$$
$$+ O((N_T - i)^3))). \quad (15)$$

Focusing on a system where all the ad hoc nodes are applied with an equal number of transmit and receive antennas, i.e. $N_T = N_R$, the total number of COs is obtained as

$$CO_{\beta \to 0}^{N_T=N_R} = \sum_{i=0}^{N_C-1} (2N_T^3 + 2N_T^2(1 - 2i) + 2N_T(i^2 - i + 1) + O((N_T - i)^3))). \quad (16)$$

Similarly, the upper complexity bound of the proposed scheme can be obtained as $\beta \to +\infty$, where all transmitting symbols at all the OFDM subcarriers are carried out by an MMSE-SIC reception, exclusively. In this case, the total number of COs are obtained as

$$CO_{\beta \to +\infty} = \sum_{i=0}^{N_C-1} (N_R(3N_T^2 + 3i^2 - 6iN_T - i + 2N_T) + N_R + N_T + O((N_T - i)^3))). \quad (17)$$

Consequently, for $N_T = N_R$, the total number of COs is obtained as

$$CO_{\beta \to +\infty}^{N_T = N_R} = \sum_{i=0}^{N_C - 1} (3N_T^3 + N_T^2(2 - 6i) + N_T(3i^2 + 2 - i) + O((N_T - i)^3))). \quad (18)$$

In order to show the fraction of saved complexity of the proposed scheme, we introduce the quotient

$$\xi = \frac{Flops_{proposed}}{Flops_{MMSE}}, \quad (19)$$

where $Flops_{proposed}$ denotes the total number of flops for the proposed hybrid scheme and $Flops_{MMSE}$ denotes the respective number of flops for the conventional MMSE-SIC. In Fig 1, the performance of ξ is depicted w.r.t. β for varying number of $N_T = N_R$ antennas, considering a MIMO-OFDM network with 128 subcarriers and 20 ad hoc nodes. As an illustrative example, in case of $N_T = N_R = 6$ and when $\beta = 3.5$, the proposed scheme requires $0.78 \times Flops_{MMSE}$ number of flops in order to complete an OFDM frame reception. Consequently, this reflects to a strong reduction in the overall computational complexity, since the proposed methodology does not produce any additional overhead to the hardware gear or to the system latency. Concluding this subsection, it is worth mentioning that the complexity efficiency of the proposed scheme is a result of the diversity of the detection approach, while the computational cost for the decision of the most appropriate equalizer depends on the calculation of S, which is negligibly small.

5.2 BER Performance

We have evaluated the performance of the proposed scheme by implementing computer simulations whereas the validity of the results has been encouraged under Monte Carlo simulation runs.

Fig 2 depicts the BER performance of the proposed hybrid SIC in a different network scenario where $N_T = N_R = 2$ and $\beta = 3$, in more detail. It is clear that a small number of system users reflects on a better BER performance due to the reduced K_u number. As K_u reduces (which indicates a higher number of system users), the variation of the power decay profile among the subcarriers assigned to different users is higher. Hence, the probability of the interference influence by the subcarriers of one user to the adjacent ones assigned to another user increases.

Fig 3 depicts the BER performance of the proposed scheme w.r.t. different SNR regions when imperfect CSI is assumed. More specifically, in this case CSI is expressed as $\widehat{\mathbf{H}} = \mathbf{H} + \widehat{\epsilon}_{\mathbf{H}}$, where $\widehat{\epsilon}_{\mathbf{H}}$ denotes the reception error upon the channel estimation in each subcarrier for every N_R and can be approached as a Gaussian approximation, i.e. $\widehat{\epsilon}_{\mathbf{H}} \propto G(0, \sigma_{\mathbf{H}}^2)$, where $\sigma_{\mathbf{H}}^2$ denotes the error variance on the channel estimation. In Fig 3, we assume a uniform network topology, where all the transmitting nodes have an equal distance from the receiver and thus, an identical decay profile. Hence, we model a simpler scenario, in which $\mathbf{P} = \mathbf{I}_{N_T}$, for each ad hoc node. It is obvious that as the channel estimation is more accurate, the BER of the proposed scheme is reduced and vice versa.

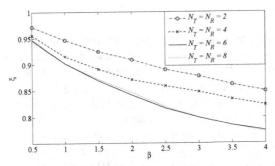

Fig. 1. Fraction of saved complexity of the proposed scheme in comparison to the conventional MMSE-SIC for different β values, in a MIMO-OFDM network with $N_U = 20$ and $N_C = 128$. A small number of transmit and receive antennas is considered in order to approach realistic scenarios, suitable for practical implementations.

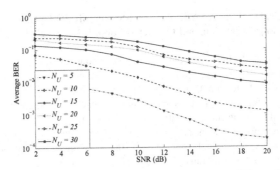

Fig. 2. Average BER performance of the proposed hybrid SIC w.r.t. different SNR system values, for a MIMO-OFDM ad hoc network with variable number of nodes, where $N_T = N_R = 2$ and $\beta = 3$

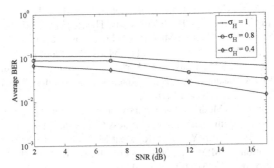

Fig. 3. Average BER performance of the proposed hybrid SIC when imperfect CSI is applied w.r.t. different SNR system values and different σ_H values, for a MIMO-OFDM ad hoc network where $N_T = N_R = 2$, $\beta = 2$ and $N_U = 10$. We consider a uniform topology where all the transmitting nodes have an equal distance from the receiver.

6   Conclusions

In this paper, we proposed a novel detection-switching scheme for SIC-based receivers in uncoded MIMO-OFDM multi-user ad hoc frameworks. This scheme is a hybrid SIC, which switches between ZF and MMSE equalization according to a certain threshold, under QPSK modulation alphabets. We, also, proposed a linear power decay profile with adaptation to fairness in order to reduce the PAPR factor, suitable for ad hoc randomly placed nodes. Furthermore, typical upper and lower complexity bounds for the proposed scheme are derived, through an extensive computational complexity analysis. Additionally, a BER performance analysis was provided. Some of our future aspects are the study of the proposed hybrid SIC under MIMO-OFCDM ad hoc networks and a definition of an appropriate threshold under QAM modulation schemes.

References

1. Haene, S., Perels, D., Burg, A.: A Real-Time 4-Stream MIMO-OFDM Transceiver: System Design, FPGA Implementation, and Characterization. IEEE J. Sel. Areas Commun. 26(6), 877–889 (2008)
2. Lee, H., Lee, B., Lee, I.: Iterative Detection and Decoding With an Improved V-BLAST for MIMO-OFDM Systems. IEEE J. Sel. Areas Commun. 24(3), 504–513 (2006)
3. Verdu, S.: Multiuser Detection. Cambridge University Press (1998)
4. Kim, E.C., Park, J.S., Kim, J.Y.: Co-channel interference cancellation based on ZF/MMSE SIC with optimal ordering for cooperative communication systems. In: IEEE 9th Int. Symp. Commun. Inf. Technol., Incheon, Korea, pp. 404–409 (September 2009)
5. Ali, O.S., Cardinal, C., Gagnon, F.: On the Performance of Interference Cancellation in Wireless Ad Hoc Networks. IEEE Trans. Commun. 58(2), 433–437 (2010)
6. Vaze, R., Heath, R.W.: Transmission capacity of ad-hoc networks with multiple antennas using transmit stream adaptation and interference cancelation. In: IEEE Conf. Record of the Forty-Third Asilomar Conf. Signals, Systems and Computers, California, USA, pp. 1709–1713 (November 2009)
7. Louie, R., McKay, M.R., Collings, I.B.: Open-Loop Spatial Multiplexing and Diversity Communications in Ad Hoc Networks. IEEE Trans. Inf. Theory 57(1), 317–344 (2011)
8. Liu, T.-H.: Some Results for the Fast MMSE-SIC Detection in Spatially Multiplexed MIMO Systems. IEEE Trans. Wireless Commun. 8(11), 5443–5448 (2009)
9. Lai, T.X., Muruganathan, S.D., Sesay, A.B.: Performance Analysis and Multi-Stage Iterative Receiver Design for Concatenated Space-Frequency Block Coding Schemes. IEEE Trans. Wireless Commun. 7(11), 4208–4214 (2008)
10. Liu, T.-H., Yeh Liu, Y.-L.: Modified fast recursive algorithm for efficient MMSE-SIC detection of the V-BLAST system. IEEE Trans. Wireless Commun. 7(10), 3713–3717 (2008)
11. Letaief, K.B., Choi, E., Ahn, J.-Y., Chen, R.: Joint Maximum Likelihood Detection and Interference Cancellation for MIMO/OFDM Systems. In: IEEE 58th Veh. Technol. Conf., Orlando, Florida, USA, pp. 612–616 (October 2003)
12. Zhou, Y., Ng, T.-S.: Performance Analysis on MIMO-OFCDM Systems with Multi-Code Transmission. IEEE Trans. Wireless Commun. 8(9), 4426–4433 (2009)
13. Stoyan, D., Kendall, W.S., Mecke, J.: Stochastic Geometry and Its Applications, 2nd edn. Wiley, Chichester (1995)
14. Jiang, H., Wang, P., Zhuang, W., Shen, X.: An Interference Aware Distributed Resource Management Scheme for CDMA-Based Wireless Mesh Backbone. IEEE Trans. Wireless Commun. 6(12), 4558–4567 (2007)

15. Weber, S.P., Andrews, J.G., Yang, X., de Veciana, G.: Transmission Capacity of Wireless Ad Hoc Networks With Successive Interference Cancellation. IEEE Trans. Inf. Theory 53(8), 2799–2814 (2007)
16. Zhuang, H., Dai, L., Zhou, S., Yao, Y.: Low Complexity Per-Antenna Rate and Power Control Approach for Closed-Loop V-BLAST. IEEE Trans. Commun. 51(11), 1783–1787 (2003)
17. Wolniansky, P.W., Foschini, G.J., Golden, G.D., Valenzuela, R.A.: V-BLAST: An architecture for realizing very high data rates over the rich-scattering wireless channel. In: Proc. URSI Int. Symp. Signals, Systems, Electronics, Pisa, Italy, pp. 295–300 (September-October 1998)
18. Nam, S.H., Shin, O.-S., Lee, K.B.: Transmit Power Allocation for a Modified V-BLAST System. IEEE Trans. Commun. 52(7), 1074–1079 (2004)
19. Nam, S.H., Lee, K.B.: Transmit power allocation for an extended V-BLAST system. In: The 13th IEEE Int. Symp. Personal, Indoor and Mobile Radio Commun., vol. 2, pp. 843–848 (2002)
20. Luo, Z., Liu, S., Zhao, M., Liu, Y.: A Novel Fast Recursive MMSE-SIC Detection Algorithm for V-BLAST Systems. IEEE Trans. Wireless Commun. 6(6), 2022–2025 (2007)
21. Whang, Y., Park, J.H., Whang, R.J.: Low Complexity Successive Interference Cancellation for OFDM Systems over Time-Varying Multipath Channels. In: IEEE 69th Veh. Technol. Conf. (VTC 2009), Barcelona, Spain, pp. 1–5 (April 2009)
22. Miridakis, N.I., Vergados, D.D.: A Survey on the Successive Interference Cancellation performance for single-antenna and multiple-antenna OFDM Systems. IEEE Commun. Surveys Tutorials (November 2010) (submitted)
23. Zijian, A., Berkmann, J., Spiegel, C., Scholand, T., Bruck, G.H., Drewes, C., Gunzelmann, B., Jung, P.: On MIMO With Successive Interference Cancellation Applied to UTRA LTE. In: IEEE 3rd Int. Symp. Commun., Control and Signal Process., St. Julians, Malta, pp. 1009–1013 (March 2008)
24. Marabissi, D., Fantacci, R., Papini, S.: Robust Multiuser Interference Cancellation for OFDM Systems With Frequency Offset. IEEE Trans. Wireless Commun. 5(11), 3068–3076 (2006)
25. Gan, Y.H., Ling, C., Mow, W.H.: Complex Lattice Reduction Algorithm for Low-Complexity Full-Diversity MIMO Detection. IEEE Trans. Signal Process. 57(7), 2701–2710 (2009)

Author Index